Presidential Leadership in Feeble Times

Presidential Leadership in Feeble Times

Explaining Executive Power in the Gilded Age

MARK ZACHARY TAYLOR

OXFORD
UNIVERSITY PRESS

Oxford University Press is a department of the University of Oxford. It furthers
the University's objective of excellence in research, scholarship, and education
by publishing worldwide. Oxford is a registered trade mark of Oxford University
Press in the UK and certain other countries.

Published in the United States of America by Oxford University Press
198 Madison Avenue, New York, NY 10016, United States of America.

CIP data is on file at the Library of Congress

ISBN 978–0–19–775074–2

DOI: 10.1093/oso/9780197750742.001.0001

Printed by Integrated Books International, United States of America

Contents

Preface

I am an unusual author for a book on the Gilded Age presidency, so some explanation is appropriate. My primary subfield of expertise is the economic competitiveness of nations. Within it, I have paid particular attention to the political economy of science, technology, and innovation. But I also deal with trade, industrial policy, defense spending, fiscal policy, even monetary policy. My previous scholarship, which is best summarized in *The Politics of Innovation* (2016), led me to suspect that political leadership plays an important, but poorly explained, role in the economic performance of nations. Public debate over President Obama's economic leadership then prompted me to perform a rough statistical analysis of all US presidents and national economic performance over the short run, published in the journal *PS: Politics & Political Science*.[1] The economic data suggested that individual presidents mattered little. But statistics miss a lot. They do not capture important factors that are difficult to quantify, like leadership, ideology, political skill, or historical contingencies. And of course, a fundamental principle of statistics warns us that correlation does not guarantee causality.

To better detect causal linkages, if any exist, I next began a qualitative investigation of every presidency. I started with an initial foundation of at least one scholarly biography of each president and several economic histories, including broad surveys and period- and issue- specific studies. I then revisited each presidency more in depth, focusing on the postbellum and modern presidents. In my research, I was struck by the unexpected drama of the Gilded Age presidency and the economy. The period seemed to defy much conventional wisdom about presidential leadership. It also provided an enormous amount of methodological leverage in that both the "independent variable" (the presidents) and the "dependent variable" (economic performance) combined elements of extreme variation and steady constancy. Such conditions intrigue us social scientists.

This book presents some of the results of this inquiry. Most experts dismiss presidents as practically irrelevant to the US economy, and we assume that the White House was at its weakest during the Gilded Age. This book turns this logic on its head. It retells the drama of America's Gilded Age political economy through the lens of the presidency. In doing so, it reveals oft-ignored subtleties of presidential power, with important lessons for us today. It attempts to use what we know about the Gilded Age to test existing hypotheses and to generate new ones about the causal role of the president in affecting the nation's economic performance. For those concerned about methodology, it applies Mills's method of agreement/differences to a set of least-likely historical cases in order to ask: What factors did the successful presidents share that the failures did not? What did the failures share that the success stories did not?

The historical chapters are based on a broad range of secondary and primary documents, including biographies, diaries, letters, public speeches, contemporary accounts, newspapers, and magazines of the era. I also pay careful attention to juxtapose our 21st-century view of the Gilded Age economy with contemporary 19th-century discussions in the *Wall Street Journal*, *The Economist*, *Quarterly Journal of Economics*, *Journal of Political Economy*, and other economic and business periodicals of the day. And although this book is partly based on original research, it also draws heavily on the outstanding work of top scholars in history, politics, economics, and sociology. Each chapter has been presented at scholarly conferences and/or circulated among presidential scholars, historians, and subject matter experts.

Accordingly, this book treats quotations and citations differently than does conventional historical research. In professional historiography, the practice is to note citations for sources not only of specific quotations but also of the information gathered in the course of one's research.[2] However, I treat citations according to the science practices of my own academic upbringing: to allow for verification, reproducibility, and independent interpretation. Provenance matters, not my personal path toward their discovery. In particular, primary sources are cited wherever I personally viewed the original source; where not, I cite either the most temporally proximate source that I viewed or the most currently reputable secondary source that I found.[3] This is not meant to dismiss or disrespect scholars who initially discovered the quote. Instead, it is meant to direct readers toward primary sources or to the most reliable secondary sources. The notes and references provide the complete list of scholarship that contributed to the evidence and arguments presented in this book.

Finally, some of the most popular attempts at presidential evaluations are either arbitrary or driven by ideology. This book is neither. It relies partly on the latest and most reliable statistical data, complemented by qualitative analysis of historical case studies. Cognizant of the "uses and abuses" of presidential rankings, this book lets the economic data do the talking.[4] I do not cherry-pick evidence to support my arguments. I do not attempt to make "heroes" or "villains" out of individual presidents. Nor do I argue that we should judge 19th-century leaders according to 21st-century expectations. I let the historical evidence speak for itself. No historical or ethical judgments are used to adjust the findings, nor is there any attempt to advance any particular political, economic, or theoretical agenda. In fact, many of my own personal a priori expectations and hypotheses were disproven in the process. In particular, I expected that experience, education, and a quiet technocratic approach to presidential leadership would produce the best economic results. What I found instead completely surprised me.

Acknowledgments

The novelist Donna Tartt once described her writing process as "painting a wall-sized mural with a brush the size of an eyelash." I now understand what that means. This book took ten years to research and three years to write, involving the synthesis of thousands of sources—books, articles, letters, diaries, speeches, and databases. Such a gargantuan task could not have been completed without the aid of dozens of scholars, librarians, editors, friends, and family.

Foremost thanks goes to David McBride and Oxford University Press for taking another risk, this time on a lengthy book about a seemingly obscure topic. Two anonymous reviewers put in valuable time during the difficult post-COVID period and provided essential guidance. Next come Dan Winship and John Dearborn, each of whom suffered through drafts of almost every chapter, offering reams of excellent advice and necessary encouragement along the way. Richard J. Ellis and the late Jeffrey Friedman were lifeboats who published early drafts of my conclusions and Benjamin Harrison chapters. For counsel on individual chapters and overarching themes, I received crucial insights from Meena Bose, Tom Cronin, George C. Edwards III, William Howell, Martin Moeller, Shannon Bow O'Brien, Jon C. Rogowski, Elizabeth Sanders, Max Skidmore, Stephen Skowronek, Stephen Weatherford, and B. Dan Wood. For their advice and encouragement at the outset, I also thank the kindest group of political scientists I have ever met: the Presidents and Executive Politics Section of the American Political Scientists, especially Lilly Goren, William Howell, Martha Joynt Kumar, David E. Lewis, Ian Ostrander, Yu Ouyang, Dan Ponder, and Andrew Rudalevige. For general suggestions and advice, much gratitude to Catherine Davies, Kurk Dorsey, Bob Kirkman, Daniel Krcmaric, Eric Schatzberg, and Stacy D. VanDeveer. In cleaning up the final draft, Brian Abolins provided useful editorial guidance.

The following political historians were among the most gracious advisors I have yet encountered in academia: Charles Calhoun, Paul Cimbala, Danny LaChance, Mark Wahlgren Summers, and Richard White. To be sure, some of these scholars remain highly critical of the application of social science methods to history. And yet, despite their objections, they provided priceless corrections, context, and suggestions and in the warmest possible terms. No less gracious or insightful were the economic historians, who understood the social science approach and helped me to apply it: Nicolas Barreyre, Charles Geisst, Douglas A. Irwin, Joshua Rosenblum, and Steven Usselman. For their insights and assistance on individual presidents, I also thank Tom Culbertson, Dustin McLochlin, Nan Card, and Joan Eckermann at the Rutherford B. Hayes Presidential Library, as well as Robert Merry.

Georgia Tech is not known for vast holdings on the Gilded Age, hence this book could not have been written without the expertise and determination of my university's librarians, who hunted down sources and access. In particular, Ameet Doshi was tireless and a master sleuth, abetted by Jay Forrest, Charlie Bennett, Marlee Givens, Rick Goodin, Bruce Henson, Patricia Kenly, and Alexis Linoski. Thanks also to Lewis Wyman at the Library of Congress.

Finally, thanks to the School of Public Policy at Georgia Tech, and especially Kaye Husbands Fealing and Cassidy Sugimoto, for their patience and encouragement. This project took far longer than expected and was probably not what they signed up for when they took me on. Nevertheless, they stood solidly by me the whole time.

A Note on Abbreviations, Data, and Sources

The presidents' names are abbreviated as follows as authors in the notes:

AJ	Andrew Johnson (1865–1869)
USG	Ulysses S. Grant (1869–1877)
RBH	Rutherford B. Hayes (1877–1881)
JAG	James A. Garfield (1881)
CAA	Chester A. Arthur (1881–1885)
SGC	Stephen Grover Cleveland (1885–1889; 1893–1897)
BH	Benjamin Harrison (1889–1893)
WMcK	William McKinley (1897–1901)

UCSB indicates primary material (e.g., speeches, executive orders, presidential messages, party platforms) sourced from the American Presidency Project at the University of California, Santa Barbara, maintained by John Woolley and Gerhard Peters: https://www.presidency.ucsb.edu/.

Unless otherwise indicated, the statistical data cited in this book came from the following sources:

1. Carter, Susan B., et al. (eds.). 2006. *Historical Statistics of the United States, Millennial Edition.* New York: Cambridge University Press (online). Indicated by *HSUS* when cited in combination with other sources. Within which, the following tables were consulted:

    Table Aa6–8. Population: 1790–2000.

    Table Aa9–14. National population and the demographic components of change: 1790–2000.

    Table Aa699–715. Urban and rural territory—population, by size of place: 1790–1990.

    Table Aa716–775. Population, by race, sex, and urban-rural residence: 1880–1990.

    Table Ab52–117. Total fertility rate and birth rate, by race and age: 1800–1998.

    Table Ab656–703. Expectation of life at specified ages, by sex and race: 1850–1998.

    Table Ab928. Infant mortality rate for Massachusetts: 1851–1998.

Table Ee362–375. Exports and imports of merchandise, gold, and silver: 1790–2002.

Table Ee416–417. Exports and imports of goods: 1869–1928.

Table Ee424–430. Merchandise imports and duties: 1790–2000.

Table Ee446–457. Exports and imports of merchandise—crude and manufactured goods: 1821–1984.

Table Ee533–550. Exports, by country of destination: 1790–2001.

Table Ee569–589. Exports of selected commodities: 1790–1989.

2. US Department of Commerce. 1975. *Historical Statistics of the United States, Colonial Times to 1970.* Washington DC: Bureau of the Census.

Series Q 321–328. Railroad Mileage and Equipment 1830–1890.

Series Q 506–517. Net Tonnage Capacity of Vessels Entered and Clears 1789–1970.

Series R 1–12. Telephones and Average Daily Conversations: 1876–1970.

Series R 46–55. Western Union Telegraph Company—Summary of Facilities, Traffic, and Finances: 1866–1915.

Series Y 457–465. Outlays of the Federal Government: 1789–1970.

3. National Bureau of Economic Research, *NBER Macrohistory Database*, https://www.nber.org/research/data/nber-macrohistory-database. Indicated by *NBER Macro* when used in combination with other sources. In particular:

Series a01005a. Index of Crop Production, Twelve Important Crops, 1866–1940.

Series a01009. US Wheat Crop, 1866–1952.

Series m04001a. US Wholesale Price of Wheat, Chicago, Six Markets, 1841–1944.

Series m04005. US Wholesale Price of Corn, Chicago, 1860–1951.

Series m04007. US Wholesale Price of Cattle, Chicago, 1858–1940.

Series m04008. US Wholesale Price of Hogs, Chicago, 1858–1940.

Series m07023. US Total Exports, 1866–1969.

Series m07028. US Total Imports, 1866–1969.

Series m08061a. US Index of Composite Wages, 1820–1909.

Series m11025a. US Index of All Common Stock Prices, Monthly, 1871–1914.

Series m12002a. US Index of Industrial Activity, 1877–1961.

Series m12003. US Index of American Business Activity, 1855–1970.

Series m12004a. US Index of Industrial Production and Trade, 1875–1915.

Series m13019. US Railroad Bond Yields, High Grade, Percent, Monthly, 1857–1937.

Series m14076a. US Monetary Gold Stock, 1878–1914.

Series m14137a. US Gold Held in the Treasury and Federal Reserve Banks, 1878–1914.

Series q13020. Municipal Bond Yields for New England, Percent, Quarterly, 1857–1914.

Other sources frequently used include:

4. For some international comparisons:

Mitchell, Brian R. 2003a. *International Historical Statistics: Europe, 1750–2000.* 5th ed. New York: Palgrave Macmillan.

Section D—Industry.

Section E—External Trade.

Table A4: Population of Major Cities.

Table C2: Output of Main Arable Crops.

Table J2: Proportions of National Product Output by Sector of Origin.

Table F1: Length of Railway Line Open.

Table F8: Postal and Telegraph Services.

Table F9: Number of Telephones in Use.

Mitchell, Brian R. 2003b. *International Historical Statistics: The Americas, 1750–2000.* 5th ed. New York: Palgrave Macmillan.

5. For price comparisons over time:

Measuring Worth = https://www.measuringworth.com/.

Throughout this book, I attempt to represent historical prices in 2020 dollars. Such interpretations are partly subjective and open to legitimate debate. Put simply, the monetary value of a good or service is difficult to measure and compare across time. This book therefore relies on the MeasuringWorth project, founded in 2006 by economists Samuel H. Williamson (Miami University) and Louis P. Cain (Loyola University Chicago). It offers a variety of alternative measures, such as consumer price index, value of consumer bundle, share of GDP (or GDP per capita), and relative earnings. When cited in this book, the measure used is also indicated in parentheses. Readers are encouraged to experiment with alternative measures.

6. For stock market performance:

Shiller, Robert. 2015. *Irrational Exuberance.* Revised and expanded 3rd ed. Princeton, NJ: Princeton University Press. http://www.econ.yale.edu/~shiller/data.htm. For stock market data.

Williamson, Samuel H. 2022. "Daily Closing Values of the DJA in the United States, 1885 to Present." *MeasuringWorth*. http://www.measuri ngworth.com/datasets/DJA/index.php.

7. For cross-national comparisons in wealth and economic growth:
   Bolt, Jutta and Jan Luiten van Zanden. 2020. "Maddison Style Estimates of the Evolution of the World Economy: A New 2020 Update." https:// www.rug.nl/ggdc/historicaldevelopment/maddison/releases/maddi son-project-database-2020. Maddison Project Database, version 2020.

8. For some data on world trade:
   Federico, Giovanni, and Antonio Tena-Junguito. 2019. "World Trade, 1800–1938: A New Synthesis." *Revista de Historia Económica/Journal of Iberian and Latin America Economic History* 37 (1): 9–41. Federico-Tena World Trade Historical Database.

9. For annual changes in industrial production:
   Davis, Joseph H.. 2004. "An Annual Index of U. S. Industrial Production, 1790–1915." *Quarterly Journal of Economics* 119 (4): 1177–1215.
   Miron, Jeffrey A., and Christina D. Romer. 1990. "A New Monthly Index of Industrial Production, 1884–1940." *Journal of Economic History* 50 (2): 321–337.

10. For assistance in dating recessions:
    National Bureau of Economic Research. *US Business Cycle Expansions and Contractions*. Cambridge, MA: NBER. http://www.nber.org/cycles/cyc lesmain.html.

1

Introduction

Presidential Leadership and the Gilded Age Economy

The Gilded Age in America (1869–1901) was a period of tremendous economic growth and political change.[1] It was also an era of extremes. There were several cycles of economic boom and depression. Financial crises were common. Years of deflation were dotted with small spurts of inflation. The rapidly growing stock market became a rollercoaster of epic bull and bear markets. Even the federal budget and trade balances brimmed with melodrama. Throughout the economy, large corporations emerged to sweep away countless small enterprises that had long been the primary mode for American business. New technologies transformed almost every kind of economic activity. Manufacturing and industry advanced from the margins to the center of the American economy. All the while, economic inequality grew to historic proportions. Industrial workers formed their first unions and then struck in record numbers. Socialists and anarchists spread dissent and violence. Around the country, a passionate fusillade of new political parties and movements flared, glittered, and faded. Even professional "political economists" struggled to explain the strange new world evolving around them—founding the modern field of "economics" in the process. In fact, the tumult of the Gilded Age was so thorough that one historian famously deemed the period "The Search for Order."[2]

In American politics and leadership studies, the Gilded Age is especially intriguing because its presidents are largely dismissed as irrelevant to the economic drama unfolding around them.[3] They were expected to be dignified, above the scrabble and dirt of daily politics. They gave few speeches of substance. They avoided the press. They rarely campaigned for specific policy programs, especially not in public. Hence, even in their own time, they were stereotyped as milquetoast backbenchers lacking in charisma or leadership capacity. Thus the British viscount James Bryce complained in the 1880s, "Europeans often ask, and Americans do not always explain, how it happens that this great office [of the US presidency] . . . is not more frequently filled by great and striking men."[4] Meanwhile, other factors supposedly drove economic policy: Congress, the parties, political machines, the courts, corporations, farmers. This is partly because the Gilded Age presidency, and the federal government itself, were allegedly too small and too frail to matter much for the nation's economy. Thus historian

Presidential Leadership in Feeble Times. Mark Zachary Taylor, Oxford University Press. © Oxford University Press 2024.
DOI: 10.1093/oso/9780197750742.003.0001

Sean Dennis Cashman has reckoned, "These are the dud presidents: Hayes, a president defied; Garfield, a president defunct; Arthur, a president dismissed; Cleveland, a president denied; and Harrison, a president derided."[5] As if to confirm these conjectures, surveys of professional historians and political scientists frequently place the Gilded Age presidents in the bottom quartiles of their rankings.[6] Or, as the great novelist Thomas Wolfe once lamented, "[T]hey were the lost Americans. . . . Which had the whiskers, which the burnsides: which was which?"[7]

Do presidents matter for America's economic performance? This book contends that they do. And it uses the most improbable executives to do so: the Gilded Age presidents. Presidents are often dismissed as mere rhetoricians with little real influence on the nation's economy.[8] This book contradicts such descriptions. In doing so, it also delivers valuable insights into leadership in the 21st century. In fact, the Gilded Age is important to us today *precisely* because its presidents seem so powerless. This book shows that, even in this unlikely period, presidents *did* affect national economic performance and that their success came from surprising sources. They could not control the economy directly, but decisive leadership could shape the environment in which the economy thrived or languished. Thus, I am also making a larger argument about presidential leadership. This book is an examination not of economic governance alone but of leadership quality overall. My point is that we can learn a lot about the evolution of the modern presidency and the exercise of presidential power from the Gilded Age.

A spotlight on the president and the economy during the Gilded Age reveals several surprises and unexpected outcomes. Ulysses Grant emerges as a curiously adamant ideologue on federal debt and deficit reduction and of returning the US dollar to the gold standard. When the Panic of 1873 struck, his dogged adherence to "hard money," and his inability or refusal to forge consensus on alternatives, allowed that financial crisis to evolve into the worst and longest economic recession in decades. Rutherford Hayes altered this approach in important ways. He championed anticorruption efforts against a combative Congress and a resistant Republican Party. He secured the nearly deserted West for settlement. With investor expectations for the US dollar having been cemented by Grant, Hayes showed consistency and ostensibly returned the dollar to the gold standard. The recession eased, and investment poured into railroads, manufacturing, economic development, and even new technologies like telephones and electricity. Hayes did not cause the economic boom, but he substantially facilitated it. James Garfield lived for only ten months after his election. But in that brief time, he maintained the Hayes economic boom by continuing the fight against corruption and by renegotiating US debt at significantly lower interest rates. Garfield's assassination then provided the fulcrum for congressional action against influence peddling. However, it also introduced the lackluster presidency of Chester Arthur. Arthur had little interest in leadership and no vision for the presidency, for the federal government, or for the country. He mostly left policy matters to his cabinet and Congress. Only rarely did he exercise executive power or even express policy preferences. Thus, when the economy drifted into depression during the period 1881 to 1885, Arthur practiced malign neglect.

Grover Cleveland ushered in a new era of presidential power, but in service of an old political-economic philosophy. In his first administration, he acted energetically to stem a brewing financial crisis. He also wrested back from the Senate the president's right to fire federal appointees. But thereafter, he receded. He stubbornly adhered to his belief that presidents, and the federal government, should play strictly limited roles. Other than issue occasional strong opinions, he did little. The result was a meandering economy. Benjamin Harrison succeeded him with the opposite belief system: the president did have a role to play in the legislative process, and the federal government should act to advance economic development. But Harrison mostly abandoned his economic vision for a staunchly partisan one. The result was an ad hoc mix of fiscal, trade, and monetary policies that severely damaged the federal balance sheet. Thus, when Cleveland returned to office in 1893, he inherited an economy barreling toward currency devaluation and financial crisis. But rather than act to prevent it, as he had before, Cleveland procrastinated. The crisis hit. It quickly turned into a great depression. And yet Cleveland stubbornly refused to provide any sort of relief or even call Congress into special session. Only when the pressure became overwhelming did he ask Congress to act. Even then, Cleveland intervened effectively to address only the monetary aspects; he then melted away on vital trade and fiscal issues. The result was one of the worst and longest economic downturns in US history. The solution was William McKinley. He quickly repaired federal revenues and formally welded the United States to the gold standard. Meanwhile, his lax approach toward antitrust enabled a massive wave of industrial consolidation that brought incredible economies of scale and scope, as well as widespread technological change. His muscular foreign policy then increased confidence in the United States, both at home and abroad, as a rising military power capable of defending its economic interests.

More generally, this book argues that a president's effectiveness as a leader flows from three sources. First, the president's vision for the country, for the federal government, and for the presidency itself is far more important than his education, training, business experience, leadership history, personal ethics, or even raw intellectual capability. In other words, ideas matter—but not necessarily the ideas of professionals or scholars, which might be eagerly consumed but are then often ignored or co-opted. This book also finds that political skill and enthusiasm matter. More specifically, leadership success appears to be partly a function of a president's willingness and ability to forge, maintain, and leverage coalitions with other important political-economic actors. These actors include Congress, the president's political party, his own cabinet and senior appointees, major interest groups, the press, and even the American people themselves. The evidence also suggests that the president's role as an educator is a significant complement to his coalition-building. Finally, trust is all-important. As economic actors, we value the predictability and reliability of others in the economy as well as that of the major political-economic institutions upon which our economic activities rely. Hence this book also suggests that a president's ability to build or maintain trust in institutions such as the financial system, the American currency, the federal government, even the presidency itself is crucial. In sum, not only do presidents matter for the nation's performance, but they matter in subtle and unexpected ways.

Why Care about the Gilded Age?

For serious scholars of the American presidency and American political development, there is much at stake here. First, even today the president is thought to be a minor player in US economic performance. After all, the United States has one of the world's most free market economic systems, which tends to minimize the role of government. Also, Congress, not the president, controls the budget and holds primary jurisdiction over legislation. The White House also has little constitutional authority over trade or regulatory matters. Even within the executive branch, the president's agenda is in the hands of thousands of career bureaucrats who have considerable independent ability to alter, delay, even ignore the president's policy agenda. Still others emphasize the power of the state and local governments in determining policy and economic outcomes.[9] Presidents just do not appear to matter much for economic performance, especially in the short run, regardless of how much credit or blame they receive.

The Gilded Age furnishes special leverage for answering the question "Do presidents matter for the economy?" because the American presidency was arguably at its weakest, making these administrations a set of least-likely cases.[10] One reason given for this period's presidential irrelevance is that the 19th-century public expected little of its executives. In an era when democracy was still rare and fragile, Americans feared powerful leaders. Nineteenth-century presidents therefore rarely dealt directly in legislative matters and almost never advocated for their own policy agenda. To do otherwise was to be a demagogue, grasping for power, and a threat to democracy. Congress was supposed to legislate. The executive branch was to administrate impartially. And the president was simply the federal government's chief administrator. Certainly 19th-century presidents had policy preferences, but unilateral action by a president was extraordinary.[11] He—and they were all "he" back then, for women were mostly barred from political office—was supposed to protect against unconstitutional activity and technical errors in legislation, but not actively promote his own programs.[12] Even within the executive branch, Gilded Age presidents typically delegated policy specifics to their cabinet members, who operated with a high level of autonomy and answered more to Congress or to their political party than to the man in the White House.

In economics, the Gilded Age presidents had no formal roster of experts to guide them in mastering difficult issues. Or, as Cleveland once complained, "[I]f the President has any great policy in mind or on hand he has no one to help him work it out."[13] This went beyond the White House. The entire executive branch was tiny during the Gilded Age. The federal budget averaged a mere 2.6 percent of gross domestic product (GDP); today that figure is closer to 22 percent.[14] The roughly 50,000-person federal workforce under Grant in 1869 may have expanded to 230,000 by McKinley's death in 1901, but never did more than 12 percent of them work in Washington, DC.[15] In fact, Britain's future ambassador to the United States marveled in 1888 that "an American may, through a long life, never be reminded of the Federal Government, except when he votes at presidential and congressional elections, lodges a complaint against the post-office, and opens his trunks for a custom-house official on the pier at New York when he returns from a tour in Europe."[16]

Nor had the "bully pulpit" or "rhetorical presidency" yet arrived to amplify the American president's influence over national opinion. Throughout much of the 19th century, presidents dared not speak directly to the nation about policy, but only to the Congress, and even then in quiet, respectful tones.[17] Even the annual "State of the Union" message was delivered in writing and blandly read into the congressional record by a clerk. All Gilded Age presidents gave public speeches. But they were mostly ceremonial sermons, heavy on patriotism but light on policy advocacy. Headline-grabbing interviews were rare. Raucous public rallies of supporters were unheard of. Even mere public comment was scarce. Presidential media events remained in the future. In fact, most Gilded Age presidents hated and feared the press. As newspapers relied ever more on advertising revenue rather than funding from a president's allies, reporters became intensely tabloid. Increasing readership via scandalous content, not thoughtful political analysis, was top priority for many Gilded Age journalists. Meanwhile, presidents were expected to be stately, aloof from the mud of everyday politics. Hence, throughout most of the Gilded Age, there were no White House daily briefings for journalists, nor even designated White House reporters posting daily reports.[18]

Instead, according to our conventional wisdom, other actors ruled national politics during the Gilded Age. State and local political machines determined who won elections and how patronage would be distributed, and therefore had an outsized influence over policy. Some have argued that the Republican Party, the courts, or American farmers were the fundamental drivers of national politics and policy during this time.[19] Still others insist that Congress was the dominant force in politics, and the president its mere "registering clerk." Even in foreign affairs, traditionally the president's domain, the Senate repeatedly thwarted White House initiatives.[20] Woodrow Wilson, then a graduate student, wrote disapprovingly in his 1885 dissertation, "[The President] is made to approach that body [the Senate] as a servant conferring with his master, and of course deferring to that master."[21] Congress certainly dominated media attention during the late 19th century. Not only did Congress generate far more news and drama, but legislators were much more inviting to the press than were the presidents.

Finally, those scholars who *do* see economic relevance in the US presidency mostly argue that it does not have much to do with the president himself. For example, some assert that institutions, not occupants, determine White House effectiveness. It is the Constitution which grants veto, appointment, and treaty powers to the president. It also gives presidents certain institutional advantages over other actors in terms of information, organizational capacity, and the ability to move first and swiftly.[22] There are additional instruments in the president's institutional "toolbox" (e.g., executive orders, memoranda, determinations, signing statements, directives, and proclamations) with which they can further leverage their constitutional position.[23] In other words, the effectiveness of the White House comes from federal law, not from the individual who occupies it. Others contend that a president's performance in office ultimately derives from personal attributes acquired long before he enters the White House: psychology, innate intelligence, character, education, or personal experience. Still others perceive a political business cycle. Here it is elections or the president's political party that matters, not the winning candidate. Finally, there are those who insist that historical circumstances and random events determine presidential effectiveness; as poet William Blake might put it, "Some [presidents] are born to sweet delight / some are born to endless night."[24] In any case, there is little place for an individual president's agency, ideas, or political skill in these descriptions.

In sum, the Gilded Age presidency is the least likely place to find effective leadership coming out of the White House. And yet this book provides evidence to moderate or contradict many of the claims just enumerated. Presidents *did* matter during the Gilded Age. They were powerful and essential actors. Their actions, or inaction, could deeply affect America's performance in the world economy. We just have to view them through the lens of Gilded Age America.

And if presidents affected national performance in this unlikely era, then there are direct lessons for understanding the effectiveness of US presidents ever since.

How Is this Relevant for the 21st Century?

In fact, the parallels and similarities between the Gilded Age and today are striking. In both the Gilded Age and our own era, we find many of the *same* issues topping the list of public priorities: globalization, technological change, immigration, race, religion, inequality, and working-class resentment.[25] In both periods, trade and monetary policy regularly make the headlines. Critics denounce today, as they did then, patterns of unbridled corruption in government. Political machines and their bosses ruled during the Gilded Age; over a century later, party elites, special interests, and large donors regularly subvert the public will.[26] Hence, today's leftists call for "Woke Capitalism," while those on right cry "Drain the Swamp!" just as political agitators of the Gilded Age excoriated "Rum, Romanism and Rebellion" and howled "Turn the Rascals Out!"[27] During the Gilded Age, Americans were whipped into political frenzies by "yellow journalism"; today "fake news" performs the same function. Familiar too are the growing crises of pollution, public health, and urban blight. And presiding over it all, in both time periods, are often inexperienced figureheads in the White House, seemingly impotent in domestic and economic policy. In both eras, instead of presidents, the most admired and influential Americans are businessmen. During the Gilded Age, we deified the great industrial monopolists: Cornelius Vanderbilt, Andrew Carnegie, J. P. Morgan, and John D. Rockefeller. Americans today similarly idolize the great high-technology monopolists: Bill Gates, Steve Jobs, Jeff Bezos, Mark Zuckerberg, and Elon Musk. And while Americans have made progress on gender and racial equality, we have yet to abandon our prejudices when voting. Finally, in both periods, we find *relatively* low threats to our national security from foreign militaries but relatively high threats from foreign economic competition and pandemic disease. Hence, we are currently living in a "new Gilded Age," according to prominent historians, political scientists, economists, policymakers, and the news media.[28]

In addition, the federal government is similarly divided in the two eras, further weakening the president's ability to get things done. Between 1875 and 1896, the same political party simultaneously held the White House *and* enjoyed clear majorities in Congress for only four years: the Republicans in 1889–1891, the Democrats during 1893–1895. Even then, Congress was deeply polarized, even fractured, often with third parties (Greenback, Prohibition, Populist, Labor) taking small but significant vote margins.[29] In our own time, during the forty years between 1981 and 2021, thirty have seen divided control of government at the national level, making the passage of legislation infamously difficult. Meanwhile, Tea Party and Democratic Socialist factions bedevil the wings of each major party in turn. As a result, recent presidents complain about many of the same divided-government problems as did the Gilded Age presidents.

Presidential elections are also uncommonly tight in both periods.[30] To date, there have been only five US presidential elections in which the winner *lost* the popular vote, two during the Gilded Age (Hayes, Harrison), two during our own time (George W. Bush, Trump). In fact, from 1876 to 1892 the Democratic nominee regularly received *more* popular votes than his Republican opponent; a similar situation occurred between 1992 and 2016.[31] More broadly, out of fifty-nine total presidential elections in US history, eleven of the fifteen closest races (by percentage of popular vote) occurred either during the Gilded Age or within our own lifetimes.[32] And in both eras, suppression of minority voters played a role in determining the outcomes of presidential and congressional elections.

Even the vast expansion of the federal government, and the impossibility of one person commanding it all, is not new. Complaints about a "deep state" that is unwieldy, byzantine, and seemingly autonomous are common today. Presidents yearn for simpler days. But back in 1885, Wilson also lamented:

> At the very first session of Congress steps were taken towards parceling out executive work amongst several departments, according to a then sufficiently thorough division of labor; and if the President of that day was not able to direct administrative details, of course the President of to-day is infinitely less able to do so, and must content himself with such general supervision as he may find time to exercise.[33]

Perhaps most surprising, intellectual debates about the economy traffic in very similar arguments during both periods. Twenty-first-century economists may be more precise and wield far better data and analytical tools, yet we can find many of the *same* basic economic arguments, often using very *similar* logics in both periods. Gilded Age discussions of monetary, trade, and fiscal policy were astonishingly well-informed. For example, our mutton-chopped ancestors understood well that tariffs made producers wealthy by driving up prices for consumers. Many of them questioned the supposed competitive advantages of trade protectionism for domestic industry. They also knew that inflationary monetary policy could help businesses with loans and credit but also risked a currency devaluation, while monetary contraction starved banks and firms of necessary cash. Proto-progressives advocated for greater government spending on welfare, education, healthcare, and environmental protection. Conservatives attacked these ideas as "Socialism!" and "Corruption!" Certainly, many assumptions and arguments popular during the Gilded Age have since been proven incorrect.

But they got a lot right. Regardless, professional economists were not much use in either period. They informed public debates but do not appear to have had much direct or independent influence over presidential decision-making. Their arguments were more often used in service of political goals than in determining them.[34]

And yet in both periods, despite all this political dysfunction, the US economy was transformed. During the Gilded Age, the country metamorphosed from a mostly agricultural economy into an industrial great power. Similarly, in our own time, the American economy went from a de-industrialization crisis during the 1980s to becoming the dominant power in a wide range of high-technology sectors by 2020. And the voyage was identically rocky in both eras: federal deficit and debt crises threatened, trade tensions were perennial, and there was widespread concern about a weak dollar. Both periods also witnessed major financial crises and deep recessions.

In short, for at least the past thirty years, US presidents have faced very similar political and economic conditions as did their predecessors during the Gilded Age. Therefore, understanding the drivers of success and failure in presidential leadership during this earlier period might be very useful for us today. Hence, this book is not just an interesting jaunt through history. Rather, it is intended as an investigation into whether and how *any* president can influence economic competitiveness during their administration, with lessons relevant for 21st-century executives, policymakers, scholars, and voters.

What's New Here?

Certainly, the US presidency and its effectiveness have been studied before; so what is new here? Most studies of the presidency focus on an individual president. They tell a story of which policies he supported or opposed, and whether he was successful in getting them through Congress and implemented by his appointees. Presidential power is emphasized at the expense of actual effectiveness.[35] Battles with other major political actors are highlighted. But studies of outcomes are sometimes superficial, especially economic ones. And there remain relatively few attempts to systematically and objectively investigate the causes of presidential success or failure over time, though this endeavor is growing rapidly.[36]

In particular, of the few scholars who reference the presidents of the Gilded Age, some tend to generalize unscientifically.[37] Grant failed because he was a poor administrator. Arthur failed because he was overwhelmed. Cleveland failed because he was uneducated and simple-minded. But these *same* charges could be leveled against some of the period's success stories: Hayes was a hands-off administrator opposed by powerful factions of his own party, even within the executive branch; McKinley was uneducated and "no brilliant genius."[38] And how do we explain Harrison? He was a superlative administrator, a policy expert, an experienced legislator, backed by his party (which also controlled Congress for half his presidency), highly intelligent, well-read, and educated— and yet he helped to create one of the greatest economic catastrophes in US history. Single-presidency studies also miss many continuities and breaks across administrations. Each administration comes across as *sui generis*. This is neither accurate nor scientific.

This book addresses these problems in several ways. First, this volume's spotlight on economic performance is new. Economics fade into the background of much presidential scholarship, which tends to focus on other, often more dramatic aspects of an administration. The Gilded Age economy in particular is often forgotten. To complicate matters, some historians and presidential scholars have little depth in economic theory, methods, analysis, or data. Hence their evaluations of presidential effectiveness or performance can lack rigor. Opinions of contemporaries and time-period stereotypes are emphasized at the expense of objective data and analysis. This book makes economic performance, based on both statistical and qualitative data, one of its central themes.

Second is this book's focus on objectivity. Most studies of presidential effectiveness and "ranking" exercises rely heavily on subjective interpretations of qualitative case studies. As presidential scholar Fred Greenstein put it, "Presidential greatness is sort of nonsensical . . . [b]ecause greatness is a value judgment."[39] The worst offenders are those hobbyists, pundits, and ideologues who cull history for support, while disregarding contradictory evidence. Such approaches, while interesting, are not terribly useful. To deal with subjectivity, this book uses considerable quantitative economic data to corroborate the qualitative evidence and to provide more precise causal explanations. Specifically, this book does not rely on infamously biased and constantly changing surveys of presidential greatness. Nor does it place much confidence in partisan editorials and opinions of 19th-century contemporaries. Instead it draws on the latest economic estimates. Sources include current data releases from the *Historical Statistics of the United States*, National Bureau of Economic Research, Maddison Project databases, and the Measuring Worth Foundation, as well as data and findings from recent studies published as scholarly books, research articles, conference papers, and doctoral dissertations. This addition of statistical data, though far from perfect, makes presidential performance less a matter of individual interpretation. With data as a reality check, historical stereotypes and hagiography cannot, say, whitewash the 1873 financial panic or mute the 1893–1897 economic collapse or ignore the late 1870s economic boom. Such relative objectivity allows us to better connect presidential backgrounds, beliefs, and leadership styles with outcomes.

Objectivity is further improved by this book's tight focus on the Gilded Age. Even decades later, many Americans today still feel passionate about the administrations of Hoover, FDR, Kennedy, Carter, Reagan, and Clinton. But the Gilded Age presidents are mostly forgotten. Grant and McKinley might generate some emotion, but few readers or scholars are willing to fall on their swords for Hayes, Garfield, Arthur, Cleveland, or Harrison. In fact, there remain tremendous gaps in our knowledge of the Gilded Age presidency, a subfield once criticized by experts as "a period that is a veritable black hole of presidential scholarship."[40] Thus we arguably have a greater likelihood of making new observations, and of unbiased analysis, when interpreting presidential performance during this time period.

Who Should Read This Book?

This book is targeted at several audiences. For scholars, it makes contributions to research on the presidency, American political development, leadership studies, and political economy. In particular, experts will want to pay special attention to the final chapter, which takes up the theoretical discussion. However, this book is *not* a complicated politics or economics text intended only for specialists. There are no mathematical equations or regression tables. It is written to be accessible to general readers interested in the evolution of the presidency and the US economy. Obviously, students at all levels seeking a better understanding of the Gilded Age should find much of interest. Voters seeking better guidelines by which to judge candidates today might find much to think about here. Policymakers can find useful lessons about the broader political context within which their daily battles occur. Executives of all types of organizations can draw lessons on how to provide more effective leadership.

Plan of the Book

This book attempts to answer the following questions: How did the US economy behave during the Gilded Age? And why did the US economy flourish under some Gilded Age presidents but flounder, even crash, under others? Chapter 2 presents some statistical data and initial hypotheses with which to begin this investigation. It suggests that Hayes, Harrison, and McKinley were each cases of relative success. In fact, they may have overseen some of the *most* prosperous economies in all US history. Meanwhile Grant (second term), Arthur, and Cleveland (second term) appear to have presided over some of the *least* successful. Somewhere in the middle sit the administrations of Grant (first term),

Garfield, and Cleveland (first term), when the economy seemed to mostly tread water.

This chapter also briefly summarizes what existing research says about the relationship between the president and the economy. There are four major families of theory: (1) presidents do not matter, and no causal relationship exists; (2) presidents who recognize and pursue the "right" policy agenda are the most successful; (3) presidential performance is a function of personal factors—character, psychology, intelligence, education, or prior experience; (4) since presidents rarely act alone, credit or blame in economic performance should go to their cabinet, staff, and advisors. Evidence with which to test these hypotheses will be presented in the chapters that follow.

Chapters 3–4 on the Civil War and its immediate aftermath start the historical journey by providing necessary background for understanding the Gilded Age. What was the American economy like, and how did it get there? What was the presidency like, and how had it evolved over time? And how did the two interact over the course of the 19th century? Also, how did Americans back then think that politics, policy, and the economy worked? How did this inform their expectations, behavior, and policy prescriptions?

The next several chapters investigate each presidency from 1869 to 1901 in chronological order. These chapters weave an examination of how the US economy evolved, together with an investigation of the actions and reactions of each US president. Interspersed between them are two "interludes" that survey broad decadal trends in the economy, business, science, technology, politics, and economic thought that simultaneously transformed American political and economic behavior during the Gilded Age.

Chapter 13 goes deep into the theoretical discussion. It analyzes the empirics of the previous chapters in the context of the major theories of presidential power and effectiveness. The evidence strongly suggests that the Gilded Age presidents affected national economic performance. The relationship is strongest in financial crises and monetary policy. And success did not depend on getting policy "right." Certainly, destructive policy choices hurt the economy, but there were usually *multiple* good policy options available to any given president on any given problem. Nor was raw executive power—the president's ability to dictate policy and personnel—the key to effectiveness. Instead, the case studies suggest that presidential vision, coalition-building, and trust-building correlate best with economic performance, at least during the Gilded Age. Of far less importance were party identification, education, business experience, economics training, leadership history, personal ethics, or intellectual capability. There were simply many men whose background or character promised effective economic leadership but then failed, and many men who had few raw materials for economic success but achieved it anyway.

* * *

Of course, in order to judge the effectiveness of the Gilded Age presidents, we first need a general idea of how the US economy performed during the final third of the 19th century. In order to do that, we need a basic grasp of how to measure a nation's economic performance and how best to assign credit, or blame, to different presidential administrations. We tackle these tasks in the following chapter.

2

The Puzzle

In order to understand whether and how the Gilded Age presidents affected the economy, we first need a basic picture of how the nation's economy performed. Even non-experts know this as a period of tremendous technological change. But it was also an era of great economic volatility. The late 19th century was awash with financial crises, economic booms, steep depressions, nauseating fluctuations in trade and fiscal balances, and wild stock market gyrations. Large corporations wiped out tens of thousands of small businesses and uprooted millions of workers. New industries emerged. Production, transportation, and distribution were modernized. Even agriculture underwent a revolution. In fact, there is hardly an aspect of the US economy that escaped turmoil. Thus, there was a substantial degree of variation in the economy's performance both across and within the presidencies of the Gilded Age. So how can we best judge the different administrations?

To answer this question, this chapter presents an index of thirty-two years of indicators and estimates of those aspects of economic performance that Americans find most important. These data are then used to approximate a rough quantitative comparison of the economy under the presidents who served from 1869 until 1901. The economic data suggest that, in terms of presidential administrations, *the US economy appears to have flourished under Hayes, Harrison, and McKinley; was mixed or floundered under Grant (first term), Garfield, and Cleveland (first term); and crashed under Grant (second term), Arthur, and Cleveland (second term).* We can also use the same data to paint an introductory picture of how the overall US economy evolved during the Gilded Age. These are not intended as perfect, or final, assays of these presidents' economic performance. Rather, this exercise is meant to construct an initial, basic ranking upon which to build additional evidence in the subsequent chapters. A full explanation of data, sources, and methods can be found in the appendix, along with an open discussion of the strengths and weaknesses of such an approach. Finally, four types of theory currently attempt to describe the relationship between the president and the economy. Since the rest of this book tests these arguments, this chapter provides a brief explanation of them. Readers primarily interested in political and economic history can skip ahead to the next chapter.

Presidential Leadership in Feeble Times. Mark Zachary Taylor, Oxford University Press. © Oxford University Press 2024.
DOI: 10.1093/oso/9780197750742.003.0002

An Economic Comparison of the Gilded Age Presidents

What is the best way to compare the presidents' economic performance?[1] Today, mainstream economists, the media, and voters generally applaud an economy that simultaneously achieves these goals: increases national wealth, minimizes unemployment and inflation, and maintains a low balance-of-payments burden, while reducing the federal deficit and debt.[2] Most also cheer decreases in economic inequality, lower real interest rates, strong stock market performance, and a strong US dollar. Such conventional wisdom has not changed much since the Gilded Age. And it gives us a list of basic indicators with which to evaluate the economic performance of a president (Table 2.1).

The Gilded Age Economy: A Basic Overview

What do these measures, however imperfect, tell us about the Gilded Age economy? Chronologically, they tell the following story (represented in Figure 2.1). After the post–Civil War slowdown, the economy entered a decade of slow and uneven growth. It expanded from the end of 1867 through mid-1869, when it entered a mild recession that lasted for around eighteen months. After the close of 1870, the economy grew steadily through autumn 1873. Then came a steep, long recession that persisted until summer 1878. A powerful economic boom then ensued, which lasted until around spring 1882. At this time, another long but less severe recession slowly crept over the economy and gradually

Table 2.1 Basic Measures
of National Economic Performance

Strong Economic Growth

Low Unemployment

Low Inflation

Trade Surplus

Deficit Reduction

Debt Reduction

Economic Inequality Reduction

Strong Stock Market

Low Real Interest Rates

Strong US Dollar

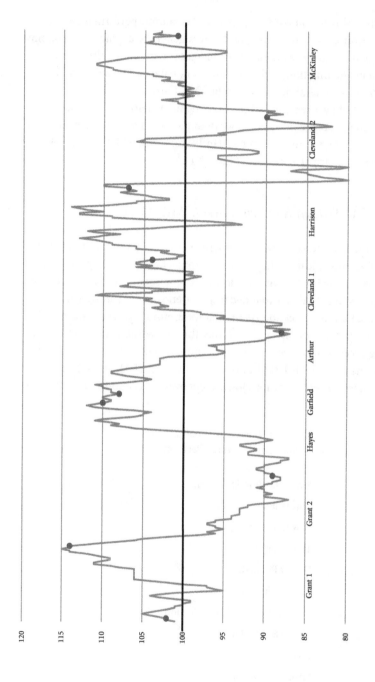

Figure 2.1 US business activity during the Gilded Age (trend = 100).

worsened until spring 1885. There was a year-long economic slowdown from spring 1887 until spring 1888, and then another from summer 1890 until spring 1891. Otherwise, the economy generally grew from spring 1885 until early 1893. Then catastrophe struck. A sudden, sharp economic decline turned into prolonged and severe economic depression that lasted until summer 1897, broken only by a shallow reprieve from mid-1894 through the end of 1895. After June 1897 the economy recovered and grew strong, interrupted only briefly by a six-month slowdown from mid-1899 until December 1900. In autumn 1901, when the Gilded Age ended,[3] the US economy had been expanding rapidly for almost a year.

Each individual indicator provides additional detail. For example, the overall trajectory was one of substantial economic growth, averaging over 4.4 percent per year. But perhaps half of this growth was due to population increases. In particular, over 9.9 million people (equivalent to just over one-quarter of the 1869 US population) immigrated permanently to the United States during the Gilded Age. Add in high domestic birth rates, and the US population doubled between 1869 and 1901, expanding an average of 2.2 percent each year. Thus, average economic growth *per capita* was only 1.9 percent annually, with some years topping 9 percent (1879, 1880, 1895, 1901), others contracting more than –2.5 percent (1870, 1874, 1888, and several years during the mid-1890s). In fact, when compared to the other rapid-growth economies of the Gilded Age, it becomes clear that the United States could have done even better (Table 2.2).

Other benchmarks illustrate the economic pressures on the country. For example, the Gilded Age was a period of overall deflation, with prices declining an average of –1.5 percent annually. There were only three years of measurable positive inflation, and even then it was small: 1880 (2.5 percent), 1900 (1.0 percent), and 1901 (1.0 percent). As corollary, the US dollar climbed in value 25 percent, regaining its pre–Civil War exchange rate against gold and the British pound by 1879.[4] Also, the federal government enjoyed budget surpluses every year, with the exceptions of the 1894–1899 period. Half of federal budget revenues came from tariffs on trade; the rest mostly came from domestic taxes on alcohol (25 percent of total) and tobacco (10 percent). Trade constituted around 12.3 percent of US GDP during the Gilded Age. And the US trade balance was rarely negative during this time, averaging an annual surplus worth 1.1 percent of GDP throughout the period. As a result, the enormous Civil War debt, still 30 percent of GDP in 1869, was paid down an average of 0.73 percentage points every year, with notable increases in debt occurring only in four years (1874, 1878, 1894, and 1896). And interest rates floated between 3.0 and 6.75 percent for high-quality borrowers, though bouts of deflation could take real rates even higher.

Table 2.2 Total Economic Growth (per Capita), 1869–1901

Switzerland	110%
Mexico*	87%
Chile	85%
Canada*	83%
Sweden	79%
USA	77%
Spain	64%
Denmark	60%
Norway	57%
Germany	54%
Finland	49%
France	41%
Belgium	40%
Japan*	37%
UK	33%
South Africa	33%
Netherlands	28%
Portugal	32%
Italy	23%

*1870–1901. Source: Bolt and Luiten van Zanden (2020), Maddison Project Database, version 2020.

An Economic Comparison of the Gilded Age Presidents

If we divide up the economic data described in Table 2.1 into an administration-by-administration comparison of the Gilded Age presidents, we get Table 2.3. *The general findings are that the US economy did relatively well under Hayes, Harrison, and McKinley; it was mixed under Grant (first term), Garfield, and Cleveland (first term); and it did relatively poorly under Grant (second term), Arthur, and Cleveland (second term).*

Of course, we should *not* conclude from Table 2.3 something like "Cleveland's first term was clearly better than Grant's first term" because of the former's small advantage in some column. Cognizant of the "uses and abuses" of presidential rankings,[5] the rankings presented here are not definitive; rather, they are

Table 2.3 Absolute Economic Performance (Chronological Order)

	Grant 1	Grant 2	Hayes	Garfield	Arthur	Cleveland 1	Harrison	Cleveland 2	McKinley
	1869–1873	1873–1877	1877–1881	1881	1881–1885	1885–1889	1889–1893	1893–1897	1897–1901
Per Capita Economic Growth	3.6%	0.4%	23.9%	1.0%	3.0%	1.6%	7.8%	1.2%	17.6%
Inflation (Prices)	−14.0%	−12.2%	−4.6%	0.0%	−4.1%	−3.4%	−4.4%	−7.3%	1.0%
Trade Balance	−0.62%	0.51%	2.06%	1.43%	0.84%	0.40%	0.79%	1.22%	2.75%
Budget (Surplus/Deficit)	0.99%	0.25%	0.32%	0.85%	0.96%	0.70%	0.36%	−0.18%	−0.06%
Federal Debt	−6.0pp	1.4pp	−5.4pp	−0.5pp	−3.8pp	−2.8pp	−2.4pp	1.7pp	−2.0pp
Inequality: Wealth-Income Ratio	10pp	39pp	−50pp	3pp	11pp	38pp	−9pp	44pp	−67pp
Stock Market	−0.6%	−38%	97%	0.20%	−30%	19%	2.30%	−21%	91%
Real Interest Rates	0.5 pp	−0.6 pp	−3.1 pp	−1.5 pp	1.3 pp	−0.4 pp	−0.01 pp	0.9 pp	−2.5 pp
US Dollar Strength	16%	2.3%	4.7%	0.2%	−0.4%	−0.2%	0%	−0.2%	−0.4%

Entries indicate change during the administration in percentage (%) or percentage points (pp). Trade, deficit, and debt are each per GDP. US dollar strength is versus the British pound. See appendix for full data description and sources.

expected to provoke constructive debate. The goal here is to create a general, albeit rough, comparison, not an exact or perfect scale of performance. In other words, my assertion is that we *can* say with relative confidence that presidents who rank high in several categories oversaw better economies than those presidents who rank at the bottom of several categories. And if we emphasize the topmost and bottommost performers across categories, then we get Table 2.4.

Again, these rankings and descriptions are *not* the final judgments, just the first steps. They build a foundation upon which to base the individual case studies that follow. Subsequent chapters tell the chronological story of the presidents, the economic issues of their day, and the politics surrounding them. The overall goal is to use both statistical data *and* qualitative evidence to test existing hypotheses and to generate a new theory about presidential power and effectiveness. Did the Gilded Age presidents matter, and if so, how? What, if anything, did the most successful administrations (those of Hayes and McKinley) share that was not present in the others? Did something change for both Grant and Cleveland between their first and second terms that might explain the dramatic change in the nation's economic performance at similar points in their respective administrations? In what ways was middle-ranking Harrison different from the economically successful presidents but similar to the failures? Or is there simply no relationship at all between these men and the economies they oversaw? Is it all a matter of luck, of being elected into an economic boom or bust? In the end, are presidents just economic bystanders who watch helplessly as the country gets tossed about by waves of prosperity and crisis? The remainder of this book attempts to answer these questions.

Major Theories of the President's Economic Performance

The debate over the relationship between the president and the economy is *not* a blank canvas. There are currently four major families of theory. The first category says simply that there is no relationship at all, and it comes in several varieties. Some describe Gilded Age presidents as weak, second-tier politicians. They were chosen more for their electability than for their political skill or policy expertise. Others argue that the presidency was then, and still is, a weak institution. Both formal and informal constraints on presidents meant that other competing actors or institutions were far more powerful than they. Still others argue that all presidents are victims of circumstance: they just happen to get elected during times of economic boom or bust. The second set of theories says simply that good economic performance is a product of the "right" set of policies; therefore, presidents who recognize and pursue the "right" policy agenda do well. A third category of theory argues that an individual president's performance in office is

Table 2.4 Relative Economic Performance

	Hayes	McKinley	Harrison	Garfield	Cleveland 1	Grant 1	Arthur	Grant 2	Cleveland 2
Economic Growth	+	+	+	–		–		–	–
Low Inflation	+	+		+	+	–		–	–
Trade Surplus	+	+		+	–	–		–	
Deficit Reduction	+	+		–			+	+	+
Debt Reduction	+			–		+	+	–	
Inequality Reduction	+	+	+		–	–	–	+	–
Stock Market	+	+			+		–	–	–
Low Interest Rates	+	+		+		–			–
Strong US Dollar	+	–			–	+		+	–

(+) TOP 3, (–) BOTTOM 3. Source: Table 2.3. Low inflation: highest scores given to administrations with annual inflation closest to 2 percent *and* between 0 and 2 percent; US dollar value declined measurably under Grant, but was similarly flat under the remaining presidents.

a function of his personal characteristics: character, psychology, experience, education, intelligence, and so on. And since presidents rarely act alone, a final set of theories awards credit or blame to the president's cabinet, staff, and advisors. Since we can test these explanations in the following chapters, let's dig deeper into them here.

No Relationship?

Perhaps the oldest and most widely held opinion, at least among experts, is that there is little relationship between the presidency and economic performance, and that Gilded Age presidents were least relevant of all. Certainly Gilded Age commentators thought this. During the late 19th century, presidents were widely criticized as being weak, ineffective, second-choice leaders, beholden to Congress or their parties.[6] In fact, the presidents themselves regularly complained about being treated like mere servants by congressmen eager for executive patronage to support their party machines.

Modern historians are often equally dismissive of the Gilded Age chief executives. For example, Richard White's recent opus on the era concludes, "Failed presidencies proliferated across the Gilded Age . . . [which] does not induce hagiography. Its presidents come from the Golden Age of Facial Hair, none of them seemingly worth remembering for any substantial achievement."[7] Lewis Gould, who held these presidents in high esteem, nevertheless lamented that "these [Gilded Age] presidents have fallen into an obscurity that makes them almost indistinguishable to modern readers"[8] Alan Peskin likewise mourned their depiction as "that gray procession of bearded politicos."[9] Some historians blame a power-hungry Congress that overstepped its constitutional bounds.[10] Others indict the corrupt spoils system that allowed the party bosses who controlled patronage to effectively select and manage America's presidents.[11] In this telling, the late 19th-century Republican and Democratic party platforms blurred together on most issues or prioritized local over national concerns. Gilded Age voters therefore divided themselves more among rival political machines than along policy lines. Presidents existed only to administrate the dole.

Many presidential scholars are similarly derisive of the Gilded Age, though for different reasons. The great Richard Neustadt famously dismissed premodern executives as mostly irrelevant because they dealt with "nothing really comparable" to the constant "emergencies in policies" faced by 20th-century presidents.[12] Arthur M. Schlesinger Jr. agreed, arguing that "there were no urgent new issues in foreign affairs to encourage a revival of the [Imperial] Presidency" during the Gilded Age.[13] More categorically, in their sweeping surveys, *The American Presidency*, Sidney Milkis and Michael Nelson have consistently argued that "the presidency remained small in scale and limited in power during the latter decades of the nineteenth century."[14] William Howell and Terry Moe likewise contend, "Until the Progressive Era, the American bureaucracy was tiny, underdeveloped, and filled with patronage employees." As a result, "American government [during the Gilded Age] was so parochial and corrupt that it had little motivation to address . . . vexing new problems, and it was so incompetent that it couldn't have even if it wanted to."[15] Andrew Rudalevige takes a different tack. He argues that premodern presidents did not have the necessary staff to process vital policy information, nor did they leverage their institutional advantages (e.g., executive orders) to have much impact.[16] As a result, "[f]or the eighteenth and much of the nineteenth centuries, Presidential leadership of government was the exception, not the rule."[17] Such unambiguous generalizations have led Richard Ellis to complain:

> In this interpretation, there is not a great deal to be gained from close investigation of pre-modern presidents because the demands placed upon them and the resources at their disposal were qualitatively unlike the expectations and opportunities for leadership in the modern presidency. Presidents of the late eighteenth, nineteenth, and early twentieth centuries are therefore largely of antiquarian interest.[18]

Economists and business and finance scholars are inconclusive. Some economic studies of the presidency and the economy do argue for a general relationship, but they tend to either omit the Gilded Age or suffer from selection bias. Most also credit a political party rather than presidential leadership as the driving force.[19] Broader studies of "political business cycles" are more comprehensive, but they report more mixed results.[20] For example, depending on the evidence and analysis used, some scholars observe such cycles,[21] while others do not.[22] Others point the finger at presidential elections or the victor's party affiliation rather than the individual president, and even these studies differ widely.[23] Still others prioritize the midterms.[24] Perhaps most important, the few studies that focus on the Gilded Age find little or no evidence of political business cycles.[25]

Political Science on the Gilded Age

Only a handful of political scientists have delved deep into Gilded Age political economy; their arguments are more subtle but similarly dismissive of presidential effectiveness. Richard Bensel has argued that the dynamics of industrialization were so complex that no single actor could manage all the intricate political deals and trade-offs necessary to provide leadership.[26] Individual presidents might occasionally exercise influence through their vetoes, but these were usually cast against minor legislation (e.g., grants of federal aid to individuals). Instead, Bensel argues, the Republican Party played the role of political-economic "broker" during the Gilded Age. Thus, only as the leader of his party might a president have real impact, and no executive achieved this until McKinley, and only after 1898.

Gilded Age presidents are likewise minor players in Elizabeth Saunders's and Samuel DeCanio's accounts of the era's politics.[27] Instead, Saunders argues that farmers were the pivotal actors. They organized into massive blocs of voters and activists who, with occasional help from organized labor, fought against the "rampaging capitalism" of northern and eastern bankers and industrialists. It was these battles that determined the political-economic evolution of late 19th-century America. DeCanio locates power more with the rampaging capitalists and party elites. In either case, presidents, and their policies, were more effects than causes.

Stephen Skowronek's deep dive into Gilded Age political development describes a premodern political-economy dominated by political parties and the courts, not presidents.[28] Administrative power was highly decentralized. As a result, "[t]he [Gilded Age] President had never risen far above the status of a clerk. . . . The only truly national officer in American government and the sensible head of the national administrative apparatus found its political and institutional resources hostage to local party bosses in Congress."[29] Over time, the forces of industrialization, mediated by battles for influence among government officials, changed these dynamics. Power would eventually accrete in the hands of professional bureaucrats in the executive branch. But this transformation would not occur until the early 20th century. Nor was the presidency a key factor in the shift. Hence Skowronek concludes, "So far as institutional politics was concerned, the particular incumbent in the office of the chief executive seemed to matter little."[30]

The Politics Presidents Make

Later, Skowronek mostly marginalized the effectiveness of presidents as individuals. Instead, he argues that presidential success is both subjective and follows historical cycles. Great "reconstructive" presidents establish new political commitments to particular ideologies and interests. They are typically followed by "articulation" presidents who flesh out and fulfill these commitments. Occasionally "preemptive" presidents will rise from the opposition, but they will be forced to govern from within the established regime as long as it remains resilient. Eventually, policy failures and crises will cause the previously established regime to lose support. It will crumble under the watch of a defensive "disjunctive" president affiliated with it. Then a new "reconstructive" president will arise to establish new political commitments to new ideologies and interests. The cycle then repeats itself. Hence, presidential performance has less to do with individual leadership and more with the historical circumstances of a president's rise to office.[31]

In fact, in his now classic discussion of "political time," Skowronek found no Gilded Age president worthy of much mention.[32] There were no high-impact "reconstructive" presidents who committed the nation to new political-economic regimes. Nor were there "disjunctive" executives who "sever[ed] the political moorings of the old regime and cast it adrift without anchor or orientation."[33] Cleveland is discussed, but only as a bizarre "anomaly" not well explained by Skowronek's theory, though still revealing of presidential power. McKinley earns attention, but only to provide background for Skowronek's much larger analysis of Theodore Roosevelt.[34]

Getting Policy "Right"

One obvious presumption is that the economy performed well when the president pursued the "right" set of policies. In other words, economic performance is less about individual leaders and more about identifying and implementing the best policy agenda for the circumstances. In particular, it is often assumed that tight monetary policy (i.e., in pursuit of rejoining the international gold standard at the dollar's pre–Civil War value) doomed the United States to recurring crises and recessions during the Gilded Age.[35] From Grant onward, most presidents favored this course of action. None supported blatantly inflationary policy. If only they had the insight, or guts, to print more money, then all those nasty financial panics and years of depression could have been avoided! A natural corollary to this argument is that the Gilded Age economy faltered because people simply misunderstood economics at the time. The field was still in its infancy. Even experts lacked the data, methods, and tools of analysis necessary to develop accurate models of how the economy worked and what government could, and should, do.

Character, Psychology, Experience, Intelligence

Harking back to essayist Thomas Carlyle's claim that "the history of the world is but the biography of great men," another set of long-held beliefs is that a president's personal characteristics determine his effectiveness.[36] Some scholars highlight presidential character, emphasizing a legion of factors, ranging from honesty to curiosity, from religiosity to work ethic.[37] All of these theoretically affect a leader's ability to identify and solve problems, create consensus, work with essential allies, communicate strategies, and implement solutions. Other research focuses on intelligence, education, or prior experience.[38] For example, economic policy is intellectually difficult. Therefore, one could argue that presidents with greater intelligence or education (especially in economics) should do better.[39] Or that executives with prior business experience should have a better understanding of the economy, and therefore of what government can do to help it.[40] Similarly, the practice of politics, policy, and legislative management is difficult. So too is administration. Leadership in these areas is arguably a skill developed over time. Therefore managerial and leadership experience should matter.[41] Still others believe that some people are just born to lead.[42] In this view, leadership is a product of genes or early environment. Hence the sources of great leadership can be found in one's youth.

Presidential Staff and Advisors

Finally, presidents do not act alone. They are rarely experts in economics. Therefore, many scholars point to the president's circle of advisors, staff, and appointees as essential for an administration's effectiveness and ultimate success.[43] Also, during the Gilded Age, cabinet members possessed ample resources and political influence with which to affect policy. More to the point, they were considered "virtually autonomous, subject to congressional oversight but not presidential control."[44] For example, the secretary of the treasury had a near monopoly on monetary policy. The secretary of the interior held sway over vast tracts of federal lands. The postmaster general controlled tens of thousands of politically valuable patronage appointments. The State Department played an influential role in trade negotiations and export promotion. The Navy and War departments had deep pockets for federal contracts and employment. Such powers could be used to aid or thwart a president's agenda. Most cabinet members were also party (or faction) leaders, influential ex-legislators, or prominent businessmen. Thus they could play essential roles in coalition-building, *if* they so chose. But they could also embarrass an administration with corruption or incompetence, or pursue their own personal interests.

* * *

The remainder of this book will chronologically explore the Gilded Age to test these theories and to generate new ones. Each chapter will either delve deep into a particular president and his administration(s) or explain broader trends affecting the presidency and the economy during the Gilded Age. The final chapter will go deeper into theory, analysis, and results. It will also offer new hypotheses about causal mechanisms: *why* and *how* presidents affected economic performance. But to start our historical journey, we need to better understand the Gilded Age. What was the American economy like, and how did it get there? What was the presidency like, and how had it evolved over time? And how did the two interact over the course of the 19th century? Also, how did Americans think about politics, policy, and the economy? How did these beliefs inform their expectations, behavior, and preferences? The next two chapters tackle these questions and guide us into the fascinating drama that was the American Gilded Age.

3

Prelude

The Civil War

What sort of economy, and political system, did US presidents inherit at the start of the Gilded Age? Technological change and globalization were the primary driving forces throughout the period. Over the years, they generated battles over tariffs, monopolies, labor, immigration, industrialization, and inequality, which dominated American politics and created pivotal moments for its presidents. But as the US economy headed into the Gilded Age, it was developments left over from the Civil War (1861–1865) that challenged Americans and their leaders most.

The Civil War and the US Economy, 1861–1865

By far the greatest impact of the Civil War was its tremendous human destruction.[1] Barely a household in the country was left untouched by some sort of suffering.[2] All told, approximately 750,000 soldiers and sailors died, constituting around 2.4 percent of the US population, but 13 percent of all white men of military age, and 22.6 percent of Confederate men aged twenty to twenty-four in 1860.[3] Another 476,000 men were wounded, while 400,000 went missing or wound up in military prisons. An additional 50,000 civilians were estimated to be killed. Meanwhile, native births declined around 10 percent, while the first years of the conflict frightened away European immigrants.[4] Between casualties, lost births, and low immigration, the Civil War likely resulted in a population deficit of 3 million by 1870.

In raw economic terms, the Civil War remains *the* most expensive endeavor in American history. Direct government expenditures totaled $3.3 billion for both sides (roughly $9 trillion in 2020 dollars).[5] Another $1.5 billion was lost in property destruction, mostly in the Confederacy.[6] Together, those losses alone put the base economic cost of the Civil War roughly equivalent to 100 percent of US GDP in 1860. We might further add to the bill the financial penalties in human lives and limbs, which economists have calculated at $1.8 billion.[7] And since most soldiers were unskilled physical laborers, the wounded survivors suffered

Presidential Leadership in Feeble Times. Mark Zachary Taylor, Oxford University Press. © Oxford University Press 2024.
DOI: 10.1093/oso/9780197750742.003.0003

income losses for decades.[8] Indirect costs (i.e., the opportunity cost of lost peaceful economic growth) add another $14.7 billion.[9] To pay the Union's share of direct war expenditures, federal spending exploded from 2 percent of GDP (1860) to 13.8 percent (1865) in just five years. The South lost over $3 billion invested in slave labor and the highly profitable plantation system built upon it.[10]

To pay for the Union's war effort, the administration of Abraham Lincoln (1861–1865) ran into financial trouble almost immediately upon his entering office. Thanks to the Panic of 1857 and the lowest tax and tariffs rates in history to date, the US federal government was already deep in deficit and debt when the Civil War began.[11] Interest rates leaped temporarily as high as 12 percent when the fighting broke out.[12] Since Southern cotton was America's primary export, accounting for perhaps half of all US exports, secession cut off the North from vital tariff revenues, but without much affecting its demand for imports. The Union also had to pay for a massive military buildup. In early 1861, the US Army had only 16,000 troops, most stationed on the western frontier, equipped with antique rifles and few small arms. In contrast, the Confederates had already mustered some 60,000 troops, with thousands more volunteering every week. Lincoln had to ramp up quickly if the nation was to remain intact. So, in mid-April, he called for 75,000 volunteer soldiers and sailors, followed in May by a request for 83,000 more recruits.[13] These men required guns, ammunition, uniforms, tents, food, wagons, horses, watercraft, and other essential supplies. How to pay for it all?

Trade and Tariffs

Tariff hikes were the Union's initial solution.[14] In late 1860, Southerners deserted Congress to join the Confederacy, thereby eliminating most political opposition to new tariff legislation.[15] This allowed protectionist Republicans to pass the Morrill Tariff of 1861 just days before Lincoln's inauguration. It levied new duties on a wide range of consumer and industrial goods. Then, once in office, the Lincoln administration embraced still higher tariffs as an "indispensable" source of wartime income.[16] Henceforth, on a regular basis, the president and Congress raised and expanded import duties in order to pay for the war. As a result, the average tariff on dutiable imports bounded from a 19th-century low of 18.8 percent (1861) to 36 percent (1862) in just the first year and eventually reached 47.6 percent by the end of the war (1865). Although the country would accept these tariffs as a necessity of war and an aid to American manufacturing, they would become a major political battleground during the Gilded Age.

Debt and Taxes

At first, most observers believed that the Morrill tariffs and traditional bond sales would cover the Union's war expenses. In fact, when conflict began, the Lincoln administration expected to quash the Confederate rebellion after a few small engagements.[17] These would not be too costly. Many in the North also assumed that most Southerners quietly opposed secession. Hence, the Union army volunteers recruited in spring 1861 were contracted to serve just ninety days. Lincoln also initially left it to the individual state governments to raise, train, clothe, house, and equip their volunteers. The federal government would take over expenses after that.[18] It would all be over by summer. "Jeff Davis & Co. will be swinging from the battlements at Washington at least by the 4th of July," promised the *New York Tribune*.[19]

However, just ten minor battles and skirmishes took place during spring 1861, resolving nothing. Nor did Southerners abandon their support for secession. Thus the military buildup dragged on. War costs quickly skyrocketed beyond all expectations, rendering inadequate the tariff revenues created earlier in the year. Only new taxes, debt, and inflation would do the job. Therefore, when the new Congress met in special session on Independence Day, July 4, 1861, it dramatically increased federal resources to fight the war. Over the next few weeks, Congress authorized the Union military to recruit 1 million men. And to pay for them, Congress increased and expanded tariffs on popular consumer goods such as sugar, liquor, cigars, iron, chocolate, fish, and coffee. Since these taxes fell most heavily on the poor and middle class, Congress also passed the nation's first income tax, directed at the wealthy, the following month.[20]

The US Treasury was further authorized to create the first national paper currency of the United States. When war broke out, Americans were using a combination of gold coins (47 percent of currency in circulation, mostly used for large transactions) and state banknotes supposedly backed by specie deposits (also 47 percent, mostly for small daily transactions) to conduct business. The new federal currency took the form of "Demand Notes," so called because they were redeemable on demand for gold coin at the Treasury. But Lincoln's gold supplies were rapidly diminishing. The nation's ample silver supply was of little help; although legal tender, silver was not used much as currency. Its value as metal had consistently exceeded its legally fixed price as coin since 1836; therefore most silver owners chose not to coin it.[21] As a result, silver constituted just 4.8 percent of US currency in 1860 and was rapidly headed lower.

The solution was mountains of new federal debt. In the first of many major debt offerings, in July 1861, Congress authorized an unprecedented $250 million in new war bonds. This was roughly equal to 5.6 percent of US GDP, or four times the previous year's federal expenditures. During summer and autumn

1861, the Treasury secretary attempted to place this extraordinary debt issue with the government's traditional funders: a handful of large banks in Boston, New York, and Philadelphia. However, he encountered considerable trouble. Some Northern bankers and wealthy families had strong financial connections to the South and firmly opposed the war.[22] Also, the surprising Confederate victory at First Manassas (First Bull Run) in mid-July, and questions about Britain's willingness to tolerate interdictions of Southern trade, worried investors that the Union war effort might fail. Moreover, the war was slow-going. To win, the North had to actively defeat armies and navies and seize territory, which it was not doing; the Confederates had only to defend and survive.[23] Lincoln needed momentum. But he was not getting it. Nor did widely expected Southern regret over secession manifest itself, only enthusiasm. Hopes for a quick end to the conflict began to fade. And with those hopes went US bond sales.

The financial axe came down in early December 1861, when the US Treasury issued a dire report on the Union's fiscal situation.[24] It described "expenditure far beyond" original limits set by Congress and warned that "the limits must be still further extended."[25] In short, the United States could no longer pay for the war under existing financial arrangements. Worried savers now began to hoard their gold coins. Fearing a run on their gold inventories, many of New York's largest banks stopped exchanging their specie for paper notes at the end of the month. The federal government immediately followed suit. The supply of paper money soon vastly exceeded the amount of gold meant to back it. Therefore paper notes could no longer be freely exchanged for gold at face value. By New Year's Day, the United States was off the antebellum gold standard![26]

Desperate for war funding, Congress took even more extraordinary action in the early months of 1862. In addition to new tariffs and domestic taxes, it authorized $500 million in interest-bearing war debt, the largest federal liability issued to date.[27] However, having just gorged on a massive tranche of war debts the previous year, few banks desired these new debentures.

The solution was Jay Cooke and the "democratization" of American debt finance.[28] An innovative banker and staunch pro-Union supporter, Cooke offered to serve as the Treasury's bond broker. Winning an exclusive contract in October 1862, Cooke set up offices nationwide and hired a few thousand salesmen to sell Treasury bonds in small amounts to everyday Americans. A marketing genius, Cooke "invoked God, country, and manifest destiny to make their purchase seem a patriotic duty" to sell Union bonds in small, affordable denominations.[29] He printed ads in newspapers. His salesmen knocked on doors and visited farms. Cooke was also the first to make extensive use of the telegraph to conduct bond transactions.[30] His sales campaign was so successful that the Treasury's entire tranche sold off by January 1864. And when Treasury officials had trouble placing a second massive bond drive worth $830 million, they again turned to Cooke.[31]

Myriad other government securities were also offered to the general public. Prior to Cooke, only the wealthy held bonds; even fewer owned stocks.[32] Hence, few Americans cared about the doings of Wall Street. But by the war's end, somewhere between 500,000 and 3 million average citizens had purchased Union war bonds, in denominations as small as $50, worth a total of $2.3 billion.[33] Now men and women who had never before been "investors" held US debt; a large secondary market for bonds emerged on the newly named New York Stock Exchange, which finally constructed its own building in which to conduct daily transactions.[34] Boston and Philadelphia also had bond and stock markets, but bankrolling the war (and the railroads) turned New York City into the nation's financial capital. In fact, during 1864 New York briefly became the only city in the world where investors could transact twenty-four hours a day.[35] Soon the country was flooded with manuals and how-to books for individual investors, while new periodicals like the *Commercial and Financial Chronicle* (1862) and *The Stockholder* (1862) appeared to satiate the popular demand for investment news and analysis.[36] These changes put the gyrations of Wall Street at the center of bank "panics" and economic recessions throughout the Gilded Age.

From 1862 onward, Congress also heaped on ever more federal taxes.[37] Certainly antebellum Americans were not unfamiliar with taxation. States, counties, and cities had taxed all sorts of goods, services, income streams, and economic endeavors since the Founding. But for around sixty years, the federal government had mostly relied on tariffs and land sales to fund its few activities. Now, with war costs mounting relentlessly higher, Congress expanded the federal tax regime. Patriotic Americans gave it widespread support, seeing their payments as demonstrating their loyalty to the Union. "It is my duty, yes . . . my privilege, to do it," bragged one wealthy Illinois taxpayer.[38]

The new wartime taxes hit a consistently broader variety of revenue sources. First came heavy "sin" taxes on alcohol and tobacco that would remain a major source of federal revenues throughout the Gilded Age. Next were controversial direct taxes on citizens. To conform with the Constitution, these levies were set according to population and left to state governments to collect. Also, the first federal corporate taxes were created. Granted, corporations were still rare.[39] Taxes on them took the form of a 3 percent levy targeted at sales of manufactured goods, railroad services, and other industrial products.

Still more taxes came. Federal income taxes were increased and expanded into the middle class. Bank assets were taxed. Corporate dividends and interest payments were taxed. Federal levies were placed on playing cards, carriages, billiard tables, medicines, insurance, and all sorts of professions. Congress even revived taxes on wills and estates, graduated by size and degree of relationship to the deceased.[40] And to administrate this enormous federal tax regime, Congress created the Office of the Commissioner of Internal Revenue within the

Department of the Treasury—the antecedent of our modern Internal Revenue Service. After the war, Gilded Age presidents would regularly demand that these taxes be reduced or eliminated. Many were, but some levies remained for decades.

The Greenback

In yet another attempt to fund the war, in early 1862 desperate legislators passed the Legal Tender Act, which authorized the Treasury to print $150 million of paper notes as a *temporary* wartime expedient.[41] Printed in green ink on their obverse to thwart counterfeiting, they became known as "greenbacks." Greenbacks were government debt, but without any premiums paid to the holder. They were interest-free loans to the government. To give them economic value, Congress made greenbacks legal for use "in payment of all taxes, internal duties, excises, debts, and demands of every kind due to the United States, except duties on imports [which were to be paid in gold]."[42] And if the bearers wished, the new law allowed them to convert larger sums of greenbacks into interest-paying bonds.[43]

During the 1870s, the paper greenback would become a major headache for presidents, policymakers, and investors alike. They were small, uniform, accepted by government, and printed in dollar denominations. In other words, greenbacks looked and acted like currency. Therefore, Americans began using them as such. And since they were plentiful, greenbacks rapidly supplanted gold, and even banknotes, in circulation.[44] But since they were backed by nothing more than the government's word and printed aggressively, their market value plummeted during the Civil War. When first issued, $100 in greenbacks could be exchanged for a similar value of gold coin; just two years later, at their nadir (July 1864), they bought just $35.09 in gold.[45] For over a decade after the war was over, whether and how to bring greenbacks back to "parity" became *the* most important economic policy debate in American politics.

Banking

The Civil War also forced a revolution in the American financial system. Antebellum banks had tended to be small, disparate, local, and poorly regulated.[46] In 1860, the United States had roughly sixteen hundred of them, most chartered by their state's government, spread throughout the country. State regulations largely prohibited branch banking. Some states banned banking altogether. Nor was there a uniform US currency. Instead, banks printed their own banknotes, supposedly backed by deposits, which operated alongside gold coins as the means of daily business transactions (silver coins having mostly fallen into disuse). Hence state banknotes varied in value against one another according to distance and trustworthiness. Merchants and tellers consulted weekly "Bank Note Reporters" to figure out exchange rates and to detect ubiquitous counterfeits.[47] As for the federal government, the US Treasury minted coins and set their price, but otherwise did little to regulate the nation's financial institutions. Instead, regulatory power was distributed among several financial centers (e.g., New York City, Boston, Philadelphia) and thirty-three state governments. All told, this meant that bank and currency regulation was spotty, usually minimal. And by 1862 these state-chartered banks, and their counterfeiters, were printing a multitude of paper notes in all sorts of denominations to compensate for shortages in specie. Partly as a result, annual inflation ran over 14 percent.

To bring order to this monetary chaos, Congress passed the National Banking Act in late February 1863, followed by important revisions a year later. With these new laws, Congress created a distinct class of federally chartered banks, or "national banks," authorized to print $300 million of their own currency.[48] These banknotes were required to be physically uniform, trade at par with one another, and be redeemable at any national bank. No longer would the market value of different $1 banknotes fluctuate against one another, at least not for national banks. These new national banknotes also had to be backed by US bonds held in reserve at the Treasury rather than by gold or the bank's word.[49] Thus, unlike state-chartered banks, if a national bank went bust, its notes could theoretically still be redeemed at the Treasury. And to privilege the notes of national banks, and gradually eliminate the kaleidoscope of dodgy state banknotes, the Act levied a tax on state banknotes in order to drive them out of circulation. This was largely achieved, but not until 1867.[50]

The Banking Acts further enhanced New York City's position as America's financial center by making *its* national banks members of a central national banking reserve. Smaller banks around the country were required to place deposits into ever larger banks, creating a pyramid of reserves with New York banks at its pinnacle. For the rest of the 19th century, this meant that reserves tended to accumulate in New York City, where they were exposed to disruptions on Wall Street.[51] In reverse, every spring and fall, millions of farmers sucked money out of New York City in the form of loans to pay for planting and harvest. Like an economic bellows pushing money back and forth across the country, both movements caused regular credit contractions, which contributed to the bank panics and recessions that became endemic to the Gilded Age.[52]

The Treasury Department was the other major benefactor. Before the war, state and private banks were the major players in markets for currency, specie, and debt. Meanwhile, Jacksonians in government worked to reduce and isolate federal finances (i.e., through "independent banking" and the "sub-Treasury" system).[53] Now those positions were suddenly reversed. The Treasury became the legal bank of issue for hundreds of millions of greenbacks, which quickly surpassed the circulation of private bank notes. Record federal debt issuance and gold collections simultaneously transformed the Treasury into *the* largest domestic player in these markets as well. And since the Treasury's financial operations powerfully influenced the amount of money and credit available to the banks, it gave the US president and his Treasury secretary unprecedented power over the nation's money supply, and hence the economy. Though few realized it at the time.

The Corruption of the Civil Service

The Civil War also transformed civil service reform into a national political-economic issue going into the Gilded Age. First, the war generated an avalanche of lucrative military contracts potentially vulnerable to graft.[54] By 1865, annual federal expenditures had reached an unprecedented 13.8 percent of GDP, while federal revenue collections had grown to roughly 3.5 percent of GDP. Other legislation sold off or gave away millions of acres of federal land for particular uses (i.e., railroads, homesteads, Indian reservations). To manage it all required a rapid expansion of the federal workforce. The Lincoln administration hired tens of thousands of bureaucrats, most steadfast Republicans. Soon accusations of fraud, corruption, and profiteering were rampant, especially against contracting middlemen.[55]

Second, the Republican Party badly needed political "glue" to keep its leaders united and their supporters loyal as the war wound down. After all, the party was a new political organization, formed just a decade earlier in 1854. At first, they had been united by antislavery, then the war became their common cause. To further broaden their support, Republicans had added trade protectionism, national banking, land grants, industrialization, and immigration to their platform. But they still lacked the deep networks of money and support that Democrats had enjoyed since the 1830s.[56] Thus, as the Civil War drew to a close, many expected, even hoped, that the Republican Party would begin to disintegrate.

So, during the 1864 campaign season, Republican leaders turned to assessments on patronage to fund election campaigns. "Patronage," a tradition since the Jackson era, was the appointment of tens of thousands of political supporters to government jobs.[57] It was a system originally created to incentivize political participation, deepen democracy, and give average citizens (rather than wealthy elites) a chance to participate in government. At the federal level, appointments were made by the president, typically at the direction of individual senators, with little regard to the education, experience, or qualifications of the appointee. Party loyalty and campaign activism were the primary requirements. Now the recipients were expected to donate 2 to 7 percent of their pay in "assessments" to the Republican Party. When first practiced by the Democrats, patronage had involved perhaps ten thousand jobs. But with the growth of wartime government, the number of federal jobs had quintupled. These jobs were also usually undemanding and sometimes quite lucrative. This made them simultaneously a valuable source of campaign funds and a breeding ground for corruption and inefficiency.

The "moiety system" was another infamous source of government waste and corruption. Moieties were a "piece of the action" given to federal revenue agents, meant to incentivize collections. That is, when a tariff, fine, or fee was collected or property confiscated, that revenue was split between the government and the collector, as well as any naval officer, port surveyor, or informer involved.[58] Together with salary, these moieties could lift the incomes of some federal collectors above that of the president himself. Hence moieties inspired widespread bribery and penalty inflation.

Political machines stood atop the entire system of patronage, moieties, and obligatory campaign donations.[59] Infamous for their influence in Boston, New York, Chicago, and Philadelphia, political machines were usually based in cities and established on a foundation of poor ethnic immigrants. They doled out jobs, government contracts, and other sources of assistance in return for votes and political support. State legislatures, controlled by the machines, also elected US senators, who then exercised their "privilege" of advising the president on federal appointments. Controlling each machine was its "boss." Powerful figures throughout the Gilded Age, they were described by one foreign contemporary thus: "He dispenses places, rewards the loyal, punishes the mutinous, concocts schemes, negotiates treaties. He generally avoids publicity, preferring the substance to the pomp of power, and is all the more dangerous because he sits, like a spider, hidden in the midst of his web. He is a Boss."[60]

In sum, these practices meant that appointments to important jobs in the executive branch were made with little regard to capabilities or character. Instead, service to the local political party determined who ran the nation's postal service, customshouses, and land management bureaus. And too often much of the money made by these appointees was either pocketed or funneled back into the machine. As a result, "professionalism was almost nonexistent in the civil service, and politics permeated it to the core," writes one scholar of the system.[61] But the rapidly modernizing economy increasingly demanded a skilled, educated bureaucracy to manage it. Hence, the incompetence and corruption of patronage appointees infuriated more and more Americans. As these problems multiplied during the Gilded Age, pressure built for reform.

The Melting Pot

Immigration provided essential fodder for the American economy but created a political can of worms. Originally, the US Constitution gave to the federal government power over naturalization, but not immigration, which was left to the states. And until the Civil War, individual state governments used this power to attract settlers, to bar criminals and the poor, and sometimes to prohibit immigrants of particular races. Meanwhile, Congress granted citizenship to free white immigrants "of good character" and who had resided in the United States for several years. At times, the federal government also assumed the authority to deport those noncitizens deemed a threat (e.g., the Alien and Sedition Acts).[62]

Since the new nation was rich in land and natural resources but scare in labor, new settlers were generally in high demand. And thanks to troubles in Europe and economic opportunities in the United States, immigration climbed to levels unsurpassed to this day (on a per resident basis) during the mid-1840s through the mid-1850s.[63] But the antebellum immigrant pool was neither particularly diverse nor widely diffused. When the Civil War began, over 90 percent of America's foreign-born were from northern and western Europe, particularly Great Britain, Ireland, and Germany, and most had settled in the Northern states.[64] Nor was antebellum immigration without controversy—Catholic arrivals in particular prompted fierce nativist animosity.[65]

The outbreak of the Civil War throttled immigration rates. Already depressed by the Panic of 1857, foreign arrivals plummeted to twenty-year lows during 1861–1862.[66] With wartime demand for labor high and in need of settlers for western development, Lincoln and the Republican Congress responded with legislation to promote mass immigration, including land grants (the Homestead Act of 1862) and the Contract Labor Act of 1864.[67] The latter of these encouraged employers to recruit foreign workers and to fund their passage to the United States in return for labor contracts, which would be enforced by state and federal courts. The legislation did the trick. Immigration recovered toward the end of the Civil War and henceforth followed the business cycle. But these contract laborers, woven together with new conceptions of work and citizenship, would ultimately prove divisive and transformational during the Gilded Age.

Western Settlement, Farmers, and the Rise of Labor during the Civil War

The Civil War altered the American economy in still other dramatic and unexpected ways. For example, in 1860 most land west of the 95th meridian—which falls roughly across Minneapolis, Des Moines, Kansas City, and

Shreveport—remained unsettled by whites.[68] Much of this was federal property. But political battles between pro- and antislavery forces had prevented legislation to open it for settlement. In 1862, the Republican Congress took advantage of secession to pass the Homestead Act. Targeted at the poor, it offered plots of 160 acres in the Midwest and Great Plains to any American family in return for a small fee and a promise to work the land for five years.[69] By the war's end, some 288 million acres had been given to fifteen thousand families, with more to come.[70] In other legislation to develop the West, another 328 million acres of federal land was given to the state governments. Meanwhile, the Pacific Railway Act of 1862 offered government bonds and vast grants of federal land to assist "men of talent, men of character, men who are willing to invest" in constructing the nation's first transcontinental railroad. The Lincoln administration considered these acts essential to maintaining western support for the Union.[71] They continued a wave of federal land grants that, between 1850 and 1871, gave some 130 million acres to the railroads, roughly the size of New England and the northern Mid-Atlantic states *combined*.[72] After considerable investment and sacrifice—the latter borne heavily by the Native Americans who lived there—these federal land grants produced enormous yields of grain and livestock, transported to market by the railroads, and therefore played a powerful role in the Gilded Age economy and politics.[73]

Thanks to military conscription, there was not enough farm labor to meet wartime demand for agricultural products; hence mechanization in agriculture leaped ahead during the Civil War and then continued for years after. Mechanical cultivators, reapers, threshers, riding plows, harrows, seed drills, forage mowers, twine binders, and other machines appeared on farms throughout the country.[74] At first, these new farm technologies were still powered by men or animals; thus productivity per acre did not increase nearly so much as did total land under cultivation. In Texas, ranching took off going into the Gilded Age, thanks in part to the advent of "spiked fencing" (barbed wire) during the late 1860s.[75] And soon after railheads were completed in Kansas and Missouri around 1865, American "cowboys" began their now iconic cattle drives to deliver enormous herds for shipment east.[76] All told, national production of wheat, corn, barley, hogs, and beef began to skyrocket, causing prices to fall throughout the postbellum period.

Meanwhile, as globalization increased, the US agricultural economy became ever more vulnerable. Output spikes and demand slumps in Europe could send American prices plummeting. Financial disruptions abroad could affect the availability of credit and loans in the United States. For many farmers, the obvious solution was cheaper machines and manufactured goods, which meant lower tariffs on imports. They also sought lower interest rates on farm loans. Or they lobbied for greater access to foreign markets. Hence political pressure for tariff reductions, anti-monopoly legislation, and "soft money" grew going into the Gilded Age.[77]

The war cut both ways for urban labor. On the one hand, jobs were plentiful and wages soared over 42 percent during the conflict, while immigration briefly fell to generational lows. However, high inflation bit into workers' purchasing power, and working conditions soured. And as the railroads knitted together the country into a national economic market, workers in Chicago factories increasingly found themselves in competition with their brethren in places like Cincinnati, New York, and Pittsburgh. Thus labor union membership increased as the war progressed. By 1864, there were an estimated 270 unions with over 200,000 members, including 32 national unions, more than at any time to date.[78] They called for higher wages, better working conditions, an end to convict labor, restrictions on Chinese immigrant labor, and, above all else, an eight-hour workday. These demands were collected by the National Labor Union, the country's first nationwide labor federation, formed in 1866.[79] It succeeded in getting the Contract Labor Act repealed in 1868, though this merely ended federal encouragement of the practice; it did not ban it. So diverse were labor's grievances, and so common their foes with other groups, that labor soon merged its cause with those of Greenbackers, anti-monopolists, land reformers, and even women's rights activists, until "no clear division" existed between them.[80] Labor would become a vibrant political force during the Gilded Age, but usually not a decisive one.

The War and the Press

The Civil War also transformed American journalism. Antebellum newspapers were typically controlled, even owned, by a particular political party, individual politicians, or their supporters. Circulations were therefore small and heavily subsidized. Government printing contracts, granted by political allies, further helped to keep them afloat. Subscription revenues were another essential lifeline. Presidents often relied on these expensive rags—of which newspapers were then made—to communicate their agenda and rally support.[81] And since news-gathering was expensive, these papers—often weeklies—focused on cheap political invective and opinion. There were few professional journalists. Correspondents were, quite literally, friends of the newspaper in distant cities who sent missives about events there. Thus, "[r]eporting of news was incidental, unorganized, and obviously subordinated to editorial partisanship."[82]

The grip of the political parties had loosened with the advent of the "penny papers" during the 1830s.[83] These daily publications cut down on political commentary in favor of far more interesting local news: important legal cases, delicious scandals, shocking crime stories, and notes on high society. They cost just 16 percent of the traditional weekly's price. And they were hawked on the street by newsboys rather than by subscription. To gather the latest stories, most hired "reporters."[84] The most prominent pennies included Benjamin Day's *New York Sun* (1833), James Gordon Bennett's *New York Herald* (1835), A. S. Abell's *Baltimore Sun* (1837), Horace Greely's *New York Tribune* (1841), and Henry Raymond's *New York Times* (1851).[85] More reliant on advertising and new steam-printing technology for profits, the penny press broke free of party control to reach a broader, more middle-class audience. In fact, Bennett's first issue of the *New York Herald* proudly declared, "We shall support no party—be the agent of no faction or coterie, and we care nothing for any election, or any candidate from president down to constable."[86] This was not quite true. The pennies could still be partisan, but at the behest of their editor rather than party leaders. Also, their news remained mostly regional in character. Only the Baltimore and Washington newspapers routinely covered Congress, and none assigned reporters to the White House.[87] Even the best-selling penny papers, which circulated nationally, still focused on local news. Hence the penny press phenomenon was mostly successful in the large eastern cities and failed to displace the party-controlled press.

Meanwhile, antebellum readers interested in business news, finance, or political-economic debate could subscribe to specialty papers and journals. These included the *Journal of Commerce* (1827), *American Railroad Journal* (1832), *American Banker* (1836), *Hunt's Merchant's Magazine and Commercial Review* (1839), *The Economist* (1843, published in London to promote free trade), *Banker's Magazine* (1846), *The Iron Age* (1859), and the aforementioned *Commercial and Financial Chronicle* (1862) and *Stockholder* (1862).[88] Most penny papers also featured a business and finance section.[89] These daily reports offered brief news stories intermixed with the latest price quotations for major commodities, bonds, and stocks. More general readers could also get political-economic news and commentary from magazines and journals such as the *North American Review* (1815, originally a literary magazine), *Harper's* (1850), and *The Atlantic* (1857).[90]

It was the Civil War and its run-up that forced newspapers into more serious reporting and increased national coverage.[91] Even before the first shots were fired, millions of Americans craved daily word of the brewing conflict and its politics. And because, over time, almost every American had a beloved family member or friend in uniform, and the personal and family fortunes of millions were bound up with the war, readers clamored for the latest and most accurate accounts of the fighting. Publishers therefore hired correspondents in Washington and sent reporters to the front lines.[92] A "Newspaper Row" of offices developed near the main telegraph station in the nation's capital.[93] Congress set up a special gallery for reporters starting in 1857.[94] Of course, most papers still had highly partisan takes, such as the Republican *Chicago Tribune* (especially under its new editor after 1855), or were founded to do so, such as the Democratic *Chicago Times* (1854). But newspapers increasingly separated out their most partisan commentary into an "editorial" page, usually placed below the paper's masthead, midway through each edition. Meanwhile, creation of the U.S. Government Printing Office in 1860 effectively muzzled the White House, cutting off the lucrative government printing contracts that presidents had leveraged for selection of, and control over, a "presidential newspaper."[95] By the end of the war, hard news and an independent (though still highly partisan) press were established parts of the American news diet.

The Civil War Presidency

The war dramatically altered the American presidency. In his conduct of the war, Lincoln vigorously expanded the power of the executive branch at the expense of Congress, the judiciary, and state and local governments.[96] In April 1861, he sent troops into battle, enlarged the military tenfold, spent $2 million of unappropriated funds, and blockaded Southern ports, all without the formal approval of Congress, and even before calling Congress into special session to debate the war.[97] That same month, Lincoln suspended *habeas corpus* and ordered military authorities to silence and imprison dissenters. When the chief justice of the Supreme Court ruled these acts unconstitutional, Lincoln simply ignored him.[98] Thereafter, some fifteen thousand to twenty thousand Americans were arrested on suspicion of "disloyal and treasonable practices," including newspaper editors, democratically elected politicians, and clergy.[99] During the war, Lincoln also declared martial law and authorized the trial of civilian defendants in military courts. His administration censored the mail and newspapers, even closed post offices deemed treasonous. When draft riots broke out in New York City in July 1863, Lincoln sent seasoned troops from the battlefield to put them down. Even his celebrated emancipation of the slaves was done without congressional approval. And in his major policy decisions, Lincoln either declined to consult his cabinet or ignored their opposition, even when it was unanimous. Thus, cabinet meetings were mostly for show. Much of this Lincoln justified on with the argument "I may in an emergency do things on military grounds which cannot be done constitutionally by Congress."[100]

However, in other important ways, Lincoln conducted a more traditional presidency. Outside of war and Reconstruction planning, he mostly left his cabinet and legislators alone to conduct domestic policy. Of course, with his fellow Republicans practically unopposed in Congress, Lincoln rarely disagreed with it on economic policy. Thus, Congress passed more major economic legislation (described above) than it had since the earliest days of the Republic.[101] Lincoln did meet with his Treasury secretary on the national bank acts, but he otherwise deferred on monetary policy, telling him, "You understand these things. I do not."[102] Nor did Lincoln resort to demagoguery to maintain his power. Instead, he respected the tradition of an aloof presidency. For example, he rarely attempted to influence American opinion through public speeches. Certainly, his inaugural addresses and Gettysburg speech have become venerated American canon; however, in practice, Lincoln instead relied on letters, written proclamations, anonymous editorials, press surrogates, and messages to Congress to put his arguments before the people.[103] And in the ultimate test of democratic leadership, Lincoln fully supported the conduct of the 1864 presidential election, despite expecting to lose.[104]

Some of Lincoln's restraint was institutional. Since the 1830s and deep into the Gilded Age, state and local parties held considerable power within the American political system.[105] Almost all politics was local. Originally crafted by "Jacksonians," the idea was to take power away from the founding elites of Virginia and New York and redistribute it more broadly among the citizenry. Presidential candidates were therefore chosen in nominating conventions made up of hundreds of local delegates whose votes were determined by local issues. In a nation of disconnected local and regional economies, this made sense. Absent cheap transportation and communications, pre-industrial Americans lived and prospered locally. Therefore, as long as the United States faced no imminent foreign threat, the focus of American parties and politics was provincial. The highly decentralized political system was a perfect fit. This meant that, in presidential elections, policy specifics were subordinated to general party values. Local parties ran the presidential campaigns and therefore highlighted local issues and preferences. As nominating delegates, they acted like gatekeepers who kept out offensive or outsider candidates. According to one scholar, "The national party appeared to be little more than a confederation of state and local parties, held together between presidential elections by a weak national committee."[106]

In such an environment, presidents generally kept their mouths shut, for any White House utterance too specific or too emphatic would inevitably offend or contradict some valuable local constituency somewhere.[107] Party unity was prioritized beyond all else. Party regulars were motivated by spoils and personal power. The mass of voters was mustered out by exciting "Hurrah!" campaigns which emphasized fireworks and cheers (or jeers) rather than policy ideas. Thoughtful debates between candidates were not conducted because parties were not held together by specific policy agendas. In fact, presidential candidates rarely campaigned for their own election. Once in office, the "spoils" of victory were similarly local. Presidential appointments to federal jobs (mostly thousands of post office, customshouse, and land or facility management workers) became favors doled out to party regulars at the behest of party elites, usually senators appointed by state legislatures. The president was merely a rubberstamp in the spoils process. And these secure, salaried federal jobs were much coveted in an era when most work was seasonal and paid with daily wages or by the piece. Most of these institutions and practices continued to hobble the power of presidents deep into the Gilded Age. They had the veto power and their ingenuity, but little else.[108]

After the Civil War was over, its memory continued to pervade American political psychology and economic behavior for decades.[109] For example, in response to Lincoln's unilateral assertion of authority, Congress became hypersensitive to expressions of executive power. And going into the Gilded Age, legislators' insistence on their congressional prerogatives only grew as the expanding federal government increasingly nourished individual and party fortunes. More generally, across the nation, one's stance on and participation in the Civil War tended to determine one's vote, party identification, and policy support, often until death. For many Americans, Gilded Age politics became war by other means. Hence, the Civil War made or broke political careers throughout the era. For presidential contenders, the conflict was such a vote-getter that war veterans won their party's nomination in almost every presidential election between 1865 and 1900.[110] Only one Gilded Age president had failed to serve in the Civil War.[111] For other politicos, military service was not quite a prerequisite for office, but it brought reputational benefits and networks of support that noncombatants could rarely rival.

What Wasn't Changed by the Civil War?

In contrast, the Civil War did *not* revolutionize the American political economy in several surprising ways. For example, unlike 20th-century warfare, it did not produce major advances in American manufacturing, nor was it even a strong driver of economic growth.[112] The country remained largely agricultural. In business, small local firms still dominated, usually sole proprietorships or partnerships; private incorporations were uncommon.[113] Railroad and telegraph firms were among the few large, multi-unit businesses or that competed across state borders. Even in manufacturing, not many firms employed more than a few dozen workers—perhaps a handful of textiles mills and the occasional iron foundry. Despite the new forays out west, net railroad building slowed to half its prewar pace during the war, and train travel saw few significant technological improvements. Domestic steel production was little changed. Of the nation's major "high-tech" systems, only the telegraph network and steamship usage expanded dramatically during the war.[114]

Outside of agriculture, scientific and technological progress were anemic throughout the Civil War.[115] Only in arms and munitions were significant advances seen.[116] Otherwise, perhaps the most memorable civilian inventions of the war years were four-wheel roller skates, tumbler locks, and ten-gallon hats. The horrors of battle did prompt the "rise of American medicine," as the nation's doctors, many poorly trained, struggled to understand and treat maladies that some had never seen before.[117] But decades would pass before American health-care would enter the modern scientific age.

Rather, the war's greatest civilian contributions to science were the institutions that it produced.[118] For example, to aid farm modernization, Congress created the Department of Agriculture in 1862. It was the country's first major federal scientific research institution. It gathered data, conducted and funded research, and disseminated its findings widely. The Morrill Land Grant Act of 1862 transferred large plots of federal land to the states to be used, or sold, to "provide colleges for the benefit of agriculture and the Mechanic arts." It would soon fund over one hundred colleges throughout the country, including The Ohio State University, Kansas State, Purdue, the University of Connecticut, and the early units of the University of California system.[119] And in early March 1863, the National Academy of Sciences was created by Congress to "investigate, examine, experiment, and report upon any subject of science or art" at the request of any government department.[120] But the scientific and economic benefits of these institutions would take years to realize.

Nor did the Civil War transform the US business environment. Interchangeable parts and mass production, the *sine qua non* of modern manufacturing, did make their way into American arms production, but not much further. The next industry to adopt them would be sewing machines, and then not until the mid-1880s.[121] Large suppliers did well during the war because military procurement officers preferred them.[122] Thanks to the railroads, American wholesalers had been growing during the 1850s and therefore had the best experience and capacity with which to meet war demands. However, after the war, most of these large firms shrank back to their previous business operations; few of their leaders would graduate to become "robber barons" or "industrial titans" during the Gilded Age.[123]

Finally, to understand the economic policy debates which confronted presidents postbellum, we first need to know a bit about American economic thought. At the time, economics was not considered an independent or scientific subject.[124] Instead, economics was widely treated as applied moral philosophy. Material gain was a function of freedom, common sense, and good behavior.[125] And to the degree that the nation's colleges taught any economics at all, it was woven into courses in philosophy, ethics, history, or politics. Even in its most secular form, economics was considered a subset of politics or history called "political economy."[126] This moral understanding of economics is what the Gilded Age presidents and their contemporaries were taught on the subject as young men, be it in the classroom, the church nave, or at the dinner table.

Economic thought was another area *not* revolutionized by the Civil War, at least not in the North. After all, the Union had won the war. Thus, to many observers, the Northern economy had been victorious because Northerners lived more pious lives, based on free labor.[127] Economic growth was God's reward to the devout. Honesty and hard work generated profits, frugal living produced savings, and thoughtful calculations of risks and costs led to wise investments. All of these together increased national wealth and prosperity. In fact, competition between free laborers forced them to become more productive, independent, and righteous.[128] On the other hand, laziness, deception, and extravagance led to bankruptcy. Many still condemned trading in stocks and bonds as unproductive "speculation" (gambling), but ownership of securities was becoming more widely accepted.[129] Slavery, in particular, resulted in aristocracy, dependency, and stagnation. Therefore, many Northerners had supported the Civil War as "a war for the establishment of free labor, call it by whatever other name you will."[130] And while the philosophical implications for trade were less clear, some insisted that this economic morality extended to banking and the currency. "Honest money" meant "hard money": gold or paper notes backed by gold.[131] To print money, like the greenback, was to create it out of thin air. It was a lie, and therefore ungodly! "Atheism is not worse in religion than an unstable or irredeemable currency in political economy," preached the *Christian Advocate*.[132] The country's leading economic thinkers—Frances Bowen (Harvard), Charles Dunbar (Harvard), Amasa Walker (Amherst), John Bascom (Williams), Arthur Latham Perry (Williams)—all taught some variation on these themes and disseminated them to the nation in articles and textbooks, which were eagerly repeated in popular periodicals such as *The Nation* and *Scribner's*.[133]

* * *

To sum up, the Civil War was a necessary prelude to the Gilded Age in that it radically changed the environment within which presidents, and indeed all Americans, operated. It put the country into massive debt and thereby called the US dollar into question. It burdened the country with taxes myriad and sundry. It threw the South into abject poverty and created a new class of Black voters, workers, and farmers. It prompted wholesale reform of the banking sector into a national financial system centered on New York City. It mushroomed the federal workforce and filled it with Republican Party hacks. It thereby grew and strengthened the practices of moieties, assessments, and patronage that fed government corruption. It freed the press from party control and focused its attention on national political, economic, and business issues. It greatly enhanced the power of the presidency and the federal government, often putting them into conflict with powerful antebellum institutions and actors. Admittedly, the war did not transform industry, science, or technology (outside of weapons, telegraphs, and steamships). But the war obliterated many obstacles that had stood in the way of industrialization and the formation of a national market economy. Thus, Americans would face a very different set of political-economic problems and opportunities going into the 1870s. The next chapter will delve into them.

Interlude: Into the 1870s

Going into the 1870s, the US economy was still mostly agricultural, the presidency was decidedly premodern, and the age was not yet gilded. The country still predominantly ran on animal power, waterwheels, wood, and human muscle. And other than railroads, telegraphs, and a handful of textile factories and mines, there were few large corporations or manufacturers. The West and Great Plains were sparsely inhabited and beckoned economic development, but long-distance transportation and communications remained skeletal and costly. Thus, even in the East, most Americans produced for local markets. The fragmented US economy badly needed investment, but historic levels of debt and taxes made lenders wary. The Confederate Army's surrender did end the debates over slavery and secession. These issues had touched almost every aspect of American political economy for a generation. Henceforth, politics would instead be dominated by battles over reunification, citizenship, economic development, debt, and the role and power of the federal government, especially the presidency, to intervene in these matters. Meanwhile, government increasingly existed to distribute the spoils among partisan loyalists. Republicans were solidly in control of the federal government and most state governments. Thus, it would be up to Presidents Grant and Hayes to return the country to financial stability, develop the West, and deliver on the promises of Reconstruction.

To produce a snapshot of the US economy at the dawn of the Gilded Age, we need to jump forward a year into Grant's presidency, for that is when we find the most reliable statistical estimates. The data tell us that, already in 1870, the US economy was the largest in the world by far, and second in wealth (per capita) only to Great Britain.[1] Forty million Americans offered a vast market for exports of European manufactured and luxury goods, while providing vital supplies of foodstuffs and raw materials. And thanks to its enormous size and dispersed population, the United States also led the world in the diffusion of transportation and communication technologies.

However, in 1870 the American economy was still decidedly farm and natural resource–based, especially compared to its European rivals.[2] Despite years of steady industrialization, just over 50 percent of Americans still worked in agriculture, another 11 percent worked in fishing, trade, or shipping; only 20 percent

Presidential Leadership in Feeble Times. Mark Zachary Taylor, Oxford University Press. © Oxford University Press 2024.
DOI: 10.1093/oso/9780197750742.003.0004

toiled away in the nation's mining and manufacturing sector.[3] And the US industrial sector (other than railroads) still mostly consisted of small companies with single factories serving local markets. In fact, the entire US economy remained one of small farms and businesses. Even "large" employers—like plantations, mines, and some factories—might employ only a few hundred workers. The railroads had begun to employ thousands, but only the federal government employed tens of thousands. Corporate America and industrial capitalism were still in their infancy.

The US economy was also geographically lopsided. Its population remained heavily concentrated in the antebellum states, with 82 percent of Americans still living east of the Mississippi River. New York City was the nation's largest city, with 1.4 million inhabitants; next up was Philadelphia with 674,000; then St. Louis and Chicago with roughly 300,000 each. But there were just ten other cities with populations over 100,000. These cities may have been wealthy, industrious, and rambunctious, but Americans were not yet urban: 80 percent of them still lived in small towns with populations under ten thousand or on farms. The West remained an unsettled, underdeveloped, and dangerous place, still home to Native American tribes fighting for their survival.[4]

Economically speaking, by 1870 the United States had split into three distinct regions: the northern and eastern states that lay east of the Mississippi and north of the Mason-Dixon line, flush with banks, manufacturing, and railroads; the West and Plains states, abounding with farmland and natural resources but in desperate need of settlers, infrastructure, and financial capital; and the ex-Confederate South, which lay ruined after the Civil War, beset by political and racial resentments that would handicap it throughout the Gilded Age. In fact, the South was starved for banks, roads, rail lines, schools, factories, and even credit. The only thing it had in good supply was labor, which was now more expensive and unruly thanks to the end of slavery. Thus, the three main prospects for rapid economic growth in the United States were the development of the Great Plains and the West, the linking of Americans to national and global markets, and developing the infrastructure (railroads, steamships, telegraph, supplies of anthracite coal) with which to do all of this.

To fund it all, Americans needed huge amounts of investment capital. Most funding came from domestic sources, though European lenders remained essential marginal investors. In fact, foreigners held investments worth 16 percent of US GDP going into the 1870s.[5] At the apex of the American financial system sat the war-era network of national banks, lightly regulated by the US Treasury and dominated by one financial center: New York City. In 1864 there had been just 167 registered bankers and brokers in New York City; by 1870, they numbered some 1,800.[6] And since these banks were bound to the US Treasury via federal charters, reserve requirements, and other regulations, the White House now had unparalleled influence over the country's monetary policy, though few understood this enormous power at the time. State-chartered banks remained widely used, but they were henceforth mostly supporting actors in the American financial drama. Europeans participated mostly through bond purchases on Wall Street. In stocks, the market remained small and quite risky. In order to increase confidence in its securities, the NYSE had set new requirements for listings (e.g., capitalization, number of shareholders, and "proven track record"), but both offerings and trading remained thin.[7] For example, the NYSE in 1870 listed just 103 firms, of which 49 were transports (mostly railroads), 31 banks, 14 industrial or other, 7 mines, and 1 utility.[8] A trading day in which more than fifty thousand shares were exchanged was considered unusual. These trades were largely unregulated by the state or federal government.[9] However, most American businesses had low capital requirements, which allowed firms to raise funds from more traditional sources: wealthy individuals, families, the business owners' own accounts, or local commercial banks.

Paying for Victory

After the war, the nation's tattered finances towered over every other public debate except Reconstruction itself.[10] Americans paid state and federal taxes on everything from their morning coffee to their evening cigar. For, by the time it was over, Washington had spent some $2.3 billion on the Civil War, equal to roughly half of all national economic output in 1860.[11] Taxes and tariffs had paid for a mere 20 percent of the Union war effort. The rest was funded by debt (70 percent of war expenditures) and printing money (10 percent).[12] The South was even worse off. Thanks to their antipathy toward government duties, the Confederates paid only around 4 percent of their war expenses with taxes and tariffs; the rest was funded by debt and money printing, most of which was rendered worthless by the defeat of the Confederacy.[13] And thanks to the extreme scarcity of goods and labor, hyperinflation devastated the Confederate economy by the end of the war.[14] Given the South's far smaller population, industrial base, and banking sector, the Union always had the financial advantage. "The Yankees did not whip us in the field, we were whipped in the Treasury Department," lamented one Confederate leader.[15]

The foremost concern of the Union victors was figuring out what to do about all those paper greenbacks. By 1865, as a result of money printing, the North was swimming in $1.08 billion worth of US currency; only 13.7 percent of it was in gold coin.[16] The rest consisted of paper notes of various origins, alongside a deluge of counterfeits.[17] As a result, annual inflation raged near 25 percent when General Robert E. Lee surrendered. It was a miracle that aggregate prices had merely doubled during the war.[18] Greenbacks were the most glaring offense. They had originally been created as a temporary expedient to fill a gap in wartime finance. Now $428 million of them flooded the country, constituting around 35 percent of all US currency, backed by nothing more than the government's promise of repayment.

Ideally, holders of greenbacks should be able to redeem them at the Treasury for gold at face value. The problem was that market forces of supply and demand dictated the greenback's price.[19] Every time the Union army had lost a major battle or new printings were approved, the greenback had lost value.[20] As a result, the greenback price of gold crept ever higher throughout the war, to $134 (1862), then $172.50 (1863), until it peaked at $285 in midsummer 1864, when just under $449 million of these "rag babies" were in circulation.[21] As the war wound down, the government began to repurchase greenbacks at market rates and then destroy them. When major hostilities ended in spring 1865, the greenback was back down to around $141 in gold, but too many of them still remained in circulation. This posed a predicament: if $1,000 was loaned in *gold* during, say, 1861, could the borrower legally pay it back later with inflated *greenbacks* at face value?

None of these issues had been discussed in the original Legal Tender Act of 1862. In fact, a handful of lawsuits had been filed questioning the constitutionality of the greenback altogether. Plaintiffs argued that Congress was empowered to coin money, not to print it. The courts generally sided with Congress, but the suits kept coming.[22] Even for those who sought to eliminate the greenback, the Act had failed to specify a means for ending its circulation.

Nor was the greenback dilemma limited to the United States. Gold was increasingly linked to the currencies of foreign economies by their own laws and market conditions. Gold's price therefore effectively set exchange rates between the US greenback and the British pound, French franc, Dutch guilder, and more. This meant that the greenback's price and legal status affected foreign decisions about whether to invest in US debt, stocks, or other assets. For those who lived off international trade, the wildly fluctuating exchange rates meant that international commerce had become "almost as uncertain as a ticket in a lottery."[23]

In addition, the federal government owed another $2.8 billion (around 30 percent of GDP) in traditional debt instruments, some at relatively high interest rates. Around 40 percent was in the form of short-term obligations due to mature within three years.[24] The annual interest charges alone amounted to $97 million. Yet, the US Treasury had only around $88 million in cash reserves at the end of the war.[25] Some of these debt obligations were payable only in gold; for others, the form of payment was unspecified. This raised the specter of partial "repudiation": federal debt might be repaid in inflated greenbacks. That is, the government might be tempted to print its way out of trouble.

Appointed in March 1865, President Lincoln's new Treasury secretary, the conservative banker Hugh McCulloch, was determined to aggressively pay down the federal debt and reduce the supply of greenbacks until they were valued at gold at one-to-one. This would mean that the exchange of paper dollars for dollar coins ("redemption") made of gold or silver ("specie") could be done again at prewar face values ("resumption"). At first, he found a ready partner in President Andrew Johnson (1865–1869), who took office a month later. Johnson was an "economic illiterate" Southerner with a "Jacksonian distrust of banks and paper currency."[26] With Johnson's support, McCulloch requested from Congress wide discretionary powers to refinance the federal debt, including contracting the supply of greenbacks.

However, the quickest solution to the mounting debt was to cut federal spending via a rapid military drawdown. President Johnson implemented this almost immediately. When Lee surrendered in April 1865, the Union had 1 million troops in the field. By early August, Union general Ulysses S. Grant and Secretary of War Edwin Stanton had discharged 641,000 troops, while the navy had shrunk its fleet from 600 vessels down to 115 by autumn. Still further reductions were to come.[27] As a result, surpluses began to accumulate in the US Treasury, even as wartime taxes continued to bring in ample revenues. Relying on these surpluses, the Treasury began to retire and destroy the excess paper notes it received, while allowing gold to flow back out into the economy.

Reconstruction

The "Reconstruction" of the Union was the other great political-economic question of the day. Lincoln had never fully articulated his terms for readmitting rebel states after the war. He was a moderate who favored presidential pardons for most ex-Confederates *if* they agreed to renounce the Confederacy, rewrite their state constitutions, and accept the end of slavery. Congress, however, wanted a Reconstruction that was longer, harsher, and under its legislative control. Nor was there yet any consensus on the legal status of the freed slaves or of the millions of rebel soldiers and their leaders. To make matters worse, Lincoln's assassination in mid-April 1865, while Congress was adjourned, put a very different executive in charge of Reconstruction at a critical juncture.

The new president, Andrew Johnson, soon emerged as an unapologetic white supremacist and an ardent supporter of small government and states' rights. As a formerly poor, Southern tailor, Johnson opposed slavery. Slavery had helped to create and maintain the Southern white aristocracy that he envied and despised. He was glad to see them both go. Johnson therefore supported the Thirteenth Amendment to abolish slavery, ratified in late 1865.[28] But he had no intention of elevating African Americans to political or social equality. He despised Blacks as having "a constant tendency to relapse into barbarism" and therefore less "capacity for government than any other race of people."[29] Johnson even believed Black slaves to have been complicit in the formation of the plantation aristocracy he hated.[30] The horrors of miscegenation became another of his obsessions.[31] Nor did he exhibit much enthusiasm for punishing the ex-Confederacy, as urged by the "Radical" Republicans soon to take control of Congress.[32] He made no mass arrests nor threats of reparations. Instead, President Johnson sought a forgiving "Restoration" of the old South under local control, rather than its "Reconstruction" into a modern multiracial society.[33] Johnson believed that the United States should remain, in his own words, "a white man's country" forever.[34]

To that end, Johnson took control over postwar Reconstruction policy during much of 1865. With Congress out of session, he granted amnesty to most rank-and-file Confederates and restored their former property rights.[35] He also single-handedly recognized the governments of several Southern states. To gain readmission to the Union, Johnson demanded only that these states renounce slavery and repudiate their Confederate war debts, but they were *not* required to grant political rights to Blacks. Johnson also installed state governors who supported his lenient version of Reconstruction and who would best guarantee the preservation of white supremacy in Southern politics. And to ensure that neither Southern "scalawags" nor Northern "carpetbaggers" could take power over Southern state governments, Johnson began to individually pardon the Southern planter aristocracy so that they could reclaim political control of their states.[36] He even allowed the formation of local Southern militia units. And despite the refusal of several rebel states to comply with his conditions, Johnson declared the Union more or less fully restored in mid-December 1865.[37] "I am of the Southern people, and I love them and will do all in my power to restore them," he told a group of Southern delegates to the White House.[38]

Meanwhile, poverty and mass unemployment plagued the vanquished Confederacy. Parts of the antebellum South had been among the wealthiest in the world. Now the entire region was destitute.[39] Over a quarter million of its working-age white males had been killed, and far more wounded, during the war. Another $2.7 billion worth of slaves had been lost to emancipation.[40] And since slavery was the *sine qua non* for the plantation economy, many Southern planters now faced bankruptcy. Even those cotton farmers who could still harvest had trouble selling. For, thanks in part to the wartime blockade, Southern cotton had been replaced in some markets by exports from Egypt, India, and Brazil.[41] And with few other goods to export, and little money to pay for imports, once-thriving Southern ports saw little traffic. In finance, Confederate debt and banknotes were worthless. Southern banks were drained of capital. In industry, much of the South's railway network lay twisted into "Sherman's neckties."[42] Its few mills and factories had been destroyed. Even horses were hard to come by. Southern governments offered little solace. With few tax revenues and scarce credit, they were incapable of providing most public goods, even basic security. Thus, crime made travel dangerous, business risky, and investors wary.

Throughout 1865, Southerners' greatest concern was the millions of ex-slaves who wandered the region, hoping for federal grants of farmland. President Johnson thwarted federal attempts to redistribute landownership in the South intended to help Blacks become economically self-sufficient, thereby ensuring that Blacks would have to work for whites. Yet some Blacks refused to work for their former masters. Many insisted on better treatment, more freedom, and higher wages than white employers were willing to grant. As a result, migrants of all shades drifted into the cities looking for work or charity. "[Y]ou will find that this question of the control of labor underlies every other question of state interest," explained a senior ex-Confederate to South Carolina's governor.[43] Some whites feared a massive "Negro uprising." That winter, to bring order and restore white supremacy, a few ex-Confederate governments created "Black Codes" which outlawed vagrancy and legalized forced labor for unemployed Blacks, while forbidding myriad other economic activities, all with the goal of "getting things back as near to slavery as possible."[44] Violence against Blacks in the South skyrocketed, even for minor transgressions. White supremacists, both as individuals and in guerrilla groups, began to terrorize and then commit violence against Blacks, which escalated severely during 1866.[45]

From a macro perspective, emancipation also removed hundreds of thousands of Blacks from the agricultural workforce. Nearly 80 percent of the slave population had worked, the highest labor participation rate in US history. However, once freed from involuntary servitude in the fields or as domestic help, many Black women, children, and the aged left the workforce. Going into the 1870s, Black labor participation had fallen to under 60 percent, roughly the same as workers in most other pre-industrial economies.[46]

Over time, economic activity would slowly return to the South in the form of sharecropping and tenant farming.[47] But this meant that small and medium farms, with their lower productivity rates, would henceforth dominate the Southern economy. Attempts were made to modernize and industrialize the South throughout the late 1860s and early 1870s. But these ambitious projects generally fell victim to poor planning, fraud, and old hatreds. As a result, for much of Reconstruction and the Gilded Age, the South would be a minor player in the economic fortunes of the country.[48]

When the 39th Congress finally came back into session in early December 1865, it sought to take back control over Reconstruction. The South's reversion "near to slavery," and Johnson's active support for it, outraged Northerners who wanted to punish the South for its rebellion and to deliver on the war's promise of free-market labor.[49] First, the new Congress refused to seat Southern representatives, eliminating their role in future Reconstruction policy. Over Johnson's veto, it also passed a Civil Rights Act in April 1866 that granted citizenship to all persons born in the United States ("excluding Indians"), as well as certain inalienable rights "without distinction of race or color, or previous condition of slavery or involuntary servitude." These included the rights to make contracts, to own property, to sue in court, and to enjoy the full protection of federal law. Congress then sought to enshrine these free labor provisions in the Constitution by sending to the states the Fourteenth Amendment, which granted African Americans citizenship and mandated equal protection under the law.[50] The Amendment, adopted in July 1868, also explicitly prohibited payment of Confederate war debts. But to reassure nervous investors and quell any talk of repudiation of Union debts, it included language guaranteeing that "[t]he validity of the public debt of the United States . . . shall not be questioned." Finally, Congress extended federal aid to freed slaves "to become self-supporting citizens of the United States, and to aid them in [defending their freedom from slavery]," again over Johnson's veto.[51]

The Recession of 1865–1867

Perhaps the only thing that Johnson and most congressional Republicans did agree upon that winter was that inflation and paper currency had to be brought under control. To that end, in December 1865, Congress formally approved Treasury secretary McCulloch's approach to winding down the greenback. However, in contracting the nation's money supply, the Johnson administration set off a cycle of deflation and recession in an economy already suffering from a postwar contraction. A downturn had likely begun with the cessation of hostilities back in April. Real GDP per capita fell 5.2 percent (1865) and then another 0.8 percent (1866). Talk of war in Central Europe, a fall in cotton prices, and higher interest rates overseas combined to scare away foreign investors and further prolong the recession.[52]

As unemployment grew and bankruptcies spread, angry voters began to protest against McCulloch's greenback withdrawals. Congressman James Blaine (R-ME) later recalled:

> The great host of debtors who did not wish their obligations to be made more onerous, and the great host of creditors who did not desire that their debtors should be embarrassed and possibly rendered unable to liquidate, united on the practical side of the question and aroused public opinion against the course of the Treasury Department.[53]

However, McCulloch remained undeterred. He was betrayed by both Johnson and Congress who, fearing for their prospects in the 1866 midterm elections, reversed course on monetary policy. In April, they carried out legislation limiting the Treasury's drawdowns to just $10 million in greenbacks until October, and then $4 million per month thereafter, or just under 1 percent of all greenbacks in circulation.[54] Yet, in order to guarantee sufficient revenues, and to protect their manufacturing constituents in the North, Republicans in Congress also refused to lower tariffs or domestic taxes for the time being.

Although McCulloch failed at contracting the currency much, he enjoyed more success with refunding the federal debt. Given the economic situation, the Treasury's short-term debt needed to be refunded at regular intervals. McCulloch dreaded the pressure of these constant payments. Nor did he relish the idea of regular judgments on the US economy and politics by the world's investors. And the kaleidoscope of diverse and ever-changing maturation dates, interest rates, and other debt provisions was confusing and difficult to manage. Therefore, McCulloch aggressively pursued refunding deals. By mid-1868, he had paid down much of these short-term obligations, while converting $1 billion of them into longer run debentures.

In the meantime, recession and deflation persisted. In May 1866, the failure of the largest discount house in London (Overend, Gurney & Company) sent damaging ripples throughout the global economy.[55] The US economic downturn accelerated. Events in Europe always had a powerful effect on American finance, but these shocks became nearly instantaneous after the installation of the transatlantic cable that summer.[56] Partly as a result, US prices fell 2.6 percent and business failures tripled in 1866, though the stock market managed to eke out a 0.5 percent gain. The following year, the situation worsened. In 1867, prices declined another 6.8 percent, business failures nearly doubled again, and stocks slumped 2.6 percent.[57] Farm prices were highly volatile and product-dependent. Thus, agricultural output leaped as farmers sought either to take advantage of price surges or to make up in volume what they lost in price.

Settling the West after the War

Out west, Americans found themselves embroiled in seemingly endless "Indian Wars."[58] In 1860, fewer than 5 percent of Americans had lived in the West or on the Great Plains, the vast majority in Texas, California, Minnesota, and Kansas. This territory was also home to several hundred thousand Native Americans. Some "Indians" had already suffered forced migrations by the US government and were wary of further depravations. When the Civil War broke out, thousands of federal troops were sent east to fight. Some Native tribes interpreted the move as a withdrawal, and attacked white settlements. With the president and Congress absorbed by the war, the military took *de facto* control of Indian policy and launched a series of brutal offenses to protect valuable supplies of gold and silver and to win western political support for the Union.

After the Civil War, US policy toward Native Americans fractured along a dozen fault lines: regional, economic interest, political party, religion, branch of government, even across executive departments. The result was a constantly changing political and economic environment out west, peppered with massacres and small wars. When violence failed or proved too costly, either Native or white leaders might pursue peaceful negotiations. But the agreements produced were violated as often as they were upheld. Meanwhile, corrupt federal and local officials proceeded to swindle peaceful Native Americans (and even white settlers) out of land, payments, and other resources due to them. The result was an inchoate patchwork of war and peace that scared off white migrants and investors. Most economically threatening were Native attacks on small settlements and on railroad and telegraph construction, which were the lifeblood of the remote western economy. Investors and settlers clamored for federal intervention. "We've got to clean the damn Indians out or give up building the [railroads]. The government may take its choice!" declared one rail entrepreneur.[59]

The Railroads

For it was the railroads that were gradually revolutionizing the American economy going into the 1870s. First, railroads slowly brought down transportation costs, especially for long-distance and bulk shipments. Second, railroads knit together disparate parts of the country into a national market for goods, services, and labor. This meant that local and regional businesses of all sorts (e.g., mining, food processing, tobacco, metals, textiles and apparel, lumber, paper, publishing) could go national. But it also meant that producers and workers increasingly had to compete against one another nationally rather than locally, bringing additional downward pressure on prices and wages. Railroads also made extensive use of the telegraph, contributing to a high-speed national market for information, and hence for financial capital. Third, railroads were natural monopolies.[60] They often controlled transportation, storage, and even banking along the routes they served, infuriating farmers, travelers, and labor alike. The tensions between them produced the first real stirrings of modern antitrust legislation.[61] Fierce debates over the constitutionality of state regulation quickly followed.[62]

Most subtly, railroads had begun to transform American business practices.[63] They were the first businesses with large numbers of geographically dispersed and interdependent subunits, whose operations had to be coordinated with relative precision. Thus railroads could *not* be run like the family enterprises, partnerships, or sole proprietorships that had comprised almost all antebellum American businesses. Rather, for railroads to function profitably, job functions had to be well-defined, strict timetables designed and enforced, organizational charts created with clear lines of authority, cost accounting and information systems implemented. Multiple layers of management were introduced. And the professional middle-manager, rather than the owner, became the essential actor. In fact, individual owners dwindled as the enormous capital demands of railroads required hundreds of bond- and stockholders. And as large enterprises arose in other industries, they too adopted the business practices of the railroads until it became the American norm.

Railroads, with their astronomical fixed costs, had also grown too large for most banks to fund.[64] Congress ended federal land grants for the railroads in 1871, further driving up expenses. So railroad owners turned to the bond and stock markets. In fact, not until the early 1890s would the stocks or bonds of *other* types of industrial corporations become as popular on Wall Street. Before then, for all intents and purposes, the American stock market *was* the railroad industry. And as interest rates on US federal debt came down, foreign investors increasingly turned to railroad stocks and bonds for better returns, especially the British. Even banks got into the act. Therefore, when railroads, or their funders, got into financial trouble due to mismanagement, overproduction, or just plain fraud, they would trigger runs on the market that could collapse the entire US financial system. These "panics" were so damaging that they dragged the US economy down into recession after recession throughout the Gilded Age.[65]

The Founding of the Grange Movement

Those most hurt by the railroads and globalization were America's farmers. In 1865, farmers remained the largest economic class in the country, employing just over half of all workers; another 5 to 10 percent worked in the transportation and commerce of agricultural goods. In fact, almost 80 percent of Americans still lived in rural communities. Farms then were small. Averaging just 170 acres (or a little over one-quarter square mile), they were also almost always owned by a single family struggling to earn a profit.[66] Most of these farms relied entirely upon the single railroad that passed closest to their land. That railroad also usually owned the grain elevators and storage facilities upon which farmers depended for shipment. Banks too, which extended precious loans and credits to farmers during planting and harvest seasons, were often affiliated with the railroad or were dependent upon infusions of railroad cash. Hence, farmers faced an assortment of charges, fees, and interest rates, all effectively controlled by the same railroad. And whenever planting or harvest season arrived, these expenses were raised at precisely the time farmers were most pressed to afford them. Then, as globalization brought farmers into competition with foreign producers, their plight worsened. Increased supply via imports brought down prices, which motivated farmers to produce still more, and thereby incur ever higher debts.

Out of this rising discontent grew the National Grange of the Patrons of Husbandry (a.k.a. "the Grange"). Founded in December 1867 by a Minnesota farmer and former Department of Agriculture bureaucrat, its original intent was to advance and disseminate effective farming methods. It also provided recreational and social outlets for isolated farmers.[67] But the Grange quickly transformed into a political movement to fight against the monopolistic be-havior of railroads. As a political force, farmers sought not modernization and concentration but to defend the small independent "yeoman" farmer idealized by Thomas Jefferson. "The farmer's enemy was not an employer but a *system*—a system of credit, supply, transportation, and marketing. To reorder such a system required political action at the highest level."[68] The farm bloc would evolve into a mighty political power, supporting third-party movements throughout the Gilded Age.[69]

The Melting Pot

In the cities and on the frontier, immigration would transform the American economy during the Gilded Age, becoming a contentious political issue that regularly demanded presidential attention. Immigration policy was fundamen-tally altered in 1868 by ratification of the Fourteenth Amendment to the US Constitution. Previously a legal assumption reserved only for whites, the new Amendment theoretically extended birthright citizenship to all.[70] In doing so, it also shifted power over citizenship, and hence immigration policy, away from the state governments. And throughout the Gilded Age, the courts interpreted the Constitution in ways that whittled down state immigration regimes, allowing federal immigration law to gradually emerge paramount. For example, in order to retain workers, Nevada's first legislature (1865) had imposed a $1 tax (roughly half a day's wages) on all persons leaving the state. But two years later, the Supreme Court linked these taxes to antebellum slavery and declared them an unconstitutional obstruction of "free access" to federal government offices.[71] To prevent paupers from immigrating, other states had required bonds or com-mutation fees from incoming passengers. The Supreme Court struck down these practices too, opining that "this whole subject has been confided to Congress by the Constitution."[72]

Chinese contract labor, in particular, became a major catalyst for change.[73] Few in number before the mid-1850s, an initial wave of Chinese immigrants had accompanied the California Gold Rush.[74] Then, in search of cheap labor, Lincoln's former ambassador to China convinced the Qing dynasty to legalize the emigration of Chinese workers in the Burlingame Treaty of 1868, triggering a much larger wave of Chinese migration to the American West. By 1870, there were over 61,400 Chinese in the United States; 82 percent of them lived in California, or around 11 percent of that state's population, highly concentrated around the city of San Francisco.[75] Other Chinese enclaves appeared in Nevada, Idaho, and Oregon. Their immigration quickly became bound up with labor issues. Compared to native whites, Chinese workers could be paid less, tolerated more dangerous conditions, could be made to work harder and longer, and were seen as passive and obedient. In particular, the Central Pacific Railroad managers found that Chinese workers could be contracted to build the transcontinental railroad on far more profitable terms than unruly whites.[76] Very quickly, Chinese contract labor composed the majority of workers on the transcontinental railroad's dangerous western half. Native-born whites rose to oppose them. An "Anti-Chinese Convention" was held in San Francisco in 1870, where white workers demanded an eight-hour workday and the exclusion of Chinese labor from the United States.[77] Thereafter, political pressures mounted until the Panic of 1873 made competition for jobs and resources a matter of economic survival, forcing Chinese immigration policy to the fore.

The immigration of "foreign agents" and "undesirables" had been contested since the 1790s, but Chinese contract workers were the first to generate federal immigration restrictions based on race. Americans were too enamored of western Europe's "cultural superiority" and too convinced by so-called race science to tolerate Chinese immigrants much. For example, few white women would fraternize with Chinese men. Yet the immigration of Chinese women only prompted widespread accusations of prostitution and polygamy. Not even Gilded Age presidents were immune to such sentiments. Grant believed the majority of Chinese immigrants had been "brought for shameful purposes."[78] Hayes called them "strangers and sojourners, and not . . . incorporated elements of our national life and growth."[79] Garfield scorned them as "an invasion to be looked upon without solicitude."[80]

The experiences of other races were mixed. Native Americans, who supposedly lived under tribal sovereignty, discovered that they were specifically excluded from US citizenship by the "subject to the jurisdiction thereof" clause of the Fourteenth Amendment.[81] And yet, in 1870, the US Supreme Court also extinguished tribal sovereignty. In a dispute over federal taxes, it held that acts of Congress superseded treaties and that Congress could legislate on behalf of all Native Americans on US soil.[82] Thereafter, the federal government simply stopped negotiating treaties with them. In contrast, the annexation of Texas, the Mexican-American War, and the Gadsden Purchase had brought US citizenship to tens of thousands of Mexicans. However, Latinos as a whole constituted just 0.5 percent of the US population in 1870.[83] Most were of Mexican descent and concentrated in the Southwest, where they were treated poorly by white settlers. Nor did their circumstances change much during the Gilded Age.[84] Non-Sino South and East Asians were vanishingly small in number, and the latter tended to get lumped in with the Chinese; migrants from the Middle East and Africa were also sparse.

Science and Technology

Science and technology would revolutionize American life during the Gilded Age, but in 1870 most Americans were still premodern. They had indoor plumbing and gaslight, and refrigeration was commonplace—always supplied by natural ice cut from rivers and lakes.[85] But human and animal power remained the dominant forms of motive energy throughout the economy. Only in railroads, watercraft, and some factories was steam, created most efficiently by anthracite coal, widely used; otherwise, wood and rivers were the main sources of inanimate power.[86] There were just fifty-three thousand miles of rail in operation, employing just under 1.8 percent of American workers, mostly east of the Mississippi and north of Kentucky and Virginia. The first transcontinental railway line across the United States was not yet a year old, and tickets were not cheap.[87] The telegraph also remained too expensive for frequent use. Rates for New York to Chicago were an exorbitant $1 per fifteen words ($20 in 2020 dollars).[88] Thus, in 1870 Americans sent an average of only twenty-five thousand telegraph messages per day over 112,000 miles of wire. Work still meant physical labor for most: on the farms, mines, forests, rails, or processing food and natural resources. Hence a cushy government desk job with a secure salary was highly attractive. For the sick, elderly, and unemployed, there was little government welfare beyond veterans payments; many had to rely on private charity. Medicine remained premodern and homespun. Modern steel, electricity, skyscrapers, and telecommunications were still a few years away.

Yet change was coming fast. When the Civil War ended, the country entered a period of gradual modernization and globalization enabled by technological change. Mass production of dynamite began in the United States (1866), vastly reducing the costs of mining and road construction. The transatlantic telegraph (1866) was quickly adopted by banks, investment houses, and international traders to conduct business. The invention of the refrigerated railcar (1867) would soon allow mass shipments of meat, dairy, and other perishables around the country. Tickertape machines appeared on Wall Street (1867), though the valuable information they carried was jealously guarded.[89] Some intrepid offices had begun to use the first staplers.[90] Arrival of the "boneshaker" velocipede from France kicked off the first bicycle craze on city streets (1868); above them, the first elevated "El" trains were built in New York City (1868). A new era in team sports began when students at Rutgers and New Jersey (Princeton) played the first American football game (1869), ten years after the first collegiate baseball game.[91] The invention of air-compressed brakes (1869) dramatically increased the safety of railroad transportation, reducing the costs, and risks, of travel and shipping. Across the Atlantic, the new Suez Canal (1869) would gradually, but considerably, lower the costs of commerce between Europe and markets farther east, which indirectly pressured, and even benefited, the US economy.

The Press in Transition: From Party to Markets

Meanwhile, thanks to the war, Reconstruction, and the diffusion of new technologies (e.g., the telegraph, steam-driven presses, paper-folding machinery, railroads), newspaper and magazine readership had exploded.[92] By 1870, the country had over 5,000 newspapers, 150 in New York City alone. Much of this was due to the popularity of daily papers, which increased 40 percent in number and 70 percent in circulation over the previous decade.[93] The *Seattle Gazette* (1863) and *San Francisco Chronicle* (1865) had appeared out west. Even small towns of a few thousand people now published some variety of local newspaper. And as readership rose, sales and advertising revenues freed newspapers from party dictates. Economies of scale were limited, though—around half the cost of producing a newspaper was for paper—so fonts were small, print was dense, and advertising was highly sought after.[94] Also, as New York City had become the top city for American manufacturing and finance, it too became the leader in newspaper advertising and advertising agencies.[95] And while papers experimented with all types of stories, interest in national politics skyrocketed. By 1870, there were over seventy reporters in Congress's official press gallery, double that of a decade prior.[96] As a consequence, newspapermen found themselves with growing, independent influence over American politics and policy.

Nevertheless, though free from direct party control, the early Gilded Age press was still deeply partisan, and politicians were wary of it. Of the major papers, perhaps only the *New York Herald*, with the nation's largest circulation, at least at first, remained independent and focused mainly on news of all varieties, especially exclusives.[97] Otherwise, Radical Republicans enjoyed the backing of Horace Greeley's—later Whitelaw Reid's—moralizing *New York Tribune* and Joseph Modell's *Chicago Tribune*. Moderate and liberal (i.e., pro-reform)

Republicans were supported by *Harper's Weekly* (and its vituperative cartoonist Thomas Nast), Murat Halstead's *Cincinnati Commercial*, Horace White's *Chicago Tribune*, the *Boston Journal*, and Samuel Bowles's *Springfield Republican* in Massachusetts. E. L. Godkin took up where *The Liberator* left off with the *The Nation* (1865), which he sought to make into America's leading voice for political commentary and reform. Conservative Republicans and many elites favored the *New York Times*. In fact, the *New York Times* was the only paper in the city to dare attack the corrupt Tweed ring, bringing both entities national attention. But it was Charles Dana's highly condensed *New York Sun*, which leaned both working-class and Democratic, that became the country's most widely read paper by the mid-1870s. Democrats could also rely on the *New York World*. In contrast, *Puck*, which began circulation in 1871, mocked them all. It became the first successful American humor magazine, full of now iconic Gilded Age cartoons, caricatures, and political satire.

Partisanship in the independent press expressed itself in new ways. For example, in return for supporting their party and its candidates, newspaper editors now expected their share of the spoils: influential postmasterships, lucrative customs jobs, advertising contracts, subscriptions, even cabinet positions. For their part, wealthy businessmen regularly paid off newspapermen for favorable coverage. And when not satisfied, the papers now struck back. Presidents Johnson, Grant, and Hayes each felt the sting of editors resentful at denial of patronage or influence. Truth and accuracy were often secondary to a newspaperman's pride, power, and circulation. And it did not help that many newspaper editors, "by experience, training, and education, often felt superior to the politicians they served."[98] Of course, the barbs cut both ways. Even papers as lofty as the *New York Times*, *Chicago Tribune*, and *Cincinnati Tribune* could suffer large drops in circulation if they betrayed their party too flagrantly, as some would discover during the 1870s.

Economic Thought Going into the 1870s

The Civil War produced fissures in the antebellum understanding of American political economy. Economics continued to be thought of as applied moral philosophy. Material prosperity still came from honesty, hard work, and common sense. However, beyond infrastructure investments—ports, canals, and roads— the prewar paradigm had envisioned a competitive market of free "yeoman" farmers and small businesses, untrammeled by the federal government. Of course, in practice, the antebellum American economy had been *heavily* regulated by state and local governments.[99] Myriad taxes and restrictions on business practices invaded Americans' daily lives. But the *federal* government had largely stayed out of it. Manufacturing had been similarly unpopular in an-tebellum America. Horrific reports of Britain's "dark satanic mills" and high start-up costs kept industry small and mostly confined to the North. But since centralized government and industrialization had clearly helped to win the war for the Union, they were reinterpreted positively. Industry was now linked with honor and prosperity. Centralization was less feared as a threat, so long as gov-ernment itself was frugal and moral. This meant a government that was honest, efficient, and run by responsible bureaucrats, which provided intellectual am-munition for civil service reformers going into the 1870s.

On the other hand, most people did not believe government was responsible for economic inequality. The formerly enslaved were now free to compete. Young men could "go west!" The poor could rise from "rags to riches," as dramatized in Horatio Alger Jr.'s popular novels that became best-sellers during the late 1860s. And if economic philosophy and popular fiction did not convince, then the extraordinary fortunes earned by ordinary men like Jay Cooke, Cornelius Vanderbilt, Jay Gould, and Daniel Drew seemed to prove it. As for Marxism, it found small footholds in a handful of immigrant urban ghettos, largely German, but it remained a fringe belief system in the United States, even among workers.[100]

There were three main challenges to this intellectual orthodoxy going into the 1870s. The first came from Europe in the form of John Stuart Mill's *Principles of Political Economy* (1848), which had become a popular textbook in American colleges. Mill conceived of political economy as a science. Its study should be based on rational thought and empirical facts, *not* interpretations of divine will or Christian morality. For example, most people believed that the value of a good or service was primarily a function of the amount of virtuous labor involved in its production. But Mill suspected that the interaction of a good's supply and demand must have some relation to its value, and that markets created equilib-rium in them by adjusting prices. He also argued that happiness, not godly be-havior, should be maximized and that government should take whatever actions necessary to achieve it. Mill generally agreed with Adam Smith and David Ricardo about the benefits of free markets. But Mill's scientific approach also convinced him to warn about destructive monopolies. They could arise wher-ever economies of scale existed, and occurred naturally in some industries, like water and gas utilities, where he recommended state control. Yet Mill fiercely disagreed with socialism, then budding in western Europe. He cautioned that, absent free-market competition, either plundering monopolies or inefficient government would dominate the economy. Also, although a free-trade sup-porter, Mill realized that trade created winners and losers within an economy, and he proposed his own argument for "infant industry" protections. Finally, he disagreed with increasingly popular race theories of his day. He argued that differences in economic outcomes were the result of different institutions and policies, not different races, cultures, or "national character." For example, he insisted this was why the Irish were far more productive in the United States than back home in Ireland.[101]

Mill's approach caught on among increasingly science-crazed Americans. Courses in biology, chemistry, and physics had been growing in popularity at American colleges since the late 1840s; people now looked for similarly scientific approaches toward social and economic issues.[102] To further this endeavor, in October 1865 a group of influential Bostonians formed the American Social Science Association, with the goal of expanding education and "the diffusion of sound principles on questions of Economy, Trade, and Finance."[103] Its members soon produced a steady stream of magazine articles for public consumption, while also advocating for adherence to the gold standard, low tariffs, and soon civil service reform. Meanwhile, new political magazines, such as *Atlantic Monthly* (1857), *Harper's Weekly* (1857), and *The Nation* (1865), appeared alongside the more established periodicals, like *North American Review* (1815), to create a national forum for the scientific debate of economic policy.

A second, equally popular challenge to orthodox American economic thought was "survival of the fittest." It retained the free markets and the self-congratulatory superiority of traditional American antebellum economic thought, but did so on scientific rather than biblical terms. The idea found its best expression in Charles Darwin's theory of biological evolution, but came to American political-economic debates via the writings of Herbert Spencer, an English biologist and amateur political-economist.[104] Spencer argued that some men (and, by extension, some firms), while locked in the competitive struggle for existence, have a natural advantage and will therefore tend to dominate.[105] Over time, these superior individuals (or firms) will thrive and survive, while the inferior will die off as "unfit." Interventions by government, and even charity, to aid the survival of struggling citizens (or firms) should therefore be discouraged. Laissez faire should rule the day. By the late 1860s, Spencer had become a household name across the United States and his theory of "Social Darwinism" was discussed widely.

Since it proscribed against "big government," Social Darwinism soon became a major component of American conservative thought during the Gilded Age, especially within the courts.[106] Its widespread adoption by the judiciary mattered. With the federal government still skeletal and permeated by party spoils and corruption, Americans increasingly turned to the state and federal courts for order and to resolve policy disputes.[107] In response, judges used the Fourteenth Amendment to enforce property rights and freedom of contract, while relying on traditional free-market and "survival of the fittest" philosophies to spawn a golden age of laissez-faire economics.[108] This created a legal environment open for big business to dominate the economic landscape at the expense of farmers, laborers, and the nascent consumer class. And once risen to power, American industrialists and financiers misappropriated Social Darwinism to explain their own personal success and to justify their cold, competitive brutality in maintaining it.

A third challenge came from Henry Carey (University of Pennsylvania), one of the most prominent American economic thinkers and a powerful dissenting voice of the era.[109] Son of early American political-economist Matthew Carey, Henry was, like his father, a Hamiltonian, a protectionist, and a fierce supporter of the "American System."[110] According to Carey, free trade helped only Britain by allowing her to dominate the world's production of processed and manufactured goods, and thereby locking all other economies into the provision of natural resources and agricultural inputs to the British manufacturing machine.[111] He therefore urged that Civil War tariffs be continued, if not raised. Meanwhile, domestic taxes should be reduced or eliminated. In fact, he linked trade and fiscal policy to the fate of American democracy. High domestic taxes and spending led to the centralization of power in government, which Carey saw as a dangerous step toward tyranny. Tariffs, on the other hand, led to economic diversification and political decentralization. America's industrialists, still in need of protection, naturally adored Carey. They circulated his essays in *Iron Age*, the widely read periodical put out by the Iron and Steel Association (created in 1855).[112] Meanwhile, a vocal minority of thinkers and activists took up Carey's arguments in favor of soft money.[113] He opposed resumption of the gold standard at prewar values, explaining that dollar depreciation acted like a beneficial tariff barrier. These ideas proved popular among a growing number of farmers, businessmen, and laborers, heavily concentrated in the central and western parts of the country, who competed for scarce loans and credit and who would eventually infuse Carey's monetary philosophy into the Greenback Labor Party platform (1874–1889).

Amateurs also had considerable influence over economic thought and policy. Often they were experts in other fields who lent their great minds to the study of urgent economic problems. For example, David A. Wells was a trained scientist and a popular science writer who took an interest in US fiscal policy. He published a widely read pamphlet in 1864 which explained how the development of America's natural resources and an open immigration policy would guarantee fiscal solvency and future economic growth.[114] President Johnson made him special commissioner of the revenue (1866-1870), where Wells contributed significantly to tax reform. His studies also led Wells, once a protectionist, to attack import tariffs as a shelter for inefficient producers and a tax on consumers

(1868). After being dismissed by President Grant to mollify protectionists, Wells went on to advise Congressman James Garfield and later Grover Cleveland. The astronomer and mathematician Simon Newcomb wrote widely read books and articles on monetary policy during the 1860s and 1870s, providing useful intellectual fodder for "hard money" policy and a rapid return to the gold standard.[115] Even Charles Dunbar, Harvard's first chair in political economy, was originally a lawyer and financial journalist. Recruited in 1869, Dunbar deferred for two years while he went to Europe to study the subject. He would prove instrumental in the evolution of economics as a field of study throughout the Gilded Age.[116]

President Johnson vs. the Republican Congress

In the meantime, President Johnson and the Republican Congress descended into a vicious political war over the power and conduct of the presidency. During spring and summer 1866, two atrocious massacres of Blacks in Memphis and New Orleans only further proved that Johnson's lenient approach toward Reconstruction was a failure. The president's program could not achieve the war goals of the Northern victors, nor his promises of safety, security, and the rule of law for Southerners. However, rather than compromise, a furious Johnson took to the stump in late August to rail against Congress's challenge to his power and to rouse support for his agenda in the autumn midterm elections. He even considered forming a new political party around his personal leadership. But Johnson's multistate speaking tour was a disaster. He bickered with audience members, publicly accused Congress of tyranny and treasonous behavior, and even implored listeners to hang senior congressmen. Many Americans were shocked. Congress objected to his "intemperate, inflammatory, and scandalous harangues," while critics called him "a braying ass."[117]

Two months later, in what became a national referendum on Reconstruction, the Republicans won big in the 1866 midterms. They took 85 percent of the Senate and 75 percent of the House, giving the 40th Congress veto-proof majorities. Talk of congressional seizure of Reconstruction policy and even impeachment soon began to circulate. Nor was the 39th Congress yet done. In January 1867, it gave Black men the right to vote in Washington, DC, and then extended that right into the territories. In March, the outgoing Congress formally took control of Reconstruction with the Reconstruction Act of 1867, again passed over Johnson's veto. It divided the South into five districts and placed them under military rule. Henceforth, Reconstruction would be run out of the War Department, not the White House. And to reenter the Union, Congress required the ex-Confederate states to pass new state constitutions and ratify the Fourteenth Amendment.

The Birth of Civil Service Reform

As Johnson escalated his battle against congressional Reconstruction, Republicans feared that he would use appointments to implement *his* policy agenda and obstruct that of the legislature. In particular, New England Protestant elites, who despised Johnson and who had traditionally played prominent roles in federal government, fulminated at the prospect of being cut out of major policy decisions. Thus demands for reform of the federal workforce rose to new heights.

The catalyst came in the form of a shocking federal government report which, in early 1866, exposed rampant "frauds, waste, and incompetency" in the New York Customs House, resulting in losses of perhaps 14 percent of all tariff revenues.[118] Soon the nation's newspapers and magazines began to call for reform of the federal revenue collections bureaucracy. "As an instrument of political and social corruption it has rarely been surpassed," declared *The Nation*. "[I]t fills the land with a swarm of employees, without either training or experience or traditions, badly paid, holding their places at the will of the Government."[119] Businessmen long weary of their tax and tariff burdens joined the reform movement.

As predicted, that autumn Johnson began to use patronage to systematically remove Radical Republicans and replace them with Democrats.[120] By early 1867, the reform movement was in full swing.[121] The popular press took up the cause. The *New York Times* blasted the civil service as "notoriously bad," describing it as full of "scamps and blockheads" and being "a contrivance for sheltering and fostering the camp-followers of the party in power."[122] *The Nation* even declared, "The diminution of political corruption . . . is the great question of our time. It is greater than the suffrage, greater than reconstruction."[123]

Congress's immediate solution was to pass, in early March, the Tenure of Office Act of 1867. It required that the president get Senate approval for the removal of any senior appointees, including cabinet members, who had been appointed by the president with the advice and consent of the Senate. This kept Reconstruction policy in the hands of men originally appointed by Lincoln, especially Secretary of War Edwin Stanton, who openly opposed Johnson.

Prelude to the Grant Presidency

After losing his battle over Reconstruction in early 1867, Johnson tried to undermine the efforts of Congress, the War Department, and the Northern Republican establishment. He continued to speak against Reconstruction, while attempting to manipulate, replace, or remove the personnel in charge of it. And in an effort to rouse popular support for his presidency and his agenda, Johnson took up the "financial issue, the issue of the national debt; whether it shall be paid or repudiated."[124] In an erratic malediction, he now described to a reporter "[a]n oligarchy of bonds and national securities in the [northern states] . . . [a]n aristocracy based on nearly $3,000,000,000 of national debt." He declared, "The war of finance is the next war we have to fight," and he warned of "a great financial crash."[125]

However, his conservative Treasury secretary refused to follow suit. Although the economy remained sluggish, McCulloch continued to reduce the number of greenbacks in circulation. In fact, McCulloch's tight monetary policy likely contributed to the stubborn recession that plagued the country throughout 1867. Backed by bondholders and conservative bankers, he even slashed the supply of greenbacks by around 3 to 4 percent during the start of the autumn harvest season, when expanded credit was needed most. Johnson considered firing McCulloch, but conservative support for the latter's deflationary monetary policy was too strong.

Indeed, the adoption of the gold standard had become something of an international *cause célèbre*. Partly in the midcentury vogue for "science" (i.e., standardizing weights and measures), and partly to promote trade and investment, international monetary deliberations of various sorts had occurred throughout the 1850s and early 1860s, including bilateral talks between the United States and Great Britain.[126] In August 1866, France, Belgium, Italy, and Switzerland created their own monetary union, with formal legal specifications for coinage.[127] Greece joined the following spring; however, its membership was limited by French insistence on a bimetallic (combined gold and silver) standard.[128] Recognizing this error, during the summer International Exposition of 1867, held in Paris, host Emperor Louis Napoleon III invited delegates from twenty nations, including the United States, to discuss movement toward an international gold standard. Expectations were high. At the conference, the participants confirmed the principle of fixed exchange rates and agreed to adopt gold as soon as possible. Plans were proposed for minting gold coins in Britain, France, and the United States of equal weights and fineness. The delegates even discussed establishing the French five-franc piece as an international unit of account. But ultimately, such specific proposals were shelved, the participants being still too protective of their nations' independent monetary systems and coinage traditions.

Back in the United States, voters pushed back against the Republican policy agenda, delivering several reversals in the 1867 off-year elections that November. Thanks to Reconstruction, Republicans managed to win elections across the South but lost badly to Democrats in the North and West. Some white voters blamed their economic troubles on McCulloch. Others were already growing tired of the Republicans' Reconstruction initiatives on behalf of Black equality. "Negro suffrage hurt us here very considerable," reported an Illinois Republican, "A great many of our party here are mean enough to want it in the South, and not in the North."[129] Still others may have been frustrated with "Seward's Folly," the Johnson administration's $7 million purchase of seemingly useless Alaska from Russia earlier that year, which came amid promises of budget austerity. Regardless, Republicans reenergized their push for votes in the South, especially among African Americans. New efforts in Reconstruction and talk of General Grant for president became part of this strategy.

The elections intensified the war between the Johnson administration and Congress. In his early December 1867 annual message, Johnson accused the Republican Congress of betraying the Constitution and railed against the granting of political rights to Blacks. "[A]t this time there is no Union as our fathers understood the term," he declared.[130] Johnson then openly pondered "making legal-tender and bank notes convertible into coin or its equivalent their present specie value in the hands of their holders," and he called for tax reform such that only luxury items purchased by the rich would be taxed. He insisted that *his* enemies were also the country's enemies—wealthy northeastern industrial and financial elites who wanted riches for themselves, rights for freed Blacks, but only poverty and subjugation for the rest of America.

As for the economy, the recession was winding down by winter 1867–1868, but the recovery was anemic. Economic growth was a mere 1.4 percent (per capita) during 1868. To arrest McCulloch's tight monetary policy, in early February Congress passed legislation that forbade the Treasury from further reductions in supplies of US notes, even though only around 12 percent of greenbacks had been retired.[131] The House even went so far as to authorize $100 million in *new* greenbacks, but the measure failed in the Senate. This left $356 million worth of US greenbacks in circulation.[132] Most of these remaining greenbacks would continue in circulation as American currency throughout the Gilded Age.

* * *

Impeachment came in early March 1868, a week after Johnson fired Secretary of War Stanton in open defiance of the Tenure of Office Act. Republicans who had long sought to remove Johnson now felt they had legal cause for it. Two months later, after a series of delays and long debates, the Senate decided against Johnson's removal by just a single vote.[133] Economic policy was partly to blame. For next in line for the presidency was Senator Benjamin Wade (R-OH), a "soft money" man who supported labor and was therefore anathema to "all the great Northern capitalists."[134] Worse yet, unless Wade proved unpopular as president, he would likely go on to win election that November. Thus for many in the Republican Party, a flaccid Johnson was more desirable than an able Wade.

Johnson thereafter ceased his interference in Reconstruction, but he still managed to lash out in economic policy. In late July, he stubbornly pocket-vetoed a moderate measure by Republicans to refund the national debt at lower rates. But otherwise, Congress overrode his vetoes and ignored his policy suggestions. Johnson's influence declined even further after he was rejected by both political parties in that year's presidential nominations. He was by now a president without a constituency, especially outside the white supremacist South.

In early December 1868, Johnson sent his final annual message to Congress.[135] It was a rabble-rouser. In it, he blasted Congress for its unconstitutional encroachments on the executive branch, states' rights, and democracy itself. He called for spending cuts. He excoriated "our public indebtedness, which has accumulated with such alarming rapidity and assumed such colossal proportions." Through this debt, Johnson claimed, Americans had "suffered themselves to become enslaved, and merely exchanged slave owners for new taskmasters in the shape of bondholders and taxgatherers." He therefore suggested that all interest payments on the federal debt be redirected to paying down the principal, thereby eliminating the debt by 1885. And he repeated his call for a partial repudiation of US war debts and a wholesale devaluation of the US dollar.[136] Republicans in Congress were so infuriated that they halted the reading of Johnson's address midway.

Yet, as president, Johnson still had cards to play. On Christmas Day 1868, in an act of defiance, he granted blanket amnesty to all Confederates who had participated in the armed rebellion. In a political slap back at Johnson, and to assuage nervous bondholders and investors, the outgoing Republican Congress passed the Public Credit Act. Backed by McCulloch and strong Republican majorities, it promised that "the faith of the United States is solemnly pledged to the payment in coin or its equivalent" of all public debts as originally contracted. One of Johnson's final acts as president was to pocket-veto it.[137]

Nevertheless, the US economy was performing well and held vast potential in 1869. In fact, unbeknownst to anyone at the time, the United States was entering into one of the fastest, but most volatile, growth spurts of any society in history. Yet it was being administered by a political apparatus designed for another time. In particular, the three pillars of the Gilded Age's infamous political corruption (patronage, the moiety system, and assessments) had become instrumental to local Republican political machines and their electoral victories. These instruments for power sat in tension with the growing demand for a modern, professional, and energetic federal bureaucracy. And presiding over the decade's commencement was a man who possessed little of the education or experience that we tend to think necessary to manage it all: Ulysses S. Grant.

4

Ulysses S. Grant, First Term

"A Great Soldier Might Be a Baby Politician," 1869–1873

The American economy under Ulysses S. Grant was unusually volatile; it was also, on average, anemic. Most historians either fault Grant or dismiss him as having been powerless or irrelevant. He is stereotyped as "lazy" and "intellectually dim."[1] He was supposedly a president "who did not know politics" and "was uninterested in domestic policy [other than Reconstruction]" and whose two terms in office were marked by scandal after scandal.[2] Recent biographies have attempted to correct this narrative, but even Grant himself regularly admitted, "Mistakes have been made as all can see" and "It was my fortune or misfortune to be called to the office of Chief Executive without any previous political training."[3] Hence presidential scholars continue to argue that Grant "had neither the detailed knowledge of the governmental process needed to perform the role of chief executive nor the political experience required to bend other leaders to his purposes."[4] Certainly the economic results appear to have been disastrous. Under Grant, there occurred two financial panics followed by two severe recessions. Together, they devastated Reconstruction in the South and severely damaged the Republican Party. Hence, the overall picture is one of an incompetent, detached, political naïf who allowed corruption to flourish while Congress, his appointees, and political machines ran the country for their own selfish purposes, sinking the economy.

However, considerable evidence suggests otherwise. First, the economy performed poorly, but not because Grant was visionless, stupid, or disinterested. In fact, Grant appears to have been consistently engaged in economic policymaking. Along with Reconstruction and foreign affairs, the economy was a top administration priority throughout his presidency. And in each of these policy realms, Grant made many of the key decisions, and did so after considerable debate and thoughtful personal deliberation. Also, many of Grant's economic accomplishments were impressive. He succeeded in reducing the massive federal debt burden and in defending the US dollar, thereby reassuring investors who continued to pour money into the US economy, despite its risks. He also backed the use of both federal funds and military might to secure the West for economic development. And he helped navigate the United States safely away

Presidential Leadership in Feeble Times. Mark Zachary Taylor, Oxford University Press. © Oxford University Press 2024.
DOI: 10.1093/oso/9780197750742.003.0005

from armed conflicts that would have severely damaged the nation's trade and financial positions.

This chapter examines Grant's background, political-economic vision for the country, and economic stewardship during his first term in office. It shows that Grant's presidency was almost entirely dedicated to settling issues left unresolved from the Civil War. In many ways, it had been *his* war, and he sought to finish it on terms that he understood. These terms included the readmission of rebel states into the Union, the expansion of civil rights and liberties to African Americans, and the settlement of wartime disagreements with the United Kingdom. For the presidency, Grant sought a reversion back to prewar traditions of a more restrained, less public-facing, and "Whiggish" chief executive.[5] On the economic side, his main goal was the reduction of wartime debt, and hence taxes, and the return of the US greenback to parity with gold. Few doubted that the United States could pay its debts. But a firestorm had erupted over how it would pay (i.e., gold or inflated paper currency), and therefore whether it would repay its debts in full. Grant insisted on full repayment. In doing so, he dedicated the country to a strict deflationary monetary policy that may have handicapped the economy and contributed to a pair of financial crises and recessions. But these were deliberate policy choices, *not* accidents committed by a disinterested, incompetent, inexperienced political amateur.

Background

For those who seek auguries of a president's performance in their upbringing or prior credentials, Ulysses S. Grant's background fails to provide much guidance. On the one hand, it reveals some enduring personality traits. Grant's personal history also provides us with useful context for understanding his rise to power and the conduct of his presidency. But it contradicts claims that a leader's character or past experience is key to their economic success or failure.

Born in 1822, Grant grew up in a small Ohio farming town around forty miles southeast of Cincinnati. The Grant family was middle class for its day. His father was a successful leather tanner and an outspoken local politician; his mother was a homemaker, a devout Methodist, and famously laconic.[6] Together Grant's parents created a caring, but stern, home for their six children. "I never received a harsh word or suffered an unjust act from my father or mother," Grant later wrote.[7] As a youth, he was "a steady, serious sort of boy who took everything in earnest."[8] In religion, he was respectful but never particularly pious.[9] Nevertheless, family and friends described him as "notably considerate and unselfish."[10] Grant was almost pathologically honest and straightforward. He seemed to fear and loathe misrepresenting himself. Unfortunately, he expected the same rectitude of others, which did not serve him well in business, nor later as president.[11] Overall, friends and family praised young Ulysses as a "stout, rugged" boy. He worked "as much . . . as grown men" but also regularly enjoyed fishing, swimming, skating, and games with his friends.[12] Hence, Grant and others have generally described his youth as "uneventful."[13] It held few portents of his future performance as either general or president.

In political economy and business, Grant never received much education. As a boy, he attended local schools for basic instruction in "Reading, 'Riting, 'Rithmetic."[14] But he later described himself as "not studious," and excelled at little other than horsemanship, which he mastered at an early age.[15] "I was fond of agriculture, and of all employment [in] which horses were used," he remembered.[16] His ambitious father, however, had other plans. After Ulysses turned seventeen, he was sent off to West Point Military Academy. There he received extensive training in mathematics, science, and engineering, as well as French, ethics, and topography. But there was little economics instruction at West Point, only some light history and political science, mostly focused on legal and military aspects.[17] Nor did Grant develop much personal interest in economic issues later in life. He was admired for his character at the military academy, but he was a lackluster student and an unenthusiastic cadet.[18] After four years, he graduated in the middle ranks of his class, with thoughts of perhaps becoming a college math professor.[19] "A military life had no charms for me, and I had not the faintest idea of staying in the army," Grant later recalled.[20]

Thus, Grant's entrée into a military career was more a product of historical accident than personal design. After his graduation in 1843, by tradition, Lieutenant Grant owed several years of service to the US Army.[21] He was sent first to central Louisiana, then to southern Texas, and thence into Mexico for the Mexican-American War, where he served as an infantry company commander and regiment quartermaster. During the conflict, Grant proved a highly effective officer.[22] On the battlefield, his fellow soldiers judged him a man of "superb courage" and preternaturally cool under fire. Back in camp, Grant remained reserved and unpretentious.[23] As a result, he quickly rose to the rank of brevet captain.[24] Yet he abhorred war. Despite his personal success in combat, privately he was "bitterly opposed" to the invasion of Mexico and regarded the conflict "as one of the most unjust ever waged by a stronger against a weaker nation."[25] Grant felt that the war of conquest contradicted American values. He also felt sympathy for the Mexican people, who endured hardships from all sides.

After the war, Grant married and drifted through a series of dull military postings to Detroit, upstate New York, Oregon, and northern California.[26] He took his army service seriously; he believed in military honor and duty. But he became bored and listless. Far from his family and friends, Grant descended into depression and bouts of binge drinking. This aggravated his commanding officer, "a[n] old S. of a B." who "was prejudiced against Grant" and made his life miserable.[27] Grant therefore resigned from the army during spring 1854. Rumors soon spread that it was alcoholism which had forced him out. Grant would battle this reputation for the rest of his life, providing useful fodder for scandal-seeking reporters, political enemies, and historians alike.[28]

Grant now entered his "wilderness years." He moved to St. Louis, where he tried his hand at farming, real estate, and even selling firewood on the streets.[29] But all his business ventures failed. The Panic of 1857 and ensuing recession not only doomed some of his endeavors, but, desperate for money and naïvely trusting, Grant was also repeatedly duped by hucksters. He even tried clerking for a federal custom house, but he "lacked administrative skills and kept untidy records."[30] He was ultimately saved from penury only by the generosity of friends and family. Eventually, to ensure steady employment, in 1860 he moved to Illinois to work in his father's leather business. Perhaps his only success during this time was his marriage and his family of four children.

Once again, history interceded. The outbreak of the Civil War in 1861 provoked Grant's enthusiastic support for the Union. He thought slavery merely "a source of irritation and shame" at the time, but he adamantly opposed secession, calling it "suicidal" to the country.[31] As a decorated war veteran, he became a local military expert in Illinois. At first, he was engaged to drill Union soldiers. He then served as a civilian advisor to the Illinois governor's office for two months. In mid-June 1861, the governor appointed Grant to a colonelship in command of his district's volunteer regiment, and he was sent off to fight in Missouri. Thereafter, Grant's career took off.

Grant proved an adept field commander. Drawing on his military training and wartime experience, he quickly gained a reputation for aggressive action and skilled, cool-headed leadership.[32] Many of the inexperienced Union officer corps consisted of less competent braggarts, men who failed at war-making but still chased after public accolades. Thus, Grant's combination of modesty and achievement stood out to his superiors. As in prior combat, contemporaries and biographers alike again describe Grant as being subdued, cold, and calculating in battle, but also dignified, fair, and compassionate, even toward his Confederate enemies.

His conversations and written communications suggest that Grant fought doggedly for reunion, not for wealth, vengeance, or personal fame. He saw the Confederacy as a rebellion launched by a small, selfish Southern aristocracy. "It does seem as if just a few men have produced all the present difficulty" he wrote.[33] The nation needed to be saved from their treachery. And while he had initially supported the war "for maintaining the integrity of the glorious old *Stars & Stripes*, the Constitution, and the Union," Grant soon also grew contemptuous of slavery.[34] "Equal rights to all. White and Black," he told a surrendering rebel general early in the conflict.[35] Beyond these general notions of national unity, freedom, and equality, he followed no particular economic philosophy in relation to the war.

Grant's wartime accomplishments gained him rapid promotion. He was made brigadier general for his effectiveness in Missouri during the summer of 1861. That August he was placed in command of all Union troops in southern Illinois and southeast Missouri. Thereafter Grant's swift victories along the Kentucky-Tennessee border elevated him to the highest ranks of Lincoln's generals. "I can't spare this man; he fights," the president supposedly told critics of Grant.[36] Regardless, by the end of the war, Grant was a national hero, having participated in some two dozen battles and risen to the rank of commanding general, the most senior position in the US Army.

As described in the previous chapter, the assassination of Abraham Lincoln in April 1865 dramatically changed the country's, and Grant's, political trajectory. The new president, Andrew Johnson, abhorred slavery and the wealthy Southern aristocracy built upon it. He therefore supported ratification of the Thirteenth Amendment to the Constitution. But Johnson despised Blacks as racially inferior and opposed awarding them political rights or social equality. He also resisted punishing the ex-Confederacy. Instead, Johnson sought to restore the old South, minus slavery, rather than to transform it.[37] In economics, when the postwar recession came, he called for a partial repudiation of US war debts and a wholesale devaluation of the US dollar.[38] This terrified banks and investors. Finally, Johnson's Reconstruction agenda and belligerent behavior came into open conflict with Congress, his generals, and even his own cabinet. Thus there ensued, from late 1865 onward, a political war between Johnson and Congress over not just domestic policy but the power and conduct of the presidency itself.

Grant's relationship with Johnson was polite and civil at first. They quarreled over surrender terms for Confederate soldiers.[39] But otherwise, General Grant was left alone to conclude the war and establish a military occupation of the South. Johnson then began to use the widely admired Grant as a political prop. Grant did his duty, but privately, his political sympathies moved toward the Radical Republicans who supported civil rights for freed slaves and a political purge of ex-Confederate leaders. Widespread violence against Blacks in the South convinced Grant of the need "to protect the rights of the freedmen"[40] and to extend "the elective franchise to her colored citizens the same as her white ones."[41] During 1867, Grant refused to become Johnson's puppet in the president's attempt to seize control over Reconstruction policy via the War Department. In private, Grant admitted that he was "disgusted" with Johnson's behavior, calling him a "disgrace" and an "infernal liar," and quietly signaled approval of the president's impeachment.[42] Otherwise, Grant remained dignified, reserved, and publicly aloof from the dirty scrum of partisan politics relished by Johnson.

1868 Elections

By the end of 1867, it was clear that Grant was the Republican favorite for the presidency.[43] He had become a symbol of strength and stability, while the rest of Washington had descended into partisan rancor. No other candidate enjoyed such wide respect among voters. Also, a sour economy that year had delivered many state and local elections to the Democrats.[44] Republicans feared that any other nominee might result in another wave of Democratic victories in 1868, thereby ending Reconstruction. This the dutiful Grant could not tolerate. "I believed that if a democratic president was elected there would be little chance for those who fought for the Union," he later explained.[45] He therefore willingly allowed himself to be drafted into politics.[46] Indeed, Republican enthusiasm for Grant was so strong that, at the May 1868 party convention, he was the only candidate and was chosen unanimously on the first ballot. He was joined a few ballots later by former House Speaker Schuyler Colfax (R-IN) as his running mate.

The economy played a major role in the 1868 electoral campaign, though Reconstruction and race dominated the headlines. The top economic concern was the $356 million of devalued greenbacks still in circulation, comprising half the nation's currency but backed by nothing more than the government's word.[47] More urgently, the greenback had lost roughly one-third of its value against gold since its creation in early 1862.[48] And there was no clear policy by which to bring it back to parity. The nation also owed over $2.58 billion in war debt, equivalent to almost one-third of annual GDP. Hence Americans still paid a panoply of taxes. Federal duties seemed to be levied on almost every economic transaction, including imports, income, property, investments, auctions, licenses, daily purchases (e.g., tobacco, alcohol, sugar), and business activities of all sorts.[49]

For their part, the Democrats wanted to repudiate some of the federal debt so as to lessen the tax burden. To that end, they proposed using inflated paper greenbacks rather than gold coin to pay off creditors, scaring investment markets.[50] Repudiation was apostasy to many Northerners. "For every dollar of the national debt, the blood of a soldier is pledged. Every bond, in letter and spirit, must be as sacred as a soldier's grave," declared a former Union army general.[51] So in Grant's brief written statement accepting the Republican nomination, he took pains to promise lower federal spending so as to "lighten the burden of taxation, while it constantly reduces the national debt,"[52] and the Republican Party platform stridently proclaimed, "We denounce all forms of repudiation as a national crime."[53]

Both parties' presidential campaigns linked the nation's tax and spending burdens to widespread corruption and incompetence in the federal bureaucracy.[54] Though long a problem, civil service reform had become a national priority. New England Republicans were particularly furious. Under Lincoln, they had enjoyed considerable influence over the executive branch, but Johnson had since cut them out of the Washington power structure. Enraged by their excommunication, these elites filled the 1868 Republican Party platform with denunciations of "the corruptions which have been so shamefully nursed and fostered by Andrew Johnson."[55] In contrast, trade policy, business regulation, and development of the West were little mentioned during the presidential race.

The 1868 elections thus became a battle over contending visions for both the country and the presidency. The Democrats declared, "This is a White Man's Country; Let White Men Rule." The Republicans answered with "Let us Have Peace," a quote from Grant's acceptance letter.[56] Holding with tradition, and his personal preference for silence, Grant declined to stump for his own election. Instead he went on vacation with his wife around the country and then quietly returned home to Illinois to wait out the contest. His opponent, Horatio Seymour, former Democratic governor of New York, failed to do likewise. Seymour launched a daring two-week speaking tour of several northern states, "not because I wish to do so, but because you have called upon me," he claimed.[57] But coming so soon after Johnson's obnoxious public speaking ventures, Seymour was "condemned by partisan opponents as demagogic and demeaning."[58] That November, Grant won one of the greatest landslides in US history, 73 percent of the electoral college, though a far more modest 52.7 percent of the popular vote.

The election of Grant was widely seen as a redemptive event. After the shocking political assassination of Lincoln and the unprecedented behavior of Johnson, the country now seemed back on track. *Harper's Weekly* boasted, "The national confidence is unbounded."[59] Businessmen and investors celebrated Grant's election as "a triumph of the conservatism and honesty of our people."[60] Civil service reformers rejoiced, "[W]e have in Grant a man who will break up the present system . . . of party charlatans."[61] In fact, so deep was public faith in him that one congressman later recalled, "The loyal people of the country looked to Grant with an almost superstitious hope. They were prepared to expect almost any miracle from the great genius who had subdued the rebellion."[62] They would be gravely disappointed.

Grant the Politician

Grant is typically described as a simple, quiet soldier who abhorred politics and had "no grand vision of his own to guide the country."[63] Other than perhaps

Reconstruction, he was supposedly indifferent to policy and politics.[64] After all, he wrote no philosophical tracts during his life, rarely gave political speeches, and appeared to avoid politics altogether. In his spare time, he had generally preferred to relax with his family or read fiction rather than take part in political activities. He had rarely even voted.[65] Thus, Grant is sometimes stereotyped as having seen the presidency as ceremonial, "a reward—a semiretirement to be enjoyed," rather than a position of true leadership.[66]

But this view is not well supported by the evidence.[67] Grant was uniquely stoic, but he was *not* disinterested in politics. Throughout his life, his friends and neighbors "were impressed by his evident mastery of, and interest in, local and national political issues."[68] He privately expressed strong views about federal policy during and after the war. And though never overtly partisan as a youth, he later told a reporter, "If I had ever had any political sympathies they would have been with the Whigs. I was raised in that school."[69] Indeed, his father, his military heroes (Generals Zachary Taylor and Winfield Scott), and his wartime commander in chief (Lincoln) had all been Whigs.[70]

Rather, Grant likely seemed apolitical because he personally loathed the infighting, selfishness, and showmanship that came with mid-19th-century politics. He also sincerely believed in modesty, self-sacrifice, and unity. All his life he had eschewed self-promotion. He also avoided personal confrontations. Finally, not only was Grant naturally reserved but, as both general and president, it was in his self-interest to appear aloof from politics. In fact, contemporaries often celebrated "his genius for silence."[71] Therefore Grant's avoidance of open politics should not be mistaken for lack of vision or interest.

Grant's vision for the country is well summarized in his first inaugural address, a brief exhortation that he wrote himself and then repeated in different versions throughout the rest of his presidency.[72] He dedicated his presidency almost entirely to settling issues left unresolved from the Civil War. His top priority was "cementing a happy union" after four years of fratricide.[73] Indeed, reunification had been Grant's initial motivation for entering the war back in 1861. And during the conflict he had consistently rejected any talk of peace short of "the complete subjugation of the South."[74] Then, in 1868, he accepted the nomination for the presidency because he feared that another candidate "would lose to us, largely, the results of the costly war which we have gone through."[75] Thus, as president, reunification of the United States under the Constitution was simply a continuation of the same war aims for which he had been fighting for eight years. And national reunification was perhaps the most consistent goal expressed in Grant's rhetoric and actions throughout his two administrations.

For Grant, the enforcement of legal protections and civil rights for African Americans was an essential part of national reunification. Initially, he had joined the war for the sake of the Union, not Black equality.[76] However, as the war progressed, emancipation gradually became a primary war objective for both Grant and many of his supporters. And by early 1869, Grant was forcefully advocating Black suffrage, proclaiming, "[T]he question should be settled now . . . by the ratification of the fifteenth article of amendment to the Constitution."[77] And throughout his presidency, the enforcement of African American rights was closely allied to national political reunification as a top concern.

As for the presidency itself, Grant rejected the independent policy activism and outspoken rhetorical style of his angry predecessor, Johnson. Grant repeatedly declared, "[A]ll laws will be faithfully executed, whether they meet my approval or not."[78] In other words, under Grant, Congress, not the White House, would legislate. The president would be reserved and dignified and stay out of the headlines. This was consistent with his pre-presidency political beliefs. It also fit the Whig principles of government that Grant had imbibed from his father and witnessed in Lincoln. He believed that good leaders relied on actions and integrity rather than words; failed leaders (like Andrew Johnson, Stephen Douglas, and Horatio Seymour) gave sensational speeches and practiced self-aggrandizement. Or as Grant put it, they "were public speakers and . . . were beaten. I am no speaker and don't want to be beaten."[79]

Nevertheless, Grant also defended his right as president to influence policy. He promised to veto measures that he opposed and to "express my views to Congress and urge them according to my judgment."[80] In his policy decisions, he claimed to take a utilitarian view, insisting "that the greatest good to the greatest number is the object to be attained."[81] He also frequently stressed his independence from either political party or special interests, especially during his early years in office. However, in practice, Grant often used arbitrary, personal moral judgments about who deserved government favor. Nor was he particularly shy about making policy recommendations.

In fact, throughout his two administrations, Grant was a strong supporter of innovative "big government" programs. For example, he advocated for the Freedman's Bureau, aid and citizenship for Native Americans, federal disaster relief, the eight-hour workday, postal savings banks, annexation of new federal territories, free primary education, federal support for agriculture, a trans-isthmus canal, and the aggressive use of federal troops to overrule Southern state governments. Here his lack of political or policy experience proved a liability. For the novelty of these schemes made him seem amateurish and impulsive to many 19th-century Americans. Critics thought him incompetent, concluding that "[a] great soldier might be a baby politician."[82]

Finally, Grant's naïve faith in the honesty of his fellow man led him into many avoidable scandals. He too often assumed that others shared his own values of honesty and integrity.[83] As a result, throughout his life, con men had repeatedly coaxed loans and investments from an overly credulous Grant, and then absconded with the funds. Such problems did not end when Grant entered the presidency. Instead, they amplified into national calamities when his own appointees, and even some friends and family, used their positions to swindle the country.

1869: "A New Strife to Which I Am Not Trained"

When Grant entered the White House in March 1869, the numbers tell the story of an economy recovering from years of postwar contraction.[84] For example, per capita economic growth strengthened to over 2.7 percent in 1869, though mostly concentrated during the first few months of the year.[85] Farm outputs were booming. Business activity was strong and accelerating. Railroad construction leaped 66 percent that year, which helped to drive up annual industrial production by 7.5 percent.[86] Yet inflation was nowhere to be seen. Meanwhile, the federal budget enjoyed a surplus totaling 14.9 percent of total federal expenditures in 1869; therefore, the federal debt was shrinking, albeit slowly, and stood at 29.6 percent of GDP. As a result, the US dollar was gradually strengthening against foreign currencies; for example, in British pounds, by 1869, the dollar had appreciated 35 percent from its wartime lows.[87] Thanks to the improving dollar and opportunities for business expansion, foreign investment neared 16 percent of GDP.[88] But the strengthening economy, foreign investment, and strong dollar translated into strong demand for foreign imports. Thus, perhaps the only blemish on the economy in spring 1869 was a steadily worsening trade deficit.

Once in office, Grant moved rapidly to fulfill his campaign promises. Debt came first. The outgoing president had called bondholders "invidious" and asked that payments to them be made in inflated greenbacks.[89] Many Democrats agreed. Thus, despite recent Republican victories, America's creditors remained nervous and looked to the new government for cues. Grant did not disappoint. The first law he signed was the Public Credit Act of 1869, passed by the Republican Congress after just two weeks in session.[90] A mere paragraph long, it "solemnly pledged" the US government to pay its debts in gold or silver, unless contracted otherwise, and "to make provision at the earliest practicable period for the redemption of the United States [paper] notes in coin."[91] It was purely aspirational. But it reaffirmed the US government's intent for paper greenbacks to, over time, become freely exchangeable for gold at face value.

In fact, throughout his presidency, Grant consistently prioritized quick repayment of the national debt and a return to the gold standard, declaring that "every dollar of Government indebtedness should be paid in gold."[92] For Grant, this was an essential part of getting back to normal after the war. But it also dovetailed with his long-held personal values. Throughout his life, Grant conscientiously kept track of his debts, and he supposedly paid back every dollar, or favor, he ever owed.[93] As president, Grant intended for the nation to do the same. He also explained that full debt repayment was necessary to restore trust in the United States as a borrower and that "it will go far toward strengthening a credit which ought to be the best in the world, and will ultimately enable us to replace the debt with bonds bearing less interest than we now pay."[94]

However, Grant knew little about the technicalities of public finance; therefore the task of achieving these goals largely fell to George Boutwell, his skilled Treasury secretary, whose policies Grant strongly supported. Boutwell adopted a multipronged strategy. On the greenback, he chose benign neglect. In order to bring the greenback's price back in line with gold, the Treasury needed to either reduce the supply of greenbacks (by withdrawing and destroying them) or grow the supply of gold (through economic growth or new gold discoveries). Boutwell's predecessor had attempted the more conservative route, aggressively retiring greenbacks, from $423 million in April 1866 to $356 million in February 1868.[95] However, reducing the money supply in the middle of a postwar recession had produced disastrous political results. And to save their seats in an election year, in February 1868 the Republican Congress had forbidden any further Treasury actions to reduce greenbacks. Then a congressman, Boutwell had supported this prohibition. Now as Treasury secretary, his strategy was to hold the quantity of greenbacks constant while letting the economy slowly "grow up to specie."[96]

As for the federal debt, Grant backed Boutwell in using budget surpluses to gradually pay it down. To this end, the Treasury set up a "sinking fund" into which excess federal revenues were regularly set aside to gradually "sink" the debt.[97] Boutwell also cleverly used excess federal gold inventories (earned through taxes, tariffs, and fees) to buy up greenbacks, and then spend those greenbacks to buy back Treasury bonds.[98] This recirculated gold back into the economy, while using inflated paper money to reduce the debt, all while obeying Congress's prohibition on greenback reductions. Boutwell also achieved several rounds of refunding at lower interest rates. When he came into the Treasury, most short-term war debt had been paid off. But there remained a mountain of long-term debt at fairly high interest rates. Boutwell managed to restructure some $1.5 billion (or roughly 70 percent) of it in two rounds, the first of which occurred in mid-July 1870, which brought down the interest on the federal debt from 6 percent to 4 to 5 percent.[99] In all of these actions, Boutwell enjoyed the hearty backing of President Grant.

Success came quickly. As early as June 1869, the federal debt was already reduced by over $13 million, or roughly 0.5 percent.[100] By the end of 1869, it would be down almost $77 million.[101] Even foreign critics hailed Grant and Boutwell for their actions, "which in a few months have lifted their country [out] of the slough of discredit into which it had fallen."[102] And thanks to Boutwell's refunding efforts, the Treasury's interest payments on public debt fell from $140 million in 1868 to $117 million by 1872, a reduction of over 16.4 percent. "Thus the dangerous figure of repudiation which had been boldly moving before the public for several years received a severe blow. . . . Creditors were no longer afraid to buy, and from that hour the national credit took a strong turn upward," wrote one contemporary.[103]

Grant supported other major economic initiatives during his first weeks in office. For example, he signed legislation that cut alcohol taxes, increased federal spending on river and harbor infrastructure, and authorized federal land grants for railroad construction (mostly in the West).[104] The *New York Times* applauded, "[I]n everything thus far he has shown unmistakable determination to do the very best he could."[105] Even the acerbic *Nation* admitted that Grant and the new Congress had "an excellent effect on the public credit at home and abroad."[106]

First-Year Blunders

Although business and financial interests praised Grant in 1869, some in the Republican establishment quickly soured on their new president. For while Grant was an asset in terms of elections and federal policy, his status as a political "outsider" also made him an unreliable patron at the top of the Republican political machine. For example, when selecting his cabinet, Grant failed to heed the preferences of party elites. He intended to demonstrate his political independence, to show that he would not be controlled by the party or its bosses. However, many influential Republicans in Congress, the party, and the press failed to get the appointments they desired. After months of promoting Grant for president, they now seethed with "wrath and indignation."[107] Infuriated congressmen called Grant "stupidly dull and ignorant"[108] and dismissed his appointees as "second rate men."[109]

It did not help that many of Grant's appointees came from the army. This gave the administration an unusual militarist flavor that many Americans found offensive. The White House "assumed the character of military head-quarters," complained a powerful Senate Republican, "[t]o the dishonor of the civil service and in total disregard of precedent."[110] Grant also ran his White House like an army general. This included senior staff who sometimes insulated him from favor-seeking congressmen and independent-minded bureaucrats, both valuable sources of information and potential allies.[111] "I thought I could run the government of the United States, as I did the staff of my army. It was my mistake, and it led me into other mistakes," he later admitted.[112]

Grant aggravated matters when, in making his senior appointments, he relied mostly on personal judgments of loyalty and character. The result was a series of public embarrassments. For example, his initial nominee for Treasury secretary, a wealthy New York merchant, was found ineligible due to potential business conflicts. His first secretary of state served only a few ceremonial days, as the brief appointment turned out to be a favor to one of Grant's political allies. The new secretary of war was so ill that he survived only six months. Grant's first navy secretary, a personal friend and political nonentity, expended much of his scant political capital renaming old naval vessels; clearly unqualified, he resigned after just three months.[113] Even supporters called Grant's cabinet fumbles "a dreadful shock to the prestige of the new administration . . . because it is such boys' play."[114] And regardless of their individual talents, Grant's senior appointees were mocked as being "chiefly distinguished for having conferred on him costly and valuable benefactions."[115] That is, they were among Grant's top financial donors.

Grant's cabinet remained unstable throughout his presidency. In eight years, over two dozen men would oversee just seven departments, and not one would serve the full duration.[116] There were two each at State and Navy, three interior secretaries, four Treasury secretaries, five war secretaries, and five attorneys general. And criticism of them could be withering. "The cabinet of Genl Grant seems to be a kind of genteel lunch, where gentlemen stop for refreshment for awhile, & if they stay too long are told to 'move on' by the police, so everybody can have a chance," mocked one Republican.[117] Few were remarkable, some were corrupt, though his second secretary of state (Hamilton Fish) and four Treasury secretaries are generally considered highly competent picks.

Grant did no better in his junior appointments. He inherited a government of some fifty thousand federal employees.[118] Some 88 percent of them worked outside of Washington, mostly in the country's extensive postal system and revenue collection offices. Like all presidents during the Gilded Age, Grant was besieged by thousands of party faithful seeking appointments to these positions. Again, too many plum positions went to members of Grant's extended family, old army buddies, and financial supporters. The New York World joked that Grant had "appointed his whole family to government posts."[119] State Department appointees were derided as "a herd of swine."[120] The Nation complained of "every office in . . . government being offered to the . . . two and three hundred thousand of the least reputable portion of the community."[121] Civil service reformers were furious at the overt nepotism, though, admittedly, the worst critics were party regulars who failed to get themselves appointed. Congressional Republicans were also frustrated that Grant's personal patronage had reduced their share of federal jobs to dole out. The Republican Party, founded upon antislavery, was still only fifteen years old when Grant assumed office.[122] And with the Civil War over, patronage appointments were seen as a vital tool for keeping otherwise disparate Republicans united and in power. Grant was now hogging that tool for himself.

Grant further disappointed his supporters when he appeared to surrender in his first major confrontation with the Senate. With the combative Andrew Johnson now safely out of the White House, Grant immediately asked Congress to repeal the Tenure of Office Act of 1867. It was specifically designed to "[tie] the hands of a hostile President" by requiring "the advice and consent of the Senate" to remove a federal officer.[123] The House quickly complied. However, covetous of their new power over the executive branch, Senate Republicans refused. In return, Grant threatened to retain Johnson's existing appointees, thereby cutting off the supply of new patronage jobs altogether. After weeks of rancorous infighting, a compromise was arranged. Grant would have free rein over cabinet removals (about which he cared most), but he would consult with the Senate over firings and appointments of other federal positions (where he rarely differed with Congress anyway). Although technically a victory, these nuances were lost on the American public. To many, Grant appeared weak and bumbling, and probably incapable of fulfilling his promises to clean up government. A disgruntled Republican conservative wrote, "The lawyers duped and cowed him. The poor devil has neither the sagacity and obstinacy for which he has credit."[124]

Grant never recovered the prestige and power lost during those first careless months in office. For there were other blunders. He failed to convince Congress to transfer the corruption-ridden Indian Bureau out of the poorly run Interior Department. He seemed powerless against supposedly entrenched cabals throughout the executive branch. Even on his own former turf, the War Department, he proved unable to prevent, or reverse, large reductions in the US military.

Every scandal or misstep of Grant's administration was henceforth amplified by his enemies, including many disgruntled Republicans. Resentment and disgust ran especially high among New England elites who felt that they, not this "political ignoramus" military general and his cadre of loyalists, should rule. A few took up lifelong grudges.[125] They proceeded to launch a fairly successful smear campaign against Grant, publicly berating him as corrupt and hopelessly unfit for office.[126] Their collective animus partly explains why Grant is so often portrayed as inept, unscrupulous, and disengaged.[127]

It did not help that Grant generally declined to speak publicly to defend himself or tout the accomplishments of his own administration. He dreaded public speaking and gave few speeches or interviews throughout his two terms.[128] He also believed that open bragging or quarreling was unpresidential. As at least one historian has found, this "often left a vacuum that his enemies eagerly and adeptly filled."[129]

The Gold Panic of 1869

Meanwhile, the worst economic debacle of Grant's first term was already brewing. During late spring 1869, the US economy began to slow. Crop harvests, especially wheat, surged to unprecedented levels, sending agricultural prices into rapid decline. Lower farm incomes meant defaults on loans and a slump in demand for farm inputs. In the cities, deflation quietly accelerated below −4 percent, pushing real interest rates up over 10 percent. Business activity began to temper. Limited national economic data were collected at the time, but by mid-June even Grant privately confessed that "he thought there was a certain amount of fictitiousness about the prosperity of the country."[130]

It was under these circumstances that the "Gold Conspiracy" was born. Partly in response to the slowing economy, a pair of wealthy railroad speculators entangled an oblivious Grant in a daring scheme to corner the US gold market.[131] The speculators' plan was to use inflated greenbacks to purchase an enormous amount of gold. They would then withhold their supplies so as to drive up gold prices. This would push down foreign prices of US agriculture (in gold terms), producing an export boom and thereby increasing the volume of traffic on their railroads headed to eastern ports. And of course the schemers would also profit directly off rising gold prices when foreign merchants bid to obtain specie for use in international trade payments.

The problem was that, under Grant, the US Treasury sporadically sold millions of dollars' worth of gold every few weeks, trading its specie for greenbacks as part of Boutwell's effort to pay down the federal debt. This unpredictable dumping of federal gold onto the private market drove down the price of gold, thereby threatening the gold corner scheme. The schemers therefore enlisted the help of Grant's brother-in-law to gain access to the president. An unsuspecting Grant met with the men several times during summer 1869. They personally lobbied Grant to slow or suspend federal gold sales, arguing that "the business interests of the country required an advance in the price of gold."[132] Grant's brother-in-law then privately urged him to comply in "the true interests of the government."[133] Grant proved unmovable. But the schemers successfully circulated rumors otherwise, even planting newspaper articles suggesting that the administration had further tightened its monetary policy.[134]

By September, many on Wall Street were duped into believing that the gold conspiracy involved "pretty much everybody in authority in the United

States, beginning with President Grant and ending with the doorkeepers of Congress."[135] Grant declined to comment publicly on the rumors, insisting instead on Whiggish presidential silence. With no clarity coming from the White House or the Treasury, the market swung in line with the scheme and the price of gold rose swiftly, increasing 25 percent over the course of a few weeks.[136] Foreign trade slowed dramatically as importers held off on buying gold.[137]

Grant and his Treasury secretary eventually caught on. On September 24, 1869, "Black Friday," Grant recommended that the Treasury flood the market with gold, thereby ruining the gold corner. In just half an hour, the price of gold plummeted from $160 to $133 per ounce and the schemers were bankrupted of their funds.[138] But so too were thousands of investors who had been lured into the market. The collapse in gold triggered bank runs, as frightened savers rushed to protect their money from potential bank failures. Worried stockholders sold off their assets in a mad rush to cash. In just days $100 million in financial wealth (equal to around 1.2 percent of GDP) was erased.[139] Several prominent banks and investment houses went under. On Wall Street, the tangled mass of trade receipts took almost a month to resolve, while import and customs transactions ground to a halt. "[F]or several weeks, business was almost entirely paralyzed," recalled one merchant.[140] Investor trust in American financial markets plummeted. A former mayor of New York City, also a prominent banker, warned Congress, "[N]ot only in this country but all over the world . . . we here are [seen as] a set of gamblers and that it is not safe to enter into any contracts to us."[141] Across the United States, money and credit supplies contracted, leaving farmers and businessmen scrambling for funds to pay their workers and suppliers.

Meanwhile, false rumors spread of Grant's complicity in the attempted gold corner. One of the schemers insisted, "The President himself was interested with us," while the newspapers speculated wildly about Grant's participation in "all these splendid dinners, balls, parties, picnics and steamboat excursions in his honor by New York financiers."[142] Grant protested his innocence in a rare interview. But otherwise, he mostly declined to comment. Thus, it appeared to many that, at best, Grant had been tricked into participating; at worst, he had abetted the swindle for his family's gain.[143] These suspicions seemed to be confirmed when Grant refused to be interrogated, or even to submit written testimony, in the Republican-led congressional investigation that followed.[144]

Grant and the Recession of 1869–1870

By winter, the "brief" financial crisis had turned into a recession. Throughout 1870, the economy shrank by 2.8 percent per capita. Overall, business activity slumped more than 9 percent, causing business failures to leap by 36 percent. Investors shunned the American market, and Wall Street trading volumes were cut in half.[145] On the nation's farms, corn and cattle prices, already in decline, fell by around 25 percent, while wheat prices collapsed over 40 percent. Wages flattened for the first time since before the Civil War. Deflation accelerated for years. Thus, real interest rates remained high. Only the railroads kept building; hence industrial production rose, albeit at the slowest rate in years.[146] Perhaps the only positive side of the debacle was that US trade deficits fell due to a surge in cheap farm exports, even though imports of industrial and manufactured products also grew.

At first, Grant did nothing. Having belatedly thwarted the gold corner, he believed that his work was done, and he now stepped back from "interfering" in the economy. When pressured to act further in the days after the crash, he declared, "This matter had been concluded and I cannot open up nor consider the subject."[147] Grant held steadfast throughout autumn. The recession was not his problem; he blamed it on the greenback, which had enabled gold speculation in the first place.

The most common explanations for Grant's inaction do not hold up well.[148] Some argue that the provision of federal relief during recessions was too innovative for Grant; that it required a more active presidency than he was willing to practice; that it was not yet in the American mindset to seek government aid during recessions. Another stereotype is that, beyond a return to the gold standard, there were few calls for a federal response other than greater honesty, restraint, and anticorruption in government. None of these interpretations is well supported by the evidence. Tax cuts and federal spending *were* openly discussed during 1869–1870. And Grant energetically *supported* federal relief in response to economic disasters later in his administration.[149]

Rather, the evidence suggests that Grant simply prioritized debt reduction and a return to the gold standard. He believed that fraud and speculation had caused the crisis; ergo, honest debt repayment and responsible government finance would solve it. Therefore, he continued to insist that Congress return the United States to the gold standard, declaring that "no substitute for it can be devised."[150] To this end, in December 1869 Grant asked Congress to hold off on tariff and tax cuts that might have eased the recession. He even pushed legislators to renew the federal income tax, albeit at a reduced rate, to bring in additional revenue for debt service. He also requested more power to speed federal debt repayments and to refinance US debt at lower rates.[151] All told, Grant refused to use expansionary fiscal, monetary, or trade policy to address the recession of 1869–1870 because he believed they were either unnecessary or inappropriate to the task. Thus, the recession ran its course.

Grant's Approach to Economic Leadership

On other issues, Grant *did* support innovative and aggressive executive action to heal and enrich the economy. For example, he moved energetically whenever his monetary policy was threatened. In early February 1870, the Supreme Court ruled that parts of the Legal Tender Acts of 1862 were unconstitutional.[152] This wartime legislation had allowed the Treasury to print notes, such as greenbacks, to fund the Union war effort. However, in *Hepburn v. Griswold* (1870), the justices decided that while Congress could mint coins, it was not authorized to declare federal notes as "legal tender" for payment of debts, even during wartime. Neither Wall Street nor the banking sector appears to have been initially worried by the ruling.[153] But Grant and many Republicans saw it as a direct threat to their control over the nation's monetary policy. If enforced, the ruling might eliminate the greenback, creating a sudden and disastrous shock to the financial system. Just two months earlier, Grant had warned Congress against similar moves.[154] Grant therefore quickly appointed two new justices to the Supreme Court with views closer to his administration's.[155] He then instructed his attorney general to refile the case. And in May 1871, the newly composed Supreme Court reversed itself, thereby saving the greenback.[156]

During these years, Grant also led on critical foreign policy issues that had major economic ramifications. In particular, his administration averted a brewing war with Spain over Cuba (1869–1870), guarded US neutrality in the Franco-Prussian conflict (1870–1871), and hammered out a grand solution with Great Britain over boundary disputes and Civil War claims (1869–1871).[157] The last involved unprecedented rounds of international arbitration. These negotiations tempered a century of US-UK animosity and formally sent the two great powers on a more peaceful trajectory.[158] Any of these disputes could have involved the United States in an armed conflict that would have driven up inflation, deficits, and debt and damaged vital trade and investment relations. In the case of a naval war with Great Britain, an American victory was unlikely. Nevertheless, many expected open conflict at the time. Hence, more than one historian of the period has argued that "the greatest legacy of Grant and [Secretary of State] Hamilton Fish's foreign policy was the avoidance of war."[159]

Reconstruction

Admittedly, it was Reconstruction policy, not the economy, that dominated Grant's attention during his first term, though the two issues quickly became intertwined. Reconstruction is where Grant's capabilities as a political leader are perhaps most clearly demonstrated. Even before becoming president, he had openly supported the Thirteenth Amendment to the US Constitution, which ended slavery (ratified December 1865), and the Fourteenth Amendment, which guaranteed citizenship and equality under the law to Blacks (ratified July 1868). And during early summer 1868, candidate Grant had celebrated the readmission to the Union of seven Southern states which had formally adopted these amendments.[160] As president, Grant hoped to usher in the remainder.[161] He also sought to enforce the rights and liberties recently granted to Blacks in postwar legislation.

Once in office, President Grant moved quickly and deliberately to move Reconstruction forward. He backed a law to eliminate race as a bar to political office or jury duty in Washington, DC. He met with representatives of the remaining ex-Confederate states to strategize on their readmission to the Union, and then convinced Congress to approve their negotiations as law. Throughout 1869, Grant followed up on developments in the South to ensure progress. When reports emerged of violence in Southern elections, Grant ordered investigations. When elected politicians in the new Southern governments faced armed resistance, he sent in federal troops. That winter, Grant also threw his weight behind ratification and enforcement of the Fifteenth Amendment, to eliminate "race, color, or previous condition of servitude" as a bar to voting (ratified March 1870).[162] And he spent much of his presidency on federal interventions and programs to aid African Americans both politically and economically.[163]

However, these activities also enlarged the economic role, and the financial expenditures, of state governments far beyond what had been considered acceptable prior to the war.[164] To pay for them, tax hikes burdened a Southern population already groaning under the costs of rebuilding and personal debt. Northern businessmen exacerbated the situation. Mocked for their shallow opportunism, these "carpetbaggers" conspicuously bought up local businesses and farms in the South and invested in newfangled technologies. Together with some forward-looking Southerners, they embraced modern railroads, factories, and diversified farming. The railroads, in particular, were seen by the hopeful as a catalyst for prosperity. Promoters promised, "A free and living Republic [will] spring up in the track of the railroad as inevitably, as surely as grass and flowers follow in the spring."[165] But the costs of building and maintaining railroads far exceeded the ability of Southern governments to pay. Instead, new government bond issues flooded the market, further increasing the South's debt burden.

Ironically, the Panic of 1869 thrust a dagger into the economic belly of Reconstruction. Northern capital dried up. European investors left for more familiar markets. The 1870 recession then proceeded to kill off demand for much Southern output. Many Southern railroads, highly leveraged, went bankrupt. With them went the promise of a modern, diversified economy. Tax revenues plummeted, leaving mountains of Southern debt that sat "like an incubus on the people."[166] Speculation and fraud abounded in unregulated markets. Hypersensitive to their rights as workers, Black laborers began to organize. Meanwhile, Black politicians revealed themselves to be just as liable to faction, spoils, mismanagement, and corruption as their white counterparts.[167] Democrats and white supremacists therefore blamed the South's economic troubles on Blacks and Republicans. The former could not be trusted with political or economic responsibility; the latter were out to victimize, defraud, and humiliate the South. Republican officials of all shades were accused by Southerners of "corrupt motives and for the accomplishment of corrupt purposes."[168] Some were run out of office before their terms were completed.[169]

Trade and Taxes

By mid-1870, with the economy clearly stuck in some sort of malaise, Grant finally moved on tariff reductions. Trade policy was one area in which he was admittedly lackluster and merely followed the political winds. Trade had not been a major issue in the 1868 campaign. And Grant had appointed both protectionists and low-tariff men to senior economic positions without prejudice. Grant had also initially asked Congress to hold off on tariff reforms until after his Treasury secretary could refinance the nation's war debt at lower interest rates.[170] This Boutwell had achieved by mid-1870. In the meantime, the last four ex-Confederate states had been readmitted to the Union. This brought trade back to the fore of national politics, for the Southern states were major exporters of agricultural products and importers of manufactured goods. They therefore strongly opposed the protectionist tariffs demanded by Northern manufacturers.[171] Republicans worried that these tariffs would become a wedge issue in the 1870 midterms. Seeking to win over Southern voters, Republicans in Congress therefore reduced tariffs on sugar, coffee, and tea, as well as iron, rubber, and lumber.[172] They would do this again in early June 1872. As a result, the average tariff level on dutiable imports declined from its record high of 49 percent (1868) down to 44 percent (1871), 41.5 percent (1872), and then to its Gilded Age low of 38 percent (1873). However, lower tariffs also sent the trade balance into annual deficits that reached –1.24 percent of GDP by 1872.[173] Grant did not lead here but, concerned about elections, he enthusiastically signed off on all of it.

Politics also forced Grant's hand on taxes. As with tariffs, he had subordinated tax cuts to his administration's monetary and debt policy, and he had asked Congress to hold off on reductions until the federal debt was under control. Now he supported major legislation in Congress, passed in mid-July 1870, to phase out or eliminate wartime taxes on inheritance, sales, occupations, incomes, and certain "stamped" items.[174] By the end of his first term, these tax cuts had reduced federal revenues from domestic sources by 27 percent and shrunk the federal budget surplus 4.9 percent from its peak.

The tax and tariff cuts came too late to rescue Republicans in the 1870 midterms. Aided by voter suppression in the South, and an economy still stuck in the doldrums up North, Democrats surged into Congress. The Republican Party still managed to maintain its majorities in both houses; in fact, six Black congressmen were elected, including four former slaves. Nevertheless, Southern Republicans warned, "It seems that we are drifting . . . back under the leadership of the slave holders."[175] After years of dominance at the polls, the reversals of fortune were ominous. Grant took the hint. Just weeks later, in early December 1870, he recommended further tariff cuts long sought by voters, suggesting that "all duty should be removed from coffee, tea and other articles of universal use not produced by ourselves."[176]

Civil Service Reform

Republican losses in the 1870 midterms were also partly due to Grant's perceived failures on corruption and intraparty relations. Admittedly, his appointees had quietly made progress instituting competitive exams for hiring in the Patent Office, Census Bureau, and Treasury Department.[177] And over at the Bureau of Indian Affairs, long infamous for its skullduggery, Grant had replaced many partisan hacks and swindlers with conscientious bureaucrats. However, it was only after Republican elites began to abandon their support for Grant, and key elections were lost in the North during 1870, that the president openly endorsed civil service reform. For the issue also hurt Reconstruction. Down South, white supremacists charged Black officeholders and Northern carpetbaggers, all Republicans, with "corruption" and "depravity" and "reckless expenditure."[178] These accusations began to attract support from civil service reformers and draw voters away from the Republican Party.

So, in early December 1870, Grant boldly admitted, "The present [civil service] system does not secure the best men, and often not even fit men, for public place."[179] He called for the wholesale reform of all federal appointments. But instead of leading a crusade for new law, he took only limited action. His Republican allies in Congress were even less enthusiastic. Rather than propose major legislation, they merely empowered Grant to create a new Civil Service Commission to study the matter. More stringent anticorruption efforts were shot down by Republican spoilsmen. Grant took the commission seriously. But its few accomplishments were generally criticized or ignored by the press.[180] In fact, the Commission's December 1871 report was used by critics to allege that over $95 million in tariffs and taxes, constituting a full 25 percent of federal revenues, was being lost each year to corruption or incompetence within the Grant administration.[181] Thus, the *New York Tribune* accused Grant of just putting up the "appearance of keeping up Civil Service Reform."[182]

The Economic Recovery of 1871–1872

During early 1871, the economy began to recover. Again, the numbers suggest a strong rebound that lasted over two years. The economy grew (per capita) in both 1871 (2.4 percent) and 1872 (1.5 percent). Overall business activity surged some 18 percent.[183] The railroad construction boom, which had been little affected by the recession, led industrial production ever higher, with increases in 1871 (5.1 percent) and 1872 (8.0 percent).[184] Exports soared 120 percent (1871), thanks in part to a surge in British demand and the end of the Franco-Prussian War.[185] Hence wheat and cotton prices recovered markedly. Prices for cattle, corn, and pork slowed their descent. Wages remained flat. Thus, severe deflation persisted throughout 1871 (–6.4 percent) and merely halted in 1872 (0.0 percent). Nevertheless, real interest rates came down from around 11 to 12 percent to 5 to 6 percent for high-quality borrowers. "From that time forward, the leading bankers of Europe and America were ready to cooperate in placing the remaining [refundings of US debt]," recalled Treasury Secretary Boutwell. "It was no longer difficult to borrow money."[186]

The West

Grant's most likely contribution to the recovery of 1871–1872 was his support for the development of the West. The region was rich in natural resources, but only around 2.6 percent of the US population lived there, and over half of them were in California.[187] Economically, these settlers were heavily dependent on the eastern half of the United States. The country's major banks and manufacturers all lay east of the Mississippi River. The largest consumer markets and ports of exports were also in the East. Linking the two regions was a single, insecure transcontinental railroad. To make matters worse, the construction of additional railroads, towns, ranches, farms, and mines regularly trespassed on Indian lands. As a result, Native American tribes harried white settlers, fighting over precious resources and transportation routes. Armed confrontations and casualties had leaped during 1867–1869, frightening many potential settlers and investors. Meanwhile, corrupt federal bureaucrats scammed both settlers and Indians out of their claims.[188]

With a fortune in untapped metals, farmland, and trade routes at stake in the West, something had to be done. Grant therefore initiated a new Peace Policy aimed at Native Americans, which promoted "conquest by kindness." He convinced Congress to provide him $2 million (roughly $30 billion in 2020 dollars) to "maintain the peace . . . promote civilization . . . [and] encourage their efforts at self support."[189] This included resources for Native Americans such as schools, supplies, and vaccines. Grant also appointed a Board of Indian Commissioners to investigate fraud and to advise him on policy, and he greatly expanded the federal Indian Service.[190] He also supported legislation to distribute federal lands and permits out west to settlers, developers, and the railroads, as well as a series of geological surveys that provided vital information to investors.[191]

But ultimately, the Grant administration's solution for Native Americans consisted of forced assimilation, militarization, and anticorruption reforms.[192] "[T]he fact is they do not harmonize well, and one or the other has to give way in the end," Grant said of the settlers and indigenous peoples.[193] He therefore stationed additional troops and constructed dozens of military forts in the West during his presidency. For the Native Americans, Grant confessed, "I see no substitute . . . except in placing all the Indians on large reservations, as rapidly as it can be done, and giving them absolute protection there."[194] Indian lands were seized. Native Americans were forced onto over a hundred reservations.[195] Resistance only brought violence from white vigilantes, local law enforcement, and federal troops. And to weaken any future legal claims, in early March 1871 Grant signed the Indian Appropriation Act. It formally made Native Americans "wards of the nation."[196] In doing so, Congress and the executive branch joined the Supreme Court in the elimination of sovereign status for Native Americans and their right to renegotiate treaties with Washington.[197]

The "Indian problem" was not solved, but it was much diminished. Armed confrontations and casualties dropped dramatically during Grant's first term. By the end of 1872, half the estimated 300,000 Native American population was thought to be "on reservations under complete control of [Bureau of Indian Affairs] agents." Another third was mostly contained, "generally roaming on or off their reservations." Just 18 percent still roamed free, "most of whom were unoffensive," concluded the commissioner for Indian Affairs.[198] Thus, the Grant administration's intolerance of native culture and economic practices secured the region for eastern investors, settlers, and industrialists. These men then developed the western economy with little regard for native populations. The indifferent brutality of Gilded Age capitalism created enormous wealth, but at great human cost.

Coalitions and Corruption

Boutwell may also deserve some credit for the 1871–1872 economic recovery, for he had taken to using the Treasury Department's monetary reserves like a central bank. Every autumn, farmers throughout the South and West demanded loans to harvest and transport their crops. This created a credit crunch for eastern banks. Likewise, in spring, farmers needed money for planting. When these credit contractions struck, Boutwell bought bonds or deposited federal funds in private banks so as to expand the available money supply. Critics complained that Boutwell was interfering in markets to benefit administration allies. But in doing so he likely prevented waves of bankruptcies, and perhaps even liquidity crises. "The degree of flexibility in the volume of the currency is essential," Boutwell explained. "This is a necessary work, and… it cannot be confided to the banks."[199]

However, the Grant administration's use of federal policy to enrich the economy only fueled new accusations of corruption. Even Grant's generally beneficial actions were increasingly viewed through this lens: his Reconstruction policy was described as favors for Northern banking and industrial interests; Boutwell's monetary policy was attacked as either rewarding supporters or pandering for votes; tariff collections served mostly to "give employment to a host of needy partisans," as well as to buy votes and campaign contributions.[200] Of course, Grant's increasing skill at handing out party patronage did not help.

For Grant had become more adept at congressional relations. The appointment fiascos and toxic battles of his first months in office had taught him valuable lessons. He soon recognized that warm relations with key leaders in Congress, built on patronage and other favors, enhanced the chances of securing policies he backed. "[A]n Executive depends on Congress," he later admitted. "If he wants to get along with Congress, have the government go smoothly, and secure wholesome legislation he must be in sympathy with Congress."[201] Therefore, Grant began to send drafts of suggested legislation to congressional allies. He met with congressmen at the White House almost daily. And he returned the favor with frequent visits to Capitol Hill to personally lobby for legislation deemed important for the administration. He wrote letters to individual legislators expressing his policy concerns and asking for their help and advice. He eagerly provided patronage appointments to his supporters in Congress, while withholding them from opponents, much to the dismay of civil service reformers. "There was no corruption in [a senator] asking me to appoint this man or the other," he later insisted. "[I]t is a condition of our representative form of government."[202]

Grant also made a serious effort to engage with the public and fellow Republicans. He genuinely enjoyed mixing with average Americans, who deeply interested him. He liked to walk the streets of Washington, often unguarded, greeting well-wishers. He hosted luncheons, dinners, parties, and social gatherings of all sorts. The long-serving White House doorkeeper later recalled, "General Grant and Mrs. Grant were certainly very popular with the people, and the number of people who called on them, socially, in the evening, was simply wonderful."[203]

Grant also extensively used the railroads, then still a somewhat dangerous mode of transportation, to tour the country for official ceremonies and personal vacations.[204] During his two terms, Grant visited twenty-two of the thirty-seven states and three territories, wisely avoiding the ex-Confederacy, while reaching as far west as Utah. This was unusual. Prior to Grant, presidents traveled sparingly. The White House was seen as the essential seat of the presidency, and time away from it was considered going "off the job," both irresponsible and selfish. Grant normalized presidential travel, paving the way for the extensive journeys of Hayes, Harrison, and McKinley. However, Grant avoided policy speeches in his travels. In fact, he avoided speeches altogether. "I am in favor of free speech, and therefore I want other people to do the talking," he joked with an audience of Omaha schoolchildren.[205] But he loved mingling with the public, and did it well. "Grant knew how to work a crowd," remarked one scholar of presidential travel.[206] He also often invited along cabinet members, congressional allies, and other political supporters, even on personal trips. And although he never openly campaigned for others, he would often time his visits to coincide with local elections for Republican allies.

Grant's extensive travel earned cries of "absenteeism" from critics eager to besmirch his presidency.[207] The *Pittsburgh Daily Post* called his trips "[o]ne of the very worst features of President Grant's administration."[208] A Missouri paper blamed government corruption on Grant's long absences from Washington, "Never before in our whole history has the public business been so culpably neglected. . . . Gen. Grant inaugurated a practice of absenteeism, the baleful effect of which has been felt through every branch of the civil service."[209] To some Americans, Grant's extravagant travel added to the perception of an irresponsible, celebrity president, wallowing in the prerogatives of office, while unsupervised government corruption ran amok.

As if to confirm accusations of Grant's "loose administration," during the first half of 1872 shocking new details of government malfeasance exploded in the media.[210] Three separate federal investigations revealed and dislodged a bribery scheme at the New York Custom House set up by two Grant appointees. Grant's enemies in Congress simultaneously launched investigations into alleged violations of US neutrality in federal arms sales during the Franco-Prussian War. The president's critics within the Republican Party now loudly denounced "Grantism" from the Senate floor, accusing him of "autocracy," "corruption," and "a scale of nepotism dwarfing everything of the kind in our history," and called for presidential term limits of just four years.[211]

The worst corruption scandal of the year was yet to come, and would not fully break until winter 1872–1873. In early September 1872, the *New York Sun* reported a scheme of "colossal bribery," involving Credit Mobilier and the Union Pacific Railroad.[212] In the scandal, a wealthy railroad construction firm paid off congressmen for years of favorable legislation. Although the bribes took place prior to Grant's presidency, some of the accused were now Grant administration officials. Those implicated included Grant's sitting vice president Schuyler Colfax, Grant's new vice presidential nominee Henry Wilson, Speaker of the House James G. Blaine, and a dozen other Republicans. The anti-Grant press went wild.[213]

The 1872 Election

Despite his faults, Grant was easily renominated for president in June 1872. Once again, he remained silent and stayed home rather than campaign.[214] But he did not go without a challenge. A group of moderate, anticorruption Republicans split off to form the Liberal Republican Party in early 1872. They composed a platform calling for civil service reform, lower tariffs, an end to Reconstruction, and the removal of federal troops from the South.[215] The Democrats, having fallen into utter disarray, abandoned their own presidential campaign. They instead threw their support behind the Liberal Republican candidates.

At first, there was considerable enthusiasm for the Liberal Republicans, but the party's presidential campaign turned into a comical farce. As their candidate, they nominated Horace Greeley, an infamously eccentric New York newspaper publisher who had criticized every president since Jackson.[216] Over his lifetime, Greeley had also enthusiastically taken up "virtually every [political] fad that came down the pike."[217] Racism and Reconstruction remained important, but serious debates about national issues faded into the background. Instead, the general campaign became an embarrassing contest of character assassination. Grant's supporters labeled Greeley a vain "office beggar" and mocked his prior support for socialism, spiritualism, and vegetarianism.[218] Greeley's men blasted Grant as a hopelessly corrupt dictator. Greeley himself joined the fray. He wrote a flurry of public letters defending himself against his critics and then desperately stumped across a handful of Northern states. Coming so soon after Andrew Johnson's embarrassing tirades, Greeley's public speaking tour struck many as similarly unpresidential.

The business community threw its support behind Grant. Ignoring the scandals and alleged corruption, in mid-October 1872 an assortment of over fifty top bankers, merchants, and businessmen in New York published a glowing endorsement of Grant in the *New York Times*, attesting that "the general welfare

of the country, the interests of its commerce and trade, and the consequent stability of its public securities would be best promoted by the re-election of Gen.
Grant."[219]

Meanwhile, during autumn 1872 a horse flu epizootic swept down from
Canada, killing tens of thousands of horses throughout the northern and eastern
states.[220] In some cities, almost *every* horse was killed or incapacitated.[221] Horses
were central to Gilded Age transportation, distribution, and emergency-response
systems; in some cases they even provided power for light manufacturing. Thus
in some cities, the local economy was virtually paralyzed. Even voter turnout was
affected in the 1872 elections. But Grant saw no role for the federal government
in combating the disease or its economic impact.

In November 1872, Grant was comfortably reelected by large margins.[222] He
received 55.6 percent of the popular vote and 81 percent of the electoral college
vote. However, it was the lowest voter turnout in any presidential election between 1852 and 1904. Although the ongoing horse epizootic played a role in the
depressed vote, the results probably reflected a rejection of Greeley more than a
vote of confidence in Grant.[223] "That Grant is an Ass no man can deny; but better
an Ass than a mischievous idiot," remarked an Ohio Republican reformer.[224] In
fact, the Liberal Republicans managed to win three Senate elections and four
House seats, while mainstream Republicans lost four additional seats in the
Senate. These results demonstrated solid support for reform in some quarters.
Nevertheless, Republicans increased their control over the House from 58 percent to 68 percent, thanks to Black voters in the South. Thus, Democrats would
remain a near powerless minority in the new Congress.

Grant was triumphant. He interpreted his reelection as an endorsement
of his leadership, and especially his Reconstruction agenda. That December,
he publicly bragged of "peace at home, peace abroad, and a general prosperity
vouchsafed to but few peoples."[225] He also saw the election as a national referendum on his character. "I have been the subject of abuse and slander scarcely
ever equaled in political history, which today I feel that I can afford to disregard
in view of your verdict, which I gratefully accept as my vindication," he told
Americans in his second inaugural address.[226]

Yet, even in victory, Grant and his Republican allies in Congress could not
stem the accusations of corruption hurled at them. During winter 1872–1873, as
Grant's first administration wound down, investigations revealed the full scope
of the Credit Mobilier bribery scandal. Meanwhile, Congress voted itself a massive raise in pay, retroactive for two years. This equated to a handsome jackpot for
every congressman, many of them outgoing. President Grant was given an even
more substantial, though less controversial, pay hike.[227] The *New York Times*
lambasted the "salary grab" as a "gross injustice" and "one of the most abomi-
nable [propositions] that ever came before Congress."[228] A new era of American

political avarice seemed to be taking shape. Disgusted by the orgy of greed, fraud, and corruption, authors Mark Twain and Charles Dudley Warner set to work on a new novel, "full of . . . spice and vigor," published the following autumn, that would give this era its moniker: *The Gilded Age: A Tale of Today*.[229]

Findings

When Grant entered office in March 1869, the US economy and the presidency were still decidedly premodern. In fact, Grant's first term is more solidly placed in the overlapping Reconstruction Era. It was concerned more with fulfilling Civil War aims and reassimilating the South than with industrialization, globalization, and technological change. At the end of it Grant explained, "It seemed to me wise that no new questions should be raised so long as that condition of affairs existed. Therefore the past four years, so far as I could control events, have been consumed in the effort to restore harmony, public credit, commerce, and all the arts of peace and progress."[230] Nevertheless, his first term offers valuable insights into the US presidency and the economy as both transitioned into the Gilded Age.

Overall, the US economy during 1869–1873 was not the worst of the period, but it was below average in many respects. Clearly, the primary economic setback during these years was the Gold Panic and the recession it produced. Together, they dragged down average per capita economic growth to just 0.9 percent per year during Grant's first term, while contributing to some of the worst deflation in the country's history. Inequality grew, albeit moderately.[231] Grant responded adroitly to the initial panic. He also backed federal aid for other economic emergencies. But his main solutions to the recession of 1869–1870 consisted of tight monetary policy, debt reduction, and support for fiscal austerity. This approach likely hobbled the economic recovery. Grant eventually supported tax and tariff cuts, both to relieve average Americans and to win elections. But this only reduced the federal budget surplus from its peak of 1.25 percent of GDP (1870) to 1.03 percent (1872), and by 1873, it was fast headed lower. Meanwhile, the US trade balance remained stubbornly negative during much of Grant's presidency.

On the other hand, the Grant administration excelled at debt reduction, at moving the US dollar back toward its prewar value, and in bringing down real interest rates.[232] "We are inclined therefore to give President Grant and Mr. Boutwell no small credit for the remarkable financial results achieved by the American Government in the last four years," applauded *The Economist* toward the end of his first term.[233] The magazine also indicated that its audience of British investors "may, we think, be very well satisfied with the result" of the

November elections, calling Grant's reelection an "extremely good omen for the future."[234] And indeed, these investors returned to the American market again and again. Had Grant supported lavish federal spending or more inflationary monetary policy, they might have fled. After all, there were lucrative returns to be had in other developing countries around the world.

Grant delivered impressive results in other areas. By 1872, western settlement was surging. Railroad construction was booming. Grant also deserves credit for keeping the country out of war with Great Britain and Spain. Many at the time expected, even desired, armed conflict. Instead, Grant and his foreign policy team skillfully guided these disputes into peaceful resolutions, even international arbitration—a first for great powers, and on highly beneficial terms for the United States. This has led many historians to conclude that while "[the] Civil War was, of course, the great event of Abraham Lincoln's presidency; the absence of civil and international war was the greatest of Ulysses Grant's."[235]

Thus, if Grant is to be blamed for the economy's miserable performance during 1869–1872, his stereotypical shortcomings are *not* likely culprits. It was not because Grant was disengaged or disinterested. In fact, he acted energetically on multiple policy fronts. Nor was he inept. It is true that he too often failed at public relations. His aversion to speech-making and his refusal to manipulate the press likely damaged public confidence in his leadership. He also mismanaged relationships with several powerful Republicans, who went on to make trouble for him in Congress and relentlessly pilloried him in the newspapers. But Grant was nevertheless repeatedly able to form consensus and coalitions so as to get things done on Reconstruction, foreign policy, and economic policy. His lack of education or business experience cannot be faulted. There is no "bad decision" by Grant that originates in them. Certainly, the taint of corruption appeared early and only grew worse over time. But political corruption seemed not to strongly affect the economy, perhaps thanks to Grant's iron dedication to paying down the debt and the eventual resumption of the gold standard. Nor did the alleged scandals appear to interfere with western development. Therefore, investors and banks remained as supportive as ever. In fact, voters in the West and Great Plains generally praised his western policy.

Rather, Grant's relative inaction in response to the financial panic and recession might be the most direct connection between the White House and the poor economy during this time. He spoiled the gold corner when he finally recognized its import. But his economic priorities for the country—debt reduction and the gold standard—led him to support contractionary economic policy thereafter. Meanwhile, his vision for the presidency—reserved, dignified, and taciturn—prevented him from the rhetorical moves that might have reassured investors and critics during the downturn.[236]

Regardless, by early March 1873, the US economy was strong again. Growth per capita was likely nearing 3 percent. Deflation had disappeared. The stock market was advancing toward new highs. Industry was expanding. The US dollar had gained around 20 percent against the British pound since Grant took office.[237] However, thanks to the vigorous recovery and lower tariffs, the US trade deficit had leaped in 1872 to its highest ever, including during wartime. And due to both tax and tariff cuts, motivated more by elections than by ideology, the country's budget surplus was contracting. Worse yet, another financial crisis was already brewing. And this time the catastrophe would devastate the US economy, Grant's Reconstruction efforts, and the ascendancy of the Republican Party.

5

Ulysses S. Grant, Second Term

Panic, Depression, and the Dawn of the Gilded Age, 1873–1877

For some historians, the second term of Ulysses S. Grant (1873–1877) heralds the true beginning of the Gilded Age, especially where the economy is concerned. During these years, business and politics were increasingly woven together into a web of greed and corruption that Americans regularly discovered blazoned across their newspaper headlines. Railroads entered a grand new phase of consolidation and political-economic influence. There also appeared new industrial corporations in steel, oil, rail manufacture, and wheat production. Silver emerged as a political rival to gold and the greenback. Democrats regained political parity with the Republicans, resulting in decades of knife-edge elections, with control over the federal government regularly split between the two parties. To get out the vote, state and local political machines mastered the arts of graft and patronage. Meanwhile, new political movements based on currency, agricultural, and anti-monopoly interests came forth to agitate the electoral waters. Each of these elements came to define the Gilded Age. Meanwhile, Civil War issues, while still useful in driving votes during election years, began to fade as national priorities. And to kick it all off, during late summer 1873 the first great industrial recession and financial crisis of the era struck, damning the remainder of Grant's presidency to economic misery.

Grant attempted to navigate these economic squalls by doggedly adhering to the same approach as in his first term. His primary concerns remained his desire to defend freedom, justice, and equality for recently freed and enfranchised African Americans, while reconciling with the ex-Confederate South, and to do so while adhering to the "hard money" ideology that he believed essential for American creditworthiness. This proved an impossible trilemma. For Grant's dedication to "hard money" eliminated monetary policy as a short-term solution to the depression. The depression eviscerated already declining political support for Reconstruction. And his determined push for Black civil rights alienated many whites, who then joined critics of his economic programs. Other ideas for federal interventions to relieve the economy, many supported by Grant, were then shot down as either too encouraging of partisan corruption or too contrary to conservative government. Grant was either unwilling or unable to form the

Presidential Leadership in Feeble Times. Mark Zachary Taylor, Oxford University Press. © Oxford University Press 2024.
DOI: 10.1093/oso/9780197750742.003.0006

political coalitions necessary to overcome these objections. The results were economically disastrous.

1873: The Dawn of Grant's Second Term

Grant's second term in office began with a political maelstrom. "[H]is success has been the success of a party which has lost public confidence with startling rapidity since last November—a party whose corruption has now become notorious," growled the *New York Herald* on inauguration day.[1] For months, the Credit Mobilier scandal had consumed the nation's attention, and most legislators' time. The story first broke during the previous year's presidential campaign. But the details awaited congressional investigations which began, with some reluctance, in December 1872. In the scheme, the managers of the famous Union Pacific Railroad, the nation's first transcontinental line, had sold stock to influential congressmen at below-market prices in return for government favors during the 1860s. Newspapers around the country now printed lurid rumors of bribery, fraud, and avarice in connection with it. Even the usually aloof *Chicago Tribune* admonished, "The issue is horrible and disgraceful."[2]

Grant himself was never incriminated. Indeed, the bribes had transpired before he entered politics. But many of the president's closest allies were implicated, including his two vice presidents and the Republican House Speaker.[3] Others suspected of involvement included future president James A. Garfield and "a covey of leading senators and representatives who scattered like so many quail for shelter."[4] Yet no one was arrested, jailed, nor forced from office. Instead, the Republican Congress merely censured two House members, including the only Democrat accused. "Every step in the proceedings revealed clearly [a] widespread reluctance to punish anybody. . . . [T]he whole debate reminded one of the efforts of a herd of sheep to find an opening in a fence through [which] they might escape a barking dog," mocked *The Nation*.[5] Such mild punishments seemed only to confirm the accusations of corruption that had beleaguered Grant, and his Republican allies, since he first entered the White House.

Then, in its final month, the outgoing 42nd Congress managed to pass two pieces of legislation that further infuriated the country.[6] The most politically devastating to Grant and the Republicans was the "Salary Grab" Act. In it, legislators voted themselves a retroactive pay raise of 50 percent.[7] Written hastily in mid-February 1873 and enacted on the last day of the session, in the thick of the Credit Mobilier scandal, it was seen as an incredible display of Republican hubris. Conspicuous among its supporters were dozens of Grant allies and lameduck Republicans, the latter of whom would now leave Washington with an extra $5,000 in pay (around $55,000 in 2020 dollars).[8] Newspapers called the Salary

Grab "a bold, defiant, flagrant robbery."[9] The tide of popular disapproval was so overwhelming that Congress retracted their portion of the pay raises a year later.[10]

More economically significant, but little noticed at the time, was the Mint Act of 1873 (a.k.a. the Coinage Act of 1873), signed by Grant just three weeks earlier. The main purpose of this mundane thirteen-page bill was to revise technical operations at the US Mint. However, among its reforms it quietly dropped provisions for the free minting of silver bullion into coins. These provisions had been created at the nation's founding to encourage specie production, but silver coins had long fallen into disuse because the metal had become more valuable as bullion than as coin.[11] Backed by Treasury officials and "hard money" men in Congress, the Act also eliminated silver's status as legal tender except for small transactions.[12] Silver could no longer be used to pay most tariffs, taxes, or government fees. The Act passed with overwhelming majorities and little debate in Congress. Grant signed it without ceremony. But by removing silver, Grant inadvertently created the grounds for a political controversy that would rock the country three years later as Americans struggled through an economic depression.[13]

Congress concluded its session by the end of March 1873, leaving Grant free to depart Washington. For the next six months, he split his time between official duties and personal affairs, traveling often from the capital. He made several trips north to Philadelphia, New York, and New England. He also took a month-long journey west to Denver. Along the way, he stopped in several central states and then returned through Chicago, still rebuilding from its catastrophic fire. He also enjoyed an occasional stay at his summer home in Long Branch, New Jersey. At no time did Grant appear to be aware of the looming financial crisis that would wreck his second term. Indeed, his new Treasury secretary, William Richardson, assured him in late August 1873, "I have devoted considerable time this summer to the investigation of the condition of the commerce of the country this year ... and am very much pleased at the favorable exhibit."[14]

The Panic of 1873 and the Currency Question

The Panic of 1873 generated an economic tsunami that devastated the United States during Grant's second term and beyond. The crisis was a textbook case of "mania-panic-crash." The "mania" was the massive rush of railroad investment which had begun back in 1869. It was fueled by excitement over the first transcontinental railroad, generous giveaways of federal lands to subsidize rail corporations and attract settlers, and a dearth of prior investment due to the Civil War. Eager for fast profits, speculators worldwide shoveled billions of dollars into the construction of several competing trunk lines across the continental United States. Investors also gambled on myriad stand-alone railroad lines.[15]

The result was a classic investment bubble. Construction of new track skyrocketed, rising annually from around 815 miles per year during the war to 7,439 miles per year by 1872. In 1869 alone, one estimate put the total value of all US rail assets at perhaps one-quarter of the nation's GDP.[16] Investors warned, "[A] great deal of [capital] has been wasted in extravagance and ill spent in wild cat enterprises such as Railroads through deserts—beginning nowhere and ending nowhere."[17] Yet the bubble grew. For investor demand created a boom cycle in which rising share and bond prices attracted still further investment that then drove asset prices ever higher. Grant briefly noted the unprecedented expansion of railroads in his December 1872 message to Congress, but he applauded it as "meet[ing] the growing demands of producers, and reflect[ing] much credit upon the capitalists and managers engaged in their construction."[18] And in his March 1873 inaugural, he repeated his dedication to "the construction of cheap routes of transit throughout the land" during his second term.[19]

Like all manias, the railroad boom bred its own destruction. Rail magnate Cornelius Vanderbilt later admitted that there were "a great many worthless railroads started in this country without any means to carry them through."[20] Even where he was wrong, many of the lowest-risk railroad projects became oversubscribed. This left only more speculative ventures to satiate still growing demand from investors. Inevitably, these risky ventures began to fail. Construction costs mounted beyond initial estimates. Frauds surfaced. Violent attacks by Native Americans delayed new rail projects. Hence business prospects faded.[21]

The fuse for the inevitable implosion was long, and it was lit in distant Europe. In autumn 1872, a similar railroad bubble in Germany burst, causing a cascade of stock and bond prices there.[22] The following May, the massive Vienna Stock Market crashed, then the largest bourse on the continent and a bazaar for European railroad stocks.[23] European investors, who held perhaps 12 percent of US rail obligations at the time, now pulled back from the US market *en masse*.[24] They needed cash quickly and feared a similar railroad collapse in the United States. Indeed, investors of all nationalities had learned from the 1869 Gold Panic to be wary of American asset booms.

As foreigners pulled out their stakes, American investors too began to shy away from US rails. As a result, those riskier railroads which needed new funds to survive soon found it difficult to attract new capital. Unable to pay their bills or recoup their creditors, these railroads began to go bankrupt in increasing numbers. Banks that had invested in these rails were caught suddenly short of funds, unable to pay depositors or redeem banknotes. They too began to go bust. A surge in bankruptcies during summer 1873 heightened fears among investors. Worries about the riskiest railroads now spilled over to tarnish all railroad investments. Yet, even as money tightened during August, the *Commercial and Financial Chronicle* warned that "the government ought not to concern itself with the money market, and that mischief must come . . . of all such intermeddling."[25]

The "panic" finally struck on September 18, 1873, when the contagion overwhelmed the famous transcontinental Northern Pacific Railroad, still under construction, forcing it to default on its loan payments.[26] Run by the widely respected investment firm Jay Cooke & Co., it had been considered too big, and too well-managed, to fail. Hence, the collapse of Cooke and his railroad hit like a "financial thunderbolt," according to the *New York Tribune*, sending Wall Street into chaos.[27] Within minutes of the news, "brokers surged out of the [New York Stock] Exchange, tumbling pell-mell over each other in the general confusion," reported the *New York Times*.[28] Investors began indiscriminately dumping assets and withdrawing deposits from banks, either to cover their losses or out of fear of financial collapse. Within a week, the stock market dropped 25 percent, forcing the NYSE to take the unprecedented step of closing for an "indefinite period."[29] And thanks in part to the National Banking Acts of 1863 and 1864, New York banks were the holders of deposits of and major lenders to smaller banks across the country.[30] Therefore, as massive withdrawals and defaults hit the New York banks, they took down with them businesses and financial institutions throughout the United States.

President Grant, who had been vacationing at Jay Cooke's estate just days earlier, was at first reluctant to act. When urged to speed government bond purchases in order to "avert a disaster," Grant resisted.[31] "All assistance of the govt. seems to go to people who do not need it but who . . . buy dividend paying securities, thus absorbing all assistance without meeting the real wants of the country at large," he complained. He also dismissed requests to call Congress into emergency session, believing that it would "have a most depressing effect upon the country . . . [and] unquestionably extend the panic and increase its violence."[32] But he nevertheless allowed the Treasury Department to buy up $10 million in bonds (roughly $220 million in 2020 dollars), an amount equivalent to 3.4 percent of the federal budget, so as to flush the financial system with currency.[33]

At the urging of his advisors, Grant then hurried to New York City with Treasury Secretary Richardson to meet with the country's top bankers and discuss options. Grant and Richardson refused the bankers' demands for direct federal loans. Both men feared that such Treasury loans were neither legal nor politically expedient.[34] But when he returned to Washington, Grant recommended another $20 million in bond purchases. His Treasury secretary disagreed, advising Grant "[not] to undertake to furnish from the Treasury all the money that frenzied people may call for," and halted the purchases after a few days and $13 million of expenditures.[35]

Nevertheless, Grant continued to look for government solutions. In an open letter to two prominent New York bankers, he declared unhesitatingly, "The Government is desirous of doing all things in its power to relieve the present unsettled conditions of business affairs, which is holding back the immense resources of the country now awaiting transportation to the seaboard and a market."[36] He also promised that $44 million then held in the US Treasury reserve would be used "to meet the demands of public necessity, as the circumstances of the country may require."[37] And when federal revenues came up short that autumn, Grant drew on this reserve to keep the government solvent. The swift and powerful monetary actions of Grant and Richardson helped to stop the panic on Wall Street. The NYSE reopened the following week. By November, markets had bottomed and began to recover.[38]

However, the fallout from the panic resulted in an economic "crash" that quickly engulfed the entire country. Perhaps two-thirds of American economic activity was then based on, or closely related to, either railroads or agriculture, which themselves were intimately linked to one another. And both sectors required bank loans to survive. For example, with record harvests already under way, railroad failures meant that farm "[w]arehouses were filled to overflowing, and transportation became slow and exceedingly difficult," according to one observer.[39] Drowning in supply, domestic prices for wheat, cotton, cattle, and hogs began to plummet. To add financial insult to economic injury, mass bank failures also meant that many farms could not acquire the loans necessary to pay for shipment to market or storage.

Nor were the hardships limited to railroads and farms. With no capital to stay afloat, national business activity slumped around 2 percent *per month* for the rest of 1873. Annual business failures surged 30 percent over those of the prior year. "[T]he general distress of the country begins to react upon us. . . . [O]perators of all kinds seem dazed and unable to act," reported the *New York Herald*.[40] Wages for unskilled labor fell 5 percent. Unemployment likely neared 1 million that winter, or roughly 20 percent of working-age males.[41] As temperatures dropped in Chicago, representatives of "thousands of suffering poor people" met with city leaders to request "bread for the hungry, clothing for the naked, and houses for the homeless."[42]

Meanwhile, critics complained that the Grant administration's bond purchases had merely saved his wealthy supporters on Wall Street, leaving the rest of the country to suffer for their speculations. Even the conservative *New York Times* asked "why the laboring man, equally honest, more productive and industrious, and as deserving of credit, should be left in narrow circumstances."[43] In off-year elections that autumn, angry voters sent Republicans packing in Ohio, New York, Virginia, and Wisconsin. "[T]heir instinct leads them just now to believe the Democrat cry that the Republican Party is responsible for the panic," explained the *Times*.[44]

The Inflation Bill of 1874

As the economy cratered throughout autumn and winter 1873–1874, Americans from all quarters pressured Grant and Congress for different forms of federal response. Letters, telegrams, newspaper articles, and editorials poured in, pleading for either progressive action or conservative patience. Congressmen on both sides of the aisle floated ideas for legislation. Business leaders, farmers, and labor representatives converged on Washington to urge their own particularistic solutions. Even Grant's own cabinet was divided. Few, if any, called for direct federal welfare to aid the sick, elderly, or unemployed. However, abundant and sundry proposals for federal spending on public works, expansionary monetary policy, trade reform, government contracts, and tax code revisions were all on the table.[45] Conservatives pushed back, urging that Americans "not be led away by fantastic theories and quack remedies."[46]

Grant listened earnestly to the proposals that swirled around him. At first, he veered erratically from eagerness on moderate inflation and public works to strict austerity and "hard money." Having failed at various business ventures during his youth, Grant understood the plight of average Americans striving to get by, but he was also wary of schemes that might damage the nation's credit or public trust in the US dollar. For Germany's endorsement of the gold standard in 1871 had set into motion a wave of gold adoptions throughout Europe. Within two years, Belgium, Denmark, Norway, Sweden, Switzerland, and France had each formally declared for gold. They joined Great Britain and Canada, which had been on the gold standard for decades.[47] In other words, by the end of 1873, most of America's key trade and investment partners had gone on gold. Hence, to suddenly reverse the US greenback's course toward gold convertibility might endanger the very recovery Grant hoped to achieve, especially since greenbacks—which were essentially IOUs—still constituted over 40 percent of US currency.

In his early December 1873 message to Congress, after much deliberation, Grant outlined his preferred course out of the worsening recession. Strangely, his discussion of the economy constituted a scant 10 percent of his lengthy address and was buried a third of the way into his missive. Also, although he acknowledged that "a financial crisis has occurred that has brought low fortunes of gigantic proportions," he also wondered "if it should not prove a 'blessing in disguise.'" Nevertheless, he had recommendations. In order to "protect the public against the many abuses and waste of public moneys which creep into appropriation bills," Grant wanted more presidential control over the federal budget. Specifically, he requested a line-item veto, a constitutional ban on last-minute logrolling, and limits on special sessions of Congress to matters determined by the president. To keep the federal government solvent, he also called for cuts in federal spending, especially infrastructure. Grant also appeared to reject inflationary monetary policy. "Undue inflation . . . while it might give temporary relief, would only lead to inflation of prices, the impossibility of competing in our own markets for the products of home skill and labor," he warned. Instead, he asked the country to stay the course on gold: "[H]owever much individuals may have suffered . . . we can never have permanent prosperity until a specie basis is reached." And he suggested various policy innovations by which Congress might enable the Treasury and national banking system to flexibly provide more or less currency as economic conditions required.[48]

With President Grant having formally weighed in, the debate over policy solutions now shifted to Congress. Most legislators blamed the ongoing economic crisis on the currency. Either too many inconvertible greenbacks had eroded investor confidence, or too few had prevented recapitalization and hence recovery. As a result, the worsening economy once again lifted dreary, arcane monetary policy to the top of the nation's political agenda. So when the new Congress convened in early December 1873, it was deluged by a flood of financial legislation. "More than 60 bills were proposed, filling over than 1700 columns of the *Congressional Record*," according to one financial historian.[49]

During the next four months, Congress considered a menagerie of schemes from across the political spectrum.[50] Conservatives wanted a reduction in greenbacks. Some even demanded immediate resumption of the gold standard. But the majority of proposals called for some version of inflationary "soft-money" policy, from printing more greenbacks to legalizing silver as national tender.[51] Any of these proposals would inject new money and credit into the US financial system, allowing banks to recapitalize. Loans could then restart, enabling businesses to grow and hire. Loans and credit were especially urgent in the still sparsely settled Great Plains and western states, which badly needed inflationary policy for investment, commerce, and jobs. Congressional debate raged throughout winter and into early spring.

The result of Congress's labors was the "Inflation Bill" of 1874, passed during the second week of April. It was brief and simple. It promised to expand the number of paper greenbacks in circulation over 12 percent, to $400 million, and to increase specie-backed national banknotes to the same level. The bill was strongly supported by farmers in the South and Great Plains, as well as eastern businessmen, railroad interests, and even a growing number of the nation's industrial labor. The main opposition came from New England and New York, where the nation's wealthy bankers and merchants were concentrated.[52]

Given its widespread popularity, Grant was expected to sign the Inflation bill, but in a move that shocked the nation, he vetoed it instead. When the bill had arrived at his desk, Grant took the full ten days allowed by the Constitution to consider it. But in the end, he could not square it with his economic vision for the country. "I read it over, and said to myself: 'what is the good of this? You do not believe it. You know it is not true,'" he later recalled.[53] He explained to his bewildered cabinet that the bill was "a departure from true principles of finance, national interest, national obligations to creditors, Congressional promises, party pledges (on the part of both political parties), and of personal views and promises made by me in every annual message sent to Congress and each inaugural address."[54] To Congressman James Garfield he was more emphatic, telling his Republican ally that he "could not help it" and that the more he studied the bill, the more convinced he became of its "dangerous character."[55] The majority of his cabinet disagreed. So did Congress. But Grant was backed by many powerful conservatives and political allies, and Congress was unable to rouse the two-thirds majority necessary to override him.

"Hard Money" and Reform

Grant's veto caused a sea change in American politics and economic policy. "Hard money" men and reformers now took the momentum. Already angry at Secretary Richardson for his use of greenbacks to expand the money supply during 1872 and 1873,[56] and resentful that this had favored Wall Street, Congress now launched a three-month-long investigation into fraudulent tax-collection contracts overseen by the US Treasury.[57] Once again, the Grant administration appeared to be stained by corruption at the highest levels. By early June 1874, Secretary Richardson was out. He was replaced by Benjamin Bristow, a "hard money" man and outspoken civil-service reformer supported by northeastern Republicans.

As for Grant, having made his decision, he now doubled-down on his advocacy for the gold standard. When the House attempted to pass other inflationary legislation that summer 1874, Grant met with congressional and party leaders to dissuade them. And to remove all doubt, he had his policy views published in the nation's newspapers.[58] "I believe it a high and plain duty to return to a specie basis at the earliest practicable day," the president declared.[59] To achieve this, Grant urged that greenbacks lose their status as legal tender by July 1875, be limited to large denominations, and be put on par with and be redeemable in gold by July 1876. How to accomplish such a task? "I would do this by rigid economy [spending cuts], and by taxation," Grant answered.[60]

Grant finally signed compromise legislation a few weeks later that set his strict monetary policy into law.[61] It established a maximum circulation of $382 million in greenbacks. It also forbade the Treasury secretary from using the federal greenback reserve to relieve tight money markets during harvest or banking contractions. This had become common practice under Secretaries Boutwell and Richardson, but it was criticized as a political favor to allies and a poorly veiled attempt to inveigle voters. In a nod to "soft money" interests, the bill agreed to lower reserve requirements for national banks and encouraged a broader redistribution of banknotes to cash-starved parts of the country. And Grant was no idle spectator during the bill's evolution. He was instrumental to its design and passage. "[P]eople who take Gen. Grant for a simpleton don't quite know the kind of man they have to deal with," reckoned the *New York Times*.[62]

That June, Grant also cooperated with Congress to enact the Moieties Repeal Bill, eliminating a major pillar of the Gilded Age spoils system. No longer would federal customs agents or tax collectors share a percentage of the revenue they brought in. Instead, the new bill replaced moieties with fixed salaries. Moieties lay at the heart of the revenue collection scandals that felled Secretary Richardson and were a constant source of aggravation for importers and shippers. They were also an irresistible source of graft. Hence, their demise was enthusiastically cheered by reformers within the administration. These reformers then proceeded to make war upon fellow Grant appointees deemed lackadaisical in their approach to corruption.[63] Soon a Democratic House would join the fray.

The Depression of 1873–1878

Grant's support for "hard money" and the end of moieties failed to repair the still worsening economy. The recession triggered by the Panic of 1873 was "the greatest crisis industrial capitalism had yet seen," according to historians and contemporaries alike.[64] "Money immediately disappeared from circulation. . . . [C]redit was gone. . . . [A] dead lock and general collapse was the result," recalled a Pittsburgh banker.[65] Banks and businesses failed in waves nationwide. In farming areas, crop and land prices plunged. Railroad construction halted throughout the country. And within three years, half of all American railroads were in some form of receivership, having defaulted on their debts.[66] The collapse of railroad construction caused drastic declines in the budding iron, steel, machinery, and coal industries, suddenly burdened with overcapacity. Half the nation's iron furnaces shut down.[67] Tens of thousands of other businesses failed across the country.[68] One historian of the period recently concluded that "the sixty-five months following the Panic of 1873 remains the longest period of uninterrupted economic contraction in American history."[69]

The effects, via trade, on the economy and the nation's finances were devastating. Although trade constituted only around 14 percent of American GDP in 1873, it was geographically specialized, and several regions were highly vulnerable to its swings. The South and Great Plains were particularly dependent on exports of agriculture and natural resources, nor could they survive long without imports of manufactured goods. The eastern ports and banks lived on flows of foreign trade and trade finance. Especially important were exports of American cotton, tobacco, and wheat. The profits from these shipments abroad kept the US trade balance in surplus, thereby bringing vital supplies of gold currency into the country. After years of annual growth, these exports flatlined in 1874 and then deteriorated over –10 percent (1875). On the other side of the trade equation, tariffs on imports, also paid in gold, were a major source of federal revenues. Hence they were essential to Grant's goals of paying down the federal debt and returning the US dollar to the gold standard. These imports now slumped for years, below –13 percent (1874), –6.2 percent (1875), –14 percent (1876), and onward, until 1878, when imports stood at one-third below pre-crisis levels. As a result, the federal surplus shrank dramatically and net paydowns of public debt were halted until 1876.[70]

American workers and their families were overwhelmed. Though we have no reliable data on unemployment during the Gilded Age, jobless numbers likely reached between 1 million and 3 million out of a working population of around 13 million.[71] Many of them had only recently sold their farms or small businesses to become wage laborers or white-collar workers in the new industrial economy. Now they had no assets of their own with which to cushion unemployment. "Families lost their homes. Wives were separated from their husbands, children from their parents as the search for employment took breadwinners farther afield."[72] Those workers lucky enough to keep their jobs suffered repeated pay cuts. Between 1873 and 1878, wages for unskilled workers dropped over 22 percent, with reductions hitting every year. Meanwhile, the cost of food dropped only 17 percent, and rents fell just 14 percent.

Without property or welfare programs, the newly unemployed were left to fend for themselves. These people suffered greatly. "The social costs of lingering hard times were incalculable, in starvation, property crime, and suicide," according to a recent historical survey.[73] The lines for Boston's soup kitchens stretched for blocks. City tenement houses bulged with overcrowding.[74] In 1874, the word "tramp" first appeared in the New York Times to describe the armies of homeless men and women that had begun to wander the country.[75] Protests and labor riots broke out in Boston, Chicago, and New York. In January 1874, police and the unemployed battled it out in Tompkins Square in New York City, where the jobless rate likely hit 25 percent.[76] Thanks in part to the rise in poverty, migration, and overcrowding, a wave of pandemic disease struck the country, including outbreaks of cholera (1873), smallpox (1875–1876), influenza (1873–1875), and diphtheria (1875–1877), all of which came at the tail end of a lingering typhoid epidemic (1865–1873).[77] As a result of the mass privation and disease, the average life expectancy for Americans dropped 3.3 years for men and 5.8 years for women by the end of the decade.

Perhaps the only silver lining of the 1873-1878 depression was the regularization of US banknote values. For almost a century, American banks had printed their own currency notes, backed by the deposits and credit of the issuing bank. These banknotes varied considerably in their "price," the notes of more trusted banks valued more highly than those of lesser banks. The resulting exchange rate risk and transaction costs burdened almost all economic activity. Worse yet, if a bank collapsed, its banknotes were rendered worthless. To address these problems, the national banking acts of the mid-1860s required banks to further back their notes with government bonds deposited with the US Treasury. To prevent inflation, quantitative limits on banknote issues were established. After 1874, banks were also required to set aside additional money equal to 5 percent of their notes. Thus, the value of the nation's banknotes became less dependent on the health of the issuing bank. For if a bank failed, federal law now guaranteed the redemption of its notes at the US Treasury. The long-detested discrepancies in banknote values finally disappeared. A dollar was worth a dollar throughout the United States. "In this respect," concluded Milton Friedman, "the Civil War and immediately post–Civil War legislation succeeded in one of its primary objectives—the provision of a uniform national currency."[78]

The Collapse of Reconstruction

The depression also dealt Reconstruction a mortal blow. It "wiped out all the hopes of . . . embarking on a gospel of prosperity in the South. The money to do so was gone."[79] Railroads, factories, experimental agriculture, and other attempts at economic modernization were devastated by the crisis. Yeoman farmers, Black and white, became unable to pay their property taxes, wages, or mortgages. Many of them were thrown into sharecropping and tenant farming, an economic abyss from which they would not escape until the next century. Banks and credit associations that served the Black community collapsed, taking the savings of tens of thousands of customers with them. In the workplace, unemployment and poverty eviscerated the bargaining power of African Americans, severely limiting their ability to influence working conditions. Meanwhile, newspapers and journals around the country increasingly portrayed Southern Blacks as "rude and unlettered . . . ignorant, thievish, immoral, stupid," while white carpetbaggers and scalawags were depicted as perpetrating all sorts of "frauds and spoliations."[80] Blacks and white interlopers were to blame, not just for their own economic fates but for mismanaging Southern state governments too. "The one is just as much of a barbarian as the other," concluded one journalist.[81] White Southerners increasingly embraced violence in order to seize back control over, and "redeem," their state and local governments.

Northerners, too, grew weary of Reconstruction battles. The causes were myriad. The leadership of the Radical Republicans had by now either died or faded into political obsolescence. And thanks to the depression, prominent societies originally created to provide aid to freed slaves went bankrupt. Business leaders, who had once championed "free labor," now feared an uncontrollable labor force, Black or white, that would either engage in "a communistic war upon vested rights and property"; turn to crime, alcohol, and prostitution; or grow lazy on charity.[82] In response, Northern governments passed antivagrancy laws, eerily similar to those enacted in the South's "Black Codes" during 1865–1866, in order to deal with armies of homeless beggars. Northern taxpayers, now facing their own economic problems, increasingly balked at paying the bill for Reconstruction. After all, the Civil War had ended a decade ago. Slavery had been successfully banished in the Constitution. Freed Blacks had been granted citizenship. Even in Boston, once a hotbed of Northern abolitionism, a crowd of protestors now mocked calls for additional federal action. "[Abolitionists] are not exactly extinct forces in American politics," observed the *New York Times*, "but they represent ideas in regard to the South which the majority of the Republican Party have outgrown."[83] Nor did constant news of armed soldiers enforcing the will of President Grant upon state and local governments "at the point of bayonet" engender widespread pride or patriotism.[84] Democracy was still a new and fragile institution in the world, and the United States remained its primary exemplar.[85] Yet Grant seemed to be drifting toward "Caesarism" and federal overreach, accusations that he generally declined to publicly repudiate. When political violence erupted in Arkansas during spring 1874, the *New York Tribune* groused, "Why not let them shoot each other down till *they* get tired of it as well as the President?"[86] With similar sentiments echoing around the country, many Northern politicians concluded that efforts to retain Black Republican governments in the South would cost them white votes at home.

1874 Midterm Elections

Disputes over the recession, the currency, Reconstruction, and corruption created troublesome fissures within the Republican Party. For over a decade since the Civil War, the Republicans had enjoyed a near lock on national, state, and even local elections across the country. However, by 1874, this grip had loosened. Grant's surprise veto of the Inflation Bill then sparked a massive voter revolt and became a rallying cry for change. Frustrations over the Salary Grab, the worsening recession, seemingly endless Republican scandals, and the usual anti-incumbent biases also played their roles. Finally, even though his presidential campaign had touted him as a "friend of the workingman," Grant offered little solace for labor or unions during the depression. He never subscribed to the view that union members were "a dangerous class" of socialist provocateurs, but he nevertheless tended to side with business against workers.[87] The latter now sought other champions, including new political parties such as the new National Independent Party (a.k.a. the Greenback Party).[88]

Political punishment came in the November 1874 midterm elections. In what has been called "the greatest reversal of partisan alignments in the entire 19th century," Republicans lost ninety-seven seats in the House of Representatives, exchanging their 70 percent supermajority for an impotent minority of just 36 percent.[89] Democrats now took control of the House for the first time since before the Civil War, and Southerners were named to several leadership positions.[90] Once in session, they would use their power to stop Reconstruction. Republicans still held the Senate. But with no major foreign treaties, Supreme Court nominations, or senior appointments for the remainder of his presidency, Grant had limited use for his Senate allies. "This election is not merely a victory but a revolution," proclaimed the *New York Herald*.[91] This proved prescient. For the next two decades, neither Republicans nor Democrats controlled the federal government for long. Divided government became the axiom of the Gilded Age.[92]

Resumption Act of 1875

The disastrous midterm results meant that Republicans had only four months left in control of Congress, and Grant meant for them to use it. In his early December message to Congress, he headlined the nation's "prostration in business and industries."[93] He then spent over a quarter of his lengthy address making diagnoses and suggesting policy remedies. Responding to rumors that he had gone soft on gold, Grant insisted that, before the 43rd Congress left office, they should legislate a date by which the greenback must achieve parity with gold. And he wanted it done before the next election. For, just as six years earlier, Grant again blamed the financial panic and economic depression on the greenback. He believed that an inflated currency had "begot a spirit of speculation involving an extravagance and luxury" and that the US currency "being of fluctuating value . . . became a subject of speculation within itself." This had scared off investors, both foreign and domestic, triggering the crash. To Grant, it was only lack of confidence in America's willingness to repay its debts in gold that could "cause any continued depression in the industries and prosperity of our people." Therefore, the way to achieve economic recovery was clear: "[I]n my judgment, the first step . . . is to secure a currency of fixed, stable value." And he dismissed as "too absurd" inflationists who urged otherwise. As long as the greenback went untethered to specie, American debt and currency were suspect. The Treasury Department followed up with an annual report strongly endorsing Grant's proposals.[94]

Divided and frightened, and with Grant driving them forward, Republicans wrote and passed the Resumption Act of 1875 in just two months. A mere single page, it required the Treasury to redeem greenbacks in specie, at parity, starting on January 1, 1879.[95] It also authorized the Treasury secretary to use surplus federal revenues and bond sales to accumulate the gold reserves necessary to meet this obligation. To further encourage redemption, it eliminated all federal fees on the conversion of gold bullion into coin. It did *not* reintroduce silver as legal tender. But, for the West's growing silver interests, it authorized the minting of small-denomination silver coins in redemption of fractional currency for daily use.[96] Also, greenbacks could still be redeemed for silver, but only in amounts not greater than $5. To further reduce the spread of greenbacks, it instructed the US Treasury to redeem federal notes in excess of $300 million in circulation, though that goal was never achieved. Finally, as a concession to inflationists and private banking interests, it loosened restrictions on banknote circulations for the national banks.

In truth, the Act was more aspirational and political than substantive. Conservatives felt it too vague, for it implemented neither a specific mechanism nor a schedule by which to achieve its goals. "[I]t is sadly inadequate in its provisions," groused one hard-money senator.[97] Business interests had not sought it. "The country needs rest," complained *Banker's Magazine*. "[T]he turmoil of congressional meddling with the currency should cease."[98] Nor was there any swell of public demand for new currency legislation. Rather it was Grant, and his new Treasury secretary Bristow, who played the pivotal roles in its passage. One journalist later insisted that "every feature of the resumption act was written in the White House under Grant's supervision."[99] This was an exaggeration. Grant preferred an even stronger bill. But he nevertheless applauded it with a rare special message, which called for still more congressional action to achieve redemption.[100]

Grant also urged the outgoing Congress to *raise* taxes and tariffs so as to ensure adequate revenues in support of redemption. Again, Congress complied. By early March 1875, Republicans had raised taxes on tobacco by 20 percent and on distilled spirits by 28.5 percent.[101] They also repealed the 10 percent tariff reductions passed in 1872. Again, Grant was instrumental in these deliberations. "Some timid Republicans were unwilling to vote increased taxes," a relieved pro-gold senator confided to his niece. "But the President saved us again."[102]

On immigration, Republicans in Congress delivered a victory for nativists. Out west, Chinese contract labor had outcompeted white workers for years, while providing ample tinder for racial violence. Immigration was not a priority for President Grant. Before the Civil War, he had briefly considered joining the anti-Catholic, anti-immigrant Know-Nothing Party, but he abandoned it after a single meeting.[103] In his presidential campaigns, he had supported the pro-immigration planks of the Republican platform.[104] As president, Grant went further, arguing for public education as a means of assimilating immigrants and preventing domestic conflict. In return, immigrant communities tended to support him.[105] Nevertheless Grant signed the 1875 Page Act. It was the first *federal* ban on immigration. It forbade contract labor. It was also the first immigration policy defined along racial lines, specifically targeting "any subject of China, Japan, or any Oriental country."[106] It also banned immigration for "lewd and immoral purposes" (i.e., prostitution), an accusation the local US consul-general might level at any woman he deemed unfit, though it was usually reserved for young, single women of East Asian descent. Thereafter the immigration of Chinese women fell dramatically, and with them went rates of Chinese family formation in the United States.[107] As for Grant, he believed that much Chinese immigration was involuntary, and he later explained, "Having [just] made those sacrifices to suppress slavery in one form, we do not feel like encouraging it in another."[108]

To defend Reconstruction, during winter 1874–1875 the outgoing Republican Congress also proposed a series of rearguard actions to protect Blacks in the South, with the zealous support of Grant. These proposals included a new civil rights bill, a fourth Force Act, a two-year military appropriation (to prevent the incoming Democrats from defunding the army's activities in the South), a bill to expand jurisdiction of the federal courts, and new federal money for the Texas Pacific Railroad. But little of it came to fruition. The Civil Rights Act did become law in March 1875. Ideally, it guaranteed equal treatment for Blacks in restaurants, theaters, and inns and on public transportation, and it prohibited their exclusion from jury service. However, it was never much enforced.[109] The judicial expansion gave federal courts greater power over civil rights cases, but few cases made it that far. The other Reconstruction proposals failed to advance by the time Congress adjourned.

Grant failed to win other important battles that winter. In order to reduce unemployment, he had wanted Congress to fund a massive program of federal transportation projects. But fiscal conservatives in Congress and his own administration checked this "foolish notion."[110] Congress also dismissed Grant's proposals for the federal government to immediately start redeeming greenbacks for gold, albeit with a small penalty, and for the creation of another federal silver mint for silver interests. And Grant's requests for renewed civil service reform funding were denied. "[I]f Congress adjourns without positive legislation on the subject of 'civil-service reform,'" he had warned them a few months earlier, "I will regard such action as a disapproval of the system, and will abandon it."[111] Congress waived action, and henceforth Grant abandoned the cause of reform.

Meanwhile, Grant's inner political circle began to implode. The infighting between reformers and Grant loyalists broke into open warfare, often propelled by Bristow, Grant's hard-driving Treasury secretary, who was a dogged anticorruptionist and a presidential aspirant. The attorney general and interior secretary were both forced out of the cabinet under suspicion of corruption. Soon Secretary Bristow would uncover the "Whiskey Ring," a massive tax evasion scheme run in collusion with Treasury officials and involving Grant's presidential secretary. Grant, however, chose to stick by his allies. He adopted a "bunker mentality," often disregarding evidence and advice.[112] He even "went so far as to perjure himself before the chief justice of the United States to keep [an] aide out of jail," concluded one biographer.[113]

The Struggle for Relevance

After March 1875, with the House lost, Grant was effectively a lame duck. As president, he could still veto legislation and issue executive orders, which he did regularly, and he could still make speeches and proclamations, which he generally avoided. He also could, and did, make headlines, though often without intending to. He occasionally rattled the swords of the US Army at Southern insurgencies which sought to violently defy Reconstruction, and he ordered the military to put down Native American uprisings out west. But without Republican control over Congress, Grant and his party were legislatively neutered for the remainder of his presidency. Even the federal budget turned into a prolonged battle, as Democrats sought to prevent the funding of Reconstruction institutions.

So, instead of politics, after Congress adjourned in early spring 1875, Grant traveled frequently. He made extended trips to New England, his New Jersey summer home, and an unprecedented journey out west, not returning to Washington until mid-October. Most Americans had never seen a president, even in photographs. Therefore crowds still gathered to catch a look at the famous general and demand speeches. But when Grant addressed the public during his travels, he rarely mentioned the economy or himself, preferring instead to promote education, civil rights, and patriotism, and always in generic terms.

Grant's tour westward took him as far as Utah and may have been done partly to reassure settlers and investors in the face of renewed violence there. Frustrated by their treatment by whites, Native Americans had launched raids in Texas, Kansas, and Oklahoma that evolved into the bloody Red River War (1874–1875).[114] To the north, a US Army expedition discovered gold deposits in the Black Hills of South Dakota during summer 1874.[115] In violation of federal treaties, thousands of gold-seekers flooded the region, laying claim to Indian lands and founding the now storied town of Deadwood. At first, Grant attempted to purchase the land. But when this failed, he simply abandoned federal treaties with Native Americans. After all, this was just the sort of gold-based, domestic monetary expansion Grant had been seeking for years. The Sioux Indians struck back. The result was a protracted war during which General George Armstrong Custer and his men were killed in the infamous Battle of the Little Bighorn in June 1876. Grant responded by sending an additional twenty-five hundred soldiers to the region, one of the few times he won funding support from the Democratic House.

The armed conflict out west was still ongoing when Grant left office. On the one hand, Grant got his Dakota specie. Domestic gold production leaped 10 percent in 1876 and another 4.9 percent the following year. And, partly as a result, gold coin in circulation increased by 16 percent (1876) and 4.4 percent (1877). However, thanks to reductions in greenbacks and state banknotes, the nation's overall money supply continued to shrink and the recession worsened.[116] Meanwhile, eastern newspapers carried stories, almost daily, about "Indians on the war path," "frontier troubles," and "recent attacks" out west, filled with gory details.[117] To many investors and settlers not already scared off by the Panic of 1873, the West now seemed a riskier economic bet.

Consequently, throughout 1875–1876 the recession spiraled downward into starvation and violence. Across the Great Plains, the US Army had begun to issue food and clothing to indigent families on the frontier during the winter of 1874–1875.[118] Such handouts of federal welfare were technically unlawful until Congress formally approved them in February. That spring, the army distributed some two million rations to over 100,000 people across four states and two territories.[119] Over in Pennsylvania, a strike by seven thousand anthracite coal miners against wage cuts, begun that same winter, dragged on through early summer. Negotiations went nowhere. Union leaders were assassinated. Masked coalmen known as "Molly Maguires" engaged in murder, arson, and pitched gun battles with corporate security men that ended only after arrests, trials, and executions. The mine owner successfully whipped up the story into a national obsession with labor terrorism. The Maguires were widely described as a "band of cut-throats . . . [which] has entered upon a systemic work of blood" and who sought to "to get by terror what cannot be obtained by honest means."[120] The newspapers also now warned of "Communists in Chicago" and "brutal violence" among disgruntled workers in large cities.[121] "The depression, it seemed, had brought European-style class conflict to America," writes one historian of the period.[122]

President Grant, however, offered little new. In December 1875, he presented Congress with a 12,200-word address, the longest annual message in fifteen years.[123] In it, he repeated his dedication to the gold standard, but otherwise he mostly ignored the recession. Instead, he headlined demands for secular education and called for taxes on church property. He then spent considerable ink on foreign policy, international telegraph regulation, and US citizenship. He also railed against Mormon polygamy in Utah, Chinese prostitution rings, and land distribution problems out west. Its reading droned on for hours. The trenchant *New York Tribune* interpreted the lengthy, often self-congratulatory agenda as a precursor to a third run at the presidency and recommended that "Congress read the message for warning rather than instruction."[124]

The new House of Representatives, gaveled into session the previous day, mostly ignored Grant's message.[125] Controlled by Democrats for the first time since before the war, committees that had been run by Northern Republicans for fifteen years were now handed over to Southern Democrats, including several former Confederate leaders.[126] "It is the first time Lee's army ever took Washington," mused one politico.[127] In the words of a Northern Democrat, their mission was to "expose [Republican] corruption, *investigate*, shake out their dirty linen before the people, keep them defending, keep them at it constantly."[128] Starting that winter and throughout 1876, around thirty committees launched inquests, producing tens of thousands of pages of reports, attacking all levels of the Grant administration. "The fury of 'investigation' in Washington has reached such a stage that it is something like the days of the French Revolution when it was enough to cry 'suspect'—& the man was ruined," wrote one of Grant's diplomats.[129] For the remainder of his term, Grant was "a president under fire."[130]

It did not help that Grant's presidency, long tarnished by corruption, continued to be plagued by ever more scandals. In his last two years alone, the abuses were legion. During 1875, Bristow's investigations of the Whiskey Ring revealed details of a massive federal tax evasion scam, in which corrupt officials in the Grant administration and whiskey makers were caught stealing millions of dollars from the government. Secretary of Interior Columbus Delano was discovered accepting bribes to secure fraudulent land grants. Attorney General George H. Williams was found to have accepted bribes not to prosecute the Pratt & Boyd Company for its fraudulent customs and tariffs reports. Then, in 1876, the secretary of war, secretary of the navy, and Grant's private secretary were each fingered in separate extortion, bribery, and cover-up plots.

Congress also made frivolous attempts to harry Grant, which nevertheless added to the atmosphere of scandal. For example, House Democrats attempted to rescind the president's salary increase. They also sought an investigation of Grant's use of military personnel for civilian executive business. They even attempted to prosecute Grant's extensive travels outside Washington as illegal, a delinquency from office. Such nuisances were generally swatted aside by the Grant administration. But the endless investigations and subsequent infighting over the Republican presidential nomination resulted in bitter discord within the administration, further hobbling its ability to act decisively during its final year. Critics inside the administration spread rumors that Grant was "drinking heavily."[131]

Meanwhile, House Democrats gutted the federal budget. They shrank discretionary spending by 15 percent in the appropriations for 1877, while still lavishing spending on river and harbor improvements in their own districts.[132] Grant railed at the former, while refusing to spend appropriations for projects he considered "purely private or local."[133] In a rare presidential impoundment of funds allocated *legally* by Congress and contradicting his own calls for infrastructure spending, he stubbornly declared, "[U]nder no circumstances will I allow expenditures upon works not clearly national."[134]

1876: Silver and the Greenback Strike Back

As the recession dragged into 1876, a presidential election year, attacks on Grant's monetary policy also heightened. Most surprising was a sudden clamor for silver coinage. The 1873 Coinage Act had eliminated the free coinage of silver, and its status as legal tender, with little controversy. However, the movement to demonetize silver and adopt the gold standard throughout western Europe reduced foreign demand for US silver exports. Meanwhile worldwide silver production rose dramatically.[135] US silver production alone rose 67 percent between 1872 and 1876, while American silver exports fell around 37 percent.[136] As a result of this silver glut, starting in 1873 the dollar price of silver had sunk annually on the private market, falling to $1.16 per ounce by 1876.[137] Many Americans now sought to take advantage of the higher $1.66 price to coin it, fixed by the Coinage Act of 1792. In other words, producers of silver bullion could now earn more from coining it at the US Mint than from sale on the free market.[138] But silver coins were no longer freely minted or acceptable as legal tender.

Americans were outraged! In early March 1876, The *Boston Globe* published an angry letter from an incensed Republican editor: "It is impossible to doubt that the laws of the country have been tampered with [in 1873] . . . the most flagrant and audacious of the manifestations of the control exercised by foreign and domestic bankers over national legislation in these recent and evil days."[139] Critics blasted the 1873 Coinage Act as "the Crime of '73," which quickly became a new rallying cry for opponents of Grant and the gold standard.[140] The demonetization of silver was excoriated as "grave wrong," a "conspiracy" born of "corrupt bargains," a "blunder which . . . is worse than a crime," and a "great legislative fraud."[141] Some even perceived the nefarious doings of a "secret agent of foreign bondholders," for gold was Britain's currency.[142] Bills to restore silver as legal tender soon appeared in Congress. For much of the next three decades, the battle between silver and gold would take center stage in American political and economic debates.

Another response was the rise of the Greenback Party. Founded in late 1874, after two years of organizing it had grown to over eighty thousand adherents.[143] Its small but passionate constituency—most numerous in the north-central states—held a presidential nominating convention, ran candidates for Congress, and published a formal platform. They urged repeal of the Resumption Act and sought to replace national banknotes with paper bonds, with every $100 note bearing 1 percent interest or less. The party also called for what we might today call the "developmental state," arguing that "[i]t is the paramount duty of government, in all its legislation, to keep in full view the full development of all legitimate business—agricultural, mining, manufacturing, and commercial."[144] There was a strong nationalist bent to the Greenback Party in that it opposed sales of gold bonds to foreigners. Yet it was no friend of silver, to them just another form of "hard money," and the party opposed the earmarking of bonds for silver purchases. Ultimately, the Greenback Party's presidential nominee would garner just 1 percent of the national vote in 1876. Though a crushing defeat, it was nevertheless the strongest performance of any third-party presidential candidate since 1860. The Greenback Party would live to fight again, and win seats, just two years later.

The Election of 1876

The Republican Party went into the 1876 elections divided and weakened. It still held the loyalty of war veterans, "hard money" men, and "old stock" white Protestants. But to many Americans, it now seemed incapable of strong leadership on economic issues or delivering economic results. Critics could, with some accuracy, cast Republicans as fiscally irresponsible, irredeemably corrupt, and unable to fulfill the economic promises of Reconstruction. In the South, this provided political cover for white supremacists to resume control of state and local governments, providing an enormous block of ex-Confederate voters who would consistently vote against Yankee Republicans for the next century. In the North, ethnic urban-based political machines rallied the Democrat vote against wealthy Republican elites.

The result was two equally matched political parties which put forward similar presidential candidates in the November elections. The scramble for the Republican presidential nomination was discouraging. After Grant dispelled speculation that he would run for a third term, a battle to succeed him ensued among senior men in his administration and the president's top allies in Congress.[145] Divided by faction, and facing widespread accusations of corruption, the Republicans wound up drafting little known Rutherford B. Hayes, an honest and dependable Ohio politician.

President Grant did not openly campaign for Hayes, but he helped in other ways. He immediately endorsed Hayes as "a good selection" and repeatedly signaled his approval of the party's choice.[146] This endorsement ensured vital campaign support from Grant's allies. Grant then proceeded to allocate federal patronage slots, allow "voluntary" party assessments on the salaries of federal appointees, and lend senior administration officials to the campaign.[147] And of course, Grant used federal resources to maximize Black voter turnout throughout the country. He also focused public attention on Reconstruction issues, warning that if the Democrats won in November, they might demand federal payment for "property" lost to the abolition of slavery. For the election itself, Grant spent federal money on thousands of federal marshals and election supervisors throughout the country, focusing on swing districts and the South.[148]

Nevertheless, the November election results were inconclusive. The Democratic candidate, New York governor Samuel J. Tilden, won just under 51 percent of the popular vote, largely thanks to the suppression of Black votes across the South. But the electoral votes remained disputed in Florida, Louisiana, Oregon, and South Carolina. The battle over these vote counts raged for four months.

As the count dragged on, the country edged toward civil conflict and the economy nosedived. The stock market fell 9 percent.[149] The greenback lost 5 percent of its value.[150] Interest rates on municipal bonds halted their monthly declines, while those on railroad bonds crept even higher. Foreign investors grew leery. For while *The Economist* in London dismissed rumors of a renewed civil war in America, it nevertheless worried that "unscrupulous and strong-willed demagogues" would "drive the Democrats, especially the exciteable and undisciplined members of that party in the South, to projects of violence and disloyalty."[151]

Grant rose to the occasion. He immediately sent the US Army "to preserve peace & good order" in the more contentious districts, while ordering that "[t]he Military have nothing to do with counting the vote."[152] He kept abreast of developments throughout the country and within his party. He organized teams of Republican elites to observe the recounts. He increased the military presence in Washington, DC, and promised to use force in response to rumors of insurrection. He supported the formation of a federal commission to resolve the standoff. And after the election was resolved in favor of Hayes, Grant had him sworn in as president, secretly, the moment it was constitutional to do so.[153] But the economy would not recover until long after Grant had left office.

Summary

When Ulysses S. Grant departed the White House in March 1877, he left behind an economic fiasco. The country remained mired in the worst depression in decades. Record unemployment and persistent wage cuts meant that economic inequality had also skyrocketed.[154] The stock market had fallen almost –40 percent from four years prior. Deflation continued to menace the country, with prices down –12 percent in his second term and almost –25 percent from when Grant initially took office. And the federal debt, as a percentage of GDP, had actually increased slightly during the same period.

Politically, Grant fared little better. By the time his presidency was over, almost every aspect of the federal government was suspected of corruption.[155] In fact, additional Grant administration scandals continued to surface for years after he left office.[156] Grant himself remained popular. He traveled the world and the country for the next two years, greeted everywhere by admiring crowds. But without the "great general" to unite them, the Republican Party lay in tatters in 1877. It divided into warring factions led by jealous state and local machine bosses who, in search of former triumphs, pushed Grant's candidacy for a third term. Meanwhile, the Democrats had achieved a political comeback. For the next two decades, Republicans and Democrats would incessantly divide control over the federal government in an electoral stalemate, in which "neither party has any principles, any distinctive tenets," according to one jaundiced observer.[157]

Admittedly, there were economic silver linings. Real interest rates had come down slightly. The trade balance had swung powerfully back into surplus, though not enough to erase the deficits of Grant's first term. And partly as a result of Grant's conservative trade and fiscal policies, the federal budget surplus increased from a measly 0.8 percent (1874) to a healthy 10.9 percent (1876). Perhaps most significant for Grant's goal of joining the gold standard, during his last two years in office the Treasury had retired almost $40 million greenbacks, reducing their circulation almost 11 percent and strengthening the US currency's value in gold by roughly the same amount.[158]

Thus, Grant may be a case of failed political-economic leadership but *not* because he was a visionless president, disinterested in politics and policy, passively implementing the will of Congress. For example, Grant's surprising inflation veto has been called "a seminal event in American history," perhaps making him "the president most responsible for putting the country on the gold standard."[159] He then drove the Resumption Act, tariff increases, and changes in tax policy, so as to bring the nation's finances into line with that goal. His steady leadership after election day 1876 may have prevented the United States from becoming a "banana republic," at least in the eyes of investors. His consistent support for Western development laid the political and security foundations for considerable investment.[160] Grant also spent substantial energy on foreign affairs and Reconstruction, often in opposition to Congress and state governments, with several major achievements in both areas, though his victories were ultimately more enduring in the former than the latter.

Nor did President Grant sit back quietly while Congress deliberated. He regularly met with congressmen in the White House, traveled to Capitol Hill, wrote letters to influential lawmakers, and threatened to block legislation of which he disapproved.[161] And when Congress failed to cooperate, Grant struck back. In total, Grant vetoed ninety-three bills, more than all presidents before him *combined*.[162] And almost all of these vetoes were cast against fellow Republicans' requests for pensions, funds, and other "relief" for individuals. Some vetoes were even for legislation strongly backed by Republicans and popular across the country (e.g., the Inflation Bill). And just four of Grant's vetoes were overturned by Congress, none of which were for major, or even significant, legislation.[163] Grant also issued hundreds of executive orders and scores of formal proclamations, many with significant policy implications.[164] Certainly his four annual messages to Congress and almost 350 special messages were replete with policy suggestions, demands, and requests.[165] Many of these were honored by Congress. This was *not* a "transitional" leader who passively let others dominate his presidency.[166]

So where did Grant go wrong, if at all? Corruption likely played a role in his poor economic performance. Throughout much of his presidency, Grant and his allies appeared to be overtly self-dealing in gold speculation, railroad stocks, land deals, tariff schemes, bond purchases, civil service appointments, tax avoidance schemes, and even raising their own salaries. Many of these schemes originated in unchecked malfeasance by Grant appointees; some continued even *after* the president had been informed of them. Some were exaggerated by critics so as to embarrass the administration. Regardless, many of Grant's own supporters believed him either corrupt or naïve. And this behavior only hardened the resistance among his opponents. For example, Grant never did win back the powerful Northern Republican elites whom he offended so badly during his first months in office. On the other hand, patronage and assessments also became an essential part of Grant's consensus-building strategy. He used them to win allies in all varieties of political battles. "You cannot call it corruption," he reasoned coyly. "In a country as vast as ours the advice of Congressmen as to persons to be appointed is useful and generally for the best interests of the country."[167] And to be fair, many of Grant's political enemies were created not by his corruption but by his failure to share the spoils with them. In other words, corruption had both positive and negative effects on his ability to forge coalitions.

More important, Grant never let corruption infect his dedication to the gold standard, western development, or stern but peaceful foreign policy.

The Grant administration might fill its pockets. Corruption might even sully Reconstruction. But Grant proved time and again that he would not betray the confidence of America's creditors, industry, or the West. Throughout myriad administration scandals, and four Treasury secretaries, the trade balance improved, the budget remained in surplus, the West was "pacified," and the US greenback reliably appreciated. "It reassured European investors, who financed railroads and heavy industry, that they could plow funds into American business and be repaid in sound money."[168] And when crises struck, the Grant administration responded adroitly to rescue the financial system. It was the recessions that hurt him most.

Grant's stubborn pursuit of the gold standard is a more tempting culprit. Throughout 1873–1875, Grant consistently pushed the country back toward greenback-gold parity, but at the expense of contracting the nation's money supply and raising taxes amid an already brutal recession.[169] In this interpretation, Grant sacrificed the nation's prosperity for that of financial conservatives, investors, and eastern bankers. However, this ignores the fact that Gilded Age financial capital was surprisingly mobile and competing markets abroad beckoned. Had Grant inflated the currency, even greater capital flight and economic collapse might have ensued. It also ignores considerable evidence that Grant himself believed deeply in "redeeming" the greenback for both economic and moral reasons. "Ultimately even the obtuse and insensitive old soldier could not deny the impelling conservative image of soft money as 'the sum of all iniquity'; specie as 'philosophy, morality and religion.'"[170] He also maintained that gambling on the greenback's value had delivered two financial panics and two recessions. Therefore, only by fixing the greenback to gold, at original parity, could he end the boom-bust cycles that plagued his administration. It is true that he could, and perhaps should, have been more flexible on gold. But Grant was neither objectively wrong on monetary policy nor a malleable novice who caved to special interests.

Furthermore, although Grant was adamant about gold, he was flexible in other areas of economic policy. He constantly floated, or entertained, ideas about nonmonetary government interventions in the economy. Some of these policies might have ameliorated the economic depression if they had been enacted. So perhaps the better question is why these other ideas never left the station.

Here it may be that Grant lacked the skills or personality "required to bend other leaders to his purposes," as some have argued.[171] Throughout his presidency, Grant got more done where a substantial constituency of support *already* existed: gold standard adoption, debt paydowns, balanced budgets, Reconstruction. In contrast, he generally failed when advocating for more innovative proposals which required him to forge a new consensus: acquisition of new territories (Santo Domingo), federal public works spending, extended federal aid to freed slaves, the eight-hour workday, and postal savings banks. In these cases, often the very same allies who supported Grant's other policy pursuits succeeded in stopping him.

Grant further complicated matters by generally failing to defend himself or support his agenda with public speeches and rhetoric.[172] Nor would he speak much with the press. When rumor and accusations roiled the nation, he simply "did not think it would comport with his dignity as President of the United States to make a statement . . . in response to the clamors of the newspapers."[173] This allowed accusations of corruption, some earned, some not, to spread uncontested by the man best able to defend himself.[174] To be sure, Grant was not an orator by nature; he had shied away from the podium all his life. Yet after he left office, he regularly gave speeches to crowds of all sizes, sometimes several per day. After some practice, he even became "an accomplished public speaker . . . able to throw off witticisms with an effortless touch and offer cogent commentary."[175] In other words, Grant could rouse an audience when he wanted to. He simply refused to perform this vital task as president. He viewed much political rhetoric as a dirty form of embellishment, misdirection, even dishonesty. Although Democrats had already begun to embrace a rhetorical presidency, Grant did not. He still believed that presidential actions spoke louder than words.

In sum, many of Grant's economic failings appear to find their origins in three aspects of his leadership: his vision for the country and of the presidency; his inflexibility in that vision as it applied to monetary policy; and his limited willingness or ability to forge coalitions, including with the American people, in support of nonmonetary economic policies. On the other hand, his education and prior experience in economics and business played little obvious role. He did take action. He could be flexible. He supported many innovative new policy ideas. He could forge consensus and rally the people. He demonstrated these qualities in several policy areas. But he chose not to in regard to gold, debt, and increases in federal spending. In the end, Grant chose stubborn loyalty to the gold standard, compromise on Reconstruction, and a general refusal to fight for countercyclical spending. He defended Wall Street, the financial system, the US dollar, and the West. But he also decreased trust in America's political institutions, including the presidency itself. The net result was an economy headed still lower and the worst civil unrest since the Civil War. Could Rutherford B. Hayes save it?

6

Rutherford B. Hayes and the Great Economic Boom, 1877–1881

President Rutherford B. Hayes (1877–1881) inherited a political-economic disaster from his predecessor, Ulysses S. Grant (1869–1877).[1] The long-promised return to the gold standard remained unfulfilled, while a new threat to this promise had arisen: silver. Out west, intermittent warfare had erupted with Native Americans, frightening settlers and investors alike. The House remained in Democratic hands, and Republicans maintained only a slight majority in the Senate. Few expected Hayes to lead. He was a political nonentity, with no political machine of his own, nor anywhere near the national gravitas of General Grant. Hayes had been chosen to win an election, not to govern. The Republican Party was already splintering underneath him. Without the great general at their head, Republican factions were bound together by little more than spoils and enmity for Democrats. Even Hayes's election was disputed. Many dismissed their new president as "his fraudulency." Worse yet, Hayes's first acts would be to abandon Blacks and Republicans in the South, while attacking the power of Republican elites in Washington and New York. It seemed that the Republican Party had gone to war with itself.

Yet the economy under President Hayes was extraordinary according to almost every measure available. Growth, employment, the trade surplus, and the US dollar all boomed, while inflation, federal deficits, and the national debt all fell. Even economic inequality declined. All told, during and soon after the Hayes administration, the United States enjoyed one of the strongest, most balanced periods of economic performance in its entire history.

Contemporaries and historians tend to dismiss Hayes as inconsequential; he has since been reduced to one of the forgotten "bearded presidents" of the Gilded Age. After all, Hayes was recruited to run for president in 1876 more for his safe, clean, honorable past than for his expected future leadership. And the suspicious conditions of his election quickly tarnished those assets. After Grant, the presidency sank to its institutionally weakest point in history. Gilded Age executives had few staff and spent most of their time dealing with job-seekers, correspondence, and ceremonial duties. Congress, on the other hand, was at the zenith of its power. It controlled the federal budget, as well as most federal appointments, and therefore had de facto control over much of the federal government.[2] Local

Presidential Leadership in Feeble Times. Mark Zachary Taylor, Oxford University Press. © Oxford University Press 2024.
DOI: 10.1093/oso/9780197750742.003.0007

political machines, party cliques, and state governments also still played powerful roles in the nation's politics.[3] And many Americans had lost faith in their
political system as hopelessly corrupt. Throw in the economy's natural rebound
after the Panic of 1873, and Hayes is perhaps the least likely case for the relevance
of the American presidency for the economy.

Nevertheless, Hayes played a valuable role in the late 1870s economic boom.
He was elected into a severely depressed economy and a notoriously corrupt
political system. Thus, his conservative vision, modest activism, and reserved
attempts at leverage and relationship-building, each discounted so heavily by
the press and historians, were from an economic leadership perspective powerful assets, not vulnerabilities. The United States during the early Gilded Age
was in a fragile state. America's extraordinary expansion was based upon the
three overlapping phenomena that simultaneously threatened to divide and
weaken the country: rapid industrialization, globalization, and natural resource
exploitation.[4] These forces created economic "winners" and "losers" on a scale
never before experienced in US history. As a result, fierce political battles raged
throughout the 1870s–1890s over monetary and trade policy, wages and prices,
the pace of technological change, and the rise of corporate power. Other 19th-
century societies slipped into war amid similar tensions (e.g., Japan, Germany).
Some became weak and decrepit from corruption and infighting (e.g., Spain,
China, Russia). Entering office under a cloud of suspicion, into a political system
beset by graft, and barely a decade after a civil war, Hayes could easily have set the
country on a path toward becoming a "banana republic," an economic mess re-
pulsive to investors and immigrants alike.

Instead, Hayes worked to return the country to normal after the chaos of the
Civil War, Reconstruction, and the scandals of Grant's administration. In doing
so, Hayes helped to steady the ship of state and navigate it through the treach-
erous waters of midstage economic development. He oversaw the formal end of
Reconstruction, which allowed the country to put Civil War issues on the back
burner and focus instead on economic development and industrialization.[5] His
severe but principled Native American policy supported westward expansion,
while improving federal treatment of the Indians and decreasing bloodshed for
all. Hayes thereby increased security for developers to tap into the vast natural
resource wealth of the West and to rapidly expand America's network of railroads
and telegraphs. On another front, Hayes successfully managed the country's
first national labor uprising. He adroitly allowed workers to vent their pent-up
frustrations over declining wages, while using small detachments of federal
troops to prevent a major strike from becoming something more revolutionary.
Meanwhile, federal corruption and incompetence risked becoming a cancer on
political and economic progress. Hayes therefore fought for civil service reform.
His efforts at the Interior Department and the New York Customs House, as

well as the reports and studies he commissioned, proved to be turning points.[6] They constituted some of the first real steps toward a professional modern bureaucracy. In an era when presidential rhetoric was frowned upon as egomaniacal and "going over the heads of Congress," Hayes also incorporated education and trust-building into his frequent travels throughout the country. He was a relentless spokesman for national unity, clean government, stable finances, and a strong currency, at a time when each was beset by doubt. Perhaps most important, Hayes staunchly supported the return of the United States to the international gold standard, ensuring that investors in the American economy would not suffer arbitrary devaluation. Thus, it is not far-fetched to assert that the Hayes presidency gradually encouraged the confidence and security of businessmen and investors, especially foreign lenders, who were then essential to America's economic development.

Background

There is little in Rutherford Hayes's background that would predict excellence in economic management. He was one of the first, and few, presidents to be a typical American of his day. He was born in a small town in central Ohio in 1822 to a middle-class family with a fairly middle-of-the-road background. In his diary, letters, and biographies, he comes across as generally compassionate, hard-working, law-abiding, and good-natured. To outsiders, he "cultivated a quiet demeanor that seemed dull."[7] He appeared stiff, formal, and humorless. But Hayes was no introvert. He was genuinely outgoing and energetic in most things: sports, social clubs, hunting, travel, public events, cultural celebrations, politics, and even simple mischief. He was also sincerely religious, but without being doctrinaire or sectarian.[8]

To the degree that Hayes excelled before politics, it was in his formal education. He graduated at the top of his high school, college, and Harvard Law. This made him was one of the best schooled presidents of the 19th century, perhaps exceeded only by John Quincy Adams. However, Hayes did not learn much economics during his school years. Nor did he ever develop much interest in economic theory, other than perhaps currency issues. Rather, Hayes likely absorbed basic economic principles from his Uncle Sardis—his surrogate father and a highly successful trader, banker, and real estate developer in Ohio. Nor did life provide Hayes much training in business. After law school, he returned to Ohio, where he passed the bar, opened a law office, and settled in Cincinnati. He also married and became a dedicated family man. But other than his law practice and personal investments, Hayes accumulated little business experience before entering office.

Hayes did have a formidable military career. An opponent of slavery and long a supporter of the Whig Party, it did not take Hayes long to volunteer to fight in the Civil War when it came in 1861, though as much for glory and adventure as for abolitionism. During the next four years, in addition to military legal assignments, Hayes's participation was "intense and ferocious" in over twenty battles; he was wounded several times and had five horses shot out from under him.[9] With a steady record of victories and a reputation for bold leadership, he was promoted up through the ranks to the position of brevet major-general.

Strangely, although Hayes was a lifelong "policy wonk" and political junkie, he was a reluctant politician. His friends in Ohio placed his name on the ballot in the 1864 congressional elections.[10] Still serving in uniform, Hayes declined a furlough to campaign and was elected *in absentia*. He then served two undistinguished years in the House. "I have no ambition for Congressional reputation or influence," he confided to his uncle. "I would like out of it creditably."[11] While there, he quietly supported Radical Republican legislation, repeatedly voted to override President Andrew Johnson's vetoes, and yet also built friendships with ex-Confederates. His main accomplishment as a congressman was to secure funding for an enlargement of the Library of Congress.[12]

Nevertheless, as a moderate Republican, respected war hero, and competent policymaker, Hayes was also a reliable vote-getter. Though reelected to Congress in 1866, he resigned the following summer when recruited by state party leaders to run for governor of Ohio. He then served two terms as governor (1868–1872), consistently opposing paper currency, strongly supporting voting rights for Blacks, and backing various education measures, prison and asylum reform, the Ohio Geological Survey, and state civil service reform (specifically, creating nonpartisan boards to manage state institutions). From the governor's office, he also supported President Johnson's impeachment and then Grant's presidential campaign, hoping in vain that Grant would "overthrow the spoils doctrine and practice."[13]

Hayes intended to retire from politics in 1872, even turning down a Senate seat offer and a regional position in the Treasury Department. After the grand battle against slavery and for Black citizenship, he found "[t]he small questions of today about taxation, appointments, etc, etc, are petty and uninteresting."[14] He was also repulsed by the spoils system. "The system is a bad one. It destroys the independence of the separate departments of the government. . . . It ought to be abolished."[15] But as a proven election winner, Hayes was soon drawn into the Republican national campaign, even to the point of an unsuccessful third run for Congress. Three years later, the Republicans in Ohio convinced Hayes to run for an unprecedented third term as governor in 1875. The party had lost big in the midterm elections thanks to the brutal recession, a wave of animosity against Grant's monetary policy, and Republican corruption. Hence they badly needed winning candidates. Hayes accepted only because he dreaded the election of Democrats, whom he still identified with "slavery, rebellion, and repression," as well as corruption and inflation.[16] He also realized, "If victorious, I am likely to be pushed for the Republican nomination for President," and he worried, "This would make my life a disturbed and troubled one until the nomination."[17]

The Disputed Election of 1876

In 1876, under assault and divided by faction, the Republicans selected Hayes to run for president. The country was still mired in a deep recession which had lasted for years. Millions had lost their savings and source of income; tens of thousands of businesses went bankrupt. Hayes himself was already in debt over $46,000 (roughly $1 million in 2020 dollars) when the recession struck, and he struggled to defend his family's investment properties against falling rents and prices.[18] Being then in power, the Republican Party was held responsible for the economic downturn and Democrats began to win elections. The Republicans realized that they needed clean, competent candidates as a remedy to the scandal-ridden Grant administration. Thus when the Republican Convention met in Cincinnati in mid-June, they nominated Hayes over several better-known and more powerful, but riskier and more controversial, party elites. The *North American Review* blandly described him as "a faithful though uninfluential member of Congress . . . [and] a respectable, though not brilliant, governor of Ohio."[19] Most important, Hayes had rarely lost an election. Otherwise, he was pleasantly boring war hero from a large swing state, generally considered "right" on the issues, who had managed *not* to offend any of the party's faction leaders. He was thus a compromise candidate. As a top supporter, Ohio senator John Sherman, put it, the Hayes nomination was "the safest . . . that could be made."[20] For himself, Hayes agreed to run because he was a good soldier, a loyal party man, and feared that "a Democratic victory will bring the [ex-Confederate] Rebellion into power."[21] As his opponent, the Democrats nominated the headline-grabbing reformer Samuel J. Tilden, from the vital swing state of New York.[22]

As presidential candidates, Hayes and Tilden supported nearly identical party platforms. The 1876 Republican agenda was an endorsement of almost every major Grant administration policy, as well as new planks endorsing women's rights and anti-monopolism.[23] Its main pillars consisted of calls for national unity under the Constitution, equal rights for all citizens, a swift return to the gold standard, and civil service reform.[24] The Democratic Party platform mirrored most of the major Republican planks, but headlined reform. It recited a vast inventory of government "abuses, wrongs, and crimes," calling them "the product of sixteen years' ascendency of the Republican party," and denounced "the financial imbecility and immorality of that party."[25] In other words, rather than major policy differences, the 1876 campaign descended into slander, graft, and voter intimidation. And of course, concerns about the future of Reconstruction lay ominously in the background.

Hayes quickly signaled that he would be a more independent and engaged president than many of his predecessors. Previous candidates had humbly accepted their nominations with brief, reserved public letters, consisting of simple platitudes and generalities. But Hayes's letter of acceptance stretched to almost fourteen hundred words and was spiked with strident policy positions.[26] He viciously attacked the spoils system and congressional control over appointments: "In every way it degrades the civil service and the character of the government." And he called their elimination his "paramount interest." Hayes also declared that he would "oppose any step backward" from a sound currency. He then took pains to strongly endorse public schools and the pacification of the South. The *New York Times* lauded the letter as "manly, frank, and explicit";[27] clean-government advocates concluded "unmistakably that it is not the work of [a] politician."[28] Liberal reformers, many of whom had abandoned the Republican Party over Grant administration corruption, were thrilled and began to return to the fold.

The result was one of the tightest presidential elections in US history.[29] Tilden won 51.5 percent of the popular vote, but the electoral college tally was almost evenly split. Closely supervised vote recounts resulted only in dueling returns of unclear legality. The standoff dragged on for months.[30] The results became so controversial that talk arose of armed conflict, rebellion, and assassination plots. Some Democrats called on Tilden supporters "to rise up in arms"; others warned that a new "Civil War would result."[31] At one point, a gunman fired into the Hayes home in Ohio while the family was at supper.[32] To defend the capitol against a potential uprising, General William T. Sherman quietly dispatched four companies of artillery to Washington.

As the threat of civil unrest mounted, Congress created a bipartisan commission of ten congressmen and five Supreme Court justices to resolve the crisis. Picking up the threads of private negotiations already underway, the commission hammered out an agreement known as the "Compromise of 1877." This deal was later affirmed, in secret, by representatives of both candidates in a Washington hotel suite. In it, the Republican Hayes won the presidency. In return, Hayes agreed to remove federal troops guarding the state houses in former Confederate states, while Republicans in Congress promised new legislation to aid industrialization in the South.[33] Concessions on federal appointments and the House speakership may also have been included in the final arrangement, which remains enigmatic to this day. Nevertheless, Tilden's supporters urged him to file suit in court; while the pro-Democratic *New York Sun* condemned Hayes's victory as one wrought by "the hands unscrupulous rogues" and the product of "monstrous crimes."[34]

Due to the controversy, confusion, and secrecy of the 1876 election's outcome, Hayes entered the presidency under a dark cloud. After having campaigned on honesty and clean government, Hayes was now scorned by critics in both parties as the benefactor of "frauds and forgeries" committed on his behalf.[35] Many Americans strongly believed that Hayes had won the presidency through chicanery and corruption and was not legally entitled to hold office. Barely a decade after the Civil War, the political stability of the United States seemed once again uncertain. These sentiments faded during Hayes's presidency, but they weakened him politically during his first two years.

Hayes: The Last Whig

Overall, Hayes was a centrist and a moderate, but he did bring into the White House a vision for America for which he consistently advocated as president, sometimes quite stridently: a sound US currency, clean and honest government, respect for the law, support for modernization, and a return to national unity. These were not novel musings, conveniently selected to score political points or to respond to problems ad hoc. Hayes had held these beliefs for decades, some since his youth.[36]

One key to understanding President Hayes's political-economic vision is that he was an old Whig. In economics, the Whig Party (1834–1854) held that the future strength and stability of the United States lay in industrialization, finance, and commerce.[37] But the infrastructure and financial demands of early industrialization were far beyond the means of the poorly capitalized American market. Therefore government needed to step in to support economic development. This put Whigs in stark opposition to the Jeffersonians and Jacksonians, who prioritized agriculture and natural resources and sought only the weak, decentralized government that these sectors required.[38]

Whig economic beliefs had enormous implications for public policy. For example, Whigs sought a central bank to foster investment and stabilize the currency. They tended to support the international gold standard, rather than paper currency or inflated silver, to improve business confidence and for moral reasons.[39] And Whigs called on Congress "to relieve the nation from a burden of debt" which they found abhorrent.[40] They nevertheless encouraged government subsidies and land grants to railroads, telegraphs, ports, roads, and bridges as essential lifelines in an industrial economy. They backed tariffs to protect American industries from foreign competition. These were all essential foundations for individual and national Christian self-betterment.[41] Whigs were *not* 20th-century progressives or liberals. They did not prescribe government as the solution to America's economic and social problems. But Whigs were "distinguished from their [Democratic] opponents, by the attribution of a beneficent and protective power to government."[42]

Hayes became a devout Whig in college and generally adhered to its economic philosophy ever after. For example, throughout his life, his letters, diary, and speeches are replete with exhortations against debt and devaluation. Even in his youth, he rejoiced in the Whigs' 1840 electoral victories, believing the country "should then have a stable currency of uniform value."[43] Decades later, Hayes believed that the Panic of 1873 was caused by irresponsible speculation and the printing of "inflated and irredeemable paper currency."[44] And when, in 1874, federal legislation was proposed to print more US dollars so as to increase lending, he protested to his uncle, "I regard the inflation acts as wrong in all ways. Personally I am one of the noble army of debtors, and can stand it if others can. But it is a wretched business."[45] Thus one of Hayes's perpetual campaign planks was that "an irredeemable paper currency, with its fluctuations of values, is one of the great obstacles to a revival of confidence and business, and to a return to prosperity."[46] In other words, gold, not paper currency, was the only trustworthy form of money.[47] The government should conduct transactions in no other. Even silver was unacceptable if it had lost value relative to gold. For "[t]o attempt to pay the public debt in depreciated silver coin is a violation of public credit and public faith and thereby [would] add to the burden of the debt."[48]

On other issues, Hayes also consistently followed Whig precepts. He was heartily pro-business, though he did not care much for the new industrial "robber-barons" who emerged during the 1870s.[49] He sympathized with the increasing plight of industrial labor, but not to the extent that he tolerated law-breaking or property destruction. Thus he tried to hew a middle course, seeking "to protect laborers in their right to work, and property owners in the use and possession of their property."[50] He believed in protective tariffs, but he generally avoided the topic because tariffs were not popular in the agricultural districts upon whose votes Republicans depended. Hayes had no such qualms about the spoils system. He despised it. "I don't sympathize with a large share of the party leaders. I hate the corruptionists . . . the appointment of unfit men on partisan or personal grounds," he repeatedly proclaimed in letters and speeches.[51] And he sought to heal the nation traumatized by war and industrialization, to "wipe out forever the distinction between the North and South in our common country," and to create "a fraternal spirit of harmony pervading the people of all sections and classes."[52] These would be the top economic priorities of his administration.

As for the presidency, Hayes unsurprisingly had a Whig view of it. That is, its powers were those defined by the Constitution—not more, not less. In his youth, he inveighed against Jacksonians who saw presidents as heroic figures, sent to exert their personal clout in public battles against perceived enemies. Hayes even once warned a political friend, "[D]on't get the Presidential mania. It makes mad every man who is at all prominent. . . . I have no knowledge of any tolerably conspicuous politician at Washington whose career is not colored and marred by his ambition to be President."[53] As with his own personal life, Hayes believed in a calm, dignified, and "proper" presidency. The executive should be professional and vigilant, but not power-grubbing or headline-seeking. He should vigorously defend his constitutional prerogatives against an acquisitive Congress and zealously exercise his duties, but avoid becoming megalomaniacal himself. True to Whig beliefs, Hayes also called for presidential term limits, even while in office, suggesting a constitutional amendment to limit presidents to a single term of six years.[54] Hayes took his own medicine here. In accepting his 1876 nomination, he stated his "inflexible purpose, if elected, not to be a candidate for election to a second term," and he never wavered from it.[55]

Fundamentally, Hayes also saw the presidency as a unifying institution. It should be used to counteract the centrifugal forces of party, economic inequality, ethnicity, and region. Thus he abhorred demagoguery. He traveled more widely than any president before him, earning the nickname "Rutherford the Rover," and spoke frequently. But he avoided fiery rhetoric.[56] "I tried to impress the people with the importance of harmony between different sections, States, classes, and races, and to discourage sectionalism and race and class prejudice," he explained.[57] To befriend Congress, foreign dignitaries, and American business and farm leaders, the Hayeses regularly entertained at the White House.[58] Nevertheless, when he left office, he confessed to his diary, "That the White House will be left 'willingly' by both Mrs. Hayes and myself is perfectly true. Indeed, 'gladly' might truthfully be substituted for 'willingly.'"[59] To Hayes, the presidency was a duty and an honor, not a coveted trophy or vehicle for personal power.

1877: Year of Conflict

Entering office in March 1877, President Hayes inherited a weak economy, still languishing in a recession caused by the Panic of 1873. Industrial production was still recovering from recession lows. Deflation, which had haunted the country for four straight years, persisted at around −2.3 percent. Food prices had improved somewhat, but prices for cotton, wool, coal, and steel continued to suffer. So too did the businesses and workers in these depressed sectors. Therefore wages for unskilled labor also stood at decadal lows. Unemployment was so high that millions of homeless roved the nation's streets and roadways. Newspapers warned of a widespread "tramp nuisance . . . swollen to the dimensions of a great and threatening social peril."[60] Nevertheless, immigrants continued to pour into eastern cities, albeit at reduced rates, driving down wages even further. Perhaps the only bright spot was trade. Poor crop yields in Europe combined with bumper harvests in the United States to send net exports soaring; even demand from Canada was strong.[61] This brought foreign gold into the American economy, providing a monetary stimulus. Meanwhile imports of foreign goods declined, reducing concerns about the American trade balance. Federal tax revenues from alcohol and tobacco had picked up during the previous year; therefore the national debt had resumed its slow but steady decline.[62]

Hayes believed that government corruption and currency speculation were preventing a recovery from the four-year-long economic slump. Therefore, once in office, he acted vigorously on his campaign promises. Thumbing his nose at party elites, he started by selecting his own cabinet with little regard for congressional preference. Republicans were shocked. Even the great Abraham Lincoln had accepted congressional leaders and party favorites into his cabinet.[63] Grant had, over time, learned to do likewise. Most expected that Hayes, politically vulnerable and faction-less, would conform to precedent in order to secure the support of his party in Congress. However, Hayes was determined to demonstrate executive independence as early as possible. He also wanted to reduce the influence of party factions on his administration. In an unprecedented act of retaliation, Senate Republicans tied up Hayes's cabinet nominations in committee. But after some adroit political maneuvering, Hayes got his cabinet approved. Historians have since described it as "the ablest presidential team between the Civil War and the 20th century."[64] The public and the press applauded Hayes's bold stand. It constituted the first major defeat of the Senate by a president in a dozen years. The *Chicago Tribune* cheered it as an early sign "that the new President is not the kind of man to yield . . . [to] the machine which it is his first duty to smash."[65]

Hayes's next act was less popular. It involved the highly controversial standdown of federal troops in ex-Confederate states, as was promised in the electoral Compromise of 1877. Perhaps only three thousand US soldiers remained in the South.[66] But they served as the last and only prop to those Republican state governments still dedicated to civil rights for African Americans. Most Americans recognized that the relocation of federal troops would be followed by a reversion to rule by white supremacists. "The negro will disappear from the field of national politics," predicted *The Nation*.[67] Violence and intimidation against African Americans in the South would follow, with few political or legal limits. To many diehards and veterans, a central purpose of the Civil War was being abandoned. Liberal Republicans and the press excoriated Hayes for deserting Southern Blacks, calling the withdrawal a surrender and themselves "deceived, betrayed, and humiliated"; ex-Confederate leaders heralded the move as "a grand opportunity" for "peace and prosperity."[68]

Hayes was therefore severely constrained as to what he could accomplish as president. As a result of overseeing the end of Reconstruction and defying Republican congressmen over patronage and cabinet appointments, he had mostly lost the support of his own party within six weeks of his inauguration. Nor did Hayes have any electoral coattails to tug on. Thanks to their growing unpopularity, and voter suppression, Republicans had performed badly in the 1876 congressional elections. The party lost six Senate seats, trimming their majority there to forty versus the Democrats' thirty-five, while the Democrats held on to a bare majority in the House (147–146). The Democratic House had spent the previous two years assailing Grant and his party, and they had little intention of stopping now. Worse yet, the still popular General Grant was no longer around to unite Republicans. Already divided, the Republican Party now imploded into warring factions, each led by powerful, proud, self-interested congressmen, which as often turned their enmity on the defiantly righteous Hayes. Hence, throughout his administration, Hayes had few strong or natural allies in Congress. Meanwhile, the White House in 1877 was minimalist. Hayes had fewer than a dozen staff, including secretaries, messengers, waiters, a valet, an usher, and a doorkeeper.[69] Thus, the veto, appointments, skilled cabinet members, and adroit political messaging would be his primary tools for leadership.

Civil Service Reform

Hayes's popular victory over the Senate in his cabinet appointments encouraged him to next tackle civil service reform.[70] He had been a critic of the spoils system since it resurfaced as a national issue during the late 1860s. Now, as president, he promised "a reform that shall be thorough, radical, and complete."[71] His pledge of a single term in office was partly done to reduce his patronage obligations to Congress.[72] For Hayes was determined to restore executive authority over all federal appointees, and thereby eliminate another pillar of the spoils edifice and a major constraint on presidential power. The elimination of federal moieties in 1874 had not been enough. To this end, Hayes openly supported an assortment of reforms: a merit- and exam-based appointments system, the abolition of mandatory political donations, the elimination of useless or unfit federal employees, and the abstention of civil servants from party or campaign management. To demonstrate his seriousness, Hayes appointed Carl Schurz as his secretary of the interior. This was an aggressive move. Schurz had been a "fearless" critic of corruption in the Grant administration, even leading the short-lived Liberal Republican Party in an attempt to drive Grant from office in 1872.[73] And the Interior Department housed the lucrative bureaus for federal lands, Indian affairs, and federal pensions, each one infamous for inefficiency, turmoil, and corruption. Schurz was expected to clean house and transform the Interior Department into a model of efficient government.

Then, in late April 1877, Hayes created the Jay Commission to investigate the infamously corrupt New York City Customs House.[74] The Customs House accounted for 70 percent of the nation's customs revenues;[75] it was also a prime source of patronage slots and graft for the state Republican Party. Hayes saw it as another beachhead from which to roll back the spoils system. His administration's stated goal was to "put the Customs House on a business footing" and to eliminate "appointments made on political influence without due regard to efficiency."[76] Soon other commissions were established to investigate the federal customs houses in Philadelphia, New Orleans, and San Francisco. Within months, these commissions were sending back reports of extensive waste, fraud, and laxity throughout the system. In response, in late May, Hayes issued an executive order which unambiguously attacked the spoils system. In it, he boldly decreed:

> Party leaders should have no more influence in appointments than other equally respectable citizens. No assessments for political purposes on [federal] officers or subordinates should be allowed. No useless officer or employee should be retained. No officer should be required or permitted to take part in the management of political organizations, caucuses, conventions, or election campaigns.[77]

He also specifically instructed the New York City Customs House to trim its patronage-bloated workforce.

However, Hayes also realized the need for flexibility. If he clamped down too hard on spoils, then he might wreck his beloved Republican Party and his own presidency.[78] Democrats and ex-Confederates would start winning elections again and gain control of federal and state offices throughout the country. Hard money, public education, government support for modernization, and Hayes's other policy priorities might all flounder. He therefore soft-pedaled on civil service exams. He backed away from removing senior spoilsmen from office. And other than Schurz, he appointed no other zealous reformers to his cabinet. Rather, Hayes's strategy was to attack high-profile cases of corruption, while allowing more general street-level practices to continue.[79]

Securing the West

A major source of economic prosperity during and after the Hayes administration was the development and exploitation of the West.[80] These new states and territories were rich with land, minerals, metals, forests, and animal resources. However, even into the late 1870s they were sparsely inhabited. Only around 2.7 percent of the US population lived west and north of Nebraska.[81] Parts of California had been well settled, and Colorado was booming, but the other states and territories badly needed investment and infrastructure in order to grow. This meant bringing in investors and migrants to establish farms and ranches, mine the earth, lay down telegraph wire and railroad track, and establish networks of communities and commerce. The Hayes administration supported western development with special permits, geological surveys, and cheap sales of federal lands to special business interests.[82]

The greatest obstacles to investment and settlers were not just the high costs and financial risks, but also physical security. Along the southwestern border, Mexican bandits and warlords regularly crossed into Texas to plunder American ranches and towns. During spring 1877, difficulties surfaced with Mexico over a surge in these raids and over confusion surrounding the rise of dictator Porfirio Díaz. Hayes refused to recognize Díaz and ordered US troops to enter Mexico to pursue raiders and pacify the border. Critics fretted that Hayes husbanded secret plans to invade and conquer. But Mexico negotiated and secured its border. By spring 1878, formal relations with Díaz had been established.[83]

Native Americans also posed a threat to settlers in the western states and territories. For the West remained the ancestral land of dozens of tribes which sought to defend themselves against perpetual invasion by white settlers.[84] The Great Sioux War, concluded during spring 1877, was supposed to have been the last stand of the now dwindling Native American resistance. But in June 1877, an uprising of Nez Perce Indians in Oregon and Idaho threatened to spark another wave of armed conflict. Eastern newspapers filled with excited reports of "Indian outrages" and settlers "wantonly murdered."[85] The *New York Times* marveled at the "remarkable . . . skill with which the Indians have fought. . . . [T]hey have in every respect proved themselves as thorough soldiers as any of our trained veterans."[86] Hayes permitted the US Army to mercilessly pursue the Nez Perce north toward the Canadian border. By October they were all either captured, killed, or driven into Canada. After years of intermittent warfare, Hayes finally won a conqueror's peace with the indigenous people that would last a dozen years.[87] It would take time to cement, but security in the West now markedly improved, at least for whites.

The Great Uprising of 1877

The greatest economic crisis of the Hayes administration struck next, just four months into his presidency, the brief but violent mass labor uprisings of July

1877.[88] Years of recession, wage cuts, and sporadic unemployment finally broke the growing class of industrial workers. The initial strike began in Martinsburg, West Virginia, when railroad workers on the Baltimore & Ohio line (B&O) walked off the job after learning of a third consecutive cut to their wages. Their incomes having already fallen 45 to 55 percent over four years, they complained, "[W]e cannot live and provide our wives and children with the necessities of life."[89] Fellow workers on the Pennsylvania, New York Central, and Erie lines took note of the B&O strike and copied it. Others followed, and strike activity spread like wildfire.

Strikes soon affected railroad lines nationwide, first along the East Coast, and then throughout the country. Within days, tens of thousands of railroad employees were on strike from coast to coast. Rail traffic was interrupted at best, completely paralyzed in many cases. Because railroads were the essential core of the US long-distance transportation and distribution system, the strikes threatened much of the American economy. Vital shipments of grain, cattle, fuel, raw materials, and industrial goods piled up on loading docks or languished in stalled railcars. Worse yet, laborers in other industries began to join the picket lines: miners, canal workers, boatmen, ironworkers, factory labor, and small armies of youths and the unemployed. At its height, some 100,000 workers were out on strike, with six thousand to seven thousand miles of track under their control.[90] This was a new phenomenon to Americans. Most had grown up in an agricultural, preindustrial economy; hence work stoppages were rare and always localized. Thus the speed, size, and national spread of the 1877 strikes seemed revolutionary. Business leaders clamored for federal action. B&O's president anxiously warned Hayes of "the greatest consequences not only upon our line but upon all the lines in the country" and urged him to immediately send in federal troops "to suppress this insurrection."[91]

At first, the American public generally sympathized with the strikers. They blamed corporations for "putting wages down to the starvation point."[92] The railroads in particular had become wealthy and powerful, and where possible, they had exploited their natural monopolies to skimp on services and working conditions. Worse yet, rail corporations had continued to pay high dividends to their already wealthy stockholders, while cutting wages for hundreds of thousands of workers and raising prices on passengers and farmers. "These men merely wanted to live," complained a sympathetic reporter.[93]

However, the strikes soon became violent, with looting, vandalism, destruction of property, fighting, and eventually shootings. In several cities, devastating riots broke out in "one of the most spectacular and frightening episodes of collective violence in American history."[94] Strikers set fires that burned down a large section of Pittsburgh. The rail strike in St. Louis transformed first into a general strike and then into near civil conflict. "We shall blow up their bridges; we shall tear up their railroads; and we shall consume their shops by fire," declared one strike manifesto.[95] Thousands of railcars were destroyed and scores of buildings burned.[96] "Madness rules the hour," one newspaper reported, ". . . so extensive and continuous a reign of anarchy."[97] Wealthy citizens in some municipalities formed vigilante posses to fight the strikers and to defend their homes and businesses. Police attacked even peaceful protestors in the major cities. Retired Civil War officers, both Union and Confederate, put on their old uniforms to lead state militias in the defense of their cities.[98] Overall, at least one hundred people were killed and countless injured, including many bystanders.[99]

State governors appealed to Hayes for military aid against rebellion. Interestingly, Hayes was more sympathetic to the strikers than most of his contemporaries. He saw no "spirit of communism" or insurrection in the strike, just a wage dispute.[100] But he also believed that strikers had no right to interfere with the right to work of other people, and violence and property destruction were beyond unacceptable. Therefore, Hayes sent the US military into West Virginia, Maryland, and Pennsylvania. This was a risky move given that the army was then skeletal, overstretched, and unpaid due to congressional wrangling over the budget.

Having previously dealt with several labor strikes while governor, Hayes adopted the following approach as president: US troops would *not* act to enforce state laws unless a formal request by state officials had been rendered to and approved by the Hayes administration. In which case, US troops would be sent into a strike area only to protect federal property "and by their presence to promote peace and order."[101] In other words, the US Army was not to break up strikes or operate the private rails, even though Hayes could have used obstruction of US mail delivery as a pretext to intervene more forcefully. Nor would Hayes be manipulated by industry heads into hasty decisions or blanket armed suppression.

Soon US troops were being directed and redirected all over the country, but always arriving after the violence had mostly dissipated. Thus, federal troops spilled no blood, even as state militias and local police killed scores of men. But the appearance of US soldiers was enough to quell additional disorder, without implicating the federal government in the fighting. Hayes did not end the crisis. But in his moderate response, and his refusal to be provoked by big business into smashing the strikers, Hayes threw cold water, rather than gasoline, onto the fire. And after two weeks, the strikes evaporated as abruptly as they had begun.

Despite its brevity, the Great Strike frightened businessmen, investors, and politicians like no other event in US history. Historians now rank these protests as the "biggest instance of labor violence anywhere on earth for the hundred years between the end of the Napoleonic Wars of 1815 and the beginning of the Great War in 1914."[102] It was also the *first* national labor uprising in America, and it seemed to come organically from nowhere. In Europe, similar mass movements had threatened to spread revolution, Marxism, and constitutional crises. Contemporaries agreed. "Communistic ideas are now widely entertained in America," warned the *Washington National Republican*, an anxiety echoed by frightened newspapers around the country.[103] Therefore some historians credit Hayes's moderation for defusing a more radical outcome.[104] Without taking sides, he allowed the strikers to express their anger. He also set a useful precedent that evolved into the federal strike injunction.[105] "[B]acked by the power of the U.S. Army [it became] one of the most effective weapons to be used against the labor movement."[106] Over the next fifty years, some eighteen hundred injunctions would be issued in a similar manner.[107]

The Gold Standard

The Great Uprising of 1877 severely damaged confidence in US credit, only recently recovered after the Panic of 1873.[108] Investors worldwide suddenly questioned anew whether the US government, fresh from a disputed election and now overseeing national upheaval, would be able to pay its debts in full.[109] The British business press warned its readers of a "declared war upon Government and upon capital" in America and that "[i]f the railway strike were to succeed in its aims, there is no saying what other attempts might not be made to 'cow' capital into submitting [to] the demands of 'labor.'"[110] In an ominous sign, for the remainder of 1877 only a paltry amount of US government bonds sold.

The currency situation did not help. The $351 million in federal notes then estimated in circulation remained untethered to gold or any other asset of value beyond the government's word.[111] Meanwhile, cash-starved sections of the West and South renewed their calls on Hayes and Congress to print even more greenbacks and to reintroduce silver currency. As silver production soared in the western states, and silver prices plummeted, urgent demands for its use as legal tender flooded Congress. These credit pressures, combined with political enthusiasm for inflationary policy, prompted widespread speculation that Hayes might give in to demands for "soft money" legislation.[112]

Therefore, after Congress reconvened in October, Democrat Richard Bland (D-MO) presented a House bill to restore federal coinage of silver. Prior to 1873, silver bullion could be presented to the US Mint for coinage into standardized silver dollars, but the Coinage Act of 1873 had quietly eliminated this service and limited the use of silver coins as legal tender to transactions not exceeding $5.[113] Henceforth, silver could be used in private transactions, but the federal government might not accept it, nor would the US Mint coin it upon demand. Bland's bill would return silver to full legal status and require the Mint to coin it. Ideally, this would allow a new supply of metal currency to reflate the US economy, aiding especially those western states where silver was mined.

The Bland proposal gained broad bipartisan support. It passed the House by a wide margin (164–34) in early November 1877. The House also narrowly voted (133–120) to repeal the Resumption Act of 1875, which was the legislative basis for the US return to the international gold standard. Hayes's entire "hard money" agenda, initially set down by the Grant administration and badly desired by American trade and financial interests, was now suddenly at risk.[114] The Republican Senate split. It declined to take up the Resumption Act repeal but responded favorably to silver coinage. Senator William Allison (R-IA) went further, amending Bland's bill so as to force the US Treasury to coin between $2 million and $4 million worth of silver dollars each month.[115] The result was nicknamed the Bland-Allison Act.[116]

Hayes removed all speculation about his views by blasting these measures in his early December annual message to Congress. Hayes argued that, as an indebted and developing nation, the United States depended heavily on the confidence of creditors everywhere. Gold was then the most trusted currency in international markets. Therefore any attempt to slow or obstruct a return to the gold standard "must end in serious disorder, dishonor, and disaster in the financial affairs of the Government and of the people."[117] Hayes himself was then still deeply in debt and would have personally benefited from the Bland-Allison Bill.[118] But he sincerely believed that inflationary policies, like silver coinage, would damage trust in America as both a trading partner and a recipient of investment and loans.

Congress ignored him and passed Bland-Allison in late February 1878; Hayes then vetoed it over the objections of some of his own cabinet members. Political conservatives reminded Hayes of the fundamental Whig axiom that presidential vetoes should be used only to defend the Constitution or to correct an obvious mistake by Congress, but not to obstruct legislation. Hayes countered that Bland-Allision was just such a legislative mistake. If allowed to pass, he later wrote, "[t]he faith of the nation was to be violated—the obligation of contracts was impaired by the law." Yet Congress immediately overrode Hayes's veto and Bland-Allison became law in February 1878.[119] Hayes then resolved to curb its effects. He ordered the US Treasury to limit silver coinage to $2 million per month ($5 billion in 2020 dollars), the smallest amount allowed under the law.[120] Partly in response, and "in view of the strong popular feeling against a contraction of the currency," Congress forbade the retirement of any more greenbacks by the US Treasury.[121] The paper greenback, initially created as a "temporary" Civil War expedient, was now a permanent fixture of American finance.

The Nadir of the Hayes Administration

It is hard to overstate the anxiety felt by the American business community during winter 1877–1878. The recession seemed never-ending. The labor uprising appeared to herald the spread of Communism in the United States. Armies of homeless continued to menace the nation's cities and towns. Western settlers nervously awaited the next Indian war. Civil service reform was in limbo. Perhaps in response to the smoldering political uncertainty and economic misery, the country was also awash in a wave of murders and assaults, some government sanctioned, prompting several historians to label 1877 a "year of violence" and "one of the blackest in the nation's annals."[122] Now gold too, the bedrock of national credit, seemed at risk. And over it all presided Hayes. He had laid the groundwork for a recovery in confidence and economic growth, but there were few signs of it yet. Frustrated critics renewed their attacks on his administration. Newspapers around the country published pages of testimony excoriating Hayes's Southern policy and questioning again his contested election. The *New York Sun* brazenly called upon "the whole American people" to impeach and cast out the "usurper in the White House!"[123]

Conditions were ripe for a major political assault on the Hayes presidency. It was finally launched in mid-May 1878, when Democratic congressmen opened an investigation into alleged voter fraud in Florida and Louisiana during the 1876 election. Hayes interpreted the investigation as an attempt to reverse his election and unsuccessfully tried to stop it. To his delight, the subsequent inquiry backfired. In mid-June 1878, the congressional committee in charge of the probe reported that Hayes was indeed the legitimate victor of the 1876 election. A resolution to this effect passed Congress by wide margins. A second Democratic effort was attempted, this time a congressional investigation to prove that the Republicans had won in 1876 by bribery. However, this scheme also backfired when, in October 1878, several New York newspapers published Democratic communications which revealed that Tilden's people were deeply involved in efforts to bribe Southern electoral officials. The Democrats in Congress now ceased their embarrassing attempts to drive Hayes from office. As a result, by autumn 1878 general suspicions over Hayes's legitimacy had dwindled to only his most diehard critics.

Bimetallism vs. Gold in 1878

Meanwhile, Hayes's monetary policy proceeded on various tracks. He sought to adhere to the gold standard as rigorously as possible, but the Bland-Allison Act required him to seek international cooperation on bimetallism. In particular,

Congress instructed him to call an international conference "to adopt a common ratio between gold and silver, for the purposes of establishing, internationally, the use of bimetallic money."[124] The driving concern was that, since the US Mint's statutory price for silver was now *higher* than the international price, silver would flood the country and gold would be driven from circulation.[125] People would hoard the more valuable metal (silver) and spend the cheaper one (gold). The United States would therefore wind up on a *de facto* silver standard, which few desired. Other supporters of the conference simply sought to spread bimetallism throughout the world. Foreign governments, likewise suffering from prolonged recession, also wanted to square inflationary policy with the reliability of fixed exchange rates.

To Hayes's relief, the conference was a failure. At his administration's request, the International Monetary Conference of 1878 met in Paris that August with the participation of twelve nations.[126] However, after lengthy discussions, the delegates rejected American proposals for bimetallism or standardized weights for gold and silver coins. Germany was dedicated to gold and refused to attend. The Swiss accused America of trying to repudiate its debt obligations and enrich its silver producers by devaluing the US dollar. Most other delegates found proposals for bimetallism simply impractical. But the conferees also refused to formally endorse an international gold standard. Each nation was to determine its own course.[127]

Nevertheless, back in the United States, many began to fear a run on gold when resumption was scheduled to begin on New Year's Day 1879. For although the Resumption Act of 1875 had set that date for the free convertibility of greenbacks into gold at face value, it had *not* created a mechanism by which to achieve it. It fell to Hayes and his Treasury secretary to figure this out. The only policy lever available to them was the Treasury's authority to sell bonds for gold (and vice versa). They could not legally destroy greenbacks nor otherwise reduce their circulation in order to boost their value. So, soon after taking office, Treasury Secretary John Sherman had begun negotiating large gold loans, attracting considerable interest from J. P. Morgan and the European Rothschild banks. By means of these loans, throughout 1877–1878 the Treasury gradually built up a special reserve of some $100 million in gold coin to service resumption.[128] Soon the business press was assuring its readers "that on or before the first day of January 1879, anyone, on application at the office of the Assistant Treasurer in New York, can obtain gold and silver for greenbacks."[129] As investor confidence grew, the greenback rose in value to within half a percent of gold parity by spring 1878. Europeans, who had been scared off by the labor uprisings and silver movement, now lost their fear of US securities and began to reinvest in America.[130] By the end of 1880, long-term foreign investment in the United States had risen from $975 million (spring 1878) to just under $1.25 billion.[131]

Economic Recovery Begins

Thanks in part to the Treasury's success in securing gold, summer 1878 finally brought signs of an improving economy. Industrial production and trade surged. Prices for railroad bonds rose.[132] Hayes was also able to point to a strengthening and reliable dollar, vast debt reduction, hugely reduced interest rates, and a rapidly improving trade balance.[133] "We have touched the bottom, and are now on the ascending grade," he triumphantly declared to a crowd in Madison, Wisconsin, in early September.[134] Even the British began to fret that "[i]n the United States . . . the conditions of industrial production have undergone such a considerable change in the last five years that possibly that country is about to become our most formidable rival."[135]

Hayes also prodded the United States to embrace a wave of globalization enabled by new transportation and communications technologies. For example, despite relentless feuds with Congress, in July 1878 Hayes was able to announce Senate approval of a new bilateral treaty with Britain on trademark recognition. The ongoing recession at home had prompted many American businesses to market their products more forcefully in foreign markets. Agriculture usually did fine business overseas, but the budding American industrial sector was vulnerable to all sorts of intellectual property infringements.[136] To leverage more open markets abroad, the Hayes administration negotiated a treaty that allowed inventors, investors, and businesses in the United States and Great Britain to equally enforce their intellectual property rights on either side of the Atlantic. At the same time, Hayes also helped finalize revisions to the three-year old Universal Postal Union with thirty other countries and their colonial possessions. It eliminated a byzantine maze of postal rates and processes, creating a single postal market with common rates on international mail. Neither agreement triggered an avalanche of trade or investment, but each was a necessary step toward greater integration of the United States with the global economy and contributed to the late 1870s economic boom.

Admittedly, Hayes rarely operated alone in economic policy. One particularly valuable ally was his Treasury secretary, John Sherman, who played a large role in the administration's economic policy decisions. Sherman and Hayes were good friends and had a strong relationship. "I ride regularly with Secretary Sherman two to three hours. We talk over affairs and visit the finest drives and scenes near Washington," Hayes wrote in his diary.[137] Sherman was a reliable gold supporter and a former Whig and therefore saw eye to eye with Hayes on most economic matters.[138] He worked closely with Hayes on monetary issues, trade policy, and the labor crisis. After six years in the House, and sixteen years in the Senate, Sherman was also an expert on Congress, with many deep ties there, and he often served as Hayes's most productive congressional liaison. When Hayes was at his weakest, it was Sherman who was often able to corral support among recalcitrant and infighting Republicans in Congress.[139] Hayes understood this well. At the end of his presidency, Hayes wrote to Sherman, "To no one am I more indebted . . . for the career in public life which is now closed, as I am to you."[140]

In July 1878, with the economy improving and challenges to his political legitimacy quashed, Hayes went on the political offensive. After months of quiescence on civil service reform, he suddenly suspended Chester A. Arthur and Alonzo Cornell, the two senior federal appointees for the New York City Customs House and port, and each a notorious spoilsman. When Hayes's replacement for Arthur was finally confirmed, the president published instructions to him: "[Y]our office shall be conducted on strictly business principles. . . . In making appointments and removals of subordinates you should be perfectly independent of mere influence."[141] Instead, new appointees were to be made on the basis of competitive exams. They would enter office at the lowest positions, while higher positions were to be filled by promotion from within. Two months later, Hayes extended these rules to cover all major postal and customs offices. As executive orders, they did not have the permanence of congressional legislation, but they were a powerful step in the direction of reform.

Thanks to the recovering economy and real achievements on civil service reform, both Hayes and the Republican Party now enjoyed a surge in popularity. Northern Republicans even began to win back seats in Congress. However, Democrats more than compensated by tightening their grip on the South. As a result, both the Senate and the House were taken by Democrats during the November 1878 midterm elections. More worrisome was the new Greenback Party, which supported paper currency and sought to reverse Hayes's pro-gold agenda.[142] Invoking patriotism, they began to portray the greenback as a home-grown "American" currency beholden to neither foreign bankers nor their governments. In a surge of popularity, Greenback candidates garnered over 12 percent of the national vote in 1878, electing thirteen of their members to the House from around the country.[143] The new 46th Congress (1879–1881) would therefore prove chaotic. It abandoned attempts to change the results of the 1876 election, but battles over corruption, patronage slots, the currency, and civil service reforms continued to rage between Hayes and Congress. Nor were Republicans entirely past feuding with their president.

1879: Resumption and Redemption

On January 1, 1879, after years of careful planning, economic distress, and raucous politics, the United States finally returned to the gold standard. US paper currency could now be freely exchanged for gold at parity.[144] Contrary to dire warnings of crisis, gold specie resumption succeeded far better than expected. Because greenbacks could now be exchanged for gold upon demand, it reduced the actual pressure to do so. Hence there was no general flight from paper currency. Nor did the much feared run on gold manifest. Of the estimated $346 million in paper notes, only $130,000 was presented for gold that day, and the greenback controversy was now settled.[145]

The final months leading up to resumption had been fraught with peril, requiring almost constant attention from the White House. Rumors circulated in the press that the Hayes administration planned to redeem greenbacks in silver. Both Hayes and his Treasury officials shut them down with vigorous denials.[146] As resumption neared, Sherman convinced the major New York banks not to rush to redeem their massive deposits of greenbacks, which could "suck up the Treasury gold as a siphon exhausts a cistern."[147] And when speculators attempted to manipulate markets during December so as to create profitable arbitrage, Sherman sold gold in order to spoil their plans.[148] With resumption achieved and panic averted, the nation was free to move on to other issues.

Hayes also signed the Pensions Arrears Act in January 1879. With the Treasury increasingly flush with funds from excise taxes and import tariffs, the Pensions Act awarded lump-sum payments to Union veterans disabled by the Civil War. The amount paid was dependent on the recipient's rank and injury. Widows and children of men killed on duty were also eligible. And the payments were retroactive, dating from time of death, disability, or discharge. This produced an immediate increase in the number of pensioners, a quarter-million Americans by 1880, and a 110 percent increase in pension expenditures. At a time when welfare programs were almost nonexistent, these military pensions were an early form of federal benefits for hundreds of thousands of Americans still struggling to recover from the recession of 1873–1878. The new pensions also constituted a small, but significant, fiscal pump to the economy. Totaling over $57 million per year by 1880 (roughly $1.4 billion in 2020 dollars), the money went toward spending on rents, food, clothing, medical care, and consumer goods.[149]

With economic concerns fading, the new Democratic-controlled Congress instead launched an attack on voting rights for recently enfranchised African Americans. Their main battleground was the federal budget. Democrats attached riders to budget appropriations bills that would strip the federal government of its power to supervise elections. This was a backdoor strategy for Southern Democrats to cripple the Fourteenth and Fifteenth Amendments to the Constitution. With Republicans now a minority in Congress, and the entire federal budget at stake, Democrats sought to pressure the isolated Hayes into submission. But Hayes fought on alone. He defiantly issued veto after veto to defend the civil rights amendments. As public opinion began to turn against them, the Democrats in Congress surrendered in late June. Republicans now rallied around Hayes, who was finally winning their respect as a clean, competent, principled president. The *New York Times* cheered, "President Hayes . . . has taken a position which the good sense of the country will heartily sustain."[150]

During 1879, the fragile economic recovery begun the previous summer solidified into a boom. Industrial production and trade stepped up in spring. Rates for wheat, cotton, wool, and coal bottomed, as did wages for unskilled labor, while prices for steel rails, bricks, and other industrial and construction materials had begun to reflate. A new expansion in railroad construction commenced, with more track laid in 1879 than during the previous two years combined, and the most since the Panic of 1873. A midsummer *Atlantic Monthly* feature celebrated President Hayes's achievements: "The honor of the nation in respect of financial obligations has been vindicated in every point. . . . [A] great burden of taxation has been lifted, the credit of the United States is as good as that of any nation in the world, and an era of sound prosperity has dawned."[151] It also applauded Hayes's victories over the spoils system: "The civil service has been purified and invigorated." And it noted a resurgence of Republican Party electoral strength: "The party is in a better position either for attack or defense than it was in two years ago."[152] Hayes concurred, writing to a close advisor, "[O] ur difficulties are over, we are moving harmoniously along."[153]

Hayes and US Foreign Policy

In comparison, US foreign policy during the Hayes administration was relatively dull. Americans at this time were focused inward, concluding Reconstruction and the assimilation of the South and West. Also, some of President Grant's foreign policy measures had proven spectacular failures.[154] Since Grant was a far more popular leader, with a far more compliant Congress, he likely soured the Hayes administration on any bold moves here.[155] Perhaps the chief foreign policy concern for Hayes was the building of a canal across Central America. Hayes opposed a venture there proposed by Fernand de Lesseps, builder of the Suez Canal, because it violated the Monroe Doctrine. But Hayes realized the strategic importance of the isthmus. In January 1880, he ordered two warships to establish US naval stations there. He and his cabinet agreed that any future canal would be under American control, which he asserted in a special message to the Senate.

Although Hayes was no imperialist—for example, he declined a Samoan request for annexation—he did see diplomacy as means to expand trade. His secretary of state, the renowned attorney William M. Evarts, zealously advanced this agenda. Evarts gave frequent speeches and interviews about opening foreign markets for American manufacturing goods. To this end, Evarts also revitalized the consular corps and instructed them to file monthly reports describing foreign economic conditions, customs, and government operations. He then published these dispatches for the American business community to study. Evarts also supported the sending of US naval vessels around the Pacific and South Atlantic to increase security for American merchants there. Like Hayes, he generally opposed imperialism of any sort and protested vigorously against any European encroachments in Latin America. Widely respected in Republican circles, Evarts was also a valuable ally in support of Hayes's domestic agenda in Congress.[156]

On immigration, Hayes generally welcomed those coming from Europe, but he was less enthusiastic about the Chinese. By 1880, there were over 104,000 Chinese immigrants living in the United States, roughly 90 percent of whom had settled in the far west. In California, for example, despite recent restrictions, Chinese immigrants still constituted 9 percent of the population and 16 percent of San Francisco's.[157] There they competed with locals for jobs and pushed down wages, especially in railroad construction, often the largest employer in the region. The Chinese also appeared strangely foreign and culturally threatening in a country flush with Christian and white supremacist beliefs.

Hayes believed that the Chinese, as one of "the weaker races," did not assimilate well and aroused violence from white nativists. In private, he called the postrecession surge in Chinese migration an "invasion," insisting that "it is not in any proper sense immigration—women and children do not come."[158] Congress agreed. In early 1879, legislators passed a Chinese Exclusion Bill. Hayes felt compelled to veto it as a flagrant violation of the Burlingame Treaty of 1868, but he promptly renegotiated the Treaty with Peking, including new assurances against trade in opium, in order to clear the legal and diplomatic paths for future immigration restrictions.[159] And a year after Hayes left office, Congress formally suspended Chinese immigration.

The Gridlock Years: 1879–1881

Hayes's final twenty months in office settled into a series of tiresome, unproductive standoffs with Congress. Undeterred by the insurmountable Democratic opposition, he continued to urge new legislation to support his agenda. In a lengthy annual message in December 1879, he pushed Congress to "suspend the coinage of silver dollars" mandated by the Bland-Allison Act and to retire federal paper currency from circulation. He also asked legislators to help him "extinguish the public debt," suggesting a new tariff on imports of tea and coffee. He recommended the study of British administrative practices as a model for additional civil service reforms in the United States.[160] And he warned against the evils of Mormon polygamy and called for support of a trans-isthmus canal across Central America. But no significant legislation resulted from his appeals.

Meanwhile, Hayes fought Congress on all sides. He vetoed Democratic bills laden with anti–federal government, pro-South riders. He waged frequent battles over civil service appointments, while pushing for new reform legislation. Congressmen on all sides of the currency issues attempted to push through new monetary legislation in their favor. And Democrats again tried to corner and embarrass Hayes into submission over budgets and federal elections. Hayes stood resolutely against them all. His consistent defiance actually further strengthened Republicans' respect for him and finally restored his relationship with his own party. Some newspapers even urged him to run again in 1880. But Hayes was now eager to leave office, telling friends, "I am now in my last year of the Presidency and look forward to its close as a schoolboy longs for the coming vacation."[161] Hayes therefore traveled for much of summer and autumn 1880.

Hayes realized early on that a president's relationship with the American people was a valuable asset. "It is public opinion that rules in this Republic," he declared.[162] Therefore, in addition to small trips throughout the eastern United States, he took four extensive tours as president, including the first presidential visit to the West Coast. All told he visited thirty states and six territories during his single term, traveling more than any president before him.[163] These trips were not empty gestures. Hayes used them as opportunities to forge a relationship with, and to educate, the American people. In small villages and large cities alike, he stopped to speak to the crowds that gathered, making over 450 speeches, from brief, dignified pleasantries to more lengthy but stately exhortations on his favorite issues: a strong currency, civil service reform, national unity, equal political and civil rights, and public education. And Hayes almost always mingled with the public, attended local fairs and events, and dined at local venues. His final trip, out west in autumn 1880, with barely twenty companions and no armed guard, made national headlines. Eastern newspapers reported "tumultuous applause on the part of the throng" and formal receptions "packed almost to suffocation."[164] The *San Jose Times* in California gloated, "Nothing so strongly illustrates the true freedom and happy security in this land of liberty . . . [as] the untrammeled movements of our worthy President in his present long journeys." Hayes's tour demonstrated not only that times were so good that the president need not fear his own people, but also that the West was safe and secure enough for the president to travel without "armed guards and lynx-eyed detectives wherever he goes."[165]

By autumn, the 1880 elections dominated the news.[166] In early November, Republican James Garfield won both the popular and electoral votes for president. Perhaps even more valuable, the Republicans won back the House and achieved parity in the Senate. Many now believed, and Hayes certainly did, that Hayes had saved the Republican Party from destruction and planted it on the solid rock of reformed government, making possible Garfield's election. After the election, Hayes continued to make federal appointments in collaboration with Garfield. It promised to be one of the smoothest transitions in history.

Hayes's final major legislative act was to veto the Bond Refunding Bill of 1881.[167] Debt refinancing was a high priority for Hayes. However, the refunding bill sent to him by Congress appeared to attack the national banking system. It contained within it a provision that would force reluctant private banks to buy federal bonds at a new, lower interest rate. And it did so by severely restricting the ability of private banks to circulate their own notes, while drastically raising their reserve requirements. Some worried that this might cause a financial panic as banks rushed to consolidate their capital; others foresaw a wave of bank failures. The bill "deranges the whole machinery of free banking," a dismayed Treasury official warned Congress.[168] Still a strong supporter of private finance, and well warned of the potential disasters, Hayes killed the bill, one of only thirteen vetoes during his presidency, arguing that it would "seriously impair the value and tend to the destruction of the present national banking system of the country."[169] A clean version would be passed soon after he departed the White House.

Hayes left office in early 1881 with one of the strongest economic performances on record. In just four years, the nation's real, per capita economic output increased by roughly 20 percent. This vaulted the United States ahead of Great Britain as the wealthiest country in the world. The rate of business failures fell over 50 percent, reaching a minimum not bested until World War I. Trade also expanded dramatically, with imports rising 34 percent, while exports boomed 47 percent. The resulting US trade surplus was some six times larger (as a percentage of GDP) than that which Hayes had inherited four years prior. And yet the superheated economy did *not* trigger new inflation, which rose to just 2.5 percent during his final year. Meanwhile, federal revenues from tariffs and excise taxes dramatically improved the nation's finances. As a percentage of GDP, the federal budget surplus rose 50 percent, while government debt fell by 25 percent and was rapidly headed lower. The burdensome war debt, which had so troubled the country at 33 percent of GDP just fifteen years earlier, was now down to around 17 percent of GDP and fast headed lower. These conditions improved confidence in the US dollar, which strengthened 10 percent against the British pound.[170] Investors at home and abroad were now eager to lend to Americans, bringing US interest rates down from around 5 percent when Hayes took office to around 4 percent when he left it. Certainly poor urban labor still suffered. But wages had bottomed and were now headed higher. In fact, wealth-income ratios (a measure of inequality) fell from their decadal high of 478 percent (1878) to 421 percent (1881) and were headed toward Gilded Age lows.[171] With mobility costs falling, tens of thousands of new migrants settled in the increasingly peaceful western states and territories. The nation's transportation and communication networks also expanded at historic rates. The American railroad network grew by over 30 percent. International shipping grew by 36 percent. Telegraph traffic increased by 53 percent, while wire mileage increased by around 68 percent. The fledgling telephone industry boomed, with ownership increasing 550 percent. In fact, overall business formation and the emergence of new industries hit record highs. In sum, the United States was transforming into an economic and technological great power.

Certainly industrialization, technological change, globalization, and western settlement were the fundamental drivers of the recovery, but Hayes played a vital role in facilitating them. In a March 2, 1881, interview, the outgoing president specified what he thought were the accomplishments of his administration. First was pacification of the South. Second was civil service reform. Third was his conservative financial policies. He also believed that he had handled the strikes of 1877 well and pointed out the lack of corruption during his term of office. The *New York Times* generally agreed. Although the newspaper faulted Hayes for letting civil service reform slip during elections, and explicitly denied him the accolades of presidential "greatness" or "heroism," its editors admitted:

> The last four years have been the period of a somewhat remarkable transition in our affairs. While sectional division and antipathy have by no means wholly disappeared, their harshest features have been softened, and it is easy to mark a decided degree of progress toward renewed nationality. The finances of the country have been restored to the basis of specie with a prospect of permanency, and the national credit has acquired a degree of strength which it never before possessed. . . . [T]he beginnings of a [civil service] reform have been made which has sufficient root to acquire a healthy growth. . . . [T]he progress which has been made in these directions is largely due to [Hayes's] clearness of conviction, steadiness of purpose, and firmness in action.[172]

As for Hayes, he later gloated in his diary, "Coming in, I was denounced as a fraud by all the extreme men of the opposing party, and as an ingrate and a traitor by the same class of men in my own party. Going out, I have the good will, blessings, and approval of the best people of all parties and sections."[173]

Hayes's Economic Leadership

By some measures, Hayes was one of the weakest presidents in US history. He was a nonentity, elected for his lack of enemies or scandal. He was not a mover and shaker in the Republican party, with his own machine, popularity, or power base. Hence once in office, he had little informal power upon which to draw, just the institutional power of the presidency. With the Civil War fading into memory, and Reconstruction mostly abandoned, little bound the Republican Party together beyond patronage and "hard money." Hayes intended to disrupt the former and guarantee the latter. But with the "great man" Ulysses S. Grant gone from the political scene, party machines based on powerful senators and local bosses were now the greatest power centers in American politics.[174] And yet Hayes managed to achieve many of his policy goals and oversee one of the strongest economic booms ever recorded.

What lessons for presidential leadership can we infer from the Hayes presidency? Obviously, we cannot draw a straight line between any particular Hayes action and a specific economic outcome. Too many variables were simultaneously at play to reach conclusions of such definitiveness. Nor does this chapter argue that Hayes somehow masterminded the late 1870s economic boom. He did not. That is not the point of this case study. Rather, the goal is to use evidence from the Hayes case is to generate new hypotheses and to disconfirm some existing ones about the relationship between the presidency and short-run economic performance.

We can say with some confidence four things based on the Hayes case. First, neither formal economic training nor personal business experience is necessary for an executive to preside over the end of a recession or a booming economy. Hayes lacked both, yet did well. Second, presidents can lead successfully without being demagogues or electrifying public speakers. For example, clarity of vision and frequency of speech, accompanied by confirmatory actions appear to have worked for Hayes. Nor are presidential moderation and flexibility a hindrance to economic performance, and are likely a help. Only on gold was Hayes a stubborn ideologue.[175] Fourth, we can also say that a friendly Congress is not necessary. Certainly Hayes achieved more with Republicans in the congressional majority and on his side. But that was rare. And Hayes was able to advance, or at least defend, his agenda when they were not.

Other assertions are more hypothetical in nature. For example, the evidence suggests that Hayes's greatest achievement may have been to restore trust in major political and economic institutions. In other words, he did not cause the economic boom, but he did substantially facilitate it. Industrialization, technological change, and globalization were the fundamental economic forces driving recovery during his administration.[176] But they work poorly in uncertain environments. When he was first nominated, opposition newspapers predicted, "Hayes is no reformer. . . . He is a man who, in the Presidency, would run the machine in as easy and unobjectionable a way as he could; but he would run it in the old ruts."[177] His controversial election and secret deals seemed only to confirm those suspicions. Then came the labor riots, Indian wars, advances for silver, and congressional infighting of his first year. Hayes also initially had a habit of making bold declarations, especially about civil service reform, but following them with caution and occasional backpedaling. All boded ill. The country seemed headed into a political and economic maelstrom. But Hayes unexpectedly took the country back to normal after years of war, Reconstruction, political corruption, and recession. His economic policy was doggedly consistent with that of his predecessor. There were no major reversals or adjustments for investors to fear.[178] His administration also proved to be remarkably scandal-free. The economic environment grew more secure, both in practice and perception, due to Hayes.

Hayes's relevance is perhaps more clear from the economy's perspective. The opening of the West created vast opportunities for farmers, ranchers, miners, and shippers. So too did increased demand in Europe for American exports. Meanwhile the promise of urbanization created threats and opportunities hitherto unseen. These could be met only by a resurgence of railroad construction, telegraph and telephone erection, agricultural development, and mine investments. This meant a surge in demand for iron, steel, copper, coal, wood, and other raw materials, as well as for intermediate and finished manufactured goods. But all this relied on trust. Trust that investors could get out dollars valued the same as they put in. Trust that settlers would not be raided or killed in the West. Trust that federal funds and soldiers would not be diverted to Reconstruction efforts in the South. Trust that the millions of elderly, widows, and disabled could afford basic necessities. Trust that private and federal monies would not be siphoned off into hairbrained schemes or corrupt political activities. The hypothesis generated by this chapter is that the Hayes administration helped to alternately create, increase, and maintain that trust.

The main counterargument is "regression to the mean": that Hayes mostly just rode an inevitable recovery from the Panic of 1873. And if the main external factor is the number, diversity, and extremity of crises that a president faces, then Hayes faced relatively few. Hence passivity worked! He was a competent, unassertive "caretaker" president with little impact and lacking in executive leadership skills. He just happened to be in office when the economy entered a boom period. Hayes lucked out.

But Hayes was neither passive nor lucky. He repeatedly acted against the status quo, and one from which he and his party might have benefited. It is true that he avoided drama and sought no headlines. Nevertheless, Hayes did innovate in his approach to presidential leadership. He spurned expectations of a weak, passive executive. Prior to Hayes, presidents tended to defer to Congress or their cabinet members on appointments. In policy, most presidents also gave their cabinet members, usually drawn from Congress, considerable autonomy in running their respective departments. But Hayes refused to be dictated to by Congress. Nor would he permit his administration to become captive of his appointees. Instead, he chose his own cabinet. He met with it regularly. He relied on it, as well as Congress, for advice and guidance. But Hayes made his own decisions, some-times even imposing his will upon influential cabinet members who disagreed with him. And he was not ad hoc in his decision-making. He entered office with a philosophy that consistently guided his actions as president. And when serious conflicts over policy or appointments arose, instead of retreating, Hayes often willfully ignored, even openly defied, Congress and his own Republican Party. All the while, he actively cultivated his relationship with the American public, educating them on his agenda. He was generally effective, as Garfield's nomina-tion and election promised a "second term" of the Hayes administration agenda. In sum, the Hayes presidency was far more consequential than we are generally led to believe. Certainly his immediate successors would be neither as capable nor as successful. For, as the next chapter will show, they faced a rapidly changing political and economic landscape that would fundamentally alter the presidency going into the 1880s.

Interlude: Into the 1880s

The United States entered the 1880s subtly, but fundamentally, transformed. The Panic of 1873 and ensuing recession had wreaked havoc on the country, but they also catalyzed American economic development, with important consequences for politics and the presidency. Bankruptcies throughout the railroad sector forced the industry to consolidate and mature. To recoup their losses, some rail investors created the first American industrial farms. Taking advantage of both these developments, the first modern manufacturing corporations emerged. Industrialization pulled people into the cities, which exploded in size and density. Much new economic activity was powered by steam, making coal the nation's primary energy source. Together these advances constituted the first wave of modern mass production in America. Meanwhile, the railways, the telegraphs, and the new telephone were quickly knitting the economy into a nationwide market, bringing competition, threats, and opportunities where previously there had been none. In response, farmers and labor organized in new ways to defend their interests. These changes were reflected in new political parties and social movements. Democrats and Republicans flexed to accommodate them, while spoilsmen battled to retain their loosening hold on patronage and elections. Even public intellectuals and scholars began to rethink their ideas about political economy as individual firms acquired unprecedented monopoly power and economic inequality grew inexplicably. The presidents of the 1880s would respond differently to these pressures and opportunities: as victor and victim (Garfield), as shrinking bystander (Arthur), as strident conservative (Cleveland).

First and foremost, by 1880 the United States had become, by far, the wealthiest economy, per capita, in the world.[1] It was also the largest. In total output, the United States now produced three-quarters more than Great Britain and over twice that of either Germany or France. Partly thanks to its enormous size and disparate, often specialized internal markets, the United States also led the world in transportation and communication technologies. The country had 115,000 miles of railways and 291,000 miles of telegraph wire (handling 31.7 million messages annually) in operation,[2] more than all of western Europe, while Americans already used 47,900 telephones, invented just four years prior. Rail freight volumes had at least tripled since 1870.[3] And to supply these expanding industries, domestic production records were being set in coal, copper, iron, and steel every few years.

Presidential Leadership in Feeble Times. Mark Zachary Taylor, Oxford University Press. © Oxford University Press 2024.
DOI: 10.1093/oso/9780197750742.003.0008

The country's population had also grown, to over 50 million, a 26 percent increase in just a decade. The vast majority of African Americans (13 percent of the population) still lived in the former Confederate states. Most of the country's 105,000 East Asians—almost double the number a decade prior—lived in the Pacific region.[4] Immigration had temporarily slumped to period lows after the Panic of 1873. Nevertheless, a full 13 percent of Americans were foreign born in 1880. And their numbers were quickly rising into what would become the greatest immigration boom of the era. These immigrants resided mostly in the northern states, especially the coastal cities. There they worked the docks and the emerging urban manufacturing centers, or they took jobs as domestic servants or wage laborers. Another 1.4 million Americans, both immigrant and native, headed out to the Great Plains and far west to try their luck at farming or ranching in the belief that "rain follows the plow."[5]

Yet, despite its great wealth, in many ways the United States was still underdeveloped. Roughly 45 percent of Americans remained on the nation's farms in 1880, while only 22 percent labored in its factories and mines.[6] In comparison, western European economies were far more concentrated in manufacturing.[7] As a result, Americans produced vital exports of foodstuffs and raw materials, but they still imported a vast amount of manufactured and luxury goods from across the Atlantic. Energy use was also primitive. Even though the United States was a top producer of coal and new petroleum products, Americans still got the majority of their power from wood, rivers, and animals. Nor was education yet modernized. Only between 33 and 50 percent of the country's children attended school on a daily basis in 1880, while around 15 percent of US population was thought illiterate. And both education and literacy were heavily skewed by race and wealth.[8] The nation's physical health was little better. Malnutrition, disease, and work injuries were tremendous burdens. In fact, the average American born in 1880 did not live to see age forty.[9]

Nor was America's wealth evenly spread. Denied slavery, the Southern states adopted sharecropping and tenant farming, whose low returns sent them ever deeper into poverty and backwardness.[10] Out west, the new states and territories boomed on cattle, silver, and grains.[11] The North thrived on industry, railroads, trade, and finance. These regional economic disparities grew sharper during the 1880s. They provided ample tinder for fiery political battles over the nation's trade and monetary policies.

The rise in manufacturing and commerce also caused American cities to swell at an alarming rate.[12] By 1880, roughly 25 percent of Americans lived in cities, around 15 percent more than a decade prior.[13] New York City remained the most populous urban area in the country, with around 1.8 million people, the third largest city in the world. Chicago was also booming, as were Pittsburgh, Buffalo, St. Louis, Omaha, Denver, San Francisco, and two dozen other major cities across the nation.[14] Yet with urban overcrowding came urban blight. Raw sewage was dumped into public waterways. Poor migrants packed into filthy tenements. Cities were therefore rife with disease, fires, pollution, and street crime.[15] Hence, the topic of sanitation, both inside the home and out, had become "a national obsession" during the 1870s.[16] Urban Americans threw themselves into the Sanitarian movement, scientific plumbing, and a craze for public sewer systems.[17] To escape the squalor, the wealthy and middle classes moved uptown. Even then, the frenetic pace of urban life drove city dwellers into "nervous exhaustion" and "hysteria," prompting medical experts to pronounce a new epidemic: "American nervousness."[18]

The Rise of Corporate Agriculture

Out west, investors poured money into a new phenomenon known as "bonanza farms" that would transform American agriculture and the economy.[19] The bonanzas originated in the 1873 collapse of the Northern Pacific Railroad, the largest and most trusted railroad venture of the era. The bankruptcy decimated the value of its corporate bonds. Eastern holders of these debentures realized that the only way to recover their money was to develop the federal land grants owned by the now insolvent railroad. To this end, they pooled their landholdings into giant farms, run like corporations and managed by experts, focused almost entirely on high-efficiency wheat production.

After a few demonstration projects in North Dakota and northern Minnesota proved successful, the bonanza farms took off.[20] By the late 1870s, over a million acres of federal lands were being turned into private corporate farms each year by eastern capitalists and foreign investors. Presidents Grant and Hayes sent the US Army to protect the region against the Native Americans from whom the land had originally been taken. Linked by rail to Minneapolis and Duluth, which soon became the nation's leading markets for grain and milled flour, the bonanza farms were able to sell their wheat to the rest of the country and, via river and ocean ports, to the world. By 1880, they sold over 200 million bushels of wheat annually, priced at around $1.25 per bushel, but at costs of just $0.50 to produce and perhaps $0.20 to ship.[21] The Dakota region alone produced around 70 percent of the nation's wheat, while wheat and wheat flour grew to comprise one-quarter of all US exports.

The bonanza farms pioneered many techniques of modern corporate agriculture.[22] First, they were capital-intensive operations. Investors equipped them with the latest plows, harrows, seeders, binders, separators, threshers, and reapers, often steam-powered. They also brought in scientific management techniques run according to modern accounting practices. The bonanzas even installed some of the nation's first telephone exchanges. They thereby "served as large laboratories for testing the most recent developments in agricultural technology."[23] Astounding reports appeared in the nation's newspapers and magazines. Foreign policymakers and agriculturists traveled from Europe to study the new phenomenon.

Given their success, the practices of large-scale industrial farming soon spread to wherever they could be applied. They diffused throughout the Great Plains, south into Texas, and west into the Pacific states. In California, the spread of mechanization led to an explosion in grain yields, as well as increased specialization in fruit ranches and vineyards.[24] In the central states, corn and oat production skyrocketed. All told, American agricultural output leaped 70 percent between 1874 to 1880, even as prices plummeted.

However, the bonanzas also created new political problems. One was immigration. So plentiful and cheap were American grains and meat products that, alongside a recovery in Southern cotton production, their export bankrupted peasant farmers in Europe. Many of these destitute Europeans then left for the United States seeking work, creating an immigration surge throughout the early 1880s. "Ironically, many of them made the journey westward on the same ships that carried to Europe the wheat that proved their undoing," notes one historian.[25] Worse yet, the export boom in American agriculture was so pronounced that, during the 1880s, the nation's expanding trade surplus would pose an embarrassing political problem for presidents and Congress alike. Cartoonists delighted in illustrating the trade surplus, which soaked up money from private circulation, as "a monster gorging on the nation's vitals."[26]

The effects of the bonanzas on local agriculture and labor markets were even more severe. Industrial agriculture in the West was far more profitable than traditional grain production east of the Mississippi River, which plummeted. Even on the fertile Great Plains, small family farms struggled to survive against the bonanzas.[27] Bonanza size and mechanization eliminated many farm jobs. And where machines proved an ill fit, the bonanzas might hire workers *en masse*, sometimes driving up wages for an entire region during planting and harvest seasons. "The result is that those who have gone into wheat-growing on a large scale are making colossal fortunes . . . while small farmers . . . are not making a comfortable subsistence," reported the *New York Times* in 1879.[28] Still worse, the bonanzas used their size and business connections to leverage favorable deals on railroad rates, bank loans, grain storage, and equipment purchases. While standard practice today, such tactics seemed shockingly corrupt to Gilded Age farmers. These arrangements also bound up the fortunes of other corporate interests (banking, railroads, manufacturing) with those of the bonanzas. Many small farmers, unable to compete, sold off their holdings to the bonanzas, which only further increased the latter's size.

The Rise of Industrial Capitalism

A similar process of consolidation and modernization was revolutionizing American manufacturing, but it took longer to manifest. Before the Panic of 1873, the US economy was dominated by small enterprises, either family-owned or sole proprietorships. These owner-operators supplied local markets. And they responded ad hoc to local business conditions as they arose.[29] Perhaps only the railroads and a few textile manufacturers could claim to be large companies. But the panic and recession sent many small manufacturers scurrying for lifelines of cash and customers. For those firms that relied on seasonal demand and loans, the situation was mortal. They made easy pickings for those few manufacturers who enjoyed fixed contracts, ready access to capital, and generous railroad rebates. In fact, for the largest manufacturing firms, the panic years were often glorious.[30]

As American firms grew in size and complexity, they were forced to adopt new business practices.[31] For example, the best-performing corporations implemented continuous year-round manufacturing that reduced the volatility of seasonal cycles and allowed them to expand even further going into the 1880s. Continuous manufacturing also forced owners into the "scientific management" of their business organizations, which created demand for a new class of professional accountants, clerks, and managers. White-collar jobs like these comprised just 3.8 percent of the workforce in 1880, but the profession was already booming.[32]

Many of the most famous names in American business history amassed their empires during the 1870s.[33] For example, in a risky move, the aspiring steel producer Andrew Carnegie introduced the new Bessemer process just a year prior to the depression, dramatically lowering the costs of mass steel production. After the panic hit, Carnegie bought up his competition at rock-bottom prices and thereby built a massive steel syndicate. Similarly, John D. Rockefeller used the opportunity to expand his oil refining and distribution operations into a national conglomerate. When he consolidated them into Standard Oil in 1882, it became America's first private monopoly of a natural resource, with control over 90 percent of the domestic oil market.[34] Philip Armour implemented a "disassembly" line which processed pork into canned and refrigerated meats with incredible efficiency; Gustavus Swift did the same for beef. Together they helped consolidate the meat industry and transform Chicago and Kansas City into the meatpacking capitals of the world. The wheat produced by the bonanza farms supplied the new C. A. Pillsbury and Company, which used the latest milling technologies to mass-produce wheat flour and turned Minneapolis into the miller to the world. Franklin Gowen bought up most of the anthracite mines that supplied his Philadelphia and Reading Railroad, creating a northeastern dynasty in both energy and transportation. The American manufacturing sector still had a long way to go, but the era of massive industrial "trusts" dominated by "robber barons" was already taking shape going into the 1880s.[35]

The Railroads

Neither the revolution in agriculture nor in manufacturing was possible without the rapidly expanding railroad system. Most major American rivers had been traversed at multiple junctions by 1880. The Great Plains and the West were increasingly connected to the Atlantic, the Mississippi River, or the port of New Orleans by new transcontinental segments and regional lines. Admittedly, the nation's rail system was still afflicted by disparate gauge sizes, insufficient bridges, unconnected systems, and somewhat primitive cars and facilities. The South still lagged behind markedly. But on average, railroad rates dropped by half during the 1870s, from 3.1 cents to 1.45 cents per ton-mile, while freight volumes increased some 350 percent and travel times on the best routes fell considerably.[36] The decade also saw the diffusion of automatic couplers and Westinghouse brakes,[37] the introduction of Pullman sleeper cars (1872), the first rail bridge across the Mississippi River (1874), the introduction of station telephones (1877), the first practical refrigerated freight cars (1878), and steam-heated passenger cars (1881). Going into the 1880s, America's railroads had matured, as demonstrated by the advent of a flourishing nationwide mail-order retail business.[38] A less chaotic, more rational, cohesive national transportation system was slowly taking shape.[39]

The 1870s also witnessed a dramatic revolution in railroad management. Once again, the Panic of 1873 played a critical role. Before the financial crisis, railroad investment was booming. Even after federal land grants ended in 1871, the money still poured in. Most railroad directors of this era saw themselves as benevolent entrepreneurs who combined historic business opportunities for investors with innovative common carriage to serve the public interest. Therefore, short-run profits and cost controls were often subordinated to rapid expansion and bond sales. Overbuilding was common practice. Even labor agitation among rail workers and coal miners garnered little concern.[40]

All this changed with the depression of 1873–1878, which bankrupted many railroads. Rail magnates like James Hill, Jay Gould, Thomas Scott, Henry Plant, and the western "Big Four" leveraged their wealth to buy up distressed lines and consolidate them into a handful of massive networks run on entirely different business premises.[41] To reduce transfer delays in New York City, Cornelius Vanderbilt began construction of Grand Central Station in 1873 to link his lines together. This new breed of railroad owner conducted business less like dashing entrepreneurs and "more as private empire builders with the authority and responsibility to draft all the enterprises along their tracks in their wars with other regional railroad empires."[42] Corporate profits and investor returns were made top priority. A new variety of engineers and professional managers implemented cost cutting, aggressive pricing schemes, modern corporate management techniques, and market segmentation which disrupted the entire rail industry.

Railroad bonds and stocks continued to play a major role on Wall Street, for they were among the few firms with capital needs large enough to justify issuance.[43] American railway shares even traded on European bourses. Certainly, the Panic of 1873 took a mighty toll, but within five years the NYSE was booming again. In 1879, it listed around 275 corporate bonds and 131 stocks, of which 94 percent and 69 percent were railroad securities.[44] And on heavy trading days, over 500,000 total shares were exchanged, ten times more than a decade prior.[45] These assets were bought mostly by banks, investment houses, wealthy individuals, and foreigners (who, for example, owned around $900 million of railroad securities in 1880).[46] Some of the largest investors insisted on management roles. But since the railroads and finance were codependent, as the rails' capital demands grew, so too did Wall Street, and the roles of investor and business manager began to separate.

Desperate to tame "ruinous competition" among themselves, many railroads turned to "pooling." For years, high fixed costs (around two-thirds of total rail costs) bred intense competition for traffic and often drove railroad rates down below profitability.[47] In response, the larger railroad corporations formed "pools" through which they colluded to fix prices, allocate freight, and split revenues between them. The first railroad pool was created back in 1870, but the practice picked up with the depression.[48]

To those Americans who increasingly relied on the rails for business, transportation, wages, or supplies, the new pricing techniques and monopolistic behavior were infuriating. Earlier in the decade, Illinois state legislators had passed a law requiring railroads to charge only "just, reasonable, and uniform rates."[49] But the law had no enforcement mechanism. Nor did the railroads accept its constitutionality.[50] Hence Illinois's antitrust moxie amounted to a mere proclamation that the powerful railroads simply ignored. Nevertheless, the anti-monopoly movement had begun, and it picked up steam during the 1870s as other states followed suit with regulations of their own.[51] Eventually the rails sued. And in several major opinions issued during 1876–1877, the Supreme Court upheld the rights of state governments to regulate transportation.[52] Going into the 1880s, the political-economic battle over monopolies would only intensify.[53]

Rise of Coal

The nation's new rails, steamships, and industrial machinery all ran on steam, and steam increasingly ran on coal.[54] In the factories, coal was also the primary input for iron and steel production. In the nation's homes, coal provided heat for cooking and warmth. So essential was the black rock that a prominent geologist proclaimed in 1873, "Coal is to the world of industry what the sun is to the natural world."[55] Its usage had doubled every decade since before the Civil War and would finally begin to supplant wood during the mid-1880s.[56] Bituminous coal was most common. It could be found scattered in seams throughout the country, but it burned neither as hot nor as clean as precious anthracite, "the highest rank coal." Most of the nation's anthracite lay buried in the mountains of central Pennsylvania and Maryland, which supplied the lion's share of coal to the East.

As coal grew in importance and profitability, the nation's industrialists moved in to control it. Many small anthracite coal producers were gobbled up by the five railroads that traversed the region. These rails then consorted to form a united front against the miners. By the mid-1870s, the corporations "had taken complete control of the economic basis of every city, town, and industrial village in the region."[57] Wages, hours, and working conditions were notoriously brutal. Yet the coal sector proved surprisingly resistant to innovation. Throughout the Gilded Age, men mined the earth much as they had for decades.[58] Thus, as collieries grew from small businesses into large corporations, coal miners formed some of the more powerful—and most notoriously violent—unions of the era.

The Rise of the Grange Movement and the Greenback Party

Farmers reacted to railroad monopolies and seemingly predatory bankers by building up the National Grange of the Patrons of Husbandry. Originally founded as an educational and social organization for farmers, the Grange expanded in both membership and purpose after 1872. Grangers formed cooperatives, created banks, worked together to improve export and shipping, and formed life and fire insurance pools. The economic recession accelerated Grange activity and, by 1875, its peak year, there were over 750,000 members organized into almost nineteen thousand local Grange societies.[59]

Although avowedly apolitical, the Grange nevertheless urged its members to vote their interests. In fact, the Grange became the first nationally successful, reform-oriented, occupation-based political movement. Grangers advanced in unexpected ways. For example, just weeks after the 1874 midterm elections, a coalition of disgruntled farmers, along with a handful of laborers and businessmen, gathered in Indianapolis to create a new National Independent Party. Though driven by anti-monopolism, they laid blame for the nation's economic troubles on the country's banks. After all, it was bank speculation that had caused the Panic of 1873. Then, with the country desperate for loans and credit, many bankers had opposed the 1874 Inflation Bill and any other expansion of the currency other than specie. One speaker at the convention "charged all bankers with being usurers, and favored classing them, as the Bible does, with thieves and murderers."[60] The National Independent platform called for "the issuing of governmental currency direct to the people in sufficient quantity to meet the requirements of the poor as well as the rich."[61] Private banknotes would be abolished. The new government money would be backed *not* by specie but by interest-bearing government bonds.[62] Since this sounded much like printing more greenbacks, the press dubbed them the "Greenback Party."[63]

The Grange leadership frankly disagreed with the Greenback Party agenda, but many rank-and-file farmers joined nevertheless. The Greenback Party fared poorly in the 1876 elections, but the following year's Great Strike produced a surge of popularity among workers. The Greenback Party therefore broadened its deliberations to include labor interests. Partly as a result, in the 1878 midterms Greenback candidates won over 12 percent of the national vote, electing fourteen members to Congress, while gaining allies in the major parties.[64] Excitement was therefore high going into 1880, when the Greenback Party (now formally renamed Greenback-Labor Party) would have its own presidential candidate, Iowa congressman James Weaver. The *New York Times* decried its "rabid platform," which now sought the elimination of private banknotes, unlimited silver coinage, greater rights for labor, an eight-hour work week, a reinstatement of the graduated income tax, and a host of anti-monopoly measures. Greenbackers proudly declared their goal of returning government to the people instead of "Government of the bondholder, by the bondholder, and for the bondholder."[65]

Meanwhile, the Grange pushed for the design and passage of early antitrust and corporate regulation legislation. In constant need of loans and credit, its members also began to lobby for the relegalization of silver as legal tender. Other items topping the Grange agenda included civil service reform, lower tariffs, and tax cuts (which then meant lower duties on tobacco and alcohol). Their political zenith came with *Munn v. Illinois* (1877). In this Supreme Court opinion, state governments *could* regulate the warehouses and grain elevators maintained by the railroads and which were essential to farmers' livelihoods. In order to further loosen industry's grip on their businesses, Grangers also experimented with their own purchasing agents, mail-order houses, and manufacturing ventures.[66] All told, farmers seemed to be enjoying a political heyday going into the 1880s.

The Melting Pot

As the American economy emerged from the depression of 1873–1878, demand for industrial labor returned and immigration soared to its highest levels of the Gilded Age, peaking in 1882 at just under 816,000, or 15.4 immigrants per 1,000 residents.[67] But the demographics changed. Wages in northern and western Europe had by now risen high enough to keep many Irish, German, and British immigrants at home. These nationalities continued to arrive in large numbers, but they were increasingly rivaled by peasant farmers and laborers from eastern and southern Europe. The rate of these so-called new immigrants jumped from just 6 percent of all arrivals (1870s) to 18 percent (1880s). The new wave was also more urban than earlier migrations.[68] Most came to work the factories, docks, and rails, not to farm or to develop the western frontier. And by 1880, the population of each of America's largest cities was roughly 70 percent immigrants and their immediate offspring.[69] Their numbers even changed the urban ethnic mix. In New York City, for example, the once Irish-dominated neighborhood around Five Points became "Little Italy," while the Lower East Side's "Little Germany" was transformed into a multinational enclave of eastern European Jews. Proponents of Social Darwinism pointed to the extreme poverty and illiteracy of these new immigrants as evidence of racial hierarchies. And although the emerging phalanx of American industrial corporations eagerly hired immigrants for cheap labor, they simultaneously vilified them in public as anti-American—especially those "foreign agitators" who dared participate in strikes or join unions—contributing to political pressure for new anti-immigration laws.[70]

All the while, the courts continued to chip away at state immigration regimes. In a series of cases going into the 1880s, the courts repeatedly struck down state laws found to be infringing on the federal government's right to regulate commerce and migration.[71] One such case forbade state taxes on new arrivals to pay for state immigration services. Cut off from these revenues, the New York Commissioners of Emigration threatened to shut down Castle Garden, the nation's largest immigration center, unless Congress created a national immigration framework.[72]

Congress responded with the Immigration Act of 1882, the nation's first comprehensive immigration reform. It reflected new thinking on immigrants as objects of commerce rather than of foreign relations, formally shifting federal authority over immigration from the State Department to the Treasury Department. Otherwise, the new federal laws were not especially novel. Rather, the Immigration Act was modeled on the very state immigration laws that it displaced. For example, to pay for federal immigration services, it levied the first head tax on immigrants (50 cents, roughly $95 in 2020 dollars).[73] It also barred from entry "any convict, lunatic, idiot, or any person unable to take care of himself or herself without becoming a public charge."[74] The states even retained immigration boards, though they were now appointed by the Treasury secretary. Meanwhile, in 1883 and 1884 the Supreme Court effectively declared *all* state immigration laws unconstitutional, "confided by the Constitution to the exclusive control of Congress."[75] Though lacking the bureaucracy to administrate it, the federal government was now firmly in control of the nation's immigration and naturalization laws.

The Chinese continued to suffer most from immigration restrictions. With the Burlingame Treaty having been renegotiated by President Hayes, the Immigration Act of 1882 now suspended altogether the immigration of Chinese laborers for twenty years. It also expressly prohibited Chinese immigrants from naturalizing.[76] Until then, there had never been legislation barring a whole nationality from immigrating to the United States.[77] Even President Arthur found the twenty-year ban on Chinese immigrants too egregious. He issued a rare veto, but the political reaction was so fierce that he relented. He quickly signed off on a ten-year ban that was energetically renewed by Congress in 1892.[78] And in contrast with European immigrants, federal officials enforced Chinese exclusion laws zealously. Chinese were refused entry at far higher rates than others, over 30 percent in some years.[79] For the remainder of the Gilded Age, Chinese immigrants became a caste of permanent aliens with few political rights and lived under constant threat of deportation.[80] Ironically, this occurred at exactly the same time that the Statue of Liberty was being erected in New York Harbor to welcome new arrivals to the United States.[81]

The experiences of other minorities varied according to skin color, literacy, wealth, and culture of origin. The vast majority hailed from different parts of Europe. Those who were white and Christian generally fared best; their economic class and social network mostly determined their fates. Catholics had a harder time of it, as did those of darker skin. A third of a million Latinos now lived in the United States, still mostly in the Southwest.[82] The majority were Mexicans who endured conditions of relative poverty and considerable prejudice. Traveling through Texas late in the 1880s, an English tourist wrote, "[I]t is difficult to convince these people that a Mexican is a human being.... [H]e is treated like a dog, or, perhaps, not so well."[83] As for those Americans of Asian or Middle Eastern descent, other than the Chinese, there numbered perhaps only ten thousand.

Freed from slavery, African Americans had entered a short-lived "golden age" of relative political and economic liberty, yet few were able to capitalize on it. Most ex-slaves were illiterate and unskilled. Few could compete with native whites or foreign immigrants for better-paid jobs or afford to purchase farms of their own. Worse yet, the emerging Northern industrial sector feared their numbers as a force for labor rights, while white workers saw Blacks as rivals, and Southerners sought to reassert white supremacy across the ex-Confederacy. Thus, African Americans were mostly restricted to subsistence farming, often as tenants and sharecroppers, and low-skilled urban work. And although theoretically "free" to roam the country in search of prosperity, ex-slaves still found themselves obstructed from economic, even physical mobility. In fact, during the 1870s only around forty thousand Blacks left the South.[84]

Nor did racism suddenly disappear. As a people, African Americans were politically and economically marginalized. Many whites simply avoided doing business with, living near, or working alongside Blacks. After all, most Northerners had fought the Civil War to end the Southern aristocracy and to free up labor and land markets, not to deliver social or political equality to the slave. And since the majority of white Americans felt that they had already sacrificed enough for Black people, support for African American civil rights and liberties evaporated. Individuals might flourish—George Washington Carver, Ida B. Wells, Frederick Douglass, and Lewis Howard Latimer are only the most well-known to us today—but the vast majority of African Americans were impoverished and marginalized.[85] Wherever they went, they encountered discrimination and violence.

African Americans were further handicapped by a succession of major Supreme Court opinions. In them, the Court eviscerated the power of the federal government to enforce the political-economic rights so recently granted to Blacks in the Constitution and the Civil Rights Act of 1875.[86] Thus, the 1880s would become a kind of "twilight zone" between Reconstruction and the Jim Crow Era.[87] And after Grant, the remaining Gilded Age presidents mostly abandoned Blacks to their fate.

Meanwhile, industrialization and urbanization were steadily driving a new economic wedge between the sexes. Back on the farm, the entire family had toiled together; rural homelife and work were fused as one. But in the rapidly industrializing cities, women stayed at home and ran the domicile, while men went out into the dirty, dangerous city to earn the wages to pay for it all. Women were therefore expected to act as the virtuous guardians of the Victorian household against the immoral temptations of the city that beckoned their husbands: alcohol, prostitution, gambling, brawling, extramarital sex, even atheism. Hence, Gilded Age women were increasingly idealized as fragile, pristine, and dangerously emotional. To aid them in proper household maintenance, new periodicals offered women plenty of "expert" advice: *Women's Home Companion* (1873), *Women's Home Journal* (1878), *Ladies Home Journal* (1883). For their part, urban men no longer chopped wood, wrangled horses, drove fence posts, or defended their homesteads against attack, so they needed other tests to prove their masculinity. Going into the 1880s, men therefore turned to fraternal organizations, exercise fads, hiking and camping excursions, and professional sporting events in which players traveled the growing rail system to compete. (The first professional sports organization was baseball's National League, formed in 1876.)[88]

The depression of 1873–1878 further endangered men's status. Wage cuts, unemployment, worsening working conditions all threatened a man's identity as the breadwinner. Many husbands resorted to drink, which squandered family funds, kept the men out late, and too often ended in marital violence. Women responded by attacking alcoholism. The Woman's Christian Temperance Union, formed in 1874, allowed women to not only defend themselves but also to become more openly political. Alternatively, evangelical Protestants, led by Anthony Comstock, chose to make war on lust, which endangered society by "corrupting the stream at the fountain-head."[89] By 1873, Comstock had convinced Congress to pass the Comstock Act, which made it illegal to mail, sell, or merely possess "obscene, lewd or lascivious" materials, including contraceptives and information about them.[90] And having won his great battle against lust, Comstock next turned his militancy against abortion.

Women had little recourse. Outside of two western territories, they still had few political or economic rights going into the 1880s.[91] At first, the granting of civil rights to African Americans and the pivotal role of women in the Civil War had helped fuel a new women's rights movement.[92] It blossomed around Elizabeth Cady Stanton (political philosopher and civil rights activist), Susan B. Anthony (who shocked the nation in 1872 when she was arrested for illegally attempting to vote), Victoria Woodhull (the first female stockbroker and presidential candidate, who campaigned with running mate Frederick Douglass in 1872), and Lucy Stone (lecturer and civil rights activist).[93] The movement attracted support from individual luminaries, but it failed to win over large swaths of the American public. Feminists themselves had divided over whether women should be included in the expansion of civil rights guaranteed in the Fourteenth and Fifteenth Amendments or focus on state-level legislation, and whether African Americans should be included at all.[94] Women also split over whether equality was better achieved within the male sphere (i.e., at work, business, and politics) or by creating their own separate space. Regardless, during the 1870s the fight increasingly focused on women's suffrage. Democrats largely ignored the issue. Republicans included "rights for women" in their 1872 and 1876 platforms, and Presidents Grant and Hayes each incrementally expanded the roles of women within the federal government.[95] In 1880, Belva Lockwood became the first female lawyer to argue a case before the US Supreme Court. But women had a long fight ahead for political equality.

Labor Strife and the American Left

Workers had a tumultuous time going into the 1880s. Labor seemed threatened from all sides: the long depression, replacement by new technology, the rise of mass production, immigration, and the competitive pressures from emerging national and global markets. The already political National Labor Union, formed in 1866 as a loose federation of workers and farmers, made the full transition into politics, becoming the National Labor Reform Party (NLRP) in 1872. It fought for workers' perennial goals: higher wages, shorter hours, better working conditions, and restrictions on immigrant labor. However, at this point, the NLRP sought not to obstruct industrial capitalism but to join it. Workers wanted to take back control over production by forming their own manufacturing cooperatives. For that, they needed access to loans and credit. Hence the NLRP put forth a platform focused mostly on currency reform. When its presidential candidate withdrew from the 1872 election, both the union and its party dissolved in failure.

As businesses fell to the panic and recession, they sent workers into unemployment and deprived the still embryonic union movement of paying members. With fewer industrial jobs and declining wages for dues, the labor unions atrophied.[96] In some cities, the unemployed protested for government spending on public works in order to provide jobs. But the disaster at Tompkins Square in January 1874 in New York City—in which swarms of police violently assaulted thousands of jobless protestors—convinced most labor leaders to abandon such demands.[97] And technically, since unions seemed to act in restraint of trade, they suffered both politically and legally. During the mid-1870s, a series of court cases seemed to make the labor union itself an unlawful criminal conspiracy. Hence, by 1880 there were perhaps only 170,000 union members nationwide out of an industrial workforce of over 3.5 million.

A few turned to Socialism. Skilled German immigrants fleeing anti-Socialist persecution by Chancellor Otto von Bismarck were among the most zealous. Other adherents found inspiration in the Paris Commune, the Socialist revolutionary movement that seized Paris for two months during spring 1871. In America, conservatives and the press had a field day with the Commune. For years, they reminded Americans of its "most infamous and bloody decrees ... [under which e]very species of outrage and persecution took place."[98] Therefore fear spread about the rising threat of Communism. In truth, Karl Marx's First International movement had divided into warring factions of violent anarchists and his own more conservative supporters who sought to work within existing state institutions. Thus, there was a burst of excitement when Friedrich Engels moved its headquarters from London to New York City in 1873 and thence to Philadelphia. But Marxism found little purchase in the United

States. American Socialists fought over who should be included in the movement (i.e., nonworkers, the middle class, women, African Americans) and whether European Socialism could be imported whole into the United States or whether it must be "Americanized" (adapted to American beliefs, institutions, and practices) in order to flourish. The German diehards purged the less orthodox from their ranks, some of whom formed the Workingmen's Party (1874), which grew and evolved into the Socialist Labor Party (1876). But neither party achieved much beyond the election of a few city aldermen in Chicago.

The Great Strike of 1877 created a fresh opportunity for American Socialism.[99] Socialists played little role in the uprising, but they seemed to flourish afterward. A new generation of workers and reformers entered the movement, energized by the surprising ferocity of the July strikes. Then, during the early 1880s, a fresh wave of German immigrants brought a new era to the movement. Many had been Socialists or union activists back home, and they transferred their passion, skills, and experience to New York and Chicago. Furious at the failures of their older brethren, they took over local Socialist newspapers, assemblies, and labor unions and shifted the movement leftward. Almost all favored more aggressive action going into the 1880s.[100] Frightened Americans in government, business, and the media cracked down on suspected Socialists. However, seeing opportunity in crisis, the established political parties and local machines quickly moved in to steal the Socialists' political thunder and policy ideas. Thus, conservative forces warned that "the infection is insidiously making its way in a disguised form even into the platforms of the [major] political parties."[101]

A few far-leftists embraced violent anarchism. Anarchists perceived government and man-made law as the means by which wealthy capitalists used force to exploit the working class.[102] "Government disinherits and enslaves the governed," explained one of its leaders, insisting that "liberty . . . will come through travail & pain, through bloodshed & violence."[103] Anarchists therefore sought to tear down the entire structure. They established a vibrant activist press, publishing *Arbeiter-Zeitung* (1877, edited by August Spies), *Freiheit* (1879, Johann Most), and *Liberty* (1881, Benjamin Tucker). Membership in anarchist groups never grew beyond several thousand nationwide, but they were passionate activists who would terrify Americans during the 1880s.

The majority of American workers dreaded being associated with violence or Communism. Most American union members during the 1870s were simply *not* revolutionaries, and they wished to avoid being seen as agents of disruption. Rather than overthrow the capitalist system, they sought more mundane improvements in wages, working conditions, and labor rights. Hence, the American incarnation of Marx's First International dwindled and died by 1876. Domestic replacements, such as the Workingmen's Party, Socialist Labor Party, and the anarchist Black International (1883) drew upon the same constituencies and fared little better.[104] Only the Greenback Party won elections to national office. Worse yet, most Americans stereotyped labor unrest as being driven by foreigners. This prevented policymakers from taking seriously the worsening plight of everyday workers. Nor did it help unions to recruit new members.

One of the few successful unions was the Knights of Labor, a secretive organization of skilled laborers founded in Philadelphia in late 1869.[105] During the 1870s, it broadened its membership to include all physical workers—white-collar professionals were denied membership—regardless of craft, skill, gender, race, or ideology. It sought to unite them into one cohesive yet highly decentralized labor organization. Shrouded in mystic rituals, it eschewed violence or revolution. Its leaders instead sought to join capitalism by forming its own worker-owned production cooperatives. "There is no good reason why labor cannot, through cooperation, own and operate mines, factories, and railroads," adduced Terrence Powderly, the Knights' "Grand Master Workman."[106] By 1879, the Knights of Labor had formed assemblies in dozens of districts around the country, with over twenty-eight thousand members, and was growing rapidly. As their influence grew, the Knights also agitated for an eight-hour workday, expanded use of the greenback, an end to prison and child labor, public lands for settlers, and gender equity in pay.

Economic Thought Going into the 1880s

The constant, unprecedented changes in the 1870s economy also forced a slow transformation in its study.[107] First, to better understand the tumult, political economists further adopted the enthusiasm for science then sweeping the country. Many prominent political economists still came from religious backgrounds (e.g., William Graham Sumner, John Bascom, Robert Ellis Thompson), and they still sought moral solutions to economic problems, but they now also insisted that "any possible application of science to this end should be invented."[108] This brought more empirical rigor to the field.

Second, although still referred to as "political economy," the field's increasing sophistication and specialization prompted a growing number of colleges to separate it out as a discipline distinct from history, politics, and philosophy and taught by specialized faculty. For advanced training, most American students who wanted a career in the subject studied in Germany, the birthplace of the modern research university. Harvard awarded the first American PhD in political economy in 1875. Amateurs continued to have more influence than scholars on policy debates in Washington, but the era of modern economics had begun.[109]

Third, too many economic problems of the early Gilded Age were just not well explained by the old models of Smith, Ricardo, Say, and Mill. The repeated panics and depressions, rising inequality, regional disparities, and growing monopolies seemed to defy classical economic thought. Certainly the mainstream colleges, like Harvard and Yale, continued to preach laissez-faire, "hard money," and the central importance of competition for economic prosperity. But some scholars, like Francis Amasa Walker, began to question whether individuals could successfully navigate the complexity and sophistication of the new industrial economy without more government regulation.[110] A few even called for "drastic changes in the organization of the economy . . . if real equality and liberty were to survive economic growth."[111] Their policy innovations included progressive taxation, the legalization of labor unions, economic cooperatives, and government supervision of land use. Of course, they were opposed by conservative thinkers like William Graham Sumner, who incorporated the lessons of Spencer and Darwin into their classical scholarship and warned "people [not] to look to government to do for them what they could only do for themselves by industry and economy."[112] Gilded Age crises were natural events, conservatives argued. Therefore government interference into free markets would only delay their resolution and create perverse results.

One crucial turning point in American economic thought, at least among academics, was imported from Britain, in the form of W. Stanley Jevons's scholarship. His *Theory of Political Economy* (1871) used complex mathematics to model economic behavior with a sophistication never before achieved. He also described a revolutionary way of thinking about prices.[113] Until then, most classical thinkers, like Smith, Ricardo, and Marx, had assumed that the value of a good or service was objective and exogenous. It was determined by the mix of raw materials and physical labor that went into the good or service being sold. Jevons, however, argued that utility of a good or service varied according to its supply and demand. In other words, prices were *not* set by nature or god; rather, we humans *created* prices through our participation in markets. Jevons even provided a causal mechanism. He posited that the last, or "marginal," good supplied had the least utility as market demand was gradually satiated by supply. That is, the first slice of bread given to a hungry man was most valuable to him; the fifth slice far less so; the twentieth not worth the effort to consume. This implied that prices might decline as either supply increased or demand fell (and prices would rise under the reverse conditions). Similar theories published by Carl Menger (Austria, 1871) and Leon Walras (France, 1874) were less widely read in the United States but nevertheless reinforced this new direction in political economy.[114]

Granted, few Americans understood, or even read, these intellectual debates, but even the illiterate got Gresham's Law. In an era when money and its behavior was perhaps *the* major economic obsession, Gresham's Law dictated that, in a market with multiple currencies, people tend to hoard the "good" currency and spend the "bad." The result, as the *Chicago Tribune* explained, was "the cheaper and inferior currency driving out the more valuable."[115] And throughout the Gilded Age, gold was the most valued currency; silver and greenbacks were clearly inferior.[116] Hence Gresham's Law often determined how average investors and policymakers thought about monetary policy during the 1880s.

Going into the 1880s, many Americans also embraced the "single tax" philosophy of Henry George described in his best-seller, *Poverty and Progress* (1879).[117] A San Francisco journalist, George blamed American poverty and widening inequality on private landownership. He argued that the rich bought up all the best land for agriculture and natural resources but developed only a fraction of it, hoping instead to profit off rising land prices. This left less productive land for the rest of Americans. Land scarcity thereby forced the poor into wage slavery, scrounging for work as day laborers. George blamed land monopolies for driving down wages, increasing inequality, perpetuating poverty, and even contributing to both depression and inflation. His solution was to tax unused land and to eliminate all other duties on the American people. He also suggested that the revenue be spent on public works, education, and transportation, in addition to healthcare and welfare and "to the payment of a fixed sum to every citizen when he came to a certain age."[118] His ideas spread like wildfire. Henry George Clubs sprang up around the country and a political movement grew around him. Even in Europe, the great playwright and activist George Bernard Shaw later recalled, "When I was thus swept into the great socialist revival of 1883, I found that five-sixths of those who were swept up with me had been converted by Henry George."[119] With great fanfare, George ran for mayor of New York for the Labor Party in 1886, winning more votes than reformer Theodore Roosevelt, but typical of the Gilded Age, both candidates were beaten by the nominee of the Tammany Hall political machine.[120]

Science and Technology

Progress in science and technology was an essential catalyst for America's surge in wealth, inequality, industrialization, and globalization going into the 1880s. Before the Civil War, science had primarily been the fascination of hobbyists and philosophers; now it seemed to enhance all aspects of America's economic development. For example, business out west was facilitated by four "Great Surveys" (1867–1879) funded by Congress, which culminated in the creation of the US Geological Survey.[121] The USGS provided essential information and analysis for the region's economic development and worked closely with investors and settlers. According to its proponents, this constituted "a turning point, when the science ceased to be dragged in the dust of rapid exploration and took a commanding position in the professional work of the country."[122] Meanwhile, a revolution in physics was occurring. The simple math of electromagnetic "fields," derived by Cambridge professor James Clerk Maxwell in 1873, not only aided new inventions but advanced an entirely new way of conceiving of the physical world.[123] The practice of American medicine was also undergoing a revolution going into the 1880s. The catalyst here was the transcontinental tour of British surgeon Joseph Lister (1876), which convinced many American physicians to accept his germ theory and the practice of "antisepsis," though not in time to save President James Garfield (1881).[124] Few Americans understood these advances in science. But they craved to. Thus, *Popular Science Monthly*, first published in 1872, found a ready audience among science-obsessed Americans; even the editors of general interest magazines such as *Harper's* and *Atlantic Monthly* added science columns to their pages.

But it was new technology that had the greatest impact on the American economy going into the 1880s. For example, while rails united the nation into a single market, advances in ship construction and steam power accelerated globalization by better linking the US economy to the world.[125] The introduction of steel cargo ships, the triple-expansion engine, and onboard refrigeration brought speed, safety, and new capability to ocean shippers. The fastest trip across the Atlantic still took just over a week, and severe weather could triple that time, but the voyage was more common and reliable by 1880. Better yet, the costs of ocean shipping eased almost every year between 1876 and 1886, falling a total of 35 percent.[126] Admittedly, the British took the technological lead here, leaving the wind-sail industry to American manufacturers.

Americans led in agricultural technology, manufacturing processes, and consumer innovations. In fact, US patent applications more than doubled during the 1870s. The greatest categories of invention were machinery, metals fabrication, manufacturing, vehicles, rubber, chemicals, instruments, and textiles. Cyrus McCormick joined his revolutionary reaper with a mechanical thresher in 1871, producing a single "combine" that would cut wheat and separate the grain at the same time. It soon became a major driver of agricultural productivity increases. Steam-driven cable cars appeared in the largest cities, starting in San Francisco (1873). Mechanical refrigeration and ice production began to replace natural ice cut from rivers and lakes.[127] Several now common products entered mass production during the 1870s. These included chewing gum (1872), barbed wire (1873), and typewriters (1873). The decade also saw major advances in pasteurization (1873), the internal combustion engine (1877), reinforced concrete (1878), and the first paper bag–making machine (1879). Some of the most iconic American consumer brands were founded during this time, including Kimberly-Clark paper goods (1872), Levi's denim pants (1873), Bulova watches (1875), Eli Lilly pharmaceuticals (1876), Quaker oats (1877), and Hills Bros. coffee (1878).[128]

To display its prowess, the United States resumed its mania for "expositions" that had obsessed Europe since London's highly successful Great Exhibition (1851).[129] America's first major effort was the grand 1876 Centennial Exposition, held in Philadelphia from May to November, which attracted 10 million visitors to view over sixty thousand exhibits sent by thirty-five countries.[130] President Grant delivered the keynote speech. The technological star of the show was the fifty-foot-tall Corliss Steam Engine, which powered a vast exhibition hall of new machinery. Within the Exposition, Americans drank their first root beer, rode their first monorail, and discovered Heinz ketchup, sugared popcorn, carbonated soda water, hamburgers, and bananas (presented as an exotic novelty to be eaten with knife and fork). Alexander Graham Bell displayed his new telephone—"My God, it talks!" exclaimed Brazilian emperor Dom Pedro when he held the receiver to his ear. The first telephone switchboards would be installed in Boston the following year. Other devices on display included the first Remington Typographic Machine (i.e., a modern typewriter with QWERTY keyboard)[131] and a hand-cranked mechanical calculator the size of a cow. Outside, the hand and torch of "Lady Liberty" were on display; attendees could climb inside for a small fee, an attempt to raise funds to pay for the statue's foundation.

Nevertheless, American innovation and entrepreneurship during the 1870s remained a remarkably small-scale affair. It was usually the purview of individuals or small firms, not large corporations or universities. Funding for "high-tech" enterprises, like manufacturing, was typically raised by the entrepreneur himself from friends, family, and wealthy individuals who might themselves take part in managing the new enterprise.[132] Local banks, trusts, and securities markets played a secondary role. They generally provided funding only *after* an innovative new firm had already begun operations.[133] And once an entrepreneur had demonstrated the profitability of a new technology, they might find themselves at the center of new overlapping business networks. The days of venture capital, corporate research labs, and initial public offerings lay far in the future. Even on college campuses, only the earliest seeds of American university research had been planted, in 1876, with the founding of Johns Hopkins University, modeled after the highly innovative research schools in Germany.

Thomas Edison is perhaps the most successful example of the early Gilded Age inventor-entrepreneur, but his experience was not atypical. His first significant commercial invention was a universal stock ticker conceived in 1870. He then proceeded to design the quadruplex telegraph (which could send four messages at once over a single wire) (1874), a long-distance telephone transmitter (1876), and a phonograph for recording sound on wax cylinders (1877). At this point, Edison funded his research with his personal savings combined with investments from business partners, wealthy individuals, clients, and the occasional bank. And he used his early successes to build a team of talented young scientists and engineers at his Menlo Park laboratory (1876–1886). Edison's uniqueness was in the volume, impact, and variety of his inventions and in that he became a "holistic conceptualizer" who thought in terms of technological systems rather than one-off inventions[134]

Partly thanks to Edison, electricity entered a new era going into the 1880s. Scientific experiments with electricity date back centuries before this time, and useful applications of electricity began to appear during the first half of the 1800s.[135] However, it was not until Edison's development of incandescent lighting (1878), and more important his centralized large-scale power generators which ran it, that electric power began to have its transformative effects on American life. "Arc-light" was his impetus. Electric arc-lighting had debuted in June 1878 on the streets of the awe-inspiring Paris Exposition and soon appeared in factories, street corners, and theaters in London and throughout the United States. But arc-lights buzzed loudly, ran hot, and emitted dangerous sparks. Thus, they were infamous sources of burns and fires, while their carbon monoxide emissions made them unsafe for indoor use. Edison studied them and believed that he could design a better, more cost-effective lighting system.[136] With funding from the Vanderbilts and J. P. Morgan, Edison constructed Pearl Street Station in lower Manhattan. From it, he strung an electricity distribution network that illuminated four hundred lamps in the homes and businesses of eighty-two customers starting in September 1882. Within a year, the station powered some ten thousand lamps for over five hundred customers and was fast on its way to profitability. Thereafter, electric lighting swept the country and modern electricity usage had begun.[137]

The Ascendancy of the Market-Driven Press

For newspapers, the depression of 1873–1878 severely damaged revenues, forcing dramatic change on the industry. For example, political parties lost influence as their funds available to subsidize, patronize, or bribe newspaper editors dried up. Control by politicians ebbed further when, in 1875, a reform-minded Congress eliminated the requirement that new federal legislation be printed in local papers. These publication contracts had been an embarrassing source of patronage and an unnecessary expense for the federal treasury. Perhaps only in the South did party-controlled newspapers still flourish thereafter. Instead of patronage, most editors in need of revenues now strove for larger audiences and more advertising dollars. And yet, while papers experimented with other types of stories, interest in national politics continued to soar. By 1880, there were over two hundred reporters in Congress's official press gallery, triple the number of a decade earlier.[138] Thus, newspapers did not necessarily become less political or less partisan; rather, their political opinions were relegated more and more to the editorial page.

The demand for readers and revenues warped the press in new directions.[139] Reporters salted their reporting from the South with noxious invocations of race and class, helping to dull Northern support for Reconstruction. Elsewhere, wealthy investors and new industrialists had begun to exercise their growing financial muscle on the press. They used bribes, subscriptions, advertising buys, and even outright ownership to influence what got printed in their city's newspapers. Stories critical of their businesses or themselves vanished from print, while editorial support for their favored policy agenda magically appeared. The prolonged economic misery of the 1870s also created audiences for new papers published by new political movements. Socialists, labor groups, Greenbackers, and reformers of all sorts started their own presses. For the wealthy and middle class, an assortment of new business-news periodicals appeared, such as the *Railroad Gazette* (1870), *Rhodes' Journal of Banking* (1874), *Bradstreet's Weekly* (1879), and *Electrical World* (1883).[140] Thus, despite the economic downturn, by 1880 in dailies alone there were 69 percent more papers and 37 percent greater circulation than a decade prior.

A new style of "western" journalism emerged in Detroit, St. Louis, Chicago, Cleveland, and Boston.[141] These newspapers printed stories that were more useful and entertaining to readers than political invective. Some cut back on political reporting altogether. Instead, the "western" style included a heightened penchant for sensational, tabloid stories. Its practitioners began to add new humor sections, feature news, and even short fiction. Investigative journalism, another novel phenomenon, also became popular. Lengthy quotations and interviews developed into regular practice. And since they depended more on sales and advertising than on political patronage, western journalism papers such as the *Detroit Evening News*, *St. Louis Globe*, and *Boston Globe* openly attacked corrupt political rings, irresponsible speculators, and business conspiracies. And after the Great Strike of 1877, even well-established newspapers began to appeal to the working class. In other words, newspapers of all kinds began to advocate for their readers as citizens, savers, consumers, and workers. Where once they had been tools of the parties and political machines, now, in their bid for wider readership, newspapers were becoming champions of the American public. Early acolytes of western journalism included Edward Scripps and Joseph Pulitzer. Going into the 1880s, eastern editors began to adopt the western style, while truly western papers, such as the new *Los Angeles Times* (1881) and the *San Francisco Examiner* (taken over by wealthy miner George Hearst in 1880), generally stuck with the more traditional partisan-political model. Either way, as newspapers grew more tabloid and revenue-driven, they threatened the traditional dignity of the

White House. The presidents of the 1880s therefore tended to view reporters as a menace rather than a mouthpiece.[142]

The President, Politics, and the Economy Going into the 1880s

The accelerating pace of political and economic change created new stresses and opportunities for American presidents going into the 1880s. Monopolies, industrialization, inequality, immigration, and technological change each provided fertile ground for action. But neither the traditional presidency nor the skeletal executive branch, the latter riddled with inefficiency and corruption, were well-equipped to deal with these new forces. In particular, problems that demanded a rigorous *national* response conflicted with the old *localized* political institutions—obsessed with patronage battles and provincial affairs—inherited from the Jackson era. Meanwhile, as the Civil War and Reconstruction faded from relevance, Republicans needed new issues to bind them together and win national elections. As the opposition party, Democrats merely had to criticize and obstruct, which they did in spades. Much of this was entirely new territory for the White House.

At the national level, monetary policy entered a new era of troubles for US presidents. Grant and Hayes had forcefully guided the US dollar back to convertibility with gold. However, throughout the 1870s the price of silver bullion on international markets gradually sank below the fixed price set by the US Mint to coin it ($1.29 per ounce). In response, silver interests in western states lobbied Congress for greater use of, and hence demand for, silver as legal tender. They were joined by farmers and small business, who were forever in need of expanded credit and loans. This spelled trouble! Political economists warned Treasury officials and Congress that, if the United States adopted bimetallism unilaterally, Gresham's Law would force the country onto a silver standard.[143] That is, "foreign nations will send in their depreciated silver in exchange for our gold."[144] America's creditors and investors would suffer a costly financial haircut. New lenders might be scared away.

One solution was to forge an international agreement on bimetallism: fix gold-silver-paper exchange rates via foreign treaty. This would eliminate dangerous exchange rate fluctuations.[145] It would also require the least compromise from any of the major American interest groups. Thus, seeking an international bimetallism agreement became the official policy of the United States from 1878 to 1897. Frustratingly elusive, it became a sort of political Shangri-La. Almost every Gilded Age president trotted it out as a promised salvation. But in reality, the much-heralded International Monetary Conferences of 1878, 1881, and 1892 accomplished little, while even mere proposals for formal negotiations in 1882 and 1897 were aborted.[146] Thus battles over monetary policy remained central to American politics.

Trade reemerged as a wedge issue going into the 1880s. Protectionists could no longer use trade deficits to argue their case. Partly thanks to the incredible agricultural output of the West and Great Plains, the US trade deficit dwindled and disappeared during the early 1870s and spent the next decade in healthy surplus.[147] But as economic disparities worsened and Northerners abandoned Reconstruction, the costs and benefits of trade naturally became the next political battleground. Put simply, protectionism benefited American industry as it struggled to compete with imports from Europe. But tariffs hurt farmers and consumers. The former feared retaliation against US agricultural exports, while both groups suffered from higher prices on manufactured goods such as farm machinery. Protectionism was a tax that raised prices and piled up revenue in the Treasury, where it sat unused, tantalizing spoilsmen. Therefore most political economists, and many businessmen, pushed for lower import duties. On the other hand, manufacturers promised disgruntled workers that high tariffs would protect their jobs by keeping foreign competition at bay. Industry leaders also argued that low tariffs, not technological change nor globalization, drove the growing inequality and myriad economic crises at home. And playing on century-old fears of English rule, some insisted that free trade was a "conspiracy" hatched in London to expand British economic power at the expense of American industry, pointing to the growing number of free-trade Cobden Clubs (which originated in England) as agents of foreign influence.[148] Though Republicans often ducked the issue during the 1870s and early 1880s, Democrats consistently blasted the tariff "as a masterpiece of injustice, inequality and false pretense."[149]

Meanwhile, the continued expansion in and improvements of railroad and telegraph networks linked the fragmented American economy into a national market. This raised demand for more cohesive national policy (trade, monetary, antitrust, public works), while simultaneously lowering the costs of national political campaigns. As a result, state and local political organizations began to lose their power—and their appeal—as voters increasingly sought a stronger federal government with a more vigorous executive branch at its head. In many realms, Americans began to assemble into new national associations for purposes of all kinds. The most prominent of the era included the American Institute of Mining and Metallurgical Engineers (1871), American Bankers Association (1875), Honest Money League (1878), American Bar Association (1878), American Society of Mechanical Engineers (1880), and National Civil Service Reform League (1881). The National Rifle Association (1871) was also founded during this time. Local political habits and networks took considerable time to break, but the process had begun.

One problem was that, especially in the cities, the boss system continued to thrive in American politics.[150] Even into the 1880s, American government and public policy remained "spoils" for partisan political machines. Sound policy and the public welfare may have made for good political speeches, but they were often neglected in practice. Instead, Gilded Age voters kept in office the machine bosses, who then doled out favors, government jobs, and contracts to reward their supporters. The system also brought personal power, wealth, and social status to ordinary Americans and immigrants who otherwise would have been marginalized. To be sure, Congress had ended the moiety system in 1874, and President Hayes had further weakened the machines by investigating corruption and implementing reforms by executive order.[151] But patronage and assessments still provided ample muscle for the machines to flex. Wrestling with this system consumed much of the energy of US presidents during the 1880s.

Finally, a seemingly minor technical change at the Republican convention in 1880 proved a critical juncture in Gilded Age politics.[152] In an effort to derail Grant's third presidential run, the Republican Party abandoned their "unit rule" requirement for presidential nominations. For decades, it had required that each state's set of convention delegates, however large, vote as a single unit, determined by their majority. "Unit rule" thereby enhanced the power of *state* party machines (many of which backed Grant at the time) at the expense of *national* campaign organizers.[153] And it all but eliminated popular outsider candidates and minority interests.[154] That same year, Republicans also began to select their convention delegates by congressional district rather than at statewide party conventions. This second change brought the presidential nomination down "to the people" and again took power away from state political machines, especially in large states like New York, Pennsylvania, Ohio, and Illinois. Together, these reforms required aspiring Republican presidential candidates to campaign more broadly for their nomination rather than to merely entice a handful of state party insiders.[155] Naturally, this made both patronage and civil service reform more valuable assets for presidents—the former as a bargaining chip, the latter as a campaign issue. Hence, conflict grew between the president's civil service priorities and those of Congress, their party, or the state political machines. And the most poignant victim of these emerging conflicts over patronage was President James A. Garfield.

7

James A. Garfield and the Economy of 1881

At first glance, President James A. Garfield seems scarcely relevant for the nation's economic performance. After all, he had an active administration of just four months during 1881, from March 4 to July 2. During this time, Congress was in session only eleven weeks, and little business of national importance presented itself. Instead, much of Garfield's presidency was spent dealing with a barrage of office-seekers, culminating in a standoff with fellow Republican and New York machine boss Senator Roscoe Conkling, which likely contributed to Garfield's assassination by a mentally ill patronage-seeker. After Garfield was shot, he was virtually incapacitated until he died in mid-September.[1] Meanwhile, the economy prospered. Growth and industrial production surged, while inflation remained negligible. Unemployment, deficits, and the debt continued to trend pleasantly downward. Overall, the unprecedented economic boom, begun three years earlier under President Hayes, seemed impervious to the political drama.

Yet Garfield was not an inconsequential president. During his brief tenure, he negotiated a major refinancing of Civil War–era bonds. He also reasserted presidential prerogative over the Senate in federal appointments and addressed the US Post Office's "Star Route" fraud, thus advancing civil service reform. In the longer run, Garfield's assassination itself was momentous. The murder of an American president at the hand of a deranged partisan office-seeker finally broke the political logjam on civil service reform. It swung the weight of American public opinion heavily in favor of major legislation and expedited the transition to a modern government. Rather than descend into a morass of inefficient corruption, lethal to economic growth and innovation, governments throughout the United States instead now pivoted toward the creation of more honest, educated, professional bureaucracies.

Background

Garfield lifted himself up from dire poverty to national prominence, an accomplishment celebrated often in his election campaigns.[2] He was born in 1831 in the northwestern Ohio wilderness to subsistence farmers. His father died when Garfield was a toddler, and he was raised mostly by his mother and other family members. As a boy, he was impulsive, rebellious, and had no formal education

Presidential Leadership in Feeble Times. Mark Zachary Taylor, Oxford University Press. © Oxford University Press 2024.
DOI: 10.1093/oso/9780197750742.003.0009

until age eighteen; when he finally entered a nearby seminary school, he became enamored with it. "Good times now. Good times," he wrote in his diary that year.[3] He developed a passion for languages, mathematics, and philosophy, but he was most excited by oratory and debate. "I love agitation and investigation and glory in defending unpopular truth against popular error."[4] After a few years excelling at local schools, he transferred to Williams College in Massachusetts, where he became the college's star pupil in almost every subject. There Garfield was also exposed to considerable economic thought for a student of this era. He even took a rare course on political economy taught by the zealous free-trader Arthur Latham Perry, one of the few professors in America who specialized in political economy at the time.[5] Yet young Garfield was unexcited by economics. Instead, at Williams he discovered politics. Like his classmates, Garfield was liberal for his time. He rejected slavery, became disenchanted with religious dogma, supported women's education, and began to attend meetings of the new Republican Party.[6]

After graduation, Garfield returned to northeastern Ohio to teach ancient languages and literature and eventually math, science, and other subjects at his old college, becoming its president at age twenty-six. A passionate abolitionist and excellent public speaker, he simultaneously got involved in local Republican politics. In 1859, he won a seat in the Ohio state senate, where he was initially dismissive of his fellow legislators. "They are not as gods," he chided a friend.[7] Garfield was also an early supporter of both Lincoln and the Civil War. When the war came, he volunteered to lead a regiment of former students and was initially awarded the rank of lieutenant colonel during summer 1861. He saw action in Kentucky, Tennessee, and north Georgia during the war, and was gradually promoted to the rank of major general. He proved a surprisingly aggressive and clever military commander, though sometimes an impetuous one.[8]

In 1862, while home on medical leave, Garfield enthusiastically, but discretely, allowed his friends to nominate him for Congress. Meanwhile, he reported to Washington, DC, for military reassignment. There he became close friends with Treasury Secretary Salmon P. Chase, a former Ohio governor. Chase mentored Garfield on economics, politics, and policy and recruited him into the fiercely "Radical" wing of the Republican Party. Thereafter, Garfield was an avid student of trade, banking, and other economic policy issues. "I have taken up the subject of currency and finance," he excitedly wrote a friend, "and have been reading the great [economic] debates."[9] That October, Garfield won his election to Congress by a wide margin. In the year-long hiatus before his term began, he was appointed chief of staff to a large Union army, a position he sought to retain until the war was over.[10] However, President Lincoln, in need of new political allies in Congress, personally petitioned Garfield to resign his military commission and assume his elected position in Washington. "I did not feel it right to consult my own preference in such a case," wrote Garfield, who left the army a war hero.[11]

For the next seventeen years, from 1863 to 1880, Garfield served in the House of Representatives. There he gained a reputation as a learned intellectual, especially on economic issues. Yet he also became known for his fierce oratory, passionate political stands, and condescending manner. For example, he felt Lincoln was far too moderate, and he evolved into one of the president's fiercest critics in Congress, referring to Lincoln as "a second rate Illinois lawyer" and advising fellow Republicans, "I think we could do better."[12] Although Garfield's performance as a speech maker and campaigner was unparalleled, to his colleagues he sometimes came across as self-righteous and "too fond of talking."[13] He was also a poor parliamentarian. He often lacked the skill or knowledge of how to successfully move legislation through Congress. Nor did he outwardly express much ambition for power. "His capacity for detachment and self-doubt at times paralyzed his will," writes one biographer.[14] He was, however, a legendary hard worker. Over time, Garfield chaired the House committees on military affairs (1867–1869) and banking and currency (1869–1871) and the powerful Appropriations Committee (1871–1875) which determined federal expenditures. He even moonlighted part time as a lawyer to earn additional income, and he argued several cases before the Supreme Court.[15]

Despite being implicated in a few corruption scandals, Garfield remained enormously popular in his home district. His vote share rarely fell below 60 percent, even as Democrats swept other Republicans out of office. Part of his success may have come from his flair for good relations with the press, a rare talent among Gilded Age politicians.[16] And yet Garfield was too meek to build his own political machine. To him, politics was about ideas and speech-making, not legislation or personal power. "I love to deal with doctrines and events," he later wrote. "[But t]he contests of men about men I greatly dislike."[17] Nevertheless, by 1875 he had become the voice of the Republican Party in a Congress increasingly filled with truculent Democrats.

He campaigned feverishly for Rutherford B. Hayes in the 1876 presidential election, despite believing that "[Hayes] certainly would not be the strongest man we could choose."[18] Garfield even ignored his own reelection campaign that year. For with Democrats already in control of the House, the election of a Democratic president would end, if not reverse, all the policies for which Garfield had worked. When the election deadlocked, Garfield was appointed to a fifteen-man bipartisan congressional committee to resolve it. He was convinced that "violence and intimidation have vitiated the result of the election [in the South]."[19] Therefore, under threat of assassination, Garfield helped lead the committee to declare a victory for Hayes. He then successfully navigated their decision through "more violence and disorder than I have ever seen in the House."[20]

At the new president's request, Garfield turned down offers to run for Senate so that he could become Hayes's legislative leader and party whip in the House.

Despite some formidable disputes with Hayes over policy and appointments, Garfield evolved to become the president's most trusted advisor in Congress. "Garfield is made by his own perseverance and industry," Hayes bragged to a journalist, testifying also to "the general's honesty and sincerity."[21] But when Democrats won control of both houses of Congress in the 1878 elections, Garfield abandoned the increasingly lame-duck Hayes and ran for Senate, winning appointment there in 1880. The desertion did Garfield no harm. Although not a faction leader with presidential aspirations, his name was already being whispered as the next Republican nominee.

1880 Election

The election of 1880 was a chaotic free-for-all.[22] Hayes was out. He had pledged a single term in office and then happily stuck by his promise. Most Republicans were relieved. They viewed the 1876 and 1878 elections as alarming failures. Those politicians who had prospered under Grant now sought "the strongest candidate who could be nominated" and a return to a trusted, winning platform.[23] Nicknamed "Stalwarts," they launched a campaign to restore their beloved General Grant to the White House.[24] Liberal Republicans were not so enthusiastic. A third term for Grant would spell an end to civil service reform. They also feared, "If Grant were to be elected [the Northern machine bosses] would hold the Administration in their hands," leaving their own factions sidelined.[25] Still other opponents wanted to avoid a renewed fight for Reconstruction, insisting, "The Southern question has been availed of to its full extent throughout the North—to a greater degree than was wise. . . . It has had its effect, but in important respects has broken down."[26] They preferred to trade concessions on civil rights for a greater focus on either reform or economic issues. Grant was a step backward, and most Republicans wanted to move on. Foremost were Senator James G. Blaine (R-ME) and Treasury Secretary John Sherman, each of whom sought to establish their own presidential dynasties. New England liberals thrust forward reformer Senator George Edmunds (R-VT) in their bid to cleanse the government of corruption. A few large Northern states added their own favorite sons to the race.

Thus, Garfield's nomination 1880 was a surprise to most.[27] He had publicly dedicated his support to fellow Ohioan John Sherman for the Republican ticket. However, Garfield was then at the peak of his popularity among Republicans. And as one of the convention managers, he had helped to block Grant's nomination by changing the nomination rules, thereby acquiring the mantle of reform.[28] Hence, when the Republican delegates proceeded to deadlock over the party's faction heads, a few began to switch their votes over to Garfield as an independent, compromise candidate. Then a stampede ensued. "The whole audience were on their feet cheering and waving banners, hats, and handkerchiefs," reported Ohio's *Cleveland Herald.*[29]

Only the Grant supporters, still a large minority, refused to change their votes. After all, these Stalwarts owed their political livelihoods to the Grant political machine and they vowed to defend it.[30] Their leaders were mostly concentrated in New York, then a vital swing state with thirty-five electoral votes (just under 10 percent of the electoral college). In an attempt to mollify them, the convention nominated as vice president Chester A. Arthur, an avowed Grant supporter and an infamous, master spoilsman in the New York Republican political machine run by Senator Roscoe Conkling (R-NY).

The subsequent election of 1880 turned on a patchwork of issues and personalities, some more local than national. To win over Civil War veterans and neutralize appeals to the "bloody shirt,"[31] the Democrats nominated former Union army general Winfield Scott Hancock from Pennsylvania. Although a popular war hero, Hancock was painfully ill-informed about politics and policy. He was neutral on gold and friendly to the South, but otherwise had little political record. Garfield adopted a watered-down version of Hayes's agenda: pro-gold, federal pensions for veterans, somewhat ambiguous on civil-service reform, but strong on tariff protectionism. After some initial haggling, Grant's Stalwarts in New York demanded a personal meeting with Garfield, during which they believed they had obtained promises for top federal appointments and perhaps even government contracts.[32]

In fact, a considerable part of the Republican campaign devolved into a battle for control between Garfield and various state faction leaders over strategy and resources, especially in swing states. The party machines still dictated politics at the local level, but they felt threatened by the loss of moieties and President Hayes's campaign for reform. Now Garfield sought to construct a national Republican constituency sometimes at odds with the local bosses.[33] He even dared to campaign personally—making stops for brief public speeches when he traveled and giving short, tailored orations from his front porch to over fifteen thousand Americans who journeyed to hear him that summer and fall.[34] Once thought "highly indecorous even for [candidates for lower offices] to speak or to take any public part in the canvas," *Harper's Weekly* now described Garfield's few activities as "a question of expediency."[35] Politics were changing, and the bosses feared for their clout.

With the electoral behemoth of New York behind him, Garfield went on to win in November. He garnered a solid 58 percent of the electoral college, but only 48.3 percent of the popular vote. It was one of the closest elections in US history. Had just over ten thousand votes in New York gone the other way, Garfield would have lost. Republicans also won back control of the House with just over 50 percent of the seats. The Senate, however, was up for grabs. The Republicans came just two seats shy of a majority there, but the election of third-party senators gave Republicans a shot at winning coalitions on many issues. In an ominous sign for economic conservatives, the pro-inflation, pro-worker Greenback-Labor presidential candidate James Weaver made a strong showing, with over 308,000 votes (3.3 percent of the popular vote), almost four times the votes received in 1876.[36]

Garfield: Power without Purpose

Thanks to his years in Congress, Garfield entered the presidency with an intimate knowledge of the budget, trade, monetary policy, and military affairs; and yet he displayed no clear, consistent "vision" for the country. For, despite his public image as a resolutely principled lawmaker, throughout his long political career he had contradicted himself on almost every major issue. "He easily changed his mind and honestly veered from one impulse to another," recalled senior Republican John Sherman.[37] A recent scholar of the period concurs, writing that "Garfield was known to have taken every conceivable measure to obfuscate his positions on issues. He seemed wishy-washy, vague, and non-committal, concerned solely on his own political survival."[38] Thus his inaugural address was a lackluster combination of bland platitudes and history lessons, laced with policy aspirations that were "strictly in accordance with the views and wishes of the [Republican] party."[39] Garfield even seemed ambivalent about the presidency. "I am not elated over the election," he wrote a friend, complaining about the "loss of liberty which accompanies it."[40]

At heart, Garfield's view of government was "to keep the peace and stand out of the sunshine of the people," but his laissez-faire principles were easily overridden.[41] He appears just as often guided by self-interest, personal morality, eagerness to make friends, or the moment's political winds. For example, although Garfield spoke frequently and fiercely in favor of gold and against inflationary monetary policy (e.g., greenbacks and silver), he suddenly expressed interest in bimetallism after investing in silver mines, and he appointed silver-backer William Windom as his Treasury secretary.[42] Windom was such an effective proponent of bimetallism that his image was printed on US silver certificates during the mid-1880s.[43] In international trade, Garfield believed in free and competitive markets, but he surrendered to trade protectionism out of political necessity. "I am for a protection which leads to ultimate free trade. I am for that free trade which can be only achieved through protection," he rationalized incredibly.[44] Although he occasionally spoke out in favor of civil service reform, Garfield was as lusty an applicant of patronage and mandatory campaign contributions as the typical spoilsman. His own presidential campaign was run by "the worst machine men in the whole party," whom Garfield urged to "do all you can" to obtain donations.[45] And reformers protested angrily when Garfield seemed to abandon the civil service reforms initiated by Hayes's executive orders. Garfield also strongly supported public education and scientific research, and he was a strong proponent of bringing the emerging fields of statistics and economics into federal policy, especially budget formulation, but he just as often neglected these priorities. Overall, he was "not executive in his talents, not original, not firm,—not a moral force," Hayes wrote years later. "His course at various times when trouble came betrayed weakness . . . [placing] him in another list from Lincoln, Clay, Sumner, and the other heroes of our civil history."[46] Hence it is not clear what doctrines, if any, President Garfield might have supported had he survived.

Presidency

Garfield inherited a "Goldilocks economy" when he was inaugurated in March 1881. The nation's adolescent industrial sector was producing at near full capacity and was poised to expand even further during the year. Record amounts of railroad track and telephone wire were being laid. Unemployment was rapidly fading. Weather extremes would reduce agricultural output during the year, but farm prices remained sturdy. And yet overall inflation was nonexistent. Also, due to rapidly expanding trade, the federal deficit and debt were shrinking. That is, surging exports resulted in record trade surpluses, while strong imports earned unprecedented tariff revenues that were used to pay down the debt and fund federal spending. In fact, the American economy was growing so strongly that *The Economist* advised its readers, "In the United States . . . the danger at present is to restrain enterprise and speculation within prudential limits."[47]

One piece of essential business left over from the Hayes administration was a major refinancing of the federal debt. The government still owed $660 million worth of bonds carrying 5 to 6 percent interest payments. With the United States back on the gold standard as of 1879, and the economy strong, interest rates had plummeted. Thus, during its final months, the Hayes administration had sought to refinance these bonds at lower interest rates. However, in Congress, critics of the national banks loaded the refunding bill with penalties and regulations so onerous that many feared it would trigger a financial crisis. The comptroller of the currency warned legislators that they "had fallen into a great error," while the *New York Times* declared the bill "wild and dangerous legislation."[48] Hayes therefore vetoed it the day before Garfield took office.

Time was now slipping by. With just months until the next bond payments were due, Garfield had to thread the needle between "enlist[ing] the active and hearty co-operation of the national banks" to refinance the bonds at favorable rates, and "sufficiently restrain[ing] the tendency of [Congress] to branch into all sorts of side ventures" that would destructively penalize the banks.[49] He also had to skirt public distrust of Wall Street corruption. Nor was it clear whether the White House had constitutional authority to proceed on its own. Nevertheless, rather than call a new session of Congress, Garfield chose to use existing legislation to execute the refunding. He then dispatched his Treasury secretary and attorney general to New York City to negotiate terms with Wall Street bankers. All the while, the administration kept the press well-informed of its deliberations. The maneuver was a "complete success."[50] With minimal wrangling, by mid-May the old 5 to 6 percent bonds were being exchanged for those with 3.5 percent interest, resulting in an annual savings to the Treasury of around $10 million to $16 million (or roughly 4 to 6 percent of total federal spending).[51] The majority of Congress tolerated the intrusion on its fiscal turf.[52] Even the *Chicago Daily Tribune* applauded Garfield's refunding coup as "much better than anything that was proposed in Congress . . . [and] more striking than any financiering accomplished by his predecessor."[53]

Garfield was far more bold, though perhaps less consistent, in his monetary policy. Gold resumption and the economic boom had not hurt popular demand for inflationary monetary policy. In fact, in the 1880 election the Greenback Party had almost quadrupled its votes since 1876 and sent nine representatives to the new 47th Congress, where they were joined by other pro-inflationists.[54] Also, because the price of silver as coin was now around 12 percent higher than as bullion,[55] demands for free silver coinage grew louder, and now included a majority of House members. In his inaugural address, Garfield had noted, "Confusion has recently been created by variations in the relative value of the two metals, but I confidently believe that arrangements can be made between the leading commercial nations which will secure the general use of both metals."[56]

A few weeks later, his administration released a joint proposal with France for a new international bimetallic monetary union. During spring and summer 1881, the United States and France partnered to convene the International Monetary Conference in Paris to debate the plan, with delegates from eighteen nations in attendance. Similar attempts had foundered in 1867 and 1878, but Garfield felt the conditions were now more favorable. An agricultural recession in Europe had stimulated new interest in bimetallism there. Also, gold-standard countries had become increasingly worried that silver-based countries were gaining a trade advantage from the steadily declining price of silver. However, the Paris negotiations ended in failure. Lengthy deliberations produced little agreement on any of the major issues, while Germany and Great Britain stood in fatal opposition to the free coinage of silver.[57]

Garfield began some promising initiatives in other areas as well. In foreign policy, he mostly supported economic globalization and sought to challenge the Great Power imperialism that confronted the United States. For example, his administration made moves to advance a trans-isthmus canal in Central America, expand US control over the Hawaiian Islands, and increase US participation in international organizations like the Geneva Convention. Closer to home, Garfield launched investigations into the recently surfaced Star Route scandals, even though they threatened to engulf his political allies.[58] "Go ahead regardless of where or who you hit," he instructed his postmaster general. "[P]robe this ulcer to the bottom."[59]

Otherwise, Garfield spent most of his short-lived presidency trying to repair political wounds and unite the divided Republican Party behind him. To do so, he had to balance his own preferences on appointments with those of the state political elites. Since Garfield had won the presidency by such narrow margins, Republican faction leaders and their political machines now expected to be rewarded handsomely for delivering the vote. His own vice president, secretary of state, and fellow Republicans schemed against him. Every faction and luminary pushed their own favorite nominees for positions in Garfield's cabinet and throughout the federal government. Garfield desperately struggled to appease them.

At the front of the line was Senator Roscoe Conkling. In return for delivering the New York vote, Conkling now demanded control over the US Treasury, including the lucrative New York City Customs House. Garfield attempted to mollify Conkling, offering him numerous lesser federal appointments for his faction. But Conkling refused to be allayed. He saw the inferior postings as either personal insults or weak beer for his proud spoilsmen. Conkling's rivals intervened and advised Garfield to appoint one of Conkling's enemies to run the New York City Customs House. Garfield agreed, writing, "This brings on the contest at once and settles the question of whether the president is registering clerk of the Senate or the Executive of the United States."[60] Conkling was furious. His allies on Garfield's cabinet threatened to resign. The battle of wills became daily fodder for the nation's newspapers, which talked of "open war" between Conkling and Garfield.[61] In a dramatic move, Conkling and his fellow Republican senator from New York resigned their Senate seats in protest, intending for the New York state legislature to reinstate them in a show of solidarity against Garfield. However, Conkling had risen to power on bullying, insults, and bribery; having now lost his influence over appointments, and having embarrassed his state with his public antics, he had little political leverage left back home.

Seeking to settle the matter, a delusional office-seeker who claimed loyalty to Conkling's Stalwart faction shot Garfield at Union Station in Washington in early July. "His death was a political necessity," wrote the assassin, who also bragged to his captors, "Arthur will be president."[62] The bullet wounds were deep but surviv able if properly treated. However, the unsterile methods and antiquated practices of Garfield's doctors produced a deadly infection. For two months, Garfield lingered in bed, dying of sepsis.[63] At first, he attempted to conduct official busi ness, or at least the appearance of it. But he was incapacitated by fever, vomiting, and pain and accomplished little. "In effect, for most of the summer of 1881, the United States of America was without a functioning chief executive," writes one biographer.[64] It did not matter much. Congress was out of session; there were no crises nor urgent legislation. Vice President Arthur sequestered himself at home and remained respectfully silent. As for Conkling, though cleared of any wrong doing, the shooting of President Garfield by a professed Stalwart, albeit an insane one, only further weakened his position. In late July, the New York state legisla ture declined to reinstate Conkling to the US Senate. Garfield, now bedridden, had won.

Garfield's assassination had little effect on the economy, even though it sat urated the nation's headlines for weeks. On the morning of the shooting, Wall Street panicked. At first, "every man who heard it believed the story to be a ca nard, a wild story set afloat . . . in order to get up 'a scene' and have some fun in the Stock Exchange."[65] When the rumors proved accurate, stocks dropped 3 to 5 percent in heavy trading. But by the end of the day, the markets had recovered from their lows. Most bankers and industrialists quickly surmised that Garfield's assassination "would not exert any permanent depressing effect on the busi ness interests of the country."[66] Over the following weeks, the markets largely shrugged off the event.[67] Some American bankers expressed concern that "the foreigner may be inclined to place us, on account of this event, in the same cat egory with Mexico, and thus injure our national and corporate credit."[68] But foreigners did not. The overseas financial press anticipated "no unfavorable ef fect on American credit, which is too firmly established to be influenced by such dastardly attempts."[69] And European investors continued to loan generously to Americans, while foreign immigration climbed ever higher.

Even when Garfield finally died in mid-September, "there was no substan tial public outpouring of grief; the public had been very well prepared for this contingency."[70] Wall Street and the business community were nonplussed, other than a "generally bearish temper in the market."[71] The financial pages admitted frankly, "It cannot be said . . . that the slightest fear was entertained of any serious disturbance in financial circles."[72] The foreign business press was similarly quies cent, dismissing "any apprehension that [Garfield's death] will be followed by any change of policy in the Government of the United States."[73]

Summary

If President Garfield had a direct impact on the US economy, it was his contribution to national financial stability. His refunding of American Civil War bonds reduced interest payments on the federal debt by over 40 percent. Taking no action would have slowed debt reduction. A venomous fight in Congress, or a poorly designed bill, might have significantly damaged American finances. Contemporaries feared damage to America's still fragile credit. Some anticipated a banking crisis. Garfield's deft negotiations with bankers and openness with the American people avoided each of these outcomes. It was Garfield's only potential economic catastrophe as president, and he handled it masterfully.

Otherwise, Garfield's administration was simply too brief and uneventful to have much economic impact in the short run, but we can nevertheless learn two lessons from it. First, training and education in economics do not necessarily determine a president's vision or policy positions. Garfield was well educated in political economy. Intellectually he was a devotee of free-market capitalism. However, none of this seemed to result in consistent ideology or policy commitments as an elected official. His positions were constantly shifting and evolving. His formal training in economics did not produce a vision, much less any sort of dogmatism.

Second, there are likely external factors that determine a president's relevance for economic performance. In Garfield's case, the economy was already robust when he entered office. And after the debt refinancing, with no significant crises to deal with, he was mostly irrelevant. For months, as he lay dying, the federal government essentially administered itself, "[e]very man running his own department . . . [with] everything in good order," according to one cabinet member.[74] In other words, when all is well, presidents may matter little. But when economic crises threaten, then presidents might be more essential actors.

Finally, although this book focuses on short-run economic performance, we should acknowledge that Garfield's assassination likely had significant medium- and long-run effects. Although his successor, President Chester Arthur (1881–1885), would drag his feet on civil service reform, Garfield's martyrdom became the fulcrum upon which long-resisted reform legislation was passed through Congress. It would take years to fully implement, but the corrupt Jacksonian "spoils system" was finally on its way out, and a professional, merit-based bureaucracy was on its way in. For a nation poised to become an industrialized, global economic power, such a transformation was essential. A more subtle transfer in political power was also taking place. For decades, disparate state and local political machines had been at the core of the American political system. The institutional pillars of that system—moieties, patronage, assessments—were gradually being eliminated. And the forces of technological change, industrialization, urbanization, and globalization were creating the conditions for a new style of politics and policy. The locus of power was therefore slowly shifting toward *national* political parties led by a more visible and active president. Garfield was both a victim and the catalyst of this tectonic change.

8

Chester Arthur and the Smoldering Depression of 1881–1885

Chester A. Arthur (1881–1885) oversaw one of the more dismal economies of any American president.[1] Almost immediately after he entered office, the country sank into a now forgotten "smoldering" depression that dragged on for four years.[2] At first, only Wall Street noticed. Stocks had been in the doldrums since the shooting of President Garfield. Soon after he died, the stock market fell into a slump that lasted almost Arthur's entire term. Industrial production and trade also began to slide during autumn 1881. Agricultural crops soon followed, descending into a deep and prolonged downturn. Thus the entire economy sagged throughout 1882–1883. The climactic paroxysm came during mid-1884, when the nation's financial system was thrown into a massive banking crisis. Thereafter severe deflation ensued. As the economy shrank and unemployment surged, labor unrest began anew. Both trade and the trade surplus fell drastically, taking down with them the federal surplus. Immigration also dropped precipitously, while emigration more than doubled. Perhaps the only bright spot was the federal debt, which continued its steady march downward, commenced at the end of the Civil War. But the overall economy would not recover until months after Arthur left office.

President Arthur did little, despite the resources at his disposal. The federal government had the means by which to avoid the 1881–1885 depression and the financial panic it produced. The US Treasury was flush with cash at the time, collecting far more tax and tariff revenues than it spent. Although countercyclical fiscal policy and the welfare state were considered eccentric concepts during the Gilded Age, other government solutions were available. The federal surplus could have been distributed to the state governments, used on infrastructure projects, spent to pay down state debts, offered as pensions to veterans, or ladled out as pork. Tariffs could have been cut. Even more potent would have been a decisive move on monetary policy. Each of these actions was well within the historical experience and political acceptability of the 1880s. In fact, Arthur himself suggested many of these ideas to Congress. But he did so only rarely, and he never followed up with any sort of action, campaign, effort to organize, or pressure on Congress. Instead, he stood by as the economy toppled. As unemployment and business failures mounted, Arthur at times spent lavishly

Presidential Leadership in Feeble Times. Mark Zachary Taylor, Oxford University Press. © Oxford University Press 2024. DOI: 10.1093/oso/9780197750742.003.0010

on himself and on transforming the White House into a fabulous social hub; at other times he appeared to fall back into unseemly meddling in state and party machine politics. Where possible, he mostly just ignored the presidency. Hence, most in Congress, and even the executive branch itself, felt comfortable ignoring him. The American public too had little regard for Arthur. Consequently, after years of economic decline, he was largely rejected by the Republican Party, and the country, in his 1884 nomination bid. Hence, Arthur reveals that presidential inactivity during crisis can have dire consequences, for both the man and the economy.

Background

Chester A. Arthur had the formal education, leadership experience, and political acumen necessary to be a great economic leader. He was born in 1829 in New England, the son of a fire-and-brimstone Baptist preacher. After wandering the region for a decade, the family settled in upstate New York. Their large household, with eight children, was rambunctious but rigid, and never far from poverty.[3] Over time, Arthur grew tired of his father's "self-righteousness and unwavering faith" and eschewed the church, resulting in a lifelong breach with his parents.[4] In the meantime, he attended the prestigious Union College in Schenectady, New York. There he was a top student, graduating with near perfect grades.[5] Arthur rejected the budding science and engineering programs at Union and instead opted for the standard undergraduate curriculum of Greek, Latin, and ancient classics; it included only marginal education in political economy. After leaving college, he taught school and studied law in upstate New York. At the age of twenty-five, he moved to New York City, where he worked at a law firm and lived a somewhat dull and isolated life. "[I] have worked pretty hard," he wrote in missives to his family, "but aside from business . . . I feel the want of near and dear friends."[6] He also became a dedicated abolitionist, even traveling to Kansas in 1856 to fight the legalization of slavery there.

Politically aware since his teenage years, Arthur became an activist within the newly formed Republican Party in New York City. There he found the camaraderie and excitement for which he had longed. He became close to his state's Republican governor, who appointed Arthur as New York's chief engineer, and later quartermaster general during the Civil War. This gave Arthur responsibility for an enormous amount of war materiel and finance, and experience with the power and influence that came with them. His wartime performance was exemplary. The governor applauded his "unbending integrity, [and] great knowledge. . . . [Arthur] can say No (which is important) without giving offence."[7] Fellow officers too remembered Arthur as having "showed unusual executive ability," despite the fact that he never saw combat and only once visited the front.[8] After the war, Arthur drew upon his experiences with the Union army, as well as his considerable network of friends and business partners gained during the war, to further build the Republican Party in New York.

Arthur loved the workings of the political machine and he delighted in mastering them. "His specialty was to be the science of gaining political office," writes one biographer.[9] More specifically, Arthur's expertise was in financial collections, winning elections for his party and faction, and then doling out the appointments, jobs, and government contracts that flowed from electoral victories.[10] Power, money, and status were the main objectives, not policy. He envisioned that "the whole [Republican] party machinery could be consolidated, unified and concentrated for any purpose . . . [to] make the party so compact and disciplined as to be practically invincible."[11] His party bosses agreed and supported him enthusiastically.

Gilded Age spoilsmen are often stereotyped as gangsters and street toughs, but Arthur was no back-alley lowlife.[12] He was a "jolly fellow" who wore the latest London fashions and preferred fine food, good cigars, and French spirits.[13] "[H]e loved the pleasures of the table . . . and could carry a great deal of wine and liquor," recalled a former crony, who also noted that Arthur was "much addicted to the game of 'poker.'"[14] Arthur especially thrived on the social aspects of the political machine. "[H]e was good company; cheery and buoyant in spirit, full of talk and anecdote," remembered a friend.[15] As he grew into a powerful party elite, he became known as "The Gentleman Boss" for his aristocratic tastes and manners. However, he abhorred the limelight, shunned elected office, and avoided the soapbox. Instead, he preferred to hold court behind the closed doors of Delmonico's Restaurant or to conduct deals in the privacy of the Fifth Avenue Hotel, which together became his *de facto* offices and the centers of New York City politics.

Over time, Arthur rose to become a powerful lieutenant in the New York Republican faction loyal to Ulysses S. Grant and led by the powerful and ostentatious Senator Roscoe Conkling (R-NY). Conkling's faction stood "stalwart" against any attempts to reform the corrupt and inefficient political-machine system. Their main opposition within the Republican Party was the "Half-Breed" faction, so named because they "were half-loyal to Grant and patronage, half-loyal to reforming it all, and fully loyal to none."[16] Arthur skillfully battled the "Half-Breeds" on behalf of Conkling, and fought the Democrats on behalf of his party. For his loyalty and finesse, in late 1871 he was rewarded with appointment as the federal collector of the Port of New York. It was the largest federal office in the country and hence the most bountiful in party patronage.[17] It also paid handsomely.[18] There, protected by President Grant and at the behest of Senator Conkling, Arthur oversaw 75 percent of all federal customs duties and several hundred federal jobs. For the next seven years, Arthur and Conkling wielded their power to divert vast sums of money, and swing scores of elections, to the Republican Party. Their misconduct became legendary. Thus, soon after the reform-minded Rutherford B. Hayes was inaugurated president), Arthur was investigated and eventually ousted from the New York Customs House in 1878.

Arthur was therefore an unexpected selection for vice president in 1880. He barely knew the Republican presidential nominee, James A. Garfield, and spoke with him little during or after the campaign. Arthur was a compromise candidate chosen to guarantee the New York swing vote in a close election. He campaigned energetically and well that year, winning pivotal support for Republicans.[19] But to anticorruption reformers, Arthur's nomination was "a miserable farce" and a manifestation of "the cowardice and infirmity of principle" that plagued the Republican Party.[20] The *Chicago Tribune* called it "a mistake" and "ill-advised," like putting a fox in charge of the hen house.[21] The editors of *The Nation* dismissed such concerns, assuring their readers that "there is no place in which [Arthur's] powers of mischief will be so small as in the Vice Presidency," while insisting that the premature death of President Garfield was "too unlikely a contingency."[22]

After winning the 1880 election, Vice President–elect Arthur set to work dividing up the spoils: cabinet positions, Senate seats,[23] postmasterships, diplomatic slots, and tens of thousands of other appointments across the federal government. He still stuck close to his faction boss, Senator Conkling, during this period, and many questioned anew his fitness for the vice presidency. Obviously, Arthur viewed members of his own Stalwart faction as first in line for the best positions. But this put him into conflict with President Garfield, who both sought to be independent of any outside influence yet also win allies and repay favors of his own. Arthur was seen openly collaborating with his Senate allies against President Garfield on several occasions. He also made indelicate remarks in front of reporters about vote-buying during the presidential election.[24] His blatant scheming was blasted in the press as "reprehensible and disgusting" and "a gross lapse of dignity [worthy of] public contempt."[25] He was widely considered to be the most disloyal vice president since John Calhoun's betrayal of Andrew Jackson in 1832.[26]

Ultimately this partisan infighting resulted in both Garfield's triumph and assassination. First, Arthur's Stalwart allies in the Senate attempted to embarrass and undermine Garfield through elaborate schemes. But their plans backfired. After much drama, the Stalwarts were left without their most powerful Senate leaders, and Garfield was free to select his own appointees.[27] However, it was a Pyrrhic victory. During Garfield's battle with the Stalwarts, a deluded office-seeker, believing himself to be wrongly denied an ambassadorship, shot Garfield at a train station, and then proudly declared, "I did it. . . . I am a Stalwart, and Arthur will be President."[28]

Most Americans now expected the presidency to pass directly under the control of the party bosses whom Arthur had long served. "Conkling will 'run' the government [just] as he has long run the 'Machine,'" predicted the *Nation*.[29] The *Chicago Tribune* agreed, calling Arthur's succession a "calamity of the utmost magnitude."[30] Certainly when Arthur gathered his advisors for guidance, they were a collection of faction loyalists and Stalwart leaders. Over the next eleven weeks, they strategized while Garfield lay dying. For while the White House would soon be Arthur's, the future of the Stalwarts remained in question. Neither the press nor the public blamed Arthur for the assassination, but they feared the corrupt patronage system which he had helped to build and upon which he thrived.

Machine Man and Accidental President

Arthur was almost completely devoid of any policy agenda or vision for the country when he entered the presidency. He cared little for public policy or economics. For decades, his portfolio had been that of a state and local party operative, happy to adopt the policy views of his superiors. In fact, even with twenty-five years of politics under his belt, Arthur's *first* public statement on national issues was his letter accepting his nomination as vice president in 1880. And this mostly just paraphrased the already established Republican platform. In it, he stated unsurprisingly, "There must be no deteriorated coin, no depreciated paper. And every dollar . . . should stand the test of the world's fixed [gold] standard." He supported public education. He advocated protective tariffs to "enable our manufacturers and artisans to compete successfully with those of other lands." He backed federal aid for national infrastructure, especially rivers and harbors. Perhaps the only hint of Arthur's own influence on the document was his *dis*approval of civil service reform, which threatened the political machine upon which his wealth and power was based.[31] Arthur was also rudderless on the great North-South divide that still vexed the country. And despite his record as a former integrationist, he provided little direction on African American rights in the ex-Confederacy.[32] This was shockingly weak policy coming from the leader of the party of Abraham Lincoln, and barely twenty years after the Emancipation Proclamation.

Nor did Arthur have any philosophy of the presidency or how to use it. He had never sought elected office of any sort, much less the White House. In fact, Arthur seems to have accepted the vice presidency out of vanity rather than political ambition.[33] And as president, he appears to have disliked and evaded the job whenever possible, often leaving controversial decisions to his cabinet or Congress. Strangely, his mastery at influencing the New York political machine did not translate into skill at, or even an inclination for, manipulating Congress. Instead, Arthur let Congress dictate legislation, budgets, and even foreign policy, an area in which the executive branch typically has seniority. He vetoed fewer bills than any president between Lincoln and George W. Bush, and only one of his major vetoes was fully successful.[34] He even tried to physically avoid the White House when he was in Washington, preferring instead to stay with friends or at a small residence on the periphery of the city.[35] An administration member summed him up as "a sensitive, almost a timid man, I mean with reference to his responsibilities . . . a man oppressed with either duties or the inversion of his natural hours, or staggering under a sense of responsibility which he does not like."[36]

Ascension, 1881

President Arthur's economic troubles began almost immediately upon entering office. The American economy had been flourishing for three years straight, but in autumn 1881 it quietly shifted toward recession.[37] After several years of bumper crops, American agriculture suffered a general setback. The wheat harvest fell 22 percent in 1881 alone, well off the historic records set in 1879. Meanwhile, fair weather in Europe and the postwar recovery of Russian farms meant a surge in European produce dumped onto international markets, forcing prices down everywhere.[38] Starting in September, US industrial activity too began an inconspicuous but sustained deceleration. Interest rates on domestic bonds suddenly plateaued, ending eight years of pleasantly gentle descents. The stock market, which had been in the dumps since early summer, continued to weaken.

Yet few seemed to notice the slowdown. Absent modern statistical reporting, there were few national data with which to evaluate the economy. Certainly newspapers carried daily stories about the "decidedly heavy tone" of the stock markets and "an absence of interest on the part of investors,"[39] but stocks were not widely held at the time.[40] Similarly, even if slackening industrial production had aroused attention, fewer than 20 percent of workers were then employed in manufacturing. Modern industry in the United States was barely twenty years old; hence slowdowns there were considered unpredictable fluctuations in an unfamiliar "high-tech" sector. Perhaps most deceiving, almost every recession in living memory had been *preceded* by a financial panic. Yet the American financial system appeared rock solid in 1881. Therefore, few recognized the beginning of the 1881–1885 economic slump. Even six months into the recession, the *New York Times* was still assuring its readers, "The era of prosperity may be said to have continued, as industrial and commercial activity have in no degree abated."[41]

Arthur therefore said and did nothing. Rather than public policy or the economy, among his first and most energetic actions as president was to remodel the White House.[42] Declaring, "I will not live in a house like this," for months he refused to move into the executive mansion until renovations were almost completed.[43] He personally managed the project, bringing in Louis C. Tiffany, of the famous New York jewelry family, to oversee interior design. This prompted critics to complain that Arthur spent more time on the remodeling than on his official duties as president.[44]

Otherwise, Arthur seemed disinterested in executive power in 1881. He gave a subdued and perfunctory inaugural address. He performed various ceremonial duties. He called Congress into special session in order to elect a president pro tempore of the Senate,[45] as well as to confirm a backlog of federal appointees. In other words, Arthur mostly just went through the motions of being president. And he gave no sign as to the future direction of his administration. "Everything is at sea about Arthur," wrote a senior Republican in October. "[A]t present the Cabinet knows nothing whatever of his intentions."[46]

As time passed, little changed. In early December, when Arthur submitted his first annual message to Congress, it was a long, rambling missive that called for tax cuts, tariff reform, Indian policy reform, civil service reform, the elimination of silver currency, and new legislation on presidential succession. Congress was nonplussed. "There were but few Senators who paid close attention to all the paragraphs," reported the *Chicago Daily Tribune*.[47]

Nevertheless, President Arthur oversaw a placid administration during his first months in office. There were no scandals. He made no major mistakes or egregious misstatements. Also, the quiet interval while Garfield lingered on his deathbed had given Arthur time to reposition himself. It also gave the press and public time to calm down. As a result, by the end of 1881 Arthur had actually earned a modicum of trust from the American people. The *New York Times* opined that "President Arthur's more recent appointments and the general conduct of his Administration have, on the whole, been such as to restore, in a measure, the feeling of confidence and hopefulness which prevailed in the early part of the year."[48] Even the hostile *New York Tribune* admitted, "President Arthur has not yet burned his bridges. . . . The feeling toward him is kindly, hopeful, and forbearing."[49]

1882: The Decline of the "Unexpected" President

During 1882, however, confidence in Arthur evaporated. In addition to his withdrawn, passive administration, he seemed increasingly incompetent and appeared to fall back into old habits. For example, in a bizarre move in late January,

Arthur suddenly canceled US participation in an ambitious Pan-American Peace Conference that had been initiated by his own secretary of state just months earlier. The partisan press and former administration officials erupted in criticism. But rather than take a stand, Arthur referred the matter to Congress. This was a remarkable abdication of executive power over American foreign affairs. Then, in late February, Arthur shocked the country by nominating his old machine boss, Roscoe Conkling, to the Supreme Court. "[Conkling's] nomination is everywhere received with astonishment," reported the *New York Times*, its editors calling it "a long step downward . . . [that goes] far toward forfeiting the respect which the President had gained."[50] Even some Republican papers called the Conkling nomination "a disastrous step" and "a surprise and mortification to those Republicans who had placed confidence in [Arthur's] good sense."[51] Worse yet, Conkling embarrassed Arthur by rejecting it.[52]

Arthur also fumbled on immigration. With the Burlingame Treaty renegotiated by Hayes, Congress was now free to restrict, but not end, Chinese immigration. And pressure to do so was mounting, especially in California and Oregon.[53] In response, Congress passed the 1882 Chinese Exclusion Act, which suspended all immigration from China for twenty years. In a rare move, Arthur vetoed it. His long, pleading message explained that the lengthy prohibition risked violating the new treaty. He also warned that "the system of personal registration and passports is undemocratic and hostile to the spirit of our institutions. I doubt the wisdom of putting an entering wedge of this kind into our laws."[54] Americans throughout the country were furious! Arthur was denounced as a "traitor" and for "being carried away by New England sentimentalism."[55] In California, he was burned in effigy. The newspapers warned, "Many prominent Republicans declare that they will no longer vote that ticket."[56] But rather than stand firm, Arthur folded. Within a month, when a new exclusion bill arrived at his desk, revised down to only a ten-year suspension on Chinese immigration, Arthur signed it without comment. Ironically, on the East Coast, European immigration from across the Atlantic would reach record highs that year.[57]

Meanwhile, the first hints of economic recession had begun to surface. In February 1882, the foreign business press noted a "collapse of the American speculation in produce" and a sudden falloff in US international trade.[58] But these were casually dismissed as "largely due to exceptional causes," such as the massive flooding of the Ohio and Mississippi rivers that month.[59] The floods had destroyed crops and livestock, blocked roads and railways, submerged river docks, inundated homes and factories, and sent hundreds of thousands of people in search of new shelter or jobs.[60] A simultaneous run on American railroad securities also occurred, as investors, especially foreign holders, "lost confidence in railway and financial management."[61] "[T]he fall has been very striking," observed *The Economist*.[62] Yet Arthur said and did nothing.

Then, during spring, a surge in European agriculture triggered an unmistakable new phase in the economic downturn. Increased exports from Europe's farms drove down food prices internationally and thereby hurt the incomes of American farmers. Starting around April, American wheat prices plunged anew for seven months, dropping over 32 percent. This bust in US agriculture both coincided with and contributed to a relative oversupply of railroad services. With too many rails to carry too few domestic goods and too little produce, the US transportation sector soon plummeted. By summer the *New York Times* was reporting regional downturns: Chicago was "on the verge of a panic" and there was already a "depression in Cincinnati."[63]

One potential palliative for the worsening recession was new federal spending on infrastructure and public works. Arthur called for "appropriations for such internal improvements as the wisdom of Congress may deem to be of public importance" in his first annual message in early December 1881.[64] In particular, he emphasized upgrades to the nation's rivers and harbors. With specific reference to "[t]he immense losses and widespread suffering of the people . . . occasioned by the recent floods," he repeated this request in a special message to Congress in April 1882, calling improvements there "of vital importance" to the entire nation.[65]

Arthur then abdicated, leaving the infrastructure bill entirely up to Congress. Without leadership from the White House, negotiations turned into a sprawling appropriation loaded with special projects. In late July 1882, after months of haggling, legislators passed the River and Harbors Bill. It sought $18.7 million (roughly $5 billion in 2020 dollars) for scores of river and harbor enhancements throughout the country.[66] This included much-needed upgrades on the Mississippi and Ohio rivers, whose flooding had devastated regional economies earlier that year. Dozens of other state and local projects were also included that might have provided a fiscal pump to regional economies suffering from the recession. Although the press and some in the public attacked it as "a scandalous misappropriation of public money for the advancement of local jobbery,"[67] it was exactly the kind of federal spending that might have boosted employment and stoked aggregate demand, all while making valuable infrastructure improvements throughout the country.[68]

Yet days later, in early August 1882, Arthur abruptly vetoed the River and Harbors Bill. Succumbing to public criticism, he now insisted that the bill was too large and too filled with pork. "My principal objection to the bill," he wrote, "is that it contains appropriations for purposes not for the common defense or general welfare, and which do not promote commerce among the States."[69] He also worried that such an "extravagant expenditure of public money" would have a "demoralizing effect" on government itself.[70] Such objections were remarkable coming from the Gentleman Boss, whose entire career had been built upon the generous ladling out of government money. Conservatives, reformers, and the press mostly applauded Arthur's "sagacity" and "courage," but Congress scoffed and passed the bill over Arthur's veto by wide margins the following day.[71]

That summer, Arthur made a far more serious political error. Rather than work together with the Republican majority in Congress on national issues, he embarrassed the presidency by continuing to play Stalwart boss in New York politics. Since entering office, Arthur had returned frequently to New York City and his old haunts, including Delmonico's and the Fifth Avenue Hotel. During mid-1882 rumors surfaced that "the old machine that Arthur brought up by hand" had set its eyes on that autumn's elections.[72] Arthur denied involvement. But he was implicated in shuffling federal appointments within New York's post offices to bolster support for the Stalwarts' slate of candidates there. Arthur was also accused of rigging the state's Republican nominating convention. In particular, he sought to unseat New York's governor, a fellow Republican, a man who was popular in the state but who had offended Arthur and the Stalwarts with his lukewarm support. The *New York Times* openly scolded the Arthur administration for "unwarranted and mischievous intrusion in a field where its agents or its influence ought never to appear" and loudly denounced the supposed "bribery and forgery, and other means equally corrupt" by which Arthur's candidates were "forced upon the convention."[73] The result was a disaster for Arthur and the Stalwarts. They got their men nominated, but proceeded to lose badly in the November elections. The New York governorship was rarely in Republican hands, and Arthur had pushed aside one of the few winning Republicans, only to lose to a newcomer and reformist Democrat, Grover Cleveland.

Back in the nation's cities, as wages dropped and unemployment mounted, labor unions began to organize. The seeds of the American Federation of Labor had been planted in Pittsburgh the previous autumn. Now, in 1882, membership in the secretive Knights of Labor accelerated past forty-two thousand, more than double the prior year, as its working cooperatives bloomed throughout the country.[74] New accounts of the defunct Molly Maguires appeared in bookstores, reminding readers of the bloodshed that angry laborers were capable of.[75] Throughout summer, perhaps 100,000 men went on strike, including some 35,000 iron workers angry over wages.[76] In early September, thousands of union members marched through the streets of lower Manhattan in the nation's first Labor Day parade. "[T]his parade coming at this time is open to suspicion," worried the *New York Daily Tribune*, which saw it as a show of political might by "certain demagogues and dishonest leaders."[77]

Arthur appeared unperturbed. In fact, throughout his presidency he refused to act as a "healer" for a country suffering from recession. Rather than assemble Congress or take executive action, he spent generously on himself.[78] He rode around Washington in an opulent carriage, the finest used by any president since

George Washington. He paid handsome sums for the latest clothing styles from New York and Europe. He traveled frequently to New York, summered in Florida or on the New England coast, and cruised the Chesapeake on the presidential yacht. And when he traveled, he eschewed a bodyguard, despite threats of assassination and Garfield's fate. Instead, a valet and a French chef accompanied Arthur on his trips.[79]

Arthur also entertained lavishly at the White House, turning it into a top-flight destination for the nation's elite. "All his ambition seems to center on the social aspect," observed a senator's wife. "Flowers and wine and food, and slow pacing with a lady on his arm."[80] Each year, he held over a dozen state dinners; each week, he threw regular dinner parties; and on special occasions, he hosted concerts, parties, and celebrations. These were usually luxurious affairs. "He wanted the best of everything, and wanted it served in the best manner," a White House attendant recalled.[81] Even small "intimate" meals with President Arthur might feature over a dozen courses, top-shelf wines and liquor, and imported cigars.[82] One attendee wrote of her experience, "The dinner was extremely elegant . . . the flowers, the damask, the silver, the attendants, all showing the latest style and an abandon in expense and taste."[83] And when rebuked for his heavy drinking by a temperance advocate, Arthur growled, "I may be President of the United States, but my private life is nobody's damned business!"[84]

Thus, 1882 was, to many Americans, a year of "dissatisfaction."[85] "There have been no brilliant achievements in finance," complained the *New York Tribune*, "[and] in administrative efficiency, there has been stagnation."[86] The recession had begun to throw people out of work and home. Charitable societies multiplied throughout the country to aid the growing numbers of impoverished. In New York City alone, public charity cost some $6.5 million (around $165 million in 2020 dollars).[87] The stock market, which had seemed to rally for a few months during summer, resumed its frustrating slide downward in early autumn. Both agriculture and industry also ended the year in the dumps.

Civil Service Reform

Civil service reform too seemed stalled. The assassination of President Garfield had been a watershed event for Americans. "The whole people was shocked by the incident," one senator professed, ". . . touched by the magnitude of the crime."[88] Arthur was not denounced for it, but the spoils system was. The weight of national opinion now shifted *en masse* toward reform. Labor unrest, bank panics, and economic recession were all linked, in the public mind, to corruption in government.

Nevertheless, President Arthur resisted change. He genuflected to clean government in his speeches but merely recommended caution and took no serious action. In fact, upon taking office, he assured the country, "No demand for speedy legislation has been heard; no adequate occasion is apparent for an unusual session of Congress."[89] Three months later, he asked Congress only for a refunding of the Civil Service Commission "for the promotion of efficiency in the different branches of the civil service."[90] Meanwhile, Congress was still packed with machine bosses and spoilsmen who rejected even that. The Arthur administration then used technicalities to avoid prosecuting the most flagrant cases of corruption in 1882.

In a wave of grassroots political advocacy, civil service reform associations appeared throughout the country to lobby for new legislation.[91] The press was widely sympathetic. For example, the New York Times openly berated a moderate anticorruption bill introduced by Senator George H. Pendleton (D-OH), calling it a "sham" which "does not strike at the root of . . . the most flagrant abuses in the civil service."[92] The anticorruption movement was so strong and widespread that many state party conventions adopted reform planks as the 1882 elections approached. Even many former spoilsmen now eagerly converted to the cause rather than be thrown out of office.[93] Yet Arthur continued to dissemble and delay. "Are you a coward?" asked a disappointed supporter. "Do you fear to face the same danger that Garfield faced?"[94]

As a result, the 1882 midterm elections were a disaster for Arthur. They evolved into a national debate over government ethics, and the Republicans lost badly.[95] Disappointed by their president's meddling, flip-flops, and failed leadership, many Republican voters simply stayed home. In one of the largest reversals in congressional history, the Republicans lost thirty-four seats in the House, collapsing from a bare majority there of 52 percent down to an impotent 36 percent minority. Thanks to a more forgiving electoral map in the Senate, they managed to defend their thirty-seven seats, which gave them a tentative grip on the seventy-five-man upper house. In the state of New York, Democrats swept the field. Not only did reformer Grover Cleveland take the governor's seat, but Democrats captured both houses of the state legislature by wide margins. Arthur, the consummate campaigner as boss and candidate, now, as president, could not even win seats for his party in his own home state.

The resounding message of the 1882 midterms forced Arthur to finally act on civil service reform. He supported Republicans in Congress who dusted off the Pendleton bill and hastily passed it in mid-January 1883. Still, Arthur was content to see the Pendleton Civil Service Act weakened by amendments and revisions so as to remove, dull, or delay its strongest dictums. The watered-down bill covered only federal positions in Washington and customs house and postal employees in the largest cities. Ninety percent of federal jobs remained exempt. So too were older veterans, blue-collar workers, and those appointments confirmed by the Senate.[96] Perhaps essential to its passage was the fact that the Pendleton Act would weaken the spoils system just as the Democrats were poised to take over the House, and possibly soon the Senate and presidency too. That is, the Pendleton reforms would prevent Democrats from removing thousands of Republican appointees or rewarding supporters, while allowing Republicans to pose as reformers. "The Congress that met in December, 1882, was thinking of 1884," writes one scholar of the period.[97]

The "Mongrel" Tariff

Meanwhile, the economy ground downward, with only occasional glimmers of hope. For example, starting in November 1882 wheat prices rose briskly; then the stock market appeared to level off during the first half of 1883. However, industrial activity told a different story. After having staged a recovery the previous autumn, the nation's industrial sector slackened again during winter and spring 1882–1883. Stagnation and decline soon returned to agriculture and the stock market. After trending upward 20 percent, wheat prices also began to sag again, from May 1883 into the close of 1884. By spring 1883, the depression had clearly spread to the iron industry.[98] A Pittsburgh manufacturer told reporters, "[F]or the past six months we have been selling coke at an actual loss. . . . [T]he only way out of the difficulty is to cease producing."[99] By the end of summer, *The Nation* was reporting several months of "over-production and consequent declining prices, resulting in an increase of business failures"[100] and a "sudden and great decline in prices on the Exchange, and . . . [m]anufacturing business has been seriously depressed."[101]

Strategic adjustments to US trade policy offered a possible solution, but Arthur mismanaged these as well.[102] As unemployment and bankruptcies rose, domestic demand plummeted. American farmers and industrialists responded by seeking help to increase exports to foreign markets, while restricting imports at home. Yet consumers wanted tariff reductions. Arthur sought compromise. On trade and tariffs, he came to believe that expanding markets for exports and reducing taxes on imports were essential for the US economy. "The present tariff system is in many respects unjust," Arthur told Congress. "It makes unequal distributions both of its burdens and its benefits."[103] After all, the US Treasury did not need the tariff income. In fact, the federal surplus had grown so large that it was becoming a public embarrassment. Also, the existing tariff protections clearly favored industry, forcing farmers and consumers to pay higher prices than would have existed under free trade.

But rather than advocate for major reforms, Arthur merely created a commission to study the problem, and only *after* gaining approval from Congress. The trade commission then took six months to investigate. Its final report roundly criticized the existing tariff structure and called for widespread reform, including a 20 to 25 percent reduction in tariffs. President Arthur declared his support, but then retired from the field of battle. He left the all-important details and negotiations to Congress. "Lobbyists [then] descended like a flock of buzzards upon Washington," transforming the tariff commission's recommendations into a confused slurry of special interest protections.[104] Without presidential leadership, the congressional haggling and horse-trading became so bogged down that the resulting bill was labeled the "Mongrel Tariff." It was a hodge-podge of compromises that wound up lowering duties on imports an average of just 1.47 percent, and therefore had little effect on the US economy. Even its supporters deemed it "half a loaf" and hardly "better than nothing."[105] Nevertheless, Arthur signed it without comment in early March 1883.[106]

Arthur's performance was in fact lackluster across all aspects of US foreign policy, the venue in which presidents have the most freedom of action and ability to innovate. He left matters almost entirely to his State Department, which then either bungled them or saw its initiatives trashed by Congress or tabled by the next administration.[107] Perhaps the only instance of relative success in Arthur's foreign policy was at the Navy Department. There, Arthur supported the first new investments to replace obsolete Civil War vessels with a modern battle fleet. But the immediate results were poor: the initial contracts went to political cronies who mismanaged ship construction. Arthur's Navy Department was later found to be so rife with corruption, partisan politics, and ossification that it had to be thoroughly reorganized by his successor. The true value of Arthur's naval decisions would not be realized for almost twenty years, until the Spanish-American War. Overall, US foreign policy under Arthur has been widely judged by historians as "uncoordinated," "stillborn," and "inept."[108] Or as one British minister of the period put it, "The result of the interference of these untrained [American] men in international affairs, which they did not fully understand, was a remarkable display of pretentious incapacity."[109]

"Making a Man President Cannot Change Him"

One perpetual obstacle for President Arthur was that he was simply not trusted. Not by political elites, nor by large swaths of the America people.[110] "To lie, to cheat, to steal, to forge, to bribe & be bribed—those are what [your friends] consider the avenues to your favor," scolded a rare admirer.[111] While president, he committed no crimes or nefarious scandals, but he was distant, self-absorbed, and cared little for his job. Other than redecorating, he made no attempt to change how things were done in the White House or within the executive branch. He continued the light hours of work to which he had grown accustomed as a state party broker. He arrived late in the morning, took long lunches, and was usually gone by late afternoon. Most of his work hours were spent greeting congressmen, meeting with his cabinet members, or receiving visitors (usually job or favor seekers, the callers he hated most). And he could be found at all hours taking long strolls with friends. Hence the media called him "sluggish," "indolent and uncertain and timid," and "given to procrastination" when it came to the serious business of the presidency.[112] Indeed, "his staff often felt it necessary to urge the President to attend to matters at hand."[113] A White House clerk later joked, "President Arthur never did today what he could put off until tomorrow."[114]

Arthur *did* inherit from President Garfield a cabinet that was capable, experienced, and widely respected. But they were of little help. Most of Garfield's men were either from rival Republican factions or leery of Arthur's reputation as a spoilsman. "The new administration will be the centre for every element of corruption," a well-regarded Republican insider warned a fellow partisan, "The outlook is very discouraging."[115] Hence, Garfield's senior appointees began to abandon Arthur soon after he was inaugurated. Despite the new president's pleas to remain, three of the seven cabinet members quit during his first weeks in office. Over the succeeding months, others followed. Of Garfield's original cabinet, only the secretary of war, Robert Todd Lincoln, would remain for the duration. The result was an unstable administration. Overall, Arthur went through nineteen cabinet members, including four men each at Treasury and the US postmaster.

Nor were Arthur's new cabinet and senior appointees strong assets. Most were leading members of the nation's various political machines who were left to run their departments with little direction or oversight from Arthur. Hence, they generally ran their departments more with an eye toward rewarding and bolstering their local party faction than with serving Arthur or the nation at large. Many were ill-qualified or poor managers. On a regular basis, the newspapers carried stories of administrative incompetence: failed federal prosecutions, botched diplomacy, neglected legislation, mismanagement in government contracting, and mischief in the administration of federal lands.[116] To many Americans, the US government, overseen by an inveterate spoilsman in the White House, had reached its nadir. The political damage was so deep that it began to threaten the party itself. "The Republican Party has outlived not merely its usefulness but its moral sense," lectured the *New York Herald*.[117]

In particular, Arthur was devoid of useful economic advice from his Treasury secretaries. Garfield's appointee resigned rather than serve under Arthur. In his place, Arthur selected a longtime friend and political ally, Charles Folger, whose expertise was in law and in arranging campaign "donations" from government employees, rather than in economics, banking, or business. Folger did implement some anticorruption reforms in Treasury Department hiring practices. He also supported Arthur's efforts to cut taxes. However, Folger became "something of a recluse, was frequently ill, and suffered spells of severe depression."[118] After he died in office, Arthur replaced him, first with an interim appointment, and finally with an experienced expert in banking and finance. But with only four months left in Arthur's lame-duck presidency, this last Treasury secretary had little influence on the US economy.

Arthur and the American People

In a broader sense, Arthur was shockingly bad at forging productive relationships with major political-economic actors. For example, his impulsive acceptance of the vice-presidential slot, against the preferences of Conkling and other Stalwart leaders, offended many within his own Stalwart faction. Of course, Democrats and Southerners felt no reason to ally with President Arthur, a Northern Republican. And to anticorruption reformers, Arthur the spoilsman had for years been a sworn enemy.

Then, once in office, Arthur proceeded to offend almost everyone with his distribution of patronage appointments. As president, Arthur had thousands of federal jobs to appoint, with myriad competing factions and subfactions jockeying for their share of the spoils. Every job meant a favor repaid or, better yet, a commitment earned for loyalty in future elections. Arthur attempted to divide these patronage positions somewhat equally among Republican Party factions.[119] But he was so closely identified with the Stalwart faction in New York that no one believed his attempts at objectivity. Each faction perceived the others as winning at its expense, and then criticized Arthur for either favoritism or disloyalty. And all were frustrated by Arthur's slowness, or outright refusal, to dismiss sitting officeholders so that loyalists could take their jobs. "[H]e has done less for us than Garfield, or even Hayes," groused one Stalwart captain.[120] Arthur even helped to destroy the remaining political base of the Republican Party in the South by withholding federal appointments from African Americans and their allies in a fruitless attempt to woo Southern whites. Thus Arthur had few reliable allies with whom to accomplish anything as president.

Nor did he make much effort to win over the American public. He mostly neglected to educate them on vital issues of the day or his rare policy preferences. When he traveled as president, it was usually to escape Washington and socialize with friends, not to campaign or meet the people.[121] The few times he did attempt to inform Americans about administration policy, he did so in writing and used well-established vehicles: his inauguration speech, his four annual messages to

Congress, his veto messages, and the occasional proclamation. These rare, formal announcements constituted the bulk of Arthur's communications strategy.

He had a dreadful relationship with the press. As a former machine boss who had always operated best in secrecy, Arthur had long learned to hate and distrust reporters. He therefore avoided them whenever possible. "I make it a habit not to talk politics with you gentlemen of the press," he told one journalist.[122] As a result, the American public relied mostly on rumors, reputation, and secondhand gossip about Arthur's presidency, with no one in the White House to set them straight.

The Road to Crisis and the Panic of 1884

Meanwhile, the economic depression worsened throughout 1883–1884. Despite some occasional bounces, industrial activity was rapidly contracting by late 1883. For the remainder of Arthur's presidency, it fell every month, eventually prompting *The Nation* to declare, "[The m]anufacturing industry is depressed to a degree hardly surpassed in our history."[123] Agricultural incomes fell further as foreign imports drove prices lower, even during periods of healthy domestic crop yields. With fewer goods to ship, railroad profits also slumped. Bankruptcies in domestic agriculture, industry, and transportation soon began to injure the banks that had invested heavily in these sectors. This pressured the stock market ever downward. And even though only the wealthy owned stocks, contemporaries observed that the effect of the constantly declining stock market "has been to produce general blueness or despondency. . . . [I]t restricts consumption in all but the necessities."[124]

As these conditions worsened, the supply of money and credit shrank, emboldening pro-silver forces and frightening "hard money" men.[125] For decades, the latter had worked to get the United States solidly on the gold standard. They included Presidents Grant, Hayes, and Garfield, each of whom had supported legislation to fix the value of the dollar to gold, and hence to other major world currencies, and to decrease the use of cheaper silver and printed paper money.[126]

However, growth in the American gold stock had slowed drastically in 1882, and then failed to make a strong recovery.[127] By 1884, gold exports were almost double those of gold imports, an exodus not seen since the depths of the 1873–1878 recession.[128] Meanwhile, silver purchases and silver prices mounted, as forces agitated anew for legislation to legalize silver for use in all private and public transactions. "The silver men are insatiable," complained the *New York Times* in early 1883. "They are not content with opposing any suspension of the coinage of silver, but are bent upon forcing in circulation the [silver] dollars already accumulated."[129] Congress began to openly debate new laws in favor of silver, as concerns grew over the Treasury's stocks of monetary gold. By early 1884, the press was reporting, "The question as to whether the Government will be compelled to pay its Clearinghouse balances in silver, instead of gold, is now a live topic of conversation among bankers."[130] Hence foreign investors feared that the United States would leave the gold standard and began to pull their gold out of the American economy.[131]

Arthur said nothing to ameliorate their concerns. In fact, throughout the depression, he restricted his commitment to the gold standard to brief and mildly favorable comments in three of his four State of the Union messages. Nor did he see any role for himself in addressing the growing economic disaster. He took no substantive actions. He issued little more than occasional, bland statements. He organized no conferences or special commissions to study the problem.[132] He made no attempts to soothe an increasingly distressed public or to reassure investors.

The conditions were ripe for a financial crisis, which finally erupted in early May 1884.[133] The trigger was the sudden and spectacular bankruptcy of Grant & Ward, a prominent brokerage house run by the son of Ulysses S. Grant. Unbeknownst to the ex-president, or his son, its success had been built on a Ponzi scheme, with new investments and loans being used to pay off the old.[134] When fresh investors dried up and its stock speculations failed, Grant & Ward collapsed. The larger problem was that the firm owed $14.5 million (perhaps $26 billion in 2020 dollars) to its creditors, including the illustrious Marine National Bank, now ruined.[135] A week later, the Second National Bank of New York was bankrupted by a similar fraud. These were quickly followed by two more bank failures and the liquidation of seven investment houses. A vicious spiral ensued with panicked selling on Wall Street, bank runs, and contagion that threatened to spread throughout the financial system. Only action by the New York Clearing House (NYCH), a private association of sixty major regional banks, saved the day.[136] The NYCH lent out $25 million in emergency funding to systematically important banks in the city, and thereby "likely short-circuited a full-scale banking panic."[137] Nevertheless, eleven national banks in New York City failed, along with a hundred state banks.

Striking at the financial center of the nation, the 1884 banking crisis in New York reverberated throughout the country. Business loans plummeted nationwide, pushing bankruptcies to record highs, totaling some $226 million (around $419 billion in 2020 dollars) in liabilities.[138] Hence, the entire US economy sagged into 1885, possibly an overall contraction of 5.5 percent since 1881, with unemployment peaking as high as 13 percent.[139] "[D]estitution was never more prevalent," reported a Michigan state government study, while broader surveys showed that factory wages declined 20 to 30 percent nationwide, as strike activity escalated.[140] Throughout the remainder of the year, the *New York Times* continued to report, "Business is dull," "Work is irregular," "Wages have been largely reduced," and "Capital is timid."[141]

By now, even the Republican Party had abandoned Arthur. Frustrated by his lack of leadership and repeated failures, some had already dismissed him as a lame duck the previous year. Meanwhile, his apathy amid the economic disaster allowed leading Democrats to blame the Arthur administration, warning Americans, "The Republican party offer no remedy for the policy which has produced the existing paralysis of industry."[142] Perhaps his only strong supporters for reelection were those business leaders who wanted a quiet, passive executive, such as he, to stay out of their way.

For his part, Arthur wanted little to do with the 1884 presidential election, and largely neglected it. He allowed his name to be floated for a second term in order to save face and to reduce suspicions about his failing health. But he was rejected for the Republican Party nomination in favor of a more powerful machine boss, Senator James G. Blaine (R-ME). Thus, the shrewd New York spoilsman, who had practically won the presidency for the Republican Party in 1881, watched from the sidelines as a Democrat took the White House for the first time in almost thirty years.

By the time Arthur left office in March 1885, the economy was in shambles. Real GDP per capita and industrial production were both down 6 to 7 percent from 1881. The stock market had fallen by 25 to 30 percent overall. Each of these metrics sat at or near their nadirs for his presidency. Deflation plagued the cities, with consumer prices falling 5 to 6 percent. Wholesale prices were also down dramatically: for steel rails (50–55 percent), wheat (40 percent), sugar (40 percent), copper (23–40 percent), wool (16–26 percent), and even inelastic coal (3–9 percent). Business failures climbed precipitously, doubling between 1881 and 1884. Labor unrest also skyrocketed, the number of strikes increasing by 45 percent between 1881 and 1885, and double the number of workers participating in them. Inequality had worsened.[143] The trade surplus shrank during 1881–1884 as imports rose around 17 percent, while exports fell around 5 percent.[144] Thanks to decreased revenues and moderate tax cuts, even the once reliable budget surplus came down, having peaked in 1883 and then fallen 22 percent by the year Arthur left office. The economic situation was so bad that America even lost its luster for foreign migrants. After hitting a record of 816,000 in 1882, immigration fell into decline, dropping by 46 percent by 1885, while alien departures surged 240 percent, reaching highs not yet seen in the postbellum era. Perhaps the only silver lining was that, thanks to Arthur's failure to ease either monetary policy or debt reduction, the dollar maintained its value against the British pound, while the public debt fell by over 20 percent.[145]

Arthur was glad to exit the presidency when it was over. Toward the end of his administration, and ever since, observers conceded that he was a far more trustworthy president than originally feared. "No [formal] duty was neglected in his administration, and no adventurous project alarmed the nation," observed the *New York World*.[146] Nevertheless, soon after leaving office, Arthur burned all of his personal papers rather than leave them for journalists and historians to investigate. He made no grand speeches. He wrote no memoirs. He granted no substantive interviews. And he "sternly advised his son never to go into politics; the price demanded of him for his office had been far too high."[147] Years after he died, former colleague and rising Republican statesman Elihu Root said of Arthur, "Surely no more lonely and pathetic figure was ever seen assuming the powers of government. He had no people behind him. . . . He had no party behind him. . . . He had not even his own faction behind him. . . . He was alone."[148]

Summary

Chester Arthur's presidency is an insightful case of failure. Our task is to understand *why* he failed. Specifically, how much blame, if any, does the president deserve? Certainly Arthur did not cause the depression of 1881–1885 or the financial crisis of 1884. Indeed, he may not have been able to prevent, or even alleviate, either collapse. But we cannot know, because Arthur never tried. His failure was his entirely passive approach to presidential leadership. His major actions over his three and a half years in office consisted of a handful of formal statements and a few vetoes. Otherwise, he left policy matters to his cabinet and Congress, even in foreign affairs. Only rarely did he exercise executive power or even express policy preferences. He evaded controversial decisions. Other than to socialize, he avoided Washington, and even the White House itself, whenever possible. In practice, he was mostly a ceremonial leader who stood by as the US economy slid into turmoil.

Arthur's passivity might be due, at least partly, to his lack of vision for either the presidency or the country. He believed the president's job was to oversee and delegate government administration and to defend the Constitution. He saw little role for himself, or the federal government, in addressing the economic downturn. "Overall, he was more reactive than active," concluded one biographer. "[H]e didn't lead the charge."[149] In fact, Arthur shrank from the presidency. He remained a city machine boss with neither interest nor experience in national policy. And he lacked the flexibility to respond to changing circumstances. Despite his elite education, as president he demonstrated little capacity to learn, to adapt, or to change his worldview. Thus, as the US economy descended into catastrophe under his watch, Arthur stuck tight to his personal inclinations *not* to act.

Moreover, Arthur had neither competent nor reliable allies to call upon. Nor did he try to cultivate any. He appointed to his administration a mix of political rivals and personal cronies, often with few qualifications. He then allowed them to run their departments with little guidance or supervision from him. The results were generally stagnation and mismanagement. His attempts to balance patronage among the factions satisfied neither friends nor foes, hurting his relationship with his own Republican Party. And when they lost badly in the 1882 midterms, Republicans resented President Arthur all the more. Also, to the extent that presidential leverage over Congress is important (to provide focus, direction, coordination, and progress), Arthur attempted little of this. Hence, on many important economic issues, Congress either failed to act, acted contrary to Arthur's wishes, or produced muddled and ineffective legislation. To the public, he was a cipher. He spurned the press. He refused to mingle with everyday Americans. He saw no reason to explain himself or his agenda, or lack thereof. In the end, only the country's industrialists and business interests loved him, but only because Arthur stayed in his place. Thus, even if Arthur had embraced presidential activism and had a vision of how to respond to the depression, it is not clear that he had the political allies or public support with which to get much done.

It did not help that Arthur was perhaps the least trusted president on record. His entire political career was steeped in backroom deals and machine politics, and his behavior as president did little to improve this perception. He occasionally spoke bold words about reform but otherwise seemed intent on perpetuating the rot and corruption that he had brought with him into office. On other issues, he could not be relied upon in a political fight, for he only rarely took strong stands, and then backed down or reversed himself when challenged. His inactivity, lack of a clear agenda, poor management skills, failure to communicate, and frequent bungling did not inspire confidence.

This distrust in Arthur may have bled out to damage public trust in broader political-economic institutions. Perhaps most important, by refusing to emphatically defend the gold standard, Arthur arguably damaged trust in the dollar, so recently hard won by the Hayes administration. On the other hand, by refusing to ease monetary policy, Arthur also failed to provide the stimulus that might have defused the financial crisis and reflated the economy. In other words, Arthur produced the worst of both worlds: the appearance of weakness on monetary policy abetted the flight of gold from the US economy (and hence a contraction in the money supply), but without the benefits of actual monetary easing, which might have provided significant economic relief.

In sum, Arthur was perhaps one of the weakest, least effective presidents in American history. His behavior as president, alongside the ailing economy, embarrassed the Republican Party and damaged trust in the presidency. Most congressmen and even many in the executive branch simply ignored him. The American public held him in low regard. Therefore, Arthur had limited ability to advance or stop legislation, respond to crises or opportunities, or even simply to administer his own government. Without that trust, there was no general sense that the president, or the federal government, was in control of the situation. Nor could Arthur be relied upon to provide solutions to economic problems or crises. We cannot "turn back the clock" and rerun the 1881–1885 depression with a more visionary, proactive, relationship-savvy, or trustworthy president and see if such changes made a difference. So any "conclusions" would more properly be labeled "hypotheses." To substantiate them further, we need to see if they are corroborated by similar administrations in other time periods.

* * *

With the benefit of hindsight, 1885 seems to mark a midway point of Gilded Age political-economic development. In many ways, the exit of Chester Arthur heralded a new phase. No longer were greenback convertibility, tax policy, or trade deficits major issues in American politics. Likewise, the Civil War and Reconstruction had by now lost their greatest spokesmen. Grant himself would expire that summer, joining a growing registry of dead Union and Confederate leaders. With them gone, the divisive conflicts over union and civil rights faded into the background of American politics. Henceforth, they might be invoked ceremoniously for election campaigns, but they were largely ignored in policy debates.

The second half of the Gilded Age had other fish to fry. For example, recent increases in silver production and the advent of industrial agriculture created a new threat to American financial stability: demand for bimetallism (and the potential inflation it implied). The railroads had ended their long entrepreneurial phase and now menaced as monopolistic behemoths. Soon industrial corporations and banks would join them to amass considerable political-economic influence. Thus, protectionism, monopoly power, and labor unrest would become central battlegrounds. In politics, the presidency had reached its 19th-century nadir by early 1885; political machines, state governments, and Congress seemed to rule the land. But Garfield's murder and Arthur's failed administration had finally shifted the battle over the civil service from spoilsmen to reformers. The end or decline of moieties, patronage, and assessments, the evolution of an independent press, and the "democratization" of Republican primaries further opened the way for a new kind of president. The question was: Should the presidency return to its traditional antebellum mores, or should it energetically lead a more interventionist and modern federal government? And if the latter, then how, exactly? These would be the challenges facing Cleveland, Harrison, and McKinley.

9

Grover Cleveland

Strict Constitutionalism and the Challenge of Recession, 1885–1889

The two administrations of Grover Cleveland (1885–1889, 1893–1897) were bookended around the one-term presidency of Benjamin Harrison (1889–1893). Together they provide us with a valuable anomaly: a natural experiment. That is, these two presidents faced nearly identical political-economic conditions, but with differing economic outcomes. In particular, both men repeatedly flirted with economic disaster, especially currency crises. Sometimes they met with success, other times with failure. And each president, in his own way, contributed to the Great Depression of 1893–1897. We can therefore compare differences in the men, their ideas and actions, and their leadership styles to look for insights into the sources of effective management of the economy. Both presidents come out poorly in this analysis, but for very different reasons. This chapter will focus on Cleveland's first term in office.

Grover Cleveland was a sternly ethical but inexperienced and poorly educated politician who entered office during the apex of the corrupt spoils system and on the tail of the smoldering depression of 1881–1885. Biographers and contemporaries alike have described him as "without genius or brilliancy" but painfully honest, straightforward, and stubbornly juridical.[1] He tended to distrust people and put his faith instead in the law. Critics thought him a political "dwarf" who lacked "the mental qualifications" for office.[2] Conservatives and pro-business interests applauded his "small government" laissez-faire doctrine. White Southerners were relieved merely to have a fellow Democrat in office.

Cleveland saw little role for presidents, or governments, in managing the economy. Before entering office, he took extraordinary actions to ward off a brewing dollar panic. Thereafter he preferred to mostly just cheer or harangue from the sidelines. Many Americans, including Cleveland himself, blamed government corruption for the nation's economic problems, which by now included recurring financial crises, economic recessions, labor strikes, monopoly abuses, and unnecessary trade protectionism. Each of these evils seemed to flow from the spoils system. Hence, Cleveland's solution, his "North Star," was to hark back to pre–Civil War democratic ideals. This meant an honest and limited federal government, run with business efficiency and strictly according to the Constitution.

Presidential Leadership in Feeble Times. Mark Zachary Taylor, Oxford University Press. © Oxford University Press 2024. DOI: 10.1093/oso/9780197750742.003.0011

And if government must act, then the intervention should be objective, non-partisan, and minimal. Hence, Cleveland's numerous vetoes were perhaps his most assertive use of executive power. He used them to strike down hundreds of spending bills that benefited individuals or special interests. But Cleveland's inflexible attachment to minimal government, and to a restrained presidency, rendered him incapable of actions that might have better grown the economy and prevented the crises that would ruin his second term.

As a whole, the 1880s were rocky years and, during his first term (1885–1889), the strictly constitutional Cleveland oversaw a merely average economy. It grew in some months and years, but not in others. Prices rose and fell in tandem with economic growth, but never approached harmful inflation. In fact, the country was plagued by persistent deflation, which meant that real interest rates remained stubbornly high. Steep interest rates were exacerbated by unreliable gold reserves, resulting in tighter than expected supplies of money and credit. And money "stringency" increased political support for the full legalization of less-valuable silver as US currency. Hence concerns about the strength of the US dollar remained a constant menace to investors, especially when Congress proposed that cheap silver be coined freely on demand. A year-long recession struck in the middle of Cleveland's first administration, mostly due to a wave of blizzards and droughts that devastated the Great Plains and paralyzed the eastern seaboard. But by spring 1888, a rapid recovery was underway. The stock market was highly volatile throughout the period. It skyrocketed a few months after Cleveland took office, but then gyrated wildly downward throughout the remainder of his first term. International trade grew at a healthy clip every year, but the trade balance collapsed as imports overran exports. Hence trade and tariffs were major campaign issues come 1888. Nevertheless, the federal debt shrank dramatically and the federal budget remained in surplus during Cleveland's first term. When all these conflicting elements are combined over four years, they sum to a relatively mediocre economy. Although individual circumstances were newsworthy, the second half of the 1880s was neither a period of overall economic decline nor one of well-balanced prosperity.

Background

Throughout his life, Cleveland was known for two things: hard work and rigid conservatism. Nicknamed "Big Steve" for his unusual height and girth, Stephen Grover Cleveland was born in 1837 to an impoverished, disciplinarian Presbyterian minister. His large family moved frequently around New Jersey and central New York in constant pursuit of a devoted flock and good-paying work. Nevertheless, Grover would always recall his childhood as idyllic.[3] As a boy, he aspired to go to college like his father, grandfather, and brothers. But after his father's unexpected death, poor family finances prohibited it.[4] Grover instead attended local academies, supplemented by homeschooling. Hence, he was among the presidents *least* educated in economics or public policy.[5] Nor was he especially brilliant. Even his sister admitted that he was "a lad of unusual good sense, who did not yield to impulses . . . but as a student Grover did not shine."[6] Throughout his political career, Cleveland was often perceived as being ignorant or simple.

Instead of intellect, Cleveland gained success through his persistence and diligent work habits. As a teenager, he worked as a store clerk, a bookkeeper, and a teacher at an asylum for the blind. Due to his lack of college training, he never gave up on self-education as a means for advancement. "Every moment of his spare time was given to the hardest kind of study," recalled a fellow teacher.[7] Yet he initially had little direction. "I am kind of fooling away my time," he confessed to his sister.[8] So, in 1855, he started off for Ohio to train to be a lawyer. He was waylaid in Buffalo, New York, by a wealthy uncle who got Cleveland hired as a clerk at a prominent local law firm. Cleveland worked long hours at the firm, studied intensely, and was admitted to the New York Bar in 1859. Three years later he had established his own law practice and was the chief provider for his mother and sisters. He continued his long office hours and assiduous study of the law, quickly becoming known for being an attorney "[of] patient industry and of downright—and always upright—hard work."[9]

When the Civil War came, Cleveland largely ignored it.[10] He took no strong stands on slavery. He spoke and wrote little about the crisis. He did not enlist to fight, and when drafted, he instead hired a legal substitute to serve in his place. He appears to have quietly backed the Union. According to friends, he admired "the genuineness of Lincoln's devotion to the country."[11] He even supported the administration's suspension of *habeas corpus*, declaring, "It seems to me that the government has a right in time of war to resort to every possible method in order to protect itself."[12] But, unlike the other Gilded Age presidents, he mostly chose not to engage in the politics of the war nor in the Reconstruction that followed.

Buffalo was then controlled by the new Republican Party, whose members included many of Cleveland's family, but he was surrounded by Democrats at work. The earnestly serious Cleveland found the Democratic Party "represent[ed] greater solidity and conservatism," and he felt "repelled" by the "flamboyant and theatrical" leading Republican candidates.[13] Therefore, the businesslike new attorney naturally gravitated toward the Democrats. In local elections, Cleveland volunteered to get men "lined up" to vote for his party. To that end, he served as a ward delegate and then a ward supervisor.[14] For his efforts, in 1863 he was appointed assistant district attorney of Erie County for two years. Once again, he was recognized for his professionalism, hard work, and an almost surgical attention to legal detail. In 1865, Cleveland was nominated by local Democrats to run for district attorney, but he was beaten in the election by a Republican.

After his electoral defeat, Cleveland returned to private practice, while continuing to hustle for local Democrats. With his growing reputation for seriousness, honesty, and effort, Cleveland was drafted in 1870 to run for Erie County sheriff, a position usually reserved for party hacks. This was an odd assignment for Cleveland. After all, he was a bachelor who enjoyed saloons, card games, and even occasional barroom fisticuffs.[15] Nevertheless, after winning election, he performed his sheriff's duties without compromise. He returned to private practice in early 1874 and methodically built his fortune over the next seven years, often working for large corporate clients. Yet again, Cleveland's integrity and industry attracted the attention of local powerbrokers in the press and politics. In 1881, when city Democrats needed a clean candidate to battle the notoriously corrupt bipartisan political ring that ran Buffalo city government, they recruited Cleveland to run for mayor. He campaigned little, relying mostly on his exceptional reputation, and he won by a landslide, even receiving support from reformist Republicans willing to cross party lines.

As mayor of Buffalo, Cleveland fought successfully against the party machines and ran an energetic, honest, and efficient city government. He shut down so much dubious legislation that he became known as "the veto mayor."[16] And rather than award lucrative city contracts to Buffalo's political bosses, Mayor Cleveland insisted on competitive bids, which were then evaluated by an independent commission of policymakers and engineers. He personally oversaw city construction projects so as to eliminate patronage, kickbacks, and bribes. Cleveland even nixed the honest shuffling of money from one holiday fund to another because he feared it might violate the public's intention.[17] Such rectitude and political independence was big news in Gilded Age New York State, which was then infamous for the Tammany Hall political machine, run by Democrats, and the corrupt politics it embodied.[18] And it won Cleveland much attention. His reforms in Buffalo sparked "nothing short of a popular revolt," recalled a former political rival. "I cannot remember a time when interest in any municipal matter[s] reached such a height."[19]

Hence, after just eleven months as Buffalo's mayor, Cleveland was recruited to run for governor of New York by reformers and a public eager for clean government. Again, he won by a landslide. His electoral coattails also brought rare Democratic majorities into both houses of the state legislature. Once in the governor's office in 1883, Cleveland again fought corruption, defied the political machines, and ran an energetic, honest, and efficient state government.[20] In just his first two months, he vetoed eight extraneous budget bills, even well-intentioned spending on veterans' monuments, library tax breaks, and money for new fire engines. In denying such government largesse, Cleveland predicted,

"I shall be the most unpopular man in the state of New York."[21] Yet many of the major newspapers, and the public, applauded him. He continued to reject his party's patronage requests, infuriating many Democrats. "Tammany was not guaranteed a single one—not so much as a night watchman at Castle Garden," groused one spoilsmen.[22] Cleveland also sought to be a nonpartisan "unifier." For example, he supported a powerful civil service reform law put forward by a young Republican legislator, Teddy Roosevelt.

Election of 1884

The cycle now repeated itself at the national level. Cleveland, the honest, efficient governor who was cleaning up New York State politics, swiftly became national news. *The Nation* praised "the well-known and respected features of the present Governor of New York," while *Puck's* political cartoonist portrayed Cleveland as enfeebling the Tammany tiger.[23] Anti-monopolists were not pleased with Cleveland's laissez-faire philosophy, however, and considered him a tool of the corporations. Nevertheless, after only eighteen months as governor, the Democrats nominated Cleveland as their presidential candidate in 1884.[24] He had proved himself in battles against the city and state bosses; reformers now wanted him to clean up Washington, DC. "They love Cleveland for his character, but they love him also for the enemies he has made," proclaimed one supporter.[25]

Cleveland's opponent, Senator James G. Blaine (R-ME), was a moderate Republican faction leader who had stridden the national political stage since the late 1860s.[26] He was far more knowledgeable than Cleveland on the major economic issues. In fact, Blaine was instrumental in leading the Republican Party away from Reconstruction issues and toward an emphasis on trade. Defying tradition, he also launched an extensive campaign tour during which he spoke almost entirely on economic questions. But after two decades in politics, Blaine now stood "accused of every roguery from shaking down a railroad to guano speculations" and had accumulated a reputation for being "a man who has prostituted public office to private gain and lied about it."[27]

The two parties' platforms were nearly indistinguishable in 1884, and neither side emphasized policy differences in their campaigns. Both called for lower tariffs, worker protections, and new limits on Chinese immigration.[28] Republicans wanted to strengthen railroad regulation. Democrats advanced a foreign policy based on a new Pan-Americanism. For the first time in twenty years, race, Reconstruction, and the Civil War were barely mentioned.[29] Rather, widespread concern with "frauds and jobbery . . . in every department of the Government" was the top issue for both spoilsmen and reformers.[30] This meant that trust, integrity, and "manliness" in battle against the political machines became top priorities for voters. Hence, the campaign rapidly descended into a series of well-orchestrated personal attacks and scandalmongering in what has been stereotyped as "the meanest and most meaningless campaign of the Gilded Age."[31] Accusations of fraud, embezzlement, adultery, bastardy, drunkenness, religious impiety, and domestic violence were regularly plastered across the nation's newspapers.

The 1884 election results were narrow and divided. Although reform appealed to some voters, many Republicans still savored power and patronage; even more feared government by Democrats, in whom they saw "the worst elements of [the] population," and Cleveland, in whom they saw an uneducated "rural sheriff."[32] In the North and Midwest, the Prohibition Party and Greenback Party each made relatively strong showings, together garnering between 3 and 11 percent of the popular vote in each of over a dozen states.[33] As a result, Cleveland won by a tiny margin, just 57,000 votes out of 10 million cast. In fact, with just under 49 percent of the popular vote, he was a minority victor. Congressional elections too were closely split. Despite losing a dozen seats, Democrats held on to 56 percent of the House, while Republicans kept their slim 52 percent majority in the Senate. Nevertheless, after enduring the "stolen election" of 1876 and the failings of Republican Chester Arthur's indifferent presidency (1881–1885), Democrats and reformers felt they finally had their man in the White House.

The Constitutional Conservative

Cleveland was neither a deep thinker nor a theorist. He had few original ideas. He was not a policy devotee. As a presidential candidate, he freely admitted that "he had not studied national questions deeply."[34] A reporter called him "curiously ignorant of federal questions and politics."[35] Even on his signature issue, civil service reform, historians report that often "his role was more passive than active; he did little to push reform measures. He simply let the public know that he favored reform and stood out of their way."[36] And having risen through the ranks of executive power in just two years, he entered the White House with few policy prescriptions and without a comprehensive program for the country.

He largely blamed the nation's economic troubles on corruption and irresponsibility.[37] Politics had fallen into "fraudulent and corrupt practices" resulting in "wasteful public extravagance," which, he thought, were the ultimate causes of the nation's economic troubles.[38] Specifically, he believed that the spoils system and government mismanagement fostered financial speculation and overinvestment in politically favored sectors. Everyday Americans then imitated government with their own foolish excesses because, Cleveland argued, "public extravagance begets extravagance among the people."[39] He also maintained that corruption and partisanship in federal spending eroded trust in the US economy, in the federal government's ability to pay its debts, and hence in the entire US financial system. Thus, he likely perceived the 1881–1885 depression as a form of mass economic judgment, akin to a financial vote of no-confidence on corrupt, inefficient government. America had gone off its constitutional rails. So, in order to mend the economy, Cleveland believed that American politics must get back on its traditional and legal tracks.

As a consequence, Cleveland possessed a near religious devotion to two beliefs about executive leadership. The first was that he should provide a government that was strictly constitutional. It must be fair and objective, above party or faction, and immune to pleas for special favors or subsidies. From his earliest political speeches to his final addresses, he held that "public office is a public trust."[40] More specifically, he insisted that "[p]ublic officers are the servants and agents of the people, [elected] to execute laws which the people have made, and within the limits of a constitution which they have established."[41] This meant strict limits on party loyalty. "Party men we *may* all well be," he wrote later in life, "but only with the reservation that thoughtful and patriotic citizens we *must* be."[42]

His second fundamental tenet was that government should be small and efficient and run more like a business. Spending should not exceed revenues. Contracts and hiring should be based on ability and fit, not on political alliances. And "all unnecessary offices should be abolished, and all employment of doubtful benefit discontinued."[43] For Cleveland believed that "the application of business principles to public affairs" would rebuild investor trust and reduce waste.[44] A small, businesslike government was also a government that could do less harm to the people and to democracy itself. Fewer actions taken by government officials meant fewer actions that could be corrupted or wasted.

Thus Cleveland tended to oppose any government expenditure, even benevolent, that was not approved by the voters and in accordance with the Constitution. To Cleveland, every spending bill stank of favors to some political machine, special interest, or individual. He particularly opposed most forms of government welfare. He insisted that public assistance "would necessarily produce more unfairness and unjust discrimination and give more scope for partisan partiality, and would result in more perversion of the Government's benevolent intentions."[45] Such convictions would forever taint him with a reputation of "indifference to human suffering and poverty."[46] Because, other than federal pensions for war veterans and their dependents, the Gilded Age had no social safety net for the elderly, sick, poor, or unemployed. The boss system, albeit inefficient and corrupt, did provide a rough form of welfare to lower-income Americans, especially recent immigrants piling into the nation's cities. And for all Cleveland's principled objections to that system, he proposed no alternatives other than private charity.

As for his administration, Cleveland sought a passive, strictly constitutional presidency. He constantly reminded Americans, "It should be remembered that the office of the President is essentially executive in its nature. The laws enacted by the legislative branch of the government, the Chief Executive is bound faithfully to enforce."[47] Policymaking would be left to legislators. The executive's job was to prevent them from making unconstitutional mistakes. If the people did not like the nation's laws or policies, then they could vote for representatives to change them. In practice, Cleveland often governed like a lawyer; he was a "stickler for legalism and the rights of property," notes one historian of the period.[48]

But in doing so, Cleveland committed himself, and the country, to a political-legal system not yet equipped to govern the powerful, often vicious forces of late 19th-century industrial capitalism.[49] For decades, railroad corporations had used anticompetitive practices to exploit farmers and small businesses.[50] "These vast and powerful corporations have inaugurated a series of abuses . . . debauched and demoralized our Courts and Legislatures . . . robbed the nation . . . flooded the land with worthless stocks . . . trampled upon individual and public rights and liberties," howled critics.[51] Now, during the mid–1880s, similarly harmful monopolies were forming in steel, copper, coal, iron, flour, sugar, telephones, and other essential industries.[52] And as business gradually displaced small agriculture, a new class of impoverished industrial labor had arisen. Hundreds of thousands of transportation, manufacturing, and mine workers now toiled long hours for subsistence wages under brutal conditions. An industrial aristocracy seemed to be forming. Yet the original US Constitution provided little recourse. It had been written for an agricultural economy of small farms and was not designed to deal with such challenges.[53]

Cleveland was also infamously rigid in his views. His lack of trust in people, with their implacable greed and self-seeking behavior, constantly led him back to the law. Historians describe him as "bull-headed"[54] and "stubborn,"[55] and even contemporary admirers called him "inflexible."[56] His critics were even less diplomatic. For example, future Republican statesman John Hay named his most ornery mule Grover Cleveland,[57] while the acerbic editor of the Texas *Iconoclast* opined, "Cleveland is a 'strong man' exactly as the hog is a strong animal. Stubborn without courage, persevering without judgment. . . . There are several other points of resemblance; but I have no desire to be hard on the hog."[58] Supporters cheered Cleveland's steadfast loyalty to his, and their, ideals. But in practical terms, such inflexibility meant that the obstinate Cleveland had trouble adapting his philosophical worldview in order to take advantage of real opportunities or avoid economic crises.

The Smoldering Depression of 1881–1885

Cleveland's election came amid the trough of the smoldering depression of 1881–1885.[59] It had started as a typical business slowdown during autumn 1881, but it was accelerated by a boom in European agriculture in 1882. As global exports of meat and grains glutted the world food supply, farm prices and incomes tumbled in America. So too fell the profits of suppliers, railroads, and the banks that catered to agriculture. The following year, mounting bankruptcies in these sectors began to injure the nation's broader loan and credit institutions. Then, in mid–1884, these conditions combined with a series of well-publicized bank failures and financial frauds in New York City, resulting in a panic on Wall Street. The entire US economy then sagged through early 1885, an overall contraction of possibly 25 percent, with nationwide unemployment running as high as 13 percent.[60]

As for Cleveland, he saw no use for intellectual theories and no duty for presidents to mend economic downturns. He never mentioned the depression during his election campaign, nor after he was inaugurated. Time and anticorruption reforms were the best remedies. Cleveland believed that corrective action by the federal government not only was unconstitutional but would just encourage more bad behavior. Rather, the surest antidote was clean, restrained, constitutional government.

1885: Silver vs. Gold

Nevertheless, Cleveland did worry about the US dollar and America's creditworthiness. Hence his first action to safeguard the economy involved the perennial contest between silver and gold. And he took it before even entering the White House.

A brief recap of history is useful here. Since the mid-1870s, Americans had waged an ongoing political battle between those who sought to join the international gold standard (often eastern financial interests, shippers, and importers) and pro-silver interests (small businesses and farmers in need of credit, western miners). The official dollar values of gold and silver coins had been set by federal law back in 1792 and were revised only occasionally, if at all.[61] Hence the free-market price of *uncoined* metal "bullion" might differ from that of *coined* specie. The wartime printing of paper greenbacks, along with vast oversupplies of domestic silver, caused silver to lose over half its value relative to gold on American markets. Meanwhile, Great Britain, Germany, and other major economic powers were gradually adopting the gold standard, making gold coins and bars the preferred currency for international trade and finance. Hence silver coins had largely fallen out of use in the United States.

In an attempt to eliminate silver coins entirely, and to hasten the United States toward adopting the gold standard, pro-gold advocates in Congress passed the 1873 Coinage Act to demonetize silver. It ended the US Mint's practice of coining silver upon demand, and it eliminated silver coins as legal tender for transactions over $5. Henceforth, silver coins could be used in private transactions, but the federal government might not accept them. The bill aroused little opposition at the time. Gold supporters cheered the Act; few others cared. But the successful exploitation of silver deposits in Nevada, Colorado, Idaho, and Montana during the 1870s changed the political calculus. Soon the United States was producing half the world's silver, but there was little demand for it at home. Meanwhile, the rapid paydown of federal war debts by Presidents Grant and Hayes, combined with the Panic of 1873, drastically reduced the supply of money and credit available in the United States. Therefore, in 1878 Congress had passed the Bland-Allison Act over the veto of President Hayes. It restored silver coins as full legal tender and *required* the Treasury to accept between $2 million and $4 million worth of silver bullion for coinage annually. This would increase domestic demand for silver, while simultaneously improving supplies of money and credit. But since silver bullion, by weight, was now worth only around 80 percent of gold, many feared Bland-Allison's effects on US creditworthiness.[62] "Will any bank, can any bank, receive from depositors silver worth eighty cents to the dollar, and pay out in gold on depositors' checks worth one hundred cents to the dollar?" fretted *The Nation* in 1884.[63] Creditors owed gold would flee the United States in fear of being paid in cheap silver. A financial panic would ensue. Trade and investment contracts with gold-standard countries would also become more difficult. The administrations of Hayes, Garfield, and Arthur had therefore kept silver coinage to its legal minimum, and no currency crisis occurred.[64]

The smoldering depression of 1881–1885 and the banking panics of 1884 threatened to wreck the situation. As the economy slowed, Americans began to use silver or paper greenbacks to pay their debts and taxes; meanwhile America's foreign creditors demanded payment in gold. With silver and paper money going into the US Treasury, and gold bleeding out, the federal government was on track to drop dangerously below the $100 million threshold in gold reserves recently legislated by Congress.[65] There was also an element of market psychology to maintaining $100 million in gold reserves, for this amount had been the basis upon which the Hayes administration had begun resumption of gold-greenback parity back in 1879. Hence many investors saw it as a symbolic "line in the sand" that the Treasury dare not fall below. By early 1885, the amount of gold held by the US Treasury had already shrunk by a third and showed no signs of slowing its descent toward that line.

America's ability to fully pay its debts now came into question.[66] US banks began stockpiling gold in expectation of a crisis. Cleveland's election provided no relief. Whether it was fears of the first Democratic administration in decades or trepidation about the nation's dwindling gold supplies, the stock market tumbled for weeks starting in mid-November 1885. Chester Arthur, still president, showed little inclination to intercede; he was by now an ineffective and disengaged lame duck.

Frightened policymakers instead reached out to the newly elected Grover Cleveland for action. A month before his inauguration, Cleveland received an urgent message from a senior congressman: "The stock of gold in the Treasury is being exhausted and cannot be replenished. . . . [A]lready the banks and trust companies are hoarding."[67] Cleveland, acting as a private citizen, signed a rare private letter to Congress warning, "It is of momentous importance . . . to prevent the increasing displacement of gold by the increasing coinage of silver." He cautioned that our danger, and our duty to avert that danger, would seem plain." He urgently recommended "a present suspension of the purchase and coinage of silver."[68] Congress overwhelmingly rejected his suggestions. Cleveland then allowed his letter to be published in the nation's leading newspapers. In an age when even sitting presidents left policy to Congress, such a strongly worded public statement from an incoming executive was striking. Critics called it a "fundamental blunder" and "flunkeyish."[69] But such an unusual declaration by the president-elect had the effect of calming financial markets for the few weeks until Cleveland's administration began.

Immediately upon entering office, President Cleveland and his secretary of the Treasury took action to defend the dollar. They suspended the previous administration's accelerated bond redemptions; this reduced the outflows of gold and allowed incoming federal revenues to pile up. Also, wherever possible, Cleveland ordered the federal government to pay out in paper greenbacks rather than in gold or silver.[70] The economic recovery, begun around May 1885, further aided inflows of specie. As a result, by early 1886 the Treasury vaults were flush with gold. The currency crisis of winter 1884–1885 was averted and soon forgotten.

But then Cleveland mostly halted his assault on silver. His negative view of government overrode his desire to take further action. He had the allies necessary, and the public sufficiently educated, to lead a repeal of pro-silver legislation passed over Hayes's veto seven years prior.[71] Cleveland might even have created an omnibus bill combining monetary reforms with tariff reductions. After all, he had the support of party members who urged precisely such action, and major newspapers predicting it to the public. One congressman observed, "[H]e had the game in his own hands. The opposition to his policy was melting away like snow in a thaw."[72] Instead, Cleveland now insisted, "[T]he most important benefit that I can confer on the country by my Presidency is to insist upon the entire independence of the Executive and legislative branches of the government"; the silver issue "was a subject which had now passed beyond his control or direction."[73] Further action by himself would tread unconstitutionally upon congressional ground. In his December 1885 annual message, he therefore strictly limited the advocacy and pressure he applied to Congress to mere policy recommendations So the issue died.[74] This refusal to act more forcefully during 1885–1886 would haunt him during his second term, when pro-silver legislation would trigger a major recession.

Reform

Instead of managing currency policy, Cleveland threw himself into rooting out corruption and waste in government, for those are what he believed to be the *true* sources of the economic recession. "Our citizens have the right to protection from the incompetency of public employees who hold their places solely as the reward of partisan service," he declared in his inaugural address.[75] Such a pledge was considerable. The federal government had grown to over 134,000 civilian employees, only 16,000 of whom were in the new "classified" civil service jobs mandated by the 1883 Pendleton Civil Service reforms. These "classified" workers had to earn their positions through civil service exams. Most of the remainder were to be appointed by the new president. Reformers were concerned that Democrats, eager to plunder federal spoils for themselves, would ignore the recent Pendleton reforms, kicking off a new cycle of corruption. Months before his inauguration, Cleveland soothed these fears. In a widely reprinted letter to the National Civil Reform League, he promised, "[P]ractical reform in the civil service is demanded. . . . I regard myself as pledged to this."[76] Even privately, Cleveland declared to colleagues, "Henceforth I must have no friends," signaling his intent to defy demands for patronage, even from political allies.[77]

He was mostly true to his word. For his cabinet, Cleveland selected few party bosses or spoilsmen.[78] He instead assembled a team that was geographically diverse but unified in their relative competence, discretion, integrity, and dedication to Cleveland's vision. There were no dynamic innovators or great leaders among them, just honest and hard-working civil servants. His cabinet was heavily drawn from conservative, pro-business communities rather than from agriculture or labor. "It is distinctively representative of the interests of the Eastern half of the country," complained the *Chicago Tribune*.[79] Hence the administration had a general tilt toward laissez-faire government that, at least since the 1870s, favored big business. Cleveland's management style was to rely upon his cabinet for advice and even to delegate considerable authority to them in their departments. But he always reserved final decisions for himself.[80]

In a bold reformist move during his first days in office, Cleveland directed his cabinet and their assistant secretaries to clean their departments of inefficiency and corruption. And, loyal to Cleveland's vision, his cabinet eagerly pursued the task. Entire departments were quickly reorganized to be run according to modern business practices rather than as sources of political favors. As early as August 1885, Pulitzer's *New York World* was proclaiming that Cleveland "has already in a little more than five months destroyed nests of corruption in the Navy Department, the Treasury, the Indian Bureau, the Land office, the Coast Survey, and the War Department."[81]

At first, the spoilsmen and political bosses revolted. After decades out of power, the Democrats now had their first president in twenty-five years; they wanted the same patronage that Republican presidents had doled out since 1861. But Cleveland stubbornly refused to promote or hire friends or political allies *carte blanche*. He even kept Republican appointees in place if they had performed well, and he gave no rewards to Democrats for mere political service or party loyalty. By summer, political observers were either celebrating or criticizing Cleveland's refusal to play the patronage game for his party. Some Democrats were furious; many feared loss of votes and supporters in the next elections. In order to prevent a schism within the Democratic Party, Cleveland began to compromise on patronage during autumn 1885, but usually only for low-level jobs in the postal service.[82]

An Unstable Economic Recovery: 1885–1886

The economy began to improve during late spring 1885. After the gold and banking crises had been resolved, and confidence restored, the depression essentially burned itself out. Inventories emptied and demand revived. After a tentative summer, industrial activity surged ahead strongly that autumn. The recovery then continued, with few interruptions, for a solid year. By March 1886, the new Bureau of Labor was reporting, "[T]he effects of the depression are wearing away, and all the indications are that prosperity is slowly, gradually, but safely returning."[83] Cleveland likely believed that the economy was responding positively to his administration's campaign to reduce waste and corruption in the federal government. For on economic policy, he had gone dormant. After his brief but energetic defense of the gold standard in early 1885, little issued forth from the White House on the economy for the remainder of the year.

Then, in early December 1885, Cleveland delivered a seventy-page Annual Message to Congress. It was the longest ever at the time, and it came packed with policy recommendations. Newspapers predicted fierce battles with Congress to enact them. Yet Cleveland assured friends, "I did not come here to legislate."[84] It was his constitutional duty to present an annual report to Congress, within which he might make suggestions. But those were his legal limits. He would lead no legislative fights. To the public he explained, "I . . . insist upon the entire independence of the executive and legislative branches. . . . I have certain executive duties to perform; when that is done my responsibility ends. . . . The Senators and members have their duties and responsibilities."[85] Strict constitutionalism was working; he would stick to a restrained presidency.

In fact, Cleveland's dogged insistence that, as president, he keep his constitutional distance from economic legislation emboldened his opponents. They launched new counterattacks on gold soon after Congress reconvened in early December 1885.[86] Angry Democrats damned Cleveland's adherence to the gold standard as "a repudiation of the policy of [the Democrats] and a complete acceptance of the financial policy of the Republican Party which had been overthrown in 1878."[87] Western states that produced silver still sought to increase demand for it. They were joined by farmers and small businessmen in perpetual want of increased silver supplies as a basis for badly needed credit and investment.[88] The *New York Herald* suggested that Cleveland might take this opportunity to resume the currency fight.[89] But Cleveland rejected the invitation. He announced that "[h]e had not the slightest wish or desire to influence in any way the consideration of congress beyond [his 1885 annual message]."[90] Gold supporters were appalled. Presidential silence would have served them far better.[91]

Pro-silver forces took Cleveland's restraint as encouragement. The leader of the Senate Democrats submitted a bill to formally place the United States on a bimetallic (silver and gold) standard.[92] To financial conservatives, it foretold disaster. Silver bullion was now legally priced in dollars at only 82 percent worth its weight in gold (i.e., undervalued) and was headed lower.[93] Under bimetallism, this discrepancy would naturally lead people to hoard gold and spend their silver, thereby driving gold out of circulation. American gold would eventually find its way overseas, where its full value would be recognized, placing the United States on a *de facto* silver standard. "[W]e shall gradually but surely be stripped of our gold and loaded down with the silver from other countries," warned the *New York Times*.[94] Problems in trade with and debts to countries on the gold standard would soon follow. The bimetallism bill was narrowly defeated in a bipartisan vote.

As silver advocates in Congress planned their next move, gold supporters implored Cleveland to act more decisively. Yet deep into summer 1886, Cleveland was still warning them, "I am not at all inclined to meddle with proposed legislation while it is pending in Congress."[95] Reassured by this, silverites in the House passed a bill designed to force the Treasury to resume accelerated bond buy-backs whenever federal gold reserves got too high.[96] Its declared intent was to pay down the national debt, reduce interest rates, and increase the availability of money and credit. But in practice, it would have forced the Treasury to spend down its gold stocks. It therefore represented an indirect, and poorly veiled, attempt to force the country onto cheap silver.[97] Cleveland merely expressed disapproval. Thus, the buy-back bill passed the House in mid-July 1886 by a large majority and with considerable Democratic support. A watered-down version then passed the Senate. Cleveland now warned that any version would "endanger and embarrass the successful and useful operation of the Treasury Department and impair the confidence which the people should have in the management of the finances of the government."[98] Nevertheless, rather than take a strong public stand, he let the bill expire quietly with a pocket veto.

With the threat of additional pro-silver legislation growing, Cleveland finally took action to defend the Treasury's holdings of gold. He ordered silver-backed certificates to be printed in small denominations (those used for most daily purchases), while gold-backed certificates were restricted to large denominations (so as to reduce demand for them). In a similar attempt to reduce the circulation of greenbacks, Cleveland began to substitute large denominations for small as they came into the Treasury. But that mostly exhausted the tools then available to the executive branch. If Cleveland wanted stronger remedies, he needed new legislation from Capitol Hill. Yet other than make occasional recommendations to Congress, Cleveland stubbornly refused to lead any battles there for the remainder of his first term in office.[99] To his mind, it was not presidential. Thus, he largely allowed pro-silver interests to fester. This would cause major problems for his successor, and worse for Cleveland during his second term.

Labor Unrest and the Haymarket Riots

Labor posed another economic problem for Cleveland. Although the depression of 1881–1885 was finally easing, its depth and duration had taken a deep toll on American workers. After years of declining wages and lengthening work hours, labor unrest peaked during 1886. Union membership temporarily soared that year to over 1.2 million, a record not surpassed until fifteen years later. "History is on the move over there at last," rejoiced Friedrich Engels in London.[100] Labor leaders had four primary demands: an eight-hour workday, steady wages, restrictions on immigrant labor, and an end to convict labor. And when they did not get them, the unions struck. In 1886, the number of strikes doubled from the previous year, involving over 600,000 workers. Operations were frequently shut down at the nation's mines, factories, and railroads. Violence erupted as strikers fought bloody street battles against law enforcement, vigilantes, and scabs. The frightened public lived in constant anxiety. The *New York Sun* warned its readers that union leaders "can at any moment take the means of livelihood from two and a half million souls . . . can shut up most of the mills and factories, and can disable the railroads."[101]

Like most executives during the Gilded Age, Cleveland was inconsistent on the emerging issues of corporate power and labor rights. In his speeches and public writings, he repeatedly scolded industrial monopolies and corporations for abuses of power. He warned that "when by combination, or by the exercise of unwarranted power, [corporations] oppress the people, the same authority which created [them] should restrain them and protect the rights of the citizen."[102] But as mayor, governor, and president, he neither took much action nor advanced much policy to do so. Likewise, he often spoke boldly about the rights of and protections for American workers. "The laboring classes constitute the main part of our population," he claimed repeatedly. "They should be protected in their efforts peaceably to assert their rights . . . and all statutes on this subject should recognize the care of the State for honest toil, and be framed with a view of improving the condition of the working man."[103] But again, he did little for labor while in office, seeing himself constrained by the Constitution and private contract rights.

His boldest action on labor as president took the form of a special labor message to Congress, the first of its kind in American history, sent in late April 1886.[104] But with his typical restraint, Cleveland asked Congress merely for "legislative care" that "[labor's] reasonable demands should be met in . . . a spirit of appreciation and fairness." In fact, Cleveland warned Congress that "any effort . . . by the Federal Government must be greatly limited by constitutional restrictions." His preferred solution was for Congress to create a permanent labor commission that could launch investigations into abuse and oversee corporate-labor negotiations. Congress, backed by industry in the North, mine owners out west, and plantation owners in the South, rejected this suggestion as too bold. It instead empowered Cleveland to appoint arbitration boards on an ad hoc emergency basis. Congress also passed legislation that set new immigration restrictions, granted an eight-hour workday to some federal postal employees, and limited prison labor. But none of these actions addressed the fundamental tensions driving labor-industry acrimony. Hence the conflicts, often violent, would continue.

Tensions boiled over in early May 1886 during labor protests in Chicago.[105] As part of a nationwide push to limit work hours, leaders of an anarchist labor association organized an evening rally in Haymarket Square. Its purpose was to protest deadly police violence and "to explain the general situation of the Eight-Hour [workday] Movement."[106] Toward the end of the Haymarket speeches, 175 policemen marched in to disperse the dwindling crowd. Suddenly, an unknown assailant hurled a bomb into the ranks of police, who began firing wildly. The workers fired back. Between the bomb and the melee that followed, eleven people were killed, while over fifty officers and an untold number of civilians were wounded. The event shocked the country. A "red scare" ensued, as the Illinois state attorney reportedly ordered his men, "Make the raids first and look up the law afterward!"[107] Suspected anarchists and Communists were rounded up indiscriminately. The criminal trials that followed became headline news, sparking a national debate over industrial capitalism and the rights of labor. Popular fears spread of "all forms of Socialism, Communism, Nihilism, and Anarchy . . . preaching their gospel of disaster."[108] Calls for action came from all quarters. But President Cleveland felt he had already done his constitutional duty and let the matter alone.

Cleveland took a similarly conservative approach toward immigrant labor. For example, he loudly denounced the brutal acts of racial violence against Chinese immigrants in the West committed by white men "engaged in competition with Chinese laborers."[109] But he took little action to protect them. Instead, seeing the Chinese as unassimilable, he encouraged new legislative restrictions on Chinese migrants and began negotiations with Peking to end Chinese migration altogether.[110] In contrast, Cleveland was much more welcoming toward European migrants. As long as they were healthy, willing to assimilate, and obeyed the law, he "encouraged those coming from foreign countries to cast their lot with us and join in the development of our vast domain."[111] Thus, when Congress passed a literacy requirement targeted at eastern and southern European immigrants, Cleveland vetoed it as "unnecessarily harsh and oppressive."[112]

The Interstate Commerce Act of 1887

The railroad monopolies had become a perennial headache for the American economy.[113] Their business practices seemed shady, if not outright exploitative. For example, in order to reduce price competition, the railroad corporations divvied up traffic among themselves and shared revenues in formal traffic "pools." To maximize profits, *different* prices were charged on the *same* routes depending on the customer. Also, special rebates were regularly awarded to the largest corporate customers on more competitive lines, but not to others or on monopolized routes. Meanwhile, "stock watering" and speculation in railroad shares contributed to recurring bank panics.[114] Some of these tactics are common practice now, but they seemed like "organized theft" to 19th-century Americans.[115] After all, most people had grown up in an economy based on small farmers and tradesmen, dealing in agricultural commodities and basic household goods, conducting exchanges in small lots in free markets. Before

1870, monopolies and large corporations had been rare. But by the mid-1880s, industrial corporations were already coming to dominate economic life in new and alarming ways. And as the oldest and largest industrial corporations, which had also grown to monopolize long-distance transportation services, railroads became a lightning rod for public discontent.

Farmers, merchants, and the ticket-paying public clamored for government regulation of the rails.[116] In response, for twenty years (roughly 1867–1887) individual congressmen had introduced over 150 bills to regulate the railroads. None passed. Railroad attorneys and property rights advocates, like Cleveland himself, ably defended corporate interests in Congress and the courts. The same rights and protections invoked by Revolutionary-era Americans to protect themselves from a predatory aristocracy were now being employed to defend private monopolies against regulation by the people. Finally, in 1876 the Supreme Court conceded that the rails "engaged in a public employment affecting the public interest" and therefore concluded that railroad rates and practices *could* be regulated by the government.[117] State governments then sprang into action with all sorts of new legislation.[118] However, while state governments might regulate railroads within their borders, the most profitable traffic was increasingly regional and transcontinental. And in 1886, the Supreme Court ruled that regulation of *interstate* routes only "should be done by the Congress of the United States under the commerce clause of the Constitution."[119] This ruling created "a twilight zone in which states could not and the federal government did not regulate railroads."[120] Meanwhile, by the mid-1880s, overbuilding had created cutthroat competition among some railroads, while consolidation created large monopolies elsewhere. Pools became ineffective, as their terms amplified in complexity and members cheated. As a result, many railroads themselves now supported federal regulation of some sort.[121]

The result was the Interstate Commerce Act of 1887. Despite his prior legal experience with the issues, President Cleveland demanded no role in its design. Congress sent it to him in late January 1887, and after two weeks of study, he signed it without comment. In principle, it banned pools, rebates, and price discrimination and mandated that rates be "reasonable and just" and be published for all to see. But the new Interstate Commerce Commission (ICC) it created to enforce these regulations had little real impact. After an initial flurry of activity, the ICC found itself virtually powerless. The language of the Interstate Commerce Act was so weak, ambiguous, and experimental that the ICC's decrees were often ignored or its mandates were reversed by the courts. Its main advantage was to publicize abuses and the need for still better federal regulation. Ninety years later, the verdict from historians remained: "Nearly everyone agrees that the Interstate Commerce Commission has failed. . . . [F]ew dispute its lack of success."[122] True antitrust enforcement would await the presidency of Theodore Roosevelt (1901–1909).

The Recession of 1887–1888

The economic recovery which initially greeted Cleveland did not last long. After late summer 1886, economic growth became sporadic and unreliable. Wheat and cotton prices remained under pressure as crop yields rebounded. By the end of the year, farm prices were headed back toward their depression lows. Net gold inflows paused. Deflation returned to the cities. Still nervous from the recent downturn, banks remained conservative in their lending, while federal debt paydowns reduced the supply of government bonds.[123] Thus real interest rates rose again toward 6 percent.

Between spring 1887 and spring 1888, a severe recession struck. It was largely caused by historic droughts and blizzards that devastated ranchers, farmers, railroads, and industry alike. The first drought hit during summer 1886, when severe heat waves and low rainfall ravaged Texas. Cattle died off. Many ranchers ate their seed corn in order to survive. Then came the "Hard Winter" of 1886–1887. Records for cold and snow were set around the country: three to four inches fell in downtown San Francisco and freezing temperatures reached deep into the South.[124] But it was the blizzards on the Great Plains that did the worst economic damage. They buried entire states in several feet of snow for weeks, while temperatures dipped below –50 degrees at times. "It was as though the Arctic regions had pushed down and enveloped us. Everything was white," wrote one Montana rancher.[125] From the Dakotas to Texas, millions of livestock, including anywhere from 50 to 90 percent of most cattle herds, froze to death.[126] Due to both the weather and the ranching bust, demand for manufactured products fell. Industrial activity contracted sharply, dropping over 7 percent, in the months following November 1886. Then, during summer 1887, droughts returned to the Great Plains and prairies, further punishing farmers and ranchers. The following winter, 1887–1888, again brought record snowfall and a "Great Blizzard," this time to the Mid-Atlantic and Northeast. Ice flows clogged the Ohio and Mississippi rivers. Roads and rails were unpassable, even in the cities. Telegraph and telephone lines were downed, snarling communications. Hundreds of ships foundered or wrecked or their docks destroyed, rendering the nation's largest eastern ports unusable. Washington, Baltimore, Philadelphia, New York, and Boston were immobilized. Even the New York Stock Exchange closed for two days. Much of the American economy was virtually paralyzed. Industrial output flatlined that winter and spring. Farmers called for aid, while the manufacturing sector clamored for trade protection, as did many American workers who believed that free trade pushed down wages and eliminated jobs.

Despite calls for federal assistance, Cleveland doggedly stuck by his constitutional ideals. For example, when suffering Texans appealed for aid, Congress passed a bipartisan bill to provide a meagre $10,000 in seed grain to save farms in selected counties in that state. Scores of federal aid packages had been granted to disaster victims for decades,[127] but President Cleveland vetoed the appropriation, arguing:

> I can find no warrant for such an appropriation in the Constitution; and I do not believe that the power and duty of the General Government ought to be extended to the relief of individual suffering. . . . [T]he lesson should be constantly enforced that, though the people support the Government, the Government should not support the people.[128]

Cleveland also struck down hundreds of spending bills for infrastructure, pensions, and regional aid. All told, he exercised his veto 414 times during his first administration, only a quarter of which were pocket vetoes. This sum is roughly twice that of *all* previous presidential vetoes combined. And of Cleveland's vetoes, only two were overridden by Congress during his first term, giving him an almost unrivaled success rate in American history. The "veto mayor" and "veto governor" had become the "veto president."

The vast majority of Cleveland's vetoes were against private pension bills for veterans of the Civil War.[129] These individual acts, written to benefit individual Americans, had become a form of patronage used to buy support for Republican congressmen. And, fearing the wrath of the "soldier vote," every president since Lincoln, all Republicans, had signed each of the thousands of pension bills which came to their desks. The expenditures became enormous. By Cleveland's time, pensions were the largest category in the annual budget, supporting some 325,000 Americans and consuming over 20 percent of federal spending.[130]

With arguably few veterans' votes to lose, the Democrat Cleveland refused to continue this practice without more serious vetting. He vetoed hundreds of pension bills that he judged fraudulent. In one such veto, he complained, "I am so thoroughly tired of disapproving gifts of public money to individuals who in my view have no right or claim to the same. . . . [T]he [freewheeling] granting of pensions invites applications without merit and encourages those who for gain urge honest men to become dishonest."[131] Northerners in Congress therefore passed a comprehensive Dependent Pensions Bill that would award pensions to any Civil War veteran disabled for any reason, even old age. Furthermore, the bill gave pensions for disabilities incurred *after* the war and provided financial incentives to physicians and towns to aid in certification.[132] Again, Cleveland vetoed it.

The economic effects of Cleveland's pension vetoes were mixed. On one hand, he reduced a persistent form of corruption and inefficient pork. For example, *The Nation* applauded Cleveland's veto of the mass pensions bill, proclaiming that he had saved the Treasury from "an outrageous scheme which was hastily passed by Congress in a characteristic fit of carelessness, folly, and cowardice."[133] And Cleveland did not veto all pensions, just those that seemed fraudulent to him. On the other hand, Cleveland's attack on pensions limited perhaps the only existing form of federal welfare. The *New York Tribune* bemoaned that Cleveland's vetoes were "sending the destitute, aged mothers of soldiers to the poorhouse, in order that the Democratic party may gain a reputation for economy."[134] But Cleveland believed that Congress was wasting money, encouraging widespread fraud and dependence, and choosing economic winners and losers, all the while treading on the authority of the executive branch; individual congressmen should either respect the judgments of the Pensions Bureau or pass legislation to change the way it made decisions.

Admittedly, Cleveland was somewhat flexible here, more opposed to specific grants of welfare than to general acts of government favor. For example, two weeks after quashing the Texas Seed Bill, he signed the Hatch Act of 1887, which provided a far greater sum, $15,000 per year, in federal funding to *each* land-grant college to support agricultural experiment stations and the circulation of information about new farming techniques. Out west, he opened up millions of acres of government land, hitherto appropriated by railroads and cattle barons, to new settlers. And he did not veto a generous rivers and harbors improvement bill, ostensibly for defense, which critics lambasted for its pork and jobs. In a blatant act of government favoritism, he even defended cattle and dairy interests by signing a bill that taxed and regulated margarine so as to make it less competitive with butter. Yet such transgressions were rare. More often, Cleveland denounced the "selfish and private interests which [convince the public] that the General Government is the fountain of individual and private aid."[135]

Trade and the Great Tariff Debate of 1888

Ultimately, it was trade that would prove Cleveland's most controversial battle.[136] The United States during the mid-1880s was relatively closed to international trade—it comprised just 12 percent of the country's economic activity—but some sectors depended heavily upon it. Southern farmers of cotton and tobacco sent large portions of their crops abroad, as did midwestern wheat farmers. Pig farmers found ready buyers of American ham and bacon in foreign markets.

Meanwhile, many struggling American consumers, and certain manufacturers, relied on imports of cheap unprocessed foods (especially sugar) and crude materials (wool, leather, and other textiles), which together constituted 75 percent of all imports.[137] In fact, the US government itself depended upon imports since tariffs brought in around 55 percent of all federal revenues.[138] These import tariffs allowed Gilded Age Americans to simultaneously afford low internal taxes, rapid debt reduction, generous pensions for Union army veterans and their dependents, river and harbor improvements, and the construction of a new, modern navy.[139]

Yet the existing tariff regime was problematic and begged for reform. First, the rates were exorbitant. Between 1875 and 1885, the overall tax rate on dutiable imports averaged above 43 percent, while tariffs on some individual goods reached far higher. Tariffs thereby "raise the price to consumers of all articles imported . . . [and] create a tax upon all our people," complained Cleveland.[140] Second, tariffs created winners and losers. Especially hurt were millions of American consumers in the lower classes, farmers, and the Democrat-dominated South (which faced reciprocal tariffs on their export crops, while paying exorbitant prices for manufactured goods). On the other hand, domestic manufacturers benefited from reduced foreign competition, which allowed them to raise prices on their own goods. "The benefits of the tariff all go one way," complained a Southern congressman, "from the consumer to the manufacturer, but not from the manufacturer to the consumer."[141] Also, customs officials were usually the agents of local party bosses; therefore tariff administration remained a source of influence for the political machines. To Cleveland, tariffs were an outgrowth of the spoils system, constituting a "vicious, inequitable, and illogical source of unnecessary taxation."[142] Finally, with the federal budget consistently in surplus, high tariffs created an embarrassment of riches in government coffers. Throughout the 1880s, the US Treasury brought in around 38 percent *more* in revenues, much of it tariffs, than Congress spent. When the Treasury invested these excess funds (i.e., purchased bonds on the open market), it drove up interest rates, while further enriching wealthy financial interests in the Northeast. And while a government surplus may not seem problematic to 21st-century Americans, the 19th-century view was that surpluses took money out of circulation, while also creating a large, irresistible reserve of pork which further tempted spoilsmen in Congress and the bureaucracy. Hence many blamed high tariffs for causing the smoldering depression of 1881–1885.

Cleveland was admittedly a latecomer to the tariff debate. Other than vague partisan support for lower tariffs shared by most Democrats since the 1840s, he had rarely spoken of them. Nor had he ever much studied the matter. "I am ashamed to say it, but the truth is I know nothing about the tariff," he admitted to a Republican reformer. "Will you tell me how to learn?"[143] He was certainly no free-trader. Cleveland recognized the value of protective tariffs for the budding American industrial sector and, he hoped, for the workingmen employed there. As a Democrat, he was also wary of causing a schism among his party in Congress; not all Democrats supported the same tariffs on the same products. And since half of all US trade was conducted with Great Britain,[144] many Americans saw free trade as a dangerous form of British imperialism, "tantamount to conspiracy: a secretive British-led attempt to stunt the growth of US 'infant' industries and foil Republican imperial designs."[145] Hence in his first annual message to Congress, Cleveland limited his recommendations to vagaries such as "I think the reduction should be made in the revenue derived from a tax upon the imported necessaries of life."[146]

Cleveland's lack of leadership on silver convinced many that he would be similarly weak on trade. For example, in early 1886, a handful of pro-reform Democrats attempted to pass new tariff legislation, but protectionist Democrats in Congress torpedoed the effort before it even made it to the House floor. As usual, the strictly constitutionalist Cleveland refused to interfere. The next plan was to ride a wave of voter frustration during the 1886 midterm elections. But the November elections failed to reveal any major shifts in public opinion, nor did they much alter the balance of power in Congress. In his December 1886 message to Congress, Cleveland therefore increased the urgency, though not the specificity, of his call for tariff reform. He even threatened to call a special session of the newly elected Congress. The threat was ignored. Again, no progress was made.

Finally, seeing tariffs as the last refuge of the spoilsmen, and with consumers and labor crying for relief amid the Recession of 1887–1888, an exasperated Cleveland dedicated his *entire* 1887 annual message to Congress to tariff reform. He may have also seen it as an opportunity to assert presidential influence over the party and thereby nationalize the organization. Election considerations likely also played a role. As one cabinet member put it, "[Cleveland] pictured the political revolution which would sweep over the Western States if the Democratic party had the boldness to wage a war in favor of a reduction of the tariff."[147] So, in unusually stark and indelicate terms, Cleveland blasted the existing tariff regime that December. He described it as an "indefensible extortion and a culpable betrayal of American fairness and justice . . . that multiplies a brood of evil consequences."[148] He demanded change, proposing a new tariff system that would lower duties on "the necessaries of life used and consumed by all the people" (such as sugar, clothing, carpets, and raw materials), while still maintaining protective tariffs for many American industries.

Coming as a surprise, for he consulted few in Congress or his party, Cleveland's trade message suddenly threw the entire country into a controversial "Great Tariff Debate" during a close election year. For months, newspaper headlines and editorial pages were consumed by trade arguments. The battle over tariffs even invaded American popular culture. In Mark Twain's new novel, published later that year, the "Connecticut Yankee" argued tariffs with a fictional blacksmith in King Arthur's Court. The Socialist Edward Bellamy, who intended to attack money and individualism, felt obligated to also lambaste customs duties in his instant 1888 classic, *Looking Backward*. Even the great American poet Walt Whitman took up the fight against protectionism, declaring, "The whole thing is hoggish—put on hoggish foundations."[149] Certainly during spring and summer, Congress debated little else. Cleveland's allies in the House drafted a new tariff bill that would reduce tariffs on iron, standardize duties on cotton, and completely abolish import taxes on hemp, flax, lumber, and wool. On average, it was a mild reform, just a 7 percent reduction in tariffs overall, but it was weighted such that Northern manufacturers would feel its sting far worse than farmers in the South or West.[150]

Immediately, the potential economic losers began to push back. Pleas for compromise came from several directions. For example, to reduce the embarrassingly large federal surplus, former House Speaker Samuel Randall (D-PA) wanted to split revenue reduction between tariff reform and cuts on internal taxes, especially the excise taxes on tobacco and whiskey produced in his part of the country. Wealthier midwestern Democrats preferred to cut taxes and tariffs on the luxury items which they consumed. The Senate Republicans drafted a counterproposal that would have *raised* duties on manufactured goods, clothing, and many of the items on Cleveland's reduction list.

Cleveland again stubbornly refused to intervene. He would neither compromise on the bill nor make side deals to attract Republican votes. This may have been a tactic to whip up votes in an election year.[151] Or Cleveland may have realized that tariff reform was not so popular as he had hoped.[152] But more than one scholar of the tariff fight has argued that "[w]here Cleveland primarily failed was in the area of public education."[153] He was willing to use a combination of threats and partisan pressure to maneuver his bill through the House, mostly along party lines. But he "considered a barnstorming tour to inspire grassroots support to be beneath the dignity of the presidential office. . . . He left to others the labors of instruction."[154] With the public confused by tariff schedule complexities and hysterical rhetoric, the bill died in the Republican-dominated Senate. Little had been accomplished.

Cleveland and Presidential Relationships

Given his resolve for a strictly "constitutional," and hence passive, presidency, Cleveland's failed attempts at relationship-building may seem irrelevant, but they might also help to explain his economic leadership problems. First, the press. Cleveland respected the democratic ideals of a free press "as a regulator and check upon temptation and pressure in office."[155] But in practice, he hated reporters. Their headline-seeking and scandal-baiting infuriated him. He regularly referred to journalists as "ghouls" and openly blasted the newspapers "for unjust and false accusations and for malicious slanders invented for the purpose of undermining the people's trust and confidence."[156] Cleveland never understood how good men could ruin his reputation for profit. Nor did journalists especially value him. "Frankly, we couldn't 'get him,'" recalled one reporter.[157] Another complained that the president was so unapproachable that news from the administration "was obtained much after the fashion in which highwaymen rob a stage-coach."[158]

Cleveland did not grasp how to campaign or mingle with the American people. One scholar of his administration has written, "[Cleveland had] little talent for mobilizing public opinion or generating publicity for his policies."[159] Instead, during his sparse free time, Cleveland went hunting and fishing, or he courted his bride-to-be, rather than rub elbows with the American people. He so much hated his lack of privacy that, after he married, he purchased a home and a small farm plot three miles northwest of the White House. The First Couple lived there for much of each year, the president commuting as necessary to the executive mansion.[160] But "[p]robably his greatest weakness," recalled one Washington journalist, "was his inability to meet men agreeably—particularly those who differed in opinion with him. He was always suspicious of them, and was too easily moved to denounce them personally."[161]

To be fair, Cleveland had few staff to help him with public relations.[162] In the White House, he was aided only by a private secretary who came with him from the New York governor's office. Another dozen clerks, stewards, and valets helped to run daily affairs. Even then Cleveland refused to delegate. A White House doorman who served ten presidents labeled Cleveland "the hardest working President I ever saw in my life."[163] Most of his peers agreed. He worked long hours, from early morning until long past midnight. He carefully vetted almost every piece of legislation and appointment that came across his desk. He would even answer the single telephone, or even the front door, himself. A skeptical senior Democrat quipped that Cleveland was "the kind of man who would rather do some thing badly for himself than to have somebody else do it well."[164]

It did not help that, as Cleveland governed like a lawyer, he spoke and wrote like one too. He "had no talent for oratory," writes one scholar. "A public speech of any kind was a heavy labor, and he had no talent for extemporaneous address."[165] Thus Cleveland gave few speeches, and when he did, he was rigidly formal and unsmiling. His prose was filled with ponderous phrases and unnecessary vocabulary that clogged endless run-on sentences to obfuscate even simple thoughts.[166] For example, he prefaced simple policy statements with long vacuous set-ups like the following:

> The laws of progress are vital and organic, and we must be conscious of that irresistible tide of commercial expansion which, as the concomitant of our active civilization, day by day is being urged onward by those increasing facilities of production, transportation, and communication to which steam and electricity have given birth.[167]

His annual messages to Congress droned on with such weighty vernacular for dozens of pages, some of the lengthiest on record. His critics saw it as subterfuge. To them, the simple-minded Cleveland was posing as an intellectual by using "archaic and obsolete words of resounding length."[168]

Cleveland even had poor relations with his own Democratic Party. He had spent few years in elected office—none of it federal—and therefore had built little in the way of a national party following. As president, he often failed to consult senior Democrats on his few policy decisions or major speeches. He refused their urgent requests for patronage and would not help them to organize in Congress. He sought neither to lead nor to influence the party.[169] As a result, "[t]he Democrats, in fact, did not recognize him as their leader, but only as their candidate for the office of President," wrote Woodrow Wilson, then a political science professor at Princeton, who explained, "Mr. Cleveland was renominated for the presidency by acclamation [in 1888], not because the politicians wanted him, but because their constituents did."[170] Rank-and-file Democrats felt little warmth for Cleveland, but they knew where he stood, and most respected him for it. And they dreaded Republicans even more.

1888 Election

Cleveland only narrowly lost his reelection bid in 1888.[171] He was renominated by his party uncontested, the first time for a Democrat in fifty years. This guaranteed that the election would be a referendum on tariff reduction and civil service reform.[172] Conservative, pro-business "Bourbon" Democrats supported him.[173] They wanted a small, clean, laissez-faire government at a time when other candidates seemed to favor special interests, Socialism, or a return to the spoils system.[174] Cleveland also carried the "solid South." He even won the popular vote, though largely due to Black disenfranchisement. But the tariff fight ultimately scuttled his chances.[175] "[T]he Republicans have got us on the run on the free trade issue," complained a Democratic organizer.[176] "There was no denying the fact that [Cleveland] had wrought his own defeat and his party's by forcing a hot fight [on tariffs] when matters were going peacefully enough," surmised Wilson.[177] He therefore lost the Northern and Western states that had been key to his electoral college victory four years earlier. He also refused to campaign vigorously, seeing it as beneath the dignity of a president.

The vote was excruciatingly close, though. Just fourteen thousand more votes in New York alone, Cleveland's home state, would have won him a second term.[178] Thus, his prospects for a return in 1892 were good. In fact, on their way out, Mrs. Cleveland blithely told a White House servant, "Now, Jerry, I want you to take good care of all the furniture and ornaments in the house . . . for I want to find everything just as it is now when we come back again. . . . We are coming back just four years from today."[179]

Cleveland left his successor a healthy, albeit erratic economy. Real GDP per capita had staggered back up to record highs. Industrial production and trade were booming again by early 1889. Agriculture had mostly recovered. Inflation for urban consumers was minimal. This was a blessing for workers, whose wages grew slowly and only toward the end of Cleveland's term. The end of deflation also meant that real interest rates dropped from 6 percent to 3.5 percent for high-quality borrowers. The wealthy enjoyed mixed returns under Cleveland. By 1889, the wild stock market had recovered from its 1885 nadir and wealth inequality rose, but both remained unreliable and significantly below their highs for Cleveland's term.[180] Fiscal conservatives were pleased, for Cleveland had mostly kept a lid on federal expenditures, which barely grew during his term despite an expanding population. As a result, in just four years, he had successfully reduced the federal debt by 15 percent. The trade story was less happy. Imports grew every year under Cleveland, for a total of over 24 percent, but exports grew only 7.2 percent and had begun to flag during his fourth year in office.[181] Nevertheless, America's stocks of monetary gold had recovered strongly from 1884 and stood at record highs, and investors trusted the US currency. Given its volatility, Cleveland's first-term economy was, taken as a whole, mediocre, but it finished on a fairly strong note.

Findings

We find in Grover Cleveland a simple, stubborn small-government constitutionalist. To the extent that he held an economic philosophy, it was his sincere belief that "[g]ood and pure government lies at the foundation of the wealth and progress of every community."[182] This made good sense at a time when governments seemed mismanaged by corrupt political machines. Cleveland's solution was a fairly negative view of the presidency, and of the federal government. The president's job was to administer and recommend, not to dictate policy. And other than his formal declarations and messages, almost always directed at Congress rather than the public, Cleveland's active use of the veto was perhaps his only forceful application of presidential power. He made plenty of suggestions to Congress, but he mostly restrained himself in politics and policy. He did use his office, and the federal government, to defend the currency and to decrease wasteful spending, but not to alleviate hardship or to proactively advance the economy. This mostly relieved Cleveland from having to leverage relationships with other major political-economic actors, or the American people, a task that he generally floundered at anyway.

One could therefore argue that Cleveland's first economic administration (1885–1889) simply benefited from good timing or suffered from bad luck. During his first months in office, the smoldering depression essentially burned itself out. Eighteen months later, a wave of droughts and blizzards brought recession. When the weather normalized, the economy recuperated. So one might reasonably conclude that, as long as Cleveland did no damage, the economy would naturally improve.

However, there *were* myriad opportunities for Cleveland to passively allow or actively produce another financial panic or recession. Instead his dedication to a stable, reliable US dollar appears to have been essential to his first administration's economic performance. He prevented a run on the US currency and destabilizing capital flight. On the other hand, he failed to effect more positive policy changes. In particular, Cleveland failed to enact major currency, tariff, welfare, or labor reforms. Also, federal aid to farmers or ranchers might have eased the 1887–1888 recession. In other words, he acted to veer the economic ship of state away from the dangerous vortex of financial crisis, but he then let it drift rather than guide it to safe harbor. Here Cleveland's problem appears to have been his negative view of government, and of the presidency, as well as his refusal to play the roles of public educator or congressional deal-maker, with all the cajoling, coercing, and sugaring that came with those vital tasks. These failures would come back with a vengeance during his second term. In the meantime, American politics and the economy were rapidly transforming in ways that would have dramatic effects on the presidency going into the 1890s.

Interlude: Into the 1890s

The breathtaking pace of globalization, industrialization, and urbanization only quickened going into the 1890s, taking the US economy and the presidency to new heights of power. This time, however, manufacturing surpassed the railroads as the driving force. And the growing management and financial demands of modern manufacturing changed the very conduct of American business. Cities became the centers of both mass production and mass consumption. Technological advances in transportation, communication, automation, and electricity created new possibilities for politics and economics, while continuing to knit the country into a national market, bringing competition, threats, and opportunities where previously there had been none. As national issues compounded, political power slipped from local control. Political machines gradually gave way to national party organizations, with the president and his men at the top. These final years of the Gilded Age would therefore see a desperate struggle between two very different conceptions of the presidency and government, from the rudimentary prototype of a national party boss leading an explicitly interventionist government (Harrison), back to a more traditional small-government, small-presidency conservatism (Cleveland), and then leaping forward to a masterful national politician at the head of a full-fledged developmental state with global ambitions (McKinley).

By 1890, the United States was an economic behemoth by almost any measure. In total output, the United States produced 60 percent more than Great Britain, over twice that of Germany, six times that of Japan, and twenty-three times more than Mexico or Canada. In wealth per capita, Britain had temporarily regained primacy (at 103 percent of US levels), but America far outperformed Belgium (82 percent), Switzerland (80 percent), Germany (58 percent), Canada (57 percent), France (57 percent), Italy (45 percent), and Spain (37 percent). In the decade since 1880, US industrial production had almost doubled and its agricultural output had increased 70 percent. Both energy consumption and production (by now mostly coal, petroleum, and natural gas rather than wood) had more than doubled. And the US had few rivals for its output of iron, steel, wheat, corn, cane sugar, cotton and cottonseed oil, tobacco, processed meats, or petroleum products. "[America] is not so much a democracy," quipped an eminent French political scientist in 1891, "as a huge commercial company for the discovery, cultivation, and capitalization of its enormous territory."[1]

Presidential Leadership in Feeble Times. Mark Zachary Taylor, Oxford University Press. © Oxford University Press 2024.
DOI: 10.1093/oso/9780197750742.003.0012

America's transportation and communication networks were the envy of the world. Rail passenger and freight volumes more than doubled during the 1880s.[2] The US telephone network expanded 475 percent during the decade, though with just 227,900 telephones in operation in 1890 they remained an elite technology, affordable only to some corporations, government offices, and the wealthy. Instead, most Americans still relied on the nation's telegraph network, which had almost tripled in size during the 1880s and handled just under 58 million messages annually by the end of the decade. In ocean shipping, dry bulk rates grew cheaper almost every year and, by 1894, were at half of 1876 prices.[3]

The US population stood at just over 63 million in 1890, yet another 25 percent increase over a decade. In one of largest waves of immigration in US history, over 5.7 million net immigrants had arrived during 1880–1890, making the foreign-born population around 15 percent of total by 1890.[4] Just under 33 percent of them migrated from Germany, 20 percent from Ireland, another 13 percent from the rest of the United Kingdom; 10 percent each were born in Canada and Scandinavia. Other large contingents traveled from Russia, Poland, Bohemia (Czech Republic), Italy, and France. In contrast, the nation's share of East Asian residents was relatively unchanged from a decade prior, while African Americans continued at around 12 percent of the total population. After they landed in the United States, just over 40 percent of the foreign-born remained in the North Atlantic states; another 40 percent made their way to the north-central states, making this region among the fastest growing parts of the country. And yet, despite the population pressures and vast lands available, the majority of Americans still lived east of the Mississippi and north of the Mason-Dixon line.[5]

Out west, 1890 marked the end of an era. Much of the most fertile, low-cost farmland west of the Mississippi had by now been bought. The populations of Washington, west Texas, and southern and central California were booming. Thus, the 1890 census famously dropped its "frontier line," which had formerly demarcated where population density fell below two persons per square mile. At the year's close, the Massacre at Wounded Knee in South Dakota marked the final large military confrontation with the Sioux and the last major battle in America's long, deadly war against the Plains Indians. Three years later, the young historian Frederick Jackson Turner famously lamented, "[T]he frontier has gone, and with its going has closed the first period of American history."[6]

The Farms

The 1880s had been a turbulent decade for American farmers. All told, American agricultural output leaped around 70 percent between 1881 and 1891, even as prices plummeted. Millions of bushels of corn, wheat, and oats became a major source of revenue for the Northern Pacific and Great Northern railroads, raising them up to profitability. Favorable weather and ample investment also profited Kansas, north Texas, Colorado, and even Oklahoma.[7] New farm machinery, often steam-powered, diffused throughout the country, as did corporate management techniques to boost production. Dairy farmers began using cream separators and butterfat testers to increase the quality and variety of their products. Greater adoption of refrigeration allowed ever more perishables to be marketed nationwide and abroad. Thus, although agriculture prices rose during the early 1880s due to economic recovery in the United States and increased demand from overseas, they generally sank after 1882 as supply swamped demand.

Nature then sought to complicate matters. Beginning in the middle of the decade, cycles of drought, plagues of locusts and grasshoppers, and increased global supplies combined to erode the tremendous farm profits earned earlier. The brutal winters of 1887 and 1888, which devastated ranchers, only added to farmers' misery. Then the rains subsided and the land dried up. And yet wages rose and interest rates remained high.[8] As a result, the "bonanza" boom faded. During the early 1890s, investors began to lease out or sell off their holdings. Small farmers dealt little better with the adversity. In fact, almost the entire US agricultural sector entered the new decade amid a vicious cycle of increasing supply and falling incomes that would persist throughout much of the 1890s.

The 1880s also saw a reversal of farmers' political fortunes. After winning battles against the railroad monopolies at the state level during the 1870s, the Supreme Court handed farmers a major loss in *Wabash v. Illinois* (1886). The ruling held that, since they conducted *interstate* commerce, most rails could be regulated only by the federal government, thereby neutering *Munn v. Illinois* (1877) in most instances.[9] In response, the farm bloc helped to design and pass the Interstate Commerce Act (1887), which ostensibly banned much monopolistic behavior. But the Act was rarely enforced. Meanwhile, the farmers' lead political organization, the Grange, declined in influence. Its membership shrank to around 115,000 by 1889 (down from a peak of over 750,000 in 1875), partly thanks to botched attempts to manufacture their own farm equipment, which proved both expensive and inadequate.[10] The remaining Grangers mostly withdrew from politics, returning the organization back to its original social and educational roots.[11] Nevertheless, the Grange had served as a model for subsequent labor and farm associations. Out of it emerged the founding members of the Greenback Party (1874–1889), the Populist Party (1887–1908), and the People's Party (1891–1908).[12]

In its place, the Farmers' Alliance grew in popularity, especially throughout the South, with membership reaching 3 million across thirty-five states by 1890.[13] Originally a small Texas collaboration, it spread like religion.[14] It created cooperatives to purchase machinery and farm goods at lower prices, constructed

independent warehouses, and built cotton gins. As it grew in power and popularity, the Alliance also helped establish the Populist Party during the early
1890s. The party platform agitated for free silver coinage, a graduated income
tax, the direct election of US senators, federal takeover of the telegraph and rail
systems, low-interest federal loans to farmers, and government-owned crop
warehouses. The Populists won seats in state legislatures throughout the South
and Great Plains, and even elected two US senators and several supportive House
members.[15] But the farm bloc could not prevent the political and economic decline of agriculture. Nor was it victorious in trade or monetary policy. Instead,
railroads and industrial corporations, both assisted by bankers, ultimately ruled
the late Gilded Age.[16]

The reckless clearing of western land prompted the country's first land preservation and natural resource conservation movements.[17] Deforestation had
long been a familiar problem for Americans. But now, with the frontier gone,
they could no longer simply "go west" to escape it. Long taken for granted, the
mountains, forests, and deserts now became a mythical repository of the nation's
values. And for the growing population of city dwellers, the wilderness had become a respite. They saw nature as a place to recover one's vigor and sanity. Men
especially desired places "to be free" from the captivity of work and family and
to prove their masculinity.[18] Recreational camping, hiking, hunting, and sport
fishing became popular pastimes, especially for the wealthy. Naturalist John
Muir therefore dubbed national parks and reservations "[t]he wildest health and
pleasure grounds accessible and available to tourists seeking escape from care
and dust and early death."[19]

The Second Industrial Revolution and the Rise of Mass Production

Instead of advances in agriculture, it was manufacturing that now disrupted the
American economy. During the early 1880s, what some called the "American
System" of modern production appeared and spread throughout the industry.[20]
It replaced men with machines and swapped out individual craftsmanship
for standardized mass production. The phenomenon was largely driven by
opportunities for mass consumption—enabled by the railroads and urbanization booms—as well as by productivity growth in other industries, all catalyzed
by technological change. For example, one of its first manifestations was in
sewing machines. The recovery of Southern cotton during the 1870s–1880s
produced a flood of cheap textiles right when demand for sewing machines was
also skyrocketing.[21] By 1881, half a million were being sold annually, often by
mail-order.[22] Companies like Singer, Wheeler & Wilson, and Willcox & Gibbs

rushed to meet demand. But sewing machines were complicated, craft devices, therefore difficult to manufacture in bulk. Meeting that demand using traditional manufacturing became untenable. Drawing lessons from the small arms industry, Wheeler & Wilson introduced interchangeable parts and machine tools, reducing the need for expert fitters and craftsmen and allowing the firm to produce over 100,000 units per year. The practice was studied and spread.

A shower of innovations produced similar revolutions in other industries. James Duke dominated the cigarette business after he began mechanized production in 1884. Within five years, Duke was manufacturing 817 million cigarettes annually, constituting 38 percent of all US sales.[23] A "new and exotic product" in the early 1880s, cigarettes were so widely consumed by middecade that they were already reviled as a "nuisance" in some cities.[24] Advances in pneumatic malting and railcar refrigeration allowed Pabst, Schlitz, and Anheuser-Busch to mass-produce and distribute beer nationally, taking business away from local brewers. The Norton brothers engineered the first "automatic line" canning factory in 1883, which was soon producing millions of cans of Campbell's soup, Heinz beans, and Borden's milk each year. The development of electric resistance welding (1886–1888) allowed manufacturers to automate, or deskill, some of the most difficult blacksmithing tasks. Studebaker Brothers used it to become the largest maker of carriages and wagons in America.[25] And after the "safety bicycle" craze arrived in 1887, annual sales gradually climbed above 1 million.[26] Hundreds of manufacturers entered the market; the most successful of them abandoned hand-bent frames and introduced metal stamping to satisfy production demands. The final major innovation of modern mass production—the assembly line—already existed in the meatpacking industry, but it would await Henry Ford to fully combine it with the others early in the next century.

The emergence of American mass production was revolutionary. Before 1880, much American business was highly fragmented. In most sectors, a free market of hundreds or thousands of individuals and small firms extracted raw materials and passed them through various cycles of processing, marketing, sales, and distribution until they were ultimately purchased by consumers. By the early 1890s, many of these economic activities were being integrated within single firms, guided by the "visible hand" of professional business managers.[27] And for those firms that could marry mass production with mass distribution, the returns were spectacular. Few such corporations existed in 1880. But during the 1890s, large, integrated business enterprises grew to dominate the heart of the nation's economy.[28]

Partly as a result of mass production, the great American industrial boom accelerated during the 1880s. Textiles still led at around 18 percent of the nation's total industrial capitalization in 1890, followed closely by industrial forestry (17 percent) and processed foods (16 percent). Among the fastest-growing industrial sectors were machinery (10 percent of total), iron and steel products (10 percent), chemicals (4 percent), and printing and publishing (4 percent). Steel output had more than doubled in a decade.[29] Most of it wound up in domestically produced locomotives and railcars, which also more than doubled, or in new track.[30] Firing the furnaces that forged the steel and ran the locomotives was coal. During the 1880s, bituminous coal production increased 119 percent, while that of precious anthracite rose 62 percent, and output of crude petroleum, though still not widely used in the United States, increased by 74 percent. Other major industries that saw rapid expansion during the decade were phosphates (140 percent increase), beer production (107 percent), processed tobacco (73 percent), refined sugar (62 percent), and wheat flour (30 percent).

The electricity industry also expanded rapidly during the 1880s, but competition here was intense.[31] The decades-old gaslight industry fought against electric lighting, while city councilmen sought to protect their neighborhoods against disruption and to fill their own pockets. Nevertheless, Edison's electric companies were soon joined by those of H. J. Rogers (1882),[32] Frank Sprague (1884), and George Westinghouse (1886), and by middecade "the battle of the systems"—between low-voltage direct current and high-voltage alternating current—had begun. By 1890, Edison's companies were providing electricity to over sixty-four thousand lamps for around seventeen hundred customers in New York City, and had opened up lighting services in Chicago, Philadelphia, Detroit, New Orleans, and St. Paul. He had even begun ventures in Milan and Berlin.[33] As more supply came on the market, the price of lighting dropped around 70 percent. In fact, so intense was competition that J. P. Morgan intervened in 1892 to form General Electric—a merger between Edison Electric Company and the Thomson-Houston Electric Company. These firms produced electricity mainly for lighting and traction. Widespread electrification of manufacturing, however, would await the new century.

The sheer volume and velocity of business at the nation's large corporations drove "scientific management" to the fore. Factories operating twenty-four hours a day to mass-produce thousands of units could no longer act like small businesses responding ad hoc to situations as they arose. Their complex and interdependent business operations (supply, production, factory maintenance, quality control, marketing, sales, and distribution) needed to harmonize like the well-oiled machines used in their factories. This required a professional managerial bureaucracy and a well-disciplined workforce. An entirely new breed of midlevel managers emerged simply to coordinate the armies of disparate low-level managers. Many manufacturers also hired professional advertising agencies, another Gilded Age innovation, to design and manage national marketing campaigns.[34] Even the highest levels of corporate management were turned over to highly trained and experienced salaried managers. Thus, white-collar jobs comprised 6 percent of the American workforce by 1890.[35] And as these professions rapidly expanded, they seeded a vibrant middle class. Company owners still collected dividends, but they no longer ran most large firms, especially not daily operations. The days in which sole proprietorships and family businesses served as the engines of the American economy were fading away; the era of modern corporate capitalism had begun.[36]

The 1880s also saw the rise of the "trust" in American business. They replaced "pools" as industry's preferred strategy for avoiding "ruinous competition." Pools were for the small and weak, and they rarely lasted long since participants often betrayed their pool agreements at the first profitable opportunity. Also, many state governments forbade cross-shareholding among firms and strictly regulated out-of-state businesses. Pools did not solve this problem. Instead, to control their far-flung enterprises, the large and powerful placed all shares of their constituent firms into the hands of a board of loyal trustees in exchange for trust certificates. Legally, the trustees did not own any property; they merely received and distributed dividends. But through control over the shares, and their voting rights, the trustees had *de facto* control over their entire portfolio. Rockefeller's Standard Oil (1882) was the first trust in America. Thereafter, trusts quickly became the model for large industrial corporations of all kinds: lead, whiskey, tobacco products, plant oils, glass, paper, and other common products.[37] The legal construction fell out of use after New Jersey gradually made cross-shareholding and cross-border corporate operations lawful starting in 1888, but the term "trust" stuck.[38]

Railroads

None of this fantastic—and sometimes destructive—economic development was possible without the railroads, which brought settlers and businesses ever deeper into the American hinterlands. By 1890, the American railroad firms were the largest companies in the world. In a tremendous building spree, the nation's rail network had grown 70 percent during the prior decade.[39] This included completion of the second and third transcontinental railroads in 1883.[40] Southern rails finally improved their connections with the North and West.[41] The diffusion of refrigerated rail cars allowed shipment of perishable goods of all kinds around the country, and to increasingly refrigerated oceanic ships for transport across the seas. The nation's disparate rail systems had also consolidated and integrated their operations. During the 1880s, 425 independent railroad companies, nearly a quarter of the total, were absorbed by mergers or leasing arrangements.[42] Innovations such as standardized time zones (1883) and the adoption of standard-gauge track (1886) further unified the nation's rails, while the spread of uniform accounting, identical signal practices, and interoperable parts and cars reduced time-consuming and costly delays.[43]

Railroad shares and bonds continued to dominate Wall Street, though they now competed with the securities of the new industrial trusts.[44] In 1893, out of 264 firms listed on the New York Stock Exchange, 66 percent were railroads,[45] and rails constituted over 92 percent of the 621 bonds offered. And although the previous five years had grown the NYSE listings (which had increased 86 percent since 1885), a day in which more than 500,000 shares were exchanged was still considered unusual.[46]

Meanwhile, the large capital demands and progressively more brutal competition between the major railroads also forced the nation's bankers—the Morgans, Loebs, Belmonts, Forbeses, and Barings—to become owner-operators. Instead of mere return on their loans, bankers now insisted on control over rail management and organization. For example, in a now famous confrontation in 1885, J. P. Morgan brought to his yacht the presidents of two warring trunk lines in which he held a financial interest. There he forged a truce that ended years of loss-making rate wars between them.[47] Morgan went on to reorganize the Philadelphia & Reading (1886) and the Chesapeake & Ohio (1887) and to merge dozens of other railroads into a massive trust controlled by his investment firm. Once in control, Morgan proceeded to ruthlessly cut debt, reduce inefficiencies, and consolidate redundant track.[48] Businessmen throughout the economy admired men like Morgan and emulated them.

The results were transformative. By the late 1880s, rail freight and passengers could move from one part of the country to another without stopping to switch cars.[49] Average rail speeds therefore doubled along many routes.[50] In fact, by the early 1890s trains reached travel times roughly equivalent to those maintained throughout much of the 20th century. Partly as a consequence, both rail freight and passenger volumes increased by almost 250 percent during the 1880s, while average rates declined 35 percent.[51] On competitive lines rates plummeted further.[52] Nevertheless, the industry was still plagued by rate wars, overbuilding, inadequate capital, and an overabundance of small firms.[53]

Cities

The nation's railroad, telegraph, and telephone networks, augmented by steam power, continued to concentrate Americans into cities. By 1890, one-third of Americans lived in urban areas, up from just over one-quarter ten years prior.[54] New York City now contained over 2.5 million people, making it the second largest city in the world, behind only London. Chicago had more than doubled in size during the decade, becoming America's "second city," with 1.1 million.

Philadelphia had also breached 1 million. Other port and transshipment cities followed in size; St. Louis, Baltimore, Pittsburgh, San Francisco, Cincinnati, Cleveland, and Buffalo were each in the 250,000 to 450,000 range. However, the fastest growing urban areas were all midwestern processers or transshipment points for agriculture or meat products: Omaha, Minneapolis, St. Paul, Kansas City, and Denver. Each had more than doubled, even quadrupled, in size during the decade following 1880, with populations ranging from 100,000 to 165,000 by 1890.

Cities were still squalid places. The larger cities had become a cacophony of foot traffic, horse-drawn vehicles, cable cars, and trolleys of various kinds. Pollution, overcrowding, and urban blight grew worse. Smokestacks blackened the air. Animal feces and carcasses littered the streets. Trash and runoff fouled the rivers and bays. Tuberculosis, diphtheria, typhoid, measles, and smallpox still raged. In fact, thanks to childhood diseases and malnutrition, the average height of native-born Americans continued its twenty-year decline.[55] But a turnaround was in sight. Death rates had already begun to fall in the better-managed cities. Fatalities from diseases of wealth and old age (e.g., heart disease and cancer) had started to rise. Life expectancies therefore began to recover, though Americans born in 1890 still lived, on average, only around forty-four years.[56]

Nevertheless, American cities had become centers of incredible innovation. The first skyscrapers appeared in Chicago in the mid-1880s. They constituted a dramatic new architecture of steel-framed, glass-enclosed, open-interior buildings equipped with innovative elevator systems and reaching as high as twenty stories. The style quickly spread to New York and other large cities. The spread of trolleys and streetcars allowed the wealthy to move further uptown or to the west side (since weather typically blew industrial pollution eastward). Electricity moved into its traction phase when the first electric trolley line opened in Richmond, Virginia, in 1888. These too would proliferate around the country during the 1890s.[57]

The growth of cities, rails, and factories also triggered a revolution in American consumerism.[58] Before the 1870s, most Americans owned relatively few belongings—even scant clothing or books—and much was produced at home; by the early 1890s, they needed closets, chests, and shelves for their myriad possessions, often mass-produced in factories. Urban shoppers flocked to "department stores." The concept had been around for decades, but now it flowered throughout the country. Every city had its own brands—Wannamaker's, Macy's, Bloomingdale's, Lord & Taylor, Filene's, Marshall Fields, Gimbels—mostly targeted at wealthy and middle-class women.[59] A handful of "chain stores" also appeared around the country, including Woolworth's Five Cent Stores and the first grocery syndicates.[60] For those living in the countryside, almost every department store offered a mail-order catalogue, as did some specialist retailers (e.g., Sears & Roebuck originated in 1888 as a popular mail-order business for watches).[61] None of this was possible without subtle, but essential, innovations in glass, paper, and cardboard packaging.[62] Together these new retail business models helped make brands like Ivory, Colgate, and Palmolive household names. Also popularized during the 1880s and early 1890s were Cream of Wheat, Aunt Jemima pancakes, Kellogg's Shredded Wheat, Hershey's chocolate, Juicy Fruit gum, Pabst Blue Ribbon beer, Quaker Oats, Coca-Cola, Jell-O, Maxwell House coffee, and Camel cigarettes.

The Melting Pot

America's burgeoning cities and factories continued to be fed by immigration.[63] Attracted by growing demand for industrial and urban labor, the number of new arrivals continued at high levels going into the 1890s, though the coming economic depression would curtail immigration for several years. The demographics also continued to shift. During the final decade of the Gilded Age, the new immigrants from southern and eastern Europe surged to constitute over half of all immigration to the United States, up dramatically from 6 percent during the 1870s.[64] And as a whole, this period's immigrants were even poorer and less educated than their predecessors. Social Darwinists like economist Francis A. Walker warned that immigration was now drawing from "every foul and stagnant pool of population in Europe, which no breath of intellectual or industrial life has stirred for ages. . . . They are beaten men from beaten races."[65] Many native Americans agreed, as did their presidents. They were joined by labor unions and striking workers, who ramped up their protests against immigration and called for bans on contract labor.

Congress responded with a series of contract labor laws, though with little effect. For example, the Alien Contract Labor Law of 1885 boasted prohibitions on the recruitment and transportation of foreigners into the United States for contract labor. However, it proved impossible to implement. Loopholes were inserted for the sake of foreign relations or at the behest of industry. Skilled immigrants working in industries not yet established in the United States were allowed in. Domestic servants of all types were also exempt, as were those immigrants who could pass as actors, artists, scholars, ministers, or lecturers. Temporary workers employed by other foreigners were also permitted. Perhaps most important, the new law failed to specify any enforcement mechanisms. Even if employers chose to obey the recruitment ban, relatives who had immigrated earlier had by now replaced them as the primary means by which foreigners arranged transportation to and employment in the United States. Subsequent legislation attempted to give teeth to the 1885 Act, while also prohibiting foreign ownership of American land and broadening the categories of "undesirables" barred from entry.[66] Nevertheless, enforcement remained lax. Out of an estimated 6 million arrivals between 1887 and 1901, fewer than eight thousand were turned away as contract workers and only 1 in 1,000 employers of contract labor was actually penalized.[67] Even laws restricting general immigration diverted just over 1 percent of all arrivals.[68]

On the other hand, the federal government's takeover of immigration management grew.[69] The Immigration Act of 1891 created new offices within the Treasury Department to administer federal policy and reserved legal jurisdiction over immigration cases for the federal court system. Over the following decade, the federal immigration bureaucracy was further expanded. Foremost was the construction of a massive immigration facility on Ellis Island in New York Harbor, which opened in 1892.[70] New congressional legislation required Chinese immigrants to carry permits at all times and deemed them unfit to serve as witnesses at trials.[71] Meanwhile, anti-immigration forces took up English literacy as their next restriction goal. Its leading advocate was the Immigration Restriction League, formed in 1894 by three Harvard graduates, who soon joined forces with the American Federation of Labor (AFL) to lobby for a literacy act. They would ultimately prove successful, but not until World War I.

Immigration radically affected American politics and the economy during the Gilded Age. Those persons coming to America grew poorer and more marginalized as Europe modernized and transportation costs fell. Rising incomes abroad also tended to keep more wealthy and skilled workers at home. In fact, those Europeans who migrated to the United States after 1880 generally had fewer skills and less wealth than their countrymen who instead sailed for Latin America or Australia.[72] And once settled in the United States, they assimilated more slowly.[73] Such wealth gaps could last well into the 1900s, even between groups of immigrants, and were especially stubborn for older migrants.[74] In regions where cultural polarization occurred, the local economy might suffer as well.[75]

Nevertheless, studies have repeatedly established that Gilded Age immigration significantly aided US economic development and output, even down to the county level.[76] In particular, immigration provided the labor crucial for industrialization and modernization during the Gilded Age: railroad construction, factory workers, dock labor, and even farm hands. For example, although immigrants accounted for just 10 percent of the total US population during this period, they constituted almost 60 percent of Gilded Age manufacturing workers, allowing factories to be built in far great numbers wherever immigrants appeared.[77] Of course, immigrants also drove up rates of illiteracy, but this only prompted many states to adopt compulsory schooling laws to assimilate migrants and to instill democratic values.[78] Immigrants even had positive effects on farm values, though more toward the end of the Gilded Age.[79] Interestingly, those states with relatively more new immigrants—those from eastern and southern Europe—would also grant women the right to vote faster.[80] In fact, far from triggering an authoritarian backlash, Gilded Age immigration expanded American democracy and concepts of citizenship.[81]

A small but vital minority of high-skilled immigrants had enormous economic influence.[82] Some brought manufacturing know-how or knowledge of advanced agricultural practices not yet adopted in the United States.[83] Even more impressive were foreign inventors, such as Alexander Graham Bell (telegraph), Conrad Hubert (flashlight), and Ottomar Mergenthaler (linotype), who made significant impacts on American industrialization and technological progress. In fact, analysis of US patents awarded to European immigrants during the Gilded Age suggests that, although relatively few in number, foreign inventors were disproportionately influential and increased in number (per immigrant) over time. More broadly, the mass immigration of labor also contributed to the adoption of the modern corporation, provided vast economies of scale for mass production and consumption, and facilitated the spread of public schools, kindergarten, and the research university.

For African Americans, the shackles of Jim Crow were forged during the 1890s. They were contrived in constitutional conventions held in states around the South, backed by white supremacists seeking to prevent "negro supremacy."[84] Out of these deliberations came new institutions designed to further restrict or eliminate the voting rights of African Americans. These new laws rarely mentioned race; instead they invoked literacy tests, poll taxes, and grandfather clauses to keep Blacks disenfranchised. African Americans now turned inward for safety, while whites regulated them out of their world. The result was the creation of almost entirely separate societies that interacted only at work, where Blacks were always in inferior positions, usually unskilled or low-skill labor. In 1896, in *Plessy v. Ferguson*, the Supreme Court found racial segregation itself to be constitutional, as long as it was "equal."[85] The ruling thereby created constitutional cover for the Southern states to isolate and exclude Blacks from American life, except as cheap labor, deep into the next century. One by one, the Southern states fell into one-party Democratic authoritarian rule.[86] Nor could Blacks physically escape. Poverty and racism meant that 91 percent of the nation's African Americans still lived in the South as of 1900, barely less than the 93 percent who had resided there back in 1860. Even Black migration between Southern states was limited during the Gilded Age.[87]

Native Americans also struck their nadir. By the 1890s, they had been driven from their homelands onto some of the most desolate, least productive lands on the continent. Their population dropped to historic lows of perhaps a quarter-million.[88] And like African Americans, they too were physically segregated;

89 percent of Native Americans lived on reservations far from cities and white settlements. No longer a security threat, and with few political rights and little material wealth, they were denied relevance in American political and economic life.[89]

White women fared somewhat better.[90] More of them completed high school and college. More of them entered the workforce. The industrial economy even drew women into lines of work previously dominated by men: clerical, retail, education, nursing, factory. The new "safety bicycle" gave them a form of mobility *not* reliant on men. The athletic, independent "Gibson Girl" soon appeared in magazines and newspapers to epitomize the "new woman," a phenomenon that set off a furious debate in the press and much satire.[91] Yet women remained barred from most labor unions, fraternal organizations, and political activities.[92] In fact, "medical science" insisted that women had frail constitutions and smaller brains. Therefore, conservatives argued, women could not play a significant role in the new industrial workforce. Nor could women absorb much education. Too much thinking might even harm their delicate reproductive systems! In response, during the 1880s and 1890s the Woman's Christian Temperance Union expanded its activities to "Do Everything" on all issues important to women, including education, childcare, healthcare, prison reform, homeless shelters, and food assistance.[93] A new push for political rights also came from the formation of the National American Woman Suffrage Association (1890) and the General Federation of Women's Clubs (1890). In arguing for the vote, women leveraged their higher average educational attainment, their superior moral position in Gilded Age culture, and their Victorian "duty" to maintain the home and family life. Who better to clean up government and deliver progressive policy? Men scoffed, but women won the right to vote in Wyoming (1890), Colorado (1893), and Utah (1896). By the end of the Gilded Age, the woman's suffrage movement was gaining momentum.

Labor

Workers paid high costs for America's rapidly expanding industrial capitalism. Throughout the 1880s and 1890s, in addition to immigration, they were cruelly battered by a prolonged wave of deskilling and skill-replacing technological change.[94] Trained artisans and experienced workers, who formerly earned high wages, were simply no longer necessary to produce the nation's iron, steel, flour, glass, shoes, or cigars.[95] New industrial technologies either replaced them altogether or split complex work processes into a series of simple tasks that could be performed, at tremendous scale, by machines operated by cheap, unskilled or low-skilled labor. The economies of scale created by mass production further eliminated jobs at all skill levels. This brought prices down for consumers. And it earned fantastic returns for investors and managers. But it devastated the artisan labor trades, while placing all industrial labor in the precarious situation of toiling in inhumane working conditions for daily wages with frequent bouts of unemployment and neither safety net nor healthcare. "Man's muscles are now made to compete with iron machines that need no rest, that have no affections, eat no bread," complained one pro-labor tract.[96]

The Knights of Labor rose to fight for workers' interests during the 1880s.[97] Their activities peaked middecade with over 700,000 members grouped into 5,892 local assemblies throughout the nation.[98] Unlike previous labor movements, the Knights successfully forged a national worker identity, with common grievances, a sense of national solidarity, and a large organization with which to flex their considerable muscle. After a victorious 1885 confrontation with Jay Gould and his Union Pacific Railroad, "the Knights of Labor appeared to have taken control of the entire labor movement and to be virtually all-powerful."[99] They won recognition and concessions hitherto unobtainable. Union activity of all kinds then reached a fever pitch during 1886, culminating in a massive 340,000-worker nationwide strike on May 1—henceforth known as "May Day"—that shocked the nation.[100] "They are, in fact, trying to introduce into modern society a new right—that is, the right to be employed by people who do not want you and who cannot afford to pay what you ask," warned *The Nation*.[101] Critics denounced the colossal 1886 strike as the work of "either foreign Socialists or native professional agitators" and therefore "probably not very effective in promoting the movement it was designed to aid."[102]

Though biased, such judgments were prescient. The May Day strike had not been approved by the Knights' senior leadership. In fact, all too frequently, local unions called strikes independently, with excessive demands and without approval from the Knights' headquarters. In doing so, they undermined their own efforts as well as those of the Knights' national organization. Industry executives decided, some willfully, that the Knights could not be trusted to keep their promises and refused to bargain with them. Some corporations even withdrew concessions previously won by the Knights.[103] Nor were the Knights' cooperatives, strikes, or political campaigns generally successful in achieving their goals of shorter working hours, higher wages, or better working conditions. Thus, the Knights fractured and disintegrated after May Day. By 1893, membership had fallen to around seventy-five thousand.[104]

In search of a more effective vehicle, skilled workers streamed into the AFL.[105] Originally part of an international cigar makers' union, its members had split from the Knights in 1881 due to disputes over the direction of the labor movement.[106] As skilled workers, they resented being lumped in with the unskilled masses. They were also frustrated with the decentralized, chaotic, and self-destructive idealism of the Knights. Instead, the AFL sought a more prac-tical and sustainable "new unionism." Like the Knights, the AFL sought to work within the existing system. But rather than lofty, long-run goals of transforming capitalism from within, the AFL prioritized wages, hours, and working conditions.[107] "We are going on from day to day. We are fighting only for im-mediate objects," declared one of its founders in 1883.[108] Its first and longest-serving president was the seemingly tireless Samuel Gompers, who recognized that "[t]rade unionism had to be put upon a business basis."[109] And whereas the Knights had been run like a secret society, with mystic rituals, underground meetings, and covert communications; the AFL was run more like a political club. This meant initiation fees, regular dues, strict accounting practices, and centralized control over the budget. In return, members received financial sup-port during hard times (e.g., sanctioned strikes, work injury, illness, or death). Though anemic in its early years, AFL membership grew to 250,000 by the early 1890s. It was not the only large union in America, but it would be the backbone of skilled labor activism for decades.

Meanwhile, inequality and poverty became a national obsession. An 1893 estimate found that just 9 percent of the country's families owned 71 percent of the nation's wealth.[110] Comprising the most affluent was the new class of industrialists, merchandisers, real estate moguls, bankers, and investors.[111] The "American millionaire" became an object of almost constant study and fascina-tion.[112] Their marriages, personal lives, and inheritances were reported daily in the nation's newspapers. To display their wealth, they erected ornate mansions in New York, Massachusetts, the Hamptons (Long Island), Newport (Rhode Island), Chicago, Pittsburgh, and whatever city, beach, or rural hamlet they might wish to call home.[113] These modern palaces featured dozens of rooms with the finest art and furnishings, maintained by squads of servants. They also hosted some of the most lavish parties in American history.[114] Some of these new patricians entered politics. In fact, by 1886 the US Senate had already become so wealthy and aristocratic that the *North American Review* referred to it as "our 'House of Lords.'"[115] Exposés regularly appeared in the press worried about "the concen-tration of wealth" and wondering, "Are we a plutocracy?"[116] Yet, William Graham Sumner, in *What Social Classes Owe Each Other* (1883), reassured his genera-tion that "[s]ociety . . . does not need any care or supervision" and told aspiring Socialists, and even philanthropists, "Mind your own business."[117] Some "robber barons," like Andrew Carnegie, likewise assured their fellow countrymen that their extreme wealth derived from "the exercise of special ability in the merchant and in the manufacturer" and that "this talent for organization management is rare among men."[118] However, when queried about the benefits to the public, rather than to the shareholder, of his mail-service railroad, magnate William H. Vanderbilt infamously responded, "The public be damned!"[119] Meanwhile, the shocking photojournalism of Jacob Riis (1890) in *How the Other Half Lives* presented the plight of the urban poor to millions of Americans and challenged them by asking, "What are you going to do about it?"[120]

The Spread of American Socialism

Americans responded with more daring forays into Socialism. While the Henry George phenomenon continued to flourish, a complementary movement formed around Edward Bellamy's (1888) political fantasy *Looking Backward: 2000–1887*. In the novel, the protagonist wakes up in Boston in the year 2000, where he finds a "nationalist" utopia of equal wages, community stores, steady jobs, gender equality, and racial harmony. Overseeing it all is a powerful central government, run by experts, which "guarantees the nature, education, and comfortable maintenance of every citizen from the cradle to the grave."[121] Bellamy's Americans participated in politics and the economy for the sake of cooperation, not profit or power. *Looking Backward* sold millions of copies and was translated into over a dozen languages.[122] Some 165 Bellamy "Nationalist" Clubs appeared throughout the country to discuss and disseminate the book's ideas. It was debated within the media, labor unions, farmers' organizations, "all [the way] down to the bootblacks as they sit on the curbstones."[123] Bellamy briefly threw his support behind the People's Party in the 1892 election. But his influence quickly faded after President McKinley's economic and military successes, and Bellamy's death in 1898.

True American Socialism was still incubating within the mind and soul of Eugene Debs.[124] A locomotive paint-scraper and coal shoveler, he helped lead his local union of "firemen" in a ten-month strike for better wages against the Chicago, Burlington and Quincy Railroad in 1888.[125] The strike was a total failure. Rather than negotiate, the CBQ called in strikebreakers and Pinkerton agents to forcefully put down the protest. The strike convinced Debs, previously in favor of labor-industry cooperation, that "[t]he paternalism of [the railroad corporations] is the same as the interest of a slave-holder in his human chattels."[126] Not happy with the AFL's more conciliatory posture, Debs also argued that industrial unions should organize along craft lines rather than as an entire class. He therefore steered rail workers into the new American Railway Union in 1893, which united all railroad labor into a single nationwide union. Debs then led the Union to boycott the handling of trains with Pullman cars in what became a nationwide strike, affecting most lines west of Cleveland and involving a quarter-million workers across twenty-seven states. Jailed for his role in the strike, Debs spent six months in his cell reading leftist theory and emerged a committed Socialist. He would go on to be a major leader of the American Socialist movement from the late 1890s until his death in 1926.[127]

Meanwhile, the anarchist movement metastasized within the immigrant labor community.[128] Overtly, the small but fanatical movement still claimed *not* to "advocate or advise the use of force," but they nevertheless insisted that "the use of force is justifiable . . . when employed to repel force."[129] Thus they sought to answer police brutality with labor violence, corporate coercion with property destruction. In fact, to anarchists, democratic capitalism *was* the institutionalized use of force. Therefore all government and law were their targets. Strikes and terrorism were the means to achieve their goals. The most organized band of anarchists split off from labor unions to form their own faction in 1883 and were generally seen to be behind the 1886 Haymarket bombing, which awoke the entire country to their cause.[130] The bombing also brought widespread public opprobrium. The media frenzy and the brutal arrest, trial, and execution of several anarchists further damaged their movement. Anarchism was thrust to the margins of American political life, even by its own Socialist and reformist brethren. Nevertheless, passionate zealots like Alexander Berkman and Emma Goldman continued their political activism, eventually inspiring the assassination of William McKinley.

During the late Gilded Age, most leftist activity centered on skilled labor enclaves in the immigrant ghettos of New York City and Chicago. It rose and fell in waves. A large influx of experienced leftist German immigrant labor during the 1880s heralded a new phase in American Socialism. They brought with them a powerful combination of ideological depth, energetic activism, organizational skill, and personal experience hitherto unmatched. They pushed aside the older generation and worked to set up unions, establish a Socialist press, organize strikes, and form alliances with non-Socialist reformers. They experienced a brief apex around the labor heyday of 1886.[131] But then, as after the 1877 strikes, "a wave of nativist hysteria whipped by the government and the press" scared off supporters. Conservatives rallied their forces. The major political parties and local machines moved in to steal the left's most appealing policy ideas.[132] And, as after 1877, American Socialists began to fight among themselves. In many quarters, the Germans were marginalized for having failed. In New York, poor immigrant Jews moved to the fore. Experienced as workers, intellectuals, organizers, and outsiders, they brought a new vigor to American Socialism. In particular, a fiercely doctrinaire Socialism issued from the typewriter of Colombia professor and activist Daniel DeLeon. His compelling vision inspired the American Socialist movement for several years during the 1890s, but his increasing dogmatism gradually alienated even his own supporters. In sum, Socialism remained at best a peripheral philosophy in American political life—its leaders quarreled over the intricacies of Marxist theory, while its followers understood little beyond simple maxims and their daily suffering—with a powerful hold on only a handful of small urban communities.

Far more appealing to Americans was the new Christian "Social Gospel" movement.[133] It attracted support from devout evangelical thinkers and social activists who held that "Christianity's purpose was . . . to save society from the injustices created by nineteenth-century capitalism."[134] Widely read religious tracts, such as Washington Gladden's (1886) *Applied Christianity* and George Herron's (1893) *The New Redemption*, repudiated both Socialism and laissez-faire capitalism, proposing instead "a call to the church to reconstruct society according to the Gospel of Christ."[135] These writers argued that, for many in the lower classes, sin came not from depravity but from inhumane working and living conditions. Poverty, the ghetto, and factory work could drive even virtuous men and women to drink, crime, sex, and violence. One response was the "settlement house" movement, led in the United States by Jane Addams and Ellen Gates at Hull House (1889). Originally conceived as a source of art and literary education in one of Chicago's lower-class neighborhoods, Hull House grew to offer a nursery and kindergarten, a public kitchen, and access to public baths and a playground to nurture the poor. During the following decade, dozens of settlement houses were created, many tied to religious bodies, to offer sanctuary, welfare, and community to poor immigrants struggling to deal with American urban life.[136]

Economic Thought Going into the 1890s: The Advent of Neoclassical Economics

The intellectual battle among America's political economists was equally fierce.[137] Still the most widely accepted view was that good things happened to good economic actors. That is, common sense and moral economic behavior (e.g., honesty, hard work, thoughtful investment, persistent saving, personal responsibility) led to prosperity. These were seen as universal laws which could be deduced logically and which applied to all peoples in all times. From this perspective, too much government was a problem. For centuries, governments had usually acted at the behest of the aristocracy or the well-connected for their own self-interest. The whole point of the US experiment in democracy was to reject government intervention beyond the safeguarding of property rights, contracts, and markets for trading them. But this "classical" political economy had a hard time explaining why *bad* things happened to good economic actors. Hence the recurring financial crises, credit stringencies, widening inequality, and growing monopoly abuses of the late Gilded Age economy were just *not* accurately described or well solved by it. Both scholars and policymakers searched for new models and theories to explain the new economy developing around them.

A "New School" of economic thought therefore developed in a handful of American universities during the 1880s. Its adherents sought a more scientific approach, rather than a purely Christian interpretation, to explain economic behavior. Led by Richard Ely, members of the New School founded the American Economic Association (1885), presided over by Francis Amasa Walker from 1886 to 1892.[138] An eager young PhD, Woodrow Wilson, joined. They sought to reform the study of political economy. Its members dismissed the doctrine of laissez-faire as "unsafe in politics and unsound in morals, and . . . an inadequate explanation of the relations between the state and the citizens."[139] Instead they sought to expand the role of history, culture, and other contingencies in economic theory, as was being taught in Germany. Classical political economists objected. Defending themselves from the ramparts of Harvard and Yale, they insisted on universal economic laws that applied equally across time and space. At Harvard, they began publication of the *Quarterly Journal of Economics* (1886) to advance their scholarship. Columbia's political economists raised their own flag with *Political Science Quarterly* (1886), as did scholars at the newly founded University of Chicago with the *Journal of Political Economy* (1892). For its part, the New School countered that economic laws were dynamic, subject to changing conditions. The New School also sought to advocate and participate in policy and legislation. They preached quasi-Socialism, right at the time of the labor union surge and the Haymarket bombing.

Outside the ivory tower, economic thinkers welcomed this turn toward data and empirical evidence and, in doing so, transformed their view of the US economy. Some observed recent history and concluded that the recurring crises of the Gilded Age were caused by "overproduction" and excessive competition. Thanks to industrialization, so much product was pouring out of the nation's farms and factories that prices simply collapsed. Waves of bankruptcy, financial panic, and labor unrest followed. A few traced this back further to an "excess of . . . enterprise.[140] David Wells, Carroll D. Wright, Edward Atkinson, Arthur Hadley, Charles A. Conant, and others in policy and business circles therefore *favored* industrial concentration. To these thinkers, monopolies were a positive good. They argued, "This waste of competition . . . can be partly saved by combination of many manufacturing establishments in one industry under one management."[141] Some observers of bank panics applied this same logic to monetary policy. Too much capital was fueling too much wasteful investment in too many speculative ventures, causing wave after wave of financial crisis.[142] Silverites countered that the quantity of money determined economic prosperity and "that the reduction of our primary money . . . reduces the value of property proportionately."[143] As the 1890s proceeded into depression, these arguments got woven into a new battle over the gold standard.[144]

Regardless, interest in economic subjects skyrocketed during the 1890s, as America's few dozen professional "economists"—the moniker by which they now referred to themselves—struggled to explain the 1890s depression, as well as the new industrialized, globally interconnected economy that had produced it.[145] The nation's presses erupted in a flood of books and articles on poverty and the unequal "distribution of wealth" and how to improve them. The few existing scholarly journals filled their pages with arguments about tariffs, taxation, and unemployment and analyses of the panic and depression.[146] Even the new *American Journal of Sociology* (1895) took up debate over monopolies, municipal reform, immigration, child labor, and the role of government in public welfare.

Among academics, a new consensus finally emerged during the 1890s: *neoclassicism*.[147] The movement was led by John Bates Clark in the United States and Alfred Marshall in Britain.[148] They, and their fellows, brought increased mathematical rigor and scientific analysis to the study of the economy. They also elevated twenty-year-old theories of *marginalism* (i.e., the effects of additional economic activity "at the margins") to a central position in their analyses.[149] In doing so, they were able to describe the complex relationships of an industrialized global economy with ever greater levels of precision. The relationships between supply, demand, and prices all made more sense now. Even the mysterious appearance and behavior of industrial monopolies could be better understood. This satisfied many New Schoolers, who promptly welcomed the classicalists into the American Economic Association, declaring, "[N]ow is the time for a love fest."[150] Henceforth, intellectual diversity and scientific rigor would be its agenda. By 1898, Marshall himself wrote, "[T]here are signs that America is on the way to take the same leading position in economic thought, that she has already taken in economic practice."[151]

However, in making economics more scientific, *neoclassicism* divorced economics from ethics, religion, and even policymaking.[152] The neoclassicals argued that the economy ebbed and flowed due to changes in impersonal variables (e.g., supply and demand), not civic virtue. Thus, unlike their predecessors, neoclassical economists could posit arguments about efficiency but *not* about morality or justice.[153] Marginal analysis also made economics more theoretical, less practical. "Economic ideas like value and utility were not real entities inherent in goods and services; they were abstractions of complex processes."[154] Recognizing this, many neoclassicalists admitted that, although they might explain the world in general terms, they could not always offer useful solutions to America's social problems. Some were embarrassed or exhausted by the political advocacy of men like Ely. Others feared termination.[155] Many top economists therefore stepped back from politics and policy. Thus, the cutting edge of 1890s economic thought was of little help to the Harrison, Cleveland, or McKinley administrations—not that these presidents paid much heed to economic theory anyway.

Science and Technology

The pace of scientific and technological progress also quickened during the late Gilded Age. Patent applications leaped by 83 percent during the 1880s. By far the greatest categories of invention were in electrical technologies, vehicles, agriculture, office machinery, and wood and minerals processing. Useful inventions of the era included the electric iron (1882), linotype (1884),[156] the ballpoint pen (1888), aluminum manufacturing (1889), smokeless gunpower (1890), and the zipper (1893). The modern automobile also saw advancement with the development of the four-stroke combustion engine (1886) and pneumatic tires (1891), though cars would not appear on the American scene until 1895, and even then mostly as playthings for hobbyists and the wealthy.[157]

Perhaps the most exciting field was electricity! The microphone (1880), dry cell battery (1887), and automatic telephone exchange (1891) are just a few examples of the myriad applications that the new energy source was already finding. In 1886, Frank Julian Sprague invented the first practical DC motor. Its key advantage was that it could run at constant speed, even as the weight it bore varied. This allowed for the wider adoption of electric motors in industrial applications. The following year, American manufacturers sold roughly ten thousand electric motors, some of which powered the first electric elevators. Then, in 1888, Nikola Tesla invented an even more powerful and cost-effective AC induction motor that was adapted by Westinghouse engineers for use in devices of all kinds—fans, pumps, crude household appliances.

Modern computing has its origins during the 1880s. In 1883, an Ohio saloon-keeper patented the "Incorruptible Cashier," which became the basis for the new National Cash Register Company, formed the following year to mass-produce the machines. As its usage spread, the cash register and the new "adding machine" (1887) displaced the need for trained bookkeepers, opening up retail jobs to less expensive female workers. Far more ambitious was the punch-card system designed by Herman Hollerith to tabulate the 1890 census. His machines reduced a task that took years to just three months, saving taxpayers $5 million.[158] And his company, which manufactured the tabulating machines, would ultimately become IBM.

Advances in visual and audio technologies gave rise to entirely new economic activities. Based on British advances in photography, in 1880 George Eastman patented "a method and apparatus for coating plates for use in photography."[159] He set up a factory for producing photographic dry plates in Rochester,

New York, and would start to mass-produce the first rolled-film "Kodak" camera by 1888. That same year, the first motion picture images, lasting just 1.6 seconds, were captured in Leeds, England. By the late 1880s, Edison's labs were experimenting with motion pictures, eventually producing the Kinetograph (a motion picture camera) and the Kinetoscope (motion picture viewer).[160] During the 1890s, further developments in motion picture technology would allow the first public viewings of films at American exhibitions, lectures, music halls, and temporary theaters.[161] Gramophones, which played flat records, were commercialized in 1889, leading to the appearance of "phonograph parlors" and early "jukeboxes" in the nation's drug stores.

Perhaps the crowning display of American technological prowess was the 1893 World's Columbian Exposition in Chicago.[162] It was a marvel of engineering and urban design that inspired city planners for decades.[163] Over just six months, it attracted 28 million visitors from around the world, including the leading minds and elites of the Americas and Europe. Its sixty-five thousand displays, submitted by fifty-one nations and thirty-nine colonies, included early motion picture devices, a new "seismograph," the cutting-edge Yerkes telescope,[164] the first moving walkway or "travelator," an electric kitchen, and the latest in steam locomotives, naval ships, turbines, textiles machines, and electric lighting displays galore. The star of the show was the first Ferris Wheel, considered by some the greatest American engineering wonder since the Brooklyn Bridge opened in 1883.

Yet corporate research remained in its infancy. Some industrial firms had begun to employ individual chemists, engineers, and later physicists to develop or test new physical structures, lubricants, compounds, metallurgical processes, and testing protocols. Standard Oil created perhaps the first permanent industrial research department in 1889.[165] But only at the turn of the century would GE build the first full-fledged industrial research facility in the United States, heralding a new era in American science.

To support the new industrial "high-tech" economy, American higher education was also being transformed.[166] Many colleges still functioned as expensive finishing schools for children of the nation's elite. But land-grant and state colleges were spreading higher education to record numbers of Americans. By 1890, there were over 157,000 college students (up from 62,000 in 1870).[167] And although only around 13,000 to 15,000 bachelor's degrees would be granted annually during the 1880s, this number would double by the end of the century, when around 2 percent of Americans born in 1877 would hold college degrees. Colleges also opened their doors wider to women, just 37 percent of schools still restricted to men in 1890 (down from 59 percent in 1870). Colleges dedicated to African Americans also grew and spread. Around twenty historically Black colleges and universities were founded during this time, including

Spelman (1881), Tuskegee (1881), Florida A&M (1887), and Winston-Salem (1892).

The very practice of higher education was also changing. The old model cast college as a "gymnasium of the mind" with a "ancient curriculum" of fixed courses in classic languages, rhetoric, history, and literature meant to stretch and exercise the intellect. Now colleges increased freedom of choice in the belief that one's mind grew best in those subjects for which the student had the most enthusiasm. Colleges therefore reduced required courses while adding electives in chemistry, physics, biology, engineering, and other fields. Students began to "major" and "minor" in distinct fields of study. Meanwhile, bankers and industrialists derided traditional college education as too focused on "the barbarous and petty squabbles of a far-distant past, or trying to master languages which are dead."[168] They instead sought to modernize higher education and make it more practical. Endowments from prominent businessmen and bankers led to the creation of Vanderbilt (1873), Stanford (1885), Georgia Tech (1885), University of Chicago (1890), Drexel (1891), Rice (1891), and other schools with modern curricula, while Congress itself established the heavily scientific and technical Naval War College (1884).[169] Colleges began to add professional schools of law, medicine, and other specialties to their standard courses of baccalaureate study. In 1881, the steel magnate Joseph Wharton created the first modern school of business on the campus of the University of Pennsylvania.[170] Within a decade or two, the University of California, University of Chicago, Dartmouth, and others would establish their own business schools. To satisfy American industry's demand for trained engineers, engineering departments were founded or enlarged at places like MIT, Purdue, Wisconsin, and Cornell. MIT offered the country's first four-year program in electrical engineering in 1882. The German model of a "research university" also spread. First established at Johns Hopkins (1876), it was core to the design of Clark University (1889), Stanford University (1891), and the University of Chicago (1890), and was soon appended to established institutions such as Harvard, Princeton, and Yale. By the turn of the century, even "several state universities had established their credentials as leading research institutions, including the universities of California, Michigan, Wisconsin, Minnesota, and Illinois."[171] Slowly, the American university was becoming an English college with a German research university grafted on top of it and multiple professional schools attached.

The Spread of Innovative Journalism

The 1880s both scrambled and savaged the press. The spread of new technologies (e.g., electric lighting, the rotary press, cheap wood-pulp white paper, typesetting and typewriting machines, and half-tone illustration techniques)[172] greatly expanded the capabilities of newspapers while bringing down their production costs. Thus, the battle for advertisements and ever larger circulations intensified.

In response, the sensationalist practices of "western journalism" spread to newspapers around the country. Joseph Pulitzer bought the *New York World* in 1883 and immediately went to war against the city's *Sun* and *Herald*. The *World* pitched itself as both nationalist and solidly Democratic—in contrast to most "western journalism" papers, which avoided overt partisanship.[173] The *World* also filled its pages with illustrations and eventually comics.[174] In fact, its editor later boasted that he "illustrated everything from advertisements to death notices and the circulation went up by leaps and bounds."[175] So successful was the *World* that other papers began to mimic its practices. Out west, William Randolph Heart took control over his father's *San Francisco Examiner*, leading it into the era of "western journalism," now called "new journalism" by its eastern acolytes.[176] During the mid-1890s, Hearst moved to New York City, where he bought the failing *New York Journal* and initiated a now infamous war with Pulitzer. In their contest for readers, Pulitzer and Hearst took "new journalism" to its most extreme form, "yellow journalism," in which newspapers printed ever bolder "scare" headlines and tabloid stories to attract readers.[177]

Meanwhile, overt partisanship became more risky as Gilded Age issues evolved and political platforms changed. For example, the pro-reform editors of the Republican-leaning *New York Times* led their paper into a near-death experience when they refused to back their party's allegedly corrupt James G. Blaine (R-ME) in the razor-close election of 1884. Thereafter, Republicans had little use for the news-light, commentary-heavy *Times*, and many Democrats still distrusted it. The paper was then nearly ruined financially by the 1890s depression, until Adolph Ochs rescued it in 1896 by promising "all the news that's fit to print." The Democratic *New York Sun* suffered a similar, but less existential, loss of readership when it refused to support Grover Cleveland (D-NY) in that same 1884 election. Nevertheless, even smaller newspapers, despite having *Republican* or *Democrat* in their name, changed their party allegiances to better fit either editor or reader preferences. For their part, investors and business readers could skip the drama and dive deep into financial news with the new *Financier* (1884) and *Wall Street Journal* (1889).[178]

The President, Politics, and the Economy Going into the 1890s

Going into the 1890s, the presidency was trapped between past constraints and emerging opportunities. For example, the federal government had grown beyond expectation. Federal expenditures as a proportion of economic output more than doubled between 1870 and 1890. Ambitious Gilded Age politicos focused on the expansion of Congress, which grew from 243 representatives and 74 senators (1870) to 332 and 88 (1890), and eventually 357 and 90 (1901). But the executive branch more than *tripled* in size during the same period. It went from 50,155 civilian employees (1871) to 150,844 (1891), and would approach a quarter-million by the close of the Gilded Age.[179] And while most federal workers were still employed by the US Post Office, its share dropped considerably throughout the period, while the proportion of employees at the War, Navy, and Treasury Departments grew significantly.[180]

However, the White House staff had barely changed. Back in 1870, Congress had provided President Grant with funding for only five assistants: one private secretary, one assistant secretary, one shorthand writer, and two clerks. Thirty years later, the president's official administrative and clerical staff stood at just thirteen.[181] Nor did technology provide much aid. The White House began using typewriters (1880) and electric lighting (1891), but the telephone remained in the basement telegraph room since it was first installed there by Hayes in 1878.[182] Most White House business was still done in pen and in person. Even then, open policy advocacy by presidents was frowned upon.

On the other hand, the growth of national issues (monopolies, inequality, tariffs, monetary policy, pandemic disease) and of a national communication and transportation system (railroads, telegraphs, telephones) brought both pressure and opportunity for a more powerful federal government, run by a more powerful president. State and local political machines dealt poorly with these issues. They rewarded votes and campaigning with jobs and basic welfare where they could, but even this was dependent on personal relationships. Nor could the weakening political machines cover skyrocketing campaign costs. For example, even in a *deflationary* environment, presidential campaign costs *increased* by leaps and bounds, from $300,000 (1872) to $1.85 million (1876) to $2.70 million (1884) to $4.03 million (1896).[183] Most of this spending went to state party organizations and national mail and pamphlet efforts. Meanwhile, the Pendleton Act (1883) had whittled away at the patronage system and the donations that came with it.[184] With moieties and assessments long abolished,[185] civil service reform was slowly freeing presidents from the grip of local machine bosses. But where to get new money and campaign workers?

The responses were myriad. Party and candidate clubs began to pop up throughout the country, working in common cause to forge a national party identity and to coordinate election efforts. As "voluntary" donations from spoilsmen dried up, bankers and corporations rushed to fill the contributions void. Average Americans joined national organizations in growing numbers to assert their political-economic interests. Some of these organizations had been around for decades; others were newly created to meet emerging policy concerns.[186] Political parties also evolved. They gradually shifted away from policy-vague, sensational "Hurrah!" campaigns and Reconstruction issues to a new educational style of campaign based on interests and specific policy demands. Local and state party operators stayed active, but they too began to surrender control to national party men who coordinated national fundraising and campaign efforts independent of the traditional machines.

This meant that presidents increasingly needed to win the support of the national electorate, not just the party faithful. Presidents had greater space and motivation to assert themselves more aggressively, both in rhetoric and action.[187] "The result was the emergence of the first truly *nationalized* party organizations, as opposed to the merely *national* network of local organizations of the Jacksonian mode."[188] Local party bosses chafed at the erosion of their power. Democrats were still united by white supremacy and their hatred of Republican government. But if the Republican Party was to flourish in this industrial era, it must continue its transformation into a national party headed by an agile president still able to appeal to local party needs. This balancing act of party versus nation was taken up by perhaps the most innovative, intelligent, and capable president of the era: Benjamin Harrison.

10

Benjamin Harrison, Patriot and Partisan

Planting the Seeds of Crisis, 1889–1893

Benjamin Harrison was, by most measures, supremely equipped to deliver a booming economy.[1] He was college educated and, for his time, exceedingly well-versed in political economy. He was also a devoted public servant, with decades of leadership experience and considerable background in public policy and legislative affairs. In fact, Harrison was one of the most competent administrators ever to enter the White House. He mastered every major aspect of domestic and foreign policy, even running several federal departments himself. In politics, he was a formidable campaigner and a paragon of decency in an indecent era. He was also a keen strategist who understood issue framing, campaigning, and political messaging. He was reportedly an amazing public speaker, "who could give five speeches a day, each one original, different, extemporaneous, and affecting."[2] And unlike most executives of the Gilded Age, he had a positive vision for the presidency and the federal government and what both could do for the American economy. Working with Harrison, Congress passed more major legislation than it had in twenty years.

However, instead of prosperity, Harrison created the conditions for a devastating financial crisis and a deep recession. For Harrison had few consistent policy preferences; rather, he was an ardent Republican partisan. As a young man, he had tirelessly stumped in the party's first political campaigns, fought in the Civil War for its ideals, and bound the Republican Party's cause with that of nation itself. He believed that Southerners continued to threaten American democracy and progress via their influence over the Democratic Party. Harrison therefore tended to support whatever policies were necessary to unify Republicans or to reward Union army veterans. The result was a haphazard mixture of fiscal, trade, and monetary policies that caused a sudden spike in spending accompanied by a rapid decrease in tax revenues that sent the country from surplus into deficit. Harrison's instability on monetary policy then scared investors into fleeing a potential dollar devaluation. When bad harvests and an economic slowdown hit during mid-1892, conditions gradually snowballed into a financial panic and the Great Depression of 1893–1897 that commenced soon after he left office.

Presidential Leadership in Feeble Times. Mark Zachary Taylor, Oxford University Press. © Oxford University Press 2024.
DOI: 10.1093/oso/9780197750742.003.0013

Background

Benjamin Harrison was as close as anyone might come to being American aristocracy. He was the son of a US congressman, grandson of the ninth president, and great-grandson of a signatory to the Declaration of Independence. Yet he benefited little from his family pedigree. Though born in his illustrious grandfather's house in Ohio in 1833, his own father was a middle-class farmer who grumbled, "My lot in this life has been to raise hogs and hominy to feed my children."[3] Benjamin's mother was also middle class, descended from low-level Scottish nobility, the daughter of a miller and merchant. Thus Harrison was "a farmer's boy, lived in a little farm house, had to hustle out of bed between 4 and 5 o'clock in the morning the year round to [do his chores]," according to one contemporary.[4] By all accounts, young Benjamin was industrious and pious, enjoyed a happy childhood, and was close to his large, devoutly Presbyterian family. But he was also a bit of a loner. He had an "introverted, sometimes self-righteous personality" and could be "terribly stubborn" and "insist upon having his own way."[5]

Harrison was one of the most intelligent and well-educated presidents of the 19th century. His parents believed deeply in education, so they provided him with a steady stream of tutors to supplement the local log-cabin schoolhouse. At age fourteen, Harrison entered the Presbyterian Farmers' College near Cincinnati, a small but surprisingly advanced institution. Its curriculum was designed, in part, by a highly respected professor of history and political economy, who personally taught Harrison about government and social relations.[6] After two years, Harrison transferred to the esteemed Miami University (of Ohio) in order to court his future wife. Again, religious instruction and scientific interpretation were central to the school's courses on history, politics, and political economy.[7] Thus, overall, Harrison received a full education, rare in its day, in political economy, but one geared toward understanding government as an organic, liberalizing instrument of the people that should foster "the growth or development of civil and religious liberty" rather than dry, technical discussions of trade or finance.[8] Harrison was judged by his classmates "an unpretentious but courageous student," often "respectable" if not "excellent" in his studies.[9] He mastered public speaking and was invited to lecture on political economy at his graduation.[10] But classmates also recalled him as being overly serious, distant, and austere; he "never seemed to regard life as a joke," while "his love of self made him careful of his time."[11]

By now a sincerely devoted Presbyterian, Harrison considered pursuing the ministry after college but chose law instead. He studied under a prominent Ohio attorney and former congressman at a law firm in Cincinnati. In early 1854, Harrison earned admission to the bar. He promptly left Cincinnati, moving with his new wife and child to the small but blossoming city of Indianapolis, Indiana.

After a year of struggling, he was invited into a law partnership with the son of the state's governor. "[H]e worked like a slave," attested his law partner, who dedicated his own time to the new Republican Party.[12] As a result of Harrison's labors, the firm flourished, as did Harrison. Yet he eschewed close friends. "I do not think he ever had an acquaintance with anyone that ripened into the hottest kind of friendship," recalled a neighbor.[13] Instead, the Harrisons, both "serious young people," intensified their Presbyterian faith, centering their lives on their church.[14] Harrison became a Sunday school teacher and "was constant in his attendance on church services."[15] Over time, he also became a church deacon and a church elder, and he kept religion the focal point of his everyday life until he died.

Though from a prominent political family, Harrison did not yet participate much in party politics, perhaps because his own father, by now in Congress, warned him that "none but knaves should ever enter the political arena."[16] After considerable thought and close attention to the political scene, young Harrison's increasingly strong antislavery views led him into the new Republican Party in 1856.[17] His religious and political beliefs began to merge. He saw the Republicans as fighting for man's God-given liberties. To him, the Republicans had come together to wage a desperate battle against the political-economic backwardness of the dangerous "slave oligarchy and the slave aristocracy" which ruled the South.[18] Although he lacked social finesse, Harrison was an adept orator. So he backed John Fremont, the Republican presidential candidate, as a busy stump speaker in that year's election. "I am Fremont all over and all the time." he proclaimed to a friend.[19] The following year, Harrison himself ran for office and won election as the city attorney of Indianapolis. He continued to do party and legal work for the Republicans in Indianapolis until the outbreak of the Civil War.

Harrison supported the war, and Lincoln, from the start, calling the president a "great simple hearted patriot."[20] He stumped for Lincoln's election and excoriated the South, swearing that he would "never, by word or thought, by mind or will, aid . . . the Everlasting Curse of Human Bondage."[21] In summer 1862, as the war dragged on, Harrison was prompted "by a high sense of Christian patriotism" to enlist in the Union army when entreated by his state's governor.[22] He volunteered to raise and train an Indiana regiment, despite having no military experience himself. Six months later, assigned the rank of colonel, he led them into three years of combat.

Over the course of the war, Harrison's regiment fought over thirty battles throughout Kentucky, Tennessee, and Georgia, eventually earning him promotion to brevet brigadier-general. He saw a divine aspect to the war, describing himself as "a good soldier of Jesus Christ," fighting "to honor my country and my friends."[23] By most accounts, Harrison was a strict but able commander who courageously led from the center of the action and participated in every aspect of combat, from daily drills to logistics, even battlefield surgery when necessary. He left the army a well-respected hero and much admired by the men who served with him. And yet Harrison was glad to be discharged when the war ended. "I am not a Julius Ceasar [sic], nor a Napoleon," he wrote his wife from the field. "[I have] no more relish for a fight than for a good breakfast."[24] Nevertheless, he resented those who had avoided military service, declaring, "I really begin to feel *contempt* for those who talk so eloquently for the Union and won't come and *fight for it*."[25] Harrison's bitterness toward the South and its sympathizers would prove an enduring disposition throughout his political career.

After the war, Harrison declined invitations to run for Congress. "[I]t would take me away from home so much," he explained to his wife. "I certainly long only for a quiet usefulness at home."[26] Instead, he returned to his family and law practice in Indianapolis. He and his wife also became heavily involved in community work, as well as church and veterans' groups. This inclination toward a tranquil life of home, church, and office, over politics, would become another lifelong tendency for Harrison. He seems to have enjoyed speech-making and administrating, but he despised the transactional aspects of politics. He also "disliked politicians" and often treated them "in a very chilly manner."[27]

The war deepened Harrison's loyalty to the Republican Party. For years, he remained furious at the disloyalty of the Confederates, as well as the Peace Democrat "Copperheads" in Indiana, who had undermined him at home while he was away in battle.[28] He long insisted, "I am willing to forget that they were rebels, at least as soon as they are willing to forget it themselves," but that time never seemed to come.[29] He therefore backed the Radical Republicans and their stern political punishments for ex-Confederates, though he gradually softened, adopting more moderate, mainstream Republican political-economic views over time. He attempted to run for governor of Indiana in 1872, but the state's Republican Party bosses failed to back his nomination.[30] The following year, the Panic of 1873 shook the Indianapolis economy, yet Harrison's law practice thrived on a steady flow of bankruptcy, foreclosure, and delinquency suits resulting from the crash. Harrison also won some high-profile legal cases around this time, bringing him national attention. And all the while he continued to work energetically for the Republican Party, for he still thought it the paramount defender of American liberty and progress.

His political prospects finally improved in autumn 1876. Caught in an election emergency, state Republican leaders drafted Harrison as a last-minute candidate to run for governor of Indiana. Harrison lost, but just barely. And he proved an enormously popular speechmaker during the campaign. Years later, an old Washington politico who had heard every president speak, from Lincoln to Coolidge, attested that "none of them equaled [Harrison] as an orator."[31] Even critics admitted that "if [Harrison] should address ten thousand men from a public platform, he would make every one his friend."[32] During the next few years, the national Republican Party featured Harrison as a speaker in cities around the eastern and central states. He campaigned for Republicans of all ranks. He also worked on state and national issues. For example, when violent railroad strikes reached Indianapolis during the explosive summer of 1877, Harrison helped to organize a peaceful resolution. He also served on the federal Mississippi River Commission, earning the admiration of President Hayes (1877–1881), who thought Harrison "a firm, sound man; his personal character is clear and high."[33] Harrison dined at the White House and even hosted Hayes in his Indianapolis home.

By 1880, thanks to his activism, distinguished reputation, and the death of a jealous political boss, Harrison had risen to become the Republican Party leader in Indiana.[34] He now ran for US Senate, which, at that time, meant lobbying the state legislature for appointment. The seat was easily won, and Senator Harrison then served in Washington from 1881 to 1887. There he specialized in problems of Indian affairs, the West, transportation, and military veterans. He strongly supported federal aid for veterans and tried to advance legislation to protect the nation's natural resources. But otherwise, Harrison mostly voted along Republican Party lines and against the hated Democrats. When Democrats increased their power in Indiana state government, he lost reappointment after a difficult political battle, and he departed the Senate.

1888 Election

By 1888, the Republicans desperately needed a clean candidate, and one independent of the party's jealous factions, to take back the White House from Democrat Grover Cleveland. Harrison was not the Republican Party's top choice.[35] However, more senior candidates either declined to run, were "wrong" on important issues (i.e., tariffs, veterans' pensions), or came from electorally unimportant states. In contrast, Harrison was a Union army general and a respected senator and hailed from the pivotal state of Indiana. He had spent decades promoting party unity and patriotism rather than divisive policies. On the issues, he was pro-pension, leaned pro-tariff, and was quietly moderate on silver. He was well-regarded by senior Republicans and an excellent public speaker. So, after considerable jousting at the convention with Ohio senator and former Treasury secretary John Sherman, Harrison won the Republican nomination on the eighth ballot.[36]

Harrison was an avid campaigner, aided by a passionate and competent team of Republican political bosses. They knew how to win elections and fought hard and dirty to do so. Many Republicans saw Democrats not just as political rivals but as enemies of American values and progress. Recognizing that open campaigning was still considered too bold and undignified, Harrison launched a clever "front porch" campaign.[37] Important interest groups and curious voters were brought to his home in Indianapolis, where he addressed the crowds, often in customized speeches informed by campaign research. He gave over ninety different campaign speeches from memory. These were then printed in papers nationwide, reaching millions of voters. In them, he capitalized on the disastrous "Great Tariff Debate" launched by President Cleveland and pounded away in support of trade protectionism. Large industrial interests (steel, iron, and manufacturing firms) donated in record amounts to elect Harrison, in what future muckraker Ida Tarbell called a "campaign for protection backed by the protected."[38] Meanwhile, Republican spoilsmen were desperate to regain their party's control over federal jobs, legislation, and government contracts. During the campaign, they spared neither fraud, threat, nor bribe to win votes.

That November, Benjamin Harrison defeated Grover Cleveland thanks to a handful of votes in pivotal states. In fact, thanks to voter suppression in the South, Cleveland won the popular vote that year;[39] but he lost the electoral college by narrow margins in New York and Indiana.[40] Third parties acted as spoilers in some states: the Prohibition Party captured nearly a quarter-million votes (2.2 percent of the popular vote), as the anti-saloon movement gained steam, while a labor-farm "union" party based in the Midwest brought in around 150,000 votes (1.3 percent of the popular vote).[41] Republicans managed to deliver razor-thin majorities in Congress, so if Harrison and the Republicans could work together, they had a rare opportunity to deliver whatever agenda they might agree upon. And Harrison was eager to forge those agreements.

For Party, Nation, and God

However, Harrison lacked a clear, coherent vision for the country. He believed deeply in representative democracy, trade protectionism, a "sound currency," education, and economic progress.[42] And he sincerely held that "God brought America into existence to serve as a model for the rest of the world."[43] But in practice, he was primarily guided by his desire to unify and strengthen the Republican Party. To Harrison, it remained locked in battle with backward-looking Democrats, whose antifederal policies were "dangerous heresy, and a deadly poison to national life."[44] Although the guns of the Civil War had fallen silent in 1865, Harrison believed, "[B]eaten by the sword, [the Confederates] will now fall back on the 'resources of statesmanship.' . . . [T]hey will steal away, in the halls of Congress, the fruits won from them at the glistening point of the bayonet."[45] His prediction proved correct. During the 1870s, Southern Democrats proceeded to suppress the Black vote and block the admission of new states and were suspected of manipulating elections in the North and West. To Harrison, they seemed intent on keeping the United States trapped in the past, as an agricultural economy run by wealthy white planters. By the 1880s, he had come to view Democrats as the enemies of democracy and "the boulder in the stream of progress, impeding and resisting its onward flow."[46] The best and only defense against them was the "high atmosphere of patriotism and pure Republicanism."[47]

Thus party unity and loyalty were more important to Harrison than policy or economic philosophy. As president, he did embrace the fiery brand of economic nationalism and trade protectionism that the Republican Party had inherited from the Whigs and which consumed the party during the 1880s and 1890s. Harrison had always leaned in this direction. But it was party unity that thrust it to his top priority. And satisfying Republican legislators and interest groups in order to stop the Democrats did *not* result in a consistent vision for the country. Here he differed drastically from Cleveland, who cared much for strict constitutionalism and laissez-faire minimalism but little for party regulars.[48] Even years into retirement, and amid a national economic crisis, Harrison continued to insist to fellow party members, "We ought not . . . to be asked to do anything that will affect the solidity, the loyalty, the discipline or the enthusiasm of the Republican party."[49]

Harrison's few consistent policy positions were all driven by his fierce partisan loyalty and his "high sense of Christian patriotism." For example, he regularly advanced Northern interests at the expense of the South. He routinely insisted that Union veterans be recognized and rewarded for their service. His Presbyterian upbringing led him to stubbornly oppose cuts in alcohol taxes, then a major source of federal revenues.[50] He believed that America's natural resources were given by God and should therefore be conserved. And his Whig tendencies told him that government should help fund education and infrastructure.[51]

But Harrison's party loyalty failed to provide him much direction on specific economic issues like tariffs, currency, and monopolies. Instead, he tended to straddle the fence on major political-economic debates. For example, despite his support for the Civil War and emancipation, he was initially lukewarm on citizenship for freed slaves. Over time, he increasingly favored civil rights for African Americans, but he led no great legislative battles there. On the spoils system, he stridently supported civil service reform in his speeches and writings, but then ignored reform when asked to find federal jobs for veterans and political allies. "[Harrison] used, but sincerely believed that he did not abuse, the spoils system," writes one biographer, "To him it was a distasteful necessity."[52] Harrison spoke out courageously against railroad monopolies, yet happily accepted their campaign donations and travel passes, and he prosecuted few corporate monopolies while in office. In regard to striking workers, he declared, "I am sympathetic with the laboring man and I shall always be found supporting such measures as are for his interest."[53] But he also insisted that the United States was *already* "a land that throws about the workingman social and political conditions more favorable than are found elsewhere."[54] Hence he did little of substance to help labor while in office. He had once blamed the impoverishment of Britain's lower classes on government welfare,[55] and yet he supported vast federal expenditures on welfare for Union army veterans and their dependents, despite clear evidence of fraudulent claims.[56] He also supported federal investment in national infrastructure, but then got distracted by the legal details.[57] Nor did he take a clear stand in the heated immigration debates of the era, choosing instead to quibble over the constitutional aspects of immigration law.[58]

Trade was perhaps *the* pivotal economic issue for Harrison's election and presidency. But over his career, his support for tariffs was uneven. He generally favored tariffs that protected American industries, but his reasoning could be tortured and illogical:

> If the tariff were lowered, our mills would close and English goods would come in, but there would be less goods all around; there would be more demand for the goods; the price would go up; and we would be just as badly off as we were before, except that the Englishman would have all the business, and our workers would be unemployed.[59]

To labor audiences, he argued that lower tariffs hurt wages by lowering prices, yet he simultaneously denied that higher tariffs much drove up domestic prices. In fact, he once mocked critics of tariff inflation, somewhat ridiculously, by saying that he was not in "sympathy with this demand for cheaper coats, which seems . . . necessarily to involve a cheaper man and woman under the coat."[60] And yet, despite all this, Senator Harrison had voted to reduce tariffs as politics demanded.[61] Only when Republicans made higher tariffs *the* wedge issue for the 1888 election did Harrison lead the fight in support of protectionism.[62]

On the equally crucial issue of money, Harrison could again be found on all sides of the debate. He reliably emphasized a "sound currency" in his speeches and writings, but, depending on the audience or situation, he might praise or criticize any type of money, while ironically attacking his opponents for inconsistency.[63] To gold men, he acknowledged that "free coinage of silver under existing conditions would disastrously affect our business interests . . . [and] produce a commercial panic."[64] To silverites, he declared, "I have been an advocate of the use of silver in our currency. We are large producers of that metal, and should not discredit it."[65] To attract the Greenback vote, he insisted, "The greenback is a promise on the part of the government to pay money . . . [and it] is a currency with which I believe the people will never consent to part."[66] To still others he claimed, "I have always believed, and do now more than ever believe, in bimetallism, and favor the fullest use of silver in connection with our currency that is compatible with the maintenance of the parity of the gold and silver dollars in their commercial uses."[67] Harrison was likely being honest, not duplicitous. He seemed to believe that gold, silver, and greenbacks could somehow coexist. But such diverse positions were not just untenable; they were economic contradictions. Because silver obtained different dollar prices as coin versus bullion, restrictions or increases in silver coinage affected metallic silver's dollar value in gold. The same applied to printed paper greenbacks. Therefore it was contradictory to simultaneously favor a "sound currency" and greater usage of all three currencies. In sum, Harrison was no inflationist, but he exhibited no specific, consistent beliefs on currency.[68]

As for the presidency, Harrison had a similarly inconsistent approach. As "ever the Whig at heart," he let legislation originate in Congress, but he provided input and applied pressure on a level hitherto unseen in 19th-century presidents.[69] On executive matters, and even much legislation, he did not take advice well. Harrison diplomatically sought input from cabinet members on bills that concerned their particular departments, but he rarely acted on it. He "was of a deliberative habit of mind and not only took his own time but kept his own counsel," said one of his senior appointees.[70] Harrison also viewed the president as a national cheerleader; thus he traveled the country giving dozens of speeches praising the nation, the US Constitution, and the American flag.

In foreign policy, Harrison was far more nationalistic, bold, and confrontational than his recent predecessors. He was no imperialist, but he wanted to see the United States respected alongside the European great powers. Thus, the Harrison administration sought to control new territories (Hawaii, Samoa), replace Britain as the primary military and economic power in the Western Hemisphere, and establish US naval stations in the Pacific. Harrison tended to be uncompromising in his negotiations with foreign governments, even using implicit threats of military force to resolve issues with Chile, Italy, Canada, and Great Britain.

Over time, Harrison proved to be one of the most "hands-on" presidents in American history. "Harrison knew more about the workings of the various departments than did their various heads," remarked one advisor.[71] He refused to delegate much. Believing himself chosen by God to lead the country, he had "a profound sense . . . that he himself could best guide the ship of state."[72] So he not only oversaw federal appointments, but he also assisted each cabinet member in determining their department's policies. At various points in his term, Harrison even took over the Departments of State, Treasury, Interior, Navy, and War when those secretaries fell ill or were incapacitated. Thus, on many issues, for all intents and purposes, Harrison *was* the executive branch.

1889: Harrison's Honeymoon Year

President Harrison's first year in office was relatively quiet. The economy fared well and there was little urgent economic business. After a lackluster spring, industrial activity surged 8 percent through late 1889. Anticipating good times, the stock market ticked up soon after Harrison's inauguration and then climbed around 6 percent during the spring and summer. Meanwhile, farmers flooded the markets with "an unprecedented crop of everything."[73] The 1889 wheat harvest alone was historic, 20 percent larger than the previous year and by far the largest to date. Thus Harrison enjoyed several months of economic honeymoon.

Nor did critical political matters call for his attention. The incoming 51st Congress was not scheduled to convene until early December, so no new legislation was possible.[74] Therefore, Harrison spent most of 1889 dealing with appointments, getting his federal departments in order, managing foreign policy,[75] organizing the Oklahoma Territory, and tending to ceremonial duties. In expectation of a renewed push for silver in Congress, he dispatched a prominent bimetallism advocate to Europe to ascertain interest in an international agreement on the "resumption of silver mintage."[76] Perhaps the only crisis to disrupt this quiet period came in May 1889, when central Pennsylvania "was desolated by floods unprecedented in the records of the great waters" after massive rainfalls caused a dam failure that deluged the region.[77] Over twenty-two hundred people died, sixteen hundred homes were destroyed, and countless businesses wiped out, while the region's railroad tracks and communication lines were washed away.[78] His predecessor, Cleveland, had refused to approve federal aid to help with local catastrophes, but Harrison quickly offered federal assistance and sent government officials to report on conditions. Harrison then presided over private fundraising efforts in Washington, DC, that delivered $30,000 in aid (roughly $1 million in 2020 dollars), telling the governor of Pennsylvania, "My heart is burdened for your smitten people."[79] The following year, Harrison visited the region and was welcomed by appreciative crowds.[80]

Civil service reform was the most immediate issue for the new Harrison administration. "Scarcely a day passed without some public debate on spoils versus merit system," notes one scholar.[81] Despite considerable progress in civil service reform, competitive exams covered just 18 percent of the almost 160,000 federal jobs in 1889. Hence Harrison and his department heads were assailed by thousands of office seekers and their intermediaries. "I was beset on all sides by dead beats & incapables," complained a senior party broker.[82] With Republicans back in office, and after an election won by historic contributions from wealthy donors, few expected Harrison's independence. Many "dolorously prophesied that [Harrison] would be the tool of [senior Republicans], the obedient servant of the imperious senatorial set . . . and the victim of faction leaders."[83] After all, the party bosses had been instrumental in getting Harrison elected, and they expected to be rewarded.

But Harrison credited himself, the party, and perhaps divine will for his election, not individual political machines. From his perspective, the Republicans had desperately recruited him to win an extremely close political battle for party and country; hence the devoutly religious Harrison owed no one but God for his success. "Providence has given us victory," he proclaimed to friends.[84] So he generally ignored the requests of the Republican machine bosses for patronage. And, despite being a former senator, Harrison also neglected "senatorial privilege" in his appointments to federal positions outside of Washington.[85] This infuriated Republican spoilsmen, who would mostly abandon Harrison in his 1892 campaign.

Nevertheless, Harrison did play the spoils game. But he played it at *his* direction, for *his* political goals. "That would be a fine appointment . . . but there isn't any politics in it!" he was known to say.[86] As usual, his primary goal was to unify the Republican Party. So, rather than blindly accept the patronage requests from party elites, Harrison personally labored over some seventeen hundred appointments to ensure that Republicans from all geographic wings of the party were appointed to his administration.[87] He quickly replaced legions of Democratic workers in the federal government with loyal Republicans. Quality and character mattered. But Harrison made some controversial appointments to high-level patronage spots, like naming a major campaign fundraiser and party operative as postmaster general. He did appoint a zealous reformer, Theodore Roosevelt, to the Civil Service Commission in charge of reform, but then generally disregarded Teddy's advice.[88] Harrison was also seen by the Republican Party as being too permissive on the collection of "voluntary" campaign donations from his appointees.[89] This relapse back into spoils seemed so egregious that, just two months into his administration, a widely respected Episcopalian bishop publicly admonished Harrison in a speech at a national ceremony, warning the new president against "[t]he conception of the National Government as a huge machine, existing mainly for the purpose of rewarding partisan service."[90]

As for Harrison's cabinet members, a contemporary journalist later described them as "neither brilliant nor exceptionally strong, and it soon became apparent that Harrison would himself attend to every important matter in the government."[91] Harrison generally did not consider party work, electoral support, or the recommendations of party bosses in his cabinet selections. He mostly selected men older than himself, of solid character, and with considerable experience. The majority of his cabinet had served in the military, four were US Army generals, most were lawyers, two were businessmen. All were loyal Republicans who agreed strongly with the party platform. All were good churchgoing Presbyterians. None was from the ex-Confederate South. In fact, most of

Harrison's cabinet consisted of men very similar in background and personality to himself. Still, much like his predecessor's cabinet, they were generally competent administrators and advisors; some were even policy innovators. Only one was a faction head and former party leader.[92]

Meanwhile, as the weather cooled, so too did the economy. The abundant crops of spring and summer resulted in a glut of grains and produce. Wheat prices fell around 25 percent by winter. Prices for beef, pork, corn, barley, and coal also slumped, as did those for steel rails and copper. As a result, deflation returned, around −2.6 percent for 1889, and real interest rates climbed toward 6 percent. The stock market flattened that autumn. The first month of winter brought unusually heavy snow and deep freezes to the West, cutting off transportation and bringing "widespread suffering, attended by appalling losses of livestock" to the region.[93] As a result, markets for transportation and equipment shrank, causing industrial activity to decelerate sharply that winter. Political pressure built for Congress and Harrison to do something about the economic issues upon which they had campaigned so fiercely.

Thus, after months of relative quiet and intense strategizing, Harrison's early December 1889 message to Congress was a widely anticipated declaration of the Republican agenda for the 1890 legislative session. After a long section reporting on foreign policy, Harrison recommended pages of legislative action: higher tariffs, a stronger military, new spending on river and harbor infrastructure, the first federal antitrust law, international copyrights, tighter immigration restrictions, a national bankruptcy law, comprehensive federal pensions for Union veterans and their dependents, the admission of new states, federal safety regulations for rail workers, civil rights protections for African Americans, and more. He also used the message to scold pro-gold, hard-money supporters. He chided them that the "evil anticipations which have accompanied the coinage and use of the silver dollar have not been realized,"[94] though he stopped short of suggesting that the Treasury coin silver on demand.

Developing Political Support

Successful passage of the Republican economic agenda depended on Harrison's ability to work with, or manipulate, the incoming 51st Congress between late 1889 and early 1891. Some issues badly divided Republicans or endangered their reelection. And much legislation depended on party-line votes, meaning that defections on either side could either jeopardize or guarantee passage. In fact, so slim were Republican majorities in Congress that reversals of just three seats in the House or one in the Senate could end them. This required Harrison to actively create and maintain allies on Capitol Hill and to foster the goodwill and support of the American public for the Republican program.

At this Harrison both excelled and failed. He could magnetize a crowd with his speeches, which he gave often. And unlike his predecessor, he regularly consulted with Congress on his major addresses and annual messages to Congress, which he used to signal paths forward. He also invited congressional leaders to special White House dinners and receptions, during which he discussed legislative design and strategy. And although Harrison used only one-tenth the vetoes of Cleveland, he used the threat of veto adroitly to shape policy, to forge Republican unity, and to assert his rare policy preferences. Indeed, he later wrote that the veto threat was his most effective legislative tool.[95] And yet Harrison generally refused to use patronage as a means to pressure Congress for legislation he favored.[96] To the press, he was more generous. In return for reporting friendly to his administration, Harrison doled out so much patronage to newspaper editors that some accused him of subsidizing the press.[97]

Unfortunately, one on one Harrison was vastly different from his magnetic public persona. While he was warm to family and friends, to most others he was alternately abrupt and rude, or silent and dismissive. "[W]henever he did anything for me," one senator recalled, "it was done so ungraciously that the concession tended to anger rather than please."[98] And when he demurred, Harrison could "say NO so loud and sharp that it will make your teeth rattle."[99] Ohio's governor simply called him "grouchy."[100] Others described Harrison as lacking personal warmth. "It's like talking to a hitching post," joked one senator.[101] "He is narrow, unresponsive, and oh, so cold!" complained a reporter.[102] Thus, Harrison soon earned the nickname "Iceberg" and his White House was scorned as an "icebox." It did not help that Harrison "believed that handshaking was both undignified and unhealthy" and avoided it by awkwardly withholding his right hand or by wearing kid gloves.[103] Visitors to the White House were warned, "Don't feel insulted by anything he may do or say. . . . [I]t is only his way."[104] Many in his party came to personally hate him. In spring 1891, a freshman senator observed, "[N]o one cares anything for him personally."[105] In particular, Harrison regularly infuriated the Republican House Speaker, who routinely excoriated him in exchange. Their "dislike was cordial and undisguised," observed one congressman.[106]

1890 and the Billion-Dollar Congress

Nevertheless, from December 1889 until March 1891, the 51st Congress would support much of Harrison's proposed economic program. At first, House

Democrats attempted to rebel, using parliamentary tactics to avoid quorums and obstruct legislation. But newly appointed House Speaker Thomas Reed (R-ME), who served simultaneously as chairman of the Rules Committee and was himself a master parliamentarian, forced through changes in the House rules to end these practices. Together, President Harrison and "Czar Reed" proceeded to pass plank after plank of the Republican Party platform. In fact, the list of legislative accomplishments made by Harrison and the 51st Congress is impressive; it was one of the most productive governments in US history.[107]

One of their earliest and perhaps greatest accomplishments, at least from Harrison's perspective, was the Dependent and Disability Pension Act, signed in late June 1890. It was the first major federal welfare program in US history. Strongly backed by Harrison, it provided federal pensions to qualified veterans, as well as their widows, minor children, and dependent parents. Within ten years, the program was consuming 30 percent of federal spending to provide support for almost 1 million Union army veterans and their families with monthly payments of $6 to $100 (in a period when monthly wages averaged around $30), depending on the case.[108] This equated to coverage for over 20 percent of all white males over the age of fifty-five.[109] Coverage was so broad that it has been described by experts as the most expensive and generous state pension program "ever passed by any legislative body in the world," eventually serving as a basis for modern Social Security, created in 1935.[110]

Next came the Sherman Antitrust Act of 1890, the first federal law to regulate large corporations.[111] Harrison had never held strong views about monopolies, but he supported the Republican Party's survival. For decades, complaints about monopoly abuses, especially by railroads, had deluged Congress. In early 1887, a bipartisan Congress had passed the Interstate Commerce Act to regulate railroads, but it did not cover other monopolies; indeed, it had failed even to govern the rails.[112] So, in response to growing public anger, Harrison and the Republicans backed the Sherman Antitrust Act. For although they may not have cared much about monopolies, the Republican Party adored trade protectionism. And they likely recognized that antitrust law was a politically necessary compromise to guarantee passage of the McKinley tariffs, which were expected to reward and further empower anticompetitive monopolies. Thus, the Sherman Antitrust Act passed the House and Senate in a rare and overwhelming bipartisan effort that spring, and Harrison signed it in early July. It seemed to be a historic step in the fight against inefficient monopolies. Ideally, it outlawed "every contract, combination in the form of trust or otherwise, or conspiracy in restraint of trade or commerce among the several states or with foreign nations."[113] But it was too vaguely worded and too poorly staffed and funded to launch many investigations. Nor did Harrison prioritize its enforcement. His attorney general initiated only seven antitrust cases, and won just one of them while still in office.

Even then, the damages were limited to only $5,000 (around $150,000 in 2020 dollars) per conviction.[114]

The Rise of the McKinley Tariffs of 1890

Trade policy was *the* major legislative battle of the 51st Congress and the focal point of its entire first session.[115] Economic nationalism and protectionist sentiment had swelled to fever pitch among top Republicans in Congress and within the Harrison administration.[116] Two years earlier, President Cleveland had whipped the country into a frenzy with his broadside attacks against high protectionist tariffs. This transformed trade into the signature issue in the 1888 elections. To Republicans, their victories in those elections appeared to deliver a ringing endorsement for higher tariffs, or at least a stinging rejection of downward revisions. So, despite his own history of flexibility on trade policy, Harrison was willing to negotiate away much legislation he *did* favor for the sake of party unity and a Republican "win" on tariffs. The problem was that almost every tariff had a different set of friends and enemies. Hence, much other legislation passed or abandoned in 1890 was done to engineer votes for higher tariffs.

In early March 1890, Republicans initiated the tariff fight with days of congressional hearings in order to generate public support. Meanwhile, representatives of the sugar, textiles, and metals industries were quietly invited to submit their own tariff schedules. Congressman William McKinley (R-OH), an arch-protectionist, managed the process. He submitted a comprehensive tariff bill in April 1890. Its goal, he proudly declared, was "to increase production here, diversify our productive enterprises . . . and increase the demand for American workmen. What American can oppose these worthy and patriotic objects?"[117] In a symbolic nod to western farmers, new duties were imposed on imports of wheat, corn, and barley, despite the fact that foreigners shipped little of these into the United States. Duties on sugar were cut, and domestic sugar subsidies were provided, to relieve the fiscal surpluses and to help sugar refineries in the Northeast. The new sugar provisions also helped consumers of all sorts of sweetened and canned goods. Duties on foreign tinplate, the basic input for the American canning industry, were jacked up in order to stimulate domestic production. Other protectionist plums and special inducements permeated the bill. It passed the House on a nearly strict party-line vote in late May.

However, when McKinley's trade bill reached the Senate, it was held hostage by opponents of pending legislation on Black suffrage, public education, and silver. Harrison, who had also come to support Black suffrage and public education, now faced a dilemma. In the South, Blacks were increasingly prevented from voting by various means, both legal and criminal. To counter Southern attempts to reverse the Fifteenth Amendment, the Federal Elections Bill of 1890 established federal supervision of congressional elections.[118] Harrison was a passionate supporter. "When and under what conditions is the black man to have a free ballot?" he demanded, "When is he in fact to have those full civil rights which have so long been his in law?"[119] While the Senate debated the McKinley tariffs, Harrison also launched an aggressive crusade to pass the Elections Bill. It proved a measure too far. Harrison had campaigned for, and won, the presidency mostly on trade protectionism, and much of the legislative session was crafted so as to forge consensus on major tariff legislation. Harrison's sudden push for the Elections Bill threatened to derail it. Not only did white Southerners oppose Black suffrage, but American industry in the North, an increasingly powerful supporter of the Republican Party, was beginning to view African Americans less as "ex-slaves" and more as cheap labor, and therefore sought to decrease their power at the voting booth. Despite great personal effort, Harrison could not get *both* the Federal Elections Bill and the McKinley Tariff. The former fell to the priority of the latter.

Another measure, the Blair Education Bill, sought to use federal aid for education in the South. Its dual objectives were to increase the economic opportunities for Blacks and to degrade the ability of literacy tests to prevent them from registering. Again, Harrison had long supported public aid for education, especially for the Black community. But he abandoned the Blair bill to soothe his party's fears about cost, constitutionality, and federal control over local education, as well as to forge bipartisan support for tariffs. Harrison instead settled for the Second Morrill Act (signed August 1890), which feebly attempted to eliminate racial discrimination in college admissions policies. More effectively, it established federal funding to support seventeen new land-grant colleges for African Americans in the Southern states.[120]

Harrison believed that these delays in Black suffrage and education were merely temporary political expedients and that African American rights would be taken up again in the next Congress. He was badly mistaken. The 1890 election and education bills would prove to be the last major efforts by any president or Congress to aid African Americans in the South until the late 1950s.

Silver Purchase Act of 1890

America's dedication to gold was Harrison's next sacrifice for party unity and protectionism. In a major enlargement of the Union during 1889–1890, he supported legislation to admit six new states in the West.[121] Harrison thereby broke a political logjam on new admissions that had existed for over thirteen years. The newly admitted states delivered a block of twelve senators and seven House members, all solid Republicans, further strengthening the party's majorities in Congress.[122] But unlike their northeastern brethren, western Republicans strongly backed silver coinage. Not only were western states home to vocal silver mining interests, but they also badly needed credit expansion for local investment. And their representatives were willing to trade support for protectionism for it. A western Republican put it bluntly:

> In all Nevada there is neither a spindle nor a loom, and the prairies of the Dakotas stretch for hundreds of miles unlit by furnace fire. How can Massachusetts expect that the people of the Northwest will continue to vote for a high protective parent tariff to sustain New England factories when both political parties in Massachusetts openly avow hostility to the great exporting industries of the Northwest?[123]

Until Harrison, all postbellum presidents had militated against the expansion of silver coinage and for progress toward the gold standard.[124] President Grant (1869–1877) had supported pro-gold legislation in Congress that eliminated silver as legal tender. Private citizens could still use silver coins, but the US Treasury might not accept them, nor would the US Mint coin silver upon demand. President Hayes (1877–1881) then reduced the supply of inflated paper currency, achieving convertibility between printed greenbacks and gold in January 1879. Nevertheless, pro-silver forces passed the Bland-Allison Act over Hayes's veto; it required the US Treasury to purchase and coin $2 million to $4 million worth of domestic silver bullion annually. Hayes used his power to ensure that only the minimum amount was minted. Neither Presidents Garfield (1881) nor Arthur (1881–1885) took strong stands on the currency issue, but no major legislation was passed under them. Then President Cleveland (1885–1889) faltered. He viewed currency and debt like any other government function—as a potential source of corruption or largesse. He therefore agreed with his "hard money" predecessors, and he initially tried to keep US finances run on the most efficient and least inflationary manner, which meant gold. But Cleveland failed to repeal Bland-Allison when given the opportunity in 1885–1886. Thus pro-silver interests felt emboldened to increase their attacks on gold.

Harrison now flagrantly betrayed the faith. He claimed to stand for a strong, reliable currency, but he had always skirted the silver issue for the sake of party unity. The new Republican silver-producing states and the tariff battle only furthered Harrison's resolve to "do something for silver" and thereby ensure harmony among Republicans, many of whom now supported bimetallism.[125] Given the composition of Congress, it is not clear that such generosity toward silver was necessary.[126] Nevertheless, toward the end of Harrison's first year in office, his Treasury secretary floated a plan in which the federal government would use government bonds to purchase *all* the silver on America's domestic market. In his first annual message to Congress, Harrison referenced this plan and came out in support of bimetallism.

This opened the floodgates to pro-silver legislation in Congress. Harrison coaxed and cajoled the Senate for a compromise, while "Czar Reed" held the party together in the Republican-dominated House. During late spring and early summer 1890, Harrison hosted a number of White House meetings with key senators and "threw his entire weight behind" a new Silver Purchase Act, along the lines his administration had proposed. The Senate finally passed it in mid-July, and Harrison signed it days later. It did not allow the free coinage of silver, nor a *de facto* shift toward a silver standard, as demanded by many silverites. But it did require the Treasury to purchase 4.5 million ounces of silver every month, or nearly the *entire* US silver output.[127] Harrison then largely ignored calls to defend the gold standard in subsequent months. The president's silence thereby "gave rise to an apprehension that if a free [silver] coinage bill should pass both Houses he would not feel at liberty to veto it," a senior Republican senator later recalled.[128]

The Passage of the McKinley Tariffs of 1890

With silver taken care of, Harrison and Congress returned to trade protection. The Senate passed the McKinley Tariff Bill in early September on a strict party-line vote. It then took over two weeks of torturous negotiations to transform the Senate and House versions into a compromise bill for President Harrison's signature.

In the meantime, however, a financial panic was brewing. Harrison may have forged Republican Party unity and won impressive legislative victories, but his economic legislation was sending the U.S. Treasury disastrously into imbalance. Throughout the summer, imports flooded into the country as Americans stocked up on foreign goods in anticipation of steep tariff hikes. The result was a sudden and severe trade deficit, hence a drawdown on US gold reserves. Massive federal spending anticipated by the Pensions Act, sugar subsidies, naval construction, and other measures, as well as the promise of pro-silver legislation, combined to pose further threats to US gold supplies. Meanwhile the British had hiked their interest rates, attracting investment out of the United States and into London. "The situation, therefore, is serious and embarrassing," fretted the *New York Times*, which blamed the brewing crisis partly on "the foolish and wicked legislation of Congress and from the policy which the Treasury . . . has chosen to follow from purely partisan and unjustifiable motives."[129]

In mid-September 1890, with demand for scarce money and credit rising during harvest season, the financial sector began to panic. Harrison, then on vacation, immediately wired the Treasury Department to increase the money supply by making early interest payments on US bonds, buying bonds, and accelerating pension payouts. He also sent senior Treasury officials to consult with, and reassure, bankers in New York City on federal action. On their combined advice, Harrison continued to increase bond sales as needed to expand the money supply and prevent a bankers' panic.[130]

Meanwhile, Congress continued its negotiations on a final trade bill, which Harrison signed in early October 1890. It was the first wholesale reform of US trade policy since the Civil War. The McKinley tariffs of 1890 raised duties on almost fifty pages of listed imports to an average of 49.5 percent, the highest duties and on the most goods since the Revolution. Within the bill, Harrison also won for the president unprecedented authority to manage America's international trade. The president was given authority to hold trade conventions, to negotiate reciprocity agreements (i.e., to offer lower duties on foreign imports in return for lower rates on American exports) "without congressional oversight, and to erect a federal bureaucracy empowered to administer the complicated details and functions of foreign trade."[131] During 1891–1892, Harrison used this new authority to negotiate trade agreements to increase US exports into Brazil, the United Kingdom, Germany, France, Austria-Hungary, and a handful of other countries. These agreements were short-lived, however, abrogated by the 1894 Wilson-Gorman Tariff.

The new McKinley tariffs were drastic and widespread, and most took effect immediately. Total imports dropped over 4 percent in October alone, then another 11 percent in November; by December, imports were over 21 percent off their summer high. Some of this falloff in trade was seasonal or due to purchases shifted earlier in the year to get ahead of the tariffs. But much of it was enduring. For example, imports of iron and steel fell immediately, dropping by half within a year.[132] Imports of other industrial materials also dropped precipitously by 1891: lead (80 percent), zinc (40 percent), sulfur (30 percent); crude foodstuffs and finished manufactured goods suffered only slightly lesser declines (20 percent and 5 percent, respectively). And since some US manufacturers combined tariffed imports with domestic inputs, the costs of their goods increased as well. The tariffs were so pervasive, complained Democrats, that "[t]he McKinley bill is with us always, at the table, at the bedside, in the kitchen, in the barn, in the churches and to the cemetery."[133] Secretary of State (and senior Republican leader) James Blaine warned that "such movements as this for protection will attack the Republican Party only into speedy retirement."[134] Even the author of the tariff bill, William McKinley, later admitted "that some [tariffs] were too high."[135]

Subsequent analysis of the McKinley tariffs has been harsh.[136] The new tariffs increased costs for nearly all American consumers, while increasing the wealth of a much smaller number of US producers. Higher tariffs shrank trade, likely shaving half a percentage point off US GDP growth.[137] Nor does the tariff appear to have provided critical protection for infant industries.[138] "[W]ould not all this growth have taken place in any case?" asked one economic analyst years later.[139] Some US industrial jobs and wages may have been protected, or at least the data suggest that they did not suffer much. But the overall costs imposed by the McKinley tariffs on American society, in the form of higher prices, were likely not worth the net benefits, if any, concentrated on relatively few producers.[140] Rather, the tariffs mostly served to transfer wealth out of agriculture and the South into industry and the North and West and to help fund the generous Pension Act for Union army veterans.[141] And since America was by now such a huge market for foreign exports, the new tariffs helped trigger economic recessions in Canada, Great Britain, Germany, Japan, Chile, and other major exporters to the United States.[142]

1890 Midterm Elections

A month later, the 1890 midterm elections were a national referendum on Harrison and the Republicans. Conservatives denounced the unprecedented expenditures of "the billion-dollar Congress." House Speaker Reed ineffectively responded, "Yes, but this is a billion-dollar country."[143] Other critics lambasted the new tariffs, silver, or failed civil service reform. In the Midwest, frustrated Populists exhorted poor farmers to "raise less corn and more hell."[144] That November, angry voters swept Republicans out of office. Democrats took 235 seats in the House, a two-to-one majority! Third parties and independents took another 10 seats. Republicans were left with a tiny minority of just 86 seats (around 26 percent) in the House. State and local issues determined the makeup of the state legislatures, which appointed men to the US Senate.[145] Hence, the Republicans retained a slim Senate majority (53 percent). But several of these surviving Republican senators had voted *against* the McKinley tariff bill, and McKinley himself lost reelection to the House. As for President Harrison, he blamed the 1890 rout on apathy. Republican voters were not angry, he explained, but "lacked interest and simply stayed away."[146]

In the week following the elections, Britain's enormous Baring Bank nearly failed, threatening a global economic crisis.[147] "The whole human race seemed to be in collapse: revolution and financial bankruptcy in Portugal and Brazil, the *coup d'etat* in Chile, war in Central America, a financial and commercial crisis in Argentina, a building crisis in Italy," recalled the new *Journal of*

Political Economy.[148] Fast action by the Bank of England saved Baring, but only by diverting European lending and investment away from the United States and into the London money centers. As money and credit rapidly contracted in the United States, the financial sector there began to panic. To increase the US money supply, Harrison again ordered the Treasury Department to buy bonds and increase pension disbursements. The president and his Treasury secretary also pressured bankers to increase lending and credit from their reserve funds. Finally, Harrison worked with a special Senate committee to legislate increases in silver and paper currency. Confidence was quickly restored and a crisis avoided.[149]

Meanwhile, with the clock now ticking on their majorities in Congress, Republicans huddled with Harrison to put together a final legislative agenda. On its last day, March 3, 1891, the lame-duck 51st Congress passed a flurry of Republican bills supported by Harrison. The Land Revision Act of 1891 reformed federal land policy to prevent the abuse, fraud, and exploitation that had run rampant under older legislation. The Forest Reserve Act of 1891 gave the president authority to conserve natural resources by withholding public lands from private development, thereby creating the legal basis for the modern national forest system. Harrison immediately used the Act to create what is now Yellowstone Park.[150] The Immigration Act of 1891 set up a new executive superintendent with direct control over immigration and established harsh guidelines against the admittance of the poor or migrants with histories of criminal behavior, "moral turpitude," or evidence of "loathsome" or "contagious" diseases. Harrison urgently requested, and Congress authorized, the construction of new battleships and other measures to continue the modernization of the US Navy begun under President Chester Arthur (1881–1885). Harrison also sought to enlarge and modernize the US merchant marine fleet. To this end, the Ocean Mail Act of 1891 subsidized US steamships to carry mail and established a series of trade routes that remained in use for decades. Harrison supported national infrastructure with a million-dollar federal improvement program of the Mississippi River. In order to gain reciprocal copyright protection abroad for US authors, the International Copyright Act of 1891 created the first protections for foreign works in the United States. The Judiciary Act of 1891 created the US Circuit Court of Appeals, thereby increasing the efficiency of the federal court system. And to resolve trade disputes with Europe, Harrison got Congress to create the first federal standards for meat inspection of exports.[151]

After an exhausting and victorious legislative session, Harrison departed for a five-week transcontinental tour during spring 1891. He visited twenty-one states and two territories across the South and West, delivering over 140 speeches touting his administration's, and the nation's, accomplishments, as well as national unity, patriotism, and the flag.[152] Harrison traveled for free on the Pennsylvania Railroad in five luxury cars, provided specially for him, "of the latest build, vestibuled, lighted by electricity, and furnished with the newest appliances of all kinds."[153] The *New York Times* questioned whether "[t]o the distressed farmer . . . this glittering, red and gold, and steel-blue parade, at no cost to the President, may seem like a mockery, as it certainly will to men who are being told that the panacea for their ills will be found in the McKinley bill, if they can live long enough to get over its first oppressive effects."[154] But generally the trip was a success, with large crowds turning out to greet their president.

The Revenge of Harrison's Economic Agenda: The Recession of July 1890 to May 1891

Harrison's economic agenda exacerbated a shallow economic recession which had begun during July 1890. Gold flight, bank failures, and nervous investors caused the stock market to drop 18 percent between May and December 1890. Worse yet, the US Treasury began paying some debts in paper rather than gold or gold certificates, further alarming investors.[155] Industrial activity stumbled in midautumn and then slumped, falling 5.3 percent from December 1890 through May 1891. For the year 1890, the economy shrank, though only slightly, around 0.6 percent, while deflation continued at –1.8 percent. Harrison then threw fuel on the financial fire in April 1891. Not yet six months after passing the Silver Purchase Act, he further emboldened free-silver proponents by writing to a major silver conference that he had "always believed, and do more now than ever believe, in bimetallism, and favor the fullest use of silver in connection with our currency."[156]

The United States was temporarily saved from major economic troubles by a freak weather event. European crops suffered a massive failure thanks to months of drought followed by frost, heavy snows, strong winds, and deep freezes during the first months of 1891. In some parts of Europe, "the winter came on so suddenly that the fields could not be well prepared before heavy snowfalls covered them up."[157] The cold persisted deep into April. "Every morning the thermometer stands close to freezing point," reported *The Economist*.[158] The harsh weather also snarled European transportation networks. As a result, that spring and summer, food prices soared across western and central Europe, while Russia declined into famine.[159] Meanwhile US farmers enjoyed record crop yields. US food exports boomed, temporarily reversing the outflows of gold and boosting the US money supply. Domestic demand for farm equipment, grain storage, and transportation soon followed. Thus, between May 1891 and May 1892, American agriculture and industry enjoyed a temporary comeback.

Homestead Strike of 1892

Meanwhile, the ongoing conflict between industry and labor entered a new stage during the Harrison administration. Strikes erupted around the country, hitting a record of 1,897 work stoppages in 1890 with some 393,000 workers participating, or around 4.2 percent of the American industrial workforce. The following year was only slightly better (1,786 strikes involving 300,000 workers, or around 3.6 percent of the workforce). Membership in labor unions, which had been in decline since their frenzied peak in 1886, resumed its upward climb. One problem was that since 1888, the average wages for unskilled labor had remained flat, while urban crowding and tariffs threatened to drive the prices of food, housing, and transportation in the cities ever higher. This was especially ominous as the 1890 census revealed that Americans were moving from the farms to the cities in record numbers. Also, for years manufacturers had replaced men with machines where possible, and cheap immigrant labor was imported where machinery would not do, all while firms demanded ever longer work hours. Unions angrily protested. "[T]he wealth of the country becomes centralized, its power increases, and the laboring classes are more or less impoverished," complained the Amalgamated Association of Iron and Steel Workers.[160] Something had to give.

Tensions climaxed in early July 1892, when an industrial lockout and strike at the Carnegie Steel plant in Homestead, Pennsylvania, turned into a massacre.[161] Striking members of the metal workers union and hundreds of private Pinkerton security agents skirmished with rifles and small cannon, while bystanders took part with stones and clubs. "[T]he town is red with blood," reported the *St. Louis* (MO) *Dispatch*.[162] Seven men died and many others were wounded. The governor of Pennsylvania mobilized the state militia to escort "scab" workers in and restart the plant. A Russian-born anarchist, supported by fellow activists, attempted to assassinate Carnegie's business partner in his Pittsburgh office. This was no longer an ordinary strike; it had become organized warfare. Private armies of industry and workers fought it out in the streets in "a momentous battle between the nation's most powerful steelmen . . . and the workers, led by the country's largest trade union," over automation, immigrant labor, and corporate power.[163] It was unlike anything the nation had seen before.

Harrison, however, did little. Vacationing in upstate New York, he added to a scheduled speech a few lines about "[o]bedience to law; deference to public authority," and he privately pressured Carnegie to negotiate. But otherwise he took no action. Instead, state militia were called in. They seized the steel plant and arrested hundreds of strikers. The local union then descended into bankruptcy as it struggled to defend them. Scabs got the Carnegie factory running again, and within a few months, the remaining strikers gave up. Rather than address worker grievances, the following year the Harrison administration successfully applied the Sherman Antitrust Act against strikers in New Orleans and in Georgia.[164]

The Cholera Scare of 1892

To be fair, Harrison was by now increasingly distracted by personal tragedy. In late December 1891, his wife contracted tuberculosis. For the next ten months she battled the disease, and mental depression, until she died. Harrison had been devoted to his wife. He lightened his official schedule during mid-1892, especially his presidential campaign, in order to care for her. "Politics and business have been crowding the day and night, and with the anxiety by your mother, makes life just now a burden and ambition a delusion," he wrote to his daughter.[165]

Yet, to his credit, Harrison plunged back into work when crisis threatened. Specifically, in September 1892 he rushed to Washington to personally coordinate the federal response to a cholera scare.[166] Over a hundred passengers on ships bound for New York had contracted the disease via a deadly outbreak in Hamburg, Germany. There, newspapers were reporting, "So great is the terror caused by the cholera . . . [b]usiness is prostrate, and shipping is going to other ports."[167] Now, several ships bearing Jewish migrants from Russia threatened to bring the disease into New York City. A cholera epidemic striking at America's financial, commercial, and transportation hub would cause an economic disaster. "READY FOR THE PLAGUE," warned a headline in the *New York Sun*.[168] Harrison endorsed a three-week quarantine on immigration, despite questionable authority to do so, thereby averting the potential pandemic. He then worked swiftly with Congress to pass legislation to create a national system of quarantines to defend against the spread of pandemic disease.[169]

In regular political matters, few legislative options remained for Harrison to advance his economic goals. When the 52nd Congress returned to its full session in early January 1892, the House was dominated by Democrats, and much of the Republican platform had already been enacted. Thus, Harrison achieved far less after spring 1891 than during the first half of his administration. He was not totally incapacitated, however, for some significant legislation was passed during this time. For example, Harrison signed the bipartisan Geary Act (May 1892), meant to aid American workers by extending the 1882 Chinese Exclusion Act for an additional ten years and requiring Chinese immigrants to carry identification papers. He helped Congress to enact an eight-hour workday for federal blue-collar workers (August 1892).[170] And he signed off on new federal mandates for safety requirements on railroads (March 1893). Nevertheless, Harrison and his Republican allies spent much of their time warding off attempts by House Democrats to rescind the work of the 51st Congress. Hence, during his last two years in office, Harrison switched his focus to foreign policy, where he achieved relatively little.

The Economy in 1892

In spring 1892, the economy began a gradual descent that lasted for the remainder of Harrison's presidency.[171] The stock market was first to show signs of weakness. It crested in March 1892, and then slowly trended downward for the next sixteen months, a decline of around 60 percent. Agriculture prices followed. After peaking at $1.08 per bushel in April 1892, wheat fell almost every month for the remainder of Harrison's presidency, hitting 74 cents the month he left office, a decline of over 30 percent. By summer, it was industry's turn to contract, though here the pullback was smaller, only around 2 percent by the close of Harrison's term.

But it was the gold-silver situation that most disturbed markets. Encouraged by Harrison's willingness to yield on currency issues, in early July 1892 the Senate passed a bill allowing free coinage of silver, spooking investors. It died in the House, but the damage was already done. Banks and the US Treasury alike began to hoard gold. For nearly six years, the use of silver in the United States had been on the rise, and a dollar devaluation now seemed only a matter of time. "[T]he general opinion seems to be that Harrison's election will bring . . . London selling," advised the *Wall Street Journal*.[172]

Harrison would lose his reelection bid in November 1892. He won just 43 percent of the popular vote, which translated into just one-third of the electoral college. Voter suppression, trade, silver, and labor issues each played a role. But Harrison's campaign was most handicapped by his own absence from it (due to his wife's illness and death) and by his single-minded approach toward federal appointments. For Harrison had lost the popular vote four years earlier and partly owed his 1888 election to a handful of machine bosses, donors, and droves of energetic and scheming supporters throughout the Republican Party. After his victory, they had eagerly awaited their spoils. But rather than enthusiastically reward their efforts, Harrison had kept silent about senior appointments for months, and then he generally failed to hand out cabinet or patronage slots according to the wishes of Republican powerbrokers. Harrison thereby frustrated Republican bosses and alienated powerful political allies. Now, four years later, the Republican political machines and party activists felt little motivation to get out the vote for Harrison. "[H]is manner of treating people who came to him had filled the country with bitter and powerful enemies," recalled an ally, "while his friends were very few."[173] In fact, some Republicans attempted a "Dump Harrison" movement, but failed to find a suitable challenger to replace him.

The business press celebrated Harrison's downfall. "Financial circles feel new hope," declared the *Commercial and Financial Chronicle*.[174] For despite the threat of low-tariff Democrats taking power, bankers and businessmen celebrated "the name and character of ex-President Cleveland . . . for the sound financial views he holds and for the adoption of those views by the convention that nominated him."[175] In fact, the *Wall Street Journal* observed that "so many good Republicans . . . voted for the Democratic party because they believe in Mr. Cleveland's modified protective ideas."[176] Even the manufacturing community seemed relieved. "The [electoral] reaction against the present tariff, strangely enough, was not so pronounced in agricultural communities as in manufacturing localities," observed *Iron Age*, which assured its readers that Cleveland would block any radical changes to protection.[177] Instead, Cleveland would restore order to America's finances. If only the economy could hold out until spring "for the assurance which conservative legislation alone can impart."[178]

The Great Depression of 1893–1897 Begins

During the final months of Harrison's presidency, the economy spiraled faster toward depression. Due to Harrison's fiscal and monetary policies, American deficits had mounted during the winter of 1892–1893, leading to a precipitous fall in the US Treasury's gold inventories.[179] The healthy budget surplus of $111 million in 1888 had dropped to an anemic $2.3 million by 1892 and was rapidly headed into deficit. Harrison backed a quixotic attempt to remonetize silver at yet another International Monetary Conference, which commenced in late November in Brussels.[180] Held at the behest of the Harrison administration, and with the participation of twenty nations, it ended in failure after a few weeks. Critics mocked the conference as "hardly . . . serious" and declared, "The whole affair should be regarded with a sense of humiliation by the people of this country."[181] The business press now regularly fretted about outflows of specie and the "real danger to our currency not remaining on a par with gold."[182] *Rhode's Journal of Banking* warned of a "storm that is likely to break at any time."[183] By early 1893, businesses and individuals were reporting difficulty in acquiring gold, while the *Commercial Bulletin* warned its readers of "the impending monetary crisis."[184]

In early 1893, conditions changed rapidly. Industrial production and trade decelerated during the first three months of the year. The stock market contracted sharply, by 8 percent, during the last five weeks of Harrison's presidency, and would not reach bottom until summer.[185] In late February, the Philadelphia & Reading Railroad collapsed, sparking further selling on Wall Street. Harrison's secretary of the Treasury considered a new bond issue to replenish federal gold stocks, but only as a last resort. He "openly expressed [his] view . . . that his responsibility ended with the fourth of March [the end of Harrison's administration] and that he cared only to avert a catastrophe up to that date."[186] With scarce money and little credit available for spring planting, and stung by a surge in European agriculture, that year's American farm situation would be among the worst of the decade. The price of wheat alone was down over 26 percent from when Harrison first took office. Overall, US real GDP per capita would shrink more than 6.7 percent in 1893. As a result, the presidential transition of 1893 would prove one of the worst economic handoffs in American history.

Harrison seemed oblivious to the growing economic danger. In his final annual message to Congress, he praised "the general prosperity of the country," bragging, "There has never been a time in our history when work was so abundant or when wages were as high."[187] And four years later, the nation mired in the depths of economic turmoil, Harrison blamed the Depression not on *his* policies but on lower tariffs passed by his successor. "Our manufacturers, left without adequate protection, have been successively and gradually closing up and putting out their fires," he argued.[188] According to him, banks and businesses had then pulled back out of fear of cheap imports, while new fiscal policies failed to bring in enough revenue to fund the government and support the dollar. Of course, Harrison ignored the fact that it was his policies that had caused the fiscal deficits, credit contractions, and fears of currency devaluation in the first place.

Summary

Harrison's record on the economy is mixed. His vigorous responses to the two budding financial crises of 1890 were exemplary. In these actions, Harrison and his Treasury Department behaved much like a modern Federal Reserve. They acted rapidly and forcefully to defend the US financial system. They did so by flooding markets with as much money and credit allowed by legislation at the time. The Harrison administration also coordinated with private bankers and Congress in serious, team efforts to respond to the crises. And their swift, vigorous, comprehensive response helped to restore confidence and trust in the US financial system. Either of these two crises could have resulted in a major recession, perhaps even economic depression, had they been ignored or dealt with in a less aggressive manner. The same can be said of Harrison's forceful reaction to the threat of a cholera pandemic during summer 1892. Had any of these emergencies been treated with the traditional passiveness of 19th-century presidents, they might have wreaked devastating short-run effects on the economy. Meanwhile, his generous fiscal and monetary policies appear to have kept the economy strong and inequality in check, at least until the end of his term.[189] Thus, if we look at 1889–1893 in isolation, Harrison did relatively well.

On the other hand, Harrison pursued a collection of policies that created the financial conditions for the Great Depression of 1893–1897. His combination of vast federal spending programs, revenue cuts, tariffs, and favor toward silver, together eroded trust in America's financial solvency and the US dollar. During the Gilded Age, the world's creditors expected to be paid in gold. Yet Harrison abruptly shifted the United States off a trajectory toward the gold standard and toward greater use of less valuable silver. Although he repeatedly insisted on maintaining the two metals' "equality in their commercial uses," investors feared devaluation and fled the US dollar when an economic slump hit in early 1893.[190] This triggered one of the deepest and longest financial crises and economic depressions in US history.

Harrison appears to have followed this path because he prioritized Republican Party unity and aid to Republican interest groups over strategic economic goals and cohesive policy. Otherwise, his economic philosophy was a hodgepodge of inconsistent and changeable views. On trade and monetary policy, he discounted the costly trade-offs and dilemmas and instead prioritized the political goal of keeping Republicans in power.[191] In fact, one scholar of the party observed in him "a streak of blind partisanship which Harrison seldom exhibited outside the arena of politics. Not only did he defend party policies that had been out of fashion for a decade, but he did so with a conviction and logic that amazed his contemporaries."[192] Harrison opposed government welfare, yet backed the Pensions Bill for US army veterans. He claimed to support a strong currency and national finances, yet he gutted the revenue streams necessary to provide them. He compromised America's dedication to gold because he wanted "to do something for silver," especially silver Republicans. His fraught personal relationships with congressmen left him few opportunities to craft less blatantly partisan and more economically constructive legislation. And while he excelled at rallying and educating the public, he tended to do so only *after* legislation had been crafted and passed. Again, this surrendered a political tool that Harrison could have used to force through more sustainable economic policy. Writing just fourteen years later, in 1907, MIT economist Davis Rich Dewey laid the currency debacle of at Harrison's feet: "No incident in our national history more forcibly illustrates the lack of determined statesmanship."[193] Thus, despite the fact that Benjamin Harrison was enormously talented, highly experienced, well-educated, deeply intelligent, and staunchly patriotic, he created conditions which plunged the country into economic disaster.

11

Grover Cleveland Returns

The Great Depression of 1893–1897

In his second administration, Grover Cleveland presided over one of the greatest economic disasters in US history. It began with an 1893 financial crisis that shook markets for months. Then came an economic downturn so deep and prolonged that, prior to the 1930s, Americans referred to it as the "Great Depression." Cleveland had ample warning that the crisis was brewing and good ideas about how to stop it, but his insistence on conservative governance and a passive presidency idled him for months while the economy toppled over. The stock market collapsed. Industrial production plummeted. Tens of thousands of farms and businesses went bankrupt. Unemployment and homelessness skyrocketed. Yet Cleveland refused to budge. Only *after* a domestic currency famine, followed by a crash in international silver markets, did Cleveland finally step in. He drove Congress to end the Sherman Silver Act, thereby shifting the United States back to the gold standard. But this only solved half the problem. He then fumbled badly in his leadership on tariff reform, leaving the US financial system bleeding specie. When he brutally cracked down on labor strikes and ignored the suffering of the homeless and unemployed, he came across as cold and uncaring. He generally lost the support of the American people, who found him detached and unreliable, and he never tried to win them back. And despite a temporary economic recovery between summer 1894 and early autumn 1895, Cleveland also lost his influence over Congress. When the economy swooned again during late 1895, his final resort was to turn to Wall Street for loan after loan to keep the US Treasury afloat. This further alienated Americans, even in his own Democratic Party. To many, Cleveland's trade, monetary, and domestic policies were actively helping wealthy bankers and British exporters to profit off the nation's economic troubles. Public confidence in the president evaporated.

Meanwhile, unemployment, deflation, economic inequality, and labor unrest plagued the country throughout Cleveland's second term.[1] Federal monies could have been disbursed to the state governments, spent on public works, or allotted as pork. Each of these had been suggested, or done, by previous administrations. Certainly, state and city governments were aggressively expanding their social welfare programs. Yet again, Cleveland's rigidity prevented him from considering any sort of federal relief. His refusal to lead, or to compromise on his strict

Presidential Leadership in Feeble Times. Mark Zachary Taylor, Oxford University Press. © Oxford University Press 2024.
DOI: 10.1093/oso/9780197750742.003.0014

constitutionalism, seemed to doom the economy, as well as his presidency. The political-economic debacle was so severe that Cleveland's departure in 1897 ended the era of small-government liberalism that had dominated the American presidency and the federal government for much of the country's first century. As a result, more than one historian of the administration has accused Cleveland of "inept tactics and wavering leadership."[2]

Ex-President Cleveland on the Sidelines, 1889–1893

Cleveland had been an exciting newcomer to politics during his first term as president (1885–1889).[3] His dogged adherence to small, constitutional government seemed fresh and invigorating during the heyday of the corrupt spoils system, especially after the Garfield assassination (1881) and the dubious Arthur administration (1881–1885). Even the Republican-leaning *New York Times* had looked forward to "the honest and safe politics represented by Mr. Cleveland," a Democrat.[4] When he first entered office, an economic recession had been underway for three and a half years. Cleveland took aggressive action to defend the dollar and the gold standard and thereby averted a brewing financial crisis in 1885. Thereafter, he retreated. To Cleveland, too much executive action and congressional legislation was driven by spoils, pork-barrel politics, and greedy partisanship. It was unconstitutional. He meant to end it! So he tended to oppose any government expenditure, even benevolent, that was not approved by the voters and in accordance with the Constitution. He also refused to interfere further in monetary policy. Thus, he allowed inexpensive silver coinage to survive and potentially undermine US commitment to the international gold standard. Nevertheless, under Cleveland, the US economy recovered from the "smoldering recession" of 1881–1885. He sought to strengthen the economy further by reducing tariffs, which he viewed as yet another form of government favoritism. But his insistence on launching a controversial trade battle in an election year, and his refusal to participate much in his own presidential campaign, resulted in his narrow defeat for reelection in 1888.

After leaving the White House in early March 1889, ex-President Cleveland observed the Republican Harrison administration (1889–1893) with rising ire. He respected Benjamin Harrison for his intelligence, patriotism, and attention to presidential duties. "I cannot see how he does it," he marveled at the new president's excellent judicial appointments.[5] But Cleveland became disturbed by what he perceived as a stream of blatantly partisan and expensive legislation backed by the White House: veterans' benefits, infrastructure spending, aid to flood victims, and scores of federal jobs handed out to Republican Party faithful.

Each bill seemed to him a special favor for some particular industry or faction that supported the Republican Party.

At first, Cleveland kept his mouth shut and his pen silent. "[T]he best way to deal with your troublesome ex-Presidents is to let them alone and give them the same chance to earn an honest living," he joked to an audience of businessmen.[6] Cleveland moved to New York City, where he reentered the practice of law and became a family man. But in 1890, he began to speak out against the Harrison administration with growing frustration. In a letter to a senior Democrat in Congress, he complained, "I have seen the Republicans getting deeper and deeper into the mire."[7] Months later, in a speech at a Democratic banquet in Philadelphia, he openly blasted the McKinley trade bill as "an unjust tariff which banishes from many humble homes the comforts of life, in order that in the palaces of wealth luxury may more abound."[8] Speaking at another political dinner, in Columbus, Ohio, Cleveland proclaimed, "[T]he expenditures of the [Harrison] government are reckless and wasteful.... [S]omething is wrong," and he called for "a vigorous and resentful defense of Americanism, by every man worthy to be called an American citizen."[9]

However, it was the Sherman Silver Purchase Act of 1890 that brought Cleveland most forcefully back into politics. To satisfy fellow Republicans in newly admitted silver states, President Harrison backed the legislation, which required the US Treasury to purchase 4.5 million ounces of silver every month, or nearly the *entire* US silver output.[10] This was a shocking handout to the silver interests. It also emboldened pro-silver forces within Cleveland's own Democratic Party. They now attempted to take over their party's platform and force the United States off the gold standard. Such action was dangerous heresy to Cleveland. As a former president, he had entered the social and business circles of the country's monied elite, including men like J. P. Morgan and Andrew Carnegie. All shared a near religious devotion to "hard money" and the gold standard. Hence, in early 1891, Cleveland wrote his now famous "silver letter," which blasted unlimited silver coinage as "the greatest peril" and a "dangerous and reckless experiment."[11] The brief letter was printed in newspapers across the country, drawing national attention.

Cleveland's increasingly public protests shook the Democratic Party and energized supporters. Indeed, "[t]hrough all the four years of Mr. Harrison's administration Mr. Cleveland was the most conspicuous man in the country out of office, and a sort of popular expectation followed him in all his movements," recalled Woodrow Wilson.[12] Talk of another presidential run spread enthusiastically. And after minor challenges from pro-silver Democrats and a few political machine bosses, Cleveland easily took his party's nomination in 1892, and then the presidency.

In one of the calmest campaign seasons in US history, Cleveland solidly beat Harrison in the 1892 election.[13] Many average Americans thought that Harrison and the Republican "billion-dollar Congress" had overstepped their bounds by passing too much, and too costly, major legislation. Republican activists and voters stayed home. The former had soured on Harrison as a notoriously difficult president who refused to reward campaigners or fundraisers with patronage. The latter were alternately satiated or overwhelmed by his avalanche of major legislation. Nor was Cleveland generous with federal patronage. Thus, in November voter turnout ranked among the lowest between 1850 and 1900. Meanwhile, disillusioned farmers in the South and across the Great Plains joined with labor groups to form an anti-industry Populist Party, which managed to win over 8 percent of the popular vote and 5 percent of the electoral college.[14]

In the end, it was Cleveland who carried twenty-three of forty-four states, with over 62 percent of the electoral vote, and beat Harrison by 3 percentage points in the popular vote. The Democrats also won powerful majorities in both the House and Senate. It was the first time since 1858 that Democrats controlled both houses of Congress *and* the presidency. If Cleveland could lead, then his party was in position to dominate US policymaking for at least the next two years. Possibly more.

The Panic of 1893

In March 1893, Cleveland reentered the White House at the start of an economic maelstrom. The economy was quietly descending into a recession, the fiscal balance was in deficit, and the US Treasury was gradually running out of gold due to Harrison's policies. Harrison and the Republicans in Congress had altered monetary policy, cut taxes, increased spending, and revised tariffs. The net result was too much gold going out of the Treasury, too little gold coming in. Meanwhile, cheap silver flooded the US financial system. Some began to fear a dollar devaluation. "The black silver cloud hangs at least as threateningly as ever over the country," warned the *Wall Street Journal*, concerned that America would soon abandon the gold standard for silver.[15] Even before he took office, Cleveland's supporters urged him to call a special session of Congress to address the silver issue and to fix the government's fiscal accounts. Several advisors explicitly warned the incoming president of "the portentous signs of a financial hurricane."[16] They wanted Cleveland to nip the crisis in the bud, just as he had back in 1885. Cleveland himself declared in his second inaugural that "nothing is more vital to our supremacy as a nation and to the beneficent purposes of our Government than a sound and stable currency."[17] But once in office, he demurred. He did not want White House policy to appear to be dictated by Wall

Street or to seem to be forcing a presidential agenda upon Congress. He also wanted the private sector to exhaust its own remedies before he took government action.[18]

Then a major financial panic struck the United States. The origins of the crisis lay partly in a glut in world agricultural produce, especially wheat.[19] Overproduction in Russia (then recovering from famine) and in Argentina (working to pay off its debts to Barings Bank) swamped global wheat markets, driving down prices. Farmers in the United States, having already broken historical production records during 1891–1892, cut back planting at first, but then began to overproduce to make up in volume what they lost in price.[20] A vicious spiral ensued. Overplanting created price declines, which led to more overplanting. In 1892 alone, wheat and corn prices dropped 20 percent from their highs. The following year, agriculture prices fell even further. As they earned less and less income, midwestern farmers failed to make payments on their mortgages, loans, and even wages to farm workers. Soon, banks which had loaned to these farmers began to fold in ever larger numbers.

Meanwhile, during early 1893, the US economy began to naturally slow after five relatively strong years. Commercial and industrial bankruptcies had been on the rise since late 1892. These bankruptcies put additional pressure on the financial institutions which had loaned to them, doubling bank liabilities during the first half of 1893.[21] During the boom years, banks had loaned precipitously and with ever lower standards, but suffered few defaults. Now they were carrying large amounts of bad loans to failing farms and businesses.[22] One harbinger of disaster appeared suddenly in mid-February 1893, when the spectacular bankruptcy of the Philadelphia and Reading Railroad made national headlines. The *New York Times* reported "the biggest day's business the [Stock] Exchange had ever had" with "big losses through Wall Street."[23] Similar railroad bankruptcies had taken down respected banks and wealthy investors, serving as omens of financial crises since the 1870s. Therefore, the failure of the Philadelphia and Reading triggered alarms throughout financial circles. Investors began to question the viability of other railroad and industrial firms.

Then, in mid-April 1893, barely a month into Cleveland's second term, the US Treasury's reserves of gold dipped below the $100 million threshold quietly set by the National Banking Act of 1882.[24] Rumors circulated that the federal government would soon stop redeeming its bonds in gold and instead pay out less valuable silver.[25] Fearing devaluation, foreign lenders began to sell off or cash in their US state, federal, and railroad bonds. New waves of selling hit the stock market. *Bradstreet's* soon reported "heavy failures in Wall Street" and "excessive declines."[26] A run on the US dollar was becoming manifest. The Cleveland administration attempted to allay any devaluation worries with official comments.[27] But without action, its pronouncements were ineffective. The occasional guarded statement from the Treasury secretary "means absolutely nothing and leaves us all in the dark," complained one bank president.[28] The problem, according to the country's bankers and finance experts, was the Silver Purchase Act.

Cleveland agreed. He believed that the summer financial crisis was caused by a combination of bad government and mass psychology.[29] The former consisted of the Harrison administration's profligate spending, partisan tariffs, and especially the Silver Act. The Act not only drained the Treasury of gold; to Cleveland, it also signaled to the world Americans' lack of commitment to the gold standard. It demonstrated the rising power of the pro-silver movement within American politics. Cleveland felt that these actions fueled a collapse in confidence in the US dollar and in the federal government's ability to pay its debts at full value. Hence the flight from US financial instruments and the ensuing panic was a psychological response. It was fear. "Our unfortunate financial plight is not the result of untoward events," he insisted, "nor of conditions related to our natural resources, nor is it traceable to any of the afflictions which frequently check national growth and prosperity."[30]

Cleveland Bides for Time

However, Cleveland still stubbornly refused to take action. He insisted that corrections by the federal government must be a last resort. "You cannot cure fright by calling it foolish and unreasonable, and you cannot prevent the frightened man from hoarding his money," he later explained to a critic of his delays.[31] Thus, as one contemporary put it, "Fearing defeat, [Cleveland] postponed the battle, gathered his reserve, marshaled his forces . . . each day showing forth stronger and better reasons why the Silver Purchase Act should be repealed."[32] Instead of rapid action, Cleveland merely briefed his new cabinet on a potential repeal of the Silver Act, while reaching out to individual congressmen to test the waters. He did order his Treasury secretary to build up federal gold supplies by requesting major banks to surrender some of their specie in exchange for other forms of currency. But this proved a weak expedient.

Throughout the spring, the signs of economic disaster compounded, but Cleveland stood his ground. Unemployment skyrocketed. Agriculture prices slumped. Factories shuttered their doors. Political pressure for action built as "Cleveland was deluged with letters, resolutions, and editorials pleading for a special session."[33] But rather than address the growing crisis, he focused on other matters: withdrawal of a treaty to annex Hawaii, new rules on civil service reform, and the usual barrage of federal appointments. And, as if to defy the ongoing catastrophe, President Cleveland attended the Columbian Exposition of 1893 in Chicago, a fantastic display of America's industrial prowess, creative design, and growing consumerism.[34] There, rather than acknowledge any economic troubles, Cleveland took the occasion to praise "the stupendous results of American enterprise and activity. . . . [W]e need not fear that these congratulations will be exaggerated."[35]

While Cleveland delayed, gold bled out of the US economy, and the economic dominoes began to tumble ever faster. In early May 1893, the National Cordage Company, a major industrial monopoly based in New Jersey, went bankrupt, throwing the stock market deeper into a tailspin.[36] In June, the panic began in earnest. The press reported "[w]ild and unfounded rumors of impending financial disaster [that] caused a senseless run on many of the banks."[37] Most damaged were banks in the western and northwestern parts of the United States, those regions home to the tens of thousands of farms ruined by the wheat glut. The bank runs continued unabated through late summer. And as these small and midsize banks got hit with wave after wave of withdrawals, they began to call upon their reserves held in the major New York City banks. Also, many smaller banks that had borrowed funds from New York now had trouble paying them back. In response, New York City banks dramatically increased their interest rates on some loans, and then restricted outflows altogether. This cut off supplies of currency in some parts of the country. *The Economist* magazine in London now warned, "[T]here can be no question as to the evil effects of the Sherman Act, and the desirability of its repeal, but something more than that will have to be done if the currency of the United States is to be put on a satisfactory basis."[38]

As the currency famine spread, major business transactions became impossible in some parts of the country. "The tides through which we are passing are phenomenal in their nature, and have never been equaled by any which have transpired during this generation," declared the president of the New York Stock Exchange.[39] Western farmers were unable to harvest or ship their crops for lack of credit. Southern farmers who managed to get their cotton to market often returned home with it unsold because buyers had no currency. In the Midwest, the Pillsbury company issued scrip to buy wheat for its flour mills.[40] The effects of these disruptions reverberated across the US economy. Overall business slumped and those savers with cash still in the banks now rushed to withdraw it. In the ensuring panic, financial institutions collapsed throughout the United States, with losses heavily concentrated in Washington state, the Midwest, and a handful of agricultural states.[41] The result was a major credit crunch, a full-blown financial crisis, and severe economic contraction.

Yet Cleveland *still* continued to stall for time. The American public had long begun to lose its enthusiasm for the Silver Purchase Act. Even in the western silver states, many called for action. "[T]he early repeal of the Silver Act is the only immediate prospect of better times. If an extra session of Congress can accomplish it, let us have an extra session," exhorted Nebraska's usually pro-silver

Omaha World Herald.[42] But Cleveland continued to believe "that the time was not yet ripe for repeal and that public sentiment must be allowed to mature."[43]

The Fight against Silver

Ultimately, it was the British abolition of free coinage of silver in India during late June 1893 that finally convinced Cleveland to act.[44] As a major consumer of American specie exports, India's abandonment of silver "sent the price of the unstable metal down with a disastrous tumble in all the world's markets."[45] Even the American silver states now clamored for federal action, as bankruptcies and unemployment there soared. Finally, "Cleveland saw that Congress must meet and face the situation at once."[46] So, at the end of the month, Cleveland formally requested a special session of Congress to convene in early August to end the nation's forced purchases of silver.

The fate of the American economy now rested heavily on Cleveland's leadership and organizational skills. But, unbeknownst to all but a few insiders, a potentially deadly oral cancer had struck the president.[47] In June, Cleveland's doctors diagnosed a growing tumor in his mouth as life threatening. He recognized that news of this, at the height of a financial panic and while attempting to rally support for major legislative change, could have a disastrous impact on both markets and politics. He therefore arranged to undergo surgery in secret. It took place on a friend's yacht during what the public was told was a five-day "fishing trip" up the East River in the first week of July. Six physicians were snuck aboard. Aware of the risks, one of the doctors quipped to the ship captain, "If you hit a rock, hit it good and hard, so that we'll all go to the bottom!"[48] Although the recovery was painful, the operation was a success.[49] Cleveland was then fitted with a rubber jaw-piece to restore his normal speech and appearance. The public would not know the truth until 1917, when one of his surgeons revealed the story to the *Saturday Evening Post.*[50]

When Congress finally met in early August 1893, the legislative battle over silver was epic. Much to his chagrin, Cleveland's long delays had been futile. Months of economic disaster and public dismay had *not* moved Congress much. The silver interests, and their representatives in Congress, responded to the president's call for action half-heartedly. They supported the repeal of the Silver Purchase Act, but they sought to replace it with full legalization of silver coinage, and therefore a *de facto* end to the gold standard. "FREE COINAGE OR NO REPEAL," they declared defiantly.[51] This was a credible threat. Early tallies suggested that while Republicans leaned heavily toward gold (hence repeal of the Silver Act), Cleveland's own Democratic Party was evenly split. Meanwhile, newspapers around the country grimly recounted the speed and depth of the ongoing economic crisis and questioned whether any agreement on repeal of the Silver Act could be reached.[52] Many Cleveland supporters agreed. The *Chicago Tribune* reported, "The great majority of the business community ... had doubt as to the ability of the President to control a majority of Congress so that they would repeal this legislation."[53] A *New York Tribune* headline was skeptical: "CONGRESS WILL MEET TO-DAY—CAN CLEVELAND CONTROL IT?"[54] Most observers predicted failure.

The utterly divided Congress debated for three months in a battle royal over monetary policy. Legislators on each side painted bleak pictures of the misery that would befall Americans if their opponents' policies won the day. "Abandon hope, all ye who enter here!" cried Representative William Jennings Bryan (D-NE) to those who would adopt the gold standard.[55] To the silverites, ex-Speaker Thomas Reed (R-ME) warned that the lack of confidence caused by abandoning gold might reverse human progress itself. He predicted "disaster, misfortune, defeat, destruction of industries, and a general paralysis of business and of labor ... a general liquidation of human affairs."[56] Emotional senators burst into tears on the floor, moved by the suffering foreshadowed in their own speeches. Senator William Stewart (R-NV) accused the Cleveland administration of a conspiracy, not just to force the gold standard on Americans but to do so over the will of voters and Congress. Gold therefore threatened democracy itself. Senator Henry Hansbrough (R-ND) agreed, arguing that the gold standard effectively surrendered US sovereignty over financial policy to Great Britain. Filibusters were launched. Insults were hurled. Several times, legislators nearly came to blows in the well of the Senate. Progress seemed hopeless.

Amid the chaos, President Cleveland moved strongly and adroitly. The day after Congress convened, he issued a firm public statement that called for immediate repeal of the Silver Purchase Act. He further called for a bipartisan effort, arguing, "This matter rises above the plane of party politics. It vitally concerns every business and calling and enters every household in the land."[57] During the remainder of the session, he continued to pressure Congress. He kept daily ledgers of which congressmen leaned for or against repeal. He used moral suasion to convince shaky allies. When weak half-measures were floated, Cleveland torpedoed them with veto threats.

But it was Cleveland's flexibility on another issue, patronage, that brought him victory.[58] Cleveland had returned to office with his old disdain for handing out jobs to party loyalists according to the dictates of the Democratic bosses. He now brushed these idealist prohibitions aside. Unlike his recent predecessors, Cleveland used patronage as a lever to force major legislation through Congress. With powerful Democrats in charge of key committees or threatening to back silver, Cleveland knew that patronage was his most effective weapon by which to coerce support. To win over the powerful chair of the Senate Finance

Committee, a former political adversary, Cleveland delegated to him the "carrot" of power over all federal patronage slots in that senator's home state. In the House, Cleveland often used the "stick" by withholding individual patronage appointments until key congressmen had declared their support for repeal of the Silver Act. As a result, during the course of the autumn congressional debate, vote by vote, Cleveland's margin of victory was achieved and then comfortably surpassed. The Silver Purchase Act was finally repealed at the end of October 1893 and the US gold supply stabilized. "We have passed through a period of fifteen years of darkness and error [of mandatory silver coinage]," proclaimed the New York Times. "That chapter in our economic history is closed."[59] But the Great Depression of 1893–1897 had only begun.

The Great Depression of 1893–1897

Though victorious, Cleveland had acted too late to prevent catastrophe. By September 1893, the currency and banking aspects of the crisis had ended,[60] but one of the worst economic calamities in American economic history was underway.[61] The stock market plummeted 30 percent from its January peak.[62] Real GDP fell roughly 6 percent in 1893, then by another 5 percent in 1894. Industrial production plunged 16 percent over eleven months following Cleveland's inauguration. Nationwide unemployment skyrocketed from roughly 4 to over 9 percent; for nonfarm labor, it peaked at over 17 percent. By 1894, wealth inequality had surged to the worst levels of the Gilded Age.[63] There was a brief recovery in 1895, but recession hit again in 1896. Over 150 railroad firms comprising some thirty thousand miles of track, perhaps one-quarter of the nation's rails, went bankrupt.[64] Countless farms failed, as did roughly 5 percent of all US banks. In some states, bank deposits did not fully recover for decades.[65]

Stories of unemployment, human misery, even starvation abounded. The New York Times told of "western towns unable to secure food for their citizens" and "appalling poverty" closer to home.[66] In Wisconsin, the homeless were allowed to sleep in empty jail cells. Many destitute Americans resorted to muggings, stealing farm animals for food, or robbing homes and small businesses.[67] In Chicago, strikers and the unemployed rioted, setting fire to the World's Columbian Exposition; barely a year old, the glorious "White City" of cutting-edge design, architecture, and technology, which took years and millions of dollars to build, was destroyed in hours.[68] In New York City, unemployed laborers of different ethnicities made open war upon one another in the streets. Around the country, attacks on Jews, Italians, and Chinese immigrants proliferated. Anarchist and Socialist activism surged. The major cities erupted with leftist rallies, demonstrations, and parades.[69] The genteel Henry Adams, a novelist and historian, wrote, "Everyone is in a blue fit of terror, and each individual thinks himself more ruined than his neighbor."[70]

Cleveland the Trust-Builder?

Restoring trust in American political-economic institutions in the face of panic and depression now became the primary objective of Cleveland's second administration. But he would rarely achieve it. One area where he failed to act entirely was fiscal policy. As the recession deepened, state and city governments got busy attacking unemployment and poverty through a variety of means.[71] They funded public works with special loans or appropriations. They provided food, fuel, clothing, and even lodging to the unemployed, though sometimes in exchange for work or after passing a "fitness for work" test. Both city governments and charities set up soup houses and inexpensive restaurants for the poor. City employment bureaus were established to more easily match job-seekers with employers. Some city governments even offered low-interest loans to their citizens. And although minimum wage laws were considered a dangerous experiment best left to foreigners, some states enacted wage laws that required corporations to pay workers on a weekly or biweekly basis rather than monthly, and the withholding of wages was outlawed.[72]

Some labor leaders and Populists suggested that the federal government might act along similar lines.[73] The Cleveland administration could provide relief via federal support for, say, a canal across Nicaragua, infrastructure improvements to the Mississippi River, or new irrigation projects out west. The more progressive elements called for food aid, housing subsidies, old-age pensions, or healthcare. These were already established policies in the German Empire and were being seriously considered in other parts of Europe and in Oceania.[74]

However, Cleveland neither sought nor supported any form of welfare or subsidies to aid those suffering from the depression. To Cleveland, such action would not only be a form of government favoritism and engender mass laziness, but it would also signal weakness. It could therefore injure the very confidence and trust that Cleveland was trying to restore in the US economy. Admittedly, many Americans agreed with the conventional wisdom, then voiced by a Southern senator, which held that "each individual citizen of the United States should look to himself, and it is not the purpose of this Government to give work to individuals throughout the United States by appropriating money which belongs to other people and does not belong to the Senate."[75] Certainly private and religious charities might provide for the poor and unemployed. Sometimes a city or county government might even legislate poor laws or initiate public works. But this was not the responsibility of the federal government.

Cleveland's Failed Tariff Battle

Instead of relief or economic stimulus, Cleveland focused next on trade.[76] His repeal of the Silver Purchase Act briefly stopped gold from bleeding out of the Treasury, but the McKinley Tariff of 1890 still supplied insufficient gold coming in. Therefore, in November 1893, Cleveland pushed for tariff reform. The result was the Wilson-Gorman Tariff of 1894. The initial bill, personally designed by Cleveland together with Congressman William Wilson (D-WV), proposed to restore tariffs on sugar (to aid revenue), reduce or eliminate them on other raw materials (to aid average American consumers), and add a small tax on corporate profits. Again, Cleveland used patronage to alternately coerce and entice support for passage in the House. But passage came only at the cost of substantial revisions: sugar was returned to the "free" list, and a personal income tax was added to restore the revenue lost from sugar, as were new taxes on corporations, gifts, and inheritances. Nevertheless, the revised bill succeeded in lowering the average tariff around 15 percent, while still returning federal government finances to solid ground. It passed the House in February 1894, in the face of small but significant Democratic opposition and without any Republican votes.

Then, to Cleveland's chagrin, the Senate butchered the bill. The free list was cut, new tariffs were added, a hundred other duties were increased. In all, over six hundred amendments were attached.[77] The final product, which came into effect in late August 1894, still reduced average duties (on total imports) to their lowest levels since 1860.[78] Therefore tariff revenues remained too small. And after the Supreme Court struck down the income tax component in April 1895, the federal government lapsed into its worst deficits since the Civil War. As for trade, few economists have been able to discern much effect of the Wilson-Gorman tariff.[79]

Contemporaries and historians largely blame Cleveland for this failure. "[His] strategy during the tariff battle was marked by poor timing, false prediction, and a confusing mixture of obstinacy and timidity," writes one scholar of the administration.[80] In stark contrast to his approach to the Silver Act repeal, with tariff reform Cleveland failed to organize and communicate effectively with key members of Congress. He also failed to rally support from the American public. A journalist of the period later wrote, "As President he could not dominate and he did not know how to persuade."[81] Hence, to many observers, the tariff debate devolved into arcane deliberations over duty rates and schedules, partly because Cleveland failed to keep the nation focused on the strategic issues of economic security, development, and inequality. He was also often insensitive to powerful interest groups that felt they needed protection in order to survive the depression. In his tariff negotiations, he failed to make minor concessions for the sake of strategic victories, yet he would occasionally concede major goals to achieve mere passage. Some have therefore accused Cleveland of "maladroit tactics," arguing that "he did not know how to strike at the weak joints in his opponents' armor, or how to enlist public sentiment in time and throw it effectively into the fray."[82] Future Republican statesman John Hay simply jeered, "What a vast, diffused, circumambient talent he has for being an ass!"[83]

As if to confirm these accusations, Cleveland refused to sign *his own* tariff bill, even though Democratic leaders in the Senate warned him, "[I]f you allow the [Democratic] bill to become law without your signature, you abdicate the leadership of the Democratic Party."[84] This warning was prophetic. The tariff debacle proved to be "one of the most painful defeats of his whole career."[85] Cleveland soon lost all influence over Congress. His relationships with his party, major interest groups, the press, and the American people also fell rapidly into decline.

During 1894–1895, with his legislative options exhausted, Cleveland turned instead to issuing debt to fix the revenue situation. Back in January 1894, he had instructed the Treasury to issue a massive $50 million tranche of ten-year bonds in exchange for gold at a rate of 5 percent. But this fix proved only temporary. Ten months later, the Treasury was forced to make a second bond offer of similar proportions. This time, the salve only lasted two months before the government was again bleeding gold. One problem was that investors were legally allowed to withdraw gold from the Treasury in order to buy the new government bonds meant to fund gold purchases. This neutered the bonds' positive effects on federal gold stocks. Simultaneously it increased the debt burden of the United States. Thus, Cleveland's temporary expedients only hurt confidence in the Treasury's ability to pay in gold. Also, with Americans hoarding gold and paying their taxes in silver, gold continued to leak out of the Treasury. Worse yet, federal laws required that any silver certificates coming into the Treasury must eventually be reissued, not destroyed. Therefore, people could repeatedly use silver to draw gold out of the Treasury.[86]

Labor Unrest in 1894

Meanwhile, workers around the country began to strike in record numbers, as businesses slashed wages and work hours while continuing to pay out dividends to stockholders. During 1894 alone, 690,000 workers, or 8.3 percent of the American labor force, went on strike in a series of work stoppages rarely surpassed in US history.[87] In these confrontations, Cleveland more often took the side of business and wealth rather than labor or the unemployed. After all, he had been a railroad attorney, as had his attorney general. Both men stridently believed that governments at all levels had a duty to protect private property, ensure commerce, and provide public order. This meant that striking workers and impoverished demonstrators faced strict limits on their activities.

Desperate for federal action, in spring 1894 quarry owner Jacob Coxey led a ragtag "army" of a few hundred unemployed from Ohio to Washington, DC.[88] For weeks, they marched the countryside for federal relief. Journalists flocked to cover the spectacle of the "ragged crowd" of "ill-starred pilgrims," judging them "a most formidable expression of the disquietude that obtains in all sections of the country."[89] Coxey's Army planned to march on the Capitol, with the demand that Congress print money to pay for a $500 million job-creating roads bill. Cleveland responded with irritation. When the marchers appeared in Washington, he had them arrested for walking on the Capitol lawn.[90]

Paramount among that year's labor uprisings was the Pullman Strike of May to July 1894. It was "more extended and convulsive than any others . . . [and] worried Americans spoke of insurrection and rebellion."[91] The Pullman Car Company prompted the massive strike and boycott by slashing wages while keeping rents and prices high in their company towns. The strike quickly spread across the midwestern railroad companies, propelling one of the strike leaders, Eugene Debs, to national fame. As the Pullman strike broadened, transportation from Chicago to the West Coast ground to a halt, threatening the entire national economy. By early July, over a quarter-million rail workers in twenty-seven states were on strike. The *New York World* called it "war against the government and against society."[92]

President Cleveland responded forcefully. Within days the administration invoked the Sherman Antitrust Act to win a federal court injunction against the strike. Then, at the behest of the railroad managers association, Cleveland sent thousands of federal troops into Chicago to prevent striker riots and to arrest dozens of strike leaders. To underscore his determination, he defiantly proclaimed, "If it takes the entire army and navy of the United States to deliver a postal card in Chicago, that card will be delivered!"[93] The arrival of troops inflamed the situation. In the confrontations that followed, over fifty people died and many more were wounded across six states. Riots broke out in which mobs burned hundreds of railcars and vandalized property. Damages reached into the tens of millions of dollars (in 2020 dollars).[94]

Many questioned the constitutionality of Cleveland's insertion of federal troops to break up the strikes, especially absent a request from state or local government. The Illinois governor was incensed. "I protest against this, and ask the immediate withdrawal of the Federal troops from active duty in this State," he repeatedly implored Cleveland. The governor insisted that the local authorities had the situation well under control and that "it is not soldiers that the railroads need so much as it is men to operate trains."[95] Cleveland dismissed the governor's objections, contending that the "obstruction of the mails . . . [and] competent proof that conspiracies existed against commerce between the States" put the situation "clearly within the province of Federal authority."[96] Congress agreed. Within days, the House and Senate each passed bipartisan resolutions in support of Cleveland's actions.[97] The following year, the Supreme Court confirmed the authority of "the [federal] government, through the executive branch and in the use of the entire executive power of the Nation," to clear the strike in the name of interstate commerce and federal mail delivery.[98]

Nevertheless, Cleveland's handling of the Pullman strike divided Americans and contributed to the political downfall of the Democratic Party. It further damaged his standing among laborers and their families, as well as states' rights advocates. To them, Cleveland had intervened in the economy at the behest of the railroad corporations and in brazen disregard of his own declared political philosophy. Historians have generally agreed. Most have criticized the Cleveland administration for unnecessary brutality, unconstitutional use of force, and antiquated thinking about worker rights and the unemployed. However, during that summer in 1894, many Americans applauded Cleveland, as did partisan newspapers from *both* major parties. Mass strikes and labor protests were rare phenomena in the United States. Americans everywhere feared anarchy. The business community and foreign investors were especially pleased to see the federal government act with speed and force to put down any threat to property or commerce and what they saw as the dangerous rise of Socialist forces in the United States. To them, Cleveland had either broken from his strict constitutionalist philosophy for the right reasons, or he had acted in line with its respect for private property and free commerce.

1894 Midterm Elections

But the accolades did not last long, as Cleveland's party suffered massive defeats in the midterm elections of November 1894. The Democrats split badly over the strike. Conservatives supported the administration, but the party's labor and states' rights wings felt betrayed. Meanwhile, congressional Republicans hammered Democrats on their negative agenda: what good were Cleveland's low tariffs and passive government while the people suffered? Ex-president Harrison even came out of retirement to campaign, telling crowds, "The Republican theory has been all along that it was right to so legislate as to provide work, employment, comfort to the American workingman."[99] The result was an electoral rout. In perhaps the largest midterm loss of congressional seats in US history, voters gave Republicans 70 percent of the House. Republicans even won a slim majority in the Senate. Thus commenced the longest stretch of Republican majorities in Congress since the party's founding in the mid-1850s. The Democratic Party splintered into warring factions and then faded as a force in national politics for almost twenty years.

With the Republicans in control of Capitol Hill, and Cleveland a reluctant legislator, the 54th Congress (1895–1897) would prove to be one of the least productive in fifty years.[100] Little major legislation passed for the remainder of Cleveland's presidency.[101] In fact, thanks to his obstinacy and failed leadership, even his own party in Congress abandoned him. "[T]here was not a single senator he could talk to in confidence. Prominent Democratic leaders had told him to his face that they would never step through the White House door again," observed one historian of the period.[102] As a result, President Cleveland was largely neutered for the next two years.[103]

His cabinet was of little help. It contained serious policymakers, loyal to Cleveland, but they possessed few ties to Congress and little experience in party politics. In fact, Cleveland's department heads were so detached from politics that their appointments made little sense to people. "His first Cabinet had contained men whom everybody knew as accredited leaders among the Democrats," explained Woodrow Wilson in 1897. "But his second Cabinet seemed chosen as if of deliberate and set purpose to make a personal and private choice, without regard to party support."[104]

Nor did Cleveland's federal appointments aid him much. In making them, Cleveland tried to remain as stringently apolitical as during his first term. In fact, he adopted additional rules: no one who served in his first administration would be reappointed, no journalists were allowed, recommendations from organized party machines were to be ignored, and evidence of extreme partisan activity was frowned upon. Cleveland did replace thousands of Harrison men with Democrats. And his willingness to use patronage to repeal the Silver Act disillusioned some reformers. But he still supported clean government. He even kept the steadfast reformer and Republican Theodore Roosevelt on the Civil Service Commission. Thus, during Cleveland's second term, the proportion of "competitive" civil service jobs in the federal government rose from 25 percent to 45 percent. (When Cleveland first entered office back in 1885, it was near 11 percent.)

Nevertheless, Cleveland seemed either unable or unwilling to repair his public image. "He did not fascinate people by the charm of extraordinary eloquence. He did not win their friendship by any magic of 'personal magnetism,'" wrote a rare Republican admirer.[105] In fact, Cleveland has been described as a "nonrhetorical" president.[106] Throughout both his administrations, he rarely gave speeches, published essays, or provided interviews to educate the public on policy matters. And when he did, Cleveland used long and laborious sentences packed with vague philosophical platitudes. This was partly because Cleveland adhered to the Victorian ideal that a virtuous and effective leader should not get into the mud of political debate. Also, Cleveland was a stubborn man who saw himself as a guardian of fair, objective, limited government against a horde of selfish, scheming partisans. He simply knew himself to be in the right. And "the right" needed neither a public defense nor a marketing campaign. Rather, Cleveland felt that quiet (in)action was more powerful than words.

"The Lamest of Lame Ducks": 1895–1897

Declines in gold supplies continued to threaten federal debt payments and the US economy.[107] By early 1895, Cleveland believed "the situation has so changed and the emergency now appears so threatening" that he asked Congress to "restore confidence in our financial soundness and avert business disaster and universal distress among our people."[108] In particular, Cleveland called for new legislation to require that US debt be repaid in gold rather than "coin," reasoning that would prevent buyers from withdrawing gold from the Treasury simply to buy bonds meant to earn gold. He also requested authority to redeem and cancel silver-based notes so as to remove them from circulation. But after months of failed leadership, Cleveland's influence over Congress was approaching its nadir. "I hate the ground the man walks on," proclaimed one Democratic senator from the floor.[109] "He is an old bag of beef," quipped another to a crowd.[110] Hence, the outgoing Congress simply ignored the president's request and his threats of crisis.

Cleveland therefore went to Wall Street for help with a third large bond issue. It succeeded in keeping the Treasury solvent for a few months. In fact, the economy seemed to stabilize, even recover, between summer 1894 and early autumn 1895. However, without protections and guarantees for its gold, the Treasury was headed toward depletion again by September 1895. As reserves fell during summer, another financial panic loomed. Cleveland again asked Congress for legislation to stop the bleeding. Again, they balked. So Cleveland issued a fourth and final massive bond issue, without protections for gold, in February 1896. This kept the Treasury stocked until September, when William McKinley's election hopes surged and short-term interest rates on gold skyrocketed, attracting European investors. The crisis was over, at least for the Cleveland administration.

However, the economic destruction was heavy and pervasive. In the four years under Cleveland, industrial production had expanded a mere 1.9 percent in *total*. But the agricultural recession meant that America's overall economic output in 1896, per capita, was roughly 6 percent *less* than that in 1892. An average of 14,360 firms had failed annually, at rates not seen since the depths of the 1873–1878 depression. The stock market lost 19.8 percent of its value.[111] Unemployment never fell below 12.5 percent and remained above 16 percent when Cleveland left office. Wealth inequality remained near historic levels.[112]

Federal government finances dropped into deficit three out of four years under Cleveland, the worst since the Civil War, while the federal debt ballooned over 26 percent. Deflation totaled 7 to 8 percent, 1894 being a particularly bad year (when price levels fell 4.6 percent). This meant that real interest rates surged near 8 percent at their peak, though by 1897 they had fallen to around 4 percent. Only exports saw improvement under Cleveland, and since imports remained relatively flat due to the depression, the US annual trade surplus surged 86 percent.[113]

The 1896 Election: America Rejects Clevelandism

Partly thanks to Cleveland, the Panic of 1893 and the depression it triggered fundamentally broke the postbellum American party system. The Democratic split that occurred in 1894 became irreconcilable. Westerners and Southerners took over the rump of the Democratic Party and led it to denounce the gold standard and high tariffs and to support "free silver."[114] They flocked to the messianic William Jennings Bryan as their candidate in 1896, who traveled the land in a blazing fury to preach his campaign against gold.[115] A small shard of "hard money" pro-business Democrats remained Cleveland's only supporters. Some even encouraged him to run for a third term. Meanwhile, hundreds of thousands of Americans abandoned both major parties. Most of them joined the new People's Party, whose platform was so close to Bryan's that they too chose him as their candidate, though with a different nominee for vice president.[116] It would be the Republicans, with William McKinley as their presidential nominee, who would sweep the elections in 1896. They also took the Senate and managed to form a working coalition to rule the House. The resolution of the Great Depression of 1893–1897 would be in their hands.

Cleveland departed the White House as politically damaged goods. According to the *New York Times*, his leadership had "provoked implacable enmities . . . evoked a tireless defamation that has poisoned the minds of multitudes of his countrymen against him . . . [and] separated him from the councils of his party"[117] Thanks to his repeated supplications to bankers and industrialists, many Americans considered him one of "[t]he greatest tools of plutocracy in this country to-day."[118] Worse yet, his dedication to the gold standard effectively surrendered US monetary policy to the Bank of England. His support for lower tariffs was seen as similarly empowering London on trade policy.[119] Some therefore called him a traitor. In the Senate, he was openly blasted as a "besotted tyrant" and an "arrogant and obstinate ruler."[120] By 1897, Cleveland was also out of step with the class warfare, budding welfare state and interventionist government ideas, and Great Power imperialism that would typify the next twenty-five years of American political practice. After he left office, Cleveland quietly retired to Princeton, New Jersey, where he quickly slipped from American memory.

Cleveland versus Harrison

Financial crises matter! This is one fairly compelling lesson to be learned from a comparison of Cleveland and Harrison. If not for the Panic of 1893 and the depression which followed, both executives would have presided over far better economic times. This observation also dovetails with the experience of the previous Gilded Age presidents. But how much can one blame either Harrison or Cleveland for the economic debacle? While assignments of responsibility are subjective, the evidence does suggest some impartial hypotheses.

First, the US economy did well, or avoided disaster, when either Cleveland or Harrison took aggressive action to defend the financial system. Cleveland did this with his 1885 silver letter, his bond redemptions and greenback payouts, and his successful entreaties to Wall Street for massive loans after 1894. His active secrecy regarding his emergency oral surgery might count as well. For Harrison, it was his use of the Treasury Department to increase liquidity during autumn 1890, much like a modern central bank. Some might also include Harrison's forceful response to the threat of pandemic disease to the nation's financial center in 1892. Certainly, some of these tactics were delaying actions rather than enduring solutions; nevertheless, they were highly successful delays.

In contrast, passiveness failed. The US economy did poorly when either president neglected or refused to address a brewing crisis. The most obvious example is Cleveland's months of inaction during 1893. He allowed a financial crisis to commence, spread unchecked, and then evolve into a historic economic depression that lasted throughout his presidency and beyond. In fact, Cleveland might have prevented the 1890s crisis if he had acted more aggressively back in 1885, during his first administration. In those early months, he had the political momentum necessary to end mandatory silver coinage and perhaps pass tariff reform. But he retreated from the fight. One might similarly blame Harrison for his refusal to confront the growing fiscal deficits, credit contractions, and fears of currency devaluation that plagued his final year in office.

So why did Cleveland and Harrison take such different approaches? Each man's vision for the country appears to have affected his likelihood of presidential action and the form that it took. In Cleveland's case, he was handicapped by his relatively inflexible belief that the executive branch, and the federal government, should be constrained. He believed that much of Gilded Age America's political and economic troubles could be traced back to violations of the Constitution's basic premises. Hence his vision for the country was to return to more strictly limited government and a passive executive of the kind practiced by most antebellum presidents. Therefore, when economic crises hit, Cleveland often resorted to the most passive responses possible. This prevented him from nipping the 1890s crisis in its bud back in 1885, or from acting earlier during the 1893 meltdown. Cleveland's strict constitutionalism was also the basis for his stubborn refusal to take any federal action on welfare or countercyclical fiscal policy, despite their implementation by many state and city governments. For, in Cleveland's view, "[government's] functions do not include the support of the people."[121]

In contrast, Harrison *did* believe in an active presidency and in a larger role for the federal government in managing the economy. However, the evidence presented in the previous chapter suggests that he valued partisanship above strategic vision, policy agenda, or political-economic philosophy. Harrison idealized the Republican Party as *the* true defender of American democracy and progress; Democrats were the enemy. Therefore, he supported almost any legislation that would keep Republicans united and in power. The result was an ad hoc combination of monetary, trade, and fiscal policies that put the United States on a direct path to the 1893 crisis. In other words, if Cleveland was too uncompromising in his philosophy, Harrison compromised far too much.

Another compelling lesson is that relationships count. Each president stumbled when he failed to cultivate and leverage his relationships with major political-economic actors. These include Congress, the party, the media, major interest groups, and even the American public. For example, Harrison's coarse personal style and refusal to budge on patronage may have played a role in his troubles. These behaviors helped to alienate key allies in Congress who might have helped him pass a less damaging legislative package. Had he better relationships with Congress, the fatal provisions of the Silver Purchase Act or McKinley tariff might have been omitted. Harrison also used too late his excellent skills as a public educator. If he had rallied public support *before* passage of the McKinley tariff, rather than after, he might have be able to craft a more constructive, sustainable economic policy agenda.

We can find similar relationship dynamics in Cleveland's approach to economic policy. In general, Cleveland held himself aloof from Congress and his own party, abhorred the press, and exerted little effort to connect with major interest groups or the American public. In fact, as one biographer has put it, Cleveland "escalate[d] the divisiveness of both party and country. . . . It almost seemed that he was determined to prove how forceful and how principled he could be, instead of how unifying."[122] The result was often failure.

The major exception for Cleveland was monetary policy. Here he actively pressured Congress, applied party patronage, made strong public statements, and even courted Wall Street when necessary in order to build support for his policies and get results. In contrast, when it came to tariff reform, Cleveland consistently failed to manage relationships in the same manner. In his second administration, he worked harder on relationship-building in the House (where he succeeded in passing a tariff reform bill), but then abandoned these efforts in the Senate (where his bill was subsequently ruined). As one historian quipped, "Like a great lethargic bear, Cleveland had bestirred himself . . . and shaken the political hive, but then he slumped back into querulous inactivity."[123] Cleveland failed when he neglected relationships.

As with previous presidents, the maintenance of trust appears to matter. Harrison's policy agenda had such a massive negative economic impact because it fatally eroded trust in American financial institutions. In creating a credible threat of a dollar devaluation, it called into question the country's ability to pay its bills, and to do so at full value. It therefore increased the perceived riskiness of the United States as an investment destination. Also, Harrison's avalanche of expensive legislation, combined with his personal mastery over patronage, seemed like graft to many Americans. Thus, Harrison seemed a backward step in the perennial Gilded Age fight against political corruption. This might have further reduced public confidence in his ability to shepherd the economy. Cleveland, by his inaction, then allowed this mistrust to fester. As the economy collapsed during 1893, his adamant refusal to act seemed irresponsible, even detached. His irregular leadership on trade provided only further evidence that he was unreliable. His stubbornness and inconsistency did not just infuriate; they damaged confidence in his ability to deliver political solutions. Calls of "traitor" and "besotted tyrant" from fellow Democrats were public manifestations of this collapse in trust.

Finally, one hypothesis that does *not* flow from the historical evidence is that there exists some particular "right" policy combination, and that presidents must implement it. We can identify any number of different monetary, trade, and fiscal policy combinations that might have averted the 1890s economic debacle. Certainly, there may be "wrong" policy combinations that should be rejected. But this was not a case of ignorance or policy error; it was a failure in presidential leadership. Specifically, a comparison of Cleveland and Harrison suggests that each president may have severely damaged the economy when he supported or allowed policies that created prolonged distrust in the American financial system. Lack of confidence in the government's ability to mend the financial system also seems to have contributed. And this distrust may have resulted, in part, from some combination of a passive approach toward the presidency and government, lack of a clear and compelling vision (or stubborn, uncompromising attachment to one), and a failure to build or leverage relationships with key political-economic actors.

12

William McKinley and the Developmental State, 1897–1901

By many measures, William McKinley (1897–1901) was one of the most economically successful presidents of any era. Elected amid the Great Depression
of 1893–1897, he ushered in a period of fantastic growth and recovery.
Agriculture prices stabilized. Industry revived and the service sector flourished.
Unemployment fell. Wages rose. Yet inflation was tame. Hence economic inequality declined significantly. Perhaps most important at the time, US debt and
deficits fell, while the trade surplus boomed. As a result, gold flowed back into
the country in record amounts and US gold inventories quickly recovered from
their fatal lows reached under his predecessor, Grover Cleveland (1893–1897).
All told, by the time McKinley was assassinated in 1901, the American economy
was not merely strong; it was back on course to becoming the mightiest economic power in world history.

But what exactly was McKinley's role? And how did his administration differ,
if at all, from the failed Gilded Age presidents? Any president elected during a
recession might simply free-ride on the inevitable return to normal economic
conditions. Also, the resolution of a tumultuous election tends to improve
market psychology, and the presidential campaigns of 1896 were historically
divisive. Long-term and international factors also played important roles in
America's *fin-de-siècle* economic performance. Industrialization and technological change, foreign demand for American exports, new gold discoveries, a
rising consumer culture, and increased globalization and urbanization each
contributed to growing the US economy. So perhaps McKinley's part in the economic boom was minor.

The evidence, however, suggests otherwise. Back in 1890, the staunchly partisan President Benjamin Harrison (1889–1893) had worked with congressional
Republicans to create an incoherent mix of monetary, fiscal, and trade policies
that favored party interests. The result was a battery of currency and financial
crises that culminated in the Panic of 1893. His successor, Cleveland (second
term), a constitutional conservative, deferred action for months, allowing
the economic crisis to escalate and spread throughout the country. Cleveland
then botched his leadership on trade reform, leaving federal revenues insufficient to prevent further panics. He also refused to provide any sort of relief to

Presidential Leadership in Feeble Times. Mark Zachary Taylor, Oxford University Press. © Oxford University Press 2024.
DOI: 10.1093/oso/9780197750742.003.0015

striking workers or the unemployed. And rather than comfort the American people, he mostly retreated into the White House or supplicated to Wall Street bankers. The result was years of economic hardship. Inequality soared. Labor strikes skyrocketed. Bank lending and business investment fell off. Gold fled the country. Cooperation broke down between the White House and Congress, while the Democratic Party split asunder. Even Cleveland's few allies in the press admitted that his leadership and its critics had "poisoned the minds of multitudes of his countrymen against him."[1]

President McKinley's solution was to embrace what political-economists today call the "developmental state": export-led industrialization shielded behind a protectionist wall and supported by strategic government intervention in finance and exchange rates.[2] He got to work soon after election day rather than await inauguration. And within a year, he had actively coordinated with Republicans in Congress to increase tariffs so as to repair federal revenues. McKinley then deftly maneuvered the United States onto the gold standard, thereby fixing the dollar's value and reassuring investors in American assets. Meanwhile, his administration held back on antitrust enforcement. This enabled a massive wave of industrial combinations that brought incredible economies of scale and scope, as well as widespread technological change. The dislocations for labor were significant, but nationwide unemployment fell, wages gradually rose, and inequality dropped to its lowest levels in fifteen years. All the while, McKinley led a campaign of education and consensus-building with party leaders, major interest groups, the press, and even the American people themselves. He thereby renewed trust in the country's major political-economic institutions, including the presidency, and he easily won reelection and with the largest vote margins in almost thirty years.

McKinley's muscular foreign policy further enhanced America's economic position. Although he abhorred bloodshed, he embraced war when it proved inevitable. His successful military action against Spain was brief, energetic, and inexpensive. The acquisitions of the Philippines, Cuba, Guam, and other island territories were controversial but boldly imperial.[3] These moves constituted a radical change in US foreign policy, ending over a century of almost purely continental focus. The principles and wisdom of American imperialism have been debated ever since. Nevertheless, McKinley's triumphant expansionism increased confidence in the United States, both at home and abroad, as a rising military power, well capable of defending its economic interests.[4]

Background

There is little in McKinley's background to suggest excellence in economic leadership. He had neither significant business experience nor much formal education before entering politics. Born into a middle-class family of Ohio iron forgers in 1843, McKinley grew up in the industrial "Silicon Valley" of his day. His large family—William was the seventh of nine children—lived in a simple rural village that supplied the "high-tech" industrial region of northeastern Ohio fed by the Erie Canal. His father managed foundries. His mother raised the children and helped run the local church. She also took responsibility for her children's religious education, imbuing them with her own zealous Christian piety. William practiced throughout his life, becoming "one of America's most intensely religious presidents."[5] Otherwise, his childhood and personality were unremarkable: school, sports, games, reading, and fishing. "He was just like other boys, except that he was of a more serious turn of mind," recalled his mother.[6]

McKinley's political and economic beliefs did not come from his formal schooling, for he had little. Certainly his parents valued education highly, even moving towns within Ohio so that their children might attend better schools. And young William was an avid reader, energetic debater, and industrious student. "It was seldom that his head was not in a book," recalled a former schoolmate.[7] McKinley aspired to higher education and a legal career. However, at age eighteen, personal illness and poor family finances forced him to drop out of Allegheny College, in northwest Pennsylvania, after his first year. Hence, McKinley is one of only four post–Civil War presidents without a college degree.[8] "William McKinley was no intellectual giant," a contemporary journalist later confirmed.[9]

Instead, in mid-1861 the teenage McKinley enlisted as a private in the Union army.[10] The McKinley family "were very strong abolitionists, and William early imbibed very radical views regarding [slavery]," his mother confessed.[11] So when the Civil War came, McKinley told a friend, "[W]e can't stay out of this war. We must get in."[12] The conflict was "a four-year nightmare of pain and destruction" for McKinley's unit.[13] He worked as a quartermaster, but *not* in safe, quiet posts. He saw combat in Virginia, Maryland, and West Virginia, where he delivered supplies under fire and even had a horse shot out from under him. His commanders, who included Colonel Rutherford B. Hayes, generally reported that "in executive ability, young McKinley was of rare capacity . . . especially for a boy of his age."[14] As a result, McKinley was steadily promoted up through the ranks to major, eventually serving as chief of staff to a major general. The brotherhood and violence of war transformed the adolescent McKinley into a confident leader. But the war also taught him humility. Even after becoming a successful congressman, governor, and president, he would instruct fellow veterans, "Call me Major. I earned that. I am not so sure of the rest."[15]

After the war, McKinley returned home to pursue a legal career. He studied law under a respected Ohio attorney, attended Albany Law School for several months, and established a legal practice in the bustling town of Canton. He was soon invited to enter, and eventually take over, a prominent local law firm. He also joined the city's civil, fraternal, and veterans' organizations. Despite his wartime hardships and serious career ambitions, McKinley was described by friends and colleagues as a "jolly" person who was "always good-natured and looked at the bright side of everything."[16] He soon met and married his wife, to whom he was thoughtfully devoted for the rest of his life, and had children.

His enduring friendship with Rutherford Hayes soon drew McKinley into Republican Party politics. He became a stump speaker for Hayes's 1867 campaign for governor of Ohio, and then a local organizer for Ulysses S. Grant's 1868 presidential campaign. The following year, McKinley himself ran for and won his own election, as the Republican attorney for Stark County, Ohio. His fierce dedication to trade protectionism gradually attracted loyal support from industry and was one key to McKinley's political success over the long run. Another was his status as a combat veteran and his support for veterans' issues. Meanwhile, a risky legal move also brought him endorsements from labor. During spring 1876, McKinley took up a high-profile case of striking coal miners who had been arrested for disorderly conduct. His thoughtfulness and professionalism during the trial earned him the respect and support of both the miners and some of the mine owners.[17] With the combined support of veterans, industry, and labor, McKinley won election to Congress in 1876, even as he fiercely campaigned for Hayes's presidential election.

McKinley served seven terms in Congress, from 1877 to 1891, giving him vast experience in the legislative process, rivaled by few other US presidents in history.[18] At first, he was pro-labor, pro-silver, anti-alcohol, and anti-monopoly, and he continued to back higher tariffs on imports. Over time, he focused mostly on trade policy, becoming known as the "Napoleon of Protection" and *the* authority on tariffs for the Republican Party.[19] But McKinley was no lackey for business interests. He also supported farmers' organizations, the 1887 Interstate Commerce Act (to regulate railroad monopolies), the 1890 Sherman Antitrust Act, and the greater usage of silver coinage as legal tender.[20] That is, rather than promote his party or a narrow interest group, McKinley sought to unify his district, and his diverse country, around an agenda of fierce economic nationalism.

McKinley's political skill and power grew together. Although passionate about his political causes, he learned not to demagogue. He "was a gentle, kindly disposed man," according to contemporaries. "McKinley preferred to please rather than to displease; to help rather than to hinder; to smile rather than to frown."[21] He was attentive to his committee work and serious about the details of legislation. As a result, McKinley rose quickly to membership, and eventually chairmanship, of the powerful Ways and Means Committee.[22] He was a strong and consistent supporter of the presidencies of fellow Republicans Hayes, Garfield, Arthur, and Harrison. And he became a skilled and influential player in Ohio's political factions. His energetic fight against President Cleveland's trade reforms in 1888 brought him national attention. He was invited to play leading roles in the formation of Republican Party national strategy, and his name was increasingly whispered as a potential House Speaker, even a presidential nominee. McKinley's political reputation was amplified further by his adroit shepherding of the protectionist McKinley Tariff of 1890. In reprisal, when Democrats gained control of Ohio politics, they gerrymandered his district so as to force him out of office in 1891.

With his eye on a future presidential run, McKinley next campaigned for and won two terms as governor of Ohio (1892–1896) on the platform "Protection Is Prosperity."[23] Admittedly, it was an all but impotent position. By constitutional design, the state's governor made few appointments and lacked even veto power. But since Ohio was a large, "high-tech" state, its governor garnered widespread publicity. It was therefore an excellent platform for political networking and useful for advertising McKinley's policy positions. Still, McKinley intended to govern too. Even though he had little power or obligation to do so, he worked actively with the state legislature to forge consensus on labor, tax, and other major legislation. He reformed the Ohio tax system on the basis of an expert report which he commissioned. He supported taxes on corporations, franchises, and intangible wealth while lowering taxes on property. He quietly supported voting rights for African Americans. He stood firm against strikes and labor violence, dispatching state militia as necessary. But he also continued to support labor with safety regulations, a labor arbitration system, and fines on firms that prevented unionization. As governor, he was invited to preside over the 1892 Republican Party national convention, which renominated President Harrison but which also strongly supported McKinley as a candidate. And all the while, McKinley gave hundreds of speeches throughout the region, often stumping for fellow Republicans, speaking in at least sixteen states to millions of listeners.[24] His speeches were frequently met with "great cheers" and "magnificent ovations"; even the mere introduction of McKinley often "brought the audience to its feet with a torrent of applause."[25]

When the country descended into the 1893 economic crisis, McKinley blamed the lower tariffs passed by President Cleveland and the Democrats in Congress. He argued that foreign imports hurt the sales of American farms and businesses and took jobs away from American workers. "The total losses to the country in business, property, and wages are beyond human calculation," he insisted in a mid-1894 speech. He excoriated Treasury Secretary John G. Carlisle for having "seized upon [the nation's gold reserve] without compunction to meet the daily expenses of the Government despite the great peril it constantly invites upon the country." And he blasted the president and his party for having promised all things to all people in order to win elections and then drifted aimlessly once in office. "The [Cleveland] administration and Congress are without compass or rudder," he scoffed.[26]

The Economy and the Realignment Election of 1896

By 1896, after years of policy activism and tireless campaigning, McKinley was one of the most well-known, and well-respected, politicians in the country.[27] McKinley himself had quietly aspired to the presidency for years.[28] When the Republican Party convention met in St. Louis in mid-June 1896, he was nominated on the first ballot in a landslide, beating the sitting House Speaker, a former vice president, and at least one powerful Republican machine boss. Tariffs had become *the* key issue by spring 1896, and McKinley was simply the best, most effective spokesman for them.[29] On the currency, he had learned to be tactically ambiguous; he either avoided the subject or spoke broadly in favor of "sound money," insisting only that American currency be "the very best money in the world."[30] This allowed listeners to impute support for either the gold standard or bimetallism as they might see fit.[31] It also helped that McKinley had been absent from Congress during the Panic of 1893 and the ensuing recession and that he hailed from a battleground state.

Meanwhile, the Democratic Party had fractured over the failed presidency of Grover Cleveland. At their July 1896 convention, struggling farmers, workers, and the poor threw their weight behind William Jennings Bryan.[32] At thirty-six, Bryan still remains the youngest presidential nominee in American history. He was also one of the most charismatic. He boldly repudiated the Cleveland administration and its conservative "Bourbon Democrat" supporters.[33] He castigated "those [wealthy bankers] who are now reaping advantage from a vicious financial system" and called upon "the avenging wrath of an indignant people" to back his campaign.[34] His principal quest was for the free coinage of silver.[35] To Bryan, the gold standard was the source of the nation's economic and social ills, and he sought to eviscerate it.[36] He argued, "A gold standard encourages the hoarding of money. . . . [I]t also discourages enterprise and paralyzes industry." He further warned that the gold standard harmed farmers through deflation while simultaneously driving up unemployment among workers.[37]

Thus, the 1896 presidential contest quickly developed into one of the most disruptive in history. The candidates offered voters an unambiguous choice between starkly different futures for America. In doing so, they pitted the country's major interest groups against one another.[38] The press then whipped the confrontation into a fever that arrested public attention throughout the year.

Bryan frightened many Americans. His arguments were considered economic heresy. He became the first popular presidential campaigner, personally touring battleground states to give speeches and meet voters.[39] Previously such behavior had been considered in bad taste, grasping, desperate, and base. But Bryan modeled his campaign on a religious revival. Farmers, unskilled labor, and silverites loved it. "So many people crowded his train that he simply spoke from the rear platform of the last car and [the whistle-stop] campaign tradition was born."[40]

The reaction against Bryan was powerful. Conservative Democrats, pro-business interests, and even many free-traders fled into the Republican camp or third parties.[41] Terrified donors directed millions of dollars to the McKinley campaign.[42] In a nationwide operation, the Republicans portrayed Bryan as an anarchist, a Socialist, and a political Antichrist who would destroy the American economy and bring chaos.[43] His "theories of government [are] crazy and positively dangerous," his critics howled.[44] The *New York Times* even suggested that Bryan was "suffering from mental disorders."[45] Nevertheless, Republicans, who had initially expected an easy presidential run, now feared the "unrest" and "communistic spirit" being tapped by Bryan.[46] McKinley, realizing he could not rival Bryan's magnetism on the stump, stayed home.[47] For weeks, he instead gave well-prepared remarks from his front porch, while a steady stream of voter delegations was brought in to hear him.[48] Eventually, over half a million Americans visited McKinley, while newspaper reprints of his speeches and Republican pamphlets reached tens of millions more.[49]

The fervor of the summer campaign had a dramatic effect on the US economy. The stock market dove after the nomination of Bryan, plummeting 12 percent in just the first week. "The [Democratic] platform of the convention is so thoroughly bad, and [Bryan] is so entirely in harmony with its worst features," complained the financial reporter for the *New York Times*.[50] As Bryan's popularity spread during the summer, foreign investors fled the US market. *The Statist*, a London business weekly, warned its readers that "so far as the investor is concerned, he will do well to keep aloof from the American market."[51] After a few weeks, the business press was reporting, "American dealers [in Europe] have very largely closed their offices and suspended business."[52] The reason, according to *The Economist*, was simple: "[T]he Democratic party stands pledged to the most predatory set of proposals for dealing with the public currency ever set forth by a body of public men. . . it is quite unnecessary to look for further sources of distrust. . . . [S]hould the Democratic party win the presidential election [the effect] would, of course, be that the moral and economic cyclone."[53] Concerns about President Cleveland's ability to fund the US Treasury only exacerbated conditions.

Back in the United States, Americans began to hoard their gold in expectation of a currency crisis. "[T]hey know what decreased purchasing power of a dollar means," explained the *Wall Street Journal*.[54] A general fear pervaded "that silver was going to sweep the country."[55] By weight, silver was then worth half that of gold.[56] Therefore, the newspapers speculated that life insurance policies, construction loans, even savings accounts would all be devalued. Contemporaries estimated that $250 million worth of domestic gold supplies, roughly equal to 1.6 percent of US GDP in 1896, drained out of the US financial system and into deposit boxes, home safes, and kitchen cupboards.[57]

As a result, business in the United States ground to a halt. Throughout the summer, agricultural prices sank. Industrial production fell 7.5 percent.[58] Some city governments had trouble funding themselves. In New York City, the usually brisk sale of municipal debt failed miserably. "[N]o one is buying bonds at present, no matter how good they may be," reported the *Wall Street Journal*.[59] It seemed that every investor and business was on hold waiting for the presidential election. And preferably a landside. "[W]e are not satisfied by a small majority," explained a prominent British investor. "We want to see Bryan defeated by such an overwhelming vote that it will plainly indicate that the American people stand for sound money and will not countenance anything [else]."[60]

In November, McKinley achieved just such a victory. He won 271 electoral votes to Bryan's 176 (224 were needed to win). McKinley won large majorities among the middle class and large-scale farmers who feared Bryan. Skilled factory workers and railroad labor also voted for McKinley, enticed by his protectionist promises. On the other hand, Bryan did well among the less wealthy farmers of the South, West, and rural Midwest.[61] Hence the popular vote was somewhat close.[62] McKinley took just 51 percent of the national tally to Bryan's 46.7 percent, with third parties picking up the remaining 2.3 percent of voters.[63] In Congress, McKinley's Republican Party swept the House, taking roughly 60 percent of the seats, and managed to win a working plurality in the Senate, with just under half the seats there.[64]

"PROSPERITY PROMISED," exclaimed the press.[65] The mere election of McKinley produced a sea change in investment and business conditions around the country. The stock market celebrated, surging 6 percent during the week following the election. Bank activity expanded rapidly.[66] "A crushing weight has been lifted and rolled away," reported the prominent investment firm R. G. Dun and Company, which now expected "a state of freedom and security [for business] which it has not known for years."[67] The *Wall Street Journal* concurred, adding, "[A]ll railroad men in the West are hopeful. . . . The election changed the business complexion in every direction."[68] When New York City next floated its midmonth bond sales, they were heralded as "a great success."[69] Industrial production rebounded by 1.6 percent during November and, after a mild December pullback, continued to grow monthly throughout the rest of winter 1896–1897. Rumors that McKinley would call an early extra session of Congress, expressly for rapid passage of a new tariff bill, only further improved confidence. Investment firms on Wall Street soon reported "[e]xpanding deposits and loans of the banks due to the reappearance of the gold which was locked up over election."[70] The newspapers began to observe drops in unemployment as soon as the election ended, though they would prove nascent. The economic revival was still tentative.[71] It awaited real legislative change. Until then, the country remained vulnerable to devaluation and partial default.

McKinley's Economic Nationalism

McKinley believed that he could both unify and save the United States through trade protectionism and industrialization. "I am a Tariff man, standing on a Tariff platform," he proudly declared.[72] Having grown up in the industrial heartland and worked in foundries as a boy, McKinley understood how foreign imports could destroy local economies.[73] The antebellum industrial sector had been fragile. Free trade might be good for wealthy consumers and those domestic farmers who could reach foreign markets, but it was devastating for budding American industry. In McKinley's experience, time and again "cheap foreign goods, invited by the low tariff . . . destroyed our manufactories, checked our mining, suspended our public works and private enterprises."[74] McKinley believed that his neighbors badly wanted the security of reliable jobs and steady wages even *more* than they desired cheap goods. "If my only means is my labor, and that is unemployed, [then] whether things are cheap or dear is of little moment to me," he reasoned.[75] In the Union army, he saw further evidence of the need for American industrial strength. The United States then had only fledgling war industries; therefore the army had relied heavily on Europe for imports of small arms and artillery pieces. As quartermaster for his regiment, McKinley regularly experienced difficulty getting high-quality supplies to his men.[76]

To McKinley, industrialization meant more than just economic benefits; it would also guarantee US civil order. He believed that a strong domestic industrial sector "protects our own people in their chosen employments" and gives them "high wages."[77] Such contented workers would have little reason for the violent strikes and labor riots that had periodically rocked the United States since the financial crisis of 1873. Because, to McKinley, even more threatening was the growing popularity of Socialists, Marxists, and anarchists. These agents of "foreign interference" were increasingly active throughout the Gilded Age. They held conferences, led parades, conducted rallies, and founded newspapers. And all of their efforts seemed aimed at undoing the fundamental institutions upon which the United States was founded: democracy, capitalism, and even Christianity. Meanwhile, decades of economic chaos had created fertile grounds for revolutionary ideas among America's growing working class.[78] McKinley believed that industrial prosperity, which could be achieved and maintained only through trade protectionism, could defuse these dangerous political trends.

Over time, his convictions about high tariffs dominated McKinley's other policy views. In fact, so thorough was his faith in protectionism that, as president, he offered few other concrete plans to deal with America's socioeconomic problems. Prosperity through tariffs would cure all. Even in foreign policy, McKinley maintained that a strong industrial America could use protectionism as a form of economic imperialism that would obviate the need for military confrontation.[79] Through the scientific study of tariff rates and their effects, protectionism could be designed as a negotiating tool in disputes with foreign governments. And McKinley truly believed "with childlike faith that all he claimed for protection was true," wrote journalist Ida Tarbell.[80]

McKinley's protectionism was partly driven by a fierce nationalism. He constantly exhorted his countrymen to "stand by the protective policy, stand by American industries, stand by that policy which believes in American wages for American laborers."[81] But his vision of nationalism was one of inclusiveness and diversity. He abhorred philosophies of racial, class, or regional supremacy. His lifelong home of Ohio had been a melting pot of millions of Americans and immigrants, from myriad origins and religious backgrounds, all seeking to take advantage of its fantastic growth. McKinley wanted the same for America. And though he genuflected to new immigration restrictions during his first presidential campaign and inaugural address, his administration did little of substance toward that end. He also believed that business and labor must work together to solve common problems in order to reap the rewards of industrialization. He even quietly supported extending voting rights and education for women. And although McKinley was a faithful Christian, "[h]is devout Methodism did not lead him to concern himself with dogma or denominational differences. . . . In a day of sharp sectarianism, McKinley was devoid of bigotry."[82] Thus, a survey of his speeches finds recurring nationalist appeals to "equal citizenship," "common cause," "unity," and "one Nation, one destiny," and he openly mocked American elites who felt they had "outgrown" their country.[83]

As for government, McKinley believed it should play an active role in promoting unity and prosperity. He dismissed as retrograde "a strict construction of the Constitution of the United States, that stood in opposition to internal improvements." He instead preferred a federal government that would intervene "for the full development of the country."[84] This was a major break from Cleveland and the laissez-faire economic thinking to which most Democrats had adhered for decades.

As a corollary, McKinley also believed in a proactive executive. For example, while in Congress he fiercely defended the veto power of the president against erosion by legislators, calling it "wisely provided by the framers of the

Constitution." He also thoroughly rejected the insistence by fellow congressmen that "[the president] has nothing to do with the legislation of this country."[85] He even defended the Democratic Cleveland administration against congressional interference in its monetary policy, declaring, "The hands of the President and [Treasury] Secretary should not be tied."[86] As president, McKinley always sought to work with Congress. He had "the greatest respect for the Legislative department, and a loyal regard for its legitimate authority," insisted a cabinet member.[87] But McKinley believed that the White House had a legitimate role in the design and passage of legislation and that the president was not restricted to mere implementation of congressional will. Thus, he rejected not just Cleveland's strict constitutionalism and Arthur's indifference to power, but also the classic Whiggish ideal of presidential restraint that had once undergirded his own Republican Party.[88]

Nevertheless, political parties were "indispensable" to McKinley's theory of democracy. He preferred to negotiate with fellow Republicans on legislation "rather than face the future with a disunited party."[89] As McKinley explained in a letter to a friend:

> The President must to a large extent rely upon his own party in the administration of public affairs. He might have a personal triumph, but that would weigh little against the demoralization and disorganization of his own party in the legislative branch of the Government upon which he must depend.[90]

McKinley's vision was not derived from abstract ideology or scholarly theories. In fact, he had little patience for economic philosophy. From the House floor, he proudly proclaimed, "I would rather have my political economy founded upon the every-day experience of the puddler or the potter . . . than the college faculty." And he routinely mocked "the influence of the professors in some of our institutions of learning, who teach the science contained in books, and not that of practical business."[91] He even once scolded Congress, then buried in a trade policy debate, "Shall we run away from the condition which we can in part relieve, or waste our valuable time now upon theory?"[92] Nor did McKinley's disdain for "theory" come from ignorance. Though limited in formal education, he was an insatiable consumer of articles, books, journals, and statistics on economics, especially trade and tariffs, amassing a considerable library at his home. He was no intellectual, but he was very well-read.

McKinley's was a flexible vision. For example, he was not a rank protectionist. Protectionism was a means to an end—American prosperity and security—not an end in itself. And as US industry grew more globally competitive and increasingly monopolistic, McKinley's support for trade reciprocity, even lower overall tariffs, grew.[93] He sought reciprocity clauses in his trade legislation, and then used them to open markets abroad.[94] Just before he died, he was openly proclaiming, "If perchance some of our tariffs are no longer needed for revenue or to encourage and protect our industries at home, [they should be bargained away] to extend and promote our markets abroad."[95] And despite being a protectionist, McKinley remained a dedicated American capitalist. He did not seek to replace the free markets with government support. He was also willing to compromise on major issues such as silver, immigration, pacificism, and anti-imperialism when necessary. Nor were his views restricted to pro-business or pro-finance measures; although he prioritized tariffs, President McKinley was a consistent supporter of railroad regulation, mine safety, labor arbitration, and respect for workers' rights. As president, his support for labor was more rhetorical than substantive. Hence, much of this broader policy agenda would await his successor, Theodore Roosevelt.

Saving the Economy: 1896–1897

After the 1896 election, the immediate economic panic subsided, but the Treasury continued to hemorrhage gold and the country remained mired in an economic depression. Hence some variation on debt default or dollar devaluation remained a possibility. McKinley immediately got to work. Unlike his predecessors, who often delayed months before taking action on major policy issues, and then got only partial measures passed as a result, President-elect McKinley began coordinating with allies in Congress for the design and passage of a new tariff bill. The central players were therefore already aligned, and the basic legislative parameters and strategy mostly agreed upon, in the weeks before he entered the White House.[96]

Then, just eleven days after taking office, McKinley called Congress into special session to deal with "the remarkable spectacle of increasing our public debt by borrowing money to meet the ordinary outlays." He further urged, "In raising revenue, duties should be so levied upon foreign products as to preserve the home market, so far as possible, to our own producers; to revive and increase manufactures . . . and to render to labor . . . the liberal wages and adequate rewards to which skill and industry are justly entitled."[97] Championed by Congressman Nelson Dingley (R-ME), the House passed McKinley's tariff bill at the end of March 1897 after just a few days of debate. McKinley mostly let the House do its work and gave all credit to Dingley, having already done his job of organizing support.

The remainder of the congressional session was consumed almost entirely by the battle over trade in the Senate. "Congress is doing nothing but sit upon the tariff egg," joked one reporter.[98] Individual senators imposed major revisions on the bill, adding 872 amendments, which raised tariffs even further.[99] Once again, McKinley judiciously avoided any public comment that might endanger the bill, but he did *not* passively await the result. The president quietly and indirectly intervened to prod, cajole, and inveigh the Senate. As a result, the bill was passed and signed by McKinley in July 1897.

The resulting Dingley Tariff regime (1897–1909) was perhaps the longest-lasting in US history and the highest tariffs in the century between roughly 1830 and 1930. In incremental hikes, the average tariff on dutiable imports rose from 40 percent (1896) to 52 percent (1899). Most important, tariffs on sugar were either reinstated or raised, re-creating a fantastic source of federal revenue. Protections on iron and steel were maintained; those on manufactured metal products and coal were increased. The bill also protected the American cotton, textiles, and carpets industries by creating tariffs on wool, silk, linen, and raw Egyptian cotton. A vast web of additional import duties filled over fifty pages.[100]

To many contemporaries, the economic results appeared to be extraordinary.[101] As the new tariffs came into effect, imports plummeted, falling by half between June and October 1897. Yet annual customs income jumped 10 percent, partly due to a surge in imports during the first half of the year (i.e., American purchasers seeking to beat the upcoming tariffs).[102] Meanwhile, American exports leaped by around 60 percent during the second half of 1897 thanks to economic improvements abroad. As a result, gold stocks recovered and the US financial position shifted rapidly into surplus.

The falloff in imports was more than offset by increased domestic economic activity. During spring 1897, quiet signs of a turnaround had already appeared. By midsummer, a full economic boom was underway. The stock market climbed over 40 percent.[103] Industrial production increased by over 3 percent. Wheat prices rose 35 percent. And as business confidence returned, total federal revenues increased 11 percent in 1897, then another 16.5 percent in 1898, and over 23 percent yet again in 1899. Many credited the recovery to McKinley because, as *The Economist* summarized, "with the outcome of that [1896] election and the passing of a Tariff Bill, much of that which had been uncertain has become certainty."[104]

Over a century's worth of new data and analysis has tempered this rosy view, but only somewhat. The new tariff revenues *did* succeed in repairing the US financial imbalance, which in turn reduced the risk of dollar devaluation. Tariffs thereby improved investor confidence in American assets and the financial system. Foreign investors took note.[105] Foreign investment in the United States rose by 15 percent (roughly $400 million) in 1897 alone, an increase roughly equal to 2 to 3 percent of the US economy (around $500 billion in 2020 dollars).[106] By 1899, foreigners had total investments worth $3.145 billion in the

US economy, or 17 percent of US GDP.[107] And the lion's share of foreign money went into funding American industrialization.[108]

Otherwise, the high tariffs probably had limited effects on the US economy, either positive or negative. First, the new tariffs likely did *not* hasten industrialization as dramatically as promised; that is, no new industries sprang up in response. Meanwhile, existing industries recovered from recession and consolidated, but their expansion continued along already existing paths with a few exceptions.[109] On the other hand, protectionism did *not* breed inefficiency or technological stagnation, as is commonly experienced today. For example, there is little evidence that the US economy, or any particular sector within it, fell behind in global competition due to the Dingley tariffs.[110] Third, for workers, McKinley's tariffs did *not* dramatically improve employment. After peaking over 16.7 percent in 1896, nonfarm unemployment declined only to 15.3 percent during 1897, and remained at 13.9 percent in 1898. And many of these gains were simply rehires of workers laid off during the nervous summer of 1896. Nor did tariffs result in higher wages, as McKinley had pledged. Average wages for unskilled labor were flat during 1897 and increased just 1 to 2 percent in 1898. Finally, tariffs did *not* create inflation, much feared at the time. On average, consumer prices actually declined 1 percent in 1897, and then remained unchanged for 1898–1899. This translated into small gains in real income for workers. In sum, tariffs provided the revenues necessary to save the US financial system, but they likely did not boost or damage the economy much in other ways.[111]

Gold versus Silver

McKinley wisely punted on the still unsettled gold-silver debate. This was no surprise to those who knew him well. Throughout his political career, whenever McKinley had spoken about money, he had either issued vague statements or hewed to the politically safe, but somewhat contradictory, middle ground of "bimetallism." Only during his presidential campaign, and only at the insistence of his campaign advisors and supporters, did candidate McKinley come out strongly for gold during summer 1896. Even then, he offered an olive branch to silver in the form of support for yet another international conference to negotiate and formalize bimetallism.

Once in office, President McKinley kept his promises. In spring 1897, he sent three prominent bimetallists off to Europe to propose a new international monetary convention. But he quietly dropped the matter after negotiations were aborted by the British and evaded by the French.[112] Otherwise, McKinley discreetly stuck by the Republican Party platform, which stood "opposed to the free coinage of silver" and which insisted that "[a]ll of our silver and paper currency must be maintained at parity with gold."[113]

His Treasury secretary, Lyman Gage, was more aggressive. A Bourbon Democrat, a rags-to-riches banker, and a staunch advocate of the gold standard, Gage proposed a detailed plan for currency reform in his annual report to Congress in December 1897.[114] That same month, a private roundtable of experts, backed by a high-profile conference of the nation's bankers and businessmen, produced a currency reform report and draft legislation for consideration by Congress.[115] It contained proposals similar to those put forward by Gage. McKinley bolstered these efforts with a prominent speech to the National Association of Manufacturers calling for "the settlement of this vital question."[116] Within Congress, attempts were made during early 1898 to advance a currency bill along these lines, but each failed to get out of committee.[117] The politics of major currency legislation were not yet ripe. So McKinley bided his time.[118]

The Great Merger Wave

The McKinley administration also brought to Washington tacit support for a new breed of industrial corporations.[119] Still referred to as "trusts," they had been given a juridical "green light" by the *E. C. Knight* (1895) decision,[120] in which the Supreme Court ruled that mergers and holding companies were not by themselves unlawful. Rather, it was the actual restraint of trade (e.g., pooling, price-fixing, price discrimination, agreements to restrict supply) that was illegal.[121] This helped kick off a tidal wave of mergers and holding companies, for if pooling and price-fixing were illegal, then only through mergers into massive single entities (i.e., trusts) could many industrial firms hope to limit "ruinous competition."[122] Previously, such business combinations had been rare, numbering only one or two dozen per year. During 1895–1896, these numbers ticked up somewhat as firms, and the courts, digested the new ruling and then awaited the outcome of the election.

Starting in 1897, with conservative Republicans safely returned to Congress and the White House, the rate of mergers rose to a sustained crescendo. At first, much of the country's anxiety was directed at the already monopolistic railroad sector. There were around 265 railroad mergers, from a base of around 750 independent railroads, and a similar number of consolidations, during McKinley's presidency, resulting in a handful of massive railroad conglomerates.[123] However, the railroad sector was seventy years old by now, and some three-quarters of all US rails had already been constructed.[124] Hence, they were no longer so profitable nor so innovative as they were at the start of the Gilded Age.

Large-scale manufacturing was quickly becoming the new "high tech," high-return sector. Investors flocked to fund exciting new ventures in processed foods and beverages, wool and cotton products, metals, wood products, leather goods, printed matter, chemicals, and dyes.[125] Mergers here were prolific. Interestingly, these consolidations were often driven by bankers in search of higher returns rather than by the industrialists themselves. Regardless, hundreds of small and medium-size industrial businesses simply disappeared, absorbed into massive trusts, many of which soon controlled 70 percent or more of their markets.[126] One study has shown that roughly half of all US manufacturing capacity was involved in mergers between 1898 and 1902.[127] No other country in the world experienced such industrial consolidation. Yet competition remained intense enough to drive efficiency and innovation forward. This was partly because a large proportion of these mergers involved small firms nearly ruined and highly indebted by the recent depression.[128]

These mergers did not assure financial success—around a third went bankrupt—but for those corporations able to achieve "bigness," the benefits were legion.[129] For the merger wave brought vast economies of scale and scope. Wasteful redundancies were eliminated. Transaction costs plummeted. More patient capital was available for innovation (e.g., the advent of early industrial research laboratories). Business processes became more streamlined and management more scientific. The division of labor became more complex, requiring more specialized workers, though often employed in repetitive tasks. Large trusts enjoyed greater ability to implement system-wide technological change. They could standardize technologies and operational procedures across their holdings. And since they were usually located in cities, trusts drove urbanization forward.[130] The merger movement also provided industrial corporations with the size and stability desired by retail investors. Henceforth, industrial shares became more popular on Wall Street.[131] The Dow Jones Industrial Average, then an index of only a dozen firms, was published in spring 1896 to keep track of them.

In almost every sector swept up by the merger wave, output per worker soared. To provide a general sense of the transformation: total US nonfarm output skyrocketed around 56 percent between 1896 and 1902; during the same time period, the American workforce increased by only 11 percent. In manufacturing, where most mergers occurred, the (real) dollar value of total US production increased by two-thirds. In many industries, the production increases were astounding (see Table 12.1).

Long a simmering issue, the nation's newspapers, magazines, and academic journals now erupted into debate over the trusts.[132] The most common fears were that, absent competition, monopolies would drive up consumer prices, lower wages, kill innovation, and capture politics and public policy to protect their own selfish interests.[133] On the other hand, Americans also recognized that

Table 12.1 Production Increases 1896 to 1902

Locomotives	246%
Steel	183%
Rails	163%
Canned food*	139%
Iron ore	122%
Coke	115%
Pig iron	107%
Zinc	93%
Coal	89%
Household appliances	72%
Clothing	62%
Cigars	54%
Liquor	48%
Refined sugar	45%
Shoes/footwear	42%
Printing and publishing	42%

Note: *Corn and tomatoes. Sources: *HSUS; NBER Macro.*

many trusts did not act this way. In fact, trusts had positive qualities. Business consolidation eliminated "wasteful duplications" and "reduce[d] the costs of production," noted the *New York Times*, which not only drove prices down but allowed American firms to compete globally. "[O]ne effect of this . . . is higher wages."[134] Nor was it clear whether trusts were the result of market forces and, therefore, the natural evolution of capitalism, or artificial corporate "monsters" forged through corruption to manipulate markets.[135] Hence, public opinion on big business was mixed.[136]

McKinley was well aware of these debates, but his administration fostered the merger mania through benign neglect.[137] Many, perhaps most of the corporate mergers carried out between 1897 and 1901 could have been stopped had the Justice Department taken action.[138] However, McKinley's attorney general filed just three antitrust cases. He repeatedly claimed that *E. C. Knight* prevented him from prosecuting mergers or holding companies, which by now were the most popular forms of monopoly. As with gold, the president waited for Congress to take the lead.[139] It is likely that McKinley simply viewed monopolies as a necessary, and temporarily acceptable, evil of industrialization. It helped that many trusts allowed their remaining competition to earn respectable profits, while still preventing new entrants.[140] The new breed of large corporations also provided national stability and prosperity via a growing middle class of white-collar workers.[141] And there is some evidence that McKinley was preparing to advance a more forceful antitrust agenda during his second term, but his assassination in 1901 left that task to his successors.[142]

The 1897 Gold Rush and Export Demand

Of course, neither McKinley nor the Republican Congress deserves all the credit for the economic boom that followed his election. For example, during July 1897 reports of "big gold strikes in Alaska" filled the nation's newspapers.[143] Rich deposits had been discovered the previous year, and tons of gold bullion now began flowing into the American financial system, creating "the greatest gold excitement since the days of [18]49."[144] As a result, US stocks of monetary gold grew rapidly and for a sustained period: 7.5 percent in 1897, then 27 percent (1898) and 7 percent (1899). The number of US gold coins in circulation rose quickly thereafter.[145] More gold flowing into more hands incentivized spending and consumption throughout the economy. And as the supply of money increased, the costs of borrowing fell by 40 to 70 percent as real interest rates plummeted. Overseas, new gold mines in the Canadian Yukon, South Africa, and Western Australia made monetary expansion a worldwide phenomenon, providing a supply-side "pump" for all countries on the gold standard. This increased foreign demand for American exports, already rising due to poor harvests in Europe.[146] All told, US exports rose 8.4 percent in 1897, then 14.8 percent (1898) and 4.5 percent (1899).

However, the effects of gold and exports should not be overstated. In 1897, the increase in US gold production constituted a monetary stimulus equivalent to roughly 0.33 percent of GDP (around $70 billion in 2020 dollars).[147] And exports then comprised just 7 to 8 percent of the US economy. Perhaps most telling is that, in 1897, US GDP per capita leaped more than 7.6 percent, far ahead of Europe, Japan, and South Africa, and more than any other country except Canada (at ~9.8 percent growth). In other words, domestic investment and business consolidations, catalyzed by McKinley's agenda, were likely the primary driving factors behind the economic boom; gold and exports were merely icing on the economic cake.

The Spanish-American War of 1898

The year 1898 was dominated by the Spanish-American War and its aftermath.[148] The conflict originated four years earlier with the imposition of American tariffs on sugar from Cuba, then a Spanish territory.[149] Spain responded with retaliatory tariffs that depressed American exports to Cuba. The trade war wreaked havoc on the Cuban economy, prompting a violent peasant insurrection against Spain and its planter-class elites. When Madrid responded with a brutal military crackdown in Cuba during 1896, Americans became incensed. "Let War Come," declared the *Chicago Tribune*.[150] Some US war hawks were fueled by democratic idealism, others by military-economic imperialism; still others simply wanted to eject a European power from the Western Hemisphere. Thus, concerns about Cuba appeared in the press almost as soon as the 1896 elections were over. For months thereafter, widely read US newspapers, like the *New York World* and the *New York Journal*, whipped American anger into a war frenzy with sensational stories of Spanish concentration camps, torture, rape, and other atrocities in Cuba.[151] After a mysterious explosion sank the battleship USS *Maine* while visiting the Havana harbor, armed conflict became almost inevitable.[152]

McKinley delayed hostilities for as long as possible. "[He] hoped that, given time, Spain would relieve the tension by freeing Cuba unconditionally," recalled one journalist.[153] To his physician, the president confided, "I have been through one war. I have seen the dead piled up, and I do not want to see another."[154] Other than tariff protectionism, McKinley had no strong foreign policy views. Many in the American business and banking communities also opposed military confrontation with a European great power. They expected war to drive up taxes and interest rates, create inflation, and thereby threaten the US commitment to the gold standard, even possibly hurt foreign investment in the United States.[155] But as Spanish offenses and stubbornness grew, the call for military action became irresistible. "Every congressman has two or three newspapers in his district, most of them printed in red ink, shouting for blood," complained one House member.[156] Finally, having exhausted all other options and facing immense political pressure, McKinley asked Congress first for a naval blockade and then, in April 1898, a declaration of war.[157]

The Spanish-American War proved to be a short, decisive victory for the United States.[158] The fighting lasted only four months, from late April to mid-August in 1898. During this time, US forces quickly seized the islands of Cuba, Puerto Rico, the Philippines, and Guam. By the war's conclusion, the four-hundred-year-old Spanish Empire lay in tatters, and the United States had established itself as a great military power. More impressive, McKinley had accomplished all this with the lowest American casualty rates suffered in any foreign war before 1990.[159] The majority of American war dead succumbed to tropical diseases; of the 306,760 US combatants, only 385 soldiers and sailors fell in battle.[160]

McKinley deserves considerable credit for the successful conduct of the war. "[He] directed every move on land and sea," recalled one journalist. "Night and day he followed closely every battleship, every regiment, and every plan. In Cuba not a move was made without approval from Washington."[161] McKinley actively participated in designing and facilitating passage of legislation relating to the war.[162] And when accusations arose of mismanagement by the War Department, he quickly appointed a high-profile independent committee to investigate.

In raw economic terms, the Spanish-American conflict was one of the most cost-effective wars in US history.[163] First, the financial burden was minor. Direct war expenses totaled roughly $270 million (~$7.4 billion in 2020 dollars), or only around 1.3 percent of GDP, making it the least expensive American war in real or relative terms after 1848, and perhaps of all time.[164] Veterans' benefits were limited, and many were not granted by Congress until decades later.[165] On the other hand, the subsequent occupation of the Philippines deteriorated into a four-year insurgency, in which thousands more American military died from bloodshed and disease, requiring years of high military spending.[166] Combat there demanded another $211 million (~$5.8 billion in 2020 dollars), or around 1 percent of GDP, spread out over 1899–1902.[167] Thus, by 1899 US military spending comprised just under half of all federal expenditures. The sudden flood of spending drove federal deficits temporarily higher: from 4.9 percent of annual expenditures (1897), to 8.6 percent (1898), then to 14.7 percent (1899). But the deficits were short-lived. Partly thanks to McKinley's tariffs and fiscal policies, the federal budget had swung back into sustained surplus by 1900.

To pay for the conflict, McKinley used a mix of taxes, debt, and inflation.[168] Federal taxes paid for just over three-quarters of war expenditures. McKinley convinced Congress to double taxes on tobacco and alcohol (a substantial source of federal revenues since the Civil War), increase inheritance taxes on large estates, and add new levies on banks and stock trading, as well as new duties on refiners of sugar and oil.[169] Americans paid new excises on places of amusement (e.g., theaters, pool halls, bowling alleys). The Treasury issued federal debt to finance another 17.6 percent of the war. As a result, public debt rose 0.5 percent (1898) and then shot up 16.5 percent (1899), but was back down to prewar levels by 1901. Money creation took care of the remaining 4.4 percent.[170] And yet much-feared inflation never materialized: consumer prices were, on average, flat for 1898–1899, while real interest rates remained low (around 3.0 to 3.5 percent for high-quality borrowers). As one congressman later bragged, "The Spanish-American War did not strain the nation in the least."[171]

However, the short-run economic benefits of the war were limited. Wartime spending stimulated growth, but it failed to provide an economic boom.[172] In fact, industrial production was flat during the lead-up and first weeks of the war, and then *fell* 4 percent throughout late spring 1898. There were initial shortages in individual items (e.g., wagons, uniforms, mess kits) and transportation, but these were gradually relieved, and the civilian economy was largely unaffected.[173] Farmers did well. They enjoyed record harvests and rising agriculture prices, as well as a surge in exports. Thus, their good fortune was due to a mix of wartime demand and increases in foreign consumption. In the end, the greatest economic benefactors from the war were probably Cuban landowners, for after the Spanish were evicted and American markets were opened, the Cuban sugar economy boomed.[174]

McKinley paid careful attention to other important matters during the conflict. In July 1898, he supported Congress in the formal annexation of Hawaii. He also helped to pass the Federal Bankruptcy Act. For over a century, the United States had suffered from a patchwork of unstable and inconsistent state bankruptcy laws that were poorly adapted for a modern, national market economy. Long sought by lenders, the Bankruptcy Act created the first enduring and uniform system of bankruptcy throughout the United States, including specially designated federal bankruptcy courts and officials.[175] The new federal bankruptcy system would endure, with few revisions, for eighty years.

1898 Midterms

The 1898 midterm elections served as a national referendum on the new administration, and they were mostly positive for McKinley. Voters had largely forgotten about the economy. "[T]he free silver sentiment has died out to a wonderful degree," bragged a Republican congressman and strategist, "... and [the people] are convinced of the wisdom of Republican tariff legislation, and they do not want to hear any more about that."[176] Instead, the elections turned mainly on the war and the ongoing peace negotiations in Paris. And rather than the usual midterm reversals, the Republican Party obtained a majority in Congress. Despite losses in the House—twenty-one seats, fewer than expected—they retained control of 53 percent of the seats there. In the US Senate, they picked up seven additional seats, one of the highest midterm Senate gains in US history, for a solid 56 percent Republican majority there. The midterms' biggest loser was the pro-silver coalition, which surrendered perhaps a dozen senators and sixteen House seats.

For the next several months, President McKinley, Congress, and the press were almost entirely fixated on foreign policy and military matters, including a major reorganization of the US Army.[177] Nevertheless, a legion of small spending bills helped to make the 55th Congress (1897–1899) the most expensive of the century. Even without war expenditures, the federal government surpassed the infamous spending spree of 1889–1891. "[T]he amount of incidental extravagance has been scandalously large," scolded *The Nation*, which placed blame almost entirely on the president.[178] Indeed, McKinley had vetoed only two bills, both minor, since his inauguration, and he urged even more spending: on the construction of a US merchant marine, on a Nicaragua canal survey, on a telecommunications cable to Hawaii, and on a massive rivers and harbors infrastructure bill.[179] "Never before was such a thing seen in this country—the Chief Magistrate leading in advocacy of reckless expenditure."[180]

Recession of June 1899 to December 1900

During spring 1899, troubling signs in the economy reappeared. The stock market peaked and then plateaued during early April. Exports flattened. Strike activity surged. The culprits appear to have been high interest rates (i.e., tight money supplies) and declines in foreign demand. Specifically, a financial panic in Russia prompted a rise in interest rates in western Europe. Then the outbreak of the Boer War in October 1899 threatened world gold supplies, prompting British bankers to call their capital back to London.

Back in the United States, conditions slowly ripened for a financial crisis. The autumn harvest brought the usual drain on domestic gold supplies. As a result, the United States slid more swiftly into recession during autumn 1899. As "stringency" in the US monetary supply worsened, banks and investors grew panicky. With the support of McKinley, Treasury Secretary Gage intervened to buy $12 million in US bonds and thereby inject money into the financial system during November.[181] But it was not enough. The following month, December, the stock market plummeted 23 percent in just two weeks, while a handful of bank and trust failures battered the financial system. As demand for cash increased, Gage announced that the Treasury would advance interest payments on US bonds and deposit $30 million to $40 million worth of federal gold into the national banks. These swift actions by the McKinley administration, combined with rescue efforts by the nation's top bankers, likely prevented a full-scale financial crisis.[182]

Instead, the country suffered only a mild, forgettable recession that lasted another year. It was partly due to disappointing crop yields, which led to equally disappointing railroad and food industry earnings. To make matters worse, Britain's financial woes set off recessions in the United Kingdom, France, and the Netherlands during 1900, all top consumers of US exports and sources of investment capital. The numbers tell a mixed story: American industrial production fell 9.8 percent, exports dropped over 25 percent, and the stock market dropped to 20 percent off its late 1899 highs. However, the job market was unaffected.

Unemployment dropped to 10.3 percent (1899), then 8.75 percent (1900) and 7.1 percent (1901). Wages rose almost 3 percent each year during the same period. Nor did deflation reappear: consumer prices were flat for 1899 and even ticked up 1 percent in each of 1900 and 1901. Even business failures increased only moderately: from 81 per 10,000 (1899) to 92 (1900), compared to 131 back in 1896. Therefore, with jobs strong and business failures limited, the press barely noticed the economic slowdown. Most observers interpreted it as a temporary lull, the bursting of a speculative bubble, and pointed out that similar economic slowdowns were hitting the major economies of Europe.

Ending the Gold versus Silver Fight

With the next presidential election looming, McKinley believed that conditions had finally ripened for a move on gold. First, American silver production (and prices) had, by now, fallen significantly from their peak.[183] Meanwhile, "[t]he silver Senators who had counted on a war with Spain to force remonetization of silver had been gravely disappointed."[184] In fact, thanks to a wildly popular US war-bond subscription, many American households now had a personal stake in dollar stability. Others had come to believe that America's new Great Power status could be maintained only on the gold standard. Hence, the political and economic might of silver had begun to fade. A massive education campaign by the Indianapolis Monetary Commission, Sound Money League, and other "hard money" groups further convinced many Americans to back gold for both prosperity and stability. As a sign of the growing shift in public opinion, many silverites were voted out of office in the 1898 midterms, eliminating their majority in Congress.[185]

Perhaps more important to McKinley, by the late 1890s the United States was one of the last major trading nations still flirting with bimetallism.[186] And the gold standard was increasingly seen as "a good housekeeping seal of approval," most countries that Americans sought to do business with transacting only in gold.[187] McKinley therefore concluded that, in order to realize his grand visions for American competitiveness in trade and industry, the country had to firmly dedicate itself to the international gold standard. To do otherwise might deprive the United States of investment and trade opportunities and leave it with fractured links to the world economy. So, in May 1899, he obliquely broached the subject by urging Congress to design "a provision that will make the so-called endless chain caused by the redemption of greenbacks with gold and consequent runs upon the Treasury reserve impossible."[188] He even considered calling a special session of Congress that autumn to enact legislation on gold. Republicans had a brief political-economic window that favored legislation, and McKinley worried that it might not last long.[189]

During the next ten months, the president worked with Congress to pass the Gold Standard Act.[190] It built upon the recommendations of the Indianapolis Monetary Commission and the Treasury secretary.[191] Enacted in mid-March 1900, it made gold the *primus inter pares* of US currency. It did so by fixing the value of gold at $20.67 per ounce and requiring that, henceforth, "all forms of money issued or coined by the United States shall be maintained at a parity of value with this standard." It thereby formally reaffirmed US commitment to the gold standard.[192] The US dollar was now *de jure* a common currency with the world's largest trading nations. This reduced exchange rate risk and trans-action costs for importers, exporters, and investors throughout the economy. American policymakers were then able to use the gold standard to further sta-bilize exchange rates and to strengthen the position of American banks in for-eign exchange markets.[193] The Act also mandated that certain US government debts be paid out in gold. This removed fears that inflated silver coin or paper currency might be used to shortchange lenders. Major investors could now trust in both American debt and the dollar over the long run. To further ensure that the Treasury would hold adequate reserves of gold to pay off its debts, the Act directed the Treasury Department to create a special gold fund, and even author-ized the sale of tax-free bonds to support it. This institutionalized the financial support necessary to maintain the US commitment to gold and thereby increased confidence in the US dollar. The Act also eliminated financial loopholes that had allowed speculators to trade in silver-denominated notes or greenbacks for phys-ical gold, which had caused the Treasury to continuously bleed out gold. Finally, the Act reduced the capital requirements for banks in rural districts in order to spread credit where demand for it remained stubbornly unmet. As a result, banking volatility fell sharply, while total currency in circulation jumped 9.3 per-cent in 1900, and then another 5.9 percent in 1901.[194]

However, the Gold Standard Act did *not* solve the problem of financial panics as it was expected to. A stock market panic would hit in 1903, then a full-fledged banking crisis in 1907. The economy remained vulnerable to these crises in part because the United States still had no central bank. Nor was the Treasury sec-retary given the tools, or the authority, to act like one. Nor did the Act formally empower the Treasury secretary to deal with the perennial "stringencies" that hit money markets every spring and fall, when the nation's farmers drew heavily on available money and credit supplies for planting and harvest seasons. What the Act did was to end the fears of dollar devaluation that had harried the US economy since the Civil War and which had prompted recurring financial panics and brutal economic depressions. It also ended the gold versus silver versus greenback political battles which had politically divided the country for decades. The Democrats would try again to take up the silver fight in the 1900 elections, but it was now a rapidly dying cause.

McKinley and Consensus-Building

One distinct difference between McKinley and other Gilded Age presidents was his comprehensive and aggressive, yet subtle, approach to building coalitions. Allies were essential to his success, and he cultivated them wherever he could. Top priority was Congress, where McKinley worked doggedly to secure useful partnerships. The Republican majorities on Capitol Hill did *not* manifest themselves as a rubber stamp for McKinley's policy agenda. Instead, the Republicans fought internally over almost every important legislation which McKinley supported. Therefore, many of McKinley's accomplishments came from his ability to convince, charm, cajole, and even coerce individual legislators in Congress to support him. McKinley excelled at this. For he understood Congress better than any president in recent memory.[195] "Having passed the greater part of his life in Congress he is, of course, a thorough parliamentarian," one of his cabinet explained.[196]

McKinley practiced a variety of techniques to win over Congress. He made himself accessible to favor-seeking congressmen from both parties. When they met with him, he was amiable; he let them do the talking while he listened patiently, even if they ranted or blustered. He always explained himself. He never made "enemies" lists. But McKinley was neither passive nor weak. "He knew how to resist pressure, and he resisted it on many occasions the public never heard about," wrote one journalist.[197] And yet he always came across as sincere and compassionate. "[H]e was as kindly disposed, as gentle-natured, as considerate of the feelings of others, and as generous and urbane as any man who has ever filled the lofty place of president," recalled one House member.[198]

Nor did he simply leave Congress alone to do its job, but became highly effective at managing Congress without offending it. He would invite senior congressmen to the White House to negotiate important legislation, sometimes with great fanfare in order to create public pressure on them to cooperate. On important votes, McKinley summoned undecided congressmen for friendly personal meetings. His allies might urge ill congressmen out of bed, even hospital, to get their votes recorded.[199] He sought input from the Senate on international treaties, recognizing that senators would be more likely to approve them later. He aggressively used threats of vetoes or special sessions of Congress in order to get his way on legislative matters. He carefully timed formal statements in order to influence legislation. McKinley even became adroit at opportune press leaks to assess public opinion or to hurry legislation. And unlike his predecessors, McKinley deliberately used his speaking tours to rouse the public for congressional action. As a metric of his success, President McKinley vetoed just forty-two bills during his presidency, fewer than Grant, Harrison, or Cleveland; almost all were of minor requests (e.g., for federal aid to individuals or matters related to an individual's military record), and not one was overridden.[200]

At a time when state legislatures appointed US senators, McKinley shrewdly applied his coalition-building tactics *outside* of Washington, DC. His administration reached out to state elected officials, pressuring them to pass state resolutions endorsing his policy agenda. Once passed, these state resolutions became explicit warning shots over the bows of senators to follow suit in Congress. McKinley was particularly adroit at using political patronage to create, even force alliances. Of course, this angered civil service reformers, who had made enormous strides in reducing what they saw as corruption, inefficiency, and blatant partisanship in public policy.

Perhaps McKinley's favorite patronage tactic was commissions. He frequently formed commissions or held conferences to study major policy problems. He then ensured that these commissions influenced policy and received national attention. And he used appointments to them to win allies in Congress, among party factions, and in geographic or interest group strongholds around the country. The commissions were not for show; McKinley used them to give diverse interests a place at his policy table, and he took their recommendations seriously. But since he made them so prestigious, appointments to these commissions became a terrific source of political allies. They became among the most highly sought-after positions in government. Hence critics recognized that commission appointments acted "to sap the independence and to influence the course of Senators and Representatives."[201] They were frequently McKinley's most powerful tool to win allies and forge consensus around his policy agenda.

Part of McKinley's effectiveness was his unique ability to act as head of the Republican Party.[202] By the 1890s, the party had become badly fractured, rarely cooperating well on national issues. McKinley realized that party cohesiveness was the *sine qua non* of long-run legislative and electoral victories. He also saw that, absent war or spoils, the president must step in to create that cohesiveness. His team therefore forged a national Republican Party with McKinley at its head.[203] Starting in 1896, they achieved this gradually through speaking tours, massive political fundraising efforts, a country-wide "campaign of instruction," and his nationalist "McKinley against the bosses" public relations campaign. With McKinley's sweeping victory in 1896, followed by hitherto unseen Republican landslides in the 1898 midterms, McKinley's team took over control of the Republican Party. He used his electoral strength to proclaim a mandate. As president, he campaigned eagerly for fellow Republicans during election season, drawing crowds and winning supporters wherever he went. This provided the local Republican candidate an implicit boost, and hence a political debt to McKinley. And if a loyal congressman found himself facing an electoral challenge, McKinley would counsel, "[L]et me know who he is, and I shall be glad to take him out of the way by giving him an appointment . . . [and] you will get the credit for having brought it about."[204] He then took action to focus Republicans on enacting the major planks of the national party platform rather than on petty local squabbles. And since McKinley proved able to carry public opinion, win elections, and raise record amounts of campaign finance, the Republican Party bosses quickly fell in line behind him. It helped that McKinley knew where to draw the line against his own power. He never overtly imposed his will upon the party. He even occasionally signed Republican legislation with which he disagreed. But these acts of self-restraint only enhanced his power. By 1899, one observer of American politics was reporting, "No man in Congress, no ambitious politician anywhere, can oppose the President's policy without 'going against his party.'"[205]

McKinley understood that good relations with the press were vital to the success of his presidency.[206] He was the first president in years, perhaps decades, to take a warm and friendly, even respectful approach toward journalists. He memorized the names of reporters. He invited them as guests to official White House social events. He even sometimes refused to attend important private events if the press was not also allowed in. In the White House, McKinley reserved for reporters a second-floor workroom in which to write. And to this press room he sent his personal secretary twice daily to speak to reporters about presidential affairs. Perhaps most effectively, when major policy problems arose, McKinley would quietly consult newspaper editors and reporters for advice. Thus many in the press respected McKinley. Some even likely felt that they held a personal stake in his administration, and perhaps even a special connection with the president himself. For reporters, this amounted to unprecedented access to a sitting president. And the press thrived on it, turning the White House into a *source* of the news rather than just its subject.[207] McKinley held no press conferences. He gave no interviews. He rarely allowed himself to be quoted directly, outside of formal speeches. Nevertheless, he mastered the 19th-century news cycle. He was therefore able to make his administration a generator of friendly news, perhaps bordering on propaganda, unlike any president since Lincoln.

Building Trust

McKinley's coalition-building seems to have been aimed at restoring public confidence in major American political-economic institutions, including the presidency itself. Certainly his policy agenda played a role here. Tariffs and the gold standard helped to restore trust in the US dollar and in the government's ability to pay its debts in gold. Reforms to the American banking sector and bankruptcy law served to reinforce confidence in the financial system. Tariffs and weak antitrust regulations likely eased investor concerns about the viability of America's fledging industrial sector. His attempts to herd Congress and unify his party also involved forging mutual trust and understanding. His conduct of the war, and the peace negotiations, excited the international community. "It must be said that the wisdom and magnanimity of President McKinley . . . have impressed most favourably the people not only of the United States, but of Europe," applauded *The Economist*.[208]

But McKinley's efforts went beyond mere policy change and congressional arm-twisting. For example, his predecessor, Grover Cleveland, had slowly closed himself off to outsiders, even posting guards about the White House. McKinley sent the sentries away and opened up the White House grounds to visitors. He invited politicians of both parties to visit him there and brought back the receptions and dinners that Cleveland had loathed. Cleveland had avoided public appearances; McKinley regularly walked the streets of Washington and traveled frequently to public events nearby. McKinley loved interacting with the American people, regardless of their background or politics. This had a mirror effect, for the people seemed to love him back. After only two weeks, the press was reporting, "Everybody seems to feel that a cloud has been lifted from over the White House."[209] Even his complainants were charmed. McKinley once met with a disgruntled tinplate worker, who later remarked, "I didn't get what I sent after, but I want to tell you that I am mighty glad there is a man in the White Houses that an ordinary fellow can talk to!"[210]

More striking, McKinley fundamentally changed the practice of presidential rhetoric in order to forge consensus around and build trust in his presidency. Most 19th-century presidents avoided speech-making, especially about policy. In contrast, McKinley constantly tutored the American people on his policies and how and why they would work.[211] He entered office having already spent years in a vast education campaign about tariffs and fiscal solvency. His subsequent efforts with reporters derived partly from his recognition that newspapers and magazines were a cheap, effective way for him to educate millions of Americans about his policy agenda. As president, he made three major tours of the United States: one throughout the Midwest in 1896, a second across the South in 1899, a third to the Pacific Coast in 1901. Each was a public affair with multitudes of events and speeches scheduled. The media was welcome to ride along with McKinley so as to amplify his visibility. Historians argue that these tours made McKinley the most viewed president elected to date.[212]

In his speeches, which McKinley wrote personally, he would synthesize broad, bold statements about American greatness, the importance of particular policies (e.g., tariffs, sound money, business-labor relations), and always supported by impressive statistics and illustrative anecdotes. His tone was not that of a dull university lecturer but that of a grand visionary supporting his aspirations with concrete policy prescriptions, clear explanations of causal linkages, and compelling evidence and anecdotes to back his claims.

Even on the stump, McKinley would listen as much as he spoke, learning from public opinion and then incorporating it into his speeches. "He led public sentiment quite as much as public sentiment led him," recalled a fellow politician.[213] Even in foreign policy, "[h]e made a systematic effort to get the reaction of the public to every feature. . . . Step by step he moved to stronger ground— always keeping ahead of public opinion but not too far ahead to be beyond its influence."[214] McKinley also took care to directly confront critical narratives and contrary opinions. Also, he generally responded to critics in a compassionate manner rather than with a dismissive tone or brutal attack. He therefore came across as calm, confident, and statesmanlike. Perhaps more important, McKinley always seemed focused on *national* prosperity and security rather using controversial wedge issues to excite his base so as to achieve *sectional* or *partisan* victories. After decades of noxious partisanship and "waving the bloody shirt,"[215] McKinley instead tried to get Americans to trust one another. Hence, people from across the political spectrum and around the country came to trust him.

In his administration, whenever scandals or policy mistakes appeared, McKinley tried to nip them in the bud *before* the press or Congress had time to gather momentum and dent trust in him or in US institutions. The largest scandal of his presidency was the deadly mismanagement practices of the US Army, revealed during the Spanish-American War. Although the "splendid little war"[216] had ended in an overwhelming American victory after just fourteen weeks, the army's logistics and medical care functions had proven utterly dysfunctional. Tens of thousands of soldiers piled up in Florida camps awaiting ships, equipment, and arms that were both antiquated and in poor supply. In Florida and Cuba, military deaths from disease were at least ten times those from combat.[217] Thousands of men perished from the Yellow Fever, typhoid, and dysentery that swept through improperly designed and poorly supplied military camps. Thousands more were made ill by the rations sent to them; the canned goods distributed were "simply rotten and filled with maggots," recalled one soldier.[218] When news of these blunders accumulated, McKinley quickly launched an investigation. The resulting Dodge Commission filed its report within months.[219] It was thorough and blistering, forcing the resignation of the secretary of the army and giving McKinley the grounds for reform. McKinley then quickly worked with Congress to enlarge the regular army, improve training and management practices, and increase federal control over it at the expense of state militia and volunteers.[220] What could have been a paralyzing scandal was turned into a political and legislative victory by McKinley's adroit action and self-criticism.

As a result, McKinley came to be widely perceived as dignified and compassionate. He managed the "narrative" of his presidency to a degree that his Gilded Age predecessors never achieved, nor even attempted.[221] McKinley certainly had critics, opponents, and eventually an assassin, but they generally trusted the man. Even Leon Czolgosz, McKinley's killer, admitted to no personal hatred against McKinley, just for the capitalist system which he led. During a weak moment, Czolgosz told a reporter, "I hated to hear about the wound [that I inflicted] and all that. . . . I felt sorry he did not live after I shot him."[222]

The Election of 1900 and McKinley's Second Administration

The elections of 1900 delivered a solid endorsement of McKinley and the Republican Party. In June, he was renominated by a unanimous vote of Republican Party delegates. Theodore Roosevelt replaced Vice President Garret Hobart, a beloved and valuable member of McKinley's leadership team, after the latter died in office the previous autumn.[223] McKinley chose not to actively campaign. Instead, he remained at work, letting Roosevelt and other surrogates far more sensational than he rouse voters with hundreds of rallies and speeches around the country.[224]

The election was also a victory for the active presidency. When Admiral George Dewey, the hero of the Philippine War, offered Democrats the alternative of a passive president, "his duties being mainly to execute the laws of Congress," he was overwhelmingly rejected.[225] Instead, William Jennings Bryan again took up the Democratic banner. And again, Bryan barnstormed the country calling for "the free and unlimited coinage of silver," attempting to whip up the same anger and fear that had energized his previous run.[226] The Democratic platform further added excoriations of McKinley for imperialism, militarism, and protectionism, while accusing Republicans of allowing the "insatiate greed" of monopolies to "destroy competition . . . in return for campaign subscriptions and political support."[227]

However, Bryan's silver message failed to rouse much support. "Nobody looks for any such demoralization this campaign as there was in 1896," explained the *New York Times*. "The reason for this is that the passage of the Currency bill at Washington has materially improved the financial situation."[228] And although many Americans rejected imperialism, they declined to punish McKinley for a short, victorious war. The solid South could be counted on; otherwise, Bryan lost votes. Even a few silver states abandoned him. That November, McKinley won with 51.6 percent of the popular vote and 65 percent of the electoral college, slightly better than his victory four years earlier. And while Republicans lost two seats in the Senate, they gained ten seats in the House, giving them comfortable majorities in Congress.

The vigorous US economy certainly played a role. In his second inaugural, the usually humble McKinley now proudly boasted, "[E]very avenue of production is crowded with activity, labor is well employed, and American products find good markets at home and abroad."[229] In fact, so strong was the American economy that a sizable stock market panic during early May 1901 failed to derail it. Triggered by a battle between rival investment moguls for control over the Northern Pacific Railway, the market plummeted over 6 percent in just a few hours. It was one of the largest single-day declines in history to date. Yet the market mostly shrugged off the event within a few days. Even the wary Treasury secretary dismissed it as "purely a speculative movement . . . nothing to warrant excitement or undue fear."[230]

After his reelection, McKinley was the most influential man in American politics, possibly the strongest executive since Lincoln. Some newspapers fretted about the new power of the presidency. In fact, so popular was McKinley that he already felt compelled to squelch talk of a third presidential run. For his new term, McKinley planned to advance US economic prosperity along several fronts. First, he proposed greater use of reciprocity treaties to pry open foreign markets for America's abundance of production, declaring, "Reciprocity treaties are in harmony with the spirit of the times, measures of retaliation are not."[231] Hence, tariffs that had served their purpose should be negotiated downward. Second, he called for construction of a trans-isthmus canal and a modern merchant marine to better foster US trade. Third, he intended to tackle the growing divide between industrial corporations and labor via a number of measures. For example, he sought a federal incorporation statute for the largest monopolies.[232] He had also begun to think about progressive corporate taxes, a permanent federal commission to investigate business practices, remedies for anticompetitive behavior, and federal mechanisms for labor arbitration. He even suggested an outright federal ban on child labor and an eight-hour workday for employees of the federal government. In other words, McKinley had begun to shift his political support toward policies that would soon typify the Progressive movement.[233]

McKinley would not live to fight these battles. The second session of the 56th Congress ended in March 1901, its time having been absorbed by thousands of bills, many necessary, but almost all mundane. In a final economic victory, McKinley convinced Congress to reduce wartime consumption taxes. But otherwise he was still mostly absorbed by foreign policy issues. He then spent much of the spring and summer traveling the United States or at his home in Ohio.

In early September 1901, he visited the Pan-American Exposition in Buffalo, New York, as a guest of honor.[234] There McKinley gave his final speech, which bragged of America's economic and technological prowess. The *London Standard* called it "the utterance of a man who feels that he is at the head of a great nation, with vast ambitions and a new-born consciousness of strength."[235] The following afternoon, against the advice of his staff, McKinley briefly shook hands with the public in a receiving line. During the event, he was shot in the abdomen by a discontented steel worker. The assassin, a sworn anarchist, later explained, "All those people seemed bowing to the great ruler. I made up my mind to kill that ruler."[236] McKinley lingered a bit, with hopes of recovery, but succumbed a week later.

Summary

William McKinley oversaw one of the most successful economies in American history. During his administrations, real GDP per capita growth averaged around 5.0 percent annually. Yearly growth in industrial production averaged 9.9 percent. And by 1901, US industry was producing over 55 percent more goods than in 1896. Yet, despite such rapid economic expansion, inflation was almost nonexistent, an average annual rate of just 0.2 percent. Unemployment gradually declined from 16.7 percent (1896) to 7.1 percent (1901), while wages rose 10 to 11 percent, all despite a strong recovery in immigration.[237] As consequence, wealth inequality fell nationwide for the first time since the Hayes administration.[238] Meanwhile, the federal balance sheet shifted from a 4.0 percent deficit (1896) to a 12 percent surplus (1901). Therefore, public debt as a percentage of GDP shrank from roughly 8 percent to 5.7 percent and was headed lower still. Farm prices stabilized. The stock market set new records regularly, rising an average of 15.5 percent each year. Total federal revenues leaped almost 75 percent. And partly thanks to McKinley's strategic avoidance of trade wars, American exports boomed 40 percent, while the US trade surplus more than doubled.[239] By 1900, the press was marveling, "It seems almost incredible that we should be sending cutlery to Sheffield, pig iron to Birmingham, silks to France, watch cases to Switzerland . . . [or] building locomotives for British railroads."[240] As a result, US gold supplies bounced back from their catastrophic lows experienced under Cleveland. Thus, stability returned to the financial system, and interest rates dropped to their lowest levels yet seen in US history.

Of course, McKinley had his failures. There were critical issues upon which he campaigned but did *not* act or achieve much. For example, he did not act to address lynching or civil rights for African Americans in the South. He was a former Union officer who detested slavery and racial hatred, but his higher priority was to construct political support in the post-Cleveland South and to reunite the country by burying the still lingering antipathies created by the Civil War. Hence his domestic policies were a tremendous disappointment to most Blacks who had supported him.[241] On corruption and civil-service reform, many accused McKinley of backpedaling. He argued that some government positions were more appropriately filled by experienced men, or even by explicit policy supporters, rather than according to objective performance on a written civil service exam. So he shuffled the federal appointments deck accordingly, infuriating reformers. Much analysis suggests that he merely reorganized the civil service.[242] Yet historians also recognize that McKinley knew how to play the patronage game and did so rigorously and well in support of his coalition-building. Finally, he did little for labor. Union membership skyrocketed and strike activity increased dramatically under McKinley, despite workers' gains in employment and wages.[243] Yet none of these failures prevented McKinley's economy, nor his presidency, from achieving dramatic and unparalleled prosperity.[244]

It is tempting to conclude that McKinley simply backed the "right" policies. His administration successfully reversed the Harrison- and Cleveland-era measures that had provoked and sustained the depression of 1893–1897. Yet McKinley's predecessors had also understood that keeping the Treasury solvent, maintaining the value of the US dollar, and recouping America's creditors in full were "good" policy. Bryan's general argument for silver was almost exactly that used by monetarists today.[245] McKinley was technically "wrong" on other major policy decisions: tariffs taxed consumers while protecting producers, resulting in suboptimal trade flows; imperialism was costly and unnecessary; and yet the economy still prospered. Thus, it was *not* that McKinley was objectively "correct" on policy, or that his challengers misunderstood economics, especially since he backed many of the *same* policies as did most Gilded Age presidents.

Instead, McKinley's greatest economic contribution may have been his efforts to *restore trust* in America's major political-economic institutions; his policy agenda was just one possible means toward that end. For example, his tariff and fiscal policies worked because they provided the revenue necessary to put US finances into surplus. They thereby repaired confidence in the US dollar and in the government's ability to pay its debts in gold. Similarly, McKinley's support for the international gold standard, together with reforms to the American banking and bankruptcy regulations, likely helped to further build trust in the American financial system and the US currency. These actions removed fears that dollar devaluation might be used to shortchange lenders or that speculators could escape their debts. They also reduced exchange rate risk and transaction costs for *all* international business conducted with American partners.

Weak antitrust enforcement may have played a similar role by reducing "ruinous competition" at home. Competition from domestic producers still existed. But the perceived destruction wrought upon American manufacturers, and their employees, by speculative domestic ventures was curtailed. Thus, in addition to its direct effects, the impact of weak antitrust rules (and protective tariffs) on late 19th-century market psychology may have been to increase confidence. Investments in new technology could be made, factories built, workmen hired, all without fear of being eviscerated at any time by a wave of cheap foreign imports or wildcat domestic ventures.

Importantly, McKinley's trust-building was neither isolated nor ad hoc; rather, it was strategically interwoven with other crucial aspects of his leadership. First, it was constructed around his vision of nationalist protectionism, industrialization, and active government. McKinley's entire political career was a continuous stream of rhetoric and activity to achieve that vision. He repeatedly communicated it in his speeches. He consistently backed it with his actions. It was clear and compelling. Both allies and opponents knew where McKinley stood and where he wanted to take the country. Nor was it ideology for its own sake. McKinley was willing to flex and change where necessary to build support and get legislation passed. Second, McKinley took a proactive view of the government, and of the presidency, to achieve his vision. He generally did not sit back and wait for the economy to recover or for Congress to legislate. He and his appointees inserted themselves into the political and policy process. They helped to design legislation, mobilize support in Congress and across the country, ingratiate the media, and educate the public. Third, McKinley took great pains to build working coalitions with key political-economic actors: Congress, the press, major interest groups, and even the American public. Usually these overtures were friendly, sometimes coercive, but often effective and always proactive.

After McKinley's death, the US presidency and the American economy would enter a different era. The political-economic fights that had defined the Gilded Age were mostly over. By 1901, the United States had formally joined the gold standard and abandoned silver. Much of the federal spoils system had been dismantled. Political machines were not dead, but they no longer dictated national politics. Instead, a national party system was now in place. Reconstruction and African American rights were all but forgotten; concerns about unions, strikes, and Socialism had replaced race as the country's headline equity issues.[246] Even the once all-mighty American farmer was now a defensive player in national politics. The future belonged to coal, steel, electricity, telephones, automobiles, and the corporations that could master and produce them. In many sectors, the "atom" of the US economy had shifted from small-scale entrepreneurial capitalism serving local markets to large industrial monopolies competing globally. Even the passive presidency, with its traditional restraint in public rhetoric, would quickly fade from memory. At the start of McKinley's second term, one political essayist even warned, "[T]he pivot upon which we revolve as a nation is no longer the Capitol, where the people's representatives assemble, but the White House, where one man sits in almost supreme power."[247] The next thirty years would pit a new generation of energetic young Progressives against a rampart of diehard American conservatives and an entirely new style of president.[248]

McKinley did not cause all of this, nor did he act singlehandedly, but he played an important role in most of these developments. And partly thanks to McKinley, by 1901 the United States had become by far the largest, wealthiest, and most technologically advanced economy in history, capable of projecting its military and economic might around the globe and possessed of a presidency far more powerful than any before in American politics.

13

Conclusions

"Talleyrand once said to the first Napoleon that 'the United States is a giant without bones,'" Congressman James Garfield told an audience in 1874, adding wryly, "Since that time our gristle has been rapidly hardening."[1] I have argued that the same can be said of the Gilded Age presidents. They were political-economic giants. They had massive reach and considerable political weight to throw around, if they chose to do so. With a word, they could influence markets around the country. Even the contemporary press described them as men who "emerge into the trying and dazzling daylight of power."[2] The problem was that these presidents had few institutional or rhetorical "bones" upon which to anchor their considerable muscle. They had to find other ways to exert their will. But throughout the Gilded Age, their "gristle" was "rapidly hardening."

Social scientists and presidential scholars will ask: How does the evidence presented thus far square with existing debates over presidential performance? And what new hypotheses, if any, are generated by the preceding case studies? This chapter attempts to tackle these questions. It begins with some important caveats and a brief review of the conventional wisdom. I then argue that presidents *do* matter for the nation's economic performance, but in four subtle ways. *In brief, presidential (in)action during economic crises appears to matter most. More tentatively, the evidence also suggests that presidential vision (and especially flexibility in achieving that vision), skill at coalition-building, and trust-building also appear to correlate strongly with economic performance.* In other words, the Gilded Age presidents have a lot to tell us about leadership and American political development in general.[3]

Hic Sunt Dracones

A few preliminary cautions are in order. First, a bit about my methodological approach. This book's historical case studies were researched and written *before* I surveyed the literature on presidential power and effectiveness. I intentionally avoided reading the theoretical canon so as not to bias my own interpretation of the data. I wanted the cases and data to speak for themselves. In my analysis, I used a basic comparative approach, inquiring which characteristics were shared by the more economically successful presidents, but not the failures (and vice-versa). Only after interpreting the empirical evidence and having drawn in-itial conclusions did I then scrutinize existing theoretical debates about the pres-idency. This process included discussions with scholars and experts, paper and poster presentations at research conferences, and talks at presidential libraries. This chapter describes the results.

Second, this book is concerned with leadership and the economy in the *short run* (i.e., during or soon after a president's term in office). It offers no opinion on the relevance of the presidency to *long-run* economic performance. There are simply too many variables changing at different rates over time to fully evaluate whether presidents matter over the long run and, if so, in what ways. How does one isolate the effects of one president versus another over the course of several administrations? And exactly how long is the long run? There is also good reason to suspect that what helps (or hurts) the economy in the short run may hurt (or help) it in the long run. These issues I leave for future research.

Third, it bears repeating that this book is not intended as a normative ar-gument about which economic ideologies or policies executives should or should not pursue, nor does it remove individual presidents from their his-torical context and judge them by 21st-century standards. Just because the president and federal government *can* do something does not mean that they *should*. These are philosophical questions that cannot be resolved scientifi-cally. Readers must judge for themselves. Rather, this book is meant to show that similar types of leadership behavior have produced similar results, re-gardless of other factors.

Fourth, this book is more about presidential performance than about pres-idential power. Powerful presidents make things happen: laws, regulations, treaties, policies. But whether or not these things help or hurt the economy (i.e., performance) is another matter. The two concepts overlap. And lessons for pres-idential power can be inferred from the evidence presented in this book. But ultimately this book is about understanding the most robust aspects and causal mechanisms of high-performance economic leadership. This is why digging through the Gilded Age is so important. Since it is the least likely time to find ef-fective economic leadership coming out of the White House, it is most revealing when we do find it.

That being said, this book does make a larger argument about presidential leadership. This is an examination not of economic policy leadership alone but of overall leadership quality. My claim is that we can learn a lot about the evolution of the modern presidency from the attempts at independent leadership by the Gilded Age presidents. It is about early indications of leadership in the modern presidency. And it implies that successful leadership in *all* times may come down to the vital importance of vision, action, coalitions, and trust-building. This book is about far more than mere fights over policy or forgotten history.[4]

Major Theories of the President's Economic Performance

The debate over the relationship between the president and the economy is *not* new. Chapter 2 highlighted the four major families of current theory. To recap: The first category says simply "no relationship at all," and it comes in several varieties. Some describe Gilded Age presidents as weak, second-tier politicians. They were chosen more for their electability than for their political skill or policy expertise. Others argue that the presidency was then, and still is, a weak institution. Both formal and informal constraints on presidents meant that other competing actors or institutions were far more powerful. Still others argue that presidents are victims of circumstance. They just happen to get elected during times of economic boom or bust. The second set of theories contends that good economic performance is a product of the "right" set of policies. Therefore, presidents who recognize and pursue the "right" policy agenda do well. A third category of theory argues that an individual president's performance in office is a function of personal characteristics: character, psychology, experience, education, intelligence, and so on. And since presidents rarely act alone, a final set of theories awards credit or blame to the president's cabinet, staff, and advisors. So, how well did these hypotheses predict or explain the economic performance of the Gilded Age presidents discussed in the previous chapters?

1. No Relationship?

The default theory is that there is little relationship between the presidency and economic performance, and that Gilded Age presidents were least relevant of all. This was my own initial expectation. *Clearly, this book disagrees. It sides with the few scholars who see strength, relevance, and effectiveness in the Gilded Age presidency.*[5] For example, it concurs with Max J. Skidmore, who has described as "warped" and "jaundiced" such dismissive views of Gilded Age presidents.[6] Along with Stan Haynes, it disputes the belief that "the Gilded Age was an era of presidential nominations decided in smoke filled rooms, where the outcome of conventions was determined by a few political bosses, and where presidents, once elected, served the bosses."[7] It agrees with Charles W. Calhoun that Gilded Age voters faced real choices between distinct political and economic paths[8] and that "the presidents of the Gilded Age presided over a gradual but undeniable accretion of authority and influence in their office."[9] I take these positions because the evidence reveals that Gilded Age presidents were often dynamic and influential and frequently rebelled against their party and Congress. They had power in ways that 21st-century presidents do not, even though they lacked many of the institutional resources and rhetorical practices of modern presidents.

Nevertheless, the presidential case studies presented here do not entirely reject the claims of critics like Neustadt, Rudalevige, Skowronek, and others. Yes, Gilded Age presidents were *sometimes* less assertive, powerful, and effective than modern presidents, while Congress, the courts, and political parties and machines were relatively more powerful than today. But not always, nor in all policy domains. For example, late 19th-century presidents were significantly more powerful in monetary policy, patronage, and spoils than are presidents today.[10] And the fact that Gilded Age presidents usually faced a Congress with at least one house controlled by their opposing party may explain their modern reputation for ineffectiveness. Therefore, I disagree with David Nichols's claim that "modern Presidents do no more—and no less—than Presidents have done in the past,"[11] while still confirming Richard Ellis in his belief that "[g]overnment has grown but the presidency has remained fundamentally as it was always intended to be, the republic's preeminent leadership position."[12]

My case studies also admit that historical circumstance mattered. For example, Cleveland was twice elected into far more challenging situations than were Hayes, Garfield, or Harrison. In many ways, Grant entered the White House under the most favorable political-economic conditions in over a decade. The nation cried out for economic leadership when McKinley took office, whereas few bothered when Arthur ascended. All presidents face challenges, but their trials are far from equal. And these differences matter when evaluating leadership ability. As Jared Bernstein, a senior economic advisor in the Obama administration, recently put it, "[P]residents in good economies are like pilots in fine weather. To test their skills, they need a storm, or downturn."[13]

However, the evidence suggests that presidents also make their own luck.[14] Presidents can choose how much they stick to "prior government commitments" once in office.[15] As historian Brooks Simpson explains, "Presidents are not total prisoners of their environment, and they themselves help determine what is, in fact, possible."[16] For example, McKinley was elected mostly on monetary issues, but he delayed action on them until deep into his first term, choosing instead to prioritize trade protectionism. Cleveland could have chosen a more aggressive response to the 1893 crisis; he might even have prevented it back in 1885. Harrison could have used his political skill to forge a more sustainable economic agenda. Arthur rarely attempted to influence, much less lead the economy. Grant's refusal to sign the Inflation Bill of 1874 can be ascribed to no one but himself. In other words, presidents are not helpless victims of their historical circumstances.

Also, while Bensel, Saunders, and Skowronek are correct that parties and the courts had unusual power during this era, they neglect considerable evidence of presidential power and independence. Several Gilded Age presidents *successfully opposed* their parties on policy and patronage. Some executives even bent the party to their will, while others zealously supported party dominance. Also, most Gilded Age presidents explicitly *supported* the power and pro-business laissez-faire ideological bent of the courts. They saw the courts "as an essential bulwark against economic radicalism and social disorder" in an era when anarchy, Socialism, and Communism seemed to threaten traditional American political-economic thought and practice.[17] Hence we cannot know whether the Gilded Age courts or parties would have been as strong *without* presidents as their champions.

2. Getting Policy Right?

Some assume that economic performance is less about individual leaders and more about pursuing the "right" policy agenda. This is a common misconception. On the one hand, economists today generally *do* agree on the most favorable conditions for balanced economic growth.[18] However, there is little consensus on how governments should create those conditions. Decades of research on and practical experience with economic policy consistently reveal that, while there may be some objectively "wrong" policies, economists and policymakers have found no single best set of "right" policies that nations must converge upon in order to achieve economic prosperity.[19] There are myriad different combinations of fiscal, trade, monetary, and regulatory approaches that can work. This was true even during the Gilded Age.[20] Or, to reverse Tolstoy: almost every happy economy is happy in its own way.[21]

In particular, it is sometimes assumed that tight monetary policy (i.e., in pursuit of rejoining the international gold standard at the dollar's pre–Civil War value) doomed the United States to recurring crises and recessions during the Gilded Age.[22] If only they had printed more money! Much economic suffering could have been prevented or at least attenuated. But this solution, so seemingly obvious and widely used by the 21st century, would not have fared well during the 19th century. For the past fifty years, the United States has faced few penalties for its debt, deficits, or inflationary policies.[23] During the Gilded Age, conditions were reversed. For centuries, feckless monarchs had debased their currencies to pay for wars, palaces, and support of powerful or favorite interest groups. Many Gilded Age investors worried that democratic leaders would follow suit to attract voters. Thus, the 19th-century gold standard was interpreted as a "good housekeeping seal of approval."[24] In international trade, adherence to the gold standard reduced transaction costs and exchange rate risk. In international finance, gold signaled to investors a responsible government and a trustworthy currency. Governments could not print their way out of problems at the expense of their, often foreign, creditors. And although foreigners were not the *primary* source of US capital back then, they were essential *marginal* investors.[25] In fact, *all* major investors had choices by the late 1860s. Modern shipping and the telegraph ushered in an era of unprecedented financial globalization.[26] So, if the United States looked risky, the markets of Argentina, Australia, Brazil, Canada, Russia, and Turkey beckoned.[27] Countries that broke their commitments to gold (e.g., Argentina in 1876 and 1885, Brazil in 1889, Chile in 1878 and 1898, Italy in 1866 and 1894) tended to suffer major financial upheavals and years of economic depression as capital fled elsewhere.[28] In other words, expansive monetary policy was not necessarily the "right" policy solution, nor was tightness objectively wrong during the Gilded Age; each came with costs and benefits.

Nor did the Gilded Age economy falter because people misunderstood economics at the time. Certainly, many economic assumptions and arguments popular during the late 19th century have since been proven incorrect. But Gilded Age thinkers got a lot right. For example, supporters of greenbacks and silver understood that growing the money supply would have an inflationary effect on the economy. Supporters of gold understood that currency devaluation and exchange rate uncertainty hurt commerce and investment. They both knew that unsustainable debts and deficits could lead to economic crises. Even average Americans had become masters of Gresham's Law; in fact, in an economy of multiple currencies, they lived it. Alternatively, late 19th-century arguments for and against trade protectionism, welfare, antitrust, and business regulation were, in fundamental ways, quite similar to the same debates in our own time. In sum, it was not that Gilded Age policymakers did not understand the economy. Their arguments may not yet have been formalized by professional economists, nor were they backed by rigorous statistical analysis of large, comprehensive data sets. But many "right" ideas about economics and policy were widely entertained during the 19th century, and the presidents and their cabinet and advisors were generally well aware of them.

3. Character, Psychology, Experience, Intelligence

For space purposes, this book did not present extensive psychological or personal portraits of the Gilded Age executives. However, in my research, I failed to find much evidence for any law-like relationship between personal attributes and economic leadership. Personality, character, and psychology all mattered; they each played a causal role in each president's particular story. But I could not find any generalizable, systematic relationship. Nor did intelligence, education, or prior experience correlate well with presidential effectiveness or economic performance.[29] For example, Grant's experience in wartime leadership did not translate into skill in economic leadership. For an American president during the late 19th century, Hayes was average by almost every dimension, except the fantastic economic boom over which he presided. Arthur's incredible skill at city and state politics did not translate to the national level. But nor did his long history of partisan malfeasance and questionable ethics manifest into corruption in the White House. The *same* tedious, dull, unschooled Cleveland both prevented a financial crisis in 1885 and then helped propagate one in 1893. Harrison was possibly the most intelligent, religious, highly educated, and experienced Gilded Age president, and one of the most competent administrators and speakers of the era. And yet he created conditions for the worst economic downturn of his time. McKinley was poorly educated and considered neither terribly bright nor outgoing by his peers, yet he led the US economy out of crisis and into prosperity. In sum, these personal factors mattered, but not in a clearly uniform way.

4. Presidential Staff and Advisors

Presidents do not act alone, even within the executive branch. This is partly because they are rarely policy experts, especially in economics. Therefore, it is natural to look to the president's circle of advisors, staff, and appointees as sources of an administration's effectiveness and ultimate success.[30] In particular, each Gilded Age president relied on his executive team, especially the Treasury secretary, for both vital advice and effective policy implementation. The case studies also suggest that incompetent or corrupt personnel in the executive branch can damage the effectiveness of a president. The administrations of Grant and Arthur were badly harmed in this way. Even McKinley suffered from incompetence in his War Department. Incompetent or corrupt appointees not only hurt performance but damaged trust in the president's leadership abilities. But ultimately it was the judgment of the president himself that mattered most. In other words, *bad* advisors, staff, and appointees were sufficient, but not necessary, for failure. Conversely, *good* advisors, staff, and appointees were necessary, but not sufficient, for success. They mattered, but only at the margins. They were tools for success, but not causal factors. Ultimately it is the person who selects and wields those tools who most determines outcomes, and that person is the president.

* * *

So what factors *do* matter most for economic performance, according to the evidence from the Gilded Age? What follows are four primary hypotheses generated by the evidence presented in the earlier chapters. *Specifically, crisis response, presidential vision (and flexibility in achieving that vision), skill at coalition-building, and trust-building, each seem to correlate strongly with economic success or failure.*

1. Economic Crises

The most compelling finding from the evidence on the Gilded Age is that finan-cial crises matter a lot for economic performance. In the 21st century, we tend to dismiss them as rare events, but during the 19th century financial panics regu-larly battered the American economy, often with devastating results. Statistically, the Gilded Age economy (per capita) shrank –2.0 percent during the years im-mediately following a financial crisis, compared to 3.9 percent economic growth during noncrisis years. In fact, almost regardless of which data one examines, the worst "hard times" of the Gilded Age find each at their core a financial crisis: the Gold Panic of 1869, the Railroad Panic of 1873, the Banking Panic of 1884, and the Devaluation Panic of 1893.[31] Two of these debacles preceded and strongly contributed to brutal multiyear economic recessions. The other two struck amid deepening recessions and probably extended the economic misery for at least another year. These events go a long way toward explaining the dismal economic rankings of Grant, Arthur, and Cleveland. In comparison, the more successful economies of Hayes and Garfield faced no financial crises.

So is it just a matter of luck, of being president when a financial crisis hits? No. If we look more closely at the evidence, we find that aggressive presiden-tial leadership likely prevented several additional financial crises. For ex-ample, Cleveland, Harrison, and McKinley each confronted budding financial crises that *never fully materialized*. These include the near meltdowns during winter 1884–1885, autumn 1890, 1894–1896, and late 1899. The difference is that in each of these *non*crises, the administration took aggressive action to diffuse the brewing financial turmoil: during his first term, Cleveland sus-pended bond redemptions and reduced gold payments, then he repeatedly went to Wall Street for loans to rescue the Treasury during his second term; Harrison and McKinley each used the Treasury like a central bank to increase liquidity during times of extreme strain on the US financial system. In compar-ison, Grant, Arthur, Harrison, and Cleveland took little or no action to prevent the Panics of 1873, 1884, or 1893. And while Grant did take action to address the Panic of 1869, he generally refused to act on the economic recession that followed.

Moreover, almost every Gilded Age president (except Garfield and Harrison) had to deal with the recessionary aftermath of a financial crisis. The US economy declined for an average of thirty-five months after each Gilded Age financial crisis, contracting an average of –4.7 percent. Once again, the "failed" presidents took little or no action to address these recessions. Grant, Arthur, and Cleveland each refused to support legislation or spending that might ameliorate the eco-nomic misery that plagued the country during their administrations. They even vetoed potential relief bills passed by Congress. In contrast, Hayes, Harrison, and

McKinley actively supported executive action, legislation, or spending intended to counteract a shrinking economy or to provide acceptable forms of welfare.

In fact, presidential action in response to *other* types of crises also likely affected economic performance. For example, with his rapid but balanced response, Hayes cut short the unprecedented labor uprisings of 1877 that had shut down America's rail transportation network and had begun to penetrate the nation's mines and factories. Harrison's swift and strong reaction to the 1892 cholera epidemic may have staved off an economic crisis in New York City, then *the* major hub for trade, finance, and manufacturing. Great Britain, Germany, France, and Russia each suffered economically when similar epidemics hit their financial and commercial centers. In comparison, Grant did little to mitigate the recessions that followed the Panic of 1869 or 1873. A decade later, as the economy sank ever deeper into recession, Arthur also did nothing, even when flooding hobbled the Ohio and Mississippi river economies in 1882. Cleveland likewise declined to act in 1886–1887, when freak weather events destroyed ranching and agriculture on the Great Plains and crippled transportation and distribution systems around the nation. Nor did Cleveland (or admittedly Harrison) respond effectively to labor strikes or the growing problem of monopolies.

In sum, the Gilded Age presidents who took action to prevent crises and to alleviate recessions enjoyed significantly *better* economies than those presidents who waited for the market to correct itself. This hypothesis is *not* meant as an indictment of free market competition, nor is it an endorsement of any particular policy response. But the evidence does strongly support the argument that presidents, and the federal government, have significant roles to play in crisis mitigation and risk management so that markets can function properly.[32]

2. Presidential Vision

The next logical question is: If crises and recessions are such powerful economic factors, *why* did some Gilded Age presidents act to address them, while others chose not to? The case studies suggest that presidential vision may have played a powerful causal role in determining presidential action.[33] This concurs with recent scholarship on the role of ideas in presidential power and performance.[34] I define presidential "vision" broadly as a set of relatively specific goals for the country, including prescriptions for the president and the federal government in achieving those goals. Vision therefore also includes the president's "theory of the presidency": his personal interpretation of his duties, responsibilities, authority, and capabilities versus those of other political-economic actors and institutions. In plain language, a president's vision answers the questions of where the president wants to take the nation and what are the things that a president and the federal government "must, can, and should do" and "must not, cannot, and should not do" in order to get it there.

The case studies in this book suggest that the Gilded Age presidents tended to act, or refrain from action, according to their vision. The successful presidents each came into office with a relatively clear, compelling, and consistent vision for the nation. Importantly, each of these visions prescribed an *active* role for the president and the federal government in achieving economic prosperity, especially during crises. Also, the successful presidents were *not* zealous ideologues who, in pursuit of their vision, damned all opposition or compromise. Instead, they were pragmatic negotiators. They were willing to be flexible enough to achieve their goals.[35] For example, Hayes advanced civil service reform without being militant. He compromised where necessary to pass legislation or keep his party in power. McKinley was a strident protectionist, but he eagerly bargained with Congress on tariffs, gold, and domestic policy in order to get his way.

The economic failures fell into two categories regarding "vision." They either had no clear, compelling, consistent vision (Arthur, Harrison), or they stuck too rigidly to one (Grant, Cleveland). For example, Grant and Cleveland were each intransigent "hard money" men. They rejected any hint of inflationary monetary policy in response to the financial crises and recessions that plagued their administrations. Otherwise, they felt that government must *not* choose sides in economic matters. They therefore held relatively passive views of the presidency and the federal government, which they stuck to doggedly, even in the face of economic disaster. One could counter that the Gilded Age was an era of laissez-faire ideology and that few Americans then prescribed federal relief during crises. But this is belied by the frequent grants of federal aid during all sorts of disasters, going back to the Founding.[36] Also, Grant had no problem advocating for newfangled "big government" ideas like federal institutions to aid freed Blacks and Native Americans, free primary education, agriculture spending, a trans-isthmus canal, the annexation of Santo Domingo, or the aggressive use of federal troops to overrule Southern state governments. Nor did Cleveland refrain from supporting federal railroad regulation. But Grant and Cleveland nevertheless stubbornly viewed federal intervention (other than pro-gold monetary policy) to correct economic crises as either unconstitutional or a form of corrupt favoritism which *caused* economic downturns.

The two other "failed" presidents suffered from a relative lack of vision. Arthur perceived the presidency mostly as a ceremonial position and occasionally as a broker of federal patronage for his party. But he saw no role for himself, nor the federal government, in actively managing the economy. Hence, he too refrained from action during the "smoldering" recession of 1881–1885 and the Panic of 1884. Harrison was different. He was an economic nationalist who had strong views about federal support for industrialization and trade protectionism.

However, Harrison feared Democratic electoral victories more than he was devoted to any particular economic philosophy. He therefore mostly abandoned his economic vision. Instead he treated the presidency and national policy as weapons in partisan warfare against the Democrats. To this end, he backed a hodgepodge of fiscal, trade, and monetary policies that won elections, but also created conditions for the Panic of 1893. In other words, if Cleveland often hurt the economy by compromising his political-economic vision too little, Harrison hurt it by compromising too much.

This is where the literature on institutional structure and rational actor models may be most relevant. The evidence from the Gilded Age dovetails with assertions that the Constitution provides the executive branch with several institutional advantages (e.g., a first-mover advantage, a collective-action advantage, and an informational advantage) over the legislative and judicial branches.[37] However, whether or not a president utilized his institutional advantages appears to have derived from his vision. Put another way, each Gilded Age president had *similar* institutional advantages but performed *differently*.[38] The successful presidents exploited their institutional advantages more often than failed presidents. And they appear to have done so in line with their presidential vision.[39] Institutions are tools, not causal forces.[40] They are sources of presidential power and effectiveness *should the president chose to use them*. And often, it was their vision that told presidents whether and how to use them.

What did presidential vision do? Vision appears to have acted like a lodestar.[41] It guided not only the chief executive but many in government, bringing cohesiveness to national policy and administration. Presidents without one floundered. The president's vision also signaled areas of cooperation to potential allies, thereby aiding in coalition building. To the public, it provided a lens through which the entire country could interpret and understand presidential actions. Policymakers, including the president himself, could use it as a reference point for crafting rhetoric and judging policy options. It may have thereby bolstered generalized trust by providing consistency and context for federal policy. People understood why an administration was taking certain actions, but not others, and how these acts were expected to solve economic problems.

Also, much like policy, it is not about presidents having the "right" vision. For there is *no* single, objectively "right" or "wrong" vision, other than perhaps inaction in the face of crisis. The argument is only that the president must have a vision, and that it must be flexible, clear, consistent, and compelling. For as long as it is flexible, then experts, interest groups, and citizens on the economic front lines can provide feedback that will push the president to modify his vision into a more curative form. Specific policy solutions will still need to be justified in terms acceptable to the president's vision. But there will be policy *solutions*. And as long as the president's vision remains clear and consistent, policymakers and economic actors will understand better what actions they must take. And they will tend to act in ways that do not contradict or counteract one another. Finally, the more compelling the vision, the less convincing, coaxing, or coercion will be necessary for people to follow it.

In sum, the evidence suggests that Gilded Age executives who had an active *and* flexible vision for the presidency and the federal government tended to enjoy better economies than those leaders who had a more passive or inflexible vision, or none at all.

* * *

A problem with this vision thesis is the concept of "flexibility." How can we objectively distinguish between artful compromise and backboneless flaccidity? Or between constructive consistency and disastrous stubbornness? Cleveland's presidency illustrates the problem well. When he first came into office, Cleveland's fast action against silver likely prevented a financial crisis. But thereafter, his strict constitutionalist vision weakened his economic leadership. He believed that legislative meddling by the president was unconstitutional and that the federal government had no legitimate role to play in economic management. As a result, he rejected opportunities to eliminate the silver question altogether through executive pressure on Congress. He similarly failed on trade reform whenever he refused to compromise his strictures against presidential action during his first term.

Cleveland was relatively more flexible in his second term. But here he seemed consistently "flexible" only for the sake of specific interest groups who backed his administration. He frequently broke from his passive leadership to support the interests of railroad corporations, eastern bankers, and wealthy consumers, many located in the Northeast. But when it came to labor, the poor, the unemployed, farmers, and others, he stuck to his strict constitutionalism and passive presidency. Those who regularly benefited trusted Cleveland's "consistent" dedication to private property, the courts, and laissez-faire; those who did not saw Cleveland as a sellout to corporate interests and no longer trustworthy. And the fact that the national economy continued to suffer, while the wealthy built mansions, only further substantiated their beliefs.

In other words, there is much subjectivity and conditionality involved in judgments of whether a president's flexibility is "good" or "bad" for the economy. To some actors, leader flexibility presents "a grand opportunity"[42] when it furthers the beholder's self-interest or ideology, while leaving opponents feeling "deceived, betrayed, and humiliated."[43] To others, flexibility is good when it is perceived to be in the *nation's* interest rather than that of some particularist group(s). And yet moralists may still approve of flexibility toward a particularist group if that group is seen as deserving, or when flexibility appears to serve higher ideals of justice, patriotism, or ethics. To still others, short-run compromise on a president's vision is acceptable if done for long-run gains. In the end, we do not yet have an objective, scientific measure of "flexibility" nor a clear boundary line between productive and destructive compromise. Clearly this an area for deeper research by leadership scholars.

3. Coalition-Building

We can observe a correlation between a president's coalition-building skills and his economic success, though the causal mechanisms here are less clear. Having a vision alone is not enough; one also needs allies in order to make it happen. In other words, politics matter! The economically successful presidents took politics seriously and played politics well. They tended to establish and maintain effective relationships with key actors: Congress, their party, and major interest groups around the country. This might involve rewards, coercion, convincing, flattery, and almost always education. Shuttle diplomacy worked. This jibes with scholars of the modern presidency who advance different versions of the argument that successful presidents must be masters of coalitional politics.[44]

For example, Hayes granted congressional Republicans enough patronage and obligatory campaign donations to retain followers and win elections. Garfield regularly huddled with Congress and important economic interest groups. Despite his prickly personality, Harrison constantly consulted or prodded congressmen on policy issues and regularly invited them to the White House for strategy sessions or social events. McKinley was a master of "hidden-hand" relationship-building.[45] He quietly built personal connections with members of Congress, party leaders, and influential political-economic interest groups. As a result, McKinley got much of his agenda passed and implemented.

The failed presidents more often neglected coalitions, allowing them to weaken and fray; some failed executives even sought combat, blasting valuable allies with public invective or private insults. Arthur only rarely made attempts to pressure Congress on legislation, and he retreated quickly when he encountered opposition. He declined even to rule his own cabinet. Cleveland, and his economy, succeeded in proportion to his willingness to play politics. When he aggressively pressured Congress, his policy agenda moved forward and the economy did well. When he withdrew from coalition-building, his policies failed and the economy faltered. It did not help that Cleveland frequently fought with the press, his party, and senior congressmen, while openly socializing with a handful of conservative eastern bankers and industrialists.

Grant exemplifies both sides of the equation. On those issues where he was willing and able build a coalition behind him (e.g., resumption of the gold standard, debt and deficit reduction, western development, peace negotiations), he was highly effective. Grant could play politics well when he wanted to. And the economic results were powerful. But where Grant was unwilling or unable to build coalitions (e.g., the acquisition of new territories, anticorruption, federal public works spending, free primary education, agricultural subsidies, extended federal aid to freed slaves, the eight-hour workday, postal savings banks), he failed.

Harrison demonstrates the limits of coalition-building. He regularly courted Congress. He doled out patronage so as to strengthen his party nationwide. He worked hard and smart to craft a legislative agenda that would unify Republicans and win elections. And he was relatively successful in these tasks. But his success at coalition-building required so many economic compromises that his policy agenda destabilized the Treasury. In other words, a coalition built more on partisan vote-buying and logrolling than on presidential vision might bring political victories, but it is not a path to national economic prosperity.

Green Lantern Theory

This emphasis on relationships conjures up the "Green Lantern Theory" of the presidency. Nicknamed by its critic Brendan Nyhan, it refers to a comic book ring whose glowing green power to affect reality is limited only "by the user's combination of will and imagination."[46] Applied to the presidency, Green Lantern Theory is "the belief that the president can achieve any political or policy objective if only he tries hard enough or uses the right tactics." In other words, if a president acts smartly and strategically to manipulate Congress, the press, the public, and others, he can get his vision implemented. Nyhan describes two types of Green Lantern approaches. The Reagan version emphasizes the power of presidential communication and education to arouse popular support: "[I]f you only communicate well enough the public will rally to your side." The LBJ variant focuses more on the president's relationship with Congress: "[I]f the president only tried harder to win over congress they would vote through his legislative agenda." Of course, this version implies that presidents with majorities in Congress will be more successful.[47] Finally, William Howell has also shown that the more unified the party in control of Congress, the more likely it is to pass "nontrivial" legislation.[48]

The Gilded Age is a good test of Green Lantern Theory. Between 1875 and 1896, the president and Congress were divided by party in all but four years. More specifically, Republican presidents sat in the White House throughout the Gilded Age *except* for Democrat Cleveland's two terms. Meanwhile, over on Capitol Hill, Republicans had working majorities in the Senate during most years, while Democrats tended to rule the House. Also, even when the *same* party controlled both Congress and the White House, that party was itself often split into warring factions.[49] These divisions made the passage of legislation difficult regardless of the partisan configuration.

	In Office	President's Party	House	Senate
1869–1874	Grant	Repub	Repub	Repub
1875–1878	Grant/Hayes	Repub	Dem	Repub
1879–1880	Hayes	Repub	Dem	Dem
1881–1884	Garfield/Arthur	Repub	Dem	Repub
1885–1888	Cleveland1	Dem	Dem	Repub
1889–1890	Harrison	Repub	Repub	Repub
1891–1892	Harrison	Repub	Dem	Repub
1893–1894	Cleveland2	Dem	Dem	Dem
1895–1896	Cleveland2	Dem	Repub	Repub
1897–1901	McKinley	Repub	Repub	Repub

The evidence from this book's case studies is mixed. On one hand, legislative victories were clearly easier during those four years when the same party controlled both the executive and legislative branches. Harrison and the Republicans passed a flood of major legislation during 1890–1891, when they controlled the federal government. However, Cleveland and the Democrats were less successful during 1893–1895. Grant and the Republicans suffered similar problems during 1869–1874. The case of Cleveland may reflect the lesser degree of ideological cohesion, as required by Howell, among Democrats during his second term.[50] The case of Harrison seems to boil down to personal feuds and factional contests over patronage and power. Nevertheless, the more relationship-oriented presidents (Hayes, Garfield, Harrison, McKinley) had much better success at legislation, policy, and appointments than those who avoided politicking (Arthur, Cleveland).[51]

Once again, a comparison of Cleveland and Harrison is perhaps most revealing. Cleveland could play the political game when he wanted to. This usually meant monetary policy. When the gold standard was at stake, Cleveland acted like the consummate relationship-oriented, transactional politician and met with great success. In contrast, he refused to play the same political games to generate support for his trade policy. Hence his trade initiatives consistently failed. Harrison should have suffered the same fate. His personality was so frigid and dismissive that many in Washington hated him outright. But he knew how to rally the public, manipulate Congress, pressure his party, and assuage major interest groups in order to get his highly erratic policy agenda passed and implemented. To this day, Harrison and the "billion-dollar Congress" rank as one of the most successful legislative teams in US history.

Otherwise, I find that political parties mattered, but they did not determine outcomes during the Gilded Age. Certainly, presidents achieved more when they fostered productive relationships with their party. However, each Gilded Age president also found his administration, and his political-economic vision, in tension with the priorities and demands of his party. Intraparty fights over patronage, civil service reform, silver versus gold, tariffs, immigration, and business regulation bedeviled every administration. Grant and Hayes often won in spite of their party. Arthur was distrusted and betrayed by the very Republicans he had served throughout his adult life. Cleveland carried the Democratic banner but constantly angered party leaders, many of whom eventually broke with him. Harrison surrendered his political-economic beliefs for the sake of party unity. McKinley was the only Gilded Age president to fully master his party and successfully impose much of his agenda on it. In other words, presidents were successful to the degree that they could lead, or at least manipulate, their party, along with other major political-economic actors.

Presidential Rhetoric and the Power to Persuade

As implied in the coalitions hypothesis, the evidence generally supports the thesis that presidential rhetoric plays an important role in executive power and effectiveness.[52] The economically successful executives understood that the public and the press were essential parts of the political coalition that they needed to build.[53] No Gilded Age president lobbied the public with the bluntness and frequency of Theodore Roosevelt and his successors.[54] But the successful ones nevertheless understood the importance of "going public" and employed subtle tactics to do so. For example, Hayes toured the country frequently, often with cabinet members, to rally the country behind his administration. He gave upbeat speeches about the importance of national unity and reconciliation for economic prosperity. Garfield had the reputation of a master rhetorician, though he had little time to use these skills as president. McKinley's public rhetoric was incrementally more partisan and policy-oriented than his predecessors'. He disliked public oratory, but nevertheless went on national speaking tours to campaign for administration policy. He did enjoy meeting the American public and press in person, and he knew well how to charm. He was also the first president to formalize a working relationship with the press, with White House facilities and regular communications between them. Finally, education, not just advocacy, seems to have been an important element of the rhetorical efforts of the economically successful presidents. They used their discourse to build support, but also to inform listeners and readers about why certain problems were national priorities and why their administration supported particular policy solutions. The "president-as-teacher" could be an effective force.[55]

In contrast, the economic failures shrank from public rhetoric. Grant, Arthur, and Cleveland each abhorred public speaking. They avoided journalists. They minimized politicking and public appearances. Grant was willing to be rolled out for ceremonial purposes, but he generally declined to make speeches about politics or policy. He also infuriated prominent journalists and intellectuals, who proceeded to instigate a fairly successful smear campaign against his administration. Arthur was about as unrhetorical as a president could be. He avoided his office, the public, and the press wherever possible. He far preferred "going private" with his lavish galas, dinners, and cocktail parties. But these were social events, with little political or educational purpose. Grant and Cleveland did occasionally deliver powerful written statements. These could be effective when done frequently and combined with sustained coalition-building. But such rhetorical moves were rare for them.

Once again, Harrison demonstrates the limits of rhetoric. During his presidency, he traveled the country, gave an unprecedented number of speeches, and subtly lobbied the public and the press. In doing so, he produced a presidential "brand" of economic nationalism and put it before the country on a more regular basis than most previous presidents. But while Harrison's rhetoric may have helped convince many in the public and Congress to support his muddled, partisan economic agenda, it did not prevent that agenda from setting the stage for a financial crisis. In other words, rhetoric is not a substitute for vision.

4. Trust

Trust appears to have been the final major factor in each president's economic performance. Trust is loosely defined here as confidence in a person or institution to act honestly and competently to do the job expected of them. As applied to leadership, it is the belief that a president says what he means and will do what he says and that his rhetoric and actions will be in the national interest as perceived by the observer (and perhaps also in the observer's personal interest). The behavior of the Gilded Age economy seems to correlate with the president's ability to build and maintain generalized trust in major political-economic institutions, including the presidency itself.

How did the Gilded Age executives affect the public trust? The most compelling evidence is for their effect on trust in the US dollar. When presidents failed to speak or act in support of the gold standard, investors feared devaluation and fled dollar-denominated assets. Banks wavered. Economic activity slowed.

Financial crises threatened. In contrast, when presidents spoke and acted in defense of the gold standard, both financial markets and the economy tended to do well.

There were other ways in which the Gilded Age presidents may have affected generalized trust with consequences for the economy. The steady drumbeat of financial corruption scandals throughout Grant's executive branch correlated with the Panic of 1873 and subsequent recession. Grant's lackluster response to these scandals, and occasional defense of their perpetrators, may have damaged economic trust across the board. Over time, Hayes's sustained anticorruption efforts may have healed these wounds. More convincingly, Hayes may have buoyed the trust of wealthy investors and lowly migrants with his military suppression of Native Americans and Mexicans, followed by his personal tour of the "wild" West, demonstrating its safety, all while speaking frequently about its economic potential. Hayes's constant reassurances that Reconstruction was over eliminated another potential flashpoint. Garfield's dexterous refunding of US debt likely brought reassurance to nervous financial markets, though his death admittedly caused only fleeting market chaos. Arthur's lifelong career as a party machine operative, and almost total disengagement as president, surely provided little confidence during the 1881–1885 recession. During his first term, Cleveland's staunch conservativism on gold and government spending most likely had a curative effect after decades of federal graft and presidential favoritism. Harrison destroyed trust through his ad hoc collection of economic policies, so clearly designed to win elections rather than promote financial or economic stability. During his second term, Cleveland seems to have damaged trust by dithering and wavering inconsistently on economic policy. McKinley may have restored that trust with his dedication to shoring up federal revenues via tariffs, followed by his swift and total military victory against Spain. Certainly his election alone relieved markets terrified of William Jennings Bryan.

Why might trust matter? As Nobel Laureate Kenneth Arrow put it, "[V]irtually every commercial transaction has within itself an element of trust, certainly any transaction conducted over a period of time."[56] Put simply, trust lowers risk.[57] In technical terms, trust reduces transaction costs and collective action problems, while increasing information sharing.[58] It therefore plays an essential role in investment decisions, financial markets, and even daily contracts and purchases.[59] There is evidence that it also contributes to skills, education, and human capital formation.[60] Many studies of political business cycles highlight the role of political uncertainty in business and investment.[61] At the macro level, trust increases investment, trade, economic activity, and therefore specialization.[62] In fact, some argue that trust is even more essential for competitiveness than industrial policy. High-trust societies tend to have more large corporations focused on high-tech industries, whereas low-trust societies tend to be dominated by small, family-owned businesses in low-tech sectors.[63] Alternatively, researchers have found that trust increases the likelihood of success in policies that reduce economic inequality.[64] In sum, the economics literature is replete with studies which show strong correlations between trust and economic prosperity.

Trust also correlates strongly with good government.[65] Among elected politicians, trust has been found to increase accountability, reduce impulsive behavior, and increase the likelihood of policy innovation.[66] All societies implicitly rely on a social contract. Government officials in high-trust nations are more inclined to respect it. Therefore, more trust results in better governance, which is a critical element for growth.[67] In fact, trustworthy governments and institutions have been found to inspire trust-intensive economic activities even where social trust is otherwise low.[68]

In contrast, distrust and fear correlate highly with financial crises, economic contractions, refusal of firms to hire, capital flight from risky assets, and the hoarding of money and specie. As John Maynard Keynes observed, people refrain from spending when they are worried about "unforeseen contingencies"; hence a government can affect economic behavior "through its effect on 'confidence.'"[69] Furthermore, low-trust societies produce a political climate that can frustrate leadership of any type.[70] Policies of extraction and rent-seeking are favored over those that support investment, innovation, and public welfare.[71] For evidence, one need only skim the extensive literature which ties low trust to corruption and bad public policy, and thence to poor economic outcomes.[72] Even in well-functioning economies, small disturbances can produce large swings in economic activity if they kick off "financial accelerators" whereby distrust suddenly shrinks national credit markets with disastrous effects.[73] In these instances, small shocks, such as the failure of the Northern Pacific Railway in 1873 or Grant & Ward in 1884, can trigger major economic collapses via financial markets. Hence maintaining the trust of banking and business elites who dominate these markets may be particularly essential.

Finally, presidents and their governments affect trust levels in the societies they govern.[74] Research has shown that trust not only reflects public confidence in the overall political process, but it also tends to be an appraisal of political leadership.[75] Institutional fairness, honesty, transparency, accountability, stability, and norm-supporting have all been found to contribute to trust at both the personal and societal level.[76] They are also areas in which the president has outsized influence and visibility. For example, trust is higher when presidents refrain from predatory actions.[77] And when politicians actively respond to their constituents, and in line with constituent preference, trust also improves. In contrast, corruption in government has been shown to degrade public trust.[78] In fact, distrust in government correlates highly with support for third parties and can therefore lead to less cohesive policymaking.[79] Thus, multiple political scientists have concluded that "trust in government responds to the performance of the president."[80]

It's Complicated

There are many theorists who make an argument akin to "It's complicated!" That is, the presidency is part of a complex system of actors, coalitions, attributes, and tasks which all must be mastered in order to achieve success and avoid failure.[81] Hence, there are no simple, general theories that can fully account for presidential power or effectiveness. This is a truism. One cannot disagree with it. The universe is a complex and complicated place, full of all sorts of variables that are in constant interaction with one another. But this approach is neither novel nor useful. The main point of science is to use data and analysis to simplify this chaos by establishing some more generalizable laws and theories that can explain much, though not all. To make an analogy, maps provide us with a simple representation of physical space. They do not show us *everything*. Nor are they perfect representations. But they generalize enough to allow us to navigate the streets successfully. The same is true of social science. We cannot explain everything about the presidency, but concluding about the presidency that "it's complicated" preempts useful attempts at partial explanation, predictability, and control, however true that statement might be.

I do *not* dismiss the importance of random or "exogenous" events as independent, causal forces. Foreign economic booms and busts, gold discoveries, weather events, epidemic disease, each affected the US economy during the Gilded Age. But different presidents, with different leadership styles, responded differently and produced different outcomes. *Any* president would have suffered economically from, say, the massive snowstorms and floods of the late 1880s. But Cleveland refused to act, while Harrison sent aid to the flood victims. In other words, random events were opportunities and crises which might favor, or frustrate, presidents in different ways depending on their vision, relationships, and trust-building. Random events test presidencies. But they do not determine their effectiveness.

Historians go further. They not only abhor the oversimplification of historical figures and events; they are also uncomfortable with the normative implications of political theories such as those put forward here. Several opined to me that these presidents had no choice, or simply made the best choices that they could. I disagree with the former. And I try to understand *why* presidents made the choices they did. "Did the best they could" takes agency away from the presidency. Presidents cease to be human actors and instead become reactive, inertial masses caroming around the political billiard table. And after all, isn't everyone "doing the best they can" all the time? Put another way, I argue that "doing," "best," and "can" varied considerably across these presidents in ways that can help us to explain success or failure. Because the driving question of this book is: Why do some presidents "win" the economic game, while others lose? Is it all just an unfathomably complicated accident that humans are powerless to explain or affect? No!

* * *

To sum up, individual presidents matter for the nation's economic performance. Presidents, and their governments, have important roles to play in making competitive markets work. Even during the late 19th century, when the White House was at its weakest, we can still find ample evidence of presidential relevance. But the sources of presidential effectiveness were not those we have come to expect. There is no evidence for a general relationship between economic leadership and the president's character, psychology, education, intelligence, or prior experience. Nor did the president's party identification or close advisors determine outcomes. And neither historical circumstance nor random events posed unsurmountable conditions for able leaders.

Rather, the Gilded Age economy appears to have performed best under visionary chief executives, who held an active view of the presidency and government; who were able to create a coalition around their vision, often through compromise, rhetoric, and education; and who built and maintained trust in major political-economic institutions, including the presidency itself, but especially financial institutions (e.g., the US dollar and the financial system). In contrast, the Gilded Age economy appears to have performed worst under presidents with no clear or consistent vision, or who stubbornly insisted on passive government; who were unable, or unwilling, to generate consensus around a legislative or policy agenda; and who failed to build and maintain trust in major political-economic institutions, especially financial institutions.

Of course, many of the assertions made in this book are better described as hypotheses, not findings. They could be products of unique conditions of the Gilded Age. They might be biased by the large number of midwestern or ex-military men who served in the White House. America's status as a "developmental state" may have been a necessary condition during this era. Nor do seven presidents constitute a large, sweeping comparison. We need to investigate further, across different presidencies and time periods, to see whether these same hypotheses are produced under different political-economic conditions. And we need to get a better idea of how vision, coalition politics, and trust-building interact to affect economic outcomes. A natural next step would be a study of the modern White House, when variations in presidential leadership styles, as well as economic outcomes, ranged even more dramatically. But we *do* now know that, when diagnosing national economic problems today, we should dismiss neither presidential leadership nor the lessons of the Gilded Age so carelessly. The Gilded Age mattered, and so did its presidents.

Appendix: Estimating Presidential Performance—Data, Sources, and Methods

Of Presidential Rankings and Economic Measures

What is the best way to compare the presidents' economic performance during the Gilded Age?[1] One may be tempted to consult any of the dozens of presidential rankings that exist today, but they are of little help to us. Most ranking systems cloud the issue with partisan bias or subjective judgments or mix economics together with other aspects of presidential performance.[2] Think tanks use presidential rankings to advance their policy agendas, while academic surveys of rank allow scholars to collectively muse over the grand sweep of history rather than produce rigorous, scientific evaluations of performance.[3] "Greatness" surveys are also infamously fickle in that they vary considerably over time and are arguably biased toward recent, wartime, or left-leaning presidents.[4] Presidential scholar James P. Pfiffner once quipped, "[R]anking and rating presidents is not very rigorous and does not tell us what we want to know."[5] Certainly, purely economic rankings of the US presidents based on objective, comprehensive, quantitative data are rare.[6]

To maximize objectivity, this book uses the most reliable statistical data for the Gilded Age economy. But which data should be used? Gross domestic product? Exports? Health and mortality? There is no objective answer to this question. Even experts disagree on precisely which indicators to include and how to weigh them. Research has further shown that perceptions of performance and responsibility can be affected by time, partisanship, and rhetoric.[7] And clearly, subjective choices about data and weights will affect the results. For example, in their ranking exercise of all US presidents, the libertarian Von Mises Institute uses only government spending as a percentage of total output.[8] Naturally, wartime big-spenders (e.g., Lincoln, Wilson, and FDR) rank near the bottom of that exercise, while their successors, all peacetime budget-slashers, come in on top (e.g., A. Johnson, Harding, and Truman). Conversely, we can assume that a left-leaning evaluation might instead select measures such as income inequality, welfare spending, or poverty levels and wind up placing some of those same big-spender presidents among the top ranks.

To minimize this kind of partisan or ideological subjectivity, this book's solution is to select those indicators most often mentioned by mainstream Western economists, the media, and voters when evaluating US economic performance. After all, it makes sense to judge American presidents using common American economic values. This does not eliminate subjectivity, but it should at least take personal political biases out of the equation. It also attempts to match the ranking criteria with popular preferences. That is, it attempts to put the American public at the judge's table, rather than some supposedly "objective" expert or group thereof.

Mainstream economists, the media, and voters generally applaud an economy that simultaneously achieves these goals: increases national wealth, minimizes unemployment and inflation, and maintains a low balance of payments burden while reducing the federal deficit and debt.[9] Most also cheer decreases in economic inequality, lower real interest rates, strong stock market performance, and a strong US dollar. This gives us the list of basic indicators used in Chapter 2 to evaluate the presidents' economic performance (Table 2.1).

An Economic Comparison of the Gilded Age Presidents

Table 2.3 presents an administration-by-administration comparison of the Gilded Age presidents using the data listed in Table 2.1. *The general findings are that the US economy did relatively well under Hayes, Harrison, and McKinley; it was mixed under Grant (first term), Garfield, and Cleveland (first term); and it did relatively poorly under Grant (second term), Arthur, and Cleveland (second term).* Of course, we should *not* conclude from Table 2.3 something like "Cleveland's first term was clearly better than Grant's first term" because of the former's small advantage in some column. Cognizant of the "uses and abuses" of presidential rankings,[10] I do not claim that the rankings presented here are definitive; rather, they are expected to provoke constructive debate. The goal here is to create a general, albeit rough, comparison, not an exact or perfect scale of performance. In other words, my assertion is that we *can* say with relative confidence that presidents who rank high in several categories oversaw better economies than those presidents who rank at the bottom of several categories. And if we emphasize the topmost and bottommost performers across categories, we get Table 2.4.

The data and calculations for Table 2.3 follow.

Per capita economic growth: Total change in GDP/capita (average of [term years] and [1 year lag]). Maddison Project Database, version 2020. See also *HSUS*, Table Ca9–19, "Gross Domestic Product," and Table Aa6–8, "Population: 1790–2000."

Inflation: Total percentage change in price levels. *HSUS*, Table Cc1–2, "Consumer Price Indexes, for All Items: 1774–2003." See also *Measuring Worth*.

Trade balance (as percentage of GDP):
Average of:

- Numerator (exports-imports nominal) from *HSUS*, Table Ee416–417, "Exports and Imports of Goods: 1869–1928."
- Denominator (GDP nominal) from *HSUS*, Table Ca9–19, "Gross Domestic Product: 1790–2002."

Budget deficit (as percentage of GDP):
Average of:

- Numerator (surplus or deficit) from *HSUS*, Table Ea584–587, "Federal Government Finances—Revenue, Expenditure, and Debt: 1789–1939."
- Denominator (GDP nominal) from *HSUS*, column Ca10 from Table Ca9–19, "Gross Domestic Product: 1790–2002."

Federal debt (as percentage of GDP): *HSUS*, Table Ea584–587, "Federal Government Finances—Revenue, Expenditure, and Debt: 1789–1939."

Inequality: Change in Wealth-Income Ratio (private wealth)/(national income). Piketty-Zucman Wealth-Income Data Set.

Stock market: Percentage change in S&P Index. Shiller 2015; for Grant 1: *NBER Macro*, American Railroad Stock Prices for United States, Dollars per Share, Monthly, Not Seasonally Adjusted. See also Goetzmann, Ibbotson, and Peng (2001).

Table A.4 Data Description (per Administration)

Measure	Source	Max	Min	Mean	Standard Dev
Economic Growth (per capita)	Maddison	23.9%	0.4%	6.2%	0.08
Inflation	Measuring Worth	2.3%	−12.5%	−5.0%	0.05
Average trade balance as % of GDP	HSUS	2.75%	−0.62%	1.04%	0.01
Average budget deficit as % of GDP	HSUS	0.99%	−0.18%	0.47%	0.004
Change in debt as % of GDP	HSUS	1.7pp	−6.0pp	−2.2pp	2.7
Inequality: Change in Wealth-Income Ratio	Piketty-Zucman	44pp	−67pp	2.1pp	39
% change in S&P	Shiller 2015	97%	−38%	15.2%	0.5
Change in real interest rates	NBER Macro, HSUS	1.3pp	−2.5pp	−0.6pp	1.5
% change in US$ price of UK£	NBERMacro	16%	−0.4%	1.8%	0.05

Real interest rates: Difference in Average Municipal Bond Yields for New England (adjusted for inflation), from previous administration. *NBER Macro,* Series q13020.

US$ strength: Percentage change in US dollar price of UK pound. Bank of England (2021).

Gathered into the separate terms/administrations (Table A.4).

Hic Sunt Dracones: Weaknesses of Statistics and Rankings

Data accuracy is an obvious concern here. Relatively few macroeconomic data were systematically collected or calculated during the 19th century. However, reliable data for the measures listed in Table 2.1 *do* exist for this time period. We have contemporary records of trade, deficits, debt, interest rates, and the US dollar, which were reported by the federal government or tracked by financial newspapers and periodicals throughout the Gilded Age. As for economic growth, inflation, and economic inequality, we rely on estimates constructed by economic historians. Unfortunately, there are no reliable estimates of national unemployment available prior to 1890, so these data are not used.[11]

Timing is also controversial. It is not clear precisely *when* a new president becomes responsible for the behavior of the macroeconomy. Some scholars have argued that presidents can affect the economy immediately upon taking office.[12] During the Gilded Age, each of Cleveland's two terms are perhaps the best examples of this. McKinley probably affected the economy even earlier, starting with his election. Others insist that the economic fallout from one president's actions can influence the economy for months, even years after they leave office.[13] Grant, Hayes, and Harrison might serve as examples here.

Since there is no consensus as to how long a "honeymoon" should be granted to incoming presidents, the ranking exercise described above was calculated only for each president's coincident term(s). That is the best we can do with statistical data. This is why the qualitative case studies of each presidential administration are so important. They allow us to make more precise and nuanced judgments. We also have three presidents with irregular terms (Garfield, Arthur, and McKinley), discussed below. The short version is the relative rankings in Tables 2.3 and 2.4 do not change when we drop Garfield or McKinley's second term or Arthur's first four months in office. Therefore, I include them all in the belief that more information is better and that, together with the case studies, their inclusion will produce useful insights into transition issues (i.e., on whom to allocate credit/blame and when).

"Multicollinearity" is another concern. Multicollinearity arises when supposedly *different* variables measure the *same* aspect(s) of the economy over and over again, and thereby bias the results. Certainly there is some natural overlap between economic measures: a rising tide lifts all boats, while an economic collapse sinks most of them. But exactly how much overlap is there? To answer this question, Table A.5 presents the statistical correlations between the different measures during the Gilded Age.

Table A.5 shows that the data selected here do likely capture *different* aspects of economic performance. As expected, we see high correlations between economic growth and stock market performance or trade balance; inflation and the trade balance; inequality and real interest rates. And there are high *inverse* correlations between economic growth and inequality or interest rates; inequality and the trade balance or stock market; and the stock market and interest rates. The dollar has its strongest relationship with the trade balance and inflation. The debt is most strongly tied to the budget deficit. None of these relationships is surprising. They represent different but interrelated aspects of the same complex machine that is the US economy. Most important for our purposes, the data are not redundant: each measure has a relatively low correlation with at least one other measure (and often several of them).

While every effort has been made to minimize error and subjective judgments in the economic rankings reported, there remain two inherent biases worth pointing out. First, the choices of measures and weightings do contain assumptions in favor of mainstream neoclassical, perhaps neo-Keynesian economics, as is taught in most American universities.[14] Therefore, even though a measure of income inequality is included in the rankings, the overall weightings will tend to favor the achievement of wealth and efficiency over economic equity or social justice. While it makes sense to judge American executives using mainstream American economic values, this does not make these values objectively correct. Second, all economic data suffer from errors. Again, we should not rely on quantitative data alone.

This book attempts to address these weaknesses in four ways. First, it communicates in an accurate and familiar way the "signal" contained in the economic data, while simultaneously being explicit about the "noise" and subjective judgments involved in interpreting the data. Second, in the rankings, the aggregation of data into four-year periods (except for Garfield) should help to eliminate some of the problems involved in making point estimates for individual years, as well as average out some of the random error. In those cases where change over time is measured, as long as the error is similar across each year (either random or systematic), it will tend to be subtracted out. Taken as a whole, this book also attempts to correct for noise and bias by using triangulation: where possible, it uses multiple, different, independent types and sources of data to measure the same

Table A.5 Correlation Matrix of Economic Indicators

	Economic Growth	Inflation	Trade Balance/ GDP	Deficit/ GDP	Debt/ GDP	Inequality	Stock Market	Interest Rates	$-Price of UK£
Economic Growth	1								
Inflation	0.51	1							
Trade Balance/GDP	0.71	0.79	1						
Deficit/GDP	−0.31	−0.15	−0.59	1					
Debt/GDP	−0.45	−0.07	0.17	−0.55	1				
Inequality	−0.87	−0.65	−0.71	0.20	0.46	1			
Stock Market	0.92	0.60	0.62	−0.25	−0.51	−0.86	1		
Interest Rates	−0.85	−0.44	−0.52	0.27	0.41	0.81	−0.92	1	
$-Price of £UK	−0.17	−0.62	−0.68	0.43	−0.44	0.14	−0.07	−0.01	1

phenomenon. Random errors should cancel out, letting the true "signal" come through. Fourth, all data are publicly available. Readers can use their own scoring rules, weights, and additional input measures (e.g., leadership, progress in science and technology, wealth redistribution) to construct their own rankings for comparison.

Finally, these rankings and descriptions are *not* the final judgment, just the first steps. They build the initial foundation upon which to base individual case studies and a qualitative comparison of the Gilded Age presidents. The overall goal is to use both statistical data and qualitative evidence to test existing hypotheses and to generate new theory about presidential power and effectiveness.

Notes

Preface

1. Taylor (2012). An updated and abbreviated version of this exercise is presented in Chapter 2 of this volume.
2. Thanks to historian Charles W. Calhoun for making this point.
3. For example, "Let us have peace" was an instantly famous statement written by Ulysses S. Grant in his 1868 letter of acceptance for the Republican nomination. As my source for this quote, I cite Grant's letter, but not the dozens of history books and articles encountered in my research that also discuss this statement.
4. Bose and Landis (2003).

Chapter 1

1. Historians disagree on the precise timing of the Gilded Age. Most end it in 1901 with the ascension of Theodore Roosevelt; however, scholars disagree on its start date, which ranges from the close of the Civil War (1865) to the end of Reconstruction (1877). See Schneirov (2006); Richardson (2017).
2. Wiebe (1967).
3. This accusation is best leveled at political scientists, economists, and the general public. In contrast, a handful of presidential historians and Gilded Age specialists, such as Charles W. Calhoun, Mark Summers Wahlgren, and Lewis Gould have done much to correct the historical record, but even they understate the economic relevance of these presidents.
4. Bryce (1888a: 100). A historian, British member of Parliament, and underssecretary of state for foreign affairs, Bryce explained to his European readers, "Both the Federal and the State legislatures [in America] contain a fair proportion of upright and disinterested men who enter chiefly, or largely, from a sense of public duty." Nevertheless, he claimed, the "best men" in America choose not to enter national politics for myriad reasons: Washington, DC, was an unattractive place to live and work; there was no natural aristocracy in America to supply political leaders; there existed only a limited number of congressional seats available to aspiring politicians; US political issues were relatively dull (tariffs, currency, internal improvement, railway regulation); there were fewer class divides to drive the contest for power; federalism made state and local politics more attractive; there were easier and more lucrative careers in the private sector; and a "distaste of . . . the bad company they would have to keep, the

general vulgarity of tone in politics, the exposure to invective or ribaldry by hostile speakers and a reckless press" (37–43).

5. Cashman (1993: 245).

6. With the exceptions of William McKinley and perhaps Grover Cleveland in his first term. Starting with Arthur M. Schlesinger's polls in 1948 and 1962, followed more recently by the C-SPAN Presidential Historian Survey, the Siena College Research Institute Presidential Expert Poll, American Political Science Association's Presidential Greatness Survey, and others.

7. Wolfe (1934: 103).

8. N. Irwin (2017); Arthur (2014); Hacker and Pierson (2012); Dolan and Tatalovich (2008); Jones and Olken (2005).

9. Thrower (2019).

10. In fact, among scholars, the conventional wisdom is that, throughout the 19th century, presidents mattered little during peacetime (e.g., Tulis 1987). Some emphasize Woodrow Wilson (1913–1921) as the pivotal figure (Knott 2019). Others emphasize the even larger expansion of presidential power and the federal government by Franklin Delano Roosevelt (1933–1945). See, for example, the scholarship of Fred I. Greenstein, William E. Leuchtenburg, Richard E. Neustadt, and James P. Pfiffner. For the opposing view, see the works of David K. Nichols and Lewis Gould. For an interesting review of the debate over the "modern" presidency, see Skowronek (2015).

11. For example, the Louisiana Purchase or the Emancipation Proclamation (Moe and Howell 1999b; Kagan (2001); Howell (2001).

12. Victoria Claflin Woodhull was the first woman to run for US president, in 1872, as the candidate of the Equal Rights Party. She was followed in 1884 and 1888 by Belva Ann Bennett Lockwood, who garnered only a few thousand votes. Thereafter, no woman would run for president until Republican Margaret Chase Smith's failed candidacy in 1964.

13. Parker (1909: 183).

14. Average for 1869–1901, though the spread was wide, ranging from 1.8 percent (1886) to 3.8 percent (1870). In comparison, since 1990 the federal budget per GDP has averaged 21.4 percent. U.S. Bureau of Economic Analysis, Federal Government Current Expenditures and GDP-Nominal, supplemented by HSUS.

15. Does not include military personnel. For comparison, in 2020 the civilian federal workforce (executive branch) totaled roughly 2.8 million, of which roughly 15 percent worked in the Washington, DC, metro area (Jennings and Nagel 2019).

16. Bryce (1888a: 411–412).

17. Lowi (1985). However, before the Civil War, several presidents used newspapers funded by allies to rally public support (Laracey 2002).

18. Smythe (2003); Kaplan (2002); Summers (1994).

19. Bensel (2000); Sanders (1999); Skowronek (1982).

20. Ellis (2012: 218); Schlesinger (1973).

21. Wilson (1885: 233).

22. See, for example, Moe and Howell (1999a); Mayer (2001); Howell (2003); Lewis (2003); Canes-Wrone (2006); Wood (2007); Beckman (2010); Posner and Vermeule (2010). For a recent review of this literature, see O'Brien (2018).

23. Howell (2003).
24. Blinder and Watson (2016); Hargrove (2014); Pious (2008); Skowronek (1997); Laing and McCaffrie (2017); Blake (1803).
25. Azari and Hetherington (2016).
26. Gilens (2012); Skocpol and Hertel-Fernandez (2016); Kalla and Broockman (2016).
27. Refers to campaign invective during the 1884 contest between Grover Cleveland (D) and James Blaine (R), and the slogan of Horace Greeley's breakaway Liberal Republican campaign against the traditional Republican, Ulysses S. Grant, in the 1872 election.
28. A few examples include Bartels (2016); Callahan (2016); McAlevey (2016); Schlozman, Brady, and Verba (2018); Wheeler (2018). For the opposing view, see Livingston (2016); Fraser (2008).
29. Lee (2016); DiSalvo (2012).
30. Azari and Hetherington (2016).
31. The exceptions being 1884, when Republican James A. Garfield eked out just 1,898 more votes than Democrat Winfield Scott Hancock, and 2004, when Republican George W. Bush received over 3 million more votes than Democrat John Kerry.
32. The fifteen closest elections in order of closeness by percentage of popular vote (Gilded Age in italics): *Garfield (1880)*, JFK (1960), George W. Bush (2000), *Cleveland (1884)*, Nixon (1968), *B. Harrison (1888)*, Polk (1844), Carter (1976), Trump (2016), George W. Bush (2004), *Hayes (1876)*, *Cleveland (1892)*, Wilson (1916), Obama (2012), *McKinley (1896)*.
33. Wilson (1885: 45).
34. For an insightful discussion on the role of ideas and ideology in politics, see Lewis (2019).
35. "Power" is defined here as a president's ability to get his legislative, policy, and/or personnel preferences implemented (Skowronek 1997). In contrast, "effectiveness" is whether the economic outcomes of these actions were those sought in the first place. That is, presidential power is more about means (i.e., "getting things done" in politics), while effectiveness is more about ends (i.e., solving problems and achieving goals in the national economy).
36. For example, in the spirit of Richard Neustadt and Fred I. Greenstein, significant advances have been made in cross-presidency scholarship by Terry Moe, James P. Pfiffner, William Howell, Richard Ellis, Andy Rudalevige, Dan Wood, Meena Bose, Julia Azari, Sharice Thrower, John Dearborn, and others. In particular, the research coming out of the Presidents & Executive Politics Section of the American Political Science Association and that appearing in *Presidential Studies Quarterly* has been notable for its scope and rigor. The Miller Center at the University of Virginia has, for years, also been a focal point for top-notch presidential scholars and research. The new Carolyn T. and Robert M. Rogers Center for the American Presidency promises likewise. Finally, the American Presidency Project at UC Santa Barbara has grown into an essential repository for documents and statistics for all presidential administrations.
37. Important exceptions include Charles W. Calhoun, Mark Wahlgren Summers, Lewis Gould, Robert Merry, Elizabeth Sanders, and Stephen Skowronek.

38. Eulogy delivered by Reverend Frank W. Gunsaulus, comparing George Washington's intellect to McKinley's (quoted in Halstead 1901: 260).
39. Greenstein (1995).
40. Ellis (1998: 112). Though recognition must also be given to recent scholarship by Charles W. Calhoun, Mark Wahlgren Summers, and Lewis Gould for filling some of these gaps.

Chapter 2

1. Parts of this discussion are taken from Taylor (2012).
2. Mankiw (2018).
3. Taking McKinley's assassination as the end of the Gilded Age. See Richardson (2017); Schneirov (2006).
4. Bank of England (2021).
5. For the scholarly debate on the development, accuracy, and consequences of different presidential ratings, see the Hofstra University symposium "The Leadership Difference: Rating the Presidents" as summarized in Bose and Landis (2003). Also instructive are Merry (2012); Felzenberg (2008).
6. For example, the widely read journalist and historian Henry Adams (1870: 41) (descended from two US presidents) wrote in 1870, "So far as Presidential initiative was concerned, the President and his Cabinet might equally well have departed separately or together to distant lands." Gilded Age senator George Frisbie Hoar (1903b: 46) (R-MA) agreed, writing later about the early years that congressmen would have taken "personal affront" if the president had asked them to support or oppose a particular bill. And moreover, "[i]f [congressmen] visited the White House, it was to give, not to receive advice. Any little company or coterie who had undertaken to arrange public policies with the President and to report to their associates what the President thought would have rapidly come to grief. . . . [Senate leaders] tolerated no intrusion from the President or from anybody else." In a similar vein, Woodrow Wilson (1879: 158–159), a budding political scientist during the Gilded Age, then described Congress as "the ruling body of the nation" and the president as "merely the executor of the sovereign legislative will." A few years later, he labeled the entire period one of "congressional government" (Wilson 1885). Even the presidents themselves concurred. Grant and Garfield openly complained that they were too often treated like mere "registering clerks" by congressmen eager for executive patronage to support their party machines. British viscount James Bryce (1888a: 109) blamed the occupants in the White House, wondering in print "why great men are not chosen presidents." Bryce's answer was that, "firstly, because great men are rare in politics; second, because the [American] method of choice does not bring them to the top; thirdly, because they are not, in quiet times [like the Gilded Age], absolutely needed." Even late in the period, in 1896, the early management theorist Mary Parker Follett argued that "the president has had so slight a share in initiating the legislative policy.

His message to Congress is really an address to the country and has no direct influence upon Congress" (Follett and Hart 1896: 325).

7. White (2017: 3).
8. Gould (2012: 94).
9. Peskin (1991: 439).
10. Remini (2006); Zelizer (2004). Robert Cherny (1997: 49) shifts the blame back to the White House, contending, "The presidents who came after [Andrew] Johnson did little to challenge congressional dominance." In contrast, Mark Wahlgren Summers (2017: 343) sees Congress as more dominant during the early Gilded Age and then "[g]radually, incrementally, presidents became more public and more energetic."
11. Bensel (2000); Summers (2004); Hoogenboom (1961).
12. Neustadt (1960: 5–6).
13. Schlesinger (1973: 76).
14. Milkis and Nelson (2019: 245). Now in its ninth edition, this text has consistently judged Grant as "transitional." The Hayes administration "has been remembered mainly for 'holding its ground, rather than for developing new frontiers.'" Garfield's tenure was too brief to have much impact. Cleveland was either too meek or, where he innovated, too ineffective. Harrison "cheerfully submitted to being practically a figurehead." McKinley often put his party and Congress ahead of the presidency and "carried into office a deep and abiding respect for congressional primacy" (Milkis and Nelson 2008: 201).
15. Howell and Moe (2016).
16. Rudalevige (2002, 2005, 2009).
17. Rudalevige (2005: 26).
18. Ellis (2012: xix).
19. Alesina (1987); Blinder and Watson (2016).
20. Political business cycles were first formally observed by Akerman (1947), though a causal model was not formalized until Nordhaus (1975). For a recent survey of the literature, see Dubois (2016).
21. Belo, Gala, and Li (2013); Yonce (2015); Pastor and Veronesi (2020).
22. Faust and Irons (1999); Grafstein and Caruson (2008); Kraeussl et al. (2014); Rohlfs, Sullivan, and McNab (2015).
23. Foerster and Schmitz (1997); Santa-Clara and Rossen (2003); Vaaler, Schrage, and Block (2005); Waisman, Ye, and Zhu (2015).
24. Chan and Marsh (2021).
25. Heckelman and Whaples (1996).
26. Bensel (2000).
27. Sanders (1999); DeCanio (2015).
28. Skowronek (1982).
29. Skowronek (1982: 169).
30. Skowronek (1982: 170).
31. To be precise, Skowronek (1997) does not entirely dismiss the causal power of individual presidents. They still "make politics," in his view. However, the role of the

individual executive is limited and highly conditioned by historical circumstances, though the power of history may be diminishing over time.

32. Skowronek (1997).
33. Skowronek (1997: 34–45).
34. An interesting new "leadership filtration theory" of presidential performance similarly gives little coverage of the Gilded Age executives (Mukunda 2012, 2022).
35. For example, Friedman (1990b); Frieden (1997); Bordo and Schwartz (1999).
36. For a recent literature review within political science, see Krcmaric, Nelson, and Roberts (2020).
37. Thompson (2010); Greenstein (2009); Barber (2009); Pfiffner (2004); Shogan (1999); George and George (1998); Simonton (1987).
38. Simonton (2018); Besley, Montalvo, and Reynal-Querol (2011); Barceló (2018); Saunders (2017); Carnes and Lupu (2016); Marchant-Shapiro (2015); Simon and Uscinski (2012); Dreher et al. (2009); Potter (2007).
39. Besley, Montalvo, Reynal-Querol (2011); Hallerberg and Wehner (2013).
40. Neumeier (2018); Pocalyko (2017); Gehlbach, Sonin, and Zhuravskaya (2010); Dreher et al. (2009); Mattozzi and Merlo (2008); Pfiffner (1999).
41. Balz (2010); Pfiffner (1999).
42. Weissing (2011); De Neve et al. (2013).
43. Bowmaker (2019); Saunders (2017); Vaughn and Villalobos (2006); Bernstein (2001); Bose (1998); Hargrove and Morley (1984). For a broader approach, see Alston, Alston, and Mueller (2021).
44. Cherny (1997: 49).

Chapter 3

1. Over 3.2 million men served in the war, including almost every eligible Southerner and around 198,000 Black soldiers. In comparison, the 1860 census reported roughly 5.62 million white men of military age out of a total US population of 31.5 million (US Census Bureau 1864). Also, slavery was not so much vanquished in the South by the Civil War as suspended for several years and then metamorphosed into a different legal and institutional form. Therefore, this volume does not consider "the elimination of slavery" as the greatest impact of the war (Blackmon 2009).
2. Faust (2008).
3. Although 750,000 military deaths is the average estimate, the high estimate suggests 850,000 possible casualties (American Battlefield Trust; Hacker (2011).
4. Between 1845 and 1931 the years 1861–1862 saw the lowest number of immigrants overall (Klein 2012).
5. Goldin and Lewis (1975); *Measuring Worth* (proportion of GDP measure).
6. Goldin and Lewis (1975).
7. Goldin and Lewis (1975).
8. Lee (2005).

9. Goldin and Lewis (1975).

10. Ransom and Sutch (1988).

11. Federal debt had leaped 225 percent in the previous three years and stood at a relatively high $64.8 million in 1860 (roughly equal to the annual federal budget).

12. Unger (1964: 13).

13. McPherson (1988: 322); Koistinen (1996).

14. Johnson (2018); Irwin (2017).

15. Customs duties had constituted the lion's share of US federal revenues since the 1790s. For example, in 1860, federal revenues came from tariffs (94.9 percent), sales of federal land (3.2 percent), and the rest in fees and penalties. Tariffs were also politically divisive. Southerners opposed them, being net importers of expensive luxury goods and manufactures. And since their wealth derived mostly from exports of cotton and tobacco, Southerners also feared reciprocal tariffs from other nations. Thus, as a rule, the antebellum South supported higher tariffs only when national defense against Great Britain was at stake. In contrast, Northern manufacturers badly wanted tariff protection to compete against cheap European imports. But US manufacturing was too small and geographically concentrated to succeed politically. Thus, Southerners in Congress had managed to pass legislation lowering tariffs on dutiable imports from an antebellum high of 62 percent (1830) down to 19 percent (1860) (Irwin 2017; Brownlee 2016; supplemented by *HSUS*).

16. Abraham Lincoln, address at Pittsburg, PA, February 15, 1861, quoted in *New York Times*, February 16, 1861.

17. Confederate leaders made similar miscalculations. Many of them expected federal troops to quickly become frustrated and return home (Rable 2015; McPherson 1988).

18. This division of funding and authority lasted only into the summer. By the end of 1861, the federal government had largely assumed control from state governments over the nation's war effort. To complete the task, in March 1863 Congress passed the Enrollment Act, which instituted a national draft placing even military recruitment under federal management (Koistinen 1996).

19. Refers to Confederate president Jefferson Davis and his fellow leaders of the rebellion. Others in the press agreed. The *New York Times* expected the South to be subdued within a month; the *Chicago Tribune* gave it two to three months. Southerners mirrored this hubris, expecting the Union to withdraw either out of cowardice or frustration (Thomas 2011: 9, 13–14).

20. The Revenue Act of 1861, signed by Lincoln in early August, imposed a 3 percent income tax on people making more than $800 per year, with an additional 2 percent tax on those earning over $10,000. At the time average household income was around $600 (Brownlee 2016; Giroux 2012; Unger 1964: 20).

21. Silber (2019); Timberlake (1993).

22. Konings (2011).

23. Or as Jefferson Davis, president of the Confederacy, told the new Confederate Congress on April 29, 1861, just days after Fort Sumter, "[W]e seek no conquest, no aggrandizement, no concession of any kind from the States with which we were lately confederated; all we ask is to be let alone" (quoted in Richardson 1905: 22).

24. US Treasury (1861: 12).
25. US Treasury (1861: 12).
26. Timberlake (1993); Konings (2011). Money printing would only worsen over time. For example, even in 1862 total US currency in circulation had grown over 39 percent in just two years. It then consisted of gold coin (47 percent), state banknotes (30 percent), zero-interest US debt notes (12 percent, a.k.a. "greenbacks"), US demand notes (8.8 percent), and silver coin (2.1 percent).
27. Paying 6 percent interest annually for twenty years, but redeemable by the government in five years, these bonds were nicknamed "5-20s" (Congressional Budget Office 2019: 20, Figure 1-8).
28. Thomson (2016).
29. Foner (2014: 22).
30. Thomson (2016).
31. This bond issue offered 7 percent interest payable over thirty years; hence they became known as "7-30s."
32. For example, in 1860 the *Financial Review* listed just twenty-two stocks on the New York Stock and Exchange Board. Earlier in the century, America's small stock markets were dominated by shares of banks and insurance companies. However, the Panics of 1837 and 1857 had bankrupted many large financial institutions and scared away investors. Hence, by the end of the Civil War, trading in financials was slim. Instead, starting in 1830, railroad shares gradually emerged as the dominant sector on US stock exchanges. And since New York City had become *the* center of railroad finance by the 1850s, it became the nation's capital for all finance. Nevertheless, stock ownership was still reserved for institutions and the wealthy, partly due to minimum transaction requirements, and the volume of stocks traded on any formal exchange was relatively small throughout the 19th century (O'Sullivan 2016).
33. Thomson (2016). This equates to as much as 13.6 percent of the Union's population of roughly 22 million.
34. It had been known as the New York Stock and Exchange Board since 1817 and had changed rental locations frequently since then due to changing fortunes. The NYSE acquired its current name and address in 1863; the existing structure dates to 1903 (Geisst 2018).
35. Davies (2018: 7).
36. Precisely how to invest was patiently explained to customers in handbooks like *Memoranda concerning Government Bonds for the Information of Investors*, published by the Fisk & Hatch banking house in New York City (White 2011). Founded by William Dana in 1865, the *Commercial & Financial Chronicle* was the first American business weekly to circulate nationally.
37. Brownlee (2016); Davis (2019).
38. Isaac Funk (Illinois rancher and politician) in a speech to Illinois legislature, quoted in *Chicago Tribune,* February 15, 1863.
39. Trachtenberg (1982).
40. Luckey (2003).

41. Notably, although Republicans sought order and stability in national finance, they remained wary of too much concentration of power. Consequently, they opted *not* to create a central bank nor prohibit private bank notes (McCulley 1992).

42. The Revenue Act of 1862.

43. Specifically, "any sum not less than fifty dollars, or some multiple of fifty dollars," or roughly equal to $1,300 in 2020 (Revenue Act of 1862; *Measuring Worth*, consumer price index).

44. Timberlake (1993); Myers (1970).

45. Mitchell (1908: 5, Table 2).

46. The legislatures of Alabama, Arkansas, Indiana, and Mississippi had established state-owned monopoly banks. Florida used the state's credit to back particular banks. In contrast, Michigan and New York adopted a laissez-faire "free banking" approach. Regardless, when bank failures proved contagious and a central bank politically untenable, the antebellum federal government had attempted to isolate its funds with an "independent" system of "sub-treasuries" in various cities (Timberlake 1993; Myers 1970; Platt 1968).

47. Dillistin (1949).

48. Few of these new "national banks" were established until after the June 1864 revisions to the law. Also, state governments could still charter and regulate their own banks. Unchartered private banks provided financial services for either small rural communities or the very wealthy. The latter type of bank was also allowed to loan and trade on its own accounts. These banks were the antecedents of JP Morgan & Company, Lehman Brothers, Goldman Sachs, Lazard, and Brown Brothers Harriman. But antebellum prohibitions on branch banking remained on the books (Markham 2002).

49. Congress also created another form of currency, Gold Certificates, with a maximum denomination of $10,000. These were given out by the Treasury in exchange for gold deposits. Hence they tended to be used mostly by importers, large businesses, and the wealthy. The first Gold Certificates would not be issued until November 1865 (Konings 2011; Timberlake 1993; Myers 1970).

50. The initial tax of 2 percent proved too low to change bank behavior. Therefore, Congress increased it to 10 percent (legislation passed in March 1865, but did not take effect until July 1866). Regardless, by the end of the war, the number of state banks had fallen by 78 percent to just 349, whereas almost 1,294 new national banks had been created (many of which were former state banks). For an alternative interpretation, see Selgin (2000).

51. For example, when New York banks had excess reserves, they lent them out as short-term loans to investors and speculators on Wall Street. Therefore, when the stock and bond markets fell, banks lost money via their bankrupt borrowers. In the reverse direction, when banks "called" back these loans, investors and speculators were forced to liquidate their investments in order to pay the banks, causing the markets to dive (Geisst 2018; Markham 2002).

52. Wicker (2000).

53. Andrew Jackson (1829–1837) and his Democrat supporters (e.g., Martin Van Buren, James Polk) believed that government had become a tool of business and banking interests largely based in the Northeast. In their view, these wealthy elites used their power to award patents of incorporation, pass legislation, and conduct fiscal, monetary, and trade policy so as to benefit themselves at the expense of average Americans. The country seemed headed toward a corrupt American aristocracy. Furthermore, to Jacksonians the financial crises of 1837, 1841, and 1857 were the result of corrupt speculators, fraudulent schemes, and irresponsible investors. Their primary solutions were to shrink government and to restrict, if not eliminate, banks and paper currency. Independent banking and the sub-Treasury system were their attempts at disconnecting state and private finance in particular (Timberlake 1993; Remini 1972).

54. In 1861, over 98 percent of the 36,672 federal civilian employees were postal workers; only 946 worked in the Departments of War or Navy combined. By 1865, the US Army Quartermaster's Department alone employed some 130,000 civilians (20,000 worked for the Navy Department, and another 10,000 were employed by various other military departments) (Wilson 2006; supplemented by *HSUS*).

55. Wilson (2006, 2003).

56. In fact, for its first several years, the Republican Party was so thoroughly associated with antislavery that many regarded it as a single-issue party. For example, in the 1856 presidential race, almost all of the Republican Party platform concerned issues related to slavery. Only a few sentences were allocated to specific policy issues, such as the banning of polygamy, federal support for a transcontinental railroad, and new federal spending on river and harbor improvements (Potter 1976; Republican Party platform of 1856, *UCSB*).

57. Summers (1993); Hoogenboom (1961).

58. Moieties were originally created by the British to incentivize customs officials and informants to crack down on smuggling. In 1789, the first US Congress copied the British system, splitting half of all confiscated goods between local customs officials and any informants (Thompson 2000: n19; Prince and Keller 1989).

59. Summers (2004).

60. Bryce (1888b: 453).

61. Hoogenboom (1961: 1).

62. Starting in 1819, Congress also attempted to regulate immigration by limiting passenger capacities and conditions on oceangoing vessels under the guise of safety.

63. Such European troubles included poverty, political revolution, and famine (Martin 2011).

64. Abramitzky and Boustan (2017; supplemented by *HSUS*).

65. Catholics then were seen by many Americans as enemies of the "true" Protestant religion and feared as loyal to the pope in Rome and therefore a threat to democracy. Irish and German Catholics, who concentrated in the major eastern cities, were especially targeted. Beyond religion, antebellum immigrants were also blamed for spreading crime, disease, poverty, and cultural division. Such anxieties led to the formation of anti-immigrant and anti-Catholic movements. These culminated in the Know-Nothing Party (1854–1860), which elected eight state governors

and over one hundred members of Congress, and nominated former president Millard Fillmore as its candidate in the 1854 presidential elections (Levine 2001; Anbinder 1992).

66. Immigration to the United States reached its historical zenith of around 15 per 1,000 residents during 1850–1854. Soon thereafter, an interval of relative peace and prosperity in Europe prompted a decline in US immigration to around 7.6 per 1,000 for several years. The Panic of 1857 and subsequent recession then drove immigration down further, to 4.3 per 1,000. In comparison, the first two years of the Civil War saw an average of 2.8 immigrants per 1,000 residents, a low not experienced again until the United States entered World War I.

67. Also known as An Act to Encourage Immigration, signed on July 4, 1864.

68. Or as historian William Cochrane (1993: 78) explains, "With the exception of a few valleys along the Pacific Coast and the Mormon settlements in Utah, all the Great West between the Pacific Ocean and a line drawn roughly from Saint Paul to Fort Worth awaited agricultural exploitation in 1860. This was the farmers' last frontier."

69. The Homestead Act also allowed settlers to buy the land in just six months for a mere $1.25 per acre.

70. Though much of the land ultimately wound up in the hands of speculators, the railroads, and wealthy investors (Brands 2019; White 2011).

71. Nevada was admitted as a state in 1864 for similar reasons (Green 2015).

72. That is, the same size as New York, New Jersey, Pennsylvania, Delaware, and Maryland (Kammer 2017).

73. Atack, Bateman, and Parker (2000).

74. Cochrane (1993); Sutherland (1989).

75. Though barbed wire would not be mass-produced until the mid-1870s (Krell 2002; Razac 2002).

76. State health legislation regarding cattle also affected the timing and routes of the cattle drives (Lehman 2018).

77. The term "soft money" refers to paper currency or paper debentures used as currency (as opposed to "hard money," which refers to gold or silver coins). During the Gilded Age, to support "soft money" meant to be in favor of printing more greenbacks and, hence, inflation. "Hard money" supporters sought to reduce or eliminate paper money and to return to the gold standard.

78. Dubofsky and Dulles (2010: 83).

79. And formally proposed in the National Labor Union's Address to the Workingman (Commons 1910: 141–169; see also Greenberg 2017).

80. Dubofsky and Dulles (2010).

81. Laracey (1998, 2002).

82. American newspapers originated during the colonial period as an adjunct of the printing business. These four-page weeklies offered "an assortment of local advertising, occasional small paragraphs of local hearsay, and large chunks of European political and economic intelligence lifted directly from London newspapers" (Schudson and Tifft 2005: 18).

83. Huntzicker (1999).

84. In 2020 dollars, a traditional party-controlled newspaper would cost roughly $1.80 versus 30 cents for a "penny" paper (*Measuring Worth*, GDP deflator).

85. The *New York Times* was originally the *New York Daily Times* before 1857. Other successful pennies included the *Philadelphia Public Ledger* (1836), the *New Orleans Picayune* (1837, named for the smallest denomination of Spanish currency), and the *Boston Herald* (1846).

86. *New York Herald*, May 6, 1835.

87. Schudson and Tifft (2005).

88. In 1870 the *Chronicle* merged with *Hunt's*.

89. The *New York Herald* was the first daily newspaper to feature regular business and financial news, including securities prices, interest rates, and dividends. Others quickly adopted this practice.

90. For a recent general treatment, see Knight (2016).

91. Sachsman and Borchard (2019); Huntzicker (1999).

92. Some political reporters were part-time congressional staffers or boarded with the legislators upon whom they reported.

93. At the corner of 14th Street and Pennsylvania Avenue.

94. Newspapermen had been allowed to reserve seats to observe Congress starting in 1841. Prior to that there had been little demand (Summers 1994).

95. Laracey (2002).

96. Calabresi and Yoo (2008); Farber (2003); Anastaplo (1999).

97. Lincoln instead relied upon "the war power of the Government" and "what appeared to be a popular demand and a public necessity" ("Special Message to Congress," July 4, 1861, *UCSB*).

98. Ex parte *Merryman*, 17 F. Cas. 144 (C.C.D. Md. 1861).

99. Farber (2003); Anastaplo (1999); Randall (1926).

100. Abraham Lincoln, comment to Zachariah Chandler (US senator, R-MI), July 4, 1864, according to John Hay (Lincoln's private secretary), quoted in Burlingame and Ettlinger (1997: 218).

101. Grant and Kelly (2008).

102. Salmon Chase (US Treasury secretary), September 11, 1863, quoted in Donald (1954: 24).

103. Ellis (2012); Holzer and Donald (2005); Laracey (2002); Harper (1951).

104. Flood (2009).

105. Summers (2004).

106. Calhoun (2008: 7).

107. Laracey (2002).

108. Klinghard (2010).

109. Marten and Janney (2021); Richardson (2020); Rose (1992).

110. The exception being the election of 1884, which pit New York governor Grover Cleveland (D) against former congressman, senator, and secretary of state James G. Blaine (R), neither of whom had ever served in the military (Summers 2000).

111. Grant was a graduate of West Point, a decorated veteran of the Mexican-American War, and the top Union military commander during the Civil War. Hayes, Garfield,

and Harrison each volunteered as civilians and fought as officers in multiple battles. Arthur saw no combat but served as military quartermaster. McKinley was the only enlisted man, but he rose to the rank of major due to his bravery and leadership ability. Only Cleveland avoided military service altogether.

112. Gordon (2016); Engerman and Sokoloff (2000).

113. Before the Gilded Age, virtually all American corporations were formed for a specific purpose prescribed in special statutes passed by state legislatures (Trachtenberg 1982).

114. Hochfelder (2013); Thompson (1947).

115. In contrast, American warfare during the 20th century produced major advances in US science and technology, even outside of armaments.

116. For example, the repeating rifle and machine gun (and machines for milling them), the ironclad ship, submarines, torpedoes, bullets, all saw major advances during the war (Hacker 2016).

117. At least two-thirds of Civil War deaths resulted from infectious diseases (Devine 2016, 2014).

118. Dupree 1957b).

119. National Research Council (1995).

120. An Act to Incorporate the National Academy of Science, March 3, 1863 (Dupree 1957a).

121. Hounshell (1984).

122. Wilson, (2003, 2006)

123. Wert (2018); Wilson (2006); Koistinen (1996).

124. In fact, in 1866 *The Nation* complained, "The study of political economy is at so low an ebb in the United States that any honest man who sits down to write about it renders a service to the public." It further observed, "The country is full of practical [and successful] men . . . [who] find it hard to believe that scholars, philosophers, and professors can have anything to tell them that they do not already know about such matters as exchange, production, profits, wages, interest, rents, and taxation" (*The Nation,* February 1, 1866).

125. For example, Reverend Joel Parker, a well-known New York clergyman and associate editor of the *Presbyterian Quarterly,* told his congregation that "the financial panic [of 1837] was a direct reproof for the 'peculiar sin' of greed, just as the flood had been a reproof for violence, famine for pride, captivity for sabbath breaking, the destruction of the temple for the rejection of Christ and, more recently, cholera for intemperance" (quoted in Fabian 1989: 131–133).

126. "Political economy" refers to how economic wealth and political power interact with one another and how they are distributed throughout society, and investigates the institutions and policies that most affect this distribution. Distinct "economics" courses and departments did not appear in American colleges until the 1890s. Since then, "political economy" has become a subfield within the broader study of political science (Farr and Seidelman 1993; Bernard 1990; Mason and Lamont 1982).

127. Foner (1970).

128. Foner (1970).

129. Davies (2018).

130. Edward Atkinson (a Massachusetts abolitionist and political activist). He further explained, "Many Northerners who did not share the Radicals' commitment to Black political rights insisted that the freedman's personal liberty and ability to compete as free laborers must be guaranteed or emancipation would be little more than a mockery" (quoted in Foner 1990: 102).

131. The term "hard money" could also refer to silver coinage, which had mostly fallen out of use in the United States long before 1870. Newspaper and book searches suggest that the term "hard money" had been common in North America since at least the mid-1700s, whereas the phrase "soft money" appears to have been popularized only during the early 1800s, possibly due to the relative scarcity of banks and banknotes in North America throughout the colonial period.

132. *Christian Advocate* (New York), August 8, 1878, quoted in Unger (1964: 121).

133. From 1837 until the mid-1860s, Francis Wayland's *Elements of Political Economy* and Jean Baptiste Say's *A Treatise on Political Economy* were widely used as introductory texts. Arthur Latham Perry's *Elements of Political Economy* began to replace them in 1866. Walker's *Science of Wealth* (1866) and Bowen's *Principles of Political Economy* (1859) were also popular (Unger 1964).

Interlude

1. Relative to the United States, the next largest economies were Great Britain (95 percent as large), the soon to be unified Germany (59 percent), France (59 percent), Italy (41 percent), Japan (28 percent), and Spain (15 percent).

2. As a proportion of total economic output, in 1870 the United Kingdom was most focused on manufacturing, with around 40 percent of its GDP in industry, followed by France (33 percent), Germany (32 percent), and Sweden (21 percent). Even tiny Denmark had greater industrial concentration than the United States (roughly 20 percent vs. 15 percent).

3. Just twenty years earlier, in 1850, over 55 percent of Americans had been farmers, while under 16 percent were industrial labor.

4. By 1870, only around 1.03 million US citizens (or just 2.6 percent of the population) had ventured west of Texas, and over half of those huddled in California. There are no reliable estimates for the western Native American population, though nationally they totaled around 300,000 (Reddy 1993; supplemented by *HSUS*).

5. This would decline to 10 percent of US GDP by 1880, largely thanks to the Panic of 1873 and subsequent recession, which affected economies around the world (Davies 2018; Wilkins 1989; supplemented by *HSUS*).

6. Thomson (2016).

7. This occurred in 1869, when the NYSE created a listing committee specifically for this purpose (O'Sullivan 2007).

8. Goetzmann, Ibbotson, and Peng (2001). In a separate tabulation, Mary O'Sullivan (2007, 2016) finds just seventy-seven firms listed on the NYSE in 1866 (not including inactive securities—stocks of firms listed, but not traded) consisting of railroads (61 percent), utilities (5 percent), miners (22 percent), industrials and miscellaneous (12 percent). Note the absence of bank or financial stocks in this inventory of actively traded shares, which O'Sullivan argues were largely wiped out by the Panics of 1837 and 1857 and stained by "double liability," which held that bank stockholders were liable for both their investment and prior investment in any shares owned. Formalized in the National Bank Act of 1864, double liability continued to stifle bank shares until it was rescinded during the Great Depression of 1929–1941.

9. *New York Times.* 1870. passim.

10. Unger (1964: 3).

11. Goldin and Lewis (1975).

12. Unger (1964: 20); Giroux (2012).

13. "All its currency, bills, bonds, treasury notes, and 'promises to pay' of very kind, became worthless to the holders" (*New York Times,* November 9, 1865). See also Ball (1991); Todd (1954).

14. Ransom (2018).

15. Quoted in Oberholtzer (1907: 574).

16. In comparison, when the war started, there had been just $435 million in US currency in circulation, divided almost evenly between specie (47.6 percent of all US currency was in gold coins, 4.8 percent in little-used silver coin) and state banknotes (47 percent). By 1865, a whopping 35 percent of US currency was in greenbacks, another 27 percent was split evenly between national and state banknotes, and just under 24 percent was in fractional and paper notes from "other" sources, 13.7 percent was in gold coin, and just 0.8 percent was in silver coin.

17. To deal with the vast scope of forgery, Congress created, in 1865, the federal government's first investigative agency, the Secret Service (Johnson 1995).

18. Throughout the war, inflation increased annually: 6.0 percent (1861), 14.2 percent (1862), 24.8 percent (1863), 25.2 percent (1864). During 1865, inflation fell to 3.7 percent.

19. Technically, the greenback was debt, not currency. Therefore, its price fluctuated on the secondary market just like any other form of debt.

20. Willard, Guinnane, and Rosen (1996).

21. Since the Treasury used cloth to make high-quality paper for greenbacks, they were ridiculed as "worthless rags" or "rag babies" (O'Malley (2008; Mitchell 1908: 4, Table 1; 6, Table 2; Friedman and Schwartz 1963: 24).

22. Unger (1964: 172).

23. *Commercial and Financial Chronicle,* November 6, 1869, quoted in Unger (1964: 153). Some of these businessmen formed the National Board of Trade in 1868 to lobby politicians and to shape national policy for business, similar to today's Chamber of Commerce or National Association of Manufacturers (Davis 2014).

24. Another 40 percent was in the form of long-run bonds.

25. Myers (1970: 176).
26. Castel (1979).
27. Another 209,000 men were home by January 1866. Most of the enormous general staff either resigned from the army or accepted demotion. By October 1866, after several rounds of dismissals, all volunteer soldiers had returned to civilian life, and Congress had set the army's strength at just fifty-four thousand (Bradley 2015; Foner 2014; McPherson 1988).
28. The bill proposing a constitutional amendment to ban slavery was initially proposed in the House in mid-December 1863. A month later, a joint resolution was submitted to the Senate. Legislation approving specific language for the amendment was passed by the Senate in early April 1864 and by the House in late January 1865. The Thirteenth Amendment then went to the states, where it was finally ratified in early December 1865. Even then, it was not formally ratified by Delaware until 1901, Kentucky in 1976, and Mississippi in 1995 (Foner 2014).
29. AJ, "Third Annual Message to Congress," December 3, 1867, *UCSB*.
30. Foner (1990, 2014)
31. Bowen (1989).
32. "Radical" Republicans were the strident antislavery faction of the new Republican Party. Led by Thaddeus Stevens (R-PA) in the House and Charles Sumner (R-MA) in the Senate, they were most powerful during the 1860s. Initially, they wanted the Confederate states to revert to the status of unorganized territories, or, even further, to be treated like provinces of a foreign nation that had been conquered by the United States. They insisted that Confederate officers above the rank of lieutenant, and nearly all civilian officials in the Confederate governments, should *not* be pardoned but should be disfranchised forever, declared "not a citizen of the United States." A few Radical Republicans even hoped for trials and executions. However, Lincoln pocket-vetoed their Reconstruction legislation in 1864. And no substantive plans for mass arrests, indictments, or executions were ever put forward. Radical Republicans were far more successful in outlawing slavery. They were instrumental in the passage and adoption of the Thirteenth, Fourteenth, and Fifteenth Amendments to the Constitution, after which their political power waned (Trefousse 1968; Foner 2014; Summers 2014).
33. Bergeron (2011); McKitrick (1960).
34. *The Spectator,* September 30, 1865.
35. Conditional upon an oath of loyalty to the Union and a renunciation of slavery (AJ, "Proclamation Granting Amnesty to Participants in the Rebellion, with Certain Exceptions," May 29, 1865, *UCSB*).
36. Seen as traitors, "scalawags" were white Southern Republicans who supported political equality and civil rights for African Americans. The term derives from 1840s slang for a worthless farm animal, and then was used to denote a "good-for-nothing" person. In practice, scalawags had diverse backgrounds and motives. Most believed that they could accomplish more personal success in a Republican South than by fighting against Reconstruction. Many had been high-ranking politicians, judges, or local officials before the war. At their peak, one-fifth of Southern whites may have

been scalawags. They therefore held considerable power until the Panic of 1873 eroded their economic and financial resources. "Carpetbaggers" were Northern investors, entrepreneurs, activists, and reformers who went south to participate in Reconstruction. Resentful Southerners viewed them as con men and speculators who had packed their few belongings in bags made of carpet remnants and gone south to prey on vulnerable Southerners laid prostrate by the war (Baggett 2003; Current 1988).

37. AJ, "Special Message to Congress," December 18, 1865, *UCSB*.

38. AJ, "Speech at the White House to Southern Delegation," September 11, 1865, quoted in *New York Herald*, September 12, 1865.

39. Dupont and Rosenbloom (2016).

40. Ager, Boustan, and Eriksson (2019).

41. Beckert (2015).

42. To destroy the South's rail system, General William T. Sherman ordered "every man of his command at work in destroying the railroad, by tearing up track, burning the ties and iron, and twisting the bars when hot. . . . [L]et a man at each end twist the bar so that its surface becomes spiral" (William T. Sherman, "Special Field Order, No. 37," July 18, 1864, Kenan Research Center, https://aspace-atlantahistorycenter.galileo.usg.edu/repositories/2/archival_objects/8901).

43. William H. Trescot to James Lawrence Orr, December 1865, quoted in Foner (1990: 92–93).

44. Legislated most thoroughly in Mississippi and South Carolina, under these "Black codes," African Americans could legally marry and own property and had limited rights to make legal contracts and sue for enforcement. However, they could not testify against whites in court, serve on juries, serve in state militia, or quit their job without permission. Some states dictated where Blacks could live, what kind of property they could own, and when they could legally rest from work. Most occupations, other than farmer or servant, were forbidden to Blacks or required Blacks to pay a tax. Unemployment was defined as "vagrancy" and made illegal. Black children could be legally forced into unpaid apprenticeships under whites. Some felonies were given harsh punishments, often death, if committed by Blacks. Even minor offenses committed by Blacks were punished by "hiring out" or the lash, while whites were rarely penalized. Restrictions were placed on Blacks regarding firearms, alcohol, even just entering the state. The selling of farm products was forbidden without written permission of a white employer, supposedly to prevent stealing. Hunting, fishing, and livestock grazing on previously public lands were made illegal, preventing Blacks from independently feeding themselves. Blacks were barred from public facilities, including parks, hospitals, and charity houses. Some states even shut down public schools rather than accept Black students. Swift and pervasive Northern backlash caused many Southern governments to revise or neglect their Black Codes (Novak 1978; Wilson 1965).

45. Parsons (2015); Southern Poverty Law Center (1998).

46. Klein (2012).

47. Carlton and Coclanis (2003); Glymph (1985).

48. US cotton production would not reach prewar levels until the mid-1870s, and then at much depressed prices. Attainment of prewar cotton export levels would await 1880; tobacco would recover more quickly, by the late 1860s.

49. Foner (2014).

50. As with the Thirteenth Amendment banning slavery, the Fourteenth Amendment also explicitly granted Congress "the power to enforce, by appropriate legislation, the provisions of this article." This was a dramatic shift from the first twelve amendments, most of which constrained the power of the federal government.

51. The Freedmen's Bureau Act of 1866 (July 16).

52. Foreigners then held 10 to 15 percent of federal debt and were important marginal investors in American railroads (Wilkins 1989).

53. Blaine (1886: 328).

54. Timberlake (1993: 90, Table 7.1; supplemented by *HSUS*).

55. Sowerbutts and Schneebalg (2016).

56. Myers (1970: 175).

57. Goetzmann, Ibbotson, and Peng (2001; supplemented by *HSUS*).

58. Utley (2003).

59. Grenville Dodge, superintendent of construction for the Union Pacific Railroad, quoted in Brands (2010: 295–296).

60. For a general treatment, see Perrow (2002); Geisst (2000).

61. In 1869, the state of Massachusetts created the first railroad commission to monitor "the actual workings of the system of railroad transportation in its bearing upon the business and prosperity of the Commonwealth" and to make suggestions "as to the general railroad policy of the Commonwealth . . . or to the condition, affairs, or conduct of any of the railroad corporations . . . as may seem to them appropriate" (Massachusetts Board of Railroad Commissioners 1870: 3). Other states followed suit during the 1870s (e.g., Iowa, Wisconsin, Nebraska, Kansas, Missouri, Georgia, and California). In 1870, Illinois went furthest, revising its state constitution to give it power to regulate railroads and grain elevators, including rate-setting authority. Also, during summer 1869, Charles Francis Adams, esteemed diplomat and descendent of two presidents, published a withering critique of railroad monopolies in the *North American Review*. In the widely read essay, Adams detailed the chicanery, greed, and corruption of the country's top railroad magnates and implicated them in the Gold Conspiracy (see Chapter 4). He warned his readers, "Modern society has created a class of artificial beings who bid fair soon to be the masters of their creator. . . . [T]hey already are establishing despotisms which no spasmodic popular effort will be able to shake off" (Adams 1869a: 104).

62. Rail owners often ignored the new state regulations and regulatory bodies. One railroad executive simply declared, "I . . . deny the right of the Legislature in any way to interfere with [the railroad's] property and franchises." Another insisted that state regulation of the rails was "unconstitutional and a violation of vested rights, and not applicable to this corporation" (quoted in Cordery 2016: 74).

63. Perrow (2002); Chandler (1977).

64. In some cases, there were also state and federal limits on loan size (Geisst 2018; Konings 2011: 50; White 2011; Summers 1984).

65. Most of which will be discussed in subsequent chapters. For a concise one-source summary, see Wicker (2000).

66. Average of 1860 and 1870 data. Farms were larger in the South (where plantation farming remained modal) and in the plentiful farmland regions of the West and Great Plains. Today, the average US farm size is 444 acres, with significant corporate ownership; small, family-owned farms account for around 21 percent of production (US Department of Agriculture 2019; supplemented by *HSUS*).

67. Bourne (2017); Lawver (1998); Nordin (1974); McCabe (1873).

68. Sanders (1999: 101).

69. Such as the Greenback Party (1874–1889), Populist Party (1887–1908), and People's Party (1891–1908) (Sanders 1999).

70. To bring immigration policy in line with the Fourteenth Amendment, the Naturalization Act of 1870 granted citizenship rights to "aliens of African nativity and to persons of African descent."

71. *Crandall v. State of Nevada*, 73 U.S. 35 (1867). Though decided a few months before ratification of the Fourteenth Amendment, the case was deliberated after the Amendment's passage by Congress (June 1866).

72. *Henderson v. Mayor of City of New York*, 92 U.S. 259 (1875).

73. Chen (2015); McKeown (2010).

74. Before the 1850s, Chinese immigration had been negligible, never rising above fifty immigrants per year. But their numbers soared during 1854, when over thirteen thousand Chinese workers arrived in response to the ongoing California Gold Rush. For the next decade, new immigrant workers from China ranged between three thousand and seven thousand per year. When gold yields diminished during 1864–1866, Chinese immigration fell in tandem. But the lull was temporary. When construction of the transcontinental railroad ran into labor trouble, Americans turned again to inflows of Chinese immigrant labor, which rose going into the 1870s. Aiding the process was the Burlingame Treaty of 1868, in which China legalized emigration (Ngai 2021; Martin 2011).

75. America's Great Migrations Project, University of Washington, https://depts.was hington.edu/moving1/; supplemented by *HSUS*.

76. Chang and Fishkin (2019).

77. Greene (2017).

78. USG, "Sixth Annual Message to Congress," December 7, 1874, *UCSB*.

79. RBH, "Veto Message," March 1, 1879, *UCSB*.

80. JAG, "Letter Accepting the Republican Presidential Nomination," July 12, 1880, *UCSB*.

81. Native Americans would later receive birthright citizenship under the Indian Citizenship Act of 1924.

82. *The Cherokee Tobacco Case* (1870).

83. The 1870 census suggests just over 208,000 Latinos living in the United States (including 6,300 Spanish), 39 percent in New Mexico, 17.6 percent in California,

16.5 percent in Texas, and roughly 5 percent each in Colorado and Louisiana; 82 percent were Mexican, 11 percent were of undetermined origin (America's Great Migrations Project, University of Washington, https://depts.washington.edu/movingl; supplemented by *HSUS*).

84. By 1900, the Latin American population had risen 240 percent but still constituted just 0.2 percent of the US population, with 34 percent living in Texas, 20 percent in New Mexico, 11 percent in California, and 7 percent in Arizona; 77 percent were of Mexican descent, 5.7 percent Cuban, and 6.4 percent of undetermined origin (America's Great Migrations Project, University of Washington, https://depts.washington.edu/movingl; supplemented by *HSUS*).

85. Gantz (2015); Rees (2013).

86. Wind had limited uses outside of watercraft (Freese 2016; Crump 2007; Righter 1996).

87. Travel from New York City to San Francisco on the transcontinental took one week in 1870. A seat on a third- or "emigrant"-class bench could be purchased for $65. Second-class tickets went for $110. First-class tickets in a Pullman sleeping car cost $136. Thus, in 2020 dollars, tickets ranged from $1,300 to $2,800 (Union Pacific Railroad Company 2020; *MeasuringWorth,* consumer price index).

88. *Measuring Worth,* consumer price index; supplemented by *HSUS*.

89. Tickers most benefited those investors, banks, and brokers who did *not* own seats on the exchange and therefore relied on messenger boys to get price information during the trading day.

90. Though early staplers could hold only one staple at a time; therefore papers were usually still bound by pins or thread.

91. Previously, horses, wrestling, boxing, racing, and swordplay had constituted most sport in North America (Borish, Wiggins, and Gems 2017; Zirin 2008).

92. Smythe (2003).

93. Summers (1994: 10).

94. After paper costs came compositors (11 percent of total), editors (8 percent), correspondence (6 percent), technical staff (5 percent), packing and distribution (5 percent), and wire service subscriptions (3.4 percent). The remaining 5.7 percent went toward rents, salaries, ink, postage, "harbor news," and glue and molasses for rollers. Cost estimates for the year 1865 for the *New York Tribune,* in Summers (1994: 13).

95. Smythe (2003); Presbrey (1929).

96. Summers (1994).

97. For example, the *New York Herald* funded the captivating and expensive search for David Livingstone, the explorer and missionary gone missing in Africa, during 1870–1872, eventually producing the instantly famous query "Doctor Livingstone, I presume?" (Jeal 2007). The *Herald* also prided itself on its coverage of foreign news and events (Smythe 2003).

98. Smythe (2003: 18).

99. Novak (1996).

100. Karl Marx fared only slightly better in Europe. He published his *Communist Manifesto* (1848) and *Das Kapital* (1867) and was adopted as the intellectual leader

of the International Working Men's Association (a.k.a. the First International). However, prior to the brief Paris Commune (1871), and by some measures not until the early 1880s, "with the partial exception of Germany, no Marxist movement of significance as yet existed, and Marx's influence was negligible" (Hobsbawm 1982: xiv). See also Buhle (2013).

101. Mill (1870).

102. The first science degree programs appeared at Yale (1851) and Harvard (1852) (Rudolph 1990).

103. American Association for the Promotion of Social Science (1865).

104. Theories of biological evolution had been discussed within the American scientific community as early as the 1840s. But Darwin's formulation was a powerful catalyst. First conceptualized in 1838, but not yet published, Darwin's theory arrived in the United States from Britain in 1857, when he shared his ideas with the widely respected Harvard botanist Asa Gray. Then came Darwin's publication of *On the Origin of Species by Means of Natural Selection* in 1859. This first edition did not use the phrase "survival of the fittest," which originated with Spencer and was used by Darwin in later editions. At first, Americans largely rejected *Origin of Species*. The Civil War then disrupted and distracted attention from the subject for several years. Nevertheless, Darwin provided a focal point for US scientific debates about evolution, which were further strengthened by his 1871 publication of *The Descent of Man*. By around 1873, some version of biological evolution had been accepted by most in the American scientific community (Numbers 1998; Hofstadter 1944).

105. Spencer (1851, 1862).

106. Hovenkamp (2015); Kennedy (2006).

107. Skowronek (1982).

108. Most prominently in the Slaughterhouse cases (1873) and later in the Civil Rights cases (1883), *In re Jacobs* (1885), and others, culminating in *Lochner* (1905). The classic study is Twiss (1942), with an update in Ely (1997). See also Schwartz (1974).

109. Morrison (1986); Green (1951).

110. Hamiltonians generally supported the political-economic agenda of former Treasury secretary Alexander Hamilton (d. 1804). This included industrialization, economic modernization, a strong financial system, a powerful standing military, and a relatively robust federal government (Green 2019; Sylla and Cowen 2018).

111. Carey (1851, 1853).

112. The American Iron Association, based in Philadelphia, was formed in 1855 mostly by eastern ironmasters "to take all proper measures for advancing the interests of the trade in all its branches." Nine years later, with the growth of steelmaking in the United States, the Association changed its name to the American Iron and Steel Association. It survives today as the American Iron and Steel Institute, headquartered in Washington, DC.

113. For example, one popular proposal was for the United States to adopt a fiat currency that paid interest and was backed by federal land holdings (Unger 1964).

114. Wells (1864).

115. Simon Newcomb's first major publication, *A Critical Examination of Our Financial Policy during the Southern Rebellion* (1865), was still celebrated by economists a century later as "the most sophisticated, original, and profound analysis of the theoretical issues involved in Civil War finance that we have encountered, regardless of date of publication" (Friedman and Schwartz 1963: 18n3). For a recent discussion of his work and influence, see Valeonti (2020).

116. Barber (1993).

117. U.S. House of Representatives (1868); Lydia Maria Child (author, abolitionist, and civil rights activist), quoted in Child and McMillen (2008: 160).

118. *Report of the Special Commission on our Revenue System,* reprinted in *New York Times,* January 30, 1866, quoted in Hoogenboom (1961: 17–18; supplemented by *HSUS*).

119. *The Nation,* February 8, 1866. See also *New York Times,* January 31, 1866; Summers 1993).

120. Hoogenboom (1961).

121. Little over a year earlier, in December 1865, a House bill appeared that would have adopted the British practice of open competitive exams for all but senior civil service appointees. It failed to gain any traction or even much newspaper coverage (Hoogenboom 1961).

122. *New York Times,* January 30, 1867.

123. *The Nation,* April 25, 1867, quoted in Hoogenboom (1961: 39).

124. AJ, interview with Charles G. Halpine, editor *New York Citizen,* March 5, 1867, quoted in McPherson (1880: 141–143).

125. AJ, interview with Charles G. Halpine, editor *New York Citizen,* March 5, 1867, quoted in McPherson (1880: 141–143).

126. The British had formally adopted the gold standard in 1821; Canada in 1853 (Meissner 2005).

127. Named the "Latin Monetary Union," it was agreed to in treaty negotiations during the close of December 1865, including a gold-to-silver ratio of 15.5 to 1 (Einaudi 2001, 2017; Redish 1993).

128. In practice, the participants conducted business mainly in gold. As in the United States, silver had faded from use as coins because of its higher value as bullion. However, the French insisted on bimetallism in the belief that it better promoted commerce; Paris was also wary that new silver discoveries might depreciate the metal and bring its coinage back into vogue (Einaudi 2001, 2017; Redish 1993).

129. Quoted in Castel (1979: 147).

130. AJ, "Third Annual Message to Congress," December 3, 1867, *UCSB.*

131. An Act to Suspend Further Reduction of the Currency, 1868 (February 4).

132. Americans also circulated banknotes issued by private banks with national charters, which remained limited by prior legislation to $300 million.

133. Stewart (2009).

134. Foner (1990: 144).

135. AJ, "Fourth Annual Message to Congress," December 8, 1868, *UCSB.*

136. Johnson suggested that interest payments on federal debt "should be applied to the reduction of the principal in semiannual installments, which in sixteen years

and eight months would liquidate the entire national debt." In other words, a reduction or elimination of interest payments. He also recommended "making legal-tender and bank notes convertible into coin or its equivalent their present specie value." That is, inflated paper greenbacks would be redeemable in gold at face value, rather than bringing them back to par by reducing their supply (or by increasing the amount of gold in the financial system by exports, inward foreign investment, and mining). AJ, "Fourth Annual Message to Congress," December 8, 1868, *UCSB*.

137. Johnson left office an angry man in March 1869. For years thereafter, he tried to make a political comeback, finally winning appointment to the US Senate by the Tennessee legislature in 1875, where he served just a few weeks before dying from a stroke (Trefousse 1989).

Chapter 4

1. Goethals (2008: 217). Here Goethals summarizes the judgements of psychologist Dean Keith Simonton (1998, 2006), who also found Grant lacking in deliberativeness, charisma, and creativity, but highly neurotic.
2. Stoddard (1927: 59); Milkis and Nelson (2019: 229).
3. USG, "Eighth Annual Message to Congress," December 5, 1876, *UCSB*.
4. Milkis and Nelson (2019: 227).
5. The Whig Party (1834–1854) was a uniquely American synthesis of political, economic, religious, and social beliefs. Reacting against President Andrew Jackson's aggressive use of presidential authority, Whigs feared executive power. They therefore held that presidents should strictly obey the Constitution, should execute the laws of Congress, and administer the federal government, but they should not legislate nor even lobby for their preferred policy agenda. This included strictures against most public speaking, which Whigs shunned as presidential demagoguery (Holt 1999; Howe 1979).
6. Chernow (2017).
7. Quoted in Garland (1898: 20–21).
8. Grant's mother, Hannah, quoted in Chernow (2017: 10).
9. Grant rarely spoke about religion and is generally believed to have held fairly basic Protestant views. One scholar summarized Grant's beliefs thus: "[A]ll persons exercised a free will and were responsible for their actions. But if those actions were harmful God would overrule those actions for the benefit of humankind. Furthermore, humans must trust in God in all of their endeavors and they must be satisfied with the outcome" (Smith 2005: 56).
10. Family and friends quoted in Garland (1898: 15).
11. Early on, Grant acquired an almost embarrassing reputation for candor and gullibility. For example, in one oft-recounted incident, when bargaining for a colt, an eight-year-old Grant immediately admitted the highest price he could pay, despite being explicitly instructed by his father to dissemble and haggle. Grant's honesty and naïveté in business dealings would become a lifelong theme (Chernow 2017: 15).

12. Family and friends quoted in Garland (1898: 10, 12, 15); Grant (1885: 30).
13. Grant (1885: 24).
14. Grant (1885: 24).
15. "He cared more for horses than for books," recalled his father (Garland 1898: 20n). See also Grant (1885: 7, 25).
16. Grant (1885: 26).
17. In the 1840s, economic subjects would have fallen under the study of political economy, ethics, or philosophy. In particular, at West Point, "[t]he Department of Ethics, chaired by the chaplain, presented a hodge-podge of courses at various times ... [including] political philosophy, ethics ... international law ... possibly some history." For its part, "[p]olitical science covered American constitutional law, Supreme Court decisions, and international law, with an emphasis on the laws of war" (Morrison 1998: 92).
18. Chernow (2017); Young (1879).
19. Grant (1885: 35–36).
20. Grant (1885: 14).
21. For the alumni of West Point, military service after graduation was customary but not obligatory by law or contract. For Grant, it was especially important if he hoped to return to West Point as a math instructor (White 2016; McFeely 1981).
22. Perret (1997).
23. Fellow officer James Longstreet, quoted in Chernow (2017: 54).
24. A British military tradition since the 17th century, the "brevet" designation was first authorized for the US Army in 1806. It constituted a promotion in rank, often temporary, awarded to an officer for exceptional service or heroism. It brought higher title and insignia, but not necessarily an increase in pay or command authority (Tucker 2013: 89).
25. Grant (1885: 37, 68) served rather than resign, later explaining, "Experience proves that the man who obstructs a war in which his nation is engaged, no matter whether right or wrong, occupies no enviable place in life or history." See also Simpson (2000); Lewis (1950).
26. Simpson (2000); Lewis (1950).
27. Rufus Ingall, former West Point roommate and fellow officer, quoted in Simpson (2000: 61).
28. Grant's struggle with alcohol is most emphasized in Chernow (2017); Smith (2001). For attempts at clinical diagnoses, see Bumgarner (1993); Heermans (1977). For the opposing view, see Simpson (2000); Ellington (1987). Historian and biographer Charles Calhoun argues that portrayals of Grant as an alcoholic are "stereotyped" and "way overdrawn." They rest "largely on rumor originating in the long-after-the-fact reminiscences of others, especially related to his early army days. There is virtually no evidence of any problem in the White House. . . . Grant's enemies exploited the drinking charge as a convenient weapon against him" (personal correspondence, December 2020).
29. Chernow (2017).
30. Chernow (2017: 104).

31. Garland (1898: xxiii). Soon after the Confederates fired on Fort Sumter, Grant wrote his father, "[W]e have a Government, and laws and a flag and they must all be sustained" (USG, letter to Jesse Grant, April 21, 1861, in Simon 1995 2: 6–7).

32. While the North was smart, agile, and resourceful, Grant ultimately relied on its overwhelming superiority in men and war materiel to win. He later told a reporter, "I used to find that the first day, or the first period of a battle, was most successful to the South, but if we held on to the second or third day, we were sure to beat them, and we always did" (quoted in Young 1879 2: 473). Grant has therefore also been characterized as a great squanderer of his soldiers' lives and limbs. See also Laver (2013); Perret (1997).

33. USG, letter, recipient unknown, December, 1860, quoted in Richardson (1868: 175–176).

34. USG, letter to Jesse Grant, April 21, 1861, quoted in Simpson (1991: 11).

35. USG, comment to Major General Leonidas Polk, February 6, 1862, quoted in Wilson (1885: 24). This was partly a taunt. Grant's full conversion to emancipation and African American equality occurred gradually during 1861–1863. See Simpson (1990).

36. Abraham Lincoln, comment to Republican powerbroker and newspaperman Alexander McClure when pushed to remove Grant after his heavy losses at the Battle of Shiloh, 1862, quoted in McClure (1892: 196). Some have dismissed this quote as willful, such as Simpson (2000: 136).

37. Bergeron (2011); McKitrick (1960).

38. In his December 1868 Annual Message to Congress, President Johnson suggested that interest payments on federal debt "should be applied to the reduction of the principal in semiannual installments, which in sixteen years and eight months would liquidate the entire national debt." In other words, a reduction or elimination of interest payments. He also recommended "making legal-tender and bank notes convertible into coin or its equivalent their present specie value." That is, inflated paper greenbacks would be redeemable in gold at face value rather than brought back to par by reducing their supply (or by increasing the amount of gold in the financial system through exports, inward foreign investment, and mining) (AJ, "Fourth Annual Message to Congress," December 8, 1868, UCSB).

39. On the battlefield, Generals Grant and Sherman had arranged more lenient surrender conditions than those preferred by President Johnson and his secretary of war. When Grant announced, "I will not stay in the army if they break the pledges I have made," Johnson conceded to most of his requests (Chernow 2017: 533–536, 550–554).

40. Quoted in Chernow (2017: 572).

41. USG, speech in Galena, IL, June 21, 1867, quoted in Rawlins (1868: 5).

42. Quoted in Chernow (2017: 578, 579, 609).

43. Prymak (2014).

44. Specifically, business activity slumped during early 1867, then again that autumn and winter, partly due to the Treasury secretary's tight money policy.

45. New York Herald, June 5, 1871, quoted in Chernow (2017: 614).

46. "I wasn't sorry to be a candidate," Grant later told a reporter (quoted in Chernow 2017: 614).

47. Congress had frozen the number of greenbacks in circulation in February 1868, at just over $356 million (as well as an additional $44 million kept in reserve at the Treasury), in order to prevent their further retirement by Johnson's "hard money" Treasury secretary, Hugh McCulloch. However, the actual number of greenbacks in use varied somewhat due to bond purchases and other financial operations of the federal government.

48. Recall that greenbacks were first circulated in March 1862 as a form a non-interest-bearing war debt. They were quickly adopted as one of many forms of currency then in use. At first, $100 in greenbacks could purchase roughly the same amount in gold. But as the US government printed more and more greenbacks to pay for war expenditures, their value in gold declined. For example, even during 1868 the market price of $100 in greenbacks ranged from $66.67 to $75.69 in gold throughout the year (Mitchell 1908: 4, Table 1).

49. Brownlee (2016); Koistinen (1996).

50. "Democratic Party Platform," July 4, 1868, UCSB.

51. Joseph Hawley, "Speech at the Republican National Convention," New York Times, May 21, 1868.

52. He also promised "economy of administration" (USG, letter to General Joseph R. Hawley, president of the National Republican Convention, May 29, 1868, in Simon 1995 19: 263–264).

53. "Republican Party Platform," May 20, 1868, UCSB.

54. Hoogenboom (1961).

55. "Republican Party Platform," May 20, 1868, UCSB.

56. USG, letter to General Joseph R. Hawley, president of the National Republican Convention, May 29, 1868, in Simon (1995 19: 263–264).

57. Horatio Seymour, New York World, October 23, 1868, quoted in Troy (1996: 70–71). Also, the Democratic Party lacked manpower, was being outspent by Republicans, and had few party newspapers at their disposal. Meanwhile, Democratic losses in key state elections earlier in October bode ill for the presidential election. Thus, Seymour wrote that "the most powerful and impressive speaker in the United States" was the party's best weapon in the presidential campaign. Finally, Seymour and the Democrats wanted a more aggressive and publicly rhetorical president, while Grant and the Republicans preferred a more aloof, reserved chief executive, as prescribed by their Whig philosophical origins (Prymak 2014).

58. Ellis (1998: 223n4).

59. Quoted in Calhoun (2017: 65).

60. Commercial and Financial Chronicle, November 7, 1868.

61. The Nation, March 4, 1869.

62. Hoar (1903a: 246).

63. Perret (1997: 416).

64. Milkis and Nelson (2020).

65. Grant had briefly dabbled in the nativist Know-Nothing Party but quickly rejected their secrecy and anti-immigrant, anti-Catholic agenda. He voted in only one presidential election before 1860. It was a spoiler vote cast against the Republican

candidate, John C. Fremont; he explained why: "I knew Fremont [and] "[i]t was evident in my mind that the election of a Republican President in 1856 meant the secession of all the Slave States, and rebellion" (Young 1879 2: 268; Grant 1885 1: 143).

66. Hoogenboom (1988: 59).

67. Waugh (2009); Smith (2001).

68. Waugh (2009: 42).

69. Young (1879 2: 269). Grant (1885: 212) also later wrote, "I was a Whig by education and a great admirer of Mr. Clay. But the Whig party had ceased to exist before I had an opportunity of exercising the privilege of casting a ballot."

70. Chernow (2017); Laver (2013); Simpson (2000); Grant (1885).

71. Strong (1952: 172).

72. Goethals (2008).

73. USG, "First Inaugural Address," March 4, 1869, *UCSB*.

74. USG, letter to General Frederick Steele, April 11, 1863, in Simon (1995 8: 49).

75. USG, letter to William Tecumseh Sherman, June 21, 1868, quoted in Simpson (1991: 246).

76. Prior to the Civil War, Grant never expressed pro-slavery or white supremacist views. In his prewar farming ventures, he overwhelmingly preferred to hire Black workers, whom he treated well and paid competitive wages. In fact, in his civilian life Grant had a reputation for being "no hand to manage negroes. He couldn't force them to do anything. He wouldn't whip them" (comment by wife of Henry Boggs, cousin to Julia Grant, quoted in Garland 1898: xxiii). But Grant had once owned a slave (whom he quickly freed rather than sold to pay off debts), and he had allowed his Southern wife to bring along four young Black slaves as house servants after he married.

77. USG, "First Inaugural Address," March 4, 1869, *UCSB*.

78. USG, "First Inaugural Address," March 4, 1869, *UCSB*. See also USG, letter to General Joseph R. Hawley, president of the National Republican Convention, May 29, 1868, in Simon (1995 19: 263–264).

79. This statement also reflects Grant's low opinion of his own rhetorical skills, especially in campaigning for office (USG, letter to Senator Roscoe Conkling, July 15, 1872, in Simon 1995 23: 200).

80. USG, "First Inaugural Address," March 4, 1869, *UCSB*.

81. USG, "First Inaugural Address," March 4, 1869, *UCSB*. Grant made similar comments throughout his life, such as at an Ohio rally in the 1880 campaign (Brands 2012: 603).

82. Adams (1907: 227).

83. Calhoun (2017); Chernow (2017); Stoddard (1927); Hoar (1903a, 1903b).

84. As military conflict wound down, the US economy fell into a recession that lasted from April 1865 until December 1867 (National Bureau of Economic Research 2021). The full quotation from which this section takes its title: "To go into the Presidency opens altogether a new field to me, in which there is to be a new strife to which I am not trained" (USG, comment to General Joseph Hawley, May 29, 1868, quoted in Balch 1885: 184).

85. In 1868, the US had managed per capita growth of just 1.4 percent.

86. America's first transcontinental railroad would be completed in May 1869.

87. Bank of England (2021).

88. By the end of 1869, long-term foreign investment in the United States totaled $1.39 billion, composed of federal debt (72 percent), railroad bonds and shares (17.5 percent), state and municipal bonds (7.7 percent), and other securities and real estate (2.8 percent) (Wilkins 1992: 233).

89. AJ, "Third Annual Message to Congress," December 3, 1867, *UCSB*.

90. Pocket-vetoed by outgoing president Johnson earlier that same month.

91. Public Credit Act of 1869 (March 18).

92. USG, "First Inaugural Address," March 4, 1869, *UCSB*.

93. Chernow (2017).

94. USG, "First Inaugural Address," March 4, 1869, *UCSB*. Grant also appears to have held a labor theory of money. He explained later in his presidency that "a currency of fixed, stable value . . . has as its basis the labor necessary to produce it, which will give to it its value." He further described gold and silver as "metals having an intrinsic value just in proportion to the honest labor it takes to produce them." From this perspective, printing money was suspect. In contrast, gold was *the* fundamental store of value, or as Grant put it, "a currency good wherever civilization reigns" (USG, "Sixth Annual Message to Congress," December 7, 1874, *UCSB*). These beliefs may have prompted Grant's enthusiastic endorsement of America's pursuit of the "precious metals locked up in the sterile mountains of the far West" in his first inaugural, in which he further suggested that the federal government might play a role in subsidizing "facilities to reach these riches" (USG, "First Inaugural Address," March 4, 1869, *UCSB*).

95. *Commercial and Financial Chronicle,* April 3, 1875.

96. Or as Boutwell himself explained, "The ability of the country to resume specie payments will not be due to any special legislation . . . but to the condition of its industries," specifically, "the development of the industry of the nation . . . to such an extent that our exports of those products should be equal substantially to our imports" (US Treasury 1869: xiii–xiv). In practice, Boutwell allowed the supply of greenbacks in circulation to grow just 5 percent during Grant's first term. As for Grant, he explained his administration's reasoning in this manner: "Immediate resumption, if practicable, would not be desirable. It would compel the debtor class to pay, beyond their contracts, the premium on gold at the date of their purchase and would bring bankruptcy and ruin to thousands. Fluctuation, however, in the paper value of the measure of all values (gold) is detrimental to the interests of trade. It makes the man of business an involuntary gambler, for in all sales where future payment is to be made both parties speculate as to what will be the value of the currency to be paid and received. I earnestly recommend to you, then, such legislation as will insure a gradual return to specie payments and put an immediate stop to fluctuations in the value of currency" (USG, "First Annual Message to Congress," December 6, 1869, *UCSB*).

97. In so doing, Boutwell finally fulfilled legislation passed by Congress on February 25, 1862, which had ordered the creation of a sinking fund for "the purchase or payment of one per centum of the entire debt of the United States, to be made within each

fiscal year" but which had never been implemented (described in Boutwell 1902 2: 125–149). For a contemporary understanding of sinking funds, see Ross (1892).

98. Recounted in Boutwell (1902).

99. The second refunding was approved by Congress during January 1871 in Act to Authorize the Refunding of the National Debt, 1870 (July 14) (Studenski and Krooss 1963; Boutwell 1902). However, the short-run benefits of Boutwell's refunding came with long-run costs. For the refunding involved conversion of the term structure of US debt from short term (mostly due during the early 1880s) into long term (mostly due in 1907) at a price fixed by law (either at par or a stated premium) or the market. And by the 1880s, US interest rates had fallen below 4 percent and would not rise again until 1907. Thus, over the long run, Grant's refunding has been deemed "a costly and irreparable mistake . . . in terms of premiums paid on bonds bought in the open market" (Patterson 1952: 422).

100. Richardson (1869).

101. Richardson (1870).

102. *The Economist,* December 25, 1869.

103. Bolles (1886: 320).

104. Congress ended federal land grants to the railroads in 1871, midway through Grant's first term.

105. *New York Times,* April 26, 1869.

106. *The Nation,* March 25, 1869.

107. Quoted in Calhoun (2017: 69).

108. Congressman Benjamin Butler (R-MA), quoted in Chernow (2017: 635–636).

109. Charles Francis Adams, quoted in Calhoun (2017: 61).

110. Sumner (1872: 10).

111. Calhoun (2017: 77–79).

112. USG, comments to John A Kasson, August 22, 1878, in Simon (1995 28: 457–458).

113. Although mostly a figurehead, Secretary of the Navy Adolph Borie did oversee the desegregation of the Washington Navy Yard and the successful resolution of a labor dispute with naval workers. But he became better known for his campaign to rename US naval vessels. A wealthy Philadelphia commodities merchant with no political or military background, Borie did not like the Native American names selected by his predecessor. He "did not think the ships had pretty names, ran down the list and replaced all of the Indian names with others out of the classic mythology—*Niobe, Castor, Colossus, Amphitrite, Circe.*" He resigned suddenly after just three months in office, and his successor changed many of them back (Pratt 1938: 347).

114. Horace White (*Chicago Tribune*) to Elihu Washburne, quoted in McFeely (2002: 302).

115. Charles Dana (*New York Sun*), quoted in Waugh (2009: 125).

116. The 1869 cabinet consisted of just seven department heads: state, treasury, war, attorney general, postmaster general, navy, and interior. There also existed a secretary of agriculture, but not yet at the cabinet level. Hamilton Fish (secretary of state) came closest to serving Grant's full tenure, just two weeks shy.

117. Ex-congressman Richard C. Parsons (R-OH), letter to Elihu B. Washburne, US minister to France, June 19, 1876, quoted in Calhoun (2017: 79).

118. Hoogenboom (1961: 1) puts the number of federal employees at fifty-three thousand.

119. Quoted in Chernow (2017: 638).

120. John Hay, secretary to the US legation in Spain, letter to John Bigelow, May 9, 1870, quoted in Hoogenboom (1961: 62).

121. *The Nation,* June 10, 1869.

122. The Republican Party's initial 1856 platform "had devoted more than half its nine brief resolutions to the slavery issue and had not addressed itself to any other public question except that of government aid for a Pacific Railroad." In 1860 and 1864, antislavery was joined by defending the Union and winning the war, in addition to protectionist tariffs for industry, a homestead act, federal spending on river and harbor improvements, and full repayment of the public debt (Potter 1976: 423; Republican Party Platforms of June 18, 1856, May 17, 1860, June 7, 1864, *UCSB*).

123. Blaine (1886: 449).

124. Gideon Welles, former secretary of the navy under Presidents Lincoln and Johnson, diary entry, March 24, 1869, in Welles (1911: 560).

125. Including the powerful Senators Charles Sumner (R-MA), Charles Francis Adams (R-MA), Carl Schurz (R-MO), and Lyman Trumbull (R-IL).

126. From the pen of Henry Adams, great-grandson of founding father John Adams, the *North American Review* published withering critiques of Grant. See, for example, Adams (1869, 1870). Other disgruntled critics included Charles Dana at the *New York Sun*, Horace Greeley and Whitelaw Reid at the *New York Tribune*, Horace White of the *Chicago Tribune*, and Murat Halstead of the still widely read *Cincinnati Commercial*. Of course, the Democratic press also leveled unceasing attacks on the Grant administration. In contrast, the *New York Times* was generally supportive. But perhaps the sole pro-Grant paper was the *Washington National Republican*, created back in 1860 to bolster Lincoln and his new party (Calhoun 2017; Maihafer 1998).

127. Political scientist and biographer Jean Edward Smith (2001) has argued that Grant's poor reputation as president is also partly the result of biased and white-supremacist scholars at Columbia University who wrote the first studies of Reconstruction.

128. Goethals (2008); Summers (1994).

129. Calhoun (2017: 91).

130. USG, comments to Jay Gould and Jim Fisk, June 15, 1869, quoted in US House of Representatives (1870: 3).

131. An in-depth history of the 1869 scheme of Jay Gould and James Fisk can be found in Ackerman (2005).

132. US House of Representatives (1870: 3).

133. US House of Representatives (1870: 155, 249.

134. *New York Times,* August 25, 1869; US House of Representatives (1870).

135. James B. Hodgskin, chairman of the New York Gold Exchange, testimony to Congress, 1870, reported in US House of Representatives (1870: 8).

136. At least one historical analysis has argued, "Had the government, the only body with the power to have maintained indefinitely a higher greenback price of gold, clearly stated its neutrality, it is likely that there would have been no Black Friday" (Wimmer 1975: 120). See also Zhylyevskyy (2010).

137. Unger (1964: 170).

138. Ackerman (2005); US House of Representatives (1870).

139. Ackerman (2005: 266).

140. William Dodge, quoted in US House of Representatives (1870: 187).

141. George Opdyke, quoted in US House of Representatives (1870: 19, 334).

142. *New York Herald,* October 8, 1869; *New York Herald,* October 5, 1869.

143. Most historians of the episode, and most biographers of Grant, agree that Grant was naïve but innocent of wrongdoing.

144. Grant did occasionally speak and correspond with journalists during autumn 1869 to defend himself against accusations (Ackerman 2005).

145. Ackerman (2005: 266).

146. Railroad construction increased in 1869 (66 percent), 1870 (37 percent), 1871 (18 percent); hence industrial production rose 1869 (7.5 percent), 1870 (2.3 percent), 1871 (5.1 percent).

147. USG, comment to brother-in-law Abel Corbin, September 26, 1869, quoted in US House of Representatives (1870: 226).

148. Chernow (2017); Calhoun (2017); White (2016).

149. For example, Grant responded adroitly to the massive fires that devastated Chicago (October 1871), Peshtigo (October 1871), and Boston (November 1872). Together they killed thousands of Americans, destroyed well over 100,000 buildings, and cost some $300 million (roughly $6.5 billion in 2020 dollars). In each case, Grant offered federal assistance, including troops to provide security and supplies of food, clothing, wagons, and equipment. He then supported Congress in the passage of tax breaks for some of the afflicted. Contemporary estimates of monetary damages taken from Grant (1969); 2020 estimate from *Measuring Worth* (consumer price index). See also USG, letter to General P. H. Sheridan, October 9, 1871, in Simon (1995 22: 159); Campbell B. (2008); Gess and Lutz (2002).

150. USG, "First Annual Message to Congress," December 6, 1869, *UCSB.* Others argued that "over-production . . . is the secret of the depression," at least in some industries, and the foreign business press continued to blame "the evils of [the American] financial and monetary system" (*The Economist,* November 20, 1869).

151. USG, "First Annual Message to Congress," December 6, 1869, *UCSB.*

152. *Hepburn v. Griswold,* 75 U.S. (8 Wall.) 603 (1870).

153. Few expected the Court's ruling to endure. Other important legal-tender cases were still outstanding, and the specific wording of the *Hepburn* decision seemed limited. Specifically, *Hepburn* stated that Congress could not require acceptance of greenbacks in payment of debts incurred before the passage of the 1862 Legal Tender Act (Calhoun 2017: 119–123).

154. In particular, Grant had urged Congress that a return to the gold standard (i.e., convertibility of greenbacks and gold, at par) "should be commenced now and reached at the earliest practicable moment." However, he also warned that it should be done "with a fair regard to the interests of the debtor class." Specifically he advised, "Immediate resumption, if practicable, would not be desirable. It would compel the debtor class to pay, beyond their contracts, the premium on gold at the date of their purchase and would bring bankruptcy and ruin to thousands" (USG, "First Annual Message to Congress," December 6, 1869, *UCSB*).

155. Grant, his attorney general, and his secretary of state each "later maintained that the [Supreme Court] nominations had been filled out and signed before the Court's announcement of its [*Hepburn*] decision," but Grant also later admitted that he "had reason to believe" that his nominees would reverse *Hepburn*, if only from their previous decisions on such matters (Calhoun 2017: 121–122).

156. In *Knox v. Lee* 79 U.S. (12 Wall.) 457 (1871); *Parker v. Davis* 79 U.S. (12 Wall.) 457 (1871).

157. On the other hand, while the nation descended into recession during mid-1869, rather than pressure Congress for economic relief at home Grant became obsessed with the acquisition of Santo Domingo (the Dominican Republic). He extolled the island's "unequaled fertility" in tropical produce and timber. Grant also noted Santo Domingo's strategic value as a "gate to the Carib[b]ean Sea." He further argued that the island was "capable of supporting the entire colored population of the United States should it choose to emigrate ... [because of] prejudice to color [in the United States]" (USG, "Memorandum: Reasons Why San Domingo Should Be Annexed to the United States," 1869, in Simon 1995 20: 74–76). In pursuit of annexation, Grant set into motion a series of secret surveys and negotiations toward a formal treaty. Congress did not find out about the bizarre scheme until late November 1869, when the American press broke the story. There ensued a fierce personal battle between President Grant and livid senior Republicans in Congress, each trying to embarrass the other. The battle lasted for months. It ended in a very public and ignominious defeat for Grant. Still not dissuaded, Grant would continue to push for Santo Domingo's annexation for the rest of his presidency, further calling into question his judgement (Calhoun 2017; Chernow 2017).

158. In an era of growing "great power" imperialism, Grant's support for international arbitration was unusually prescient. In fact, just months after he left the presidency, Grant told a British audience that he hoped that "at some future day, the nations of the earth will agree upon some sort of congress, which will take cognizance of international questions of difficulty, and whose decisions will be as binding as the decision of our Supreme Court is binding on us" (USG, "Address to the Midland International Arbitration Union," October 10, 1877, quoted in Young 1879 1: 120).

159. McCullough (2014). See also Calhoun (2017); Herring (2008); McFeely (1981).

160. Readmission occurred during June and July 1868 for Alabama, Arkansas, Florida, Georgia, Louisiana, North Carolina, and South Carolina. However, white supremacists in Georgia subsequently expelled Blacks from the state legislature, prompting the incoming 41st Congress to eject Georgia's congressional

representatives from their seats (March 1869) and to reimpose federal military rule (December 1869). After grudgingly accepting reforms, Georgia was again readmitted to the Union in mid-July 1870, the last former Confederate state to do so.

161. At the time of Grant's inauguration in 1869, Virginia, Mississippi, Texas, and a lapsed Georgia were the only ex-Confederate states still not readmitted to the Union.

162. Grant later regretted this move, telling a journalist in June 1879, "In giving the South negro suffrage, we have given the old slave-holders forty votes in the electoral college. They keep those votes, but disenfranchise the negroes. This is one of the gravest mistakes in the policy of reconstruction" (quoted in Young 1879 2: 362).

163. When Southern white supremacists violently resisted the implementation of the new constitutional amendments, Grant worked with the Republican majority in Congress to pass three "Force Acts" during 1870–1871. The Force Acts gave Grant greater authority to fight white vigilantes and defend voter rights in the South. See Foner (2014); Summers (2014). To further aid the president, Congress also created the Department of Justice under the direction of the attorney general, partly to implement the Force Acts. It was formally established in August 1870 to meet the growing inventory of federal cases resulting from the Civil War and associated legislation. The new department was also intended to professionalize, and thereby diminish, the federal government (Shugerman 2014; Calabresi and Yoo 2008; Kaczorowski 2005).

164. Before the Civil War, Southern plantation owners had either provided public goods for their own locale or simply blocked state and local governments from doing so altogether (Foner 2014).

165. *New Orleans Tribune,* January 8, 1869, quoted in Foner (2014: 379). See also Summers (1984).

166. Quoted in Foner (2014: 374).

167. Also, in those states where white Republicans directed the spoils and corruption, such as North Carolina and Georgia, Blacks often silently accepted it "either from fear of weakening the Republican party or because notorious corruptionists shrewdly took steps to enhance their standing among the black electorate" (Foner 2014: 388).

168. *Augusta* (GA) *Chronicle,* September 9, 1869. Though most Southerners were far more vociferous. For example, the *Atlanta Constitution* (1872) described its state's Republican governor as "a picture of bold, evil rule not often seen, and admirable in its malicious and tyrannically consistency" (both quotes in Duncan 1994: 119, 122).

169. For example, the most prominent being Governors Rufus Bullock (Georgia), Adelbert Ames (Mississippi), Daniel Chamberlain (South Carolina) (Foner 2014; Summers 2014).

170. USG, "First Annual Message to Congress," December 6, 1869, *UCSB*. Nevertheless, iron manufacturers had convinced the newly inaugurated Grant to get rid of David Wells, a special revenue commissioner, whose troublesome public reports attacking protectionism made headlines that fanned the flames of tariff reduction, partly by asserting links between political corruption and high tariffs (Johnson 2018).

171. Recall that representatives from the Southern states had successfully blocked tariff hikes during the decades before the war. Immediately after the South left the Union, the Republican Congress passed the wartime Morrill Tariff of 1861, strongly supported by Lincoln. Thereafter, Republicans in Congress had regularly increased average tariff levels on dutiable imports, taking them from around 19 percent (1861) to around 49 percent (1868), the highest in almost forty years. Protections for iron and wool were especially generous.

172. Revenue Act of 1870 (July 14).

173. To add insult to injury, a misplaced comma in the tariff law cost American taxpayers roughly 1 percent of the government's tariff income by accidentally changing "fruit-plants," to "fruits, plants," on the free list. This error has since been celebrated as the "most expensive" comma ever printed (*New York Times*, February 17, 18, 1874; Oldfield 1891: 116).

174. Revenue Act of 1870 (July 14); Studenski and Krooss (1963). Many wartime stamp taxes, originally passed in 1862 and placed on a variety of goods, services, and legal dealings, were also reduced or repealed in 1872.

175. Quoted in Foner (2014: 444).

176. USG, "Second Annual Message to Congress," December 5, 1870, *UCSB*.

177. Calhoun (2017); Hoogenboom (1961).

178. Foner (2014); Summers (2014).

179. USG, "Second Annual Message to Congress," December 5, 1870, *UCSB*.

180. Initially received with much ballyhoo and staffed by Grant with well-respected reformers, the Civil Service Commission did not meet until late June 1871. For months they debated reforms. But in the end, the Commission merely recommended to Grant that the federal civil service be divided into hierarchical grades and that competitive exams and probationary periods be required for the lowest grade of entry as was *already* being done in some departments. Grant agreed and implemented the Commission's recommendations on New Year's Day 1872. But without additional appropriations from Congress or new funding requests from the president, the Commission then faded into obscurity (Hoogenboom 1961).

181. Civil Service Commission (1871: 8). This allegation was challenged in *Harper's Weekly* (1872) and by the Civil Service Commission itself, which wrote that the figure was based on 1866 data: "[W]e selected the fact of [the civil service's] worst condition as the most forcible illustration of the mischiefs of the system" (Civil Service Commission, letter to John A. Logan, September 4, 1872, quoted in *Portland* [ME] *Daily*, October 1, 1872).

182. *New York Tribune*, April 17, 1872, quoted in Calhoun (2017: 373).

183. From January 1871 to January 1873.

184. New railroad construction increased in 1871 (18 percent) and 1872 (12 percent).

185. The war in central Europe had disrupted trade there; hence its conclusion brought back stability and demand for US exports (Dedinger 2012).

186. Boutwell (1902: 143–144).

187. US Census Bureau (1872).

188. Brands (2019); Utley (2003).

189. Calculated as a percentage of total federal budget expenditures (41st Congress, 1st Session, April 10, 1869, cited in Calhoun 2017: 267).

190. Reddy (1993); Stuart (1987); Utley (1984).

191. For example, Grant backed the Timber Culture Act of 1873, which gave away federal lands to timber developers. In his second term, he also signed the Desert Land Act of 1877, which sold federal lands at low prices to anyone who would irrigate their plot within three years. On the role of geological surveys, see Bartlett (1962). For a more general treatment, see Robbins (1994).

192. Brands (2019); Calhoun (2017); Utley (2003).

193. USG, "First Annual Message to Congress," December 6, 1869, *UCSB*.

194. USG, "First Annual Message to Congress," December 6, 1869, *UCSB*.

195. Reddy (1993: 8, Table 9).

196. USG, "First Annual Message to Congress," December 6, 1869, *UCSB*.

197. Just three months earlier, in a dispute over federal taxes, the US Supreme Court had held, "An act of Congress may supersede a prior treaty [with Native Americans]," thereby extinguishing tribal sovereignty (*Cherokee Tobacco Case*, 1870).

198. "Opinions expressed by the Commissioner of Indian Affairs (or his agents) on the condition of Indians in 1872" (Reddy 1993: 8, Table 9).

199. US Treasury (1872: xx–xxi).

200. *New York Herald,* March 30, 1872.

201. Young (1879 2: 265).

202. Young (1879 2: 265).

203. Pendel (1902: 64).

204. Ellis (2008).

205. USG, quoted in *New York Times,* October 10, 1875.

206. Ellis (2008: 99).

207. See, for example, House Resolution 1876 (April 3), which was responded to with Memorandum of Absences of the Presidents of the United States 1876 (May 4).

208. *Pittsburgh* (PA) *Daily Post,* September 8, 1875.

209. *People's Tribune* (Jefferson City, MO), July 21, 1871.

210. *People's Tribune* (Jefferson City, MO), July 21, 1871.

211. Sumner (1872).

212. *New York Sun,* September 4, 1872.

213. Although historians concur that the optics of Credit Mobilier were dreadful, they disagree about the extent to which illegal or corrupt activities actually occurred. See Mitchell (2018); White (2011); Summers (1993).

214. Though Grant did meet with campaign visitors and allocated patronage jobs so as to win votes in battleground states (Troy 1996: 73; Prymak 2014).

215. Slap (2006).

216. Lundberg (2019); Williams (2006).

217. Quoted in National Portrait Gallery (2008).

218. *Hartford* (CT) *Courant,* September 21, 1872, quoted in Troy (1996: 76).

219. *New York Times,* October 16, 1872.

220. Law (1874).

221. Mohl (1997).
222. Prymak (2014).
223. Ultimately, Greeley proved so obviously unfit for office that even party supporters called his nomination "the triumph of quackery, charlatanry and recklessness" (Edwin L. Godkin, editor of *The Nation*, letter to Senator Carl Schurz [R-MO], May 19, 1872, quoted in Hoogenboom 1961: 114).
224. Quoted in Foner (2014: 503).
225. USG, "Fourth Annual Message to Congress," December 2, 1872, *UCSB*.
226. USG, "Second Inaugural Address," March 4, 1873, *UCSB*.
227. The president's annual salary had been fixed at $25,000 since 1789. It had therefore not kept up with either inflation (average consumer prices had arisen around 35 percent by 1873) or the increased expenses of the presidency. Hence the salary raise to $50,000 per year was generally not considered egregious.
228. *New York Times*, February 10, 1873.
229. *Lawrence* (KS) *Daily Journal*, November 15, 1873.
230. USG, "Second Inaugural Address," March 4, 1873, *UCSB*.
231. The earliest available data suggest that the ratio of private wealth to national income rose from 421 percent (1870) to 429 percent (1872), while private wealth to average disposable income went from 466 percent (1870) to 474 percent (1872) (Piketty and Zucman 2014).
232. During his first term, Grant successfully cut federal spending by over 26 percent and the federal debt by over 14 percent.
233. *The Economist*, December 21, 1872.
234. *The Economist*, November 9, 1872.
235. McFeely (1982: 332).
236. It is also possible that, had Grant forged a consensus in Congress and among the American people to successfully annex Santo Domingo during 1869, the economy may have recovered sooner. However, Grant instead proceeded in secret and produced only confusion, distrust, acrimony, and failure.
237. Bank of England (2021).

Chapter 5

1. *New York Herald*, March 4, 1873.
2. *Chicago Tribune*, January 29, 1873.
3. Grant's first vice president, Schuyler Colfax, had announced in September 1870 his intent to retire from politics, declaring his "eighteen years of continuous service at Washington . . . long enough for any one; and my ambition is gratified and satisfied." This was likely a feint to generate support for his renomination. But Colfax's unpopularity with the press, and perhaps with Grant himself, contributed to his loss in the 1872 nomination process. He was replaced by Henry Wilson, who had been a US senator from Massachusetts since 1855, a Radical Republican, a reformer, and a

"rags-to-riches" shoemaker. Wilson was therefore expected to appeal simultaneously to New England elites, liberal reformers, and labor (Chernow 2017; Hatfield 1997).

4. White (2011: 64).

5. *The Nation,* March 6, 1873.

6. The final reports were submitted during the second half of February 1873. For a contemporary account see Crawford (1880).

7. Congressional salaries were raised from $5,000 per year to $7,500 (or from around $115,000 to $170,000 in 2020 dollars), made retroactive to March 4, 1871, the first day of the 42nd Congress. President Grant's salary was also doubled, to $50,000 (around $1.1 million in 2020 dollars), but this was far less controversial. The presidential salary had not changed since George Washington entered office, while the expenses of the office, and average prices, had greatly increased. The justices of the Supreme Court also received a raise (*Measuring Worth,* consumer price index).

8. *Measuring Worth,* consumer price index. In early 1873, the outgoing Congress had 114 lame ducks out of 243 House members and 16 of 74 senators. However, recent analysis has shown that "Republicans and lame ducks were no more likely to support the salary increase than Democrats or returning members of Congress." Rather, the true division was between elite liberal reformers and Jacksonian spoilsmen of both parties (Alston, Jenkins, and Nonnenmacher 2006).

9. *Defiance* (OH) *Democrat,* March 15, 1873, quoted in Alston, Jenkins, and Nonnenmacher (2006: 681).

10. The president and Supreme Court justices got to keep their raises, which were largely deemed justified.

11. The Coinage Act of 1792 had fixed the legal value of silver coins at $1.29 per fine ounce. This was the price that the US Mint would pay for silver bullion, which it cast into US coins at no cost to the depositor (a.k.a. "free silver coinage"). Since financial capital was scarce in the early Republic, this made good policy at the time. However, the free-market value of silver bullion fluctuated according to supply and demand, rising above $1.29 during 1833 and hitting a maximum of $1.36 by 1859 (5.4 percent above the US Mint price). At these prices, those who dealt in silver preferred more valuable bullion over coins, and the latter largely faded from use during the 1830s (Myers 1970; Timberlake 1993; Silber 2019).

12. Silver coins could still be used as legal tender "for any amount not exceeding five dollars in any one payment," or roughly $100 in 2020 dollars (*Measuring Worth,* consumer price index).

13. Friedman (1990b).

14. Secretary George Boutwell had left the Treasury in mid-March to take an open Massachusetts seat in the US Senate. Richardson had previously served as assistant secretary of the Treasury (1869–1872) and acting attorney general (1870). His missive concludes, "The [Treasury] Department and Department business are very quiet," with "few matters . . . of consequence enough to to [sic] trouble you about" (William Richardson, telegraph to USG, August 28, 1873, in Simon 1995 24: 214–215).

15. These were highly speculative rail projects which linked two individual cities, but without necessarily connecting them to a trunk line or even providing feeder lines to surrounding towns.

16. "[T]he stock, mortgage bonds, equipment, obligations, etc. of US railways in 1869 were valued in total at just over $2 billion" (Platt 1984: 161; supplemented by *HSUS*).

17. James Lee, letter to William Ralston (Bank of California), December 7, 1872, quoted in White (2011: 78).

18. USG, "Fourth Annual Message to Congress," December 2, 1872, *UCSB*.

19. USG, "Second Inaugural Address," March 4, 1873, *UCSB*.

20. *New York Herald,* September 19, 1873.

21. Meanwhile, some European investors began to shift their money into the now booming, closer, and better understood, German economy (White 2011; Davies 2018).

22. Germany's victory in the Franco-Prussian War in January 1871, and the massive 5 billion franc war indemnity paid to Berlin by the French, turned the ongoing German economic boom into an asset bubble.

23. With 378 stocks listed, and up to 90,000 trades daily among 2,941 authorized traders, the Vienna Stock Exchange was the largest speculative market in Europe in 1873. The growing bubble in neighboring Germany had inflated it by spilling money into an Austrian railroad mania. However, swindles and fraud were common in the region's relatively unregulated markets. Thus, European investment markets began to falter starting in autumn 1872. And after the crowning event of the World Exhibition in Vienna was over (May 1873), investors fled the continent in droves (Resch and Stiefel 2011; Davies 2018).

24. Platt (1984: 161); Davies (2018).

25. *Commercial and Financial Chronicle,* September 6, 1873. The American business press was generally nonplussed through most of summer 1873. After all, trade in agricultural goods and manufactured products seemed healthy. Money markets were pleasantly dull. The flat stock market was interpreted as seasonal. Even railroad earnings seemed robust for most participants.

26. This episode is well-documented in Lubetkin (2006); see also White (2011).

27. *New York Tribune,* September 19, 1873.

28. *New York Tribune,* September 19, 1873.

29. It remained closed for ten days.

30. In 1873, just seven large New York banks held between 70 and 80 percent of the nation's bankers' deposits (Nitschke 2018).

31. Senator Oliver P. Morton (R-IN), telegram to USG September 19, 1873, in Simon (1995 24: 213–214).

32. Grant and others in the Republican Party may also have been dissuaded from government involvement by the Credit Mobilier scandal, still fresh in the public mind (USG, letter to Senator Oliver P. Morton, September 19, 1873, in Simon 1995 24: 213–214).

33. *New York Times,* September 20, 1873. The Grant administration had already started buying bonds to relieve "stringency" in the market that summer. The money came from federal gold sales, which Richardson and his predecessor, Boutwell, conducted

regularly during spring and summer to raise funds for use during the autumn harvest to counteract monetary contractions (Hacket 1898; Davies 2018; *Measuring Worth,* consumer price index; supplemented by *HSUS*).

34. *New York Times,* September 23, 1873.

35. William Richardson, telegram to USG September 24, 1873, in Simon (1995 24: 214); US Treasury (1873: xv).

36. USG, letter to Horace B. Claflin and Charles L. Anthony, September 27, 1873, in Simon (1995 24: 218–219); see also *New York Times,* September 23, 1873.

37. USG, letter to Horace B. Claflin and Charles L. Anthony, September 27, 1873, in Simon (1995 24: 218–219).

38. Shiller (2015).

39. O. O. Merick, letter to the editor, *Chicago Tribune,* December 25, 1873.

40. *New York Herald,* November 8, 1873.

41. US Census Bureau (1872: Table XXIII).

42. *New York Times,* December 23, 1873.

43. *New York Times,* December 26, 1873.

44. *New York Times,* November 6, 1873.

45. Calhoun (2017: 425–426); Chernow (2017: 778–779); Unger (1964: 215–217).

46. *The Nation,* November 13, 1873.

47. Britain had been on gold since 1821, Canada since 1853. Other early adopters include Australia (1852), Portugal (1854), and the Ottoman Empire (1863). These dates are often inexact. Even after formally declaring adoption of the gold standard, countries proceeded at different paces toward fulfillment, some with glaring reversals or with concurrent usage of different currencies. For example, Germany formally declared adoption of the gold standard in 1871, but took over a year to fully implement it. France sharply cut demand for silver starting in 1873, but was not fully on gold until 1878. Switzerland had a similar experience (Meissner 2005; Eichengreen and Flandreau 1994).

48. USG, "Fifth Annual Message," December 1, 1873, *UCSB.*

49. Myers (1970: 192).

50. Documented well in Unger (1964).

51. The term "soft money" had been used on and off for decades to describe paper currency or expansionary monetary policy, but it became especially popular during 1874–1876, used regularly by the press to refer to greenbacks and other inflationary policies.

52. California, Nevada, and Texas also voted against (Rosenthal 2007: 130–132; Barreyre 2011).

53. Young (1879: 264–266). See also Atkinson (1892: 119).

54. Hamilton Fish, US secretary of state, diary entry, April 21, 1874, quoted in White (2011: 546).

55. Congressman James A. Garfield (R-OH), diary entry, April 23, 1874, in Brown and Williams (1967: 316).

56. In October 1872, while assistant secretary of the Treasury, Richardson continued the practice, in Boutwell's absence, of buying up Treasury bonds so as to expand the

money supply during the harvest season, temporarily increasing greenback circulation to $360 million. But Richardson had acted without any financial or economic crisis to justify doing so. In autumn 1872, the economy was booming. Therefore, House members accused Richardson of violating the February 1868 law, which had set limits on greenback circulation, and suspected corrupt motives. A subsequent Senate investigation concurred. But Richardson was neither punished nor dismissed from office at the time (Mannen 2018).

57. Specifically, the schemes of John D. Sanborn, a private tax collector from Massachusetts. Legally contracted by Secretary Richardson in 1872, Sanborn was initially celebrated for his ability to bring in federal revenues and identify tax cheats. However, since he received 50 percent of all delinquent taxes that he reported, Sanborn began to pad his reports with the names of hundreds of firms and individuals whom the Treasury was *already* pursuing. For months, the Grant administration either unwittingly aided Sanborn or ignored complaints against him. Congress started an investigation in early 1874. Its report, issued in May 1874, found that Sanborn had claimed $427,000 in tax revenues that would have been collected anyway. Sanborn was indicted for corruption but never prosecuted since technically he had not violated the word of the law (Thorndike 2004; Burg 2014).

58. In the form of a letter responding to the new Republican senator from Nevada, John P. Jones.

59. USG, letter to Senator John P. Jones (R-NV), June 4, 1874, quoted in *New York Times*, June 6, 1874.

60. USG, letter to Senator John P. Jones (R-NV), June 4, 1874, quoted in *New York Times*, June 6, 1874.

61. An Act Fixing the Amount of United States Notes, 1874 (June 20).

62. *New York Times*, June 13, 1874.

63. Webb (1969).

64. Brown (2008: 27). Banker Thomas Mellon (1885: 410), father of Andrew Mellon, called it the "most disastrous and extensive panic and collapse since that of 1819." For the counterargument, see Rothbard (2002); Wicker (2000).

65. Mellon (1885: 411).

66. Foner (2014).

67. Foner (2014).

68. Business failures by year: 5,183 (1873), 5,830 (1874), 7,740 (1875), 9,092 (1876), 8,872 (1877), 10,478 (1878).

69. Foner (2014: 512–513).

70. Also due in part to a decline in alcohol and tobacco sales, the other major sources of federal tax revenues.

71. US Census Bureau (1872: Table XXIII; supplemented by *HSUS*). Some estimates reach as high as 3 million unemployed (Morris 2003: 24).

72. Summers (2014: 339).

73. Summers (2014: 339).

74. McFeely (1981: 393).

75. Beatty (2007: 293); *New York Times*, January 7, February 19, 1874.

76. Gutman (1965); Smith (2018).

77. LeMay (2012: 51–52, Table 3.1; supplemented by *HSUS*). For a contemporary account, see Woodworth (1875).

78. Friedman and Schwartz (1963: 22–23).

79. Summers (2014: 351).

80. Pike (1874: 47, 95).

81. Pike (1874: 47).

82. *Chicago Tribune*, September 26, 1873; *New York Times*, January 20, 1874; Foner (2014); Summers (2014).

83. Quoted in Foner (2014: 554).

84. Quoted in Foner (2014: 554).

85. During the early 1870s, the only other democracies were Belgium, Canada, Colombia, Greece, Liberia, New Zealand, Switzerland, and by some measures the United Kingdom (Marshall and Gurr 2018).

86. *New York Tribune*, May 9, 1874, quoted in Summers (2014: 334).

87. *New York Times*, January 20, 1874.

88. Ritter (1997); Unger (1964).

89. Foner (2014: 523).

90. Foner (2014: 524).

91. *New York Herald*, November 4, 1874.

92. Specifically, the Democrats would control the 46th and 53rd Congresses (1879–1881 and 1893–1895); Republicans would control the 51st and 54th Congresses (1889–1891 and 1895–1897). Within each period, the Republicans would also control the White House only in 1889–1891 (Harrison); Democrats in 1893–1895 (Cleveland) (Martis, Rowles, and Pauer 1989).

93. USG, "Sixth Annual Message to Congress," December 7, 1874, *UCSB*.

94. US Treasury (1874).

95. Though it only required these redemptions "at the office of the assistant treasurer of the United States in the city of New York, in sums of not less than fifty dollars [roughly $1,200 in 2020 dollars]" (An Act to Provide for the Resumption of Specie Payments, 1875 [January 14], 43rd Congress, Session II; *Measuring Worth*, consumer price index).

96. As a result, circulation of silver coins in the United States would leap by half in just a year, though they still constituted only around 2.5 percent of American money.

97. Senator Carl Schurz (R-MO), December 22, 1874, quoted in US Congress (1875: 205).

98. *Banker's Magazine*, January 1875, quoted in Unger (1964: 260).

99. Stoddard (1927: 71).

100. USG, "Special Message to Congress," January 14, 1875, *UCSB*.

101. In 1874, these two categories brought in just over 30 percent of all federal revenues (Calhoun 2017; supplemented by *HSUS*).

102. Senator Timothy Howe (R-WI), letter to Grace Howe, March 8, 1875, quoted in Calhoun (2017: 484).

103. Though some historians see Grant as leaning nativist throughout his life (Anbinder 1997).

104. In 1868, the Republican Party formally declared, "Foreign immigration, which in the past, has added so much to the wealth, development of resources, and increase of power to this nation . . . should be fostered and encouraged by a liberal and just policy." Four years later, they were less fervent. But the Republican platform continued to highlight "immigration protected and encouraged" under their rule and urged "continued careful encouragement and protection of voluntary immigration" (Republican Party Platforms of 1868 and 1872, *UCSB*).

105. Luconi (2007).

106. Contract labor from other countries was left unregulated.

107. As late as 1890, the Chinese immigrant male-to-female ratio was still only around 27 to 1. Thus, at least one scholar has called America's policy toward the Chinese "the only successful instance of ethnic cleansing in history of American immigration" (Parker 2015; Zolberg (2009: 192).

108. Though Grant also admitted, "[T]he Chinese have been of great service to our country. I do not know what the Pacific coast would be without them. They came to our aid at the time when their aid was invaluable" in building the West's transportation system (USG, comments while visiting Tientsin, China, June 12–14, 1879, quoted in Simon 1995 29: 159).

109. Partly because it left responsibility to initiate legal procedures with Black litigants, few of whom dared to risk life or limb on legal complaints that might never bear fruit. Never popular, the Civil Rights Act of 1875 would be struck down as unconstitutional by the Supreme Court in 1883. Congress would not pass another civil rights act for over eighty years (Friedlander and Gerber 2019; McPherson 1965).

110. Calhoun (2017: 482).

111. USG, "Sixth Annual Message to Congress," December 7, 1874, *UCSB*.

112. Calhoun (2017: 524).

113. McFeely (1981: 415).

114. Haley (1976).

115. These initial gold discoveries were made by a US Army expedition in French Creek, but they proved to be minor deposits. Far larger veins were discovered nearby during November 1875, and again during April 1876 (McClintock 2000).

116. Friedman and Schwartz (1967; supplemented by *HSUS*).

117. *New York Times,* July 18, 1875; *(Philadelphia) Times,* April 26, 1875; *Boston Post,* September 10, 1875.

118. Cochrane (1993: 97); Simon (1995 26: 47–48).

119. Cochrane (1993: 97).

120. *New York Times,* September 4, October 9, 1875.

121. *New York Times,* June 15, 1875; *Chicago Tribune,* June 5, 1875.

122. Foner (2014: 515).

123. USG, "Seventh Annual Message to Congress," December 7, 1875, *UCSB.* As with all Gilded Age presidential messages, it was not delivered orally by Grant, but read into the record by a clerk with Congress in attendance.

124. *New York Tribune,* December 8, 1875.

125. As the reading of it stretched into its second hour, most House members "gradually left their seats, retiring to the cloak rooms, or standing in the aisles [to] engage in conversation with each other . . . [as if] the House was indulging in a recess" (*New York Herald,* December 8, 1875).

126. For example, the former vice president of the Confederacy, Alexander Stephens (D-GA), became chair of the Committee on Coinage, Weights and Measures; former Confederate general Alfred Scales (D-NC) became chair of Indian Affairs; the former Confederate minister to Russia, Lucius Lamar II (D-MS), became chair of Pacific Railroads; former Confederate general Robert Vance (D-NC) became chair of the Patents Committee. In fact, the cohort of Southerners elected to the 44th Congress was suffused with former Confederate military officers and political leaders.

127. Quoted in Calhoun (2017: 512).

128. Quoted in Calhoun (2017: 512).

129. Robert R. Hitt, first secretary of the US Legation in France, letter to Oliver Morton, April 21, 1876, quoted in Calhoun (2007: 241).

130. Calhoun (2017: 511). Though Calhoun contends that the political onslaught against Grant had begun by autumn 1875.

131. Quoted in Calhoun (2017: 544).

132. Discretionary payments on the interest and veterans' pensions are not included (Calhoun 2017: 545; supplemented by *HSUS*).

133. USG, "Special Message," August 14, 1876, *UCSB*.

134. Quoted in Calhoun (2017: 545). Presidential impoundment was then rare but not unprecedented. Studies of impoundment have concluded that almost every president prior to Grant had "almost certainly impounded appropriated funds . . . largely attributable to the fact that, unlike today, appropriations bills 'were quite general in their terms and, by obvious . . . intent, left to the President . . . the [power] for determining . . . in what particular manner the funds would be spent.'" Grant's impoundment did break new ground, however. It left $2.7 million of a $5 million appropriation unspent, which provoked a House resolution demanding legal justification. When it failed to win much political support, the matter was dropped (Stanton 1974: 5–6; Middlekauf 1991).

135. Reti (1998: 192, Table 7).

136. The export number is taken from the 1873 peak.

137. A US silver dollar had 371.25 grains (0.773 ounces) of pure silver, as dictated by the Coinage Act of 1792. There are 480 grains per 1 troy ounce. Price data from US Treasury Department (1927: 119).

138. Silver coins had fallen out of use during the 1830s, when the value of silver as bullion rose above its use as coins.

139. George M. Weston, letter to the editor, *Boston Globe,* March 2, 1876.

140. Friedman (1990a). Though gold supporters stuck by their president.

141. Quoted in Friedman (1990b: 1160). See also Barnett (1964).

142. Barnett (1964: 178).

143. Especially in Kansas, Indiana, Iowa, Illinois, Michigan, Minnesota, and Oregon. Based on 1876 elections turnout.

144. Adopted at the Greenback Party Convention in Indianapolis, IN, May 18, 1876. Reprinted in *Chicago Tribune,* May 19, 1876.

145. Rumors that Grant would seek an unprecedented third term in office had begun just months after his 1873 inauguration, and by the end of 1874, politicians and newspapers around the country were openly debating it (Chernow 2017). For example, *Harper's Weekly,* November 7, 1874, published a Thomas Nast cartoon titled "The Third Term Panic," which depicted Republicans as an elephant stumbling into a pit, and Democrats as a braying donkey, the first usage of these now iconic party symbols (Halloran, 2012). Such rumors were a combination of tabloid journalism meant to drive up readership, fearmongering by Grant's opponents, and the sincere hopes of those Republicans who still saw Grant as their best chance for remaining in power and retaking the House. For who else could keep the fracturing party united, while attracting enough votes from even more divided Americans? However, others in the Republican Party worried that such a break in tradition would scare voters into third parties or the Democratic camp. Even Grant realized this risk. Therefore, in late May 1875, Grant penned an open letter mostly dismissing the idea of his renomination (USG, letter to Harry White, chair of the Pennsylvania Republican Convention, May 29, 1875, quoted in *New York Times,* May 31, 1875). However, Grant still defended the constitutionality of a third run. As a result, schemes to renominate him for president were floated in both 1880 and 1884, nearly succeeding in 1880 (Calhoun 2017).

146. *New York Herald,* June 17, 1876, quoted in Morris (2003: 99). However, there was a private kerfuffle when Hayes publicly declared that he intended to serve only a single term as president, an implicit insult to Grant, whom many had supported for a third term and who himself argued for its constitutionality (Holt 2008; Morris 2003).

147. These "voluntary" campaign contributions amounted to 1 percent of the appointee's salary, "for the laudible purpose of maintaining the organization of the republican party" as Grant put it (USG, letter to Hamilton Fish, July 2, 1875, in Simon 1995 26: 177).

148. Holt (2008: 149).

149. Shiller (2015).

150. Mitchell (1908: 332–333, Table 1).

151. *The Economist,* January 6, 1877.

152. USG, message to General Philip Sheridan, November 11, 1876, in Simon (1995 28: 37).

153. Grant's term formally ended on March 4. But being a Sunday, the inauguration ceremony for Hayes was not scheduled until Monday, March 5. To avoid the uncertainty of an interregnum, Grant invited Hayes to dine at the White House on the night of March 3 and had him quietly sworn in by the chief justice of the Supreme Court with several witnesses attending (Morris 2003).

154. The available data suggest that the ratio of private wealth to national income increased from 427 percent (1873) to 474 percent (1877), while private wealth to average disposable income jumped from 472 percent (1873) to 525 percent (1877). Each constituted a record not beat until the mid-1890s (Piketty and Zucman 2014).

155. Calhoun (2017: 4–5) argues that "many of those who raised allegations of corruption against his administration really aimed to discredit his methods of governing" because they were jealous of Grant's accomplishments or angry at their meager rewards or influence. Nevertheless, while much of this suspicion may have been the result of rumor, innuendo, and exaggeration by Grant's political enemies, it affected the public perception of the Grant administration and the federal government at the time.

156. Such as the Star Route scandal, in which federal postal contracting was discovered to be plagued by bribes and corruption.

157. Bryce (1888b: 653).

158. Mitchell (1908: 327, 333; supplemented by *HSUS*).

159. Smith (2001: 581); Scaturro (1998: 60).

160. Robbins (1994).

161. Calhoun (2017); McFeely (1981); Chernow (2017); Smith (2001).

162. Forty-eight vetoes in his first term, forty-five in his second term (*UCSB*).

163. The vast majority of Grant's vetoes were for bills of relief or pensions for named individuals. Of the four that were overridden, three bills provided relief or pensions to four individuals (one widow's pension, one tax rebate for two individuals, one absolving a Union soldier of desertion), and one bill allowed the sale of portions of reserved Indian tribal land.

164. *UCSB*. Admittedly, counts of executive orders and proclamations prior to the 1930s are incomplete, rendering their use in cross-presidency comparisons problematic (Mayer 2001).

165. Roughly 217 special messages in his first term and 125 in his second term (*UCSB*).

166. Milkis and Nelson (2019: 227).

167. Young (1879: 264–266).

168. Chernow (2017: 781).

169. Friedman and Schwartz (1967).

170. Unger (1964: 243).

171. Milkis and Nelson (2020: 227).

172. Goethals (2008).

173. *National Republican* (Washington, DC), October 28, 1874. This particular statement was made in response to rumors of his seeking a third term in office, but it also reflects Grant's attitude toward defamatory political gossip more generally.

174. Summers (1994).

175. Chernow (2017: 881).

Chapter 6

1. Unless otherwise indicated, all speeches, letters, and diary entries for Hayes are sourced from Rutherford B. Hayes Presidential Library and Museum Home, http://resources.ohiohistory.org/hayes/. See also Williams (1922).

2. Recall that the Tenure of Office Act of 1867 had mostly stripped the president of his power to dismiss federal appointees without the consent of the Senate. Congress had also passed a measure which limited the president's role as commander in chief. Specifically, it required that all military orders be issued through a commanding general who could be removed only by the Senate. Together, these acts gave Congress, or at least its leadership, tremendous influence over the executive branch and the military. Federal workers were now effectively appointed and fired by Congress, not the president, while the senior army commander answered to Congress, not the president. Even cabinet members were often drawn from Congress, supported by powerful factions there.

3. White (2017); Summers (2004); Cherny (1997).

4. Natural resources are broadly defined here to include agriculture (White 2017; Klein 2007; Shannon 1977).

5. Sadly, the drawdown of federal troops came at the expense of African Americans in the South, who were soon forced back into near slave status with few true political or economic rights. Others have argued that, *de facto*, Reconstruction had already ended throughout most of the South; Hayes simply ended it *de jure*. See Culbertson (2013); Palen (2014); Foner (2014).

6. One prominent example was the *Report concerning Civil Service in Great Britain*, written in 1879 by Dorman Eaton at Hayes's request. Eaton was a former member of the first US Civil Service Commission and later a central figure behind the Pendleton Act. The *Report* sold widely the following year as Eaton (1880). Scholars of the era have called it "the single most important piece of civil service reform propaganda" (Skowronek 1982: 48).

7. Morgan (1969: 8).

8. Though Hayes would play upon popular anti-Catholic fears in order to win elections (DeCanio 2005).

9. According to future president William McKinley, one of Hayes's enlisted men during the war (quoted in Bruce 1989: 86).

10. This was not his first elected office. In late 1858, Hayes was chosen by the Cincinnati City Council to serve as city solicitor. He was reelected the following spring and served a full two-year term (Hoogenboom 1988).

11. RBH, letter to his uncle Sardis Birchard, February 2, 1867, quoted in Culbertson (2016: 97).

12. Hoogenboom (1995); Culbertson (2016).

13. RBH, letter to his Uncle Sardis Birchard, March 7, 1869.

14. RBH, diary entry, March 16, 1871.

15. RBH, speech in Glendale, OH, September 4, 1872, quoted in Howard (1876: 129).

16. Hoogenboom (1995: 257).

17. RBH, diary entry, October 12, 1875. Though recent scholarship suggests that such sentiments were more artful pretense by an ambitious Hayes who was actually eager to break onto the national political stage (DeCanio 2015).

18. RBH, diary entry, September 13, 1873; Hoogenboom (1995); *Measuring Worth*, GDP Deflator.

19. Adams and Adams (1876: 441).
20. Sherman (1896: 452).
21. RBH, letter to Carl Schurz, August 9, 1876.
22. Samuel Tilden had a long and storied career in New York politics and law. As a teenager, he had campaigned for Democrat Andrew Jackson. Tilden served in the New York State Assembly during the 1840s, where he became a legislative leader. There he helped to break up New York's huge manorial estates that had existed since colonial times; he was also delegated to reform the New York state constitution. During the 1850s, he became strongly allied with antislavery Democrats and supported the Union during the Civil War, though as a strident critic of Lincoln. He then chaired the Democratic Party in New York from 1866 to 1874. He was also a conservative corporate attorney who had built up great personal wealth defending railroad corporations. Tilden's national fame, and his candidacy for president, sprang from his sudden and spectacular anticorruption campaign in New York City. He saw it as a way to compete with Republicans for votes and to save his own party from destruction. So, in late 1869, after years of working alongside the city's powerful Tammany Hall political machine, Tilden began to assail it, earning the nickname "Slippery Sam." Almost single-handedly at first, but with growing numbers of supporters, Tilden launched a campaign to topple Tammany and its infamous Boss Tweed. He exposed millions of dollars in fraudulent contracts, hidden payments and kickbacks, false overages, forged city documents, and a small army of corrupt judges and city officials. The media celebrated the public trials in which Boss Tweed and his top lieutenants were convicted of hundreds of felonies. As a result, in the 1871 state elections almost every Tammany Hall member was swept from office. Then, in the 1874 elections, Tilden was overwhelmingly voted governor of New York. He became national news, instantly positioning himself as the top Democratic candidate for president in 1876. His momentum increased when Governor Tilden further shocked the country by busting the "Canal Ring"—an Albany-based conspiracy of government contractors who for years had colluded with corrupt state and local officials to defraud New York taxpayers out of millions of dollars of canal funding. Thus, with only slim opposition from a few party rivals and old Tammany allies, the Democratic national convention, held in late June 1876, quickly nominated Tilden at the top of their ticket, with Indiana governor Thomas Hendricks as his vice president (Calhoun 2010; Holt 2008; Morris 2003).
23. In fact, despite his shortcomings and treatment by the press, Grant himself remained enormously popular with the American public.
24. "Republican Party Platform," June 14, 1876, *UCSB*.
25. "Democratic Party Platform," June 22, 1876, *UCSB*.
26. RBH, letter of acceptance of the Republican nomination for president, July 8, 1876).
27. *New York Times*, July 10, 1876.
28. George William Curtis, civil service reform leader, letter to RBH, July 13, 1876, quoted in Hoogenboom (1995: 266).
29. Holt (2008); Morris (2003); Haworth (1927).

30. Although Tilden, the Democratic nominee, needed just one electoral vote to win, his party suffered from irreconcilable divides. Southerners demanded federal subsidies, especially to fund new railroads. In contrast, Northerners, like Tilden himself, sought to rein in government spending on industry and corporate subsidies. As result, many Southerners abandoned Tilden for the more pro-development agenda of the Republican platform. They sought a federal government large enough to resuscitate and modernize the Southern economy, yet simultaneously too weak to prevent them from reestablishing white rule in the South. Southern Democrats believed Hayes would support industrialization more strongly than Tilden. Hence they could trade their support for patronage and "benign" neglect in racial matters (Miller 2019).

31. Albert Maher, letter to Samuel J. Tilden, February 20, 1877, quoted in Holt (2008: 242); Congressman Abram S. Hewitt (D-NY), DNC chair, letter to the National Democratic Committee, March 3, 1877, reprinted in Bigelow (1908: 511). Others argued that the recentness of the Civil War, and the near complete withdrawal of Union forces from the South, provided a powerful disincentive against civil violence. See, for example, Hoar (1903b).

32. Williams (1928: 1–2).

33. Hayes did not participate personally in the "compromise" meetings. Rather the Republican delegates appear to have made these promises on his behalf. Hayes subsequently removed federal troops from the state house lawns in South Carolina and Louisiana, thereby ending the Republican governorships in these states. But there was no general outflow of troops from the South, where they were already thinly spread and of little use for enforcing civil rights. Nor was much legislation in support of Southern industrialization forthcoming (Foner 2005; Culbertson 2013, 2016).

34. *The Sun* (New York), March 3, 1877.

35. *The Sun* (New York), March 3, 1877.

36. Although Hayes wrote no lengthy tracts or led much on national economic issues before he became president, his political-economic principles are well outlined and repeated in his diary, letters, and speeches, stretching across almost sixty years of his life. These same themes are corroborated by his words and actions as Whig and Republican Party member, congressman, governor of Ohio, president, and into his post-presidency.

37. Holt (1999); Bernard (1990); Howe (1979).

38. Mccoy (1980); Bernard (1990).

39. To Whigs, repayment in printed paper money or inflated silver of a debt initially transacted in gold was a form of theft and dishonesty (Holt 1999; Howe 1979).

40. "Whig Party Platform," June 7, 1848, *UCSB*.

41. At the Whig Party's ideological foundation lay a now forgotten liberal, evangelical Christian postmillennialism which originated in the Second Great Awakening (c. 1790–1840). These doctrines held that Christ would return to Earth only after a golden "Millennium" during which Christian society prospered. For many American Protestants of this time, the driving idea became that they must better themselves, and their country, in order to gain God's grace and hasten the arrival of Christ. That is, Americans should not await the Millennium but were destined to create it themselves

in the United States. Recent advances in American democracy, law, science, technology, and industry were each interpreted as signs of a divine plan and America's special place in it. Scientists, inventors, innovators, and even investors during the mid-1800s regularly spoke of themselves as divine agents, working to create a Christian democratic republic and bring forward the day when Christ would reign. So too were American military victories and geographic expansion widely interpreted as signs of "manifest destiny." In contrast, lawlessness, violence, corruption, alcoholism, intellectual and economic stagnation, and demagoguery were signs of decline. The Whig Party became the political manifestation of and vehicle for many of those evangelical Christians, like young Hayes, who sought to influence public policy (Holt 1999; Howe 1979, 2007).

42. *American Review* (1849): 443.

43. RBH, diary entry, September 6, 1841.

44. RBH, speech delivered at Marion, Lawrence County, OH, July 31, 1875.

45. RBH, letter to Uncle Austin Birchard, April 21, 1874.

46. RBH, letter accepting the Republican Party nomination, Columbus, OH, July 8, 1876. See also RBH, speech in Marion, OH, July 31, 1875. Similar statements by Hayes can be found throughout his life.

47. Hayes was so consistently dedicated to hard money that, by June 1876, he was telling Republican ally Carl Schurz, "I do not expect to say anything on the specie resumption plank. I am so pronounced and well known on that question that I feel like saying, that the man who wants other interpretation of our platform . . . is pretty likely to vote against me [anyway]" (RBH, letter to Carl Schurz, June 27, 1876). As president, he wrote in his diary "[I]n my opinion, (1) [greenbacks] are not, in time of peace, a constitutional currency, and (2) they are a dangerous currency, depending as they do wholly on congressional discretion as to their amount, their issue, and all of their functions" (RBH, diary entry, July 24, 1879).

48. RBH, diary entry, November 5, 1877.

49. During his post-presidency, Hayes became far more progressive. He attacked the "giant evil and danger" of economic inequality and called for redistributive "changes in the laws regulating corporations, descents of property, wills, trusts, taxation" (RBH, diary entry, December 4, 1887).

50. RBH, speech in Columbus, OH, on the Stark and Wayne Country mining strikes, April 19, 1876.

51. RBH, letter to George Curtis, editor, *Harper's Weekly*, March 1875, quoted in Hoogenboom (1988: 142).

52. RBH, letter accepting the Republican Party nomination, Columbus, OH, July 8, 1876.

53. RBH, letter to Guy Bryan, Texas politician and former classmate, July 11, 1855, quoted in Culbertson (2016: 41).

54. Speculation during 1874–1875 that Grant would seek a third term had sparked a national backlash, which Hayes and the Republicans sought to diffuse, even though it risked insulting the still widely esteemed Grant. Grant rejected the invitation to run again, but he defended the legality of a third term, stating that unless the Constitution was amended, "the people cannot be restricted in their choice." This led critics to fret

about the rise of "Caesarism" in the United States (RBH, inaugural address, March 5, 1877, *UCSB*; Eschner 2017; USG, letter to Harry White, chair of the Pennsylvania Republican Convention, May 29, 1875, quoted in *New York Times,* May 31, 1875; Klinghard 2010; Calhoun 2017).

55. A single term also increased Hayes's power over civil service reform, freeing him from the need to kowtow to Congress over patronage in return for their political support in 1880 (RBH, letter accepting the Republican Party nomination, Columbus, OH, July 8, 1876).

56. Ellis (2008).

57. RBH, diary entry, August 26, 1877.

58. To satisfy his wife, the temperance community, and the growing Prohibition Party, Hayes infamously avoided serving alcohol while in office, but he usually compensated with lavish spreads of food (Culbertson 2016; Hoogenboom 1995).

59. RBH, diary entry, January 16, 1881.

60. "A War with the Tramps," *Georgia Weekly Telegraph,* September 18, 1877, quoted in Bellesiles (2010: 113).

61. Friedman and Schwartz (1963) argue that "accidents of weather . . . produced two successive years of bumper crops in the United States and unusually short crops elsewhere . . . [which] led to a large inflow of gold." In other words, favorable rain patterns led, via agriculture supply and demand, to a monetary expansion that caused the Hayes economic boom. However, the data do not correlate well with the strong version of this hypothesis. The American wheat supply surge occurred in 1877–1880, at least a year before the Hayes boom commenced, while poor crops in Europe began as early as 1873 (with a particularly bad harvest in 1879) and ended by 1880. Also, US wheat prices peaked in May 1877 at over 158 cents per bushel, then plummeted over 50 percent (to 82 cents) through November 1878, then recovered to 127 cents per bushel by the following winter, after which they fell again to 80 cents by August 1880. For comparison, the average price for wheat during 1874–1884 was 105 cents, while the average during the Hayes boom (1878–1881) was 99 cents. In sum, the fortunes of agriculture did contribute to the Hayes boom, but they were not alone (Veblen 1892; supplemented by *NBER Macro*).

62. Taxes on alcohol and tobacco then constituted around 90 percent of federal internal (i.e., nontariff) tax revenues.

63. Goodwin (2005).

64. Trefousse (2002).

65. *Chicago Daily Tribune,* March 11, 1877.

66. Of the roughly twenty-five thousand soldiers in the US Army in 1877, most were stationed out west to defend against and subjugate Native Americans, or to guard the still perilous border with Mexico. Only around three thousand were used in what we might term "occupation" or Reconstruction duties in the ex-Confederate South.

67. Quoted in Foner (2014: 245).

68. Radical Republican and former US senator Benjamin F. Wade, 1877, quoted in Hoogenboom (1995: 315); Alexander H. Stevens, former vice president of the Confederate States of America, quoted in *Atlanta Constitution,* April 13, 1877.

69. Hoogenboom (1988).
70. Hoogenboom (1961, 2014).
71. RBH, inaugural address, March 5, 1877, *UCSB*.
72. Klinghard (2010).
73. *New York Times,* March 8, 1877.
74. Headed by John Jay, grandson of the first US chief justice and an eminent New York jurist in his own right. Long an antislavery activist, Jay had helped found the Republican Party and served President Grant as the US minister to Austria-Hungary (1869–1875).
75. Hoogenboom (1988: 132).
76. John Sherman, US Treasury secretary, quoted and paraphrased in *New York Times,* April 18, 1877.
77. RBH, "Executive Order" (directed at Treasury Secretary John Sherman), May 26, 1877, *UCSB*.
78. Ex-president Ulysses S. Grant, an enthusiastic spoilsman, lambasted Hayes for his "Utopian ideas . . . of running a government without a party" (quoted in Calhoun 2017: 83).
79. Hayes put it this way: "The end I have chiefly aimed at has been to break down congressional patronage, and especially Senatorial patronage. . . . It has seemed to me that as Executive I could advance the reform of the civil service in no way so effectively as by rescuing the power of appointing to office from the congressional leaders" (RBH, diary entry, July 14, 1880).
80. For general treatments, see Robbins (1994); Strom (2003); Barber (2004); White (2011); Kornblith and Zakim (2011); Brands (2019).
81. US Census Bureau (1883: Table I).
82. For example, the Timber and Stone Act of 1878 authorized sales of valuable timber and stone lands in the far west, while the Timber Cutting Act of 1878 allowed timbering on federal lands without charge, if used for domestic purposes (rather than exports). On the role of geological surveys, see Bartlett (1962).
83. Schoultz (1998).
84. Some of these lands were less "ancestral" than others. For example, the nomadic tribes on the Great Plains relied on horses, which had been introduced by Europeans. Once mounted, these Native Americans pursued the great buffalo herds, creating a new horseback culture during the mid-1700s and reaching its zenith during the 1830s (Utley 2003).
85. *New York Times,* July 2, 15, 1877.
86. *New York Times,* August 14, 1877.
87. Countless smaller clashes occurred sporadically, particularly in Arizona. Also, Hayes did not seek genocide or expulsion, but pacification and forced assimilation. He defended the civilian management of Indian affairs against the War Department's assertion of control. His administration also worked to increase funding and reduce corruption in the federal treatment of Native Americans (Hoogenboom 1988; Danziger 2007).
88. Foner (1977); Bruce (1989); Stowell (2008).

89. Quoted in Bellesiles (2010: 147, 149).
90. Foner (1977); Bruce (1989); Stowell (2008); Davin (2014).
91. John W. Garrett, telegram to RBH, July 18, 1877, quoted in Brands (2010: 122).
92. *Martinsburg Statesman,* July 17, 1877, quoted in Bellesiles (2010: 149).
93. *National Labor Tribune,* quoted in Foner (1977: 58).
94. Stowell (2008: 2).
95. Quoted in Bellesiles (2010: 150–151).
96. Davin (2014).
97. *Missouri Republican,* July 23, 1877, quoted in Foner (1977: 66).
98. Davin (2014).
99. Foner (1977).
100. And he thought that education and regulation, rather than force, were the real remedies (RBH, interview with the *National Republican,* July 23, 1877, quoted in Hoogenboom 1995: 331; RBH, diary entry, August 5, 1877).
101. RBH, 1877, quoted in Hoogenboom (1988: 86).
102. Davin (2014: 452). A similar conclusion is reached by Oestreicher (1988: 1260).
103. *Washington National Republican,* August 4, 1877, quoted in Bellesiles (2010: 144).
104. Though others argue that the United States never had the raw materials (e.g., a peasant class, inherited aristocracy, limited agricultural land) for a mass Communist movement or Socialist revolution. See Lipset and Marks (2000).
105. A strike injunction is a court order, issued by a federal judge, that prohibits an individual or a labor union or other type of organization from engaging in strike-related activities.
106. Foner (1977: 196).
107. Beatty (2007: 292); Stewart and Townsend (1966). In order to deter future riots and speed the government response, Hayes also supported a new movement to build state armories in cities around the country, many of which still stand today (Fogelson 1989).
108. Grant's defense of the financial system and strong dedication to the gold standard after the Panic of 1873 had reassured investors that American debts would not be inflated away. Thus, after the initial crash, interest rates had gradually dropped below pre-crisis levels, despite the fact that the US economy was still stuck in recession in 1877.
109. The Resumption Act of 1875 may have set the date for the free convertibility of greenbacks into gold, but it had not created a mechanism by which to achieve it. It fell to Hayes and his Treasury to make it happen. And that date for gold "resumption" or "redemption" was looming fast—January 1, 1879.
110. *The Economist,* July 28, 1877.
111. Also, although the Grant administration had made considerable progress toward gold-greenback parity by "growing the economy towards specie," when Hayes was inaugurated greenbacks still remained around 5 percent cheaper than gold, and their price regularly fluctuated by 1 to 2 percentage points each month (Mitchell 1908). For estimates of greenbacks in circulation: in its annual reports, the US Treasury reported $367,535,716 notes in circulation in June 1876 and $351,340,288

in June 1877. The most recent HSUS puts the 1877 figure at $338 million (where the term "in circulation" refers to currency held outside the US Treasury) (US Treasury 1876: xv; 1877: xii).

112. Hoogenboom (1988).
113. At the time, silver currency had fallen into disuse; also, the backers of the Coinage Act of 1873 sought to eliminate it entirely and move the United States toward the international gold standard. Hence there was little congressional debate over or public opposition to these aspects of the 1873 bill. See Weinstein (1967); Silber (2019).
114. Key trade and investment partners Great Britain and Canada had been on the gold standard for decades. And Germany's declaration for gold in 1871 had triggered a wave of gold adoptions throughout western Europe (Eichengreen and Flandreau 1994).
115. The Bland-Allison Act also created a new federal currency: the silver certificate. These were not legal tender for private transactions but could be used to pay federal taxes and tariffs.
116. An Act to Authorize the Coinage of the Standard Silver Dollar, and to Restore Its Legal-Tender Character, 1878 (February 28).
117. RBH, "First Annual Message to Congress," December 3, 1877, *UCSB*.
118. Hoogenboom (1988, 1995).
119. Even more than the vote to override Grant's veto of the Inflation Act of 1874, the 1878 override was based almost entirely on region rather than party or ideology. From New England and New York, home to the nation's bankers, only ten House members voted to override Hayes's veto, while *all* the region's senators supported Hayes. The override votes came from the West and South, where only seven House members and four senators supported Hayes's veto (Poole and Rosenthal 2007).
120. *Measuring Worth,* proportion of GDP.
121. Previously, the US Treasury had been instructed by the Resumption Act of 1875 to redeem federal notes in excess of $300 million in circulation. Therefore, some financial conservatives interpreted the new legislation as an attempt to thwart the resumption of gold-greenback parity in January 1879 (*New York Times,* June 2, 1878; An Act to Forbid the Further Retirement of United States Legal-Tender Notes, May 31, 1878; US Treasury 1878: ix).
122. Bruce (1989); Nevins (1927: 304). See also Bellesiles (2010)
123. *The Sun* (New York), January 1, 1878.
124. An Act to Authorize the Coinage of the Standard Silver Dollar, and to Restore Its Legal-Tender Character, 1878 (February 28).
125. Reti (1998: 65).
126. Austria-Hungary, Belgium, France, Great Britain, Greece, Italy, the Netherlands, Russia, Sweden and Norway, Switzerland, and the United States.
127. To most observers, however, the results of the conference were unsurprising. The steady march of the world toward gold had proceeded apace since the previous such conference, in summer 1867. Great Britain, Germany, Canada, and most Nordic nations were already on gold, and they had been joined by the Netherlands (1875) and Finland (1877); large parts of Latin America were also on gold (Argentina,

Uruguay, Colombia) and even Indonesia (1877) had joined (Eichengreen and Flandreau 1994).

128. In creating such a large reserve, Sherman also increased the Treasury's (and hence the president's) power over monetary policy and its role as a quasi-central bank (McCulley 1992).

129. *Commercial and Financial Chronicle,* April 13, 1878.

130. Unger (1964).

131. The majority of it going into a new railroad construction boom (Wilkins 1989: 147, Table 5.4).

132. Trading volumes on the nation's stock markets and the number of firms listed also recovered starting in 1878 (O'Sullivan (2016: 29; supplemented by *NBER Macro*).

133. RBH, speech in Toledo, OH, September 19, 1878.

134. RBH, speech in Madison, WI, September 4, 1878.

135. *The Economist,* July 27, 1878.

136. Dalzell (1987); Bracha (2016).

137. RBH, diary entry, March 18, 1878.

138. Weaver (1987). Sherman was not a "hard money" zealot. He had favored the greenback during much of the 1860s. He had even supported various inflationary schemes during the late 1860s in an effort to defeat the Democrats in Ohio. But under President Grant, he became the author, and political champion, of major pro-gold legislation, including the Resumption Act, which some called the "Sherman Financial Bill." So, although militant gold bugs considered him unreliable, "the more practical conservatives . . . [considered him] an augury of safe and steady progress toward resumption" (Unger 1964: 323).

139. Though Sherman's desire to appease Republican silverites also led him to occasional gaffes that damaged confidence in the administration's dedication to achieving strict gold-greenback parity (Unger 1964).

140. RBH, letter to John Sherman, March 6, 1881.

141. RBH, letter to General Edwin A. Merritt, February 4, 1879.

142. Ritter (1997); Unger (1964).

143. In addition to one Independent, but likely Greenback supporter, in the US Senate (David Davis, I-IL). Still other supporters of paper currency remained as Democrats or Republicans but declared allegiance to the Greenback caucus on monetary issues. Formal Greenback candidates were elected to the House from Iowa, Maine, Pennsylvania, Alabama, Illinois, Indiana, Missouri, North Carolina, Texas, and Vermont (Martis, Rowles, and Pauer 1989).

144. Timberlake (1993).

145. Timberlake (1975). Contemporary accounts estimated $346,681,016 in federal legal tender notes (all issues). See, for example, *New York Times,* January 1, 1879. But more recent analysis suggests that the number of greenbacks in circulation (i.e., outside the US Treasury) was in the range of $300 million to $320 million.

146. Though Secretary Sherman was often the source of these rumors, thanks to his fear of alienating Republican silver interests or unnecessarily antagonizing greenbackers (Unger 1964).

147. *Chicago Tribune,* November 15, 1878.

148. Unger (1964).

149. Skocpol (1993); Glasson (1900); *Measuring Worth,* GDP Deflator.

150. *New York Times,* April 30, 1879.

151. Allen (1879: 198).

152. Allen (1879: 198).

153. RBH, memo to William Henry Smith, Ohio politician, political ally, and reformer, May 25, 1879, quoted in Hoogenboom (1995: 402–403).

154. Namely Grant's politically disastrous attempt to annex Santo Domingo (Dominican Republic), as well as his failure to establish a naval base on Samoa or to get traction on a trans-isthmus canal (Calhoun 2017).

155. Hayes was likely also dissuaded by the tortured passage of the Alaska acquisition treaty, and the subsequent corruption associated with it, ten years earlier (Zakaria 1998).

156. Pletcher (1998); Dyer (1933); Barrows (1941).

157. The Page Law of 1875 had placed a federal ban on Chinese contract labor and a *de facto* end to the immigration of Chinese women, thereby obstructing the formation of Chinese families in the United States (Chan 1984).

158. RBH, diary entry, February 20, 1879.

159. In exchange for prohibitions on trade in opium in China, the United States was allowed to supervise, limit, or even suspend the immigration of Chinese workers.

160. RBH, "Third Annual Message to Congress," December 1, 1879, *UCSB.*

161. RBH, 1880, letter to Guy Bryan, quoted in Trefousse (2002: 118–119).

162. RBH, speech in St. Joseph, MO, September 1879, quoted in Hoogenboom (1995: 410).

163. Ellis (2008).

164. *New York Times,* October 3, 1880.

165. *San Jose* (CA) *Times,* September 15, 1880, quoted in Ellis (2008: 103).

166. Arrington (2020).

167. Otherwise, Hayes spent much of his final legislative session dealing with minor issues, such as the trans-isthmus canal, racial animus at West Point, and polygamy legislation.

168. John Jay Knox, testimony to the Senate Finance Committee, January 25, 1881, quoted in Knox (1900: 167–168); Laughlin (1882); *School Herald,* February 1, 1882.

169. RBH, "Veto Message," March 3, 1881, *UCSB.*

170. Bank of England (2021).

171. Ratio of private wealth to national income (the ratio of private wealth to average disposable income went from 525 percent [1877] to 466 percent [1881]). The average for the Gilded Age was 454 percent, with a minimum of 417 percent (1882) and maximum of 509 percent (1894) (Piketty and Zucman 2014).

172. *New York Times,* March 2, 1881.

173. RBH, diary entry, January 23, 1881.

174. Grant not only departed Washington after his presidency; in May 1877 he departed the United States for a two-year-and-four-month trip around the world (Young 1879).

175. This is not an endorsement of fixed exchange rates or zero-inflation policy. For example, had Hayes taken a similar stance five decades later, his inflexibility on gold would likely have produced the same dire consequences as it did for Herbert Hoover.
176. Engerman and Gallman (2000: passim).
177. *The Sun* (New York), June 17, 1876.
178. In trade, monetary policy, fiscal matters, and western development, Hayes's presidency might even be described as the third term of the Grant administration.

Interlude

1. Having surpassed Great Britain during the early 1870s. If US wealth is set at 100 in 1880, it was followed by the United Kingdom (96), Belgium (78), Netherlands (75), Switzerland (62), Denmark (56), France (54), Germany (51), Canada (46), Italy (45), and Spain (40).
2. This constituted growth of over 85 percent in rail mileage and 319 percent in telegraph traffic since 1870.
3. White (1993).
4. Most heavily in California, Oregon, Nevada, Idaho, and Washington.
5. During the late 1870s and early 1880s, heavy downpours east of the Mississippi River, and a perceived rise in the Great Salt Lake following the nearby Mormon settlements, seemed to buttress such claims. These rumors were formalized and spread via the widely discussed book *Mission of the North American People, Geographical, Social, and Political*, written by William Gilpin (1873). See also Smith (1947); Mock (2000). Numbers are for migration to states west of the Mississippi River during the years 1870–1880. Over half the migrants went to Kansas, Texas, Nebraska, Minnesota, or California.
6. Just twenty years earlier, in 1860, over 56 percent of Americans had been farmers, while under 14 percent were industrial labor.
7. As a proportion of total economic output, the United Kingdom dominated with 40 percent of GDP in industry, followed by France (35 percent) and Germany (33 percent). Even tiny Denmark still had greater industrial concentration than the United States (20 percent vs. 18.7 percent).
8. US Census Office (1885: 1633–1656).
9. Average US life expectancy in 1880 was 39.7 years, the lowest peacetime lifespan since perhaps 1850, though partly due to high infant and toddler mortality.
10. Wright (1986).
11. The United States was a major producer of corn, wheat, oats, and, to a lesser extent, potatoes and barley.
12. The railroads, telegraphs, and new telephone systems made cities the most profitable locations in which to concentrate industry and commerce. The switch from water power to steam power also allowed factories and merchants to relocate closer

to urban ports and transshipment points. And as these fast-growing industries clustered in urban areas, new residents streamed in from both the countryside and overseas in search of work.

13. Measures and definitions of urbanization differ. The *HSUS* puts the urban population at 26.3 percent in 1880. Using this as a base, urbanization may have been around 23 percent in 1870, 17 percent in 1860.

14. The New York City tabulation includes Brooklyn, although it was legally a separate entity at the time. In 1880, Philadelphia was still the nation's "second city," with just under 850,000 residents, followed by Chicago (503,000), St. Louis (351,000), Baltimore (332,000), and Cincinnati (255,000). No other US cities had populations above 250,000. Only fifteen others had breached 50,000. Of these, Pittsburgh and San Francisco were each around 235,000; Washington DC, Cleveland, Buffalo, Louisville, Detroit, and Milwaukee were all over 115,000; next were Albany, Rochester, Indianapolis, Kansas City (MO), Columbus, Syracuse, and Toledo, which had each risen to between 50,000 to 90,000 (Mitchell 2003b).

15. White (2017); Hanlon (2015).

16. Ogle (1996: 4).

17. Duffy (1992).

18. Beard (1881: 1).

19. Drache (1964); Hammer (1979); Robbins (1994); Strom (2003).

20. Specifically the Red River Valley.

21. Hammer (1979).

22. Drache (1964: 13, Table 5); Hammer (1979).

23. Robbins (1994: 73).

24. Olmstead and Rhode (1988).

25. Wolf (1982: 319).

26. "One chief danger they saw in the surplus was the implicit temptation to indulge in extravagance and wasteful spending of the people's money, much of which ought not to have been collected in the first place" (Calhoun 2008: 16–18).

27. *Atlantic Monthly,* December 1879.

28. *New York Times,* December 16 1879.

29. Nitschke (2018: 233).

30. Nelson (2011).

31. Chandler (1977); Hounshell (1984); Kornblith and Zakim (2011); Perrow (2002).

32. Up from 2.9 percent in 1870 (Edwards 1934). Charles Morris (2005: 167) is more generous, arguing, "Between 1870 and 1880, the number of clerks and copyists in offices quadrupled, the number of bookkeepers and accountants doubled, insurance office staffs doubled, bank and railroad office staffs nearly doubled, and the number of commercial travelers quadrupled. Clerical workers were overwhelmingly male. While entry pay was often very low, advancement could be rapid."

33. Morris (2005); Porter (2006b).

34. Standard Oil was originally founded in 1870 by Rockefeller in Cleveland, Ohio. He merged his disparate, multistate operations into a single "trust" in 1882.

35. The term "robber baron" had been around for decades, but during the 1880s it was increasingly applied to the great industrialists and their bankers (Tipple 1959). For a general treatment of the evolution of monopolies, see Geisst (2000); Perrow (2002).

36. US rail freight rose from around 9 billion ton-miles (1870) to over 32 billion ton-miles (1880). Due to safety issues and delays (e.g., transshipment, congestion, maintenance, accidents), fast freight travel during the early 1870s averaged around five miles per hour and often slowed to only around one mile per hour. By 1880, most average fast freight speeds remained around five to six miles per hour, though on some routes trains could average thirteen to fourteen, while slow rates had improved to two to three miles per hour (White 1993).

37. In particular, the Miller automatic coupler (on some lines, called the "knuckle" coupler) replaced dangerous and time-consuming link-and-pin coupling. The new systems allowed railcars to be joined by simply pushing them together, and then separated with a platform lever. The new couplers also employed a buffer, which prevented fatal telescoping in railroad collisions (Clark 1972).

38. The pioneer in mass mail-order retail was Aaron Montgomery Ward of Chicago. Ward did not invent mail-order catalogues—Tiffany's 1845 *Blue Book* of exquisite gems and jewelry may have been first—but his discount prices and wide-ranging inventory became the model to emulate for decades. For while many retailers offered specialized purchases by mail, Ward was the first to offer a general catalogue. His first, sent out in 1872, was a single-page price list of 163 clothing and household items. It originally catered to growing urban markets and rural cooperatives. Within ten years, the Ward catalogue numbered over 240 pages, filled with pictures for over ten thousand items, and was distributed all over the country (Morris 2005: 174; Cherry 2008).

39. White (1993).

40. Veenendaal (2002); Arnold (2014); Usselman (2002).

41. The "Big Four" consisted of the California merchants Leland Stanford, Collis Huntington, Mark Hopkins, and Charles Crocker (Rayner 2009).

42. Arnold (2014: 16–17).

43. On the NYSE, formal listing requirements also played a role in the railroads' dominance. The NYSE's conservatism "precluded it from admitting issuers other than the largest and most well-established companies and, at that time, such companies in the United State tended to be railroads" (O'Sullivan 2007: 495).

44. Utilities comprised just 5 percent of the remaining bonds, with only two industrial firms offering debentures on the NYSE. On the stock market, the railroads were followed by mines (18 percent of firms listed on the NYSE), industrials and miscellaneous (18 percent), and utilities (5 percent) (O'Sullivan 2016: 29).

45. *New York Times*, 1880, passim.

46. Wilkins (1989: 147).

47. Chandler (1977).

48. When informal pools proved inadequate to control their members' activities, the railroad corporations resorted to formal federations to coordinate activities between them, complete with executive, legislative, and judicial functions. However, the

ultimate solution was either merger or predation so as to reduce or eliminate competition (Chandler 1977).

49. In 1870, Illinois even revised its constitution to give the state government power to regulate railroads and grain elevators, including rate-setting authority.

50. One railroad vice president declared, "I ... deny the right of the Legislature in any way to interfere with [the railroad's] property and franchises," while others insisted that any state regulations were "unconstitutional and a violation of vested rights, and not applicable to this corporation" (Cordery 2016: 74).

51. Iowa, Wisconsin, Nebraska, Kansas, Missouri, Georgia, and California also passed railroad regulations during the 1870s (Porter 2006a: 21–22; McCraw (1984).

52. *Peik v. Chicago & Northwestern Railway Company,* 94 U.S. 164 (1876); *Chicago, Burlington & Quincy Railroad Company v. Iowa,* 94 U.S. 155 (1876); *Munn v. Illinois,* 94 U.S. 113 (1876).

53. Geisst (2000); Perrow (2002).

54. Petroleum did not compete with coal as a major energy source during the Gilded Age. The commercial use of oil in the United States began with the 1859 discoveries at Titusville, Pennsylvania. In subsequent years, it gradually replaced whale fat as lamp fuel or was used as an industrial lubricant. Only with the appearance of automobiles and the internal combustion engine during the early 20th century did petroleum find large markets. Even then, petroleum and natural gas would not surpass coal as an energy source until World War II (Yergin 2008).

55. MacFarlane (1873: 1); Lesley (1886).

56. During the 1870s, the nation's output of bituminous coal skyrocketed 247 percent, while anthracite production increased 43 percent.

57. Long (1989: 107).

58. Technological backwardness persisted in American coal mining into the 1930s. As historian Keith Dix (1988: 1) wrote, "[T]he advance in technology and management, which gave modern industry is momentum, bypassed the one industry on which most others depended."

59. Sanders (1999: 105–106); Buck (1913: 60–62). Cochrane (1993: 95) puts peak Grange membership at 1.5 million in 1874.

60. Reuben A. Riley, quoted in *Chicago Tribune,* November 26, 1874.

61. *Shelby County Herald* (Shelbyville, MO), January 27, 1875.

62. *New York Times,* March 13, 1875.

63. Unger (1964); Ritter (1997).

64. Greenback candidates were elected to the House from Iowa, Maine, Pennsylvania, Alabama, Illinois, Indiana, Missouri, North Carolina, Texas, and Vermont, in addition to one likely Greenback supporter in the US Senate (David Davis, I-IL) (Martis, Rowles, and Pauer 1989).

65. National Greenback-Labor Party Platform of 1880, quoted in *New York Times,* June 11, 1880.

66. Nordin (1974).

67. *HSUS* estimate. Calavita (1984) puts immigration at 790,000, or 14.9 immigrants per 1,000 residents in 1882.

68. Klein (2012).
69. Calavita (1984).
70. This began soon after the Civil War, when American businessmen began to link immigrants to labor strife in the growing US industrial sector. The Paris Commune of 1871, in particular, frightened and alerted Americans to the latent power of wage laborers. Thus, when the Great Strike of 1877 erupted, employers across the country were long accustomed to blaming labor unrest on foreign agitators (Zeidel 2020).
71. For example, *Chy Lung v. Freeman* (1875) held that California's bond requirements on immigration infringed upon the federal government's authority to conduct foreign affairs. *Henderson v. Mayor of New York* (1876) held that New York's immigration policy violated federal control over international commerce. In the *Head Money Cases* (1884), the Supreme Court then affirmed federal authority to regulate immigration by approving a federal head tax on ship owners to pay for federal immigration aid and services (Parker 2015).
72. Castle Garden had served as America's busiest immigration hub since it opened in early August 1855. When it closed in 1890, over 8 million arrivals had been processed there, roughly two-thirds of all US immigrants (Parker 2015).
73. Calculated using the relative cost of unskilled labor. In comparison, a simple consumer price index measure would make the equivalent around $13 in 2020 (*Measuring Worth*).
74. Statutes at Large (22 Stat. 58, Chap. 126). Official Title: An act to execute certain treaty stipulations relating to Chinese
75. *People v. Compagnie Generale Transatlantique*, 107 U.S. 59 (1883), in which the city and county of New York sought, unsuccessfully, to recover arrival taxes on immigrants levied by an 1881 statute. This judgment was reinforced by the *Head Money Cases*, 112 U.S. 580 (1884) decision, wherein the Supreme Court held that Congress had "the power to pass a law regulating immigration as a part of the commerce of this country with foreign nations," thus overriding state immigration policies.
76. This was another federal adoption of state laws. In 1878, a California court held that Chinese immigrants could not naturalize because they were of the "Mongolian race" (Parker 2015).
77. Parker (2015).
78. An Act to Prohibit the Coming of Chinese Persons into the United States (a.k.a. Geary Act), 1892 (May 5).
79. Lee (2003).
80. Parker (2015).
81. The Statue of Liberty was first proposed in 1865 by French liberals inspired by the abolition of American slavery. Her spiked crown suggests the sun's rays radiating freedom. Her tablet is inscribed with the date of America's independence. A broken shackle and chains at her feet symbolizes the abolition of slavery. Emma Lazarus's poem "The New Colossus" (1883), written to raise money for the pedestal, was later cast into bronze and mounted at the base. But the monument took decades to fund and erect. Construction of the statue was completed, in France, only in July 1884; the pedestal in New York took another two years. Meanwhile, the statue was broken

down into 350 components and shipped across the Atlantic. Final reassembly was not completed until October 1886, when President Grover Cleveland formally dedicated it in front of an admiring crowd.

82. America's Great Migrations Project, supplemented by *HSUS*.

83. Jaques (1889: 361).

84. Many traveling to settle in Kansas (Parker 2015; America's Great Migrations Project).

85. As might be expected, the most successful African Americans of the Gilded Age lived outside of the South.

86. Especially the *Slaughterhouse Cases*, 83 U.S. 36 (1872); *United States v. Cruikshank*, 92 U.S. 542 (1875); and *United States v. Reese*, 92 U.S. 214 (1875). In these opinions, the Supreme Court held that the Constitution protected those rights "which owe their existence to the Federal government" against deprivation by the *federal* government, but not by state governments or private actors. These guaranteed federal rights included such activities as interstate commerce, candidacy for federal office, and activities on the high seas. However, those rights provided by state and local governments (e.g., business regulation, labor laws, criminal codes) were *not* protected. Nor did the Constitution guard Blacks against predation by *private* individuals. Finally, the Court decided that state governments could legally determine which citizens were qualified to vote and how elections would be conducted, so long as they did not explicitly discriminate by race. These judgments removed the legal justification for presidents to use federal troops to enforce the Fourteenth and Fifteenth Amendments in many cases, and severely damaged the political will to do so in others (Goldman 2001; Kousser 1974).

87. For example, Blacks continued to vote in many parts of the South during the 1880s. There was violence against them, but African Americans still held political office. Civil rights laws remained on the books. The 1875 Civil Rights Act theoretically mandated equal treatment in public facilities, though it was little enforced and the Supreme Court declared it unconstitutional in 1883. Nevertheless, white Southern Democrats began to take back their states one by one and legally push Blacks back toward near-servitude. The "Jim Crow" era was a period during which rigid anti-Black laws (poll taxes, literacy tests, grandfather clauses, antivagrancy laws, and other restrictions) and fiscal policy denied African Americas their civil rights, civil liberties, and basic public goods and government services, making them second-class citizens. It lasted until the civil rights movement of the 1950s–1960s.

88. These trends would accelerate during the 1890s (Hilkey 1997; Gorn and Goldstein 2004). The popularization of recreational camping during the 1870s is credited to Murray (1869).

89. Comstock (1883: 242).

90. Beisel (1998); Werbel (2018).

91. In an attempt to attract more female settlers, Wyoming's territorial government expanded voting rights to women in 1869. In Utah, since female suffragists defended polygamy, the Territory enacted women's voting rights in 1870 to enlarge support for the Mormon church (Enss 2020).

92. McCurry (2019).

93. Other important participants in the women's rights movement during this time were Jane Addams, Leonora Barry, Charlotte Hawkins Brown, Florence Kelley, Julia Ward Howe, Lucy Craft Laney, Mary Elizabeth Lease, Anna Garlin Spencer, Ellen Gates Starr, Mary Church Terrell, and Frances Willard. See Evans (1997).

94. Some "women's rights activists led by Lucy Stone, Henry Blackwell, and Frederick Douglass agreed that 'this hour belongs to the negro,' fearing that the debate about woman suffrage at the federal level would introduce additional controversy and endanger the passage of the Fourteenth and Fifteenth amendments." To which Stanton replied, "Do you believe the African race is composed entirely of males?" (Evans 1997: 122).

95. Grant appointed thousands of women as US postmasters, including Anna M. Dumas, the first African American woman in the position. Grant also signed legislation that broadened property rights and legal equality for women within Washington, DC, and which set wage requirements for female employees of the federal government. He met with Susan B. Anthony in 1872 and pardoned her associates when she broke the law by voting for Grant in that year's presidential election. Hayes's infamously dry White House was in response to pressure from his wife and the Woman's Christian Temperance Union. He also appointed women to the Agriculture Department and the Patent Office (1872 and 1876 Republican Party platforms; Andrews 1977; supplemented by *UCSB*).

96. Only nine of thirty national labor unions survived, and aggregate union membership dropped from around 300,000 to perhaps 50,000 (Dubofsky and Dulles 2010: 100).

97. Then twenty-four years old, Samuel Gompers (1925: 96–98) later described it as "an orgy of brutality": "I was caught on the street and barely saved my head from being cracked by jumping down a cellarway." The incident convinced the future labor leader that strict ideology was a poor foundation for labor activism: "I saw how professions of radicalism and sensationalism . . . nullified in advance normal, necessary [labor] activity. . . . I saw the danger of entangling alliances with intellectuals who did not understand that to experiment with the labor movement was to experiment with human life."

98. *New York Times,* February 5, 1880.

99. Buhle (2013).

100. In late 1880, "boycott" also entered into common practice and American parlance. It derived from embargos of products from the farms of absentee Irish landlord Charles Cunningham Boycott following a wage dispute that year. See *New York Tribune,* October 31, 1880; *Brooklyn Daily Eagle,* November 15, 1880; *Atchison* (KS) *Daily Champion,* November 16, 1880; *Buffalo* (NY) *Morning Express,* November 19, 1880.

101. *New York Times,* June 16, 1878.

102. Marshall (2010).

103. Parsons (1887).

104. The Black International originated in London as the International Working People's Association in 1881. Johann Most, August Spies, and Albert R. Parsons created an

American wing in 1883. It recruited several thousand members, but the organization mostly melted away after the Haymarket riots and the execution of anarchist leaders in 1887.

105. Phelan (2000); Fink (1983).

106. Quoted in Dubofsky and Dulles (2010: 124).

107. Dorfman (1949); Barbour, Cicarelli, and King (2018); Barber (2004).

108. Sumner (1874: 333).

109. As an example of amateur influence, a major plank of the Greenback Party platform in 1876 sought to repeal the Resumption Act and to replace national banknotes with paper bonds, with every $100 note bearing 1 percent interest or less. This derived from the thinking of wealthy real estate mogul and armchair political-economist Edward Kellogg (Unger 1964).

110. Walker (1876).

111. Bernard (1990: 137).

112. Sumner (1877: 53).

113. Anne Robert Jacques Turgot made less sophisticated, but similar, arguments about the relations between supply, demand, and prices during the mid-1700s. But his writings were eclipsed by those of Adam Smith and blemished by Turgot's association with the Physiocrat school. A few other Europeans also proposed various utility theories of value during the 18th century, but they failed to gain a wide audience (Rothbard 1995).

114. Bernard (1990); Samuels, Biddle, and Davis (2003); Screpanti and Zamagni (2005).

115. *Chicago Tribune,* January 6, 1879.

116. This was abetted by Germany's endorsement of the gold standard in 1871, which triggered a wave of similar adoptions throughout Europe. By 1880, Canada and most of Europe (except Italy and Russia) had demonetized silver as currency and adopted the gold standard.

117. George (1879). See also O'Donnell (2015).

118. Henry George, interview with D. D. Field, *North American Review* 141. 344 (1885 July): 6.

119. Shaw (1905); D'A. Jones (1988). Even former president Rutherford Hayes gave his grudging approval, writing in 1887 that "Henry George is strong when he portrays the rottenness of the present system," but adding, "We are, to say the least, not yet ready for his remedy." Instead, Hayes suggested, "We may reach and remove the difficulty by changes in the laws regulating corporations, descents of property, wills, trusts, taxation, and a host of other important interests, not omitting lands and other property" (RBH, diary entry, December 4, 1887).

120. The victor, Abram Hewitt, was a lifelong Democrat, a highly successful iron manufacturer, and a former four-term congressman He was actually a staunch reformer who had managed New York governor Samuel Tilden's unsuccessful run for the presidency in 1876. Nevertheless, Tammany Hall was a Democratic organization that feared Roosevelt and George far more than it did Hewitt, with whom Tammany leaders had personal relationships (Post 1976; Guerin 2012).

121. Bartlett (1962).

122. King (1880: 4).

123. English physicist Michael Faraday first introduced the concept of "fields" in the 1840s, but it was widely rejected by scientists who sought a material conduit of magnetism and electricity. In translating Faraday's empirical findings into general mathematical formulas, Maxwell was responsible for "turning Faraday's heresies into the orthodoxy of classical field theory" (Williams 1966: 121). Other thinkers began to apply the concept of fields to other areas of inquiry. Perhaps the most famous was Albert Einstein's work on space, time, and gravity (Kuhn 1962; Williams 1966; Hunt 1991).

124. And perhaps William McKinley, who died from septic shock due to bacterial infection along the path of an unrecovered bullet after being shot by an assassin in September 1901 (Adler 1963). Lister arrived in New York back on September 3, 1876, invited to speak at the International Medical Conference in Philadelphia by Samuel Gross, an ardent critic of germ theory intent on humiliating him. At the time, most American surgeons ignored hygiene as a contributor to success. For example, the head surgeon at Massachusetts General Hospital banned Lister's system, calling it "hocus-pocus." From Philadelphia, Lister traveled west to San Francisco and back, lecturing to students and surgeons along the way. Over the next several months, he convinced a substantial number of physicians to experiment with carbolic acid to sterilize surgical instruments and wounds. However, Lister's theory of "antisepsis" took decades to gain full acceptance in American medical circles (Rutkow 2013; Fitzharris 2017).

125. Crump (2007); Smith (2018).

126. Jacks and Stuermer (2021).

127. At first, only a few ammonia absorption machines provided mechanical refrigeration, usually for industrial ice manufacturers or for large shipments of perishable food. But going into the 1880s, the natural ice industry was in decline, thanks in part to concerns over water pollution and health risks, while mechanical ice machines and cleanable iceboxes (with removeable linings) began to enter the mainstream (Gantz 2015; Rees 2013).

128. Americans had not yet acquired a taste for milk chocolate, which was invented in Switzerland in 1875 but not mass-produced in the United States until the Hershey Chocolate Company (founded in 1894) introduced it in 1900.

129. The American Institute Fair, held annually in New York City since 1829, is often considered the first world's fair to be convened in the United States. However, the early AI fairs were relatively small and "financially unsuccessful; the receipts not meeting the expenses" (American Institute of the City of New York 1872: 120). The first major American world's fair, with over 1 million attendees, was the Exhibition of the Industry of All Nations, held in New York during 1853–1854. The United States also hosted the Philadelphia Technological Exhibition (1858) and Franklin Institute Exhibition (1874), the latter of which attracted around 270,000 visitors over five weeks.

130. Giberti (2015).

131. Exhibited in hopes of increasing sales of the Remington, which first sold the model in 1874, but it was expensive and broke down often. It would not take off until the new 1878 model featured improvements.

132. Lamoreaux, Levenstein, and Sokoloff (2007: 40).

133. Lamoreaux, Levenstein, and Sokoloff (2007: 40).

134. Hughes (1983: 18).

135. Weak-current technologies, such as the telegraph, teleprinter, and electric clocks, had been in use since the 1840s, and the first stock tickers appeared on Wall Street in 1867. These were *technically* revolutionary systems, but electric power in these forms had only limited social or economic impact compared to what was to come. Starting in 1873, electric motors began to enjoy commercial success. At that year's World's Fair in Vienna, the accidental discovery of reversibility in dynamos showed that electric motors could also be used as generators, inspiring Belgian engineer Zenobe Gramme to begin production of them (Hughes 1983: 18).

136. Edison also competed with gaslight, which had been developed in England in the 1790s and gradually spread throughout Europe. It first went into service in the United States on the streets of Baltimore in 1816 and remained popular into the early 20th century, though primarily with industrial and commercial customers (Nye 2018; Tomory 2012).

137. Hughes (1983); Jonnes (2003).

138. Though partly because the Associated Press, through which member newspapers freely shared national news content since 1846, did not cover Washington, DC. A fall in rail and telegraph prices between Washington and major cities further incentivized more reporting from the nation's capital (Summers 1994).

139. By 1880, advertising constituted half of newspaper income, rivaling sales, even as newspaper prices plummeted. Patent medicines, soaps, and baking powder companies were the most prolific advertisers of the decade. And as department stores proliferated, so too did their adverts (Summers 1994; Smythe 2003).

140. For a general treatment of financial news, see Knight (2016).

141. Originally called "western," the term changed to "new" during the mid-1880s as these practices spread east (Smythe 2003).

142. Only James Garfield demonstrated some success at mastery over Gilded Age press relations, and mostly while in Congress (Summers 1994).

143. In other words, Americans would hoard gold and spend it only on imports, for which silver and paper were usually not accepted. Hence, gold would slowly but surely bleed out of the US financial system. Thus, "gold would be driven out of circulation, and out of the Treasury's reserves. This would imperil the Treasury's ability to maintain convertibility into gold, which in turn would cast doubt on the value of paper currency" (Reti 1998: 95).

144. *Chicago Tribune,* January 6, 1879.

145. The logic was that money printing produced gluts of cash, which fed financial speculation, which then caused financial panics (such as those of 1869 and 1873). By fixing exchange rates and limiting the supply of money to specie (i.e., an international gold or bimetallic standard), such imbalances would be curtailed. "[T]here could never be too much or too little money in any one nation, since the laws of supply and demand would guarantee an efficient distribution of the world's gold [or bimetallic] resources" (Davies 2018: 147).

146. Reti (1998).
147. The *HSUS* puts 1873 as the last year of deficit.
148. Palen (2016).
149. "Democratic Party Platform," June 22, 1876, *UCSB*.
150. Golway (2014); Hoogenboom (1961); Summers (2004).
151. Hayes even bragged to a reformer, "[Mine] is the first Administration in half a century that has not employed its office holders to promote its own political purposes" (RBH, letter to Republican leader Wayne MacVeagh, October 30, 1878, quoted in Klinghard 2010: 62).
152. Klinghard (2010); Arrington (2020).
153. That is, since state party leaders sat atop statewide networks of power and patronage, they had both the incentives and resources to advance the Republican Party's *state* interests rather than its *national* interests, which often differed. For example, religious education, an important cultural issue in Ohio during the 1870s, played an important role in Hayes's rise to power as the state's governor, but played less of a role in his presidential election.
154. For state party leaders naturally used their considerable power to reward insiders and marginalize outsiders. An example here is Benjamin Harrison, who inadvertently crossed Indiana's state machine boss, Oliver P. Morton. Harrison was virtually banished from politics until Morton died in 1877 (Fuller 2017).
155. Klinghard (2010).

Chapter 7

1. Garfield's only concrete presidential act, between his shooting and his death, was the signing of an extradition treaty with Canada (Rutkow 2006).
2. See, for example, his presidential campaign biographies, McClure (1880); McCabe (1880).
3. JAG, diary entry, August 24, 1849, in Brown and Williams (1981: 22).
4. JAG, diary entry, September 5, 1850, quoted in Smith (1968: 39).
5. Peskin (1978); Bernard (1990); Palen (2016).
6. Leech and Brown (1978); Peskin (1978).
7. JAG, letter to J. Harrison Rhodes, January 1, 1860, quoted in Smith (1968: 144).
8. Leech and Brown (1978); Peskin (1978).
9. JAG, letter to J. Harrison Rhodes, November 2, 1862, quoted in Smith (1968: 256).
10. Rutkow (2006: 19).
11. JAG, letter to Mark Hopkins, president of Williams College, December 1863, quoted in Smith (1968: 355–356).
12. JAG, letter to Lucretia Garfield, September 27, 1862; JAG, letter to Harmon Austin, March 4, 1864, quoted in Peskin (1978: 153, 237).
13. Reid (1895: 759).
14. Peskin (1978: 396).

15. Smith (1968); Young (2017).

16. Summers (1994).

17. JAG, diary entry, March 14, 1881, in Brown and Williams (1981: 558).

18. JAG, letter to lifelong friend Charles E. Henry, January 27, 1876, quoted in Peskin (1978: 398).

19. JAG, diary entry, November 23, 1876, quoted in Smith (1968: 618).

20. JAG, diary entry, March 1, 1877, in Brown and Williams (1973: 452).

21. RBH, letter to William Henry Smith, June 18, 1880, quoted in *The Dial*, September 1880.

22. Arrington (2020); Clancy (1958).

23. *New York Times*, May 31, 1880.

24. Peskin (1984–1985).

25. *New York Tribune*, May 29, 1880.

26. *Springfield* (MA) *Republican*, November 5, 1880.

27. Though not all. As early as May 1879, the Pennsylvania press opined that Garfield was the best candidate (*Penn Monthly*), while Ohio's *Cleveland Herald* reported in early June that "a Garfield tide is rising in the west" (quoted in Dehler 2011: 43; Smith 1968: 965).

28. As chairman of the Rules Committee for the 1880 convention, Garfield had helped mortally weaken the "unit rule" requirement for presidential nominations. For decades, it had required that each state's set of convention delegates, however large, vote as a single unit, determined by their majority. Unit rule thereby tended to "stack the deck" in favor of state party leaders, like the New York Stalwarts, and all but eliminate popular minority interests and outsider candidates. "The results were decisive. In the eight states closely associated with the Grant boom (Alabama, Arkansas, Illinois, Louisiana, Mississippi, New York, Pennsylvania, and Texas would have given him 250 votes), the rule changes cost Grant 90 votes. . . . On the first ballot, with 379 votes necessary to win, Grant received 304—the votes he lost from the enforcement of the new rules would have secured his victory" (Klinghard 2010: 200; Arrington 2020).

29. *Cleveland* (OH) *Herald*, June 9, 1880, quoted in Smith (1968: 983).

30. Journalist Murat Halsted more accurately described them as Republicans "who represented the Democratic States and [the Democratic] Districts of the Republican States." In other words, they sought to save their own political careers by resurrecting Grant's (*Cincinnati* [OH] *Commercial*, January 6, 1882, quoted in Peskin 1984–1985: 714).

31. To "wave the bloody shirt" was a common Republican campaign tactic. It meant invoking the Civil War and insinuating that Democrats remained the party of Southern rebellion, and therefore of the Confederacy, against whom many likely Republican voters, their families, and friends had fought and died (Calhoun 2010).

32. Peskin (1978); Jordan (1971).

33. Klinghard (2010).

34. Arrington (2020); Bourdon (2019).

35. *Harper's Weekly*, August 28, 1880.

36. In addition to their original agenda of money printing, to support domestic labor Greenbackers now fiercely opposed Chinese immigration. They also supported a progressive income tax, federal labor standards, federal regulation of the railroads, an eight-hour workday, and the reservation of public lands for settlers (Lause 2001).
37. Sherman (1896: 634).
38. Dehler (2011: 60).
39. *The Sun* (New York), March 5, 1881.
40. JAG, letter to former student Burke A. Hinsdale, January 5, 1881, quoted in Smith (1968: 1043).
41. JAG, letter to H. N. Eldridge, December 14, 1869, quoted in Peskin (1978: 262).
42. Peskin (1978: 429). Garfield's inconsistency on monetary and financial policy, combined with his personal scandals, prompted Murat Halstead (editor, *Cincinnati (OH) Commercial*) to editorialize in 1878, "The trouble with Gen. Garfield is not dishonesty or greed, but *greenness* in money matters" (quoted in Summers 1994: 170).
43. Salisbury (1993).
44. JAG, Speech in the US House of Representatives, 39th Congress, 1st Session, July 10, 1866. Over time, Garfield came to support a combination of high tariffs and "reciprocity," which might protect budding industries and industrial labor but not punish consumers and farmers with exorbitant import taxes, and would hopefully incentivize American businessmen to invest in domestic manufacturing. But he never made much progress in implementing such policies (Skrabec 2018).
45. John Murray Forbes, railroad magnate and Republican reform activist, letter to JAG, July 1, 1880, quoted in Peskin (1978: 486, 496).
46. RBH, diary entry, February 21, 1883.
47. *The Economist*, March 12, 1881.
48. *New York Times*, February 1, March 3, 1881.
49. *New York Times*, March 22, 1881.
50. JAG, diary entry, March 23, 1881, in Brown and Williams (1981: 598).
51. The refunding measure was declared in a US Treasury circular issued on April 11, 1881.
52. Though a few critics blasted it as an "unconstitutional usurpation of authority" (*Daily Morning Times* [Brooklyn, NY], April 19, 1881). Several other newspapers reprinted an editorial, "The United States of Windom," which insisted that "the Secretary of the Treasury without authority of Congress had no power to negotiate a loan on behalf of the government, or to renew a loan," therefore the Treasury secretary acted "without a shadow of authority of law and in absolute violation of legislative prerogative" (*Cincinnati* [OH] *Inquirer*. April 1881).
53. *Chicago Daily Tribune,* May 14, 1881. The conservative business-oriented *Commercial and Financial Chronicle,* April 16, 1881, concurred, calling it "a remarkably clever and favorable arrangement for the Government . . . [while also] doing the fair thing toward the bondholder . . . [and] wisely conceived so as to disturb as little as possible the industries of the country." Perhaps more revealing, in a long, gushing editorial, the

Democrat-leaning *New York Sun,* May 11, 1881, admitted to its largely working-class readership that "[the financial] returns virtually remove any doubts that may have existed as to the success of Secretary WINDOM's funding scheme." Though it also scolded, "But for all that, the procedure is not one of which the country can be proud, nor one which we would like to see repeated."

54. Including independents, allies in the Republican and Democratic parties, and members of the new Readjuster Party from Virginia (Martis, Rowles, and Pauer 1989).

55. US Treasury Department (1927: 119).

56. JAG, "Inaugural Address," March 4, 1881, *UCSB.* Garfield did, however, in consultation with his cabinet, prohibit banks from exchanging US bonds for greenbacks which they had retired at the Treasury, though these bonds could be exchanged for new circulating banknotes (decided and announced on March 11, 1881) (Brown and Williams 1981: 556n88).

57. Reti (1998).

58. The Star Route scandal was a massive scheme by which a handful of Republican appointees had accepted bribes for awarding millions of dollars in inflated contracts for US Postal delivery on particular ("starred") mail routes (Calhoun 2017; Doenecke 1981).

59. Savidge, Eugene Coleman (1891) *Life of Benjamin Harris Brewster* (Philadelphia: J.B. Lippincott Company), 138.

60. JAG, letter to Burke A. Hinsdale, April 4, 1881, quoted in Smith (1968: 1109).

61. *Chicago Daily Tribune,* March 30, 1881.

62. He also explained, "The President's tragic death . . . will unite the Republican Party and save the Republic" (Charles Guiteau, letter to General Sherman, July 2, 1881; letter to the White House, July 2, 1881, both quoted in *New York Times,* July 3, 1881.

63. For the best coverage of Garfield's injuries, illness, and medical treatment, see Rutkow (2006) and Millard (2011).

64. Rutkow (2006: 122).

65. *New York Times,* July 3, 1881.

66. *New York Times,* July 3, 1881.

67. The stock market peaked during June 1881. It then drifted lower throughout the next twelve months, losing over 13 percent of its value. However, this was mostly a result of declining earnings and a correction from "irrationally exuberant" highs rather than any political event.

68. *New York Sun,* July 3, 1881.

69. *Bourse Gazette* (Paris), July 5, 1881, quoted in *New York Times.*

70. Dehler (2011: 68).

71. *New York Times,* September 20, 1881.

72. *New York Times,* September 21, 1881.

73. *The Economist,* September 24, 1881.

74. Robert Todd Lincoln, US secretary of war, letter to friend Norman Williams, July 28, 1881, quoted in Emerson (2012: 229–230).

Chapter 8

1. Even Friedman and Schwartz (1963: 92) have described Arthur's 1881–1885 economic slump as "unusually long and fairly severe."
2. "Smoldering depression" is not a historical term but one employed by the author.
3. Reeves (1975: 5).
4. Greenberger (2017: 15).
5. Greenberger (2017). Though years later, associates of Arthur would generally describe him as "never brilliant and in no way intellectual" (Adam Badeau, writer and diplomat in the Grant administration, quoted in Reeves (1975: 41).
6. CAA, letter to Annie Arthur, March 11, 1855, quoted in Greenberger (2017: 24–25).
7. Burt (1902: 145); Edward Morgan, governor of New York, December 1, 1881, quoted in Reeves (1975: 30).
8. Reeves (1975).
9. Reeves (1975: 39).
10. The system of financial "assessments" regularly imposed on government workers who gained employment via the party is described in Hoogenboom (1961); Summers (1993).
11. CAA, quoted in Greenberger (2017: 77).
12. As portrayed in Riordon (1905) and in films like *Gangs of New York* (Miramax Films, 2002).
13. Silas Burt, civil service reformer, December 1886, Box 1: 154, Silas Burt Papers, New York Public Library.
14. Silas Burt, quoted in Reeves (1975: 33); Greenberger (2017: 81).
15. Adam Badeau, quoted in Reeves (1975: 41).
16. Karabell (2004:19); Peskin (1984–1985).
17. Reeves (1975: 62).
18. A friend and colleague of Arthur's estimated that in just "two and a half years ... [Arthur] received as his share [of moieties and perquisites] $90,802.74 in addition to his salary of $6,000 for annum. He also received a commission for collecting the official fees of certain State officials ... which netted him about $4,000 per annum" (equivalent to roughly $2.75 million in 2020 dollars over two years) (*Measuring Worth*, CPI measure; Silas Burt, December 1886, Box 1: 49–50, Silas Burt Papers, New York Public Library.
19. Reeves (1975).
20. Charles Elliot Norton, Massachusetts author and social commentator, quoted in Karabell (2004: 42); William Henry Smith, June 15, 1880, letter to RBH.
21. *Chicago Daily Tribune*, June 9, 1880.
22. Reeves (1975: 183).
23. During the Gilded Age, US senators were chosen by state legislatures at the behest of the state political machines. Only after the passage of the Seventeenth Amendment to the Constitution in in 1913 were senators chosen by popular vote.
24. *New York Times*, February 12, 1881.

25. *Evening Journal* (Albany, NY), April 8, 1881, quoted in Reeves (1975: 226); *New York Tribune*, May 26, 1881, quoted in Greenberger (2017: 144).

26. Calhoun had distrusted the former general since Jackson's insubordination during the First Seminole War (1817–1818), while Calhoun was serving as secretary of war. Nevertheless, Calhoun, a southerner, allowed himself to be drafted as vice president in order to defeat John Quincy Adams and his northeastern supporters. However, Calhoun had become a fervent supporter of states' rights and a seeker of power. This put him in tension with Jackson's agenda and ambitions. Once in office, Vice President Calhoun appeared to openly disparage President Jackson and his allies and then machinate against them. Jackson therefore removed Calhoun's supporters from his administration, while Calhoun used his deciding vote in the Senate to oppose his president. Their final breaking point came when Calhoun took South Carolina's side during the Nullification Crisis of 1832 against Jackson's trade agenda. Jackson saw such open opposition to federal policy as treasonous and a plot by Calhoun to increase his own personal power, which it likely was. Rather than complete his second term as vice president, Calhoun resigned and entered the Senate, from where he continued to harass the Jackson administration (Karabell 2004; Niven 1993).

27. Specifically, New York senators Roscoe Conkling and Thomas Platt, both Stalwart Republicans, resigned their Senate seats in mid-May 1881 in protest over Garfield's federal appointments within their state. Their plan was for their state's legislature to quickly reappoint them to the Senate in a public show of defiance against Garfield. This failed to occur, effectively ending Conkling's political career and severely weakening the Stalwart faction. See Jordan (1971).

28. Charles Guiteau, July 2, 1881, quoted in *New York Times*, July 3, 1881.

29. *The Nation*, July 7, 1881.

30. *Chicago Tribune*, July 3, 1881.

31. CAA, letter accepting the Republican nomination for vice president, July 15, 1880, printed in *New York Times*, July 19, 1880.

32. Greenberger (2017).

33. When nominated for the ticket, Arthur had immediately sought the approval of Conkling, who bluntly instructed him to "drop it like a red hot shoe from the forge." Offended, Arthur retorted, "The office of the Vice-President is a greater honor than I ever dreamed of attaining" (Hudson 1911: 98). The vanity argument is also supported by Arthur's recognition that a Garfield-Arthur ticket might fail; nevertheless, he still contended that even "[a] barren nomination would be a great honor" (98). Arthur probably also sought to reclaim his political relevancy, which had faded quickly after his removal from the New York Customs House. Hence the vice presidency was both a personal honor and a means of political survival for Arthur. Regardless, after his nomination, campaign collections and patronage were his only concerns. When news of Garfield's assassination reached him in New York, Arthur was unnerved. He immediately huddled with Conkling and the Stalwart captains to strategize, while telling reporters, "I am overwhelmed with grief over the awful news" (*New York Times*. July 3, 1881). As a behind-the-scenes political broker, Arthur appears to have been terrified at the thought of becoming president. The few existing sources report seeing

him visibly shaken and often in tears during this period. "He is overwhelmed by the magnitude of the calamity and of the task which he may be called upon to perform," wrote one reporter (quoted in Greenberger 2017: 163). During most of Garfield's convalescence, Arthur secluded himself in his New York City brownstone, venturing out only to strategize with Conkling and the party machine. When Garfield finally died, Arthur's butler informed reporters that the new president was "sitting alone in his room sobbing like a child, with his head on his desk and his face buried in his hands" (*New York Times*, September 20, 1881). Arthur's cherished private life, largely free from responsibility, was over.

34. The only exception is Garfield, who vetoed no bills during his abbreviated term, mostly because Congress was in session for just ten weeks of it and passed little significant legislation. Arthur vetoed a total of twelve bills, nine of which were for pensions or other rewards for individual persons. His veto of the River and Harbors Bill was quickly overridden. His veto of the Chinese Exclusion Act was countered weeks later by a somewhat less restrictive act, which he signed. His only legislative veto to survive unaltered was his July 1882 veto of a bill to regulate the carriage of passengers by sea.

35. Doenecke (1981).

36. Reeves (1975: 273).

37. National Bureau of Economic Research (2021) dates the peak of the economy as March 1882. However, it is not clear upon what this judgment is based, nor when it was made. Nor does it appear to be corroborated by the most recent statistical data available. It is possible that the NBER dating is decades old and unrevised. Author exchanges with current members of the NBER Business Cycle Dating Committee support this interpretation and suggest that revisions of older recession dates are being considered.

38. Refers to the Russo-Turkish War of 1877–1878 (Veblen 1892; supplemented by *NBER Macro*).

39. *New York Times*, August 2, 16, 1881.

40. Data on stock ownership prior to the 1920s is sparse to nonexistent. During the Gilded Age, stocks were used more for speculative investment and short-term trading than for long-term investment. On average, in 1881 only around 450,000 shares were traded daily on the New York Stock Exchange. Currently, trading volume is considered low when it dips below 6.5 billion shares on a daily average (Geisst 2018; supplemented by *HSUS*).

41. *New York Times*, December 31, 1881.

42. Bailey (1970).

43. Sage (1909: 246).

44. Arthur brought his taste for finery into the remodeling. He insisted on gold leaf, Limoges china, Japanese leather, Indian brass work, and jeweled Tiffany glass from New York. And as a "thorough connoisseur of music," he even commissioned a brand new McKnabe concert grand piano (Doenecke 1981; Seale 2008; *New York Times*, December 18, 1882).

45. And thereby repair the line of presidential succession.

46. John Hay, letter to Whitelaw Reid, editor, *New York Tribune*, October 1881, quoted in Cortissoz 1921: 76).

47. *Chicago Daily Tribune*, December 7, 1881.

48. *New York Times*, December 31, 1881.

49. *New York Times*, December 31, 1881.

50. All quoted in *New York Times*, February 25, 1882.

51. *Cleveland* (OH) *Herald*, quoted in *New York Times*, February 25, 1882.

52. Conkling felt betrayed by Arthur for not appointing more Stalwarts to his administration and for retaining enemies of Conkling's. It is also likely that Conkling preferred the high salary, personal autonomy, and lavish lifestyle of a private attorney in New York City, where he did quite well (Jordan 1971).

53. Opposition to the Act mostly came from New England, New York, and the north-central states.

54. CAA, "Veto message," April 4, 1882, *UCSB*.

55. *Sacramento Daily Record Union*, April 6, 1882.

56. *Sacramento Daily Record Union*, April 5, 6, 1882; *Los Angeles Daily Herald*, April 11, 1882.

57. Roughly 790,000 immigrants in total, or around 1.5 per 100 residents (Martin 2011).

58. *The Economist*, February 18, 1882.

59. *The Economist*, February 18, 1882.

60. *Chicago Tribune*, February 12, 1882; *Cincinnati* (OH) *Enquirer*, February 21–23, 1882; *Daily Arkansas Gazette*, March 14, 17, 23, 1882; *New Orleans Times-Democrat*, March 29, 1882.

61. Friedman and Schwartz (1963: 100).

62. *The Economist*, February 25, 1882.

63. *New York Times*, July 30, 1882.

64. CAA, "First Annual Message to Congress," December 6, 1881, *UCSB*.

65. CAA, "Special Message to Congress," April 17, 1882, *UCSB*.

66. *Measuring Worth* (per capita GDP measure).

67. *New York Times*, July 27, 1882.

68. Countercyclical fiscal policy at the federal level was still controversial. But state and local government spending on public works as a local economic boost was commonly discussed in newspapers and among policymakers, albeit in basic terms. In other words, the short-run economic effects of government spending on infrastructure were well accepted in some quarters. It was the long-run wisdom (and politics) that remained much disputed, especially at the federal level.

69. CAA, "Veto Message," August 1, 1882, *UCSB*.

70. CAA, "Veto Message," August 1, 1882, *UCSB*.

71. *New York Times*, August 2, 1882.

72. *Cincinnati Enquirer*, June 1, 1882, quoted in Reeves (1975: 314).

73. *New York Times*, September 20, 22, 1882. After the election, the editors of the *New York Times* scolded Arthur, "Cease trying to be a ward politician and the Executive of the Nation at the same time" (November 8). Though historians debate how much Arthur actually participated.

74. Dubofsky and Dulles (2010: 121).

75. Lucy (1882). The Molly Maguires were a violent, secret society of laborers which organized against mine and railroad owners, mostly in Pennsylvania during the 1870s. It was believed that they conducted assassinations, kidnappings, arson, property destruction, and beatings to achieve their goals.

76. Skrabec (2015); see also comments to the Senate by John Tyler Morgan (D-AL), June 21, 1882, in *Congressional Record,* 47th Congress, 13.5 (1882): 161.

77. *New York Daily Tribune,* September 6, 1882.

78. To his credit, Arthur did sign off on the creation of the Bureau of Labor Statistics (BLS) within the Department of Interior. It was the only federal agency concerned with labor issues from 1884 until the establishment of the Department of Labor in 1913. Its first commissioner, Carroll D. Wright, appointed by Arthur, was a visionary technocrat and experienced statistician who ran the BLS for twenty years. The BLS served as a bastion of scientific data gathering, objective analysis, and professionalism on the very sensitive issues of labor-industry relations and the conditions of working Americans. It gathered the first statistics, conducted analyses, and offered labor policy suggestions. Its leadership also aided in strike negotiations and advised the federal government on myriad labor issues (Norwood 1985; Goldberg and Moye 1985).

79. Hochschild (1998).

80. Beale (1908: 8).

81. Rood (1911: 163).

82. Bailey (1970).

83. Beale (1908: 4–5).

84. Reeves (1975: 274).

85. *New York Times,* December 31, 1882.

86. *New York Times,* December 31, 1882.

87. Rezneck (1956: 296); *Measuring Worth* (consumer price index).

88. George Pendleton (D-OH), 47th Congress, 1st Session, December 13, 1881.

89. CAA, "Address upon Assuming the Office of President of the United States," September 22, 1881, *UCSB.*

90. CAA, "Special Message to Congress," February 28, 1882, *UCSB.*

91. Hoogenboom (1961).

92. *The Sun* (New York), December 29, 1882.

93. Hoogenboom (1961).

94. Julia Sand, letter to CAA, January 7, 1882, Chester Alan Arthur Papers: Series 1, General Correspondence and Related Manuscripts, 1843–1938; 1882, Jan. 1–1925, Apr. 27, Library of Congress.

95. Summers (2000).

96. Doenecke (1981) estimates a total of 131,000 federal employees at the time, of which only 14,000 fell under the purview of the Pendleton Act when it was first passed.

97. Hoogenboom (1961: 237).

98. *New York Times,* May 30, 1883.

99. *New York Times,* June 15, 1883.

100. *The Nation,* August 9, 1883.

101. *The Nation,* September 6, 1883.

102. Irwin (2017); Johnson (2018).

103. CAA, "Second Annual Message to Congress," December 4, 1882, *UCSB.*

104. Josephson (1938: 330); quoted in Irwin (2017: 239).

105. *New York Times,* March 4, 1883.

106. In a related episode, both France and Germany banned imports of American pork products in 1881 and 1882 due to a mix of public health concerns (i.e., trichinosis) and trade protectionism. American pork producers, meatpackers, and shippers were furious. The American pork titan Philip Armour declared that the ban would be a "disaster to the farming interests of Illinois and the Northwest" (quoted in Doenecke 1981: 136). Arthur created a Pork Commission in early 1883 to study the matter and sent his newly appointed envoy to Berlin to negotiate. The Commission equivocated, while the envoy proceeded to offend Chancellor Bismarck so greatly with threats and bluster that Arthur was forced to recall him. Thereafter, Arthur declined to take up the fight, and the bans remained. Partly as a result, hog prices fell by 46 percent between summer 1882 and Arthur's departure from office in March 1885 (Hoy and Nugent 1989; Webb 1982; Doenecke 1981; supplemented by *NBER Macro*).

107. Arthur's first secretary of state, James Blaine, was himself a machine boss who tried to build up a record of achievement so as to boost his own presidential chances. Blaine tried to force a renegotiation of the Clayton-Bulwer Treaty with Great Britain; insert the United States into peace negotiations to end a war between Chile, Peru, and Bolivia; moderate a boundary dispute between Mexico and Guatemala; settle a trade dispute over US pork exports to Europe; free Irish American prisoners held in Britain; and host a grand Pan-American conference in Washington, DC. In each case, Blaine mismanaged matters in a way that not only embarrassed the United States but also angered the other countries involved. His successor at the State Department, Fredrick Frelinghuysen, was more responsible, conservative, and orthodox but spent much of his time trying to clean up after Blaine. Where Frelinghuysen innovated was in his attempts to open up new markets for American products, which mostly failed (Reeves 1975; Doenecke 1981; see also Herring 2008).

108. For just one case study of Arthur's bungling in foreign policy, see Hochschild (1998).

109. Quoted in Doenecke (1981: 62).

110. The subhead's quotation is from Julia Sand, letter to CAA, August 27, 1881, Chester Alan Arthur Papers: Series 1, General Correspondence and Related Manuscripts, 1843–1938; 1843, Aug. 31–1881, Dec., Library of Congress.

111. Julia Sand, letter to CAA, October 9, 1882, Chester Alan Arthur Papers: Series 1, General Correspondence and Related Manuscripts, 1843–1938; 1882, Jan. 1–1925, Apr. 27, Library of Congress.

112. Reeves (1975: 275).

113. Reeves (1975: 273).

114. Reeves (1975: 273).

115. Henry Adams, letter to Henry Cabot Lodge, November 15, 1881, quoted in Greenberger (2017: 184). Adams was not only an esteemed historian and political observer; he also lived across the street from the White House.

116. Reeves (1975); Doenecke (1981); Karabell (2004); Greenberger (2017).

117. *New York Herald,* June 21, 1883, quoted in Grana (2015: 50).

118. Reeves (1975: 354).

119. Others have argued that "Arthur's patronage appointments were not directed towards reconciliation. Instead he used patronage to reward his followers and the independents in the south for breaking with the bourbon Democrats, and above all else, gain the Republican renomination of 1884" (Dehler 2011: 103).

120. *Cincinnati* (OH) *Enquirer,* November 22, 1883, quoted in Greenberger (2017: 217).

121. For example, Arthur was criticized in 1883 when he failed to greet the crowds gathered to see him during his trip to Wyoming. The *Chicago Journal* scolded, "We think President Arthur made a mistake when passing through the country on his recent trip in persistently refusing to appear at the railroad stations where the people had assembled to pay their respects to the chief magistrate. Many of these persons had travelled a considerable distance in order to get a sight of a live President, and were no doubt sorely disappointed when the train stopped and there was no response to their urgent appeals" (quoted in Ellis 2008: 297n15).

122. *Chicago Tribune,* August 3, 1883, quoted in Greenberger (2017: 219).

123. White (1884: 112).

124. *The Nation,* August 16, 1883, quoted in Rezneck (1956: 286).

125. Although *nominal* interest rates remained relatively low and steady during the recession, in the neighborhood of 4 percent, increasing deflation meant that *real* interest rates headed up toward 10 percent.

126. Fixing the dollar to gold would boost investor confidence, for anyone who invested in the United States could get out dollars worth the same as those put in. Eliminating alternative forms of money (paper, silver) meant that the government could not print its way out of debt, nor could cheap and abundant silver be substituted in deals originally made in precious gold.

127. The three primary causes of the gold stock deceleration were changing trade patterns, severe drops in investor confidence, and Gresham's Law. First, as American exports fell, so too did incoming foreign payments in gold. Second, as the returns on land development and railroads declined, foreign investors began to pull back on their investments, thus fewer gold inflows and more outflows. Third, whenever given the option, Americans paid their bills, fees, taxes, and tariffs in the weaker currency (silver and paper) and hoarded the stronger (gold). Nor were new discoveries of domestic gold deposits large enough to make up the difference. Thus, gold slowly bled out of the US Treasury and out of the country. See Studenski and Krooss (1963); Timberlake (1993); Friedman and Schwartz (1963).

128. In relative terms, the leakage was not large, only 2 to 5 percent of the total monetary gold stock, but it called into question the ability of the United States to maintain its commitment to the gold standard over time. Looking back, we can see that, between

1881 and 1884, the US gold stock grew only around 11 percent, just barely ahead of population growth and not enough to maintain the economic boom begun in mid-1878. Meanwhile, gold in circulation shrank.

129. *New York Times,* February 5, 1883.

130. *New York Times,* February 26, 1884.

131. Friedman and Schwartz (1963: 128–132).

132. In 1882, Arthur made a minor attempt to revive discussions with Europe for an international monetary regime that had been initiated by Garfield, but he quickly dropped the matter when nothing came of it (Reti 1998).

133. Geisst (2018: 103–104); Skrabec (2015: 103–104).

134. Ward (2012).

135. *Measuring Worth* (per capita GDP measure). In comparison, the largest hedge fund in 2020 managed $98 billion.

136. The NYCH was a private association of around sixty major New York banks that acted as a central clearinghouse for the "adjustment and payment of the daily balances due to and from each other at one time and in one place on each day." Originally founded in 1853 as a "labor-saving device," by 1884 it had "become a medium for united action among the banks," such as acting as a lender of last resort during liquidity crises (Cannon 1911: 1).

137. Anderson and Bluedorn (2017); Cannon (1911: 90).

138. Skrabec (2015: 103–104); *Measuring Worth* (per capita GDP measure). A total output measure puts the 2020 figure closer to $389 billion.

139. Calculated as change in GDP/capita using *HSUS*; unemployment data from Skrabec (2015: 103); Sorkin (1997: 150).

140. Michigan Bureau of Labor Statistics, 1885, quoted in Rezneck (1956; supplemented by *HSUS*).

141. *New York Times,* October 28, November 1, December 4, 1884, quoted in Rezneck (1956: 303).

142. Abram S. Hewitt, letter to the *Argus,* December 26, 1883, quoted in *New York Times,* December 29, 1883.

143. The ratio of private wealth to national income rose from 421 percent (1881) to 443 percent (1885), while private wealth to average disposable income went from 466 percent (1881) to 490 percent (1885) (Piketty and Zucman 2014).

144. Federico-Tena World Trade Historical Database (Federico and Tena-Junguito 2019).

145. Bank of England (2021), supplemented by *HSUS*.

146. *New York World,* November 20, 1886, quoted in Reeves (1975: 423).

147. Reeves (1975: 418).

148. Elihu Root, address at the unveiling of a statue of President Arthur in Madison Square, New York City, June 13, 1899, quoted in Root (1917: 111). Elihu Root was supposedly present when Arthur received news of Garfield's death. Arthur appointed him as a US attorney in New York (1883–1885). Root served later Republican presidents as secretary of war (1899–1904) and secretary of state (1905–1909).

149. Karabell (2004: 2, 140).

Chapter 9

1. Wilson (1897).
2. William Bourke Cockran, Democratic politician and orator in New York City, comments at the Democratic National Convention, July 1884, quoted in Golway (2014: 139).
3. Graff (2002).
4. Often in poor health, Richard Cleveland died of a stomach malady in October 1853, when SGC was sixteen years old (Tugwell 1968).
5. Cleveland was also one of only three post–Civil War presidents who received no formal higher education, the others being William McKinley (1897–1901) and Harry S. Truman (1945–1953).
6. Margaret Cleveland memo, quoted in Nevins (1932: 18–19).
7. Crosby (1909: 581).
8. SGC, letter to Mary Cleveland, 1853–1854, quoted in Tugwell (1968: 18).
9. Bissell (1909: 583).
10. Nevins (1932a: 51).
11. Gilder (1910: 190).
12. Quoted in Brodsky (2000: 27).
13. Brodsky (2000: 26).
14. Nevins (1932a: 45).
15. At the Buffalo saloons, Cleveland even became notorious for leading ceaseless rounds of the drinking song "There's a Hole in the Bottom of the Sea" (Lachman 2011).
16. Brodsky (2000).
17. He instead headed a movement to raise the money anew via private donations (Brodsky 2000).
18. Riordon (1905); Myers (1971); Golway (2014).
19. John Weber, New York Republican Party activist and future US congressman, quoted in Armitage (1926: 101–102). Specifically refers to Cleveland's veto of corrupt street-cleaning contract.
20. Historian Mark Wahlgren Summers (2000: 122), however, argues that Cleveland's "reputation as a machine smasher was slightly misleading. Cleveland fought Tammany. He got along much better with the Brooklyn machine."
21. This quote specifically references Cleveland's veto of a bill to halve and standardize elevated railway fares (Nevins 1932a: 116).
22. *Buffalo* (NY) *Commercial*, May 7, 1883.
23. *The Nation*, May 29, 1884; *Puck*, March 26, 1884.
24. An excellent and thorough account of the 1884 election can be found in Summers (2000).
25. Congressman Edward S. Bragg (R-WI), July 10, 1884, quoted in Nevins (1932a: 153).
26. Calhoun (2000). Blaine's political-economic philosophy is well described in his own autobiography: Blaine (1884).
27. Summers (2000: xi); *New York Times*, October 31, 1884; Schurz (1884).

28. Though, while the Republican Party "pledge[d] itself to correct the inequalities of the tariff, and to reduce the surplus," it also promised that any tariff revisions "shall be made, not 'for revenue only,' but that in raising the requisite revenues for the government, such duties shall be so levied as to afford security to our diversified industries and protection to the rights and wages of the laborer" (*UCSB*). Democrats made similar promises in their official platform but had a long history of advocacy for lower tariffs. Also, the parties differed little on labor issues in part because Republicans and Democrats had not yet split along capital-labor lines; such fissures would await the next decade.

29. Debate on these issues would have split Democrats, while Northern Republicans still hoped to court Southern voters, and neither presidential candidate had served during the war. Therefore, they were generally neglected.

30. "Democratic Party Platform," 1884 (July 8), *UCSB*.

31. Summers (2000: 312); Rosenberg (1962).

32. John Hay, letter to Richard Watson Gilder, editor *The Century* magazine, formerly *Scribner's Monthly,* July 11, 1884, quoted in Clymer (1975: 54). Democrats were then seen by Republicans as representing the rabble of uneducated, uncultured Americans, including recent immigrants with values "alien" to traditional Protestant hard work and moral rectitude (Golway 2014).

33. Albeit not enough to earn any electoral votes or to send more than a single representative to Washington. In fact, third parties won only 1.83 percent of the *national* vote. Still, it was a historically strong turnout for third parties that may have cost Blaine his victory. Thus, many Republicans now viewed party factions and third parties as serious threats in the North and West. Meanwhile, intimidation and fraud throughout the South drove many Republican and third-party voters away from the polls in the ex-Confederate states (Summers 2000; Martis, Rowles, and Pauer 1989; Andersen (2013).

34. Stoddard (1927: 143).

35. Charles Nordhoff, letter to David Wells, *New York Herald,* 1885, quoted in Calhoun (2008: 32).

36. For example, in 1884, 10.5 percent of federal jobs were "classified" as competitive (i.e., hiring was based on exams). After four years of Cleveland, not quite eighty-eight hundred jobs had been added to the classified list. Thus, in 1888, the ratio had increased only to 15 percent. Perhaps the major exceptions were Cleveland's fights to repeal the Tenure of Office Act and to lower tariffs (Summers 2000; supplemented by *HSUS*).

37. Welch (1988).

38. SGC, "Letter Accepting Nomination for Governor of New York," October 7, 1882, in Goodrich (1888: 194); SGC, "Second Annual Message to Congress," December 6, 1886, *UCSB*.

39. SGC, "First Inaugural Address," March 4, 1885, *UCSB*.

40. This particular wording became a campaign catchphrase created by a journalist after studying Cleveland's speeches and consulting him. See Brodsky (2000: 41–42).

41. SGC, "Letter Accepting Nomination for Governor," October 7, 1882, quoted in Goodrich (1888: 194).

42. Cleveland (1897: 30).

43. SGC, "First Message to the New York Legislature," January 2, 1883, quoted in Goodrich (1888: 229).

44. SGC, "First Inaugural Address," March 4, 1885, *UCSB*.

45. SGC, "Veto of Military Pension Legislation," February 11, 1887, *UCSB*.

46. Welch (1988: 18).

47. SGC, "Letter of Acceptance of the Nomination for President," August 18, 1884, in Goodrich (1888: 381).

48. Summer (2000: 121).

49. Summer (2000); Welch (1988).

50. Usselman (2002).

51. McCabe (1873: 7).

52. Enabled in part by the economic downturns of 1873–1878 and 1881–1885, which allowed the major producers to either buy up or drive out their smaller competitors.

53. McCraw (1984); Geisst (2000).

54. Summers (2008).

55. Brodsky (2000: 24).

56. Charles Evans Hughes, future New York governor, US secretary of state, and Supreme Court justice, quoted in Hugins, (1922: 92).

57. Clymer (1975: 58).

58. Clymer (1975: 58); William Cowper Brann, journalist and playwright, quoted in Flemmons (1998: 26).

59. The trough is believed to have occurred sometime during the second quarter of 1885, likely in May (Glasner 1997: 732–733; supplemented by *NBER*).

60. Glasner (1997: 150); Skrabec (2015: 103).

61. The value of federally minted US silver coins was set by Congress at $1.29 per ounce in 1792 and remained there until silver was demonetized in 1879. The value of federally minted gold coins was slightly less constant, but also set by Congress at $19.39 (1792), $20.69 (1834), and then $20.67 (1837). Otherwise, gold and silver *bullion* (i.e., uncoined, bulk metal) was traded freely on private markets, where prices were determined by supply and demand until 1933, when President Franklin D. Roosevelt pulled gold from circulation and made private ownership of gold currency illegal.

62. Later estimates put 1878 silver at around 89 percent of gold, by weight (US Treasury Department 1927: 119).

63. *The Nation*, April 3, 1884.

64. Though Milton Friedman (1990b) has argued that demonetizing silver created economic instability; hence the 1873 Coinage Act was "a mistake that had highly adverse consequences." For an opposing view, see Velde (2002).

65. According to the National Bank Act of 1882, "the Secretary of the Treasury shall suspend the issue of such gold certificates whenever the amount of gold coin and gold bullion in the Treasury reserved for the redemption of United States notes falls below one hundred millions of dollars."

66. When in, early 1885, the US Treasury paid some of its debts in silver, possibly to test the market's reaction, the foreign business press erupted, warning its readers that any

further debt payments in silver "would be tantamount to a confession on the part of the [US] Government that it is unable to maintain payments on the gold basis" (*The Economist*, February 14, 1885).

67. Abram S. Hewitt, chairman of the House Ways and Means Committee, letter to SGC, February 2, 1885, quoted in Nevins (1932a: 202).

68. SGC, letter to Hon. A. J. Warner and others, members of the 48th Congress, February 24, 1885, printed in *New York Tribune, New York Sun,* and others, February 28, 1885.

69. *New York Sun,* March 1, 1885; *New York Tribune,* February 28, 1885.

70. Benson (2010).

71. Specifically, the 1878 Bland-Allison Act, which mandated federal purchase and coinage of silver.

72. *New York Herald,* January 6, 1886. In an opposing view, biographer Richard E. Welch (1988: 82) has argued, "Even had Cleveland acted more forcefully or with more political finesse, it is doubtful that he could have gained victory, so numerous were the silver men in both houses of Congress."

73. *New York Herald,* January 5, 1886.

74. Pro-silver forces took Cleveland's public statements as encouragement, while the "hard money" faction in Congress fell into disarray. "[I]f only he had said nothing," complained one pro-gold legislator. "We should have presently had a united party, confident and happy. . . . [I]t makes me sick" (*New York Herald,* January 6, 1886).

75. SGC, "First Presidential Inaugural Address," March 5, 1885, *UCSB.*

76. SGC, letter to George William Curtis, president of the National Civil Service Reform League, December 25, 1884. Printed in *New York Times* December 30, 1884.

77. Quoted in Quoted in McElroy (1923: 100).

78. For example, his Treasury secretary, Daniel Manning, was a former newspaper man and powerful party boss in New York. He had led the Tilden faction of the state Democratic Party during the 1870s and even served as state party chairman. Thus reformers considered him "the Machine incarnate" (Calhoun 2008: 34). Yet, the conservative *New York Times,* December 25, 1887, described Manning as "unflinchingly" a reformer and "not a seeker for office." In fact, "many of the schemes of reform proposed [under Governor Tilden] were credited to the fertile brain of [Manning]."

79. *Chicago Tribune,* March 15, 1885.

80. Welch (1988); Nevins (1932a).

81. *New York World,* August 13, 1885, quoted in Nevins (1932a: 215).

82. Cleveland explained, "My idea has been that those officials who have held their places for four years should as a rule give way to good men of our party, that those who have been guilty of offenses against our political code should go without regard to the time they have served, and that we should gladly receive all resignations offered" (SGC, letter to Treasury Secretary Daniel Manning, June 20, 1885, in Nevins 1933: 64). Ultimately, Cleveland was relieved of violating his principles, or of breaking campaign promises about defying patronage, when in 1886 his Republican predecessor's appointees began to cycle out of their federal appointments, allowing Cleveland to send more Democrats into the federal government.

83. Wright (1886: 290).

84. SGC, letter to Wilson Bissell, friend and former law partner, December 27, 1885, quoted in Nevins (1932a: 270).

85. SGC, *Chicago Tribune.* January 6, 1886.

86. *New York Times,* December 14, 17, 21, 1885; Timberlake (1993). Particularly unnerving to financial markets was a pro-silver speech on December 21, 1885, by Senator James B. Beck (D-KY), chairman of the Senate Democratic Caucus.

87. Congressman David B. Culberson (D-TX), quoted in *New York Times,* March 28, 1886.

88. Investment capital was still far more accessible in the northeastern states, with their thriving trade, industry, and financial sectors, than in the West, which was still being settled (Murtazashvili 2013).

89. *New York Herald,* 1885–1886, passim.

90. *New York World,* January 4, 1886.

91. Benson (2010: 43).

92. Senator James B. Beck (D-KY), chairman of the Senate Democratic Caucus 1885–1890, submitted the resolution on January 12, 1886 (*New York Times,* January 13, 1886).

93. US Treasury Department (1927: 119).

94. *New York Times.* (March 18, 1886).

95. SGC, letter to Congressman Samuel J. Randall (D-PA), July 14, 1886, quoted in Nevins (1932a: 271).

96. Known as the Morrison Resolution, it mandated that the US Treasury retire bonds whenever federal gold reserves rose above $100 million. (At the time, they were estimated at $228 million.)

97. Objections from the banking community can be found summarized in *Rhodes Journal of Banking,* 1886, 13(8): 585–587; *New York Times,* July 22, 1886.

98. SCG, "Memorandum on the Morrison Surplus Resolution," August 5, 1886, printed in the *New York Tribune,* August 17, 1886.

99. For example, in his December 1886 Annual Message to Congress, Cleveland briefly repeated his opposition to compulsory silver coinage (i.e., urged repeal of the 1878 Bland-Allison Act) (SGC, "Second Annual Message to Congress," December 6, 1886, *UCSB*).

100. Friedrich Engels, letter to German Communist leader Friedrich Sorge, August 8, 1887, quoted in Green (2006: 145–146).

101. Quoted in Dubofsky and Dulles (2010: 128).

102. SGC, "Letter Accepting Nomination for Governor," October 7, 1882, in Goodrich (1888: 194).

103. SGC, "Letter Accepting Nomination for Governor," October 7, 1882, in Goodrich (1888: 194); repeated in SGC, "Letter Accepting Nomination for President," August 18, 1884, in Goodrich (1888: 381).

104. SGC, "Special Message to Congress," April 22, 1886, *UCSB*.

105. Avrich (1984); Green (2006).

106. Spies (1886: 3).

107. Avrich (1984: 221).

108. Schaack (1889: v, 687).

109. SGC, "First Annual Message to Congress," December 8, 1885, *UCSB*.

110. For example, Cleveland signed the Scott Act (1888), which prohibited the return of any Chinese migrant who left the United States, explaining, "The experiment of blending the social habits and mutual race idiosyncrasies of the Chinese laboring classes with those of the great body of the people of the United States, has proved by the experience of twenty years . . . to be in every sense unwise, impolitic, and injurious to both nations" (SGC, "Special Message to Congress," October 1, 1888, *UCSB*).

111. SGC, "Veto Message," March 2, 1897, *UCSB*.

112. SGC, "Veto Message," March 2, 1897, *UCSB*.

113. Usselman (2002).

114. "Stock watering" was the practice of issuing shares at a much higher value than the underlying assets, usually to defraud investors. The term was likely borrowed from ranchers who would force their cattle to drink large amounts of water before taking them to market, where they would be sold by weight (Pratt 1903; Geisst 2018).

115. Adams (1869b: 146).

116. Hoogenboom (1961); Usselman (2002); White (2011).

117. *Munn v. Illinois*, 94 U.S. 113 (1877).

118. These were not the first state-level laws to regulate the railroads. As a result of Grange lobbying, between 1871 and 1874 four midwestern state legislatures (Illinois, Minnesota, Wisconsin, and Iowa) passed the first laws requiring governments to regulate private industry. They fixed rates on railroads and the nearby grain warehouses which served them (often owned by the railroads) and prohibited free rail passes for public officials. Corporate lawsuits against these "Granger Laws" evolved into the March 1877 *Munn v. Illinois* Supreme Court decision, which provided constitutional cover for the surge in state railroad regulations that followed (Bourne 2017).

119. *Wabash, St. Louis & Pacific Railway Company v. Illinois*, 118 U.S. 557 (1886).

120. Hoogenboom and Hoogenboom (1976: 12).

121. Kolko (1965).

122. Hoogenboom and Hoogenboom (1976: ix).

123. Friedman and Schwartz (1963: 127–128).

124. US War Department (1887). See also Clark (2015); St. Martin (2009).

125. Granville Stuart, quoted in Fletcher (1930: 125).

126. With death precluding any roundups, cowboys nicknamed it "the Great Die-Up" (Boardman 2015).

127. Dauber (2013).

128. SGC, "Veto Message," February 16, 1887, *UCSB*.

129. During the Civil War, Congress had expanded the Federal Pensions Bureau to provide for disabled Union army veterans and for the widows and dependents of Union soldiers killed during the war. Individuals disqualified by the Pensions Bureau (some 28 percent of all applicants) could ask their congressman to support a bill to override the Bureau's ruling (Skocpol 1992, 1993).

130. In 1885, total federal outlays were $260 million, of which $42.7 million went for the army, $16 million for the navy, $51.4 million for interest on the public debt, and $56.1 million on veterans compensation and pensions (Nevins 1932a: 327; supplemented by US Department of Commerce 1975).

131. SGC, "Veto Message," June 21, 1886, *UCSB*.

132. Skocpol (1993).

133. *The Nation*, February 17, 1887.

134. Quoted in Nevins (1932a: 329).

135. SGC, "Fourth Annual Message to Congress," December 3, 1888, *UCSB*.

136. For excellent recent discussions of Gilded Age tariff politics, see Irwin (2017); Johnson (2018).

137. US Department of Commerce and Labor (1908: 694, Table 266).

138. Another third of federal revenues came from internal taxes on tobacco and alcohol, the remaining ~15 percent came from land sales, fees, and other excise taxes.

139. In federal expenditures, in 1888 for example, almost 30 percent was spent on pensions for Union veterans; only 20 percent went toward military spending, another 16 percent went to interest payments on federal debt.

140. SGC, "Third Annual Message to Congress," December 6, 1887, *UCSB*.

141. Roger Mills (D-TX), April 17, 1888, quoted in Irwin (2017: 245).

142. SGC, "Third Annual Message to Congress," December 6, 1887, *UCSB*.

143. SCG, letter to Carl Schurz, late 1884 or early 1885, quoted in Stoddard (1927: 152).

144. Another 15 percent of US trade was with Germany and France combined, and another 15 percent with the Americas.

145. Palen (2016).

146. SGC, "First Annual Message to Congress," December 8, 1885, *UCSB*.

147. William Collins Whitney, secretary of the navy, 1885–1889, quoted in Klinghard (2010: 165).

148. SGC, "Third Annual Message to Congress," December 6, 1887, *UCSB*.

149. Palen (2016: 145–147); Walt Whitman, September 13, 1888, quoted in Traubel (1906: 313).

150. Welch (1988: 88).

151. In particular, Cleveland may have sought to energize western farmers to vote Democrat (Welch 1988; Calhoun 2008).

152. Calhoun (2008).

153. Welch (1988: 89). For the opposing view, see Klinghard (2010), who argues that Cleveland did support a campaign of education, but ultimately failed due to desertions and betrayals by protectionist Democrats in the North, especially New York.

154. Welch (1989: 89).

155. SGC, "Speech at the 250th Anniversary of the Founding of Harvard College," November 8, 1886, in Winsor (1887: 269)

156. SGC, quoted in Charles W. Eliot, Harvard president, letter to William Gorham Rice, 1886, in Nevins (1932: 309–310); SGC, "Speech at the 250th Anniversary of the Founding of Harvard College," November 8, 1886, in Winsor (1887: 269).

157. Stoddard (1927: 143).

158. Barry (reporter for the *New York Sun*) (1897: 283).

159. Welch (1988: 89). Once again, Klinghard (2010: 159–163) opposes this view, arguing that "Cleveland used executive messages [as well as letters and rare interviews] to grab public attention and assert the executive's ability to articulate party commitments."

160. Whitcomb and Whitcomb (2000).

161. Stoddard (1927: 152).

162. Welch (1988).

163. Pendel (1902: 148).

164. Samuel Tilden, quoted in *Outlook* (1909: 807).

165. Welch (1988: 22, 35).

166. Summers (2008).

167. SGC, "First Annual Message to Congress," December 8, 1885, *UCSB*.

168. Unknown author, quoted in Summers (2008).

169. For the opposing view, see Klinghard (2010), who interprets Cleveland's approach to patronage and tariffs as an attempt to lead, control, and unify the Democratic Party.

170. Wilson (1897).

171. Calhoun (2008).

172. Other issues, such as labor troubles, Chinese immigration, and a recent dust-up with Great Britain over fishing rights in Canadian waters, as well as a handful of local concerns, also played significant, but less prominent, roles (Calhoun 2008).

173. "Bourbon Democrat" was originally a pejorative term used by machine politicians to refer to reformist, conservative Democrats who yearned to return to pre–Civil War practices of minimal government. In New York, Bourbons led the fight against the Tweed Ring and Tammany Hall and for civil service reform. Since many reformers were wealthy, educated elites, the term was meant to evoke the elitist, royalist, anti-democratic views of the Bourbons in France before the 1789 Revolution who had "learned nothing and forgot nothing." Over time, "Bourbon" referred more generally to all political-economic conservative Democrats, often from the South, from roughly 1876 to 1904. Bourbon Democrats favored both small government and big business. Thus, they supported the gold standard and laissez-faire capitalism, while opposing state subsidies and trade protections. In foreign policy, they opposed US expansion overseas (Witcover 2003; Feldman 2013).

174. Other parties running candidates included the Prohibition Party and the Union-Labor Party. The latter was an offshoot of the Greenback-Labor Party, which mixed farmers, labor, and "a sprinkling" of Socialists. The National Equal Rights Party renominated Belva Lockwood in 1888, the third presidential run by a woman, but received few votes from the all-male electorate.

175. "[Cleveland] missed his chance; *instead of striking the [British] lion, he kicked the donkey;* America was laughed at; Cleveland was defeated" (*Record* [Columbia, SC], quoted in Sievers 1960: 8n10).

176. William B. Ivins, letter to Daniel S. Lamont, private secretary to SGC, August 1888, quoted in Nevins (1932a: 423).

177. Wilson (1897).
178. Third parties did their usual damage: the Prohibition Party took 2.2 percent of the popular vote, the Union-Labor Party won 1.3 percent. "In the end, [Benjamin] Harrison edged out Cleveland in a victory so narrow that any number of factors could have made the difference," concludes the most recent study of the 1888 contest (Calhoun 2008: 3).
179. Rood (1911: 198).
180. The ratio of private wealth to national income rose from 443 percent (1885) to 453 percent (1889), while private wealth to average disposable income went from 490 percent (1885) to 501 percent (1889) (Piketty and Zucman 2014).
181. Federico-Tena World Trade Historical Database (Federico and Tena-Junguito 2019).
182. SGC, speech in Buffalo, NY, September 7, 1882, in Bergh (1909: 111).

Interlude

1. Boutmy (1891: 128).
2. Some 520,000 Americans rode the rails in 1890, which also carried over 79 billion ton-miles in freight.
3. Ocean shipping rates (dry freight) spiked briefly in 1886-1889, but then tumbled again thereafter (Jacks and Stuermer 2021). Also, due to tariffs, recession, and increases in individual ship capacity, the total number of ships clearing American ports fell during the 1880s and were only just recovering going into the 1890s.
4. Another 4.18 million net immigrants would arrive during 1891–1901. Thus, as a proportion of the population, Gilded Age and early Progressive immigration was outdone only by the years 1847–1854 and has had no equivalent since the outbreak of World War I (US Census Bureau 1895; supplemented by HSUS).
5. US Census Bureau (1895; supplemented by HSUS).
6. In particular, Turner (1894: 1–2) feared that the closing of the American frontier would bring an end to "the vital forces that call [American institutions, culture, and intellect] into life and shape them to meet changing conditions." By the mid-1890s, the "Wild West" era had also ended due to the subjugation of the Native Americans, the formal organization of new states and territories, and the spread of barbed wire, the railroads, and telecommunications.
7. Strom (2003).
8. During the 1880s, wages for both unskilled labor and farm labor (with board) rose 19 percent, while bank rates on short-term business loans ranged between 8 and 12 percent in the South and Plains states, but reaching as high as 20 percent in the West (compared with the northeastern states, where they averaged just 6 to 7 percent).
9. In *Munn v. Illinois* (1877) the Supreme Court had decided that state governments could regulate the warehouses and grain elevators maintained by the railroads but essential to farmers.

10. Sanders (1999: 105–106). Cochrane (1993: 95) puts peak Grange membership at 1.5 million in 1874.

11. Grangers did manage to win federal support for agricultural research stations (1887), but their few political efforts during the 1890s mostly focused on government subsidies for Rural Free Delivery of the mail (Benedict 1953: 104).

12. Sanders (1999: 101).

13. Benedict (1953: 106).

14. Benedict (1953: 106) places the origins of the Farmers' Alliance equally in mid-west and southwest settlers' alliances which sought to "resist the encroachment by the railroads on pre-empted lands."

15. The Farmers' Alliance was also instrumental in the passage of the Hatch Act for federal aid for agricultural research (1887); the elevation of the Department of Agriculture to the cabinet level (1889), which raised the profile of scientific research among farmers; and the passage of the Sherman Antitrust Act (1890). And it would join the Grangers in advocacy for Rural Free Delivery of the mail. Many of the Alliance's other causes (e.g., increased popular democracy via state referendums and initiatives, secret ballots, and the direct election of US senators) would be taken up by the Progressive movement early in the next century (Benedict 1953: 106).

16. Sanders (1999).

17. A transformation in the American politics of conservation began with George Perkin Marsh's (1864) treatise, *Man and Nature*, which awoke the nation to the real dangers of deforestation and environmental degradation. It arguably had far more policy impact during the Gilded Age than more famous environmentalists of the period (e.g., David Thoreau, John Muir). See Lowenthal (2000). For more general treatments, see Taylor D. (2016); Jacoby (2014); Montrie (2011). For a White House perspective on environmental politics and policy, see Graham (2015).

18. Or, for those who could afford it, to maintain their physical and mental health. For "[t]he very men who most benefited from urban-industrial capitalism were among those who believed that they must escape its debilitating effects" (Cronon 1995: 78). See also Montrie (2011).

19. Muir (1901: 12). See also Montrie (2011).

20. Hounshell (1984).

21. The poor and middle classes bought sewing machines either to make their own clothes or to tailor and spruce up new lines of made-to-wear garments then being mass-produced. The wealthy sought expensive handmade clothing to distinguish themselves from others, and thereby drove demand for seamstress work (Stamper, Condra, and Severa 2010; Harris 2005).

22. Hounshell (1984: 122).

23. American Tobacco Company (1960: 28; supplemented by *HSUS*). Cigarette machines were extremely efficient: "By the late 1880s, one machine was turning out over 120,000 a day. At that time the most highly skilled hand workers were making 3,000 a day. Fifteen such machines could fill the total demand for cigarettes in the United States in 1880, and thirty could have saturated the 1885 market" (Chandler 1977: 249).

24. *Boston Globe,* April 17, 1881; *New York Times,* October 22, 1886.
25. Though the need for annual model changes, many unnecessary, to maintain sales kept expert fitters and craftsmen on the payroll and slowed automation in the wheeled vehicle industry.
26. First developed in England and called the "safety bicycle" for its relatively lower height, it was the first mass-produced bicycle to approximate our modern bike.
27. Chandler (1977).
28. Even in 1891–1892, there were few industrial corporations with a capitalization greater than $10 million (around $300 million in 2020 dollars). By 1902, almost one hundred firms had grown to this size (Livingston 1986: 56).
29. Steel industry expansion during 1880–1890 differed by production method. For example, open-hearth steel increased by 401 percent, while Bessemer steel went up 243 percent. All told, raw steel production increased by 242 percent.
30. Between 1880 and 1890, passenger car production rose over 140 percent, freight car production increased over 125 percent, locomotive manufacturing rose 63 percent.
31. During the 1880s, electricity was still mostly used in lighting, telegraphy, and telephones and was only beginning to find applications to urban trams and trolleys, but it was not yet used much in manufacturing. In 1889, electric motors comprised just 2.5 percent of US manufacturing power; this would increase to just 4.5 percent by 1899. In fact, total US electricity use in manufacturing in 1890 was equal to only 447,000 horsepower.
32. Rogers constructed the first hydroelectric dam, in Appleton, Wisconsin, on the Fox River.
33. Hughes (1983: 46).
34. Corporations also increasingly turned to credit agencies in order to further reduce the risks of unreliable suppliers or retailers.
35. Increasing to 7.5 percent by 1900 (Edwards 1934). See also Kocka (1980).
36. Kornblith and Zakim (2011); Perrow (2002); Hounshell (1984); Chandler (1977).
37. Chandler (1977) argues that the most successful trusts were concentrated in the refining and distilling industries: petroleum, cottonseed oil, linseed oil, sugar, whisky, and lead. Others, such as cattle and rope, did not survive long after formation or functioned at the regional level, not nationally.
38. Grandy (1989).
39. Following a similar 85 percent expansion during the 1870s that had been interrupted by the depression of 1873–1878.
40. A southern line from Los Angeles to New Orleans and a northern line from Tacoma to Duluth. Work on a fourth transcontinental line (the Atlantic & Pacific) would be completed in 1893.
41. Often built by nominally free African Americans who had been arrested for petty crimes and turned into prison labor on the rails down south (Blackmon 2009).
42. Wolmar (2012: 256).
43. Time zones would eventually become federal law in the Standard Time Act of 1918 (a.k.a. Calder Act).

44. The dominance of the stock market by the railroad sector would continue until World War I propelled industrial and utilities stocks to the fore henceforth (O'Sullivan 2007: 503).

45. Another 27 percent were large industrials (of which just under one-third were miners), and 7 percent were utilities (i.e., traction, telephone, telegraph, electricity, gas) (O'Sullivan 2016: 29; Navin and Sears 1955:106; O'Sullivan 2007).

46. *New York Times*, 1890, passim. The stock market remained small because many American business sectors still had relatively low capital requirements. These firms did not need to issue stock or bonds, but raised funds from more traditional sources: wealthy individuals, families, the owners' own accounts, or local commercial banks. Meanwhile, on the retail investing side, before 1890, those Americans with excess savings were more likely to buy real estate, life insurance, or bonds (O'Sullivan 2007, 2016).

47. The Pennsylvania Railroad and New York Central Railroad, two of the largest railroads in 1885, viciously competed on their trunk routes, each trying to beggar the other, severely damaging their profits and stock prices in the process. J. P. Morgan sat on the Central's board. His partners at Drexel & Company had financed the Pennsylvania Railroad. Morgan explained to his guests that their war not only hurt business at home but was damaging American access to European investment capital. The business press applauded his successful negotiations, declaring, "[B]y one act, not only will every cause of discord between the trunk lines have been removed, but also the chief source of discord to the whole railroad system of the country will be out of the way" (*Commercial and Financial Chronicle*, July 25, 1885.

48. Nor did Morgan restrict himself to railroads. During the 1880s, he expanded his reach into the electricity, telegraph, telephone, and machinery sectors (Sinclair 1981).

49. Chandler (1977: 123).

50. In 1880, railroads were capable of top speeds of 60 to 80 miles per hour under ideal conditions. However, the *average* "fast freight" speed was only around 5 to 6 miles per hour due to delays, congestion, and frequent stops, though some routes could maintain 13 to 14 mph. Average slow rates were often 2 to 3 miles per hour. A decade later, in the early 1890s, average freight speeds of 16 mph were not uncommon, while a handful of special service routes could maintain 26 mph (White 1993).

51. Total US rail freight rose from around 32 billion ton-miles (1880) to over 79 billion ton-miles (1890) (White 1993; supplemented by *HSUS*). Older estimates by Fishlow (1966) have freight rates down 29 percent, passenger rates down 12 percent.

52. For example, between 1880 and 1889 the price of rail shipment from California to the East Coast fell by almost 50 percent and rates to New York City in particular were reduced by over 50 percent. However, in those regions monopolized by a single line, rates were more expensive (Benedict 1953).

53. Martin (1992); Wolmar (2012).

54. Existing urbanization data for the Gilded Age puts it at 26.3 percent (1880), 32.9 percent (1890), 37.3 percent (1900).

55. The average height of native-born American males declined roughly four-fifths of an inch between 1870 and 1890.

56. Life expectancy was 44.8 (1890) and 47.1 (1900), partly due to continued high infant and toddler mortality rates.

57. "The electric streetcar system was cheaper to install than cable car systems and al-most as flexible to operate as the horse-drawn car. After the first system installed in Richmond, Virginia in 1887 [sic] had proven itself, electric traction quickly replaced other modes of urban transportation. By 1890, 15 percent of urban transit lines in the United States were already using electric-powered streetcars and by 1902, 94 per-cent were. By then only 1 percent still employed horses and another 1 percent cable cars. . . . [T]he [electric] cars moved at greater speed and could carry greater loads" (Chandler 1977: 192–193; Duffy 2003).

58. Witkowski (2018); Livingston (1994); Bronner (1989).

59. Aided by advances in plate glass manufacture, expanded storefront window displays alerted shoppers to the latest fashion trends.

60. Frank Woolworth opened his first five-and-dime store in Utica, New York, in 1879.

61. Originally, the R. W. Sears Watch Co. catalogue issued by Richard Sears featured only watches and jewelry. Sears sold his firm in 1889 to become a rural banker, but then rejoined former employee and watchmaker Alvah Roebuck in the A. C. Roebuck & Company in Minnesota, which then became Sears, Roebuck and Company and moved to Chicago in 1893.

62. Twede (2012, 2015).

63. Eriksson and Ward (2022).

64. Klein (2012).

65. Walker (1896: 828).

66. Adding "idiots, insane persons, paupers or persons likely to become a public charge, persons suffering from a loathsome or a dangerous contagious disease, persons who have been convicted of a felony or other infamous crime or misdemeanor . . . [and] polygamists." The Alien Contract Labor Law of 1885 also introduced "moral turpi-tude" as justification for refusing admittance. Purposely vague, it was used against travelers accused of adultery and women traveling alone, especially if pregnant.

67. Calavita (1984).

68. Parker (2015).

69. Greene (2017).

70. In a terrible loss to historians and genealogists, the original Ellis Island facility burned down five years later, in June 1897. There were no deaths, but reams of fed-eral and state immigration records dating back to 1855 were incinerated (New York Times, June 15, 1897; Cannato (2010).

71. The Geary Act of 1892.

72. Hatton (2021).

73. Perez (2021).

74. Ward (2020); Alexander and Ward (2018).

75. Ager and Bruckner (2013).

76. Fulford, Petkov, and Schiantarelli (2020); Sequeira, Nunn, and Qian (2020); Ager and Bruckner (2013). These benefits extend into the present day. Recent statistical analysis has found that "counties with more historical immigration [during the Gilded Age]

have higher income, less poverty, less unemployment, higher rates of urbanization, and greater educational attainment today. The long-run effects seem to capture the persistence of short-run benefits, including greater industrialization, increased agricultural productivity, and more innovation" (Sequeira, Nunn, and Qian 2020: 382).

77. Sequeira, Nunn, and Qian (2020).
78. Bandiera et al. (2019).
79. Sequeira, Nunn, and Qian (2020).
80. Wong, Clark, and Hall (2018).
81. Currarino (2011).
82. Wegge (2002); Long and Ferrie (2013); Abramitzky and Boustan (2017); Sarada, Andrews, and Ziebarth (2019); Akcigit, Grigsby, and Nicholas (2017).
83. Sequeira, Nunn, and Qian (2020).
84. The phrase "Jim Crow" likely originated from "Jump Jim Crow," a song-and-dance caricature of Blacks first performed by white actors in blackface in 1828. It quickly became a disrespectful term used to refer to Americans of African descent (Lewis and Lewis 2009).
85. Will not be overturned until *Brown v. Board of Education*, 347 U.S. 483 (1954).
86. Kousser (1974).
87. Klein (2012).
88. Excluding Alaska and Hawaii.
89. Utley (2003).
90. Evans (1997).
91. The Gibson Girl was the product of artist Charles Dana Gibson, who sought to capture the new feminine ideal of beauty and independence (Patterson 2008). For a contemporary debate over the "new woman," see Grand (1894a, 1894b); Ouida (1894); *British Medical Journal* (1894). For literature and theater, see Denison (1895); Hamblin (1895); Hall (1895).
92. The welcoming Knights had fallen; the AFL banned them. Women were also barred from the wave of fraternal organizations which Gilded Age men joined in record numbers in what some scholars have dubbed "the Golden Age of Fraternalism," such as the Knights of Columbus (1882), Loyal Order of Moose (1888), and Woodmen of the World (1890). See Clawson (1989).
93. Willard (1893).
94. James and Skinner (1985); Acemoglu (2002a, 2002b).
95. Laurie (1989).
96. McNeill (1887: 100).
97. Fink (1983); Phelan (2000); Weir (1996).
98. Dubofsky and Dulles (2010: 127).
99. Dubofsky and Dulles (2010: 127).
100. Labor historian Gerald Friedman has estimated over 1.2 million union members in 1886, during which time Joshua Rosenblum has tabulated 1,572 work stoppages involving 610,000 workers on strike (Biggs 2002; supplemented by *HSUS*).
101. *The Nation*, April 1, 1886; see also Dubofsky and Dulles (2010: 130). *The Nation*'s antilabor sentiment at this time might surprise modern readers. Founded by

abolitionists in 1865, *The Nation* supported the gold standard, free trade, civil service reform, and limited government during much of the Gilded Age. Its leftward turn came after 1900, when it was inherited by Oswald Garrison Villard (1872–1949), a passionate liberal who transformed the periodical into a current affairs publication with a strident Socialist orientation (Grimes 1953).

102. *New York Times*, May 2, 1886.

103. To complicate matters, the Knights' leader, Terence Powderly, leaned conservative. He generally opposed strikes and confrontation and instead pressured his members to work within the existing system: to join capitalism by forming their own manufacturing cooperatives, to vote pro-labor candidates into office, and to support pro-labor legislation in federal, state, and local government. None of this was especially popular with the Knights' impatient and newly empowered workers.

104. Dubofsky and Dulles (2010: 132).

105. Greene (1998).

106. This first attempt at a coalition of skilled labor unions called itself the Federation of Organized Trades and Labor Unions of the United States and Canada, established in mid-November 1881. It proved neither popular nor successful, partly due to its intense rivalry with the Knights of Labor. During 1886, in response to the destructive infighting among unions and in the wake of the disastrous Haymarket Riot, labor leaders held a series of "peace" negotiations. In these deliberations, the Knights effectively drove the craft unions from their ranks and into the Federation, which, in December 1886, reorganized itself into the American Federation of Labor.

107. Hallgrimsdottir and Benoit (2007); Cornfield and Fletcher (1998).

108. Adolph Strasser, (testifying before the Senate Committee on Education and Labor, August 21, 1883, quoted in US Senate (1885: 460). At the time, Strasser was head of the Cigar Makers' Union and would be one of the founders of the American Federation of Labor.

109. Kaufman (1973).

110. Boutmy (1891: 128).

111. Rockoff (2008).

112. Just a few examples: *New York Times*, November 26, 1882; *Philadelphia Times*, November 20, 1887; *Indianapolis* (IN) *Journal*, June 26, 1892.

113. The crown jewels were The Breakers, built between 1893 and 1895 in Newport, Rhode Island, and the ostentatious Biltmore, constructed between 1889 and 1895 near Asheville, North Carolina—the largest private residence ever built in the United States.

114. Homberger (2004).

115. *North American Review* (1886) 142 (354): 454–465.

116. Holmes (1893); Howells (1894).

117. Sumner (1883: 119–120).

118. Carnegie (1889: 655).

119. *Chicago Tribune*, October 17, 1882; Gordon (1989).

120. Riis (1890: 3).

121. Bellamy (1888: 74).

122. Patai (1988); Bowman (1986, 1962).

123. Lloyd (1894: 528).

124. Salvatore (1982); Cain (2019).

125. "Firemen" were those workers responsible for maintaining the fire that heated a locomotive's steam engine. The job required considerable physical labor, such as shoveling coal, under arduous conditions.

126. Eugene Debs, speaking in Kensington, IL, during the American Railway Union's Pullman Strike, May 16, 1894, quoted in Stead (1894: 177).

127. Salvatore (1982).

128. Marshall (2010).

129. Parsons (1887: 33).

130. Some date the formal institutionalization of anarchists in America to the October 1883 meeting of the Congress of the International Working People's Association in Pittsburgh, PA.

131. Biggs (2002).

132. Buhle (2013: 44).

133. Evans (2017).

134. Evans (2017).

135. Herron (1893).

136. Barbuto (1999).

137. Dorfman (1949); Barbour, Cicarelli, and King (2018); Barber (2004).

138. Bracketed by the American Historical Association (1884) and the American Political Science Association (1902) (Coats 1960).

139. Ely (1886: 16).

140. Wells (1889: 71).

141. Jenks (1900: 36).

142. Two variations evolved: a Republican one, which sought greater federal control over monetary policy and later a central bank; a Bourbon Democrat version, which blamed the US Treasury and preferred a return to more Jacksonian laissez-faire "free banking" practices (McCulley 1992).

143. Harvey (1894: 147).

144. Livingston (1986).

145. "By the 1890s, the term *economics* had replaced *political-economy* as the most commonly used name for the discipline" (Bernard 1990: 197). At the time, the membership lists of the American Economic Association suggest that a handful of university professors alongside several bureaucrats, businessmen, and hobbyists were considered "economists."

146. The scholarly economics journals then consisted of *Quarterly Journal of Economics* (started 1886), *Economic Journal* (UK, 1891), *Journal of Political Economy* (1892). During the 1880s and 1890s, economists also published in nominally "political science" journals such as *Political Science Quarterly* (1886) and *Annals of the American Academy of Political and Social Science* (1890).

147. Screpanti and Zamagni (2005); Breit and Ransom (2014); Samuels, Biddle, and Davis (2003).

148. Bernard (1990). Also emerging as significant figures in the discipline during this time were John R. Commons (in labor economics, regulatory economics, evolutionary economics), Irving Fisher (in mathematical economics, money, interest rates, prices), and the Austrian economist Eugen von Bohm-Bawerk (in theories of capital, investment, and interest rates).

149. Previously, the classical political economists, like Smith, Ricardo, and Marx, had struggled to explain from where goods and services got their value. Was value inherent in the good itself? Or realized when the good was used? Or when the good was exchanged? *Marginalists* focused on the value provided by one additional unit of a particular good (i.e., at the margins) rather than whether a good provides more satisfaction in total. To this "marginal utility" question, the answer depends on how much of each good one already has (i.e., the first bread roll consumed is of enormous value to a hungry person, but the utility of additional, or marginal, bread rolls decreases as one continues to eat). Marginal analysis first emerged during the early 1870s in the academic work of William Jevons, Leon Walras, and Carl Menger. However their influence had been confined to a handful of mathematical political economists. With Clark and Marshall, this analytical focus on comparing marginal utilities and marginal costs evolved into the modern field of *microeconomics.*

150. Richard Ely, political economist, letter to Edwin Seligman, Columbia University faculty and founder of the American Economic Association, October 22, 1890, quoted in Bernard (1990: 199).

151. Marshall (1898: 68).

152. Neoclassicism also succeeded in marrying hitherto opposing schools of economics: classical (which assumed that economics follows external and unchanging laws) and "new school" (which assumed that economic behavior is subject to history and culture). The neoclassicals were able to show that some economic behavior was "static" and unchanging, while other behavior was "dynamic" (Bernard 1990; Breit and Ransom 2014).

153. Bernard (1990); McCoy (1980); Sklansky (2002).

154. Bernard (1990: 246).

155. For some of the more vocal academic supporters of labor unions or "soft money" were persecuted or drummed out by their universities, such as Richard Ely (University of Wisconsin), E. Benjamin Andrews (Brown), Edward Bemis (University of Chicago), Edward Ross (Stanford), eventually leading to the formation of the American Association of University Professors (1915).

156. In July 1886, the first commercially used Linotype was installed in the printing office of the *New York Tribune*. Linotype was a hot-metal typesetting machine that cast lines of type, entered on a keyboard, onto a metal printing block. It became the primary method for typesetting in newspapers and magazines until the development of phototype and computerization during the 1970s–1980s.

157. Americans had experimented with motorized vehicles since the early 1800s, but they remain a mostly 20th-century technology. For example, the first American gasoline-powered automobile was not produced until 1893, and not sold commercially until early 1896. Interest in them peaked after the first auto race in the United States took

place on Thanksgiving Day 1895; of the eighty-three cars entered, only six started and just two completed the race. Four years later, automobile manufacturing was still an infant industry, with thirty small firms producing just twenty-five hundred automobiles in the United States in 1899 (Flink 1988).

158. Austrian (1982). Different sources provide different estimates, ranging from six weeks to three years depending on method of calculation.

159. Eastman (1880).

160. Patented in 1897, but working prototypes were developed years earlier. The first Kinetoscope parlor would open in New York City in 1894. Dedicated movie halls and theaters (in which motion pictures were projected onto a screen) began to appear in 1896 (Phillips 1997; Thompson and Bordwell 2019).

161. Kobel (2009).

162. Initially launched as an effort to outdo the widely acclaimed Paris Exposition of 1889 (Rosenberg 2008; Bolotin and Laing 1992; Muccigrosso 1993; Larson 2003).

163. In comparison, the 1876 Philadelphia Exposition, though a fantastic display of new science and technology, was considered something of an architectural and design flop. Looking back on it, the great historian and philosopher of cities and urban architecture Lewis Mumford (1931: 16) declared, "It is hard to conceive anything lower than the architecture of the Centennial Exposition." Pulitzer Prize–winning historian Oliver Larkin (1949: 241) called the 1876 fair "[t]he oddest collection of structures that had ever been assembled in America, and assembled in that rather careless way which was still a convention in landscape architecture." *Harper's* editor Russell Lyons (1954: 115) later added, "Critics today look back upon the Centennial Exhibition as an architectural and artistic calamity that produced not a single new idea but was, rather, the epitome of accumulated bad taste of the era that was called the Gilded Age, the Tragic Era, the Dreadful Decade, or the Pragmatic Acquiescence, depending on which epithet you thought most searing."

164. The Yerkes telescope was a forty-inch refracting telescope, the largest ever at the time. After its 1897 installation at the University of Chicago's observatory in Wisconsin, it was used in astronomical research for over a century (Osterbrock 1997).

165. The modern industrial research laboratory would await those created by General Electric and AT&T in 1900.

166. Rudolph (1990); Lucas (1994).

167. Lucas (1994: 140).

168. Sheldon (1892: 191).

169. In contrast to West Point, which had been established in 1802 to instill Democratic-Republican values in the nation's military officer corps (Crackel 1987).

170. Business education had existed in the United States since at least the 1830s, but usually not as part of the standard college curriculum. In 1886, Frenchman Eugene Leautey counted 165 business colleges and 104 commercial colleges in the United States. The former were vocational schools that focused on practice; the later included theory. Wharton sought to elevate the prestige and quality of business education (Conn 2019).

171. Atkinson and Blanpied (2008).

172. In "halftone" newspaper illustration, monochromatic ink dots of different sizes or spacing (or both) were used to reproduce a visual image.

173. Pulitzer even ran for Congress as a Democrat in 1884 and won by a landslide. But after a year in office, he realized that he had greater influence as a newspaper editor and resigned his seat. During the 1890s, with the emergence of William Jennings Bryan and the pro-silver wing of the Democratic Party, Pulitzer grew less enthusiastic about the Democrats and withdrew his support for the party (Smythe 2003).

174. *The World* followed the *Chicago Inter-Ocean*, which began printing comics in the early 1890s. These early comics were originally intended for adult readers and not yet in the standard comic "strip" format targeted at children.

175. John Cockerill, 1898, quoted in Smythe (2003: 115).

176. New Yorkers began calling it "New Journalism," supposedly because they "could hardly endorse a regional journalism other than their own" (Smythe 2003: 107).

177. The term "yellow press" derives from the "Yellow kid" character in the *World's Hogan's Alley* color comics, which first appeared in 1895 and was then poached by the *Journal*. "Yellow press" was an extreme form of "western journalism," with a focus on crime, vice, scandal, and other sensational stories intended to attract readers (Spencer and Spencer 2007).

178. For a general treatment of the era's financial news, see Knight (2016).

179. The executive branch would employ 231,056 in 1901.

180. The percentage of executive branch workers employed by the US Post Office declined from 73 percent (1871) to 63 percent (1891) to 59 percent (1901). Civilian employees at the Departments of War, Navy, and other defense-related functions increased from 2.4 percent of the total (1871) to 14 precent (1891) to 19 percent (1901). See US Treasury (1869, 1901; supplemented by *HSUS*).

181. Neither the 1870 nor the 1900 figure includes perhaps a dozen others (stewards, ushers, messengers, doorkeepers, cooks, watchmen, and firemen) who managed the physical operation of the executive mansion on a daily basis (Hart 1995: 17–18).

182. A telephone would not arrive on the president's desk until Herbert Hoover's administration, in March 1929.

183. Johnson and Liebcap (1994: 23, Table 2.2).

184. By 1891, one in five federal employees was required to pass a competitive civil service exam; this would double to two in five by 1901. The executive branch would employ 231,056 in 1901.

185. Assessments were the "voluntary" campaign donations of 2 to 7 percent of their salaries demanded from federal appointees (Hoogenboom 1961; Summers 1993).

186. Among the most powerful of the newly formed clubs were the American Institute of Electrical Engineers (1884), American Protective Association (1887), American Tariff Reform League (1888), Sierra Club (1892), National Association of Manufacturers (1895), Sound Money League (1897), and National Congress of Mothers (1897).

187. Klinghard (2010).

188. Klinghard (2010: 99).

Chapter 10

1. An earlier, abbreviated version of this chapter was published as Taylor (2021).
2. Calhoun (2005: 2).
3. John Scott Harrison, letter to John Cleves Short, January 21, 1856, quoted in Sievers (1960: 21).
4. Congressman Benjamin Butterworth (R-OH), quoted in Sievers (1960: 23).
5. Calhoun (2005: 5); Harriet Root, tutor, quoted in Sievers (1960: 25).
6. Refers to Robert H. Bishop (Huston 1900).
7. "Miami University . . . could not have been more Presbyterian if founded by John Knox," the school's historian later wrote (Havighurst 1958: 46).
8. Rodabaugh (1935: 132).
9. Quoted in Sievers (1960: 52); Lewis W Ross, Illinois congressman and schoolmate of Harrison, 1892, quoted in Wallace and Halstead (1892: 61n).
10. Harrison's graduation speech focused on explaining "the poor of England," which he blamed on a shift away from private charity to government welfare.
11. Ross (1892).
12. William P. Fishback, quoted in Sievers (1960: 108).
13. John Kitchen, *Indianapolis* (IN) *News,* March 15, 1901, quoted in Sievers (1960: 92).
14. Sievers (1960: 55).
15. Quoted in Sievers (1960: 113).
16. John Scott Harrison, letter to BH, December 28, 1855, quoted in Sievers (1960: 117).
17. Harrison's choice may also have been driven by the strong Presbyterian bent of the early Republican Party; the greater chances for a young neophyte to move up in a new party versus the long established Democratic organization; and the unique networking opportunities provided by his new law partner, William Wallace (a Republican, son of a former governor, and a candidate himself, with strong connections to the local party organization) (Sievers 1960).
18. BH, speech at Lawrenceburg, IN, June 1860, quoted in Sievers (1960: 147).
19. BH, letter to J. A. Anderson, November 5, 1856, quoted in Sievers (1960: 125). John Fremont, a former governor and senator from California, was the Republican Party's first presidential candidate.
20. Harrison (1901: 473).
21. BH, 1860, quoted in Calhoun (2005: 20).
22. BH, letter to Caroline Harrison, December 24, 1862, quoted in Ringenberg (1986: 179).
23. BH, letter to Caroline Harrison, August 21, 1862, quoted in Sievers (1960: 190).
24. BH, letter to Caroline Harrison, August 20, 1864, quoted in Sievers (1960: 264).
25. BH, letter to Caroline Harrison, August 24, 1864, quoted in Sievers (1960: 273).
26. BH, letter to Caroline Harrison, May 21, 1865, quoted in Ringenberg (1986: 180).
27. Mayer (1964: 221); Ellis (2008: 100).
28. In 1860, Harrison had won election as Supreme Court reporter of Indiana. "The post was not only a dignified one, but most lucrative," notes his biographer. And during the war, Harrison relied heavily on its income to support his family. But in August 1862,

the Democrats forced his replacement with one of their own (Sievers 1960: 136–137, 208–209).

29. BH, "Speech to the Marquette Club Banquet," Chicago, March 20, 1888, quoted in Hedges (1892: 22).

30. Harrison had eschewed a congressional run just six years earlier. But by 1872, he had established his law firm and built up his family finances. Also, the governorship would allow him to remain home in Indianapolis, close to his family, friends, and church community. Thus, Harrison was now more enthusiastic about seeking elected office (Calhoun 2005).

31. Depew (1923: 140).

32. Cullom (1911: 248).

33. RBH, diary entry, June 24, 1888.

34. Harrison's rise in Indiana politics during the late 1870s was aided by the death of Republican governor and state machine boss Oliver P. Morton (1823–1877). The two men had been friends and allies until 1872, when Harrison revealed in court the shady financial practices of several Republican Party operatives, including Morton's brother-in-law. The powerful and tyrannical Morton considered Harrison disloyal and thereafter blocked his political progress. Harrison chose not to fight back and accepted years of near political exile until Morton died in late 1877 (Fuller 2017).

35. Calhoun (2008).

36. James Blaine (R-ME), Republican Party leader and US senator, also had a strong showing as a shadow candidate (Calhoun 2008).

37. Harrison was not the first Republican presidential candidate to openly campaign, but he was the most systematic to date. During the 1880 presidential campaign, James A. Garfield lived close to a major rail line and therefore received delegates at his home, speaking to them from his front porch. Four years later, Senator James A. Blaine toured for six weeks to meet voters, but then lost the election partly due to comments by a warm-up speaker about "rum, Romanism, and rebellion" that offended Irish and Catholic voters. It was these types of incidents that Harrison sought to avoid. Thankfully, Harrison's "home in Indianapolis was so accessible that he could not discourage visitors, so he deliberately planned his campaign around many voter pilgrimages" (Socolofsky and Spetter 1987: 11; Bourdon 2019; Calhoun 2008).

38. Johnson (2018: 121).

39. In 1888, Cleveland received 5,534,488 (48.6 percent) of the popular vote, Harrison won 5,443,892 (47.8 percent) (Calhoun 2008; supplemented by HSUS).

40. Such an unusual event had occurred only twice before in American history (in 1824, John Quincy Adams lost by 44,804 votes to Andrew Jackson; in 1876, Rutherford B. Hayes lost by 264,292 votes to Samuel J. Tilden) and would not occur again until the 2000 election (when George W. Bush lost the popular vote by 543,816 votes to Al Gore).

41. The latter was the Union Labor Party, consisting of remnants of the Greenback-Labor Party and Henry George enthusiasts. Its platform called for George's single tax on land, a shorter workday, federal control over all railroads and telegraphs, the abolition of child labor and convict labor, and mandatory federal inspections of factories, tenements, and mines.

42. Calhoun (1993).

43. Ringenberg (1986:182). A book-length statement can be found in Harrison (1901).

44. BH, "Speech at the Indianapolis Tabernacle," October 19, 1864, quoted in Sievers (1960: 275).

45. BH, speech in Indianapolis, IN, August 1865, quoted in *Indianapolis Journal*, August 12, 1865, reprinted in Sievers (1959: 13–14).

46. BH, "Speech to the Michigan Club Banquet," Detroit, February 22, 1888, quoted in Hedges (1892: 11).

47. BH, "Speech to the Michigan Club Banquet," Detroit, February 22, 1888, quoted in Hedges (1892: 11).

48. Some have argued that Cleveland did not favor ideology over party, but merely saw reform as essential for the Democratic Party's future success (Klinghard 2010). Labor issues constituted one problem with which both Cleveland and Harrison dealt similarly: a combination of neglect, sympathy for the workers, and support for the occasional use of force (or threat thereof) to quell striker violence and arrest strikers.

49. BH, "Address on the Issues of the Campaign," Carnegie Hall, New York City, August 27, 1896, quoted in *New York Times*, August 28, 1896.

50. Federal taxes on alcohol then constituted roughly 75 percent of internal federal revenues.

51. Sievers (1959); Graham (2015).

52. "Harrison played a similarly unimpressive role in the reform movement" (Sievers 1959: 220).

53. BH, letter to Kentwell, February 18, 1886, quoted in Sievers (1959: 284).

54. BH, "Gates of Castle Garden Speech," Indianapolis, IN, July 26, 1888, quoted in Hedges (1892: 61).

55. In particular, the 1834 Poor Laws under which "the charitable offering is snatched from the kind hand of the benevolent giver [e.g., the church and fellow citizens]" and placed under control of a faceless, "soulless" government and funded with "compulsory" taxes which allowed employers to reap a "princely magnificence" while providing workers with only "a starving portion" (BH, "The Poor of England," commencement address, Miami University, June 24, 1852, quoted in Sievers 1960: 65; Calhoun 2005: 14).

56. As a US senator, Harrison introduced over one hundred pension and relief bills for veterans, and he rarely blocked those proposed by others in Congress, even though many of these bills turned out to be fraudulent or undeserved (Sievers 1959: 210).

57. For example, Harrison argued that federal appropriations for *river* improvements were fine, but money for related *land* reclamation and levees was unconstitutional on a states' rights basis, despite the fact that he otherwise dismissed states' rights and accepted that river-land boundaries were poorly demarcated (Sievers 1959).

58. Harrison was more consistent on immigration during his presidency. In his 1888 presidential campaign, his rhetoric was fiercely anti-immigrant. He came out against the recruitment of contract labor and the admittance of "paupers and criminals" (BH, "Letter of Acceptance for the Republican Nomination," September 11, 1888, quoted in Hedges 1892: 111). As president, he lodged public, formal objections to Russia's

persecution of its Jews because it drove them to the United States impoverished and in large numbers and where they faced growing anti-Semitism. As a presidential candidate, he declared, "We are . . . clearly under a duty to defend our civilization by excluding alien races whose ultimate assimilation with our people is neither possible nor desirable" (111). As president, he encouraged further legislation to prohibit Chinese immigration and greater power to enforce bans on contract labor, which Congress delivered. And throughout his administration, Harrison generally stuck to these positions.

59. The problem here is that, if American production were replaced by imports from Britain, then there should not be "less goods all around." Even if there were, a change in supply would not necessarily affect demand, at least not in the direction indicated by Harrison. (Even during the Gilded Age, many believed in Say's Law, which suggests that supply and demand should move together, not in opposing directions.) Finally, if domestic prices increased so dramatically, they would draw domestic producers back into the market (Latham 1939: 30, quoted in Sievers 1959: 212–213).

60. BH, "Speech to the Marquette Club Banquet," Chicago, March 20, 1888, quoted in Hedges (1892: 22).

61. For example, he supported President Chester Arthur's efforts to reduce tariffs in 1882–1883 (Sievers 1959: 210–214, 227–228).

62. In his 1888 campaign, Harrison simplified his tariff logic: "[Economic] competition with foreign countries, without adequate discriminating and favoring duties, means lower wages to our working people. . . . [F]ree trade, means larger importations of foreign goods, and that means less work in America" (BH. speech in Indianapolis, IN, October 20, 1888, quoted in Hedges 1892: 179).

63. See, for example, his speech on the currency issue, reported in *Indianapolis* (IN) *News,* August 21, 1876.

64. BH, "Third Annual Message to Congress," December 9, 1891, *UCSB.*

65. BH, "First Annual Message to Congress," December 3, 1889, *UCSB.*

66. BH, speech at Danville, IN, August 18, 1876, quoted in Wallace (1888: 279).

67. BH, letter to H. B. Kelly, chairman of the Western States Commercial Congress, April 7, 1891, quoted in Hedges (1892: 289).

68. He most likely favored some form of bimetallism (Socolofsky and Spetter 1987).

69. Socolofsky and Spetter (1987: 47).

70. Whitelaw Reid, quoted in Sievers (1968: 4). Reid was also Harrison's running mate in the 1892 election campaign.

71. Louis T, Michener, former Indiana attorney general and advisor to BH, letter to US Attorney Eugene Hay, March 23, 1901, quoted in Sievers (1968: 276).

72. Sievers (1968: 5).

73. Senator William B. Allision (R-IA), letter to BH, September 8, 1889, quoted in Sievers (1968: 129).

74. Harrison considered summoning Congress into special session to work on Republican legislation, but a few unresolved House seats made him worry that "any combination of accidents or misfortunes . . . [could] leave us without a Republican quorum at the special session" (BH, letter to Senator George F. Hoar (R-MA), August 26, 1889, quoted in Calhoun 2005: 83).

75. In particular, a serious confrontation with Canada over seal fishing, and presiding over a long-sought-after Pan-American Conference to promote trade and investment. See Socolofsky and Spetter (1987); Herring (2008).

76. Soon after assuming office, his new Treasury secretary had warned, "It is believed that an attack in Congress on the existing restrictions on silver mintage will begin on its reassembling. Hence it is of the first importance that the Executive have results in Europe to show before that day" (William Windom to BH, March 1889, quoted in Horton 1891: 16).

77. Johnson (1889).

78. Johnstown Area Heritage Association (1889).

79. McCullough (1987); *Measuring Worth,* consumer price index; BH, wire to Governor J. A. Beaver of Pennsylvania, c. June 11, 1889, quoted in Sievers (1968: 77).

80. *Pittsburgh Daily Post,* July 25, 1890.

81. Sievers (1968: 78).

82. Benjamin H. Bristow, letter to Judge Walter Gresham, March 22, 1889, quoted in Sievers (1968: 41).

83. *New York Herald,* March 17–18, 1889, quoted in Sievers (1968: 48).

84. Quoted in Socolofsky and Spetter (1987: 16); Sievers (1959: 426). Harrison was likely willfully convinced by those who believed his victory had been "a graceful sweep over hill and dale along the lakes and from two oceans. . . . It has come so honestly, and so full of good will toward all, so free from abuse that the campaign leaves no sting" (David Swing, former classmate, letter to BH, November 12, 1888, quoted in Sievers 1959: 427). See also Klinghard (2010), who interprets Harrison's actions in light of the ongoing battle between presidents and state leaders over spoils and control of the party. Calhoun (2005, 2008) disputes this interpretation, arguing that Quay's quotation was more a venting of frustration by a disappointed Quay than the sincere belief of Harrison, and that the quote may even be apocryphal.

85. "Senatorial privilege" refers to the tradition of deferring to a senator's preferences and requests for federal appointments in his home state.

86. Quoted in Socolofsky and Spetter (1987: 33).

87. Socolofsky and Spetter (1987: 31).

88. Roosevelt complained that "the little gray man in the White House [looked on him] with cold and hesitating disapproval" (Morris 1979: 441).

89. Armbruster (1958).

90. Henry Codman Potter, "Address on the Centennial of George Washington's Inauguration," April 30, 1889, quoted in *New York Times,* May 1, 1889.

91. Dunn (1922: 10).

92. The former party leader in Harrison's cabinet was Senator James Blaine, a.k.a. "the Plumed Knight," whom Harrison reluctantly appointed secretary of state. Thrice a candidate for president, a Senate leader, a former secretary of state, and a party boss, Blaine was an ambitious political diva throughout the Gilded Age. But by 1893 he was in physical decline. For much of the Harrison administration, severe illness and the deaths of several of his children kept Blaine on the sidelines. On foreign policy, the two men agreed on much; at times, Harrison even took significant advice from Blaine. But Harrison served as his own secretary of state for much of his administration.

93. Oliphant (1932: 4).

94. BH, "First Annual Message to Congress," December 3, 1889, *UCSB*.

95. Socolofsky and Spetter (1987: 48).

96. Socolofsky and Spetter (1987: 43).

97. Ponder (1998).

98. Senator Shelby Cullom (R-IL), quoted in Socolofsky and Spetter (1987: 33).

99. *Boston Traveller,* April 22, 1889, quoted in Sievers (1968: 49).

100. Foraker (1916: 425).

101. According to Walter Wellman, *Chicago Tribune,* March 20, 1889; letter to Walter Q. Gresham, US Circuit Court judge and former cabinet member under CAA, in Sievers (1968: 43).

102. Wellman, Walter (*Chicago Tribune*). 1889. Letter to Walter Q. Gresham. (March 20). Quoted in Sievers (1968: 43).

103. During the war, Harrison had developed a rash, perhaps scarlet fever, which supposedly rendered his skin extremely sensitive (Moore 2006; Ellis 2008).

104. Morgan (1969: 229).

105. Senator William Washburn (R-MN), letter to E. G. Hay, May 20, 1891, quoted in Sievers (1968: 199).

106. Representative Joseph G. Canon (R-IL), quoted in Socolofsky and Spetter (1987: 80).

107. The first session alone lasted 303 days and has been compared with the ambitious 37th "Civil War" Congress (under Lincoln), 1861–1863, and the 63rd "Progressive" Congress (under Wilson), 1913–1915. Over 2,250 bills and resolutions were passed overall during the 51st Congress, more than any other Congress in the 19th century (and most of the 20th century). See Socolofsky and Spetter (1987: 47; supplemented by *HSUS*).

108. Applicants had to prove that they had served in the Union army for ninety days or more, had been honorably discharged, and that their disability was not due to addiction or sexual promiscuity (i.e., "vicious habits") (Costa 1998; Blanck and Millender 2000: 4).

109. Costa (1998).

110. Skocpol (1993).

111. Also perhaps the world's first national antitrust law (Kovacic 2010).

112. Hoogenboom and Hoogenboom (1976).

113. Sherman Antitrust Act (1890), Section 1.

114. Hauberg (1999: 8). True antitrust action would await the early 1900s and the presidencies of Theodore Roosevelt (1901–1909) and Howard Taft (1909–1913).

115. Excellent surveys can be found in Johnson (2018); Irwin (2017); Palen (2016).

116. Palen (2016).

117. WMcK, speaking to the US House of Representatives, May 7, 1890, in McKinley (1893: 422).

118. Calhoun (2006).

119. BH, "First Annual Message to Congress," December 3, 1889, *UCSB*.

120. It not only guaranteed the survival of the existing land-grant colleges, created under the First Morrill Act (1862) but put them on a new trajectory toward becoming world-class universities.

121. North and South Dakota (November 1889), Montana (November 1889), Washington (November 1889), Idaho (July 1890), and Wyoming (July 1890). Congress had passed, and the outgoing President Cleveland had signed, enabling legislation for the first four admissions in late February 1889, but their formal admission as states awaited Harrison's signature seven months later. Cleveland and the Democrats had opposed these admissions but gave way in light of victories by pro-statehood candidates in the 1888 elections. In addition, Oklahoma was formally organized into a territory by Congress in the Oklahoma Organic Act (May 1890).

122. Not for long, though. Of the new states admitted during 1889–1890, only Wyoming (and perhaps Washington) remained solidly Republican over time. The others began to elect "Silver" Republicans, Democrats, Populists, Progressives, and Independents within a few election cycles.

123. Thomas Fitch, ex-congressman, R-NV, speech at First National Silver Convention, St. Louis, MO, November 1889, quoted in Frieden (1997: 387).

124. President Andrew Johnson (1865–1869) was a bimetallist while silver was still legal tender and he died before its demonetization became controversial. But he generally spoke against depreciation of US currency, including that of silver coins. See, for example, his February 2–3, 1853, "Speech Opposing Change in Coinage" in Graf et al. (1970: 129–132). Where Johnson rebelled, it was in his support for the partial repudiation of US war debts during the late 1860s. For he described debt as the means by which an elite financial aristocracy exerted their control over American politics (Bergeron 2011; Castel 1979).

125. Dunn (1922: 36).

126. While support for silver coinage was rising in both parties, only one-third of state-level Republican Party platforms then supported it (just under two-thirds in the Democratic Party). And while no party explicitly endorsed the gold standard, the House reliably voted against silver. It was senators from the newly admitted silver states who were the major obstacle to gold. They wanted nothing less than the free coinage of silver, hence the end of the gold standard. But only around 20 percent of the Senate was from silver-producing states. Therefore Harrison might have used his veto power, and perhaps patronage, to win their support for tariffs, pensions, and so on. But Harrison instead prioritized Republican Party unity (Bensel 2000: 136).

127. Payment would be in the form of Treasury certificates, which could be redeemed in silver or gold. There was also considerable leeway for the president, and market forces, to prevent rampant silver coinage (Timberlake 1993; Friedman and Schwartz 1963).

128. Sherman (1896: 1070). Historian Charles Calhoun suggests that Sherman was being "disingenuous" here: "Rather than grandstanding in a fashion that could paint the silverites into a corner, Harrison [had] worked behind the scenes [on monetary policy]." Calhoun therefore contends that "there was little doubt" that Harrison would veto silver free-coinage legislation (personal correspondence with the author, July 2020).

129. *New York Times*, September 12, 1890.

130. Socolofsky and Spetter (1987); Sievers (1968).

131. An Act to Reduce the Revenue and Equalize Duties on Imports, and for Other Purposes, 1890 (October 1).
132. Johnson (2018: 123).
133. Donald Dickson, former postmaster general, 1890, quoted in Bolt (1970: 50).
134. Secretary of State James Blaine, quoted in Irwin (2017: 269). A Republican from Maine, Blaine had served as US House member (1863–1876), US House Speaker (1869–1875), US senator (1876–1881), and secretary of state (1881, 1889–1892) and had made three runs at the presidency (1876, 1880, 1884).
135. Quoted in Olcott (1916: 127).
136. Irwin (2017); Johnson (2018).
137. Irwin (2017: 284).
138. For example, see Pursell (1962).
139. Taussig (1915: 153); confirmed in subsequent analysis by Irwin (2017).
140. Irwin (2000).
141. Skocpol (1992).
142. Birnie (2006); Berend (2012); Easterbrook and Aitken (1956); Tolliday (2001).
143. Peck (1906: 198).
144. Mary Ellen Lease, Populist speaker and political activist, 1890, quoted in Cochrane (1993: 311).
145. During the 1890s, state and local elections tended to focus on race and ethnicity, religion, and party loyalty (Bensel 2000; Nichols and Unger 2017).
146. After all, the 52nd Congress (1891–1893), though flush with Democrats, spent even *more* heavily and enthusiastically than the thoroughly Republican one it replaced (BH, comments to Frank Tibbott, Harrison's stenographer and private secretary, in diary entry, November 8, 1890, quoted in Sievers (1968: 181).
147. Michener and Weidenmier (2008).
148. Wirth (1893: 234).
149. Socolofsky and Spetter (1987); Sievers (1968).
150. President Grant had signed a law establishing Yellowstone in March 1872. But illegal hunting, poaching, vandalism, and reckless campfires beset it for years. Harrison's action expanded the park by 1.2 million acres and designated it as a national reserve, protected by the executive branch. See Graham (2015).
151. The 1891 legislation on meat inspections built upon a similar bill supported by Harrison the previous year. It ended a devastating "pork war" begun by France and Germany during the early 1880s, which had been fumbled by Arthur and neglected by Cleveland. Partly as a result, by the time Harrison left office, American hog prices had risen 80 percent.
152. Dozer (1948).
153. *New York Times,* April 14, 1891.
154. *New York Times,* April 14, 1891.
155. Friedman and Schwartz (1963: 106n25).
156. BH, letter to the Western States Commercial Congress meeting in Kansas City, MO, April 7, 1891, quoted in Sievers (1968: 59).
157. *The Economist,* April 25, 1891.

158. *The Economist,* April 25, 1891.

159. Alfani and Gráda (2017).

160. Constitutions of the Amalgamated Association of Iron and Steel Workers, June 1892, quoted in Demarest and Weingartner (1992: 17).

161. Krause (1992); Wolff (1965); Demarest and Weingartner (1992).

162. *St. Louis* (MO) *Dispatch,* July 6, 1892, quoted in Demarest and Weingartner (1992: 75).

163. Krause (1992: 3).

164. *Blindell v. Hagan,* 54 F. 40 (Louisiana, February 9, 1893); *United States v. Workingmen's Amalgamated Council of New Orleans,* 54 F. 994 (Louisiana, March 25, 1893); *Waterhouse v. Comer,* 56 F. 149 (Georgia, April 1893).

165. BH, letter to Mary McKee, July 30, 1892, quoted in Sievers (1968: 241–242).

166. Markel (1997).

167. *New York Sun,* August 26, 1892.

168. *New York Sun,* August 27, 1892.

169. National Quarantine Act of 1893.

170. Congress had set an eight-hour day for federal workers back in 1868, but its results were disappointing. Federal wages were cut along with hours, private contractors were not covered, and private industry chose not to follow suit. Nor was the law well-enforced. The 1892 law extended the eight-hour workday to all federal workers, including contractors and subcontractors on public works projects. But again, enforcement would prove lax.

171. Strangely, the National Bureau of Economic Research (2021) does not record this period as recessionary, or at least not until January 1893.

172. *Wall Street Journal,* November 5, 1892.

173. Depew (1923: 134–135).

174. *Commercial and Financial Chronicle,* November 12, 1892.

175. *Commercial and Financial Chronicle,* November 12, 1892.

176. *Wall Street Journal,* November 10, 1892.

177. *Iron Age,* November 17, 1892.

178. *Commercial and Financial Chronicle,* November 12, 1892.

179. Steeples and Whitten (1998; supplemented by *NBER Macro*).

180. Reti (1998).

181. Congressman George F. Williams (D-MA), 1892, quoted in *New York Times,* December 6, 1892.

182. *Wall Street Journal,* December 17, 1892. After some encouraging discussions with foreign governments about bimetallism, the Harrison administration enthusiastically participated in a November–December 1892 international monetary conference to discuss a coordinated move toward silver. When the conference ended in failure, speculators who had bid up the price of silver in anticipation of an international agreement now sold off. Wall Street pressured the Treasury Department for new bond sales so as to avert a panic and to defend federal gold inventories. This time, Harrison refused. He saw in the demand a financial scheme to drive up interest rates. The stock market remained unperturbed. However, these events increased

the air of uncertainty and rising risk around the US currency (Reti 1998; Sievers 1968: 252).

183. Even despite a strong Christmas season in 1892 (*Rhode's Journal of Banking* 20 [January 1893]: 97).

184. Quoted in *Wall Street Journal,* February 15, 1893.

185. Williamson (2022).

186. *Commercial and Financial Chronicle,* March 4, 1893, quoted in Steeples and Whitten (1998: 32).

187. BH, "Fourth Annual Message to Congress," December 6, 1892, *UCSB*.

188. BH, "Address on the Issues of the Campaign," Carnegie Hall, New York City, August 27, 1896, quoted in *New York Times,* August 28, 1896.

189. The ratio of private wealth to national income was relatively flat during much of Harrison's term: 453 percent (1889), 462 percent (1890), 465 percent (1891), 458 percent (1892). It jumped to 475 percent only in 1893, likely in connection with that year's financial crisis soon after he left office. The ratio of private wealth to average disposable income tells a similar story (Piketty and Zucman 2014).

190. BH, "Letter Accepting the Presidential Nomination," September 3, 1892, *UCSB*.

191. For example, in a letter to W. W. Slaughter (March 14, 1885) concerned about Republican losses in the South, BH wrote, "[A] division of the white vote in the South furnishes the only possible solution . . . [using] the tariff or some other financial question [to divide them]." Or on the currency: "Cleveland's silver letter has produced a wide and bitter break in his party in Congress. . . . If we are left half a chance, we can beat them in 1886" (BH. letter to Louis T. Michener, February 7, 1885, both quoted in Sievers (1959: 275, 269).

192. Mayer (1964: 221).

193. Dewey (1907: 227).

Chapter 11

1. Immigration policy was not a priority for Cleveland during his second term, a rare intermission for an otherwise chronic inflammatory issue during the Gilded Age. Thanks to the Great Depression of 1893–1897, new arrivals plummeted to just 30 percent of their 1882 highs, near the lowest rates of the entire Gilded Age (on a per resident basis). Thus, immigration shrank dramatically in the 1890s, both as a physical phenomenon and as a political problem.

2. Welsh (1988: 137).

3. See Chapter 9 on Cleveland's first administration.

4. *New York Times,* November 5, 1885.

5. Parker (1909: 246).

6. SGC, "Speech to the New York Chamber of Commerce Banquet," November 19, 1889, in Parker (1892: 158).

7. SGC, letter to former House Speaker John G. Carlisle (D-KY), April 7, 1890, quoted in Nevins (1932: 462).

8. Nevins (1932b: 464).
9. SGC, "Comments at the Thurman Birthday Banquet," Columbus, OH, November 13, 1890, in Parker (1892: 158).
10. Timberlake (1993); Friedman and Schwartz (1963).
11. SGC, letter to E. Ellery Anderson, chairman of the Reform Club, February 10, 1891, quoted in *New York Times*, February 12, 1891.
12. Wilson (1897).
13. The dignified Cleveland refused to stump, while the sickness and death of Harrison's wife during the height of campaign season sapped his enthusiasm for politics. Thus the *New York Herald* on October 26 described the 1892 campaign season as being "marked by an exceptional calmness . . . an unprecedented absence of noisy demonstration, popular excitement and that high pressure enthusiasm." See also Knoles (1942).
14. The Populists supported silver coinage, income taxes on the wealthy, the nationalization of the railroads, tax cuts, the creation of government banks, and new barriers to immigration (Populist Party Platform of 1892, *UCSB*; Knoles 1942).
15. *Wall Street Journal*, March 18, 1893. The "silver cloud" refers to the threat of the United States leaving the international gold standard in favor of either a bimetallic silver-gold standard or a *de facto* silver standard for the US dollar.
16. Villard (1904: 363).
17. SGC, "Second Inaugural Address," March 4, 1893, *UCSB*.
18. Nevins (1932b); Welsh (1988).
19. Wheat was pivotal to the depression of 1893 due to its massive price fluctuations and the effects of declining wheat prices on the prices of other important commodities (those for which wheat could substitute), and hence on wages and the daily costs of living. See O'Connor (1970); Lewis (2010).
20. Dupont (2009).
21. Lauck (1907); Carlson (2013).
22. Sprague (1910).
23. *New York Times*, February 21, 1893.
24. Back in July 1882, Congress had passed, with only passive support from President Arthur, new national banking legislation. Its main purpose was to extend the federal charters of already existing national banks; it also attempted to rein in the printing of paper money by eliminating small denominations of greenbacks. More fatefully, it also forbade the US Treasury from issuing gold certificates (essentially paper money backed by gold, with a dollar-gold exchange rate fixed by law) if its reserves of physical specie fell below $100 million. This prohibition was so little noticed at the time, and so poorly enforced thereafter, that much debate ensued as to whether the statute existed at all. On April 17, 1893, the *New York Sun* called it "most absurdly misinterpreted," and historians of the period have fallen on either side of the debate. Nevertheless, the $100 million floor on US Treasury gold inventories exerted a powerful effect on market psychology throughout the 1880s and 1890s. It was perceived as a monetary Rubicon that must not be crossed. And whenever the federal gold supply fell near $100 million, fearful newspaper headlines appeared and bank runs and financial panics loomed.

25. For example, *New York Times,* April 22, 1893.

26. *Bradstreet's,* May 6, 1893, quoted in White (1982: 11).

27. For example, *Commercial and Financial Chronicle.* April 22, 1893.

28. J. Edward Simmons, president of the Fourth National Bank, New York City, quoted in *New York Times,* April 22, 1893.

29. Nevins (1932b); Welch (1988); Brodsky (2000).

30. SGC, "Special Message to Congress," August 8, 1893, *UCSB.*

31. SGC, letter to Governor William J. Northen of Georgia, September 25, 1893, quoted in Bergh (1909: 353).

32. Alfred de Cordova, letter to *New York Times,* dated April 29, printed May 1, 1893.

33. Nevins (1932b: 526).

34. Silla (2018); Downey (2002); Larson (2003).

35. SGC, "Speech at the Columbian Exposition of 1893," Chicago, May 1, 1893, quoted in *New York Tribune,* May 2, 1893.

36. At the time, industrial corporations were perceived by investors as highly speculative. National Cordage had been formed, in part, to address such concerns. It was considered too big, too well-run, and too well-vetted to fail. Therefore, its bankruptcy was shocking. It "raised questions about the stability of the entire class of industrial securities and contributed to a collapse in investor interest in them" (O'Sullivan 2016: 109; Dewing 1913).

37. *New York Tribune,* June 6, 1893.

38. *The Economist,* June 10, 1893.

39. Frank Knight Sturgis, quoted in *Wall Street Journal,* July 22, 1893.

40. Steeples and Whitten (1998).

41. In Washington, 35 percent of existing liabilities were lost; also leading the list of most financially damaged states were Kansas (23 percent), Montana (18.5 percent), Louisiana (12.3 percent), Colorado (10.8 percent), Minnesota (9.7 percent), and Idaho (9.0 percent) (Carlson 2013; Ramírez 2009).

42. *Omaha* (NE) *World Herald,* May 7, 1893, quoted in White (1982: 11).

43. Nevins (1932b: 524).

44. Nevins (1932b); Wilson (1897).

45. Wilson (1897).

46. Wilson (1897).

47. Cleveland first noticed the malignancy in May 1893 (Algeo 2011).

48. Nevins (1932b: 530).

49. A second follow-up surgery was performed two weeks later to remove suspect tissue (Algeo 2011).

50. Keen (1917).

51. *New York Times,* August 3, 1893.

52. Steeples and Whitten (1998); White (1982).

53. *Chicago Tribune,* August 6, 1893.

54. *New York Tribune,* August 7, 1893.

55. William Jennings Bryan, speech in the House of Representatives, August 16, 1893, in Bryan (1913: 81). This was not his famous "Cross of Gold Speech," which Bryan

would present three years later at the Democratic Party's convention to win the presidential nomination.

56. Congressman Thomas B. Reed (R-ME), speech in the House of Representatives, August 26, 1893, reprinted in *Boston Evening Transcript,* August 26, 1893.

57. SGC, "Message on the Repeal of the Sherman Silver Purchase Act," August 8, 1893, *UCSB.*

58. Welch (1988); Nevins (1932b).

59. *New York Times,* October 31, 1893.

60. The high interest rates in New York City lured back European investors and repaired bank balance sheets; the repeal of the silver purchase requirements of the Sherman Silver Act restored confidence in the US adherence to the gold standard; and regulators conducted examinations of banks so as to sort out healthy from risky banks for potential depositors. See Carlson (2013).

61. Hoffmann (1970).

62. And by 1894, trading volumes on the NYSE had fallen by just under two-thirds from their 1892 peak (O'Sullivan 2016: 138; supplemented by Shiller 2015).

63. The ratio of private wealth to national income exploded from 458 percent (1892) to 509 percent (1894), while private wealth to average disposable income went from 506 percent (1892) to 562 percent (1894). These were the steepest increases and the highest levels of the Gilded Age (Piketty and Zucman 2014).

64. Ramírez (2009).

65. Ramírez (2009).

66. *New York Times,* July 9, 1894; December 19, 1893.

67. Steeples and Whitten (1998).

68. Larson (2003).

69. McSeveney (1972).

70. Henry Adams, letter to Elizabeth Cameron (wife of Senator J. Donald Cameron, niece of William Tecumseh Sherman and John Sherman), August 8, 1893, quoted in Steeples and Whitten (1998: 1).

71. Grant (1983). For contemporary accounts, see Shaw (1894); Closson (1894).

72. New Zealand enacted the first minimum wage law in 1894. In 1912, Massachusetts passed the first American minimum wage law, applicable only to women and children under eighteen. Meanwhile, women and children were legally prohibited from working in manufacturing and mining in some states (Starr 1993).

73. McSeveney (1972).

74. Skocpol (1992).

75. Senator James Berry (D-AR), December 19, 1893, quoted in White (1982: 25).

76. Welch (1988); Irwin (2017); Johnson (2018).

77. For examples, see Williams (1973); Schlup (1978).

78. Average duties on tariffed goods dropped to 1880s levels.

79. Perhaps the only noteworthy penalty was that the abolition of wool tariffs may have severely hurt the American sheep and wool industry. See Bensel (2000).

80. Welsh (1988: 137).

81. Stoddard (1927: 208).

82. Nevins (1932b: 583–584).
83. John Hay, letter to Whitelaw Reid, August 4, 1894, quoted in Clymer (1975: 58).
84. Senator John McAuley Palmer (D-IL), communication to SGC, August 23, 1894, quoted in McElroy (1923: 115).
85. Nevins (1932b: 587).
86. Timberlake (1993); Friedman and Schwartz (1963).
87. Surpassed only in 1916 (8.4 percent), 1919 (20.8 percent), 1922 (8.7 percent), and 1946 (10.5 percent).
88. Alexander (2015); Schwantes (1985).
89. *New York World,* May 1, 1894, evening edition; *Los Angeles Herald,* March 9, 1894; *Lincoln* (NE) *Courier,* April 21, 1894.
90. Alexander (2015); Schwantes (1985).
91. Papke (1999: xiii). See also Schneirov, Stromquist, and Salvatore (1999).
92. *New York World,* July 1894, quoted in Dubofsky and Dulles (2010: 156).
93. Quoted in Nevins (1932b: 628).
94. *MeasuringWorth,* Consumer Price Index measure.
95. Governor John P. Altgeld of Illinois, letter to SGC, July 5, 1894, quoted in *Railway World,* July 14, 1894.
96. SGC, telegram to Governor John P. Altgeld, July 5, 1894, in Nevins (1933: 360). Cleveland (1913) later published a book-length defense of his actions.
97. July 11 (Senate) and July 16 (House), 1894.
98. *In re Eugene V. Debs*, 158 U.S. 564 (1895).
99. Quoted in *The Nation,* February 22, 1894.
100. Grant and Kelly (2008).
101. Lapinski (2013).
102. Summers (2008).
103. Summers (2008).
104. Wilson (1897: 296).
105. Schurz (1897).
106. Leff (2008). See also Tulis (1987).
107. The title of this section is from Summers (2008).
108. SGC, "Message to Congress on the Need for Action to Restore Confidence in Financial Soundness," January 28, 1895, *UCSB.*
109. Senator John Morgan (D-AL), 1894, quoted in Brodsky (2000: 356).
110. Governor Ben Tillman (D) of South Carolina, June 1894, quoted in Brodsky (2000: 356).
111. Williamson (2022).
112. The ratio of private wealth to national income was still 502 percent in 1896, while private wealth to average disposable income was 555 percent (Piketty and Zucman 2014).
113. (Federico and Tena-Junguito 2019).
114. Ware (2006).
115. Williams (2010).
116. Former Democrat, Congressman Thomas E. Watson (GA).

117. Miller (1897).
118. Howard (1895).
119. Brodsky (2000); Palen (2016). Possibly to combat this image of weakness, Cleveland triggered a war scare in mid-December 1896, when he threatened military action against Great Britain if London failed to respect the Monroe Doctrine in managing the border dispute between British Guyana and Venezuela. See Cleaver (2014).
120. Tillman, Ben (Senator, D-SC). Quoted in *Twentieth Century Magazine* 16 (11): 6 (March 12, 1896).
121. SGC, "Second Inaugural Address," March 4, 1893, *UCSB*.
122. Brodsky (2000: 291).
123. Garraty (1968: 295).

Chapter 12

1. Miller (1897).
2. The concept of the "developmental state" originated in late 20th-century explanations of the rapid development of East Asian nations put forward by Chalmers Johnson, Meredith Woo-Cumings, T. J. Pempel, Ben Ross Schneider, Megan Greene, Gordon White, and others. For a survey see Woo-Cumings (1999). However, in the 20th-century version, the developmental state often *depreciates* its currency in order to boost exports, while offering a cheap, but disciplined, domestic labor force to attract investment in manufacturing, often via foreign subsidiaries. The 19th-century American version involved currency *appreciation* in order to reassure investors, who put vital marginal financial capital into manufacturing and infrastructure, despite a relatively expensive labor force. See also Link and Maggor (2020); Maggor (2017).
3. Other territories acquired by the United States under McKinley included Hawaii, Puerto Rico, Wake Island, and American Samoa (Herring 2008).
4. Herring (2008); Kennedy (1987); May (1961).
5. Smith (2015: 160); Leech (1959).
6. Quoted in Morgan (2003: 8).
7. Russell (1896: 57).
8. The others are Andrew Johnson (1865–1869), Grover Cleveland (1881–1885, 1893–1897) and Harry S. Truman (1945–1953).
9. Stoddard (1927: 229). Several in McKinley's cabinet agreed. For example, his Treasury secretary later wrote, "He was not a scientist, nor a poet, nor distinguished in literature or philosophy. He was related in his thought to practical affairs. . . . He understood men, and perceived clearly the springs of action, noble and ignoble, by which they were moved" (Gage 1937: 110–111).
10. Armstrong (2000).
11. Quoted in Morgan (2003: 10).
12. Quoted in Morgan (2003: 13).

13. Morgan (2003: 14).
14. RBH, "Address to the Ohio Farmer's Alliance," Lakeside, OH, July 30, 1891.
15. Quoted in Morgan (2003: 26).
16. Olcott (1916: 57).
17. In particular, Mark Hanna, a mine owner and shrewd Republican Party powerbroker, would later become an invaluable political ally. An ardent campaigner for McKinley, Hanna was later described by longtime congressman and senator James E. Waston (R-IN) as "the greatest field marshal of political hosts that ever led his forces into battle in this country since the Civil War" (Watson 1936: 52). See also Horner (2010).
18. All told, McKinley's roughly thirteen years in Congress are exceeded or rivaled only by six other US presidents: Joe Biden (thirty-six years), LBJ (twenty-four years), Ford (twenty-four years), Garfield (eighteen years), Polk (fourteen years), and JFK (thirteen years). McKinley failed to complete one of his terms in Congress: he was seated in the 48th Congress and served from March 4, 1883, to May 27, 1884, when he was replaced by Jonathan Wallace (D-OH), who had successfully contested McKinley's election. But McKinley won his next election and served in the 49th Congress, as well as two subsequent Congresses (March 4, 1885–March 3, 1891) (US House of Representatives. History, Art, & Archives, https://history.house.gov/People/Detail/17980).
19. For contemporary descriptions, see, for example, Wichita (KS) Daily Eagle, July 15, 1888; Helena (MT) Weekly Herald, December 26, 1889; New York Times, September 20, 1890; see also Morgan (2003: 61); Skrabec (2008).
20. Gould (1980).
21. Dunn (1922: 207); Stoddard (1927: 230).
22. The primary tax-writing committee in the House of Representatives, from which the Constitution mandates that "[a]ll Bills for raising Revenue shall originate." Ways and Means has long been a stepping stone to higher federal office. As of 2020, eight presidents and eight vice presidents have served on it, along with twenty-one House Speakers and four Supreme Court Justices.
23. Merry (2017: 85).
24. Morgan (2003: 137).
25. St. Louis (MO) Globe Democrat, October 26, 1892; Minneapolis (MN) Star Tribune, March 30, 1893.
26. WMcK, speech on the Gorman Tariff in Bangor, ME, September 8, 1894, reprinted in Ogilvie (1896: 151).
27. The section relies on Williams (2010); Durden (2015). One journalist called McKinley "beyond doubt the most popular man in the country" at this time (Dunn 1922: 207).
28. For example, McKinley once told a Boston luncheon party, "I have never been in doubt since I was old enough to think intelligently that I should sometime be made president" (quoted in Powers 1925: 164). Fellow Ohio congressman Theodore Burton later remarked, "No one except those who were close to him ever knew how anxious Mr. McKinley was for an office when he went after it" (Theodore Burton, April 11, 1906, quoted in Merry 2017: 74).

29. Wolman (1992).
30. WMcK, "Speech Accepting the Republican Nomination for Governor," Columbus, OH, June 17, 1891, reprinted in McKinley (1893: 531). As for McKinley's support for silver while in Congress, Mark Hanna later explained, "He did not pretend to be a doctor of finance and had followed the popular trend of that time." That is, McKinley's district strongly backed bimetallism, therefore McKinley did too (quoted in Morgan 2003: 47).
31. Though less so for free silver. In fact, so strong was public trust in his stance on "sound currency," that, despite McKinley's earlier support for bimetallism, even many Bourbon Democrats pledged their votes to him. For example, John Palmer, the pro-gold Democratic splinter candidate for president, himself declared, days before the 1896 election, "I promise you, my fellow Democrats, I will not consider it any very great fault if you decide next Tuesday to cast your ballot for William McKinley" (quoted in *Kansas City* [MO] *Journal*, November 2, 1896.
32. Bensel (2008).
33. Active since the late 1870s, Bourbon Democrats yearned to return to pre–Civil War practices of minimal government. By 1896, "Bourbon" referred more generally to all political-economic conservative Democrats, often from the South. Bourbon Democrats favored both small government and big business. Thus, they supported the gold standard and laissez-faire capitalism, while opposing state subsidies, regulation, and trade protections. In foreign policy, they opposed US expansion overseas, such as the acquisition of Hawaii (Witcover 2003; Feldman 2013).
34. William Jennings Bryan, "Speech Accepting the Democratic Nomination for the Presidency," August 10, 1896; "Cross of Gold" speech at the Democratic National Convention in Chicago, July 9, 1896, both reprinted in Bryan (1913: 268, 246).
35. "The 1896 Democratic party platform, written by silverites, was a nearly point-by-point refutation of the Cleveland years; attacks on the Republican party were practically an afterthought" (Klinghard 2010: 154).
36. Recall that, during the 1790s, Congress had legislated the free minting of silver bullion into coins to encourage specie production in the capital-sparse United States. These provisions had been quietly dropped by the Mint Act of 1873 (a.k.a. the Coinage Act of 1873). Backed by Treasury officials and "hard money" men in Congress, the Mint Act also eliminated silver's status as legal tender except for small transactions. At the time, silver coins had fallen into disuse because the metal's price was higher as bullion than as coin. Thus, the Mint Act passed with overwhelming majorities and little debate in Congress. President Grant had signed it without fanfare. But in subsequent years, the market price of silver bullion fell. Americans also found themselves struggling through recession after recession, in dire need of expanded loans and credit, especially farmers. Thus, the "free silver" movement was born. See preceding chapters for more detail.
37. William Jennings Bryan, "Speech Accepting the Democratic Nomination for the Presidency," August 10, 1896, reprinted in *New York Sun*, August 13, 1896.
38. As historian Barbara Tuchman (1966: 160) put it, "The [1896 presidential] campaign roused the country to extremes of emotion and reciprocal hate. It was Silver

against Gold, the People against the Interests, the farmer against the railroad oper-ator who siphoned off his profits in high freight charges, the little man against the banker, the speculator and the mortgage holder. Among Republicans there was real fear that a Democratic victory, coming after the violence of Homestead and Pullman, would mean overturn of the capitalist system." Similarly, historian James Livingston (1986: 100–103) described the period as a battle over "a new way of seeing, and so of defining, America," and whether the nation would adopt the policies "critical to the maintenance and further development of a modern civilization . . . [and] support an advanced system of production and exchange."

39. The McKinley campaign also innovated, featuring the first presidential film "spot," which was shown in the few public cinemas around the country (Auerbach 1999).
40. Chandler (1998).
41. Palen (2016).
42. The vast reduction in "spoils" had mostly neutered that practice as a campaign tool by 1896. Therefore campaign donations, especially from business corporations and the wealthy, had become an increasing potent financial weapon (Mutch 2014). See also Parker (2008).
43. See, for example, Chandler and Quincy (1896).
44. Dr. Collins, quoted in *Meriden* (CT) *Republican*, October 3, 1896.
45. *New York Times*, September 27, 1896.
46. Williams (2010: 129).
47. "I cannot stump against that man," McKinley told his campaign team. "I might as well put up a trapeze on my front lawn and compete against some professional athlete as go out speaking against Bryan." He also feared that mere appearances might produce a public relations disaster: "[I]f I took a whole train, Bryan would take a sleeper; if I took a sleeper, Bryan would take a chair car; if I took a chair car, he would ride a freight train" (quoted in Williams 2010: 130; Troy 1996: 105).
48. McKinley was not an innovator here. Front-porch campaigns had been used by James Garfield (1880) and Benjamin Harrison (1888). See Bourdon (2019). Other than his front-porch speeches, McKinley's (1896) only major contribution was his election-year tome *The Tariff of Henry Clay and Since*. It is a windy, chapter-less history of US tariff policy and its supposed benefits for Americans, with considerable space dedi-cated to McKinley's own contributions to the cause.
49. Williams (2010); Harpine (2005).
50. *New York Times*, July 13, 1896.
51. *Wall Street Journal*, September 12, 1896.
52. *Wall Street Journal*, September 26, 1896.
53. *The Economist*, July 11, 1896.
54. *Wall Street Journal*, July 29, 1896.
55. *Wall Street Journal*, July 29, 1896.
56. US Treasury Department (1927: 119).
57. *Wall Street Journal*, October 24, 1896.
58. From March to October 1896.

59. *Wall Street Journal,* July 30, 1896.

60. *Wall Street Journal,* September 23, 1896.

61. In raw economic terms, Bryan won those counties where interest rates (and therefore mortgage rates) were high, railroad penetration was low, and farm prices had recently declined (Eichengreen et al. 2017).

62. In fact, state by state, the vote was so close that myriad local factors and campaign choices might have altered the result (Eichengreen et al. 2017; Williams 2010).

63. The best-performing third parties included the National "Gold" Democratic Party (0.97 percent of the popular vote), the Prohibition Party (0.94 percent), and the Socialist Labor Party (0.26 percent).

64. In the House elections, Republicans took 206 seats, Democrats won 124, and Populists took 22. The remaining seats went to Silver Republicans (3), a Silver Party candidate (1), and an Independent Republican (1). Of the 90 Senate seats available, Republicans won 43, Democrats won only 33, and Populists took 5. The remaining 7 Senate seats were split between the ephemeral Silver Republican Party (5) and the Silver Party (2) (Martis, Rowles, and Pauer 1989).

65. *Wall Street Journal,* November 4, 1896.

66. Fulford and Schwartzman (2020).

67. *Wall Street Journal,* November 7, 1896. R. G. Dun was the first successful commercial and credit reporting agency in America and pioneered the industry. It merged with a competitor in 1933 to form the Dun & Bradstreet Corporation.

68. *Wall Street Journal,* November 10, 1896.

69. *Wall Street Journal,* November 10, 1896.

70. Robert Goodbody and Co., letter to *Wall Street Journal,* November 21, 1896.

71. For example, the failure of the high-profile Illinois National Bank in late December 1896 set off "a financial shaking up . . . such as has not been felt since the panic of [1893]" (*New York Times,* December 22, 1896).

72. WMcK, June 1896, quoted in Olcott (1916: 321). This changed little over his political career. McKinley's first speech as a congressman on the House floor was in support of higher tariffs.

73. Skrabec (2008).

74. WMcK, "A Reply to Mr. Cleveland. Address at the Lincoln Banquet," Toledo, OH, February 12, 1891, quoted in McKinley (1893: 487).

75. WMcK, "Address before the Home Market Club," Boston, February 9, 1888, quoted in McKinley (1893: 294).

76. At first, many Union soldiers were supplied with obsolete equipment or nothing at all. McKinley's own infantry regiment was initially provided no uniforms and given muskets "of an old-fashioned sort," perhaps forty years old. They had such severe problems getting adequate equipment that McKinley's commander had to intervene to quell a soldiers' strike (Koistinen 1996; Keegan 2009; Wilson 2006; Armstrong 2000).

77. WMcK, speech in the House of Representatives (on the Mills Tariff Bill), May 18, 1888, quoted in McKinley (1893: 294).

78. Dubofsky and Dulles (2010); Weinstein (2003); Buhle (2013).

79. Based partly on the writings of Immanuel Kant, the belief that trade policy could be a powerful lever in the conduct of US foreign policy had a considerable history in American thought, dating back to Thomas Jefferson (Herring 2008).

80. Tarbell (1911: 186).

81. WMcK, campaign speech at the Academy of Music, Petersburg, VA, October 9, 1885, quoted in McKinley (1893: 194).

82. Leech (1959: 12); Skrabec (2008: 44).

83. McKinley liked to tell a story about "[a] college-bred American . . . who had travelled much in Europe [on] inherited wealth . . . [and who] said to me a few years ago, with a sort of listless satisfaction, that he had *outgrown his country*. What a confession! Outgrown his country! Outgrown America! Think of it!" (WMcK, "Address before the Home Market Club," Boston, February 9, 1888, quoted in McKinley 1893: 260).

84. WMcK, campaign speech in Cleveland, OH, October 5, 1889, quoted in McKinley (1893: 368).

85. WMcK, speech in the House of Representatives (on free elections), April 18, 1879, quoted in McKinley (1893: 49). Though McKinley did push back against the idea that "the Cabinet of the President . . . [t]hat body, unknown to the Constitution, with no legislative power, is to prepare a bill and the Congress is to accept and adopt it" (WMcK, "Address to Ohio Republican League," Columbus, February 14, 1893, quoted in McKinley 1893: 635).

86. WMcK, speech in the House of Representatives (on the Treasury surplus), April 18, 1886, quoted in McKinley (1893: 205).

87. John Hay, letter to Joseph Choate, US ambassador to the United Kingdom, June 15, 1899, quoted in Morgan (2003: 344).

88. Many of the founding members of the Republican Party had come from the dying Whig Party during the 1850s. Whigs feared presidential overreach. They had originally formed in reaction to the unprecedented executive actions of Andrew Jackson and advocated a more passive president who deferred to Congress and the American people (Holt 1999; Howe 1979).

89. WMcK, campaign Speech in Cleveland, OH, October 5, 1889, quoted in McKinley (1893: 368); WMcK, Comment to a friend, 1900, quoted in Olcott (1916: 218).

90. Quoted in Gould (1980: 209).

91. WMcK, speech in the House of Representatives (on the Mills Tariff Bill), May 18, 1888, quoted in McKinley (1893: 303).

92. WMcK, speech in the House of Representatives (On a Senate tariff bill), January 26, 1889, quoted in McKinley (1893: 357).

93. In fact, just months into his presidency, McKinley argued, "Domestic conditions are sure to be improved by larger exchanges with the nations of the world. . . . Reciprocity of trade promotes reciprocity of friendship" (WMcK, "Speech at the Commercial Club," Cincinnati, OH, October 30, 1897, quoted in McKinley 1900: 54). See also Palen (2016); Wolman (1992).

94. As president, McKinley appointed a special ambassador who negotiated reciprocity treaties with eleven Latin American economies, as well as France, Germany, Italy,

Portugal, and Spain, though the protectionist US Senate refused to approve them. What he railed against was "sham reciprocity," in which "what these other countries want is a free and open market with the United States . . . [but not] reciprocity that shall give us our share in the trade or arrangement that we make with the other nations of the world" (WMcK, speech in the House of Representatives [on the Tariff of 1890], May 7, 1890, quoted in McKinley 1893: 408; Irwin 2017).

95. WMcK, "Speech Delivered at the Pan-American Exposition," Buffalo, NY, September 5, 1901, *UCSB.*
96. Merry (2017); Morgan (2003); Gould (1980).
97. WMcK. "Special Message to Congress." (March 15 1897). *UCSB.*
98. *The Economist,* correspondent's report, dated May 15, 1897, printed May 29, 1897.
99. Irwin (2017: 296).
100. An Act to Provide Revenue for the Government and to Encourage the Industries of the United States, 1897 (May).
101. The expert debate was more measured. There was general consensus that consumers bore the burden of the tariff, but many also claimed benefits for industry and industrial labor. See, for example, the debates between Charles Beardsley, F. W. Taussig, C. R. Miller, Herbert J. Davenport, Thomas Nixon Carver, Chauncey Ford, and others published in the *Quarterly Journal of Economics, Economic Journal, Journal of Political Economy,* and other periodicals during this time.
102. In anticipation of higher tariffs, imports had surged 75 percent during the seven months following McKinley's election in November 1896.
103. From late May to early September 1897, prompting one reporter to wax, "[T]he upward movement in the prices of shares is like a team of wild horses which has got beyond the control of the driver" (*The Economist,* letter from US correspondent, dated August 7, 1897, printed August 28, 1897). Increased trading activity may also have been a sign of growing investor confidence thanks to new NYSE requests for annual reports from listed corporations starting in 1895. In 1899, they would become a formal requirement for listing on the NYSE (O'Sullivan 2016: 149).
104. *The Economist,* letter from US correspondent, dated July 31, 1897, printed August 14, 1897.
105. Newspapers of the day suggest that the 1896 election alone reassured foreign investors by signaling strong political support, at least in Washington, DC, for industry and the banking sector.
106. Wilkins (1989: 147, Table 5.4); *Measuring Worth,* total output per GDP.
107. The British led the way (79 percent of total foreign investment), followed by the Dutch (7.6 percent), Germans (6.4 percent), and Swiss (2.4 percent) (Wilkins 1989: 159, Table 5.8).
108. For example, British investment went largely into railroads and other transportation (62 percent), manufacturing (7.4 percent), utilities (7.3 percent), and mining (5.7 percent) (Wilkins (1989: 164, Table 5.9; supplemented by *HSUS*).
109. At best, tariff protectionism may have played a role in establishing or maintaining America's lead in tin plate and canning, or speeding its ascendency in iron, steel, rails, and possibly textiles (especially woolens). Otherwise, the concurrent increase

in manufacturing exports was more likely due to America's competitive advantage in natural resources (notably iron and coal) and labor (especially immigrants), as well as its unprecedented merger wave, none of which was matched by other trading nations (Irwin 2017).

110. Irwin (2017).

111. Even some of the most rigorous critics of McKinley's trade policies have also admitted that "it is difficult to argue that the high tariff policy was costly and inefficient" (Irwin 2017: 284).

112. The British saw no gain for themselves in bimetallism; the French, another essential participant, dithered over trade concessions (Reti 1998; Morgan 2003; Gould 1980).

113. "Republican Party Platform," June 18, 1896, *UCSB*.

114. US Treasury (1897).

115. Frightened by the meteoric rise of Bryan, and encouraged by the 1896 election results, a group of Indianapolis businessmen sought an end to the damaging gold-silver wars. Two weeks after the election, they urged the city's Board of Trade to call a regional conference on currency reform. The idea of a conference quickly won support from boards of trade, chambers of commerce, and other business and banking groups throughout the country, but most heavily in the central and western states, which suffered most from credit and currency shortages. The conference convened in Indianapolis during mid-January 1897. Some five hundred delegates from twenty-six states and Washington, DC, attended, representing over one hundred cities. They established the Indianapolis Monetary Commission, composed of experts charged "to make a thorough investigation of the monetary affairs and needs of the country in all relations and aspects, and to make proper suggestions as to the evils found to exist and the remedies therefor" (Memorial to the Board of Governors of the Indianapolis Board of Trade, November 16, 1896, quoted in Laughlin 1898: 3). It began work in late September 1897. In mid-December, the Commission's preliminary draft was circulated; the final full report was published a few months later as Laughlin (1898).

116. WMcK, "Speech at the Banquet of the National Association of Manufacturers of the United States," New York City, January 27, 1898, in McKinley (1900: 64).

117. The *New York Times*, January 16, 1898, explained that the various currency proposals were "progressively better to all members of the Congress who are open to [currency reform].... So far, however, neither the President, the Secretary of the Treasury, nor the Monetary Commission appear to have made any converts [of those opposed to reform]."

118. Tariffs were McKinley's first priority; then came the brewing confrontation with Spain. In the meantime, the president insisted that "no action [on currency reform] could be taken until 'the receipts suffice to pay the expenses of the government'" (quoted in *The Economist*, December 18, 1897).

119. Peritz (2001); Porter (2006b); Sklar (1988).

120. Technically, trusts were created when "[o]wners of several competing corporations put all their stock in the hands of a board of trustees and received trust certificates of equivalent value. Boards of trustees became, in effect, boards of directors with

full powers of management, and holders of trust certificates were converted into shareholders. The constituent corporations were managed as a single unit and the chairman of the board of trustees had the power to consolidate and rationalize production by closing inefficient factories and enlarging and modernizing the most efficient or best located factories" (Seavoy 2006: 241).

121. The Supreme Court ruling also suggested that regulatory oversight of large corporations was best left to the state governments via their incorporation laws. In fact, some have argued that incorporation statutes were more powerful tools than antitrust laws at the time. This might explain why some in the McKinley administration developed an interest in passing legislation for *federal* incorporation. See Lamoreaux (1985: 165–168).

122. Economist Naomi R. Lamoreaux (1985: 86) has also shown that, in most cases, Gilded Age pools and price-fixing agreements failed on their own accord. Instead, it was devastating price wars, triggered by the 1893–1897 depression, that drove the "Great Merger Movement." *E. C. Knight* merely gave them legal cover. She also finds that "[t]he industries most likely to erupt into price wars [and therefore mergers] were those in which fixed costs were high and in which expansion had been rapid and recent."

123. Both "merger" and "consolidation" are defined as the contractual and statutory combination of two or more firms. Hence the terms are often used interchangeably. However, the data cited in this paragraph treat them separately. Technically, a *merger* generally involves a takeover: one firm acquires the assets and liabilities of another. The company taking over remains in operation, but the other one ceases to exist. In a *consolidation*, two or more firms join together to become an entirely new entity. The original corporations cease to exist altogether (Interstate Commerce Commission 1892–1902).

124. American rail operation would peak in 1929–1930 (counting main track and including lessors, proprietary, unofficial, and circular companies; does not include yard tracks and sidings).

125. US Census Bureau (1902: 66, Table XII).

126. Lamoreaux (1985: 2–4).

127. Bittlingmayer (1985); Nutter (1951).

128. Peritz (2001); Lamoreaux (1985).

129. Another one-fifth of the era's mergers achieved only meager profits (Seavoy 2006: 242). For a discussion of benefits of business consolidation, see Chandler (1977); Peltzman (1977); Hounshell (1984); Clarke, Davies, and Waterson (1984); Daughety (1990); for a contemporary account, see Moody (1904).

130. Kahan (2017).

131. Prior to the early 1890s, railroad shares dominated Wall Street, followed by a handful of mining, utilities, and textile firms. Most manufacturers were either too small or too risky for most investors. This began to change as the industrial merger movement, combined with new NYSE requirements for annual statements, helped to boost both supply and demand for shares of industrials. Ultimately, it would take World War I to displace railroads and install industrials as the dominant sector in

the US stock market. But industrials experienced a surge in popularity starting in late 1898. Meanwhile, for average Americans, real estate was still the preferred investment of the late Gilded Age. Even by 1900, just under 6 percent of Americans owned stocks (O'Sullivan 2016; Bunting 1986; Navin and Sears 1955; Means 1930).

132. For a contemporary survey, see Bullock (1901).

133. Holt (1899).

134. *New York Times*, January 31, 1899.

135. The lack of consensus about trusts extended into the Ivory Tower. For example, the economist John Bates Clark (Columbia University) too was unsure. While he admitted that trusts "do not kill men in a literal way, but to a large extent they do kill competition," he concluded, "Whether in the long run they will prove to be benevolent or malevolent we cannot know." Clark's main concern was that the trusts would discourage innovation. He therefore recommended that government regulate trusts where necessary to encourage competition (Clark 1900: 181–182; Clark and Clark 1901). Richard Ely (1900) (University of Wisconsin, Madison) went further, implying that powerful trusts could threaten freedom and democracy. In contrast, William Graham Sumner (1901, 1913) (Yale) and others generally applauded trusts for their superior economic performance, declaring, "There is no evil or danger in trusts" and urging that they be given "maximum freedom" (Gunton 1899: 237). Their only concern was that trusts should emerge naturally, and not be favored government intervention. More than a few economists noted that, since big business benefited most from the trade protectionism, there may be a pernicious trust-tariff axis that influenced the nation's trade policy. Jeremiah Jenks (1900: 235–236) (Cornell) led one of the most extensive investigations of the era, which concluded, "Trusts have become fixtures in business life; their power for evil should be destroyed, their means for good preserved." His remedies consisted of greater transparency and reporting, increased accountability to stockholders, and fines for discriminatory or predatory practices (including stock manipulation).

136. Galambos (1975).

137. Merry (2017); Morgan (2003); Gould (1980).

138. Sklar (1988).

139. For example, in his Third Annual Message to Congress (December 5, 1899), McKinley included a substantial section on trusts that warned, "Combinations of capital organized into trusts to control the conditions of trade among our citizens, to stifle competition, limit production, and determine the prices of products used and consumed by the people, are justly provoking public discussion, and should early claim the attention of the Congress." After a year of little legislative activity, he reminded Congress of his concerns in his Fourth Annual Message (December 3, 1900). But McKinley himself took little action to advance antitrust beyond organizing an expert commission on the matter.

140. Lamoreaux (1985).

141. Zunz (1990); Sklar (1988).

142. Merry (2017); Morgan (2003); Gould (1980).

143. *New York Times*, July 15, 1897.

144. *New York Times,* July 17, 1897.
145. By 14 percent (1897), 27 percent (1898), and 3 percent (1899).
146. In 1897 alone, US exports surged to the United Kingdom (19 percent increase), Germany (28 percent), France (23 percent), and Canada (8.3 percent), as well as to China (71 percent), Japan (62 percent), Mexico (21 percent), Australia/Oceania (35 percent), and even Africa (21 percent). US exports made similar gains in 1898.
147. As a percentage of GDP, the gold stimulus would increase to 1.28 percent in 1898, then return to 0.4 percent (1899) (*Measuring Worth,* total output per GDP; supplemented by *HSUS*).
148. For a complete history, see O'Toole (1984); Musicant (1998).
149. The Wilson-Gorman Tariff of 1894, passed over the objections of President Grover Cleveland, placed a 40 percent effective tariff on sugar from Cuba, while keeping duties lower on American sugar firms located in Hawaii.
150. *Chicago Tribune,* December 19, 1896.
151. Spencer and Spencer (2007).
152. The USS *Maine* had been dispatched to Havana by McKinley in late January 1898, ostensibly on a "friendly call." Initially thought to be a sunk by a Spanish mine, the destruction of the USS *Maine* in mid-February has since been attributed to an onboard accident: an internal ammunition magazine explosion, possibly caused by a nearby coal bunker fire (Hansen and Wegner 1998; Samuels and Samuels 1995).
153. Stoddard (1927: 252).
154. Quoted in Morgan (2003: 274).
155. Kirshner (2007).
156. Charles Boutelle (R-ME), quoted in Gillett (1934: 195–196).
157. For a more hawkish interpretation of McKinley's war decision, see Kapur (2011).
158. O'Toole (1984); Musicant (1998).
159. All told, the US side of the conflict suffered 2,446 military deaths and 1,662 wounded. Another 260 Americans died in the USS *Maine* explosion (Brum and DeBruyne 2020).
160. Brum and DeBruyne (2020).
161. Stoddard (1927: 252). This judgment has been widely supported by subsequent scholars. See Merry (2017); Morgan (2003); Musicant (1998); O'Toole (1984); Gould (1980); Koistinen (1997).
162. Including troop limits, war taxation and expenditure measures, the peace settlement, and more.
163. Edwards (2014); Rockoff (2012); Koistinen (1997).
164. This includes a $20 million payment to Spain for the Philippines, or roughly $23 billion in 2020 dollars (*Measuring Worth,* total output per GDP; Rockoff 2012; Hansen and Wegner 1998).
165. In later years, the Spanish-American War (1898) would become extremely expensive in terms of veterans' benefits, which ultimately accounted for 78 percent of all war costs (compared to the US historical average of 35 percent) (Edwards 2014).
166. Linn (2000); Silbey (2007); Rockoff (2012: 83–84, 88).

167. Rockoff (2012: 88, Table 4.1). Does not include veterans' benefits, most of which were legislated decades later.
168. Rockoff (2012); Bank (2010).
169. Brownlee (2016).
170. Rockoff (2012).
171. Watson (1936: 310).
172. The infant motion picture industry was a prominent exception. See Hooper (2012).
173. On the whole, the military supply agencies "rapidly and efficiently conduct[ed] business ventures virtually free of graft, fraud, and corruption." However, severe bottlenecks in distribution emerged, "and the [military] supply system as a whole ran into serious trouble and for a time nearly broke down." Specifically, railroad co-ordination and setting up base depots proved embarrassingly problematic. "At one point, boxcars were backed up halfway to the nation's capital," while thousands of soldiers suffered from malaria, dysentery, and typhoid in Florida base camps while awaiting transportation (Koistinen 1997: 79–88).
174. Lebergott (1980).
175. Congress had passed federal bankruptcy acts in 1800, 1841, and 1867 in belated response to the economic crises of 1793, 1837, and 1857, respectively. But each proved unpopular and was repealed within a few years. Battles over the rights of state governments, creditors, and debtors, as well as between contending ideologies, political parties, and economic interests, doomed each attempt. The result was an in-coherent patchwork of state bankruptcy laws. The system provided little recourse for handling out-of-state debtors and was poorly adapted to the increasingly national market. During the 1870s–1890s, the development of local chambers of commerce, boards of trade, and other business organizations gradually created a nationwide political movement for federal bankruptcy law that eventually persuaded Congress to act. In the 1898 legislation, US district courts were made into bankruptcy courts and given original jurisdiction. The Supreme Court and the US circuit courts of ap-peals were given appellate jurisdiction. The Act also created bankruptcy referees, appointed by the court, who would carry out various bankruptcy functions, subject to review by a district judge. The 1898 bankruptcy system remained in place, with few revisions, until 1978 (Hansen 1988; Skeel 2001).
176. Congressman Joseph W. Babcock (R-WI), quoted in *New York Times,* August 25, 1898.
177. The Spanish-American War had revealed systemic inefficiencies and antiquated practices that hindered the army's performance (Barr 1998; Koistinen 1997).
178. *The Nation,* March 9, 1899.
179. However, fiscal conservatives in Congress rejected many of the president's larger spending requests. Perhaps the only major piece of domestic economic legislation to pass that winter was the massive Rivers and Harbors Appropriation Act of March 1899. It allocated tens of millions of dollars in federal spending to twenty-eight pages of infrastructure projects around the country. It also authorized funding and personnel for the survey of a canal across the Isthmus of Panama. Finally, it estab-lished an innovative system of federal permits for the pollution, construction, or

modification of America's ports, harbors, channels, and navigable streams, rivers, and their tributaries. It remains today perhaps the oldest federal environmental law in the United States.

180. *The Nation,* March 16, 1899.
181. The US Treasury offered to purchase up to $25 million in bonds, but when the program ended in late December, just over $18.4 million had been bought (*New York Times,* November 25, 1899; US Treasury 1900: 22).
182. *New York Times,* December 15, 19, 1899; Friedman and Schwartz (1963: 141).
183. Annual US silver production during the Gilded Age peaked in 1892 at 1,974 metric tons and had fallen 13 percent to 1,718 metric tons by 1899. Similarly, silver exports had crested in 1897, while silver imports were flat from 1897 through 1899.
184. Myers (1970: 221).
185. Livingston (1986); McCulley (1992).
186. In October 1897, Japan had adopted the gold standard. Russia followed that winter.
187. Bordo and Rockoff (1996).
188. *New York Tribune,* May 10, 1899.
189. Merry (2017); Morgan (2003); Gould (1980).
190. An Act to Define and Fix the Standard of Value, to Maintain the Parity of All Forms of Money Issued or Coined by the United States, to Refund the Public Debt, and for Other Purposes, 1900 (March 14).
191. The Indianapolis Monetary Commission played a prominent role in the design and passage of the Gold Standard Act of 1900. Its December 1897 proposals were very similar to those made by the Treasury Department, both of which sought to "take the government out of the banking business." However, initial attempts to advance a more laissez-faire currency bill, based on Commission propositions, had failed during 1898. These efforts ended in January 1899 with the death of the McCleary Bill. Nevertheless, many of the Commission's technical recommendations were incorporated into the 1900 Act, though with the federal government playing a powerful role in monetary and banking policy. See McCulley (1992); Livingston (1986).
192. Though its final section promised silverites that "the provisions of this Act are not intended to preclude the accomplishment of international bimetallism whenever conditions shall make it expedient and practicable to secure the same by concurrent action of the leading commercial nations of the world and at a ratio which shall insure the permanence of relative value between gold and silver." In other words, bimetallists could have their system, but only if it was indistinguishable from the international gold standard in practice.
193. Rosenberg (1985).
194. Fulford and Schwartzman (2020); supplemented by *HSUS.*
195. Before McKinley, perhaps only Polk, Tyler, and Madison had more experience in Congress before becoming president. Garfield also outranked McKinley in this regard. But Garfield lasted only four months as president before being incapacitated by an assassin's bullet, and during that time Congress was in session just eleven weeks at the beginning of Garfield's term.

196. John Hay, US ambassador to the United Kingdom 1897–1898, secretary of state 1898–1901, quoted in Morgan (2003: 344).
197. Stoddard (1927: 230).
198. Watson (1936: 48).
199. Gould (1980: 210).
200. Though McKinley vetoed more bills than any pre–Gilded Age president. Total vetoes (regular and pocket) of Gilded Age presidents: Grant (93), Hayes (13), Garfield (0), Arthur (12), Cleveland (584), Harrison (44), McKinley (42).
201. Pulitzer (1899: 890).
202. Klinghard (2005).
203. Klinghard (2010); Gould (2014); Kazin (2008).
204. Watson (1936: 53).
205. Pulitzer (1899: 889).
206. Ponder (1994: 823). Ponder (1998) further emphasizes the catalyst of the Spanish-American War, which rapidly escalated McKinley's reliance on press relations to rally popular support and manage public expectations.
207. McKinley also formalized processes for releasing speeches and presidential messages so that all reporters would be treated equally. His practices were continued by subsequent presidents, eventually evolving into the modern White House press room, press secretary, and presidential press conference. McKinley even became adroit at timely leaks so as to prepare the public for major legislation or policy changes. But he was also careful to keep reporters from getting too close or familiar so as not to breed contempt or provide opportunities for scandalmongering (Merry 2017; Morgan 2003; Gould 1980).
208. The magazine continued, "It is felt that . . . [the United States] will not prove, if it enters into the vast sphere of European interests, an unscrupulous or meddling Power. That is so much gained for the international morality of the world, which stands in need of all the additional moral force it can acquire" (*The Economist*, August 20, 1898).
209. Quoted in Gould (1980: 37).
210. Watson (1936: 49).
211. Laracey (2002).
212. Morgan (2003: 246).
213. Charles Emory Smith, US postmaster, minister to Russia, October 11, 1902, quoted in Gould (1980: 136).
214. Stoddard (1927: 254–255).
215. Invoking the Civil War in order to whip up the soldier and veteran vote, which formed a loyal base for the Republican Party.
216. John Hay, letter to Theodore Roosevelt, July 27, 1898, quoted in Thayer (1915: 337).
217. O'Toole (1984); Musicant (1998).
218. Quoted in McCaffrey (2009: 139).
219. Zais (1974).
220. Ultimately, the reforms were neither as thorough nor as far-reaching as desired. The bill's own sponsor criticized it as "the worst kind of patchwork," Theodore Roosevelt

labeled the reforms "a miserable makeshift." But they did provide the foundation for a major reorganization and reforms in subsequent years (Cosmas 1971; Barr 1998; Koistinen 2017).

221. Medhurst (2008); Tulis (1987).

222. Leon Czolgosz, comments to reporters, September 27, 1901, quoted in Halstead (1901: 462).

223. An energetic Washington politico, Hobart became both master of the administration's social calendar and its key liaison to the Senate. Until he died in late 1899, Hobart was the president's alter ego, and was so trusted and influential that some even nicknamed him the "Assistant President" (Magie 1910; Connolly 2010).

224. Hilpert (2015); Horner (2010).

225. Dewey also opined that "the office of President is not such a very difficult one to fill" and then admitted that he had "never voted in my life" (New York Times, April 5, 7, 1900).

226. William Jennings Bryan, speech at Madison Square Garden, New York City, August 10, 1896, quoted in Bryan (1913: 269).

227. "Democratic Party Platform," July 9, 1900, UCSB.

228. New York Times, July 8, 1900.

229. WMcK, "Second Inaugural Address," March 4, 1901, UCSB.

230. Lyman J. Gage, May 9, 1901, quoted in New York Times, May 10, 1901.

231. WMcK, "Speech to the Pan-American Exposition," Buffalo, NY, September 5, 1901, UCSB.

232. This would empower the federal government to directly regulate large corporations rather than await lengthy and uncertain litigation of antitrust behavior in the judiciary (Lamoreaux 1985; Morgan 2003; Gould 1980).

233. Merry (2017); Morgan (2003); Gould (1980).

234. Pickenpaugh (2016).

235. Quoted in Merry (2017: 8).

236. Leon Czolgosz, statement to police, quoted in New York Times, September 8, 1901.

237. Net immigration dropped at first, from 205,000 (1896) to 105,000 (1897), and then rose steadily: 121,000 (1898), 201,000 (1899), 385,000 (1900), and 288,000 (1901).

238. Specifically, the ratio of private wealth to national income decreased from 502 percent (1896) to 435 percent (1901), while private wealth to average disposable income went from 555 percent (1896) to 481 percent (1901) (Piketty and Zucman 2014).

239. Federico-Tena World Trade Historical Database (Federico and Tena-Junguito 2019).

240. "Our Commercial Expansion" (1900). Munsey's Magazine 22 (4): 538.

241. For the counterargument, see Justesen (2020).

242. Merry (2017); Morgan (2003); Gould (1980).

243. From its 1896 low, union membership rose around 135 percent by 1901, strikes rose 183 percent in total number and 128 percent in total workers involved, and 64 percent in workers as a percentage of total employment (with a temporary lull in 1898 due to the Spanish-American War).

244. In addition, McKinley was never able to get his merchant marine legislation passed by Congress. He constantly argued that a large, modern merchant marine was

essential to American exports. For after McKinley protected and strengthened American industry, he meant to expand its global reach through trade. That was the purpose of his inserting presidential reciprocity power into his 1897 tariff bill. Yet for all his efforts, Congress refused to fund it (Merry 2017; Morgan 2003; Gould 1980).

245. It was also based on principles similar to those by which the Federal Reserve is currently run. Bryan and the silverites did not formalize their views into mathematical equations nor rigorously test them using extensive data sets or sophisticated statistical models. But their fundamental observations were nonetheless "correct" from a 21st-century economics perspective.

246. Partly due to a combination of poll taxes, literacy tests, ballot manipulations, and physical terror that had eliminated most Blacks from politics in the South.

247. West (1901: 23–24).

248. To some, McKinley himself marked the beginning of a new kind "imperial presidency" (Schlesinger 1973).

Chapter 13

1. JAG, "Speech on the Railway Problem," June 22, 1874, quoted in Ridpat (1881: 240).

2. *Commercial and Financial Chronicle*, November 7, 1868.

3. An earlier, abbreviated version of this chapter was published as Taylor (2021).

4. Thanks to Meena Bose for making this point.

5. Calhoun (2002). For investigations of presidential power before the Gilded Age, see Cash (2018); Prakash (2015); Bessette and Tulis (2009); Cronin (1989).

6. Skidmore (2014).

7. Haynes (2016: 3).

8. Calhoun (2010).

9. Calhoun (2002: 256).

10. Rogowski (2016: 325).

11. Nichols (1994: 7).

12. Ellis (2012: 17).

13. Bernstein (2020).

14. See also O'Brien (2018); Hargrove (2014).

15. Skowronek (1997: 411).

16. Simpson (1998: 5).

17. Ellis (2012: 375).

18. Most scholars of economic growth, development, and competitiveness concur that governments seeking to foster balanced economic growth should act to create a competitive economic environment that is rich in resources; solve classic market failures and network failures that prevent efficient and innovative economic behavior; reduce transaction costs; attract investors into high-return sectors; increase the labor supply in high-wage jobs in high value-added sectors and in geographic regions characterized by familiar social networks and freedom of mobility; provide infrastructure for transportation, communication, and finance; increase skill levels;

create and diffuse new technology; allow modest inflation (and either free capital flows or fixed exchange rates); and subsidize the supply and demand of those new goods and services with increasing returns over time where appropriate (Mankiw 2018; Jones 1998; Aghion and Howitt 1998; Grossman and Helpman 1991).

19. Rodrik (2007); Taylor (2016).

20. See, for example, Irwin (2017); Friedman (1990a, 1990b).

21. "All happy families are alike; each unhappy family is unhappy in its own way" (Tolstoi 1886: 5).

22. For example, Friedman (1990b); Frieden (1997); Bordo and Schwartz (1999).

23. By the late 20th century, the United States was well-established as the world's most innovative nation and the largest wealthy consumer economy, and the dollar had become the world's reserve currency, all backed by the most powerful military in history. Hence, US inflation and exchange rate risk were well compensated by the relative liquidity, safety, low transactions costs, and higher rates of return of US stocks and bonds. Thus American policymakers for the past fifty years have enjoyed the "exorbitant privilege" of *not* facing a balance of payments crisis for printing money. In fact, many countries in Asia and the Middle East eagerly loan money to the highly indebted United States in order to support their own export sectors. None of this was true during the 19th century. The United States was still a developing nation then, competing with others for investment capital (Eichengreen 2011).

24. Bordo and Rockoff (1996). See also Bordo (1999, 2012).

25. Wilkins (1989).

26. Eichengreen (2019); Williams and Armstrong (2012); Fayle (1933).

27. Goetzmann and Ukhov (2006).

28. Bordo and Rockoff (1996); Bordo (2012).

29. See also Balz (2010).

30. Bowmaker (2019); Saunders (2017); Vaughn and Vilalobos (2006); Bernstein (2001); Bose (1998); Hargrove and Morley (1984). For a broader approach, see Alston, Alston, and Mueller (2021).

31. Grant (second term), Arthur, and Cleveland (second term).

32. Stern (2009); Pious (2008). Perhaps also Pfiffner (1999). In foreign policy, this argument is further developed in Boettcher (2005); Farnham (1992).

33. This is consistent with those scholars of the modern presidency who see presidential vision as critical for power or effectiveness: Weatherford (2009); Greenstein (2009); Stam, Van Knippenberg, and Wisse (2010).

34. Dearborn (2019a, 2019b). For the opposing view, that ideas are more effect than cause, see Lewis (2019).

35. See also Arnold, Doyle, and Wiesehomeier (2017); Abbott (2013); Wolf, Strachan, and Shea (2012); Gutmann (2012); Mycoff, Pika, and Sole (2008); Gardner, Avolio, and Walumbwa (2005); Badaracco and Ellsworth (1989).

36. Dauber (2013).

37. See, for example, Moe and Howell (1999a); Mayer (2001); Howell (2003); Lewis (2003); Canes-Wrone (2006); Wood (2007); Beckman (2010); Posner and Vermeule (2010). For a recent review of this literature, see O'Brien (2017).

38. In fact, one could argue that these institutional advantages *increased* over time as the Gilded Age presidents whittled away at the Tenure of Office Act, the spoils system (which privileged Congress and state political machines), and norms restraining presidential campaigns and rhetoric (Klinghard 2010).

39. For example, the Gilded Age presidents were constantly battling their party's faction heads and state machine leaders for control over appointments, campaigns, and fundraising. These battles got more intense as the institutional pillars of state party power fell (moieties, patronage appointments, mandatory campaign donations). They demanded a more public and aggressive president. But Harrison failed to master these institutional changes, in part because he prioritized the settlement of intraparty distributional issues (patronage, policy, etc.) over the achievement of a consistent, unifying vision. Cleveland also failed, partly because he rarely tried. He exploited his institutional advantages well over monetary policy, but otherwise chose not to assert them in accordance with his belief in a restrained presidency and federal government. Only McKinley succeeded. And he did so, I argue, because he quietly put his institutional advantages in service of a well-articulated national vision and in accordance with his belief in a more active presidency.

40. An argument proven more explicitly in Taylor (2016); Rodrik (2007).

41. As one presidential scholar has put it, "The president cannot master the job simply by resolving to respond promptly as new economic contingencies arise. To keep the national economy on an even keel . . . he needs to have a clear idea of his own goals" (Weatherford 2009: 551).

42. Alexander H. Stevens, former vice president of the Confederate States of America, commending the decision by President Hayes to withdraw federal troops from the state houses of Louisiana and South Carolina as part of the "Compromise of 1877," quoted in *Atlanta Constitution,* April 13, 1877.

43. Benjamin F. Wade, former Radical Republican leader in the US Senate, blasting President Hayes's compliance with the "Compromise of 1877," quoted in Hoogenboom (1988: 315).

44. See, for example, Potter (2019); Milkis and Tichenor (2019); Pika, Maltese, and Rudalevige (2017); Hacker and Pierson (2012); Hargrove (2014); Jones (1999); Peterson (1993); Edwards (1990); Bond and Fleisher (1990).

45. For individual case studies, see Levin, DiSalvo, and Shapiro (2012); Scully (2018); Greenstein (1982). For more generalized work, see Edwards (2009); Tsebelis (2002); Cheibub, Przeworski, and Saiegh (2004); Hacker and Pierson (2012); Acs (2019); Hickey (2014).

46. The term "Green Lantern Theory" was originally coined by Matthew Yglesias (2006) to critique the George W. Bush administration's emphasis on "will, resolve, and perceptions of strength and weakness" as its primary guide for national security policy. Brendan Nyhan (2009) then pejoratively reapplied "Green Lantern Theory" to describe a similar belief in the president's power to influence Congress through his will and resolve (Klein 2014).

47. For a recent survey of this literature, see Beckman (2017).

48. Though "nontrivial legislation" may not necessarily implement the president's vision (and where "nontrivial" consists of landmark, important, and ordinary laws) (Howell 2003).
49. DiSalvo (2012).
50. Howell (2003).
51. Grant falls into both categories. He could be quite successful at politicking when he wanted. And he got better at it over time. But he found distasteful the flattery, coercion, cajoling, and tribute required to sway some men; he especially avoided public rhetoric. Therefore, he sometimes shied away from politics where it could have done much good.
52. Neustadt (1960); Tulis (1987); Medhurst (1996); Hargrove (2014); Campbell K. (2008); Ponder (2017); Kernell (2006); Cohen (1999). For a powerful critique of the "power to persuade" thesis, see Edwards (2009).
53. Wood (2007).
54. Tulis (1987); Medhurst (2008).
55. Neustadt (1960); Cronin (2009); Smith (1973); Silberman (1970).
56. Arrow (1972: 357).
57. Some argue that trust simplifies economic life by reducing the number of contingencies involved in any given economic transaction (Luhmann 2017).
58. Dyer and Chu (2003); Putnam (2001); LaPorta et al. (1997).
59. Bjornskov (2012).
60. Papagapitos and Riley (2009); Coleman (1988).
61. Francis, Hasan, and Zhu (2021); Mnasri and Essaddam (2021); Yonce (2015); Waisman, Ye, and Zhu (2015).
62. Zak and Knack (2001); Greif (1998); Greif, Milgrom, and Weingast (1994); Guiso, Sapienza, and Zingales (2009).
63. Fukuyama (1995a, 1995b).
64. Perhaps because nations with greater generalized trust are able to develop larger government sectors without damaging the economy. See Habibov, Cheung, and Auchynnikava (2017); Camussi, Mancini, and Tommasino (2018); Bergh and Henrekson (2011).
65. As George Shultz (2020), economist and former US secretary of labor, treasury, and state (as well as former director of the Office of Management and Budget), wrote toward the end of his life, "Trust is fundamental, reciprocal and, ideally, pervasive. If it is present, anything is possible. If it is absent, nothing is possible." For an extensive look at the role of trust and its effects in politics, economics, and business, see the Russell Sage Foundation's multivolume series on trust research (2001–2014).
66. Bjornskov (2012); Heinemann (2008); Knack and Zak (2003); Dollar and Kraay (2003); Rodrik, Subramanian, and Trebbi (2004); Putnam (2001).
67. Bjornskov (2012).
68. Bergh and Funcke (2019).
69. Keynes (1936).

70. Hetherington (1998). Though Dan Ponder (2017) has shown that when Americans trust the president more than government itself, the White House has considerable leverage to get things done.

71. Acemoglu and Robinson (2012).

72. The seminal work is Mauro (1995). For recent general reviews, see Arnone (2014); Rose-Ackerman (2016); Fisman (2017). For more recent analysis, see Dutta and Sobel (2016); Liu, Moldogaziev, and Mikesell (2017).

73. Bernanke, Gertler, and Gilchrist (1996).

74. For recent reviews of the causes and effects of political trust, see Uslaner (2018); Zmerli and Van der Meer (2017).

75. Keele (2005).

76. Rothstein and Stolle (2008); Farrell and Knight (2003); Knight (2001); Rothstein (2000); Sztompka (1999); Braithwaite and Levi (1998).

77. Knack and Keefer (1997).

78. Serritzlew, Sonderskov, and Svendsen (2014).

79. Peterson and Wrighton (1998).

80. Keele (2007); Citrin and Green (1986).

81. See, for example, Kellerman (2016); Miroff (2016); Kamarck (2016); Hacker and Pierson (2012); Jones (1994); perhaps also Pfiffner (1999).

Appendix: Estimating Presidential Performance—Data, Sources, and Methods

1. Some of this discussion is taken from Taylor (2012).

2. Eland (2009); Merry (2012).

3. Eland (2009); Vedder and Gallaway (2001).

4. Bailey (1966); Bose and Landis (2003).

5. Pfiffner (2003: 27).

6. The only long-run, nonpartisan, scholarly, data-based, and purely economic ranking of the US presidents is Taylor (2012) Another is limited to eleven post–World War II presidents: Dolan, Frendreis, and Tatalovich (2009).

7. This also applies to judgments of which data to include, weights to assign, and algorithms to use when constructing an index or ranking (Tilley and Hobolt 2011; Uscinski and Simon 2011; Bose and Landis 2003; Emrich et al. 2001).

8. Vedder and Gallaway (2001).

9. Mankiw (2018).

10. For the scholarly debate on the development, accuracy, and consequences of different presidential ratings, see the Hofstra University symposium "The Leadership Difference: Rating the Presidents," as summarized in Bose and Landis (2003). Also instructive are Merry (2012); Felzenberg (2008).

11. Confirmed by author's discussions with labor historians and historical data experts Susan Carter (UC Riverside), Joshua Rosenbloom (Iowa State), Matthew Sobek (University of Minnesota), and David Weir (University of Michigan) during January 2020.
12. Examples might include Fillmore, Wilson, Harding, FDR, Reagan, JFK, and Obama.
13. Samuels (2004).
14. Mankiw (2018).

References

Abbott, Philip. 2013. *Bad Presidents: Failure in the White House*. New York: Palgrave Macmillan.

Abramitzky, Ran, and Leah Boustan. 2017. "Immigration in American Economic History." *Journal of Economic Literature* 55 (4): 1311–1345.

Acemoglu, Daron. 2002a. "Directed Technical Change." *Review of Economic Studies* 69 (4): 781–809.

Acemoglu, Daron. 2002b. "Technical Change, Inequality, and the Labor Market." *Journal of Economic Literature* 40 (1): 7–72.

Acemoglu, Daron, and James A. Robinson. 2012. *Why Nations Fail: The Origins of Power, Prosperity, and Poverty*. New York: Crown.

Ackerman, Kenneth D. 2005. *The Gold Ring: Jim Fisk, Jay Gould, and Black Friday, 1869*. New York: Carroll & Graf.

Acs, Alex. 2019. "Congress and Administrative Policymaking: Identifying Congressional Veto Power." *American Journal of Political Science* 63 (3): 513–529.

Adams, Charles Francis, Jr. 1869a. "A Chapter of Erie." *North American Review* 109 (224): 30–106.

Adams, Charles Francis, Jr. 1869b. *A Chapter of Erie*. Boston: Fields, Osgood.

Adams, Henry Brooks. 1869. "Civil-Service Reform." *North American Review* 109 (225): 443–475.

Adams, Henry Brooks. 1870. "The Session." *North American Review* 111 (228): 29–62.

Adams, Henry. 1907. *The Education of Henry Adams*. Washington, DC: Henry Adams.

Adams, Henry, and Charles Francis Adams Jr. 1876. "The 'Independents' in the Canvass." *North American Review* 123 (253): 426–467.

Adler, Selig. 1963. "The Operation on President McKinley." *Scientific American* 208 (3): 118–131.

Ager, Philip, and Markus Bruckner. 2013. "Cultural Diversity and Economic Growth: Evidence from the US during the Age of Mass Migration." *European Economic Journal* 64: 76–97.

Ager, Philip, Leah Platt Boustan, and Katherine Eriksson. 2019. "The Intergenerational Effects of a Large Wealth Shock: White Southerners after the Civil War." Working Paper No. 25700. Cambridge, MA: NBER.

Aghion, Philippe, and Peter Howitt. 1998. *Endogenous Growth Theory*. Cambridge, MA: MIT Press.

Akcigit, Ufuk, John Grigsby, and Tom Nicholas. 2017. "Immigration and the Rise of American Ingenuity." *American Economic Review* 107 (5): 327–331.

Akerman, Johan. 1947. "Political Economic Cycles." *Kyklos* 1 (2): 107–117.

Alesina, Alberto. 1987. "Macroeconomic Policy in a Two-Party System as a Repeated Game." *Quarterly Journal of Economics* 102 (3): 651–678.

Alexander, Benjamin F. 2015. *Coxey's Army: Popular Protest in the Gilded Age*. Baltimore, MD: Johns Hopkins University Press.

Alexander, Rohan, and Zachary Ward. 2018. "Age at Arrival and Assimilation during the Age of Mass Migration." *Journal of Economic History* 78 (3): 904–937.

Alfani, Guido, and Cormac Ó Gráda. 2017. *Famine in European History*. New York: Cambridge University Press.

Algeo, Matthew. 2011. *The President Is a Sick Man*. Chicago: Chicago Review Press.

Allen, Walter. 1879. "Two Years of President Hayes." *Atlantic Monthly* 44 (262): 190–199.

Alston, Eric, Lee J. Alston, and Bernardo Mueller. 2021. "Leadership and Organizations." Working Paper 28927. Cambridge, MA: NBER.

Alston, Lee J., Jeffery A. Jenkins, and Tomas Nonnenmacher. 2006. "Who Should Govern Congress? Access to Power and the Salary Grab of 1873." *Journal of Economic History* 66 (3): 674–706.

America's Great Migrations Project. University of Washington. Retrieved February 8, 2023. https://depts.washington.edu/moving1/.

American Association for the Promotion of Social Science. 1865. (October 4). "Constitution." Boston.

American Battlefield Trust. "Civil War Casualties." Retrieved February 8, 2023. https://www.battlefields.org/learn/articles/civil-war-casualties.

American Institute of the City of New York. 1872. *Annual Report of the American Institute 1871–1872*. Albany, NY: Argus Co. Printers.

American Review: A Whig Journal. 1849. "Organization of the Party." 23 (November): 443.

American Tobacco Company. 1960. *The American Tobacco Story*. New York State: American Tobacco Co.

Anastaplo, George. 1999. *Abraham Lincoln: A Constitutional Biography*. Lanham, MD: Rowman & Littlefield.

Anbinder, Tyler G. 1992. *Nativism and Slavery: The Northern Know Nothings and the Politics of the 1850's*. New York: Oxford University Press.

Anbinder, Tyler. 1997. "Ulysses S. Grant, Nativist." *Civil War History* 43 (2): 119–141.

Andersen, Lisa M. F. 2013. *The Politics of Prohibition: American Governance and the Prohibition Party, 1869–1933*. New York: Cambridge University Press.

Anderson, Haelim Park, and John C. Bluedorn. 2017. "Stopping Contagion with Bailouts: Micro-evidence from Pennsylvania Bank Networks during the Panic of 1884." *Journal of Banking & Finance* 76: 139–149.

Andrews, William D. 1977. "Women and the Fairs of 1876 and 1893." *Hayes Historical Journal* 1 (3). Retrieved June 22, 2023. https://www.rbhayes.org/research/hayes-historical-journal-women-and-the-fairs/.

Armbruster, Carl Joseph. 1958. "Problems and Personalities of the Civil Service Reform in the Administration of Benjamin Harrison." Master's thesis, Loyola University, Chicago.

Armitage, Charles H. 1926. *Grover Cleveland as Buffalo Knew Him*. Buffalo, NY: Buffalo Evening News.

Armstrong, William H. 2000. *Major McKinley William McKinley and the Civil War*. Kent, OH: Kent State University Press.

Arnold, Andrew B. 2014. *Fueling the Gilded Age: Railroads, Miners, and Disorder in Pennsylvania Coal Country*. New York: New York University Press.

Arnold, Christian, David Doyle, and Nina Wiesehomeier. 2017. "Presidents, Policy Compromise, and Legislative Success." *Journal of Politics* 79 (2): 380–395.

Arnone, Marco. 2014. *Corruption: Economic Analysis and International Law*. Cheltenham: Edward Elgar.

Arrington, Benjamin T. 2020. *The Last Lincoln Republican: The Presidential Election of 1880*. Lawrence: University Press of Kansas.

Arrow, Kenneth J. 1972. "Gifts and Exchanges." *Philosophy & Public Affairs* 1 (4): 357.

Arthur, C. Damien. 2014. *Economic Actors, Economic Behaviors, and Presidential Leadership: The Constrained Effects of Rhetoric*. Lanham, MD: Lexington Books.

Atack, Jeremy, Fred Bateman, and William N. Parker. 2000. "The Farm, the Farmer, and the Market." In *Cambridge Economic History of the United States*, vol. 2, edited by Stanley L Engerman and Robert E Gallman, 245–284. New York: Cambridge University Press.

Atkinson, Edward. 1892. "Veto of the Inflation Bill of 1874." *Journal of Political Economy* 1: 117–119.

Atkinson, Richard C., and William A. Blanpied. 2008. "Research Universities: Core of the US Science and Technology System." *Technology in Society* 30: 30–48.

Auerbach, Jonathan. 1999. "McKinley at Home: How Early American Cinema Made News." *American Quarterly* 51 (4): 797–832.

Austrian, Geoffrey D. 1982. *Herman Hollerith: Forgotten Giant of Information Processing*. New York: Columbia University Press.

Avrich, Paul. 1984. *The Haymarket Tragedy*. Princeton, NJ: Princeton University Press.

Azari, Julia, and Marc J. Hetherington. 2016. "Back to the Future? What the Politics of the Late Nineteenth Century Can Tell Us about the 2016 election." *Annals of the American Academy of Political and Social Science* 667 (1): 92–109.

Badaracco, Joseph L., Jr., and Richard R. Ellsworth. 1989. *Leadership and the Quest for Integrity*. Boston: Harvard Business School Press.

Baggett, James Alex. 2003. *The Scalawags: Southern Dissenters in the Civil War and Reconstruction*. Baton Rouge: Louisiana State University Press.

Bailey, Howald. 1970. "Le Grand Chester." *History Teacher* 3 (3): 50–55.

Bailey, Thomas A. 1966. *Presidential Greatness: The Image and the Man from George Washington to the Present*. New York: Appleton-Century.

Balch, William Ralson 1885. *Life and Public Service of General Grant*. Philadelphia, PA: Aetna.

Ball, Douglas B. 1991. *Financial Failure and Confederate Defeat*. Chicago: University of Illinois Press.

Balz, J. 2010. "Ready to Lead on Day One: Predicting Presidential Greatness from Political Experience." *PS-Political Science & Politics* 43 (3): 487–492.

Bandicra, Oriana, Myra Mohnen, Imran Rasul, and Martina Viarengo. 2019. "Nation-Building through Compulsory Schooling during the Age of Mass Migration." *Economic Journal* 129 (617): 62–109.

Bank of England. 2021. "A Millennium of Macroeconomic Data: US/UK Foreign Exchange Rate in the United Kingdom." FRED Database, Federal Reserve Bank of St. Louis. https://fred.stlouisfed.org/series/USUKFXUKA.

Bank, Steven A. 2010. *From Sword to Shield: The Transformation of the Corporate Income Tax, 1861 to Present*. New York: Oxford University Press.

Barber, James David. 2009. *The Presidential Character: Predicting Performance in the White House*. 4th ed. New York: Pearson Longman.

Barber, William J. 1993. *Economists and Higher Learning in the Nineteenth Century*. New Brunswick, NJ: Transaction.

Barber, William J., ed. 2004. *The Development of the National Economy: The United States from the Civil War through the 1890s*. Vols. 1–4. London: Pickering & Chatto.

Barbour, Samuel, James Cicarelli, and J. E. King. 2018. *A History of American Economic Thought: Mainstream and Crosscurrents*. London: Routledge.

Barbuto, Domenica M. 1999. *American Settlement Houses and Progressive Social Reform: An Encyclopedia of the American Settlement Movement*. Phoenix, AZ: Oryx Press.

Barceló, Joan. 2018. "Are Western-Educated Leaders Less Prone to Initiate Militarized Disputes?" *British Journal of Political Science* 50 (2): 535–566.

Barnett, Paul. 1964. "The Crime of 1873 Re-examined." *Agricultural History* 38 (3): 178–181.

Barr, Ronald J. 1998. *The Progressive Army: US Army Command and Administration, 1870–1914*. New York: St. Martin's Press.

Barreyre, Nicolas. 2011. "The Politics of Economic Crises: The Panic of 1873, the End of Reconstruction, and the Realignment of American Politics." *Journal of the Gilded Age and Progressive Era* 10 (4): 403–423.

Barrows, Chester L. 1941. *William M. Evarts: Lawyer, Diplomat, Statesman*. Chapel Hill: University of North Carolina Press.

Barry, David. 1897. "News-Getting at the Capital." *The Chautauquan* 26 (3): 282–286.

Bartels, Larry M. 2016. *Unequal Democracy: The Political Economy of the New Gilded Age*. Princeton, NJ: Princeton University Press.

Bartlett, Richard A. 1962. *Great Surveys of the American West*. Norman: University of Oklahoma Press.

Beale, Harriet S. Blaine, ed. 1908. *Letters of Mrs. James G. Blaine*. Vol. 2. New York: Duffield.

Beard, George Miller. 1881. *American Nervousness, Its Causes and Consequences*. New York: G. P. Putnam's Sons.

Beatty, Jack. 2007. *Age of Betrayal: The Triumph of Money in America, 1865–1900*. New York: Alfred A. Knopf.

Beckert, Sven. 2015. *Empire of Cotton: A Global History*. New York: Alfred A. Knopf.

Beckman, Matthew N. 2010. *Pushing the Agenda: Presidential Leadership in U.S. Lawmaking, 1953–2004*. New York: Cambridge University Press.

Beckman, Matthew N. 2017. "A President's Decisions and the Presidential Difference." In *Leadership in American Politics*, edited by Jeffrey A Jenkins and Craig Volden, 65–87. Lawrence: University Press of Kansas.

Beisel, Nicola Kay. 1998. *Imperiled Innocents: Anthony Comstock and Family Reproduction in Victorian America*. Princeton, NJ: Princeton University Press.

Bellamy, Edward. 1888. *Looking Backward: 2000–1887*. Boston: Ticknor.

Bellesiles, Michael A. 2010. *1877: America's Year of Living Violently*. New York: New Press.

Belo, Frederico, Vito D. Gala, and Jun Li. 2013. "Government Spending, Political Cycles, and the Cross Section of Stock Returns." *Journal of Financial Economics* 107 (2): 305–324.

Benedict, Murray R. 1953. *Farm Policies of the United States, 1790–1950: A Study of Their Origins and Development*. New York: Twentieth Century Fund.

Bensel, Richard F. 2000. *The Political Economy of American Industrialization, 1877–1900*. New York: Cambridge University Press.

Bensel, Richard. 2008. *Passion and Preferences: William Jennings Bryan and the 1896 Democratic National Convention*. New York: Cambridge University Press.

Benson, Joel D. 2010. *The Presidency of Grover Cleveland*. Hauppauge, NY: Nova Science.

Berend, T. Ivan. 2012. *An Economic History of Nineteenth-Century Europe: Diversity and Industrialization*. New York: Cambridge University Press.

Bergeron, Paul H. 2011. *Andrew Johnson's Civil War and Reconstruction*. Knoxville: University of Tennessee Press.

Bergh, Albert Ellery, ed. 1909. *Letters and Addresses of Grover Cleveland*. New York: Unit Book.

Bergh, Andreas, and Alexander Funcke. 2019. "Social Trust and Sharing Economy Size: Country Level Evidence from Home Sharing Services." *Applied Economic Letters* 27 (19): 1592–1595.

Bergh, Andreas, and Magnus Henrekson. 2011. "Government Size and Growth: A Survey and Interpretation of the Evidence." *Journal of Economic Surveys* 25 (5): 872–897.

Bernanke, Ben, Mark Gertler, and Simon Gilchrist. 1996. "The Financial Accelerator and the Flight to Quality." *Review of Economics and Statistics* 78 (1): 1–15.

Bernard, Paul Roger. 1990. "The Making of the Marginal Mind: Academic Economic Thought in the United States, 1860–1910." PhD dissertation, University of Michigan.

Bernstein, Jared. 2020. "How Can We Have a Bad Economy with Such a Terrible Leader?" *Washington Post*, February 18.

Bernstein, Michael A. 2001. *A Perilous Progress: Economists and Public Purpose in Twentieth-Century America*. Princeton, NJ: Princeton University Press.

Besley, Timothy, Jose G. Montalvo, and Marta Reynal-Querol. 2011. "Do Educated Leaders Matter?" *Economic Journal* 121 (554): 205–227.

Bessette, Joseph M., and Jeffrey K. Tulis, eds. 2009. *The Constitutional Presidency*. Baltimore, MD: Johns Hopkins University Press.

Bigelow, John, ed. 1908. *Letters and Literary Memorials of Samuel J. Tilden*. Vol 2. New York: Harper & Brothers.

Biggs, Michael. 2002. "Strikes as Sequences of Interaction: The American Strike Wave of 1886." *Social Science History* 26 (3): 583–617.

Birnie, A. 2006. *An Economic History of Europe 1760–1930*. London: Routledge.

Bissell, Wilson S. 1909. "Cleveland as a Lawyer." *McClure's Magazine*, March.

Bittlingmayer, George. 1985. "Did Antitrust Policy Cause the Great Merger Wave?" *Journal of Law & Economics* 28 (1): 77–118.

Bjornskov, Christian. 2012. "How Does Social Trust Affect Economic Growth?" *Southern Economic Journal* 78 (4): 1346–1368.

Blackmon, Douglas A. 2009. *Slavery by Another Name: The Re-enslavement of Black Americans from the Civil War to World War II*. New York: Knopf Doubleday.

Blaine, James G. 1884. *Twenty Years of Congress*. Vol. 1. Norwich, CT: Henry Bill.

Blaine, James G. 1886. *Twenty Years of Congress*. Vol. 2. Norwich, CT: Henry Bill.

Blake, William. 1863. "Auguries of Innocence" (1803). In Alexander Gilchrist, *Life of William Blake: "Pictor Ignotus."* Vol. 2, 94–97. London: Macmillan:.

Blanck, Peter David, and Michael Millender. 2000. "Before Disability Civil Rights: Civil War Pensions and the Politics of Disability in America." *Alabama Law Review* 52 (1): 4.

Blinder, Alan S., and Mark W. Watson. 2016. "Presidents and the US Economy: An Econometric Exploration." *American Economic Review* 106 (4): 1015–1045.

Boardman, Mark. 2015. "The Great Die-Up: The Winter of 1886–87 Took the Crown off King Cattle." *True West Magazine* 63 (1): 12.

Boettcher, William A., III. 2005. *Presidential Risk Behavior in Foreign Policy: Prudence or Peril?* New York: Palgrave Macmillan.

Bolles, Albert S. 1886. *The Financial History of the United States from 1861 to 1885*. Vol. 3. New York: D Appleton.

Bolotin, Norman, and Christine Laing. 1992. *The World's Columbian Exposition: The Chicago World's Fair of 1893*. Washington, DC: Preservation Press.

Bolt, Jutta, and Jan Luiten van Zanden. 2020. "Maddison Style Estimates of the Evolution of the World Economy. A New 2020 Update." Maddison Project Database v.2020. https://www.rug.nl/ggdc/historicaldevelopment/maddison/releases/maddison-proj ect-database-2020.

Bolt, Robert. 1970. *Donald Dickinson*. Grand Rapids, MI: W. B. Eerdmans.

Bond, Jon R., and Richard Fleisher. 1990. *The President in the Legislative Arena*. Chicago: University of Chicago Press.

Bordo, Michael D., ed. 1999. *The Gold Standard and Related Regimes: Collected Essays*. New York: Cambridge University Press

Bordo, Michael. 2012. *Credibility and the International Monetary Regime: A Historical Perspective*. New York: Cambridge University Press.

Bordo, Michael D., and Hugh Rockoff. 1996. "The Gold Standard as a 'Good Housekeeping Seal of Approval.'" *Journal of Economic History* 56 (2): 389–428.

Bordo, Micahel D., and Anna J. Schwartz. 1999. "Monetary Policy Regimes and Economic Performance: The Historical Record." In *Handbook of Macroeconomics*. Vol. 1, edited by John B. Taylor and Michael Woodford, 149–234. New York: Elsevier.

Borish, Linda J., David K. Wiggins, and Gerald R. Gems, eds. 2017. *The Routledge History of American Sport*. New York: Routledge.

Bose, Meena. 1998. *Shaping and Signaling Presidential Policy: The National Security Decision Making of Eisenhower and Kennedy*. College Station: Texas A&M University Press.

Bose, Meena, and Mark Landis, eds. 2003. *The Uses and Abuses of Presidential Ratings*. New York: Nova Science.

Bourdon, Jeffrey Normand. 2019. *From Garfield to Harding: The Success of Midwestern Front Porch Campaigns*. Kent, OH: Kent State University Press.

Bourne, Jenny. 2017. *In Essentials, Unity: An Economic History of the Grange Movement*. Athens: Ohio University Press.

Boutmy, Emile. 1891. *Studies in Constitutional Law: France—England—United States*. London: Macmillan.

Boutwell, George S. 1902. *Reminiscences of Sixty Years in Public Affairs*. New York: McClure, Phillips.

Bowen, David Warren. 1989. *Andrew Johnson and the Negro*. Knoxville: University of Tennessee Press.

Bowmaker, Simon W. 2019. *When the Presidency Calls: Conversations with Economic Policymakers*. Cambridge, MA: MIT Press.

Bowman, Sylvia E. 1962. *Edward Bellamy Abroad: An American Prophet's Influence*. New York: Twayne.

Bowman, Sylvia E. 1986. *Edward Bellamy*. Boston: Twayne.

Bracha, Oren. 2016. *Owning Ideas: The Intellectual Origins of American Intellectual Property, 1790–1909*. New York: Cambridge University Press.

Bradley, Mark L. 2015. *The Army and Reconstruction 1865–1877*. Washington, DC: Center of Military History, US Army.

Braithwaite, Valerie, and Margaret Levi, eds. 1998. *Trust and Governance*. New York: Russell Sage Foundation.

Brands, H. W. 2010. *American Colossus: The Triumph of Capitalism, 1865–1900*. New York: Random House.

Brands, H. W. 2012. *The Man Who Saved the Union: Ulysses Grant in War and Peace.* New York: Random House.

Brands, H. W. 2019. *Dreams of El Dorado: A History of the American West.* New York: Basic Books.

Breit, William, and Roger L. Ransom. 2014. *The Academic Scribblers.* 3rd ed. Princeton, NJ: Princeton University Press.

British Medical Journal. 1894. "A New Light on the 'New Woman.'" 2 (1758): 548.

Brodsky, Alyn. 2000. *Grover Cleveland: A Study in Character.* New York: St. Martin's Press.

Bronner, Simon J., ed. 1989. *Consuming Visions: Accumulation and Display of Goods in America, 1880–1920.* New York: Norton.

Brown, Harry James, and Frederick D. Williams, eds. 1967. *The Diary of James A. Garfield.* Vols. 1–2. East Lansing: Michigan State University Press.

Brown, Harry James, and Frederick D. Williams, eds. 1973. *The Diary of James A. Garfield.* Vol. 3. East Lansing: Michigan State University Press.

Brown, Harry James, and Frederick D. Williams, eds. 1981. *The Diary of James A. Garfield.* Vol. 4. East Lansing: Michigan State University Press.

Brown, Joshua. 2008. "The Great Uprising and Pictorial Order in Gilded Age America." In *The Great Strikes of 1877*, edited by David O. Stowell, 15–54. Chicago: University of Illinois Press.

Brownlee, W. Elliot. 2016. *Federal Taxation in America: A Short History.* 3rd ed. New York: Cambridge University Press.

Bruce, Robert V. 1989. *1877: Year of Violence.* Chicago: Ivan R Dee.

Brum, David A., and Nese F. DeBruyne. 2020. "American War and Military Operations Casualties: Lists and Statistics." Washington DC: Congressional Research Service.

Bryan, William Jennings. 1913. *Speeches of William Jennings Bryan.* New York: Funk & Wagnalls.

Bryce, James. 1888a. *The American Commonwealth.* Vol. 1. New York: Macmillan.

Bryce, James. 1888b. *The American Commonwealth: The State Governments—The Party System.* Vol. 2. New York: Macmillan.

Buck, Solon J. 1913. *The Granger Movement: A Study of Agricultural Organization and Its Political, Economic and Social Manifestations, 1870–1880.* Cambridge, MA: Harvard University Press.

Buhle, Paul. 2013. *Marxism in the United States: A History of the American Left.* 3rd ed. New York: Verso Press.

Bullock, Charles J. 1901. "Trust Literature: A Survey and a Criticism." *Quarterly Journal of Economics* 15 (2): 167–217.

Bumgarner, John R. 1993. *The Health of the Presidents: The 41 United States Presidents through 1993 from a Physician's Point of View.* Jefferson, NC: McFarland.

Bunting, David. 1986. *The Rise of Large American Corporations 1889–1919.* Princeton, NJ: Princeton University Press.

Burg, Robert W. 2014. "Scandal, Corruption." In *A Companion to the Reconstruction Presidents 1865–1881*, edited by Edward O. Frantz, 581–600. West Sussex: John Wiley & Sons.

Burlingame, Michael, and John R. Turner Ettlinger, eds. 1997. *Inside Lincoln's White House: The Complete Civil War Diary of John Hay.* Carbondale: Southern Illinois University Press.

Burt, Silas W. 1902. *My Memoirs of the Military History of the State of New York during the War for the Union, 1861–65.* Albany, NY: J. B. Lyon.

Cain, William E. 2019. "The End of Capitalism: Eugene V. Debs and the Argument for Socialism in America." *Society* 56 (5): 466–480.

Calabresi, Steven G., and Christopher S. Yoo. 2008. *The Unitary Executive: Presidential Power from Washington to Bush*. New Haven, CT: Yale University Press.

Calavita, Kitty. 1984. *U.S. Immigration Law and the Control of Labor, 1820–1924*. New York: Academic Press.

Calhoun, Charles W. 1993. "Civil Religion and the Gilded Age Presidency: The Case of Benjamin Harrison." *Presidential Studies Quarterly* 23 (4): 651–667.

Calhoun, Charles W. 2000. "James G. Blaine and the Republican Party Vision." In *The Human Tradition in the Gilded Age and Progressive Era*, edited by Ballard C. Campbell, 19–35. Wilmington, DE: Scholarly Resources.

Calhoun, Charles W. 2002. "Reimagining the 'Lost Men' of the Gilded Age: Perspectives on the Late 19th Century Presidents." *Journal of the Gilded Age and Progressive Era* 1 (3): 225–257.

Calhoun, Charles W. 2005. *Benjamin Harrison*. New York: Times Books.

Calhoun, Charles W. 2006. *Conceiving a New Republic: The Republican Party and the Southern Question, 1869–1900*. Lawrence: University Press of Kansas.

Calhoun, Charles W. 2007. "Public Life and the Conduct of Politics." In *The Gilded Age: Perspectives on the Origins of Modern America*, 2nd ed., edited by Charles W. Calhoun, 239–264. Lantham, MD: Rowman & Littlefield.

Calhoun, Charles W. 2008. *Minority Victory: Gilded Age Politics and the Front Porch Campaign of 1888*. Lawrence: University Press of Kansas.

Calhoun, Charles W. 2010. *From Bloody Shirt to Full Dinner Pail: The Transformation of Politics and Governance in the Gilded Age*. New York: Hill and Wang.

Calhoun, Charles W. 2017. *The Presidency of Ulysses S. Grant*. Lawrence: University Press of Kansas.

Callahan, David. 2016. *Givers: Wealth, Power, and Philanthropy in a New Gilded Age*. New York: Random House.

Campbell, Ballard C. 2008. *Disasters, Accidents, and Crises in American History: A Reference Guide to the Nation's Most Catastrophic Events*. New York: Facts on File.

Campbell, Karlyn Kohrs. 2008. *Presidents Creating the Presidency: Deeds Done in Words*. Chicago: University of Chicago Press.

Camussi, Silvia, Anna Laura Mancini, and Pietro Tommasino. 2018. "Does Trust Influence Social Expenditures? Evidence from Local Governments." *Kyklos* 71 (1): 59–85.

Canes-Wrone, Brandice. 2006. *Who Leads Whom? Presidents, Policy, and the Public*. Chicago: University of Chicago Press.

Cannato, Vincent J. 2010. *American Passage: The History of Ellis Island*. New York: Harper Collins.

Cannon, James Graham. 1911. *Clearing Houses*. Publications of the National Monetary Commission. Vol. 6. Washington, DC: Government Printing Office. Originally 61st Congress, 2nd Session, Senate Document 491.

Carey, Henry. 1851. *The Harmony of Interests: Agricultural, Manufacturing & Commercial*. New York: Myron Finch.

Carey, Henry. 1853. *The Slave Trade, Domestic and Foreign*. Philadelphia, PA: A. Hart, late Carey & Hart.

Carlson, Mark. 2013. "The Panic of 1893." In *Routledge Handbook of Major Events in Economic History*, edited by Randall Parker and Robert Whaples, 40–50. New York: Routledge.

Carlton, David L., and Peter A. Coclanis. 2003. *The South, the Nation, and the World: Perspectives on Southern Economic Development*. Charlottesville: University of Virginia Press.

Carnegie, Andrew. 1889. "Wealth." *North American Review* 148 (391): 653–664.

Carnes, Nicholas, and Noam Lupu. 2016. "What Good Is a College Degree? Education and Leader Quality Reconsidered." *Journal of Politics* 78 (1): 35–49.

Cash, Jordan T. 2018. "The Isolated Presidency: The Institutional Logic of Constitutional Presidential Power." PhD dissertation, Baylor University.

Cashman, Sean D. 1993. *America in the Gilded Age: From the Death of Lincoln to the Rise of Theodore Roosevelt*. 3rd ed.. New York: New York University Press.

Castel, Albert. 1979. *The Presidency of Andrew Johnson*. Lawrence: University Press of Kansas.

Chan, Kam Fong, and Terry Marsh. 2021. "Asset Prices, Midterm Elections, and Political Uncertainty." *Journal of Financial Economics* 141 (1): 276–296.

Chan, Sucheng. 1984. "Chinese Livelihood in Rural California: The Impact of Economic Change, 1860–1880." *Pacific Historical Review* 53 (3): 273–307.

Chandler, Alfred D., Jr. 1977. *The Visible Hand: The Managerial Revolution in American Business*. Cambridge, MA: Harvard University Press.

Chandler, D. Aaron. 1998. "A Short Note on the Expenditures of the McKinley Campaign of 1896." *Presidential Studies Quarterly* 28 (1): 88–91.

Chandler, W. E., and Josiah Quincy. 1896. "Issues and Prospects of the Campaign." *North American Review* 163 (477): 175–194.

Chang, Gordon H., and Shelley Fisher Fishkin, eds. 2019. *The Chinese and the Iron Road: Building the Transcontinental Railroad*. Stanford CA: Stanford University Press.

Cheibub, Jose, Adam Przeworski, and Sebastian M. Saiegh. 2004. "Government Coalitions and Legislative Success under Presidentialism and Parliamentarism." *British Journal of Political Science* 34 (4): 565–587.

Chen, Joyce J. 2015. "The Impact of Skill-Based Immigration Restrictions: The Chinese Exclusion Act of 1882." *Journal of Human Capital* 9 (3): 298–328.

Chernow, Ron. 2017. *Grant*. New York: Penguin Press.

Cherny, Robert W. 1997. *American Politics in the Gilded Age: 1868–1900*. Wheeling, IL: Harlan Davidson.

Cherry, Robin. 2008. *Catalog: An Illustrated History of Mail-Order Shopping*. New York: Princeton Architectural Press.

Child, Lydia Maria, and Sally McMillen. 2008. *Seneca Falls and the Origins of the Women's Rights Movement*. New York: Oxford University Press.

Citrin, Jack, and Donald Philip Green. 1986. "Presidential Leadership and the Resurgence of Trust in Government." *British Journal of Political Science* 16: 431–453.

Civil Service Commission. 1871. *The Reform of the Civil Service: A Report to the President*. Washington, DC: Government Printing Office.

Clancy, Herbert John. 1958. *The Presidential Election of 1880*. Chicago: Loyola University Press.

Clark, Charles H. 1972. "The Development of the Semiautomatic Freight-Car Coupler, 1863–1893." *Technology and Culture* 13 (2): 170–208.

Clark, John Bates. 1900. "Trusts." *Political Science Quarterly* 15 (2): 181–195.

Clark, John Bates, and John Maurice Clark. 1901. *The Control of Trusts*. New York: Macmillan.

Clark, Laura. 2015. "The 1887 Blizzard That Changed the American Frontier Forever." *The Smithsonian*, (January 9).

Clarke, Roger, Stephen Davies, and Michael Waterson. 1984. "The Profitability-Concentration Relation: Market Power or Efficiency." *Journal of Industrial Economics* 32 (4): 435–450.

Clawson, Mary Ann. 1989. *Constructing Brotherhood: Class, Gender, and Fraternalism*. Princeton: Princeton University Press.

Cleaver, Nick. 2014. *Grover Cleveland's New Foreign Policy: Arbitration, Neutrality, and the Dawn of American Empire*. New York: Palgrave Macmillan.

Cleveland, Stephen Grover. 1897. *The Self-Made Man in American Life*. New York: T. Y. Crowell.

Cleveland, Stephen Grover. 1913. *The Government in the Chicago Strike of 1894*. Princeton, NJ: Princeton University Press.

Closson, Carlos C., Jr. 1894. "The Unemployed in American Cities." *Quarterly Journal of Economics* 8 (4): 453–477.

Clymer, Kenton J. 1975. *John Hay: The Gentleman as Diplomat*. Ann Arbor: University of Michigan Press.

Coats, A. W. 1960. "The First Two Decades of the American Economic Association." *American Economic Review* 50 (4): 556–574.

Cochrane, Willard Wesley. 1993. *The Development of American Agriculture: A Historical Analysis*. Minneapolis: University of Minnesota Press.

Cohen, Jeffrey E. 1999. *Presidential Responsiveness and Public Policy-Making: The Publics and the Policies That Presidents Choose*. Ann Arbor: University of Michigan Press.

Coleman, James S. 1988. "Social Capital in the Creation of Human Capital." *American Journal of Sociology* 94: s95–s120.

Commons, John R., Ulrich B. Phillips, Eugene A. Gilmore, Helen L. Sumner, and John B. Andrews, eds. 1910. *A Documentary History of American Industrial Society: Labor Movement*. Vol. 9. Cleveland, OH: Arthur H. Clark.

Comstock, Anthony. 1883. *Traps for the Young*. New York, Funk & Wagnalls.

Congressional Budget Office. 2019. *The Budget and Economic Outlook: 2019 to 2029*. Washington, DC: Government Printing Office.

Conn, Steven. 2019. *Nothing Succeeds Like Failure: The Sad History of American Business Schools*. Ithaca, NY: Cornell University Press.

Connolly, Michael J. 2010. "'I Make Politics My Recreation': Vice President Garret A. Hobart and Nineteenth-Century Republican Business Politics." *New Jersey History* 125 (1): 20–39.

Cordery, Simon. 2016. *The Iron Road in the Prairie State*. Bloomington: Indiana University Press.

Cornfield, Daniel B., and Bill Fletcher. 1998. "Institutional Constraints on Social Movement 'Frame Extension': Shifts in the Legislative Agenda of the American Federation of Labor, 1881–1955." *Social Forces* 76 (4): 1305–1321.

Cortissoz, Royal. 1921. *The Life of Whitelaw Reid*. Vol. 2. New York: Charles Scribner's Sons.

Cosmas, Graham A. 1971. "Military Reform after the Spanish-American War: The Army Reorganization Fight of 1898–1899." *Military Affairs* 35 (1): 12–18.

Costa, Dora L. 1998. *The Evolution of Retirement: An American Economic History, 1880–1990*. Chicago: University of Chicago Press.

Crackel, Theodore. 1987. *Mr. Jefferson's Army: Political and Social Reform of the Military Establishment, 1801–1809*. New York: New York University Press.

Crawford, Jay Boyd. 1880. *The Credit Mobilier of America: Its Origin and History.* Boston: C. W. Calkins.

Cronin, Thomas E., ed. 1989. *Inventing the Presidency.* Lawrence: University Press of Kansas.

Cronin, Thomas E. 2009. *On the Presidency: Teacher, Soldier, Shaman, Pol.* Boulder, CO: Paradigm.

Cronon, William. 1995. "The Trouble with Wilderness: or, Getting Back to the Wrong Nature." In *Uncommon Ground: Rethinking the Human Place in Nature,* edited by William Cronon, 69–90. New York: W. W. Norton.

Crosby, Fanny J. 1909. "Cleveland as a Teacher in the Institution for the Blind." *McClure's Magazine,* March.

Crump, Thomas. 2007. *A Brief History of the Age of Steam: The Power that Drove the Industrial Revolution.* New York: Carroll & Graf.

Culbertson, Thomas J. 2013. "Did Rutherford B. Hayes End Reconstruction?" Hayes Lecture on the Presidency. Fremont, OH: Hayes Presidential Center, February 17. https://www.rbhayes.org/hayes/did-rutherford-b.-hayes-end-reconstruction/.

Culbertson, Thomas. 2016. *Rutherford B. Hayes: A Life of Service.* New York: Nova Science.

Cullom, Shelby Moore. 1911. *Fifty Years of Public Service.* Chicago: A. C. McClurg.

Currarino, Rosanne. 2011. *The Labor Question in America: Economic Democracy in the Gilded Age.* Urbana, IL: University of Illinois Press.

Current, Richard Nelson. 1988. *Those Terrible Carpetbaggers.* New York: Oxford University Press.

D'A. Jones, Peter. 1988. "Henry George and British Socialism." *American Journal of Economics and Sociology* 47 (4): 473–491.

Dalzell, Robert F. 1987. *Enterprising Elite: The Boston Associates and the World They Made.* Cambridge, MA: Harvard University Press.

Danziger, Edmund J., Jr. 2007. "A Native American Resistance and Accommodation during the Late Nineteenth Century." In *The Gilded Age: Perspectives on the Origins of Modern America,* edited by Charles W. Calhoun, 167–186. Lantham, MD: Rowman & Littlefield.

Dauber, Michaele Landis. 2013. *The Sympathetic State: Disaster Relief and the Origins of the American Welfare State.* Chicago: University of Chicago Press.

Daughety, Andrew F. 1990. "Beneficial Concentration." *American Economic Review* 80 (5): 1231–1237.

Davies, Hannah Catherine. 2018. *Transatlantic Speculations: Globalization and the Panics of 1873.* New York: Columbia University Press.

Davin, Eric Leif. 2014. "The Shattered Dream: The Shock of Industrialization and the Crisis of the Free Labor Ideal." In *A Companion to the Reconstruction Presidents, 1865–1881,* edited by Edward O. Frantz, 452–474. West Sussex: John Wiley & Sons.

Davis, Cory. 2014. "The Political Economy of Commercial Associations: Building the National Board of Trade, 1840–1868." *Business History Review* 88 (4): 761–783.

Davis, John Martin. 2019. *Civil War Taxes: A Documentary History, 1861–1900.* Jefferson, NC: McFarland.

Dearborn, John A. 2019a. "The Foundations of the Modern Presidency: Presidential Representation, the Unitary Executive Theory, and the Reorganization Act of 1939." *Presidential Studies Quarterly* 49 (1): 185–203.

Dearborn, John A. 2019b. "The 'Proper Organs' for Presidential Representation: A Fresh Look at the Budget and Accounting Act of 1921." *Journal of Policy History* 31 (1): 1–41.

DeCanio, Samuel. 2005. "State Autonomy and American Political Development: How Mass Democracy Promoted State Power." *Studies in American Political Development* 19: 117–136.

DeCanio, Samuel. 2015. *Democracy and the Origins of the American Regulatory State.* New Haven, CT: Yale University Press.

Dedinger, Beatrice. 2012. "The Franco-German Trade Puzzle: An Analysis of the Economic Consequences of the Franco-Prussian War." *Economic History Review* 65 (3): 1029–1054.

Dehler, Gregory J. 2011. *Chester Alan Arthur: The Life of a Gilded Age Politician and President.* New York: Nova Science.

Demarest, David P., and Fannia Weingartner. 1992. *"The River Ran Red": Homestead 1892.* Pittsburgh, PA: University of Pittsburgh Press.

De Neve, Jan-Emmanuel, Slava Mikhaylov, Christopher T. Dawes, Nicholas A. Christakis, and James H. Fowler. 2013. "Born to Lead? A Twin Design and Genetic Association Study of Leadership Role Occupancy." *Leadership Quarterly* 24 (1): 45–60.

Denison, Thomas S. 1895. *The New Woman: A Comedy of A.D. 1950.* Chicago: Denison.

Depew, Chauncey Mitchell. 1923. *My Memories of Eighty Years.* New York: Charles Scribners Sons.

Devine, Shauna. 2014. *Learning from the Wounded: The Civil War and the Rise of American Medical Science.* Chapel Hill: University of North Carolina Press.

Devine, Shauna. 2016. "'To Make Something Out of the Dying in This War': The Civil War and the Rise of American Medical Science." *Journal of the Civil War Era* 6 (2): 149–163.

Dewey, Davis Rich. 1907. *National Problems, 1885–1897.* Vol. 24. New York: Harper and Brothers.

Dewing, Arthur S. 1913. *A History of National Cordage.* Cambridge, MA: Harvard University Press.

Dillistin, William H. 1949. *Bank Note Reporters and Counterfeit Detectors 1826–1866.* New York: American Numismatic Society.

DiSalvo, Daniel. 2012. *Engines of Change: Party Factions in American Politics, 1868–2010.* New York: Oxford University Press.

Dix, Keith. 1988. *What's a Coal Miner to Do? The Mechanization of Coal Mining.* Pittsburgh, PA: University of Pittsburgh Press.

Doenecke, Justus D. 1981. *The Presidencies of James A. Garfield and Chester A. Arthur.* Lawrence: Regents Press of Kansas.

Dolan, Chris J., John Frendreis, and Raymond Tatalovich. 2008. *The Presidency and the Economic Policy.* Lanham, MD: Rowman & Littlefield.

Dolan, Chris J., John Frendreis, and Raymond Tatalovich. 2009. "A Presidential Economic Scorecard: Performance and Perception." *PS: Political Science and Politics* 42: 689–694.

Dollar, David, and Aart Kraay. 2003. "Institutions, Trade, and Growth." *Journal of Monetary Economics* 50: 133–162.

Donald, David Herbert, ed. 1954. *Inside Lincoln's Cabinet: The Civil War Diaries of Salmon P. Chase.* New York: Longmans.

Dorfman, Joseph. 1949. *The Economic Mind in American Civilization: 1865–1918.* Vol. 3. New York: Viking Press.

Downey, Dennis B. 2002. *A Season of Renewal: The Columbian Exposition and Victorian America.* Westport, CT: Praeger.

Dozer, Donald Marquand. 1948. "Benjamin Harrison and the Presidential Campaign of 1892." *American Historical Review* 54 (1): 49–77.

Drache, Hiram M. 1964. *The Day of the Bonanza: A History of Bonanza Farming in the Red River Valley of the North*. Fargo: North Dakota Institute for Regional Studies.

Dreher Axel, Michael J. Lamla, Sarah M. Lein, and Frank Somogyi. 2009. "The Impact of Political Leaders' Profession and Education on Reforms." *Journal of Comparative Economics* 37 (1): 169–193.

Dubofsky, Melvyn, and Foster Rhea Dulles. 2010. *Labor in America: A History*. 8th ed. New York: Wiley-Blackwell.

Dubois, Eric. 2016. "Political Business Cycles 40 Years after Nordhaus." *Public Choice* 166: 235–259.

Duffy, John. 1992. *The Sanitarians: A History of American Public Health*. Champaign: University of Illinois Press.

Duffy, Michael C. 2003. *Electric Railways: 1880–1990*. London: Institution of Electrical Engineers.

Duncan, Russell. 1994. *Entrepreneur for Equality: Governor Rufus Bullock, Commerce, and Race in Post–Civil War Georgia*. Athens: University of Georgia Press.

Dunn, Arthur Wallace. 1922. *From Harrison to Harding: A Personal Narrative, Covering a Third of a Century 1888–1921*. Vol. 1. New York: G. P. Putnam's Sons.

Dupont, Brandon R. 2009. "Panic in the Plains: Agricultural Markets and the Panic of 1893." *Cliometrica* 3: 27–54.

Dupont, Brandon, and Joshua Rosenbloom. 2016. "The Impact of the Civil War on Southern Wealth Holders." Working Paper No. 22184. Cambridge, MA: NBER.

Dupree, A. Hunter. 1957a. "The Founding of the National Academy of Sciences: A Reinterpretation." *Proceedings of the American Philosophical Society* 101 (5): 434–440.

Dupree, A. Hunter. 1957b. *Science in the Federal Government: A History of Policies and Activities to 1940*. Cambridge, MA: Belknap Press of Harvard University.

Durden, Robert F. 2015. *The Climax of Populism: The Election of 1896*. Lexington: University Press of Kentucky.

Dutta, Nabamita, and Russell Sobel. 2016. "Does Corruption Ever Help Entrepreneurship?" *Small Business Economics* 47 (1): 179–199.

Dyer, Brainerd. 1933. *The Public Career of William M. Evarts*. Berkeley: University of California Press.

Dyer, Jeffrey H., and Wujin J. Chu. 2003. "The Role of Trustworthiness in Reducing Transaction Costs and Improving Performance: Empirical Evidence from the United States, Japan, and Korea." *Organization Science* 14 (1): 57–68.

Easterbrook, William T., and Hugh G. J. Aitken. 1956. *Canadian Economic History*. Toronto: Macmillan.

Eastman, George. 1880. "Method and Apparatus for Coating Plates for Use in Photography." U.S. Patent No. 226,503. Washington, DC: US Patent and Trademark Office.

Eaton, Dorman. 1880. *Civil Service in Great Britain: A History of Abuses and Reforms and Their Bearing upon American Politics*. New York: Harper & Brothers.

Edwards, Alba M. 1934. "The 'White-Collar Workers.'" *Monthly Labor Review* 38 (3): 501–505.

Edwards, George C., III. 1990. *At the Margins: Presidential Leadership of Congress*. New Haven, CT: Yale University Press.

Edwards, George C., III. 2009. *The Strategic President: Persuasion and Opportunity in Presidential Leadership*. Princeton, NJ: Princeton University Press.

Edwards, Ryan D. 2014. "U.S. War Costs: Two Parts Temporary, One Part Permanent." *Journal of Public Economics* 113: 54–66.

Eichengreen, Barry J. 2011. *Exorbitant Privilege: The Rise and Fall of the Dollar.* New York: Oxford University Press.

Eichengreen, Barry J. 2019. *Globalizing Capital: A History of the International Monetary System.* 3rd ed. Princeton, NJ: Princeton University Press.

Eichengreen, Barry, and Marc Flandreau. 1994. "The Geography of the Gold Standard." Working Paper C94–042. Berkeley, CA: Center for International and Development Economics Research.

Eichengreen, Barry, Michael R. Haines, Matthew S. Jaremski, and David Leblang. 2017. "Populists at the Polls: Economic Factors in the US Presidential Election of 1896." Working Paper 23932. Cambridge, MA: NBER.

Einaudi, Luca. 2001. *Money and Politics: European Monetary Unification and the International Gold Standard (1865–1873).* New York: Oxford University Press.

Einaudi, Luca. 2017. "A Historical Perspective on the European Crisis: The Latin Monetary Union." In *The Political Economy of the Eurozone*, edited by Ivano Cardinale, D'Maris Coffman, and Roberto Scazzieri, 78–95. New York: Cambridge University Press.

Eland, Ivan. 2009. *Recarving Rushmore: Ranking the Presidents on Peace, Prosperity, and Liberty.* Oakland, CA: Independent Institute.

Ellington, Charles G. 1987. *The Trial of U.S. Grant: The Pacific Coast Years 1852–1854.* Glendale, CA: Arthur H. Clark.

Ellis, Richard J. 1998. *Speaking to the People: The Rhetorical Presidency in Historical Perspective.* Amherst: University of Massachusetts Press.

Ellis, Richard J. 2008. *Presidential Travel: The Journey from George Washington to George W. Bush.* Lawrence: University Press of Kansas.

Ellis, Richard J. 2012. *The Development of the American Presidency.* New York: Routledge.

Ely, James W., Jr., ed. 1997. *Property Rights in the Age of Enterprise.* New York: Garland.

Ely, Richard T. 1886. "Report of the Organization of the American Economic Association." *Publications of the American Economic Association* 1 (1): 16.

Ely, Richard T. 1900. *Monopolies and Trusts.* New York: Macmillan.

Emerson, Jason. 2012. *Giant in the Shadows the Life of Robert T. Lincoln.* Carbondale: Southern Illinois University Press.

Emrich, Cynthia G., Holly H. Brower, Jack M. Feldman, and Howard Garland. 2001. "Images in Words: Presidential Rhetoric, and Charisma, and Greatness." *Administrative Science Quarterly* 46 (3): 527–557.

Engerman, Stanley L., and Robert E. Gallman, eds. 2000. *The Cambridge Economic History of the United States.* Vol. 2. New York: Cambridge University Press.

Engerman, Stanley L., and Kenneth L. Sokoloff. 2000. "Technology and Industrialization, 1790–1914." In *Cambridge Economic History of the United States*, Vol. 2, edited by Stanley L. Engerman and Robert E. Gallman, 267–401. New York: Cambridge University Press.

Enss, Chris. 2020. *No Place for a Woman: The Struggle for Suffrage in the Wild West.* Lanham, MD: Rowman & Littlefield.

Eriksson, Katherine, and Zachary Ward. 2022. "Immigrants and Cities during the Age of Mass Migration." *Regional Science and Urban Economics* 94: 1–8.

Eschner, Kat. 2017. The Third-Term Controversy that Gave the Republican Party Its Symbol. *Smithsonian Magazine* (November 7).

Evans, Christopher H. 2017. *The Social Gospel in American Religion*. New York: New York University Press.

Evans, Sara M. 1997. *Born for Liberty: A History of Women in American*. New York: Free Press.

Fabian, Ann. 1989. "Speculation on Distress: The Popular Discourse of the Panics of 1837 and 1857." *Yale Journal of Criticism* 3 (1): 127–142.

Farber, Daniel A. 2003. *Lincoln's Constitution*. Chicago: University of Chicago Press.

Farnham, Barbara. 1992. "Roosevelt and the Munich Crisis: Insights from Prospect Theory." *Political Psychology* 13 (2): 205–235.

Farr, James, and Raymond Seidelman, eds. 1993. *Discipline and History: Political Science in the United States*. Ann Arbor: University of Michigan Press.

Farrell, Henry, and Jack Knight 2003. "Trust, Institutions, and Institutional Change: Industrial Districts and the Social Capital Hypothesis." *Politics & Society* 31 (4): 537–566.

Faust, Drew Gilpin. 2008. *This Republic of Suffering: Death and the American Civil War*. New York: Alfred A. Knopf.

Faust, Jon, and John Irons. 1999. "Money, Politics and the Post-war Business Cycle." *Journal of Monetary Economics* 43 (1): 61–89.

Fayle, C. Ernest. 1933. *A Short History of the World's Shipping Industry*. New York: Dial Press.

Federico, Giovanni, and Antonio Tena-Junguito. 2019. "World Trade, 1800–1938: A New Synthesis." *Revista de Historia Económica/Journal of Iberian and Latin America Economic History* 37 (1): 9–41.

Feldman, Glenn. 2013. *The Irony of the Solid South: Democrats, Republicans, and Race, 1865–1944*. Tuscaloosa: University of Alabama Press.

Felzenberg, Alvin S. 2008. *The Leaders We Deserved (and a Few We Didn't): Rethinking the Presidential Rating Game*. New York: Basic Books.

Fink, Leon. 1983. *Workingmen's Democracy: The Knights of Labor and American Politics*. Urbana: University of Illinois Press.

Fishlow, Albert. 1966. "Productivity and Technological Change in the Railroad Sector, 1840–1910." In *Output, Employment, and Productivity in the United States after 1800*, edited by Dorothy S. Brady, 583–646. New York: National Bureau of Economic Research, Columbia University Press.

Fisman, Raymond. 2017. *Corruption: What Everyone Needs to Know*. New York: Oxford University Press.

Fitzharris, Lindsey. 2017. *The Butchering Art: Joseph Lister's Quest to Transform the Grisly World of Victorian Medicine*. New York: Farrar, Straus and Giroux.

Flemmons, Jerry. 1998. *O Dammit! A Lexicon and Lecture from William Cowper Brann, the Iconoclast*. Lubbock: Texas Tech University Press.

Fletcher, Robert S. 1930. "That Hard Winter in Montana, 1886–1887." *Agricultural History* 4 (4): 123–130.

Flink, James J. 1988. *The Automobile Age*. Cambridge, MA: MIT Press.

Flood, Charles Bracelen. 2009. *1864: Lincoln at the Gates of History*. New York: Simon & Schuster.

Foerster, Stephen R., and John J. Schmitz. 1997. "The Transmission of US Election Cycles to International Stock Returns." *Journal of International Business Studies* 28 (1): 1–27.

Fogelson, Robert M. 1989. *America's Armories: Architecture, Society, and Public Order*. Cambridge, MA: Harvard University Press.

Follett, Mary Parker, and Albert Bushnell Hart. 1896. *The Speaker of the House of Representatives*. New York: Longmans Green.

Foner, Eric. 1970. *Free Soil, Free Labor, Free Men: The Ideology of the Republican Party before the Civil War*. New York: Oxford University Press.

Foner, Eric. 1990. *A Short History of Reconstruction 1863–1877*. New York: Harper and Row.

Foner, Eric. 2005. *Forever Free: The Story of Emancipation and Reconstruction*. New York: Knopf.

Foner, Eric. 2014. *Reconstruction: America's Unfinished Revolution, 1863–1877*. New York: Harper Collins.

Foner, Phillip S. 1977. *The Great Labor Uprising of 1877*. New York: Pathfinder.

Foraker, Joseph B. 1916. *Notes of a Busy Life*. Vol. 1. 2nd ed. Cincinnati, OH: Stewart & Kidd.

Francis, Bill B., Iftekhar Hasan, and Yun Zhu. 2021. "The Impact of Political Uncertainty on Institutional Ownership." *Journal of Financial Stability* 57 (100921).

Fraser, Steve. 2008. "The Gilded Age, Past and Present." *Salon*, April 28. https://www.salon.com/2008/04/28/gilded_age/.

Freese, Barbara. 2016. *Coal: A Human History*. New York: Basic Books.

Frieden, Jeffry A. 1997. "Monetary Populism in Nineteenth-Century America: An Open Economy Interpretation." *Journal of Economic History* 57 (2): 367–395.

Friedlander, Alan, and Richard Allan Gerber. 2019. *Welcoming Ruin: The Civil Rights Act of 1875*. Boston: Brill.

Friedman, Milton. 1990a. "Bimetallism Revisited." *Journal of Economic Perspectives* 4 (4): 85–104.

Friedman, Milton. 1990b. "The Crime of 1873." *Journal of Political Economy* 98 (6): 1159–1194.

Friedman, Milton, and Anna Jacobson Schwartz. 1963. *A Monetary History of the United States, 1867–1960*. Princeton, NJ: Princeton University Press.

Fukuyama, Francis. 1995a. "Social Capital and the Global Economy." *Foreign Affairs* 74 (5): 89–103.

Fukuyama, Francis. 1995b. *Trust: The Social Virtues and the Creation of Prosperity*. New York: Free Press.

Fulford, Scott, Ivan Petkov, and Fabio Schiantarelli. 2020. "Does It Matter Where You Came From? Ancestry Composition and Economic Performance of US Counties, 1850–2010." *Journal of Economic Growth* 25 (3): 341–380.

Fulford, Scott L., and Felipe Schwartzman. 2020. "The Benefits of Commitment to a Currency Peg: Aggregate Lessons from the Regional Effects of the 1896 U.S. Presidential Election." *Review of Economics and Statistics* 102 (3): 600–616.

Fuller, A. James. 2017. *Oliver P. Morton and the Politics of the Civil War and Reconstruction*. Kent, OH: Kent State University Press.

Gage, Lyman J. 1937. *Memoirs*. New York: House of Field.

Galambos, Louis. 1975. *The Public Image of Big Business in America, 1880–1940*. Baltimore, MD: Johns Hopkins University Press.

Gantz, Carroll. 2015. *Refrigeration: A History*. Jefferson, NC: McFarland.

Gardner, William L., Bruce J. Avolio, and Fred O. Walumbwa. 2005. *Authentic Leadership Theory and Practice: Origins, Effects and Development*. Boston: Elsevier JAI.

Garland, Hamlin. 1898. *Ulysses S. Grant: His Life and Character*. New York: Doubleday & McClure.

Garraty, John Arthur. 1968. *The New Commonwealth, 1877–1890*. New York: Harper & Row.

Gehlbach, Scott, Konstantin Sonin, and Ekatrina Zhuravskaya. 2010. "Businessman Candidates." *American Journal of Political Science* 54 (3): 718–736.

Geisst, Charles R. 2000. *Monopolies in America: Empire Builders and Their Enemies from Jay Gould to Bill Gates*. New York: Oxford University Press.

Geisst, Charles R. 2018. *Wall Street: A History*. 2nd ed. New York: Oxford University Press.

George, Alexander L., and Juliette L. George. 1998. *Presidential Personality and Performance*. Boulder, CO: Westview Press.

George, Henry. 1879. *Progress and Poverty: An Inquiry into the Cause of Industrial Depressions and of Increase of Want with Increase of Wealth: The Remedy*. N.p.: National Single Tax League.

Gess, Denise, and William Lutz. 2002. *Firestorm at Peshtigo: A Town, Its People, and the Deadliest Fire in American History*. New York: Henry Holt.

Giberti, Bruno. 2015. *Designing the Centennial: A History of the 1876 International Exhibition in Philadelphia*. Lexington: University Press of Kentucky.

Gilder, Richard Watson. 1910. *Grover Cleveland: A Record of Friendship*. New York: Century.

Gilens, Martin. 2012. *Affluence and Influence: Economic Inequality and Political Power in America*. Princeton, NJ: Princeton University Press.

Gillett, Frederick H. 1934. *George Frisbie Hoar*. Boston: Houghton Mifflin.

Gilpin, William. 1873. *Mission of the North American People: Geographical, Social, and Political*. Philadelphia, PA: J. B. Lippincott.

Giroux, Gary. 2012. "Financing the American Civil War: Developing New Tax Sources." *Accounting History* 17 (1): 83–104.

Gladden, Washington. 1886. *Applied Christianity: Moral Aspects of Social Questions*. Boston: Houghton Mifflin.

Glasner, David. 1997. *Business Cycles and Depressions*. New York: Garland.

Glasson, William H. 1900. "History of Military Pension Legislation in the United States." PhD dissertation, Columbia University.

Glymph, Thavolia, and John J. Kushma, eds. 1985. *Essays on the Postbellum Southern Economy*. College Station: Texas A&M University Press.

Goethals, George R. 2008. "Resolute Commander for Just Peace: The Rhetoric of President Ulysses S. Grant." In *Before the Rhetorical Presidency*, edited by Martin J. Medhurst, 213–242. College Station: Texas A&M University Press.

Goetzmann, William N., Roger G. Ibbotson, and Liang Peng. 2001. "A New Historical Database for the NYSE 1815 to 1925: Performance and Predictability." *Journal of Financial Markets* 4 (1): 1–32.

Goetzmann, William N., and Andrey D. Ukhov. 2006. "British Investment Overseas 1870–1913: A Modern Portfolio Theory Approach." *Review of Finance* 10 (2): 261–300.

Goldberg, Joseph P., and William T. Moye. 1985. *The First 100 Years of the Bureau of Labor Statistics*. Washington, DC: Bureau of Labor Statistics.

Goldin, Claudia, and Frank Lewis. 1975. "The Economic Costs of the American Civil War: Estimates and Implications." *Journal of Economic History* 35: 299–326.

Goldman, Robert Michael. 2001. *Reconstruction and Black Suffrage: Losing the Vote in Reese and Cruikshank*. Lawrence: University Press of Kansas.

Golway, Terry. 2014. *Machine Made: Tammany Hall and the Creation of Modern American Politics*. New York: W. W. Norton.

Gompers, Samuel. 1925. *Seventy Years of Life and Labor*. New York: E. P. Dutton.

Goodrich, Frederick Elizur. 1888. *The Life and Public Services of Grover Cleveland.* Springfield, MA: Winter.

Goodwin, Doris Kearns. 2005. *Team of Rivals: The Political Genius of Abraham Lincoln.* New York: Simon & Schuster.

Gordon, John Steel. 1989. "The Public Be Damned." *American Heritage* 40 (6). https://www.americanheritage.com/public-be-damned.

Gordon, Robert J. 2016. *The Rise and Fall of American Growth: The U.S. Standard of Living since the Civil War.* Princeton, NJ: Princeton University Press.

Gorn, Elliott J., and Warren Goldstein. 2004. *A Brief History of American Sports.* Urbana: University of Illinois Press.

Gould, Lewis L. 1980. *The Presidency of William McKinley.* Lawrence: University Press of Kansas.

Gould, Lewis L. 2012. *Grand Old Party: A History of the Republicans.* New York: Oxford University Press.

Graf, LeRoy P., and Ralph W. Haskins, eds. 1970. *The Papers of Andrew Johnson, 1852–1857.* Vol. 2. Knoxville: University of Tennessee Press.

Graff, Henry F. 2002. *Grover Cleveland.* New York: Henry Holt.

Grafstein, Robert, and Kiki Caruson. 2008. "Surprise Party: Estimating the Consequences of Unexpected Presidential Election Results." *Public Choice* 137 (1–2): 315–328.

Graham, Otis. 2015. *Presidents and the American Environment.* Lawrence: University Press of Kansas.

Grana, Mari. 2015. *On the Fringes of Power: The Life and Turbulent Career of Stephen Wallace Dorsey.* New York: Rowman & Littlefield.

Grand, Sarah. 1894a. "The Man of the Moment." *North American Review* 158 (450): 620–627.

Grand, Sarah. 1894b. "The New Aspect of the Woman Question." *North American Review* 158 (448): 270–276.

Grandy, Christopher. 1989. "New Jersey Corporate Chartermongering, 1875–1929." *Journal of Economic History* 49 (3): 677–692.

Grant, J. Tobin, and Nathan J. Kelly. 2008. "Legislative Productivity of the U.S. Congress, 1789–2004." *Political Analysis* 16 (3): 303–323.

Grant, Roger. 1983. *Self-Help in the 1890s Depression.* Ames: Iowa State University Press.

Grant, Ulysses S. 1885. *Personal Memoirs of U.S. Grant.* Vol. 1. New York: Charles L. Webster.

Grant, Ulysses S., III. 1969. *Ulysses S. Grant: Warrior and Statesman.* New York: William Morrow.

Green, Arnold W. 1951. *Henry Charles Carey: Nineteenth-Century Sociologist.* Philadelphia: University of Pennsylvania Press.

Green, James. 2006. *Death in the Haymarket: The Story of Chicago, the First Labor Movement and the Bombing That Divided Gilded Age America.* New York: Pantheon Books.

Green, Michael S. 2015. *Nevada: A History of the Silver State.* Reno: University of Nevada Press.

Green, Richard T. 2019. *Alexander Hamilton's Public Administration.* Tuscaloosa: University of Alabama Press.

Greenberg, Brian. 2017. *The Dawning of American Labor: The New Republic to the Industrial Age.* Newark, NJ: John Wiley & Sons.

Greenberger, Scott. 2017. *The Unexpected President: The Life and Times of Chester A. Arthur.* New York: DeCapo Press.

Greene, Julie. 1998. *Pure and Simple Politics: The American Federation of Labor and Political Activism, 1881–1917*. New York: Cambridge University Press.

Greene, Julie 2017. "Race, Immigration, and Ethnicity." In *A Companion to the Gilded Age and Progressive Era*, edited by Christopher McKnight Nichols and Nancy C. Unger, 137–148. New York: John Wiley & Sons.

Greenstein, Fred I. 1982. *The Hidden-Hand Presidency: Eisenhower as Leader*. New York: Basic Books.

Greenstien, Fred I. 1995. Interview with *New York Times*.

Greenstein, Fred I. 2009. *The Presidential Difference: Leadership Style from FDR to Barack Obama*. 3rd ed. Princeton, NJ: Princeton University Press.

Greif, Avner. 1998. "Historical and Comparative Institutional Analysis." *American Economic Review* 88 (2): 80–84.

Greif, Avner, Paul Milgrom, and Barry R. Weingast. 1994. "Coordination, Commitment, and Enforcement: The Case of the Merchant Guild." *Journal of Political Economy* 102 (4): 745–776.

Grimes, Alan Pendleton. 1953. *The Political Liberalism of the New York Nation, 1865–1932*. Chapel Hill: University of North Carolina Press.

Grossman, Gene, and Elhanan Helpman. 1991. *Innovation and Growth in the Global Economy*. Cambridge, MA: MIT Press.

Guerin, Polly. 2012. *The Cooper-Hewitt Dynasty of New York*. Charleston, SC: History Press.

Guiso, Luigi, Paolo Sapienza, and Luigi Zingales. 2009. "Cultural Biases in Economic Exchange?" *Quarterly Journal of Economics* 124 (3): 1095–1131.

Gunton, George. 1899. *Trusts and the Public*. New York: D. Appleton.

Gutman, Herbert G. 1965. "The Tompkins Square Riot in New York City on January 13, 1874: A Re-examination of Its Causes and Its Aftermath." *Labor History* 6 (1): 44–70.

Gutmann, Amy. 2012. *The Spirit of Compromise: Why Governing Demands It and Campaigning Undermines It*. Princeton, NJ: Princeton University Press.

Habibov, Nazim, Alex Cheung, and Alena Auchynnikava. 2017. "Does Trust Increase Willingness to Pay Higher Taxes to Help the Needy?" *International Social Security Review* 70 (3): 3–30.

Hacker, Barton C. 2016. *Astride Two Worlds: Technology and the American Civil War*. Washington, DC: Smithsonian Institution Scholarly Press.

Hacker, J. David. 2011. "A Census-Based Count of the Civil War Dead." *Civil War History* 57 (4): 307–348.

Hacker, Jacob S., and Paul Pierson. 2012. "Presidents and the Political Economy: The Coalitional Foundations of Presidential Power." *Presidential Studies Quarterly* 42 (1): 101–131.

Hacket, Frank Warren. 1898. *A Sketch of the Life and Public Services of William Adams Richardson*. Washington, DC: privately printed.

Haley, James L. 1976. *The Buffalo War: The History of the Red River Indian Uprising of 1874*. Garden City, NY: Doubleday.

Hall, George F. 1895. *A Study in Bloomers or The Model New Woman: A Novel*. Chicago: American Bible House.

Hallerberg, Mark, and Joachim Wehner. 2013. "The Technical Competence of Economic Policy-Makers in Developed Democracies." *SSRN Electronic Journal* DOI: 10.2139/ssrn.2191490.

Hallgrimsdottir, Helga Kristin, and Cecilia Benoit. 2007. "From Wage Slaves to Wage Workers: Cultural Opportunity Structures and the Evolution of the Wage Demands of the Knights of Labor and the American Federation of Labor, 1880–1900." *Social Forces* 85 (3): 1393–1411.

Halloran, Fiona Deans. 2012. *Thomas Nast: The Father of Modern Political Cartoons.* Chapel Hill: University of North Carolina Press.

Halstead, Murat. 1901. *The Illustrious Life of William McKinley: Our Martyred President.* Chicago: P. A. Stone.

Hamblin, Jessie DeFoliart. 1895. *A New Woman.* Chicago: C. H. Kerr.

Hammer, Kenneth M. 1979. "Bonanza Farming: Forerunner of Modern Large-Scale Agriculture." *Journal of the West* 18 (4): 52–61.

Hanlon, W. Walker. 2015. "Pollution and Mortality in the 19th Century." Working Paper No. 21647. Cambridge, MA: NBER.

Hansen, Bradley. 1988. "Commercial Associations and the Creation of a National Economy: The Demand for Federal Bankruptcy Law." *Business History Review* 72 (1): 86–113.

Hansen, I. S., and D. M. Wegner. 1998. "Centenary of the Destruction of USS Maine—A Technical and Historical Review." *Naval Engineers Journal* 110 (2): 93–104.

Hargrove, Erwin C. 2014. *The Effective Presidency: Lessons on Leadership from John F. Kennedy to Barack Obama.* 2nd ed. Boulder, CO: Paradigm.

Hargrove, Erwin C., and Samuel A. Morley, eds. 1984. *The President and the Council of Economic Advisers: Interviews with CEA Chairmen.* Boulder, CO: Westview Press.

Harper, Robert S. 1951. *Lincoln and the Press.* New York: McGraw-Hill.

Harper's Weekly. 1872. "Senator Trumbull and the Revenue." 16 (819): 690.

Harpine, William D. 2005. *From the Front Porch to the Front Page: McKinley and Bryan in the 1896 Presidential Campaign.* College Station: Texas A&M University Press.

Harris, Beth, ed. 2005. *Famine and Fashion: Needlewomen in the Nineteenth Century.* Burlington, VT: Ashgate.

Harrison, Benjamin. 1901. *Views of an Ex-President.* Indianapolis, IN: Bowen-Merrill.

Hart, John. 1995. *The Presidential Branch: From Washington to Clinton.* Chatham, NJ: Chatham House.

Harvey, W. H. 1894. *Coin's Financial School.* Chicago: Coin.

Hatfield, Mark O. 1997. *Vice Presidents of the United States.* Washington, DC: Government Printing Office.

Hatton, Timothy J. 2021. "Emigration from the United Kingdom to the United States, Canada and Australia/New Zealand, 1870–1913: Quantity and Quality." *Australian Economic History Review* 61 (2): 136–158.

Hauberg, Robert E., Paul Taylor, James A. Backstrom, Donald C. Klawite, Ronland M. Slover, and Gary Spratling, eds. 1999. *Sentencing Guidelines in Antitrust: A Practitioner's Handbook.* Chicago: American Bar Association.

Havighurst, Walter. 1958. *The Miami Years, 1809–1969.* New York: Putnam.

Haworth, Paul Leland. 1927. *The Hayes-Tilden Election.* Indianapolis, IN: Bobbs-Merrill.

Haynes, Stan M. 2016. *President-Making in the Gilded Age: The Nominating Conventions of 1876–1900.* Jefferson, NC: McFarland.

Heckelman, Jack, and Robert Whaples. 1996. "Political Business Cycles before the Great Depression." *Economics Letters* 51 (2): 247–251.

Hedges, Charles. 1892. *Speeches of Benjamin Harrison, Twenty-third President of the United States.* New York: United States Book Company.

Heermans, Harry W. 1977. "Ulysses S. Grant." *British Journal on Alcohol and Alcoholism* 12 (4): 174–176.

Heinemann, Friedrich. 2008. "The Impact of Trust on Reforms." *Journal of Economic Policy Reform* 11 (3): 173–185.

Herring, George C. 2008. *From Colony to Superpower: U.S. Foreign Relations since 1776*. New York: Oxford University Press.

Herron, George Davis. 1893. *The New Redemption: A Call to the Church to Reconstruct Society according to the Gospel of Christ*. New York: T. Y. Crowell.

Hetherington, Marc J. 1998. "The Political Relevance of Political Trust." *American Political Science Review* 92 (4): 791–808.

Hickey, Patrick. 2014. "Beyond Pivotal Politics: Constituencies, Electoral Incentives, and Veto Override Attempts in the House." *Presidential Studies Quarterly* 44 (4): 577–601.

Hilkey, Judy. 1997. *Character Is Capital: Success Manuals and Manhood in Gilded Age America*. Chapel Hill: University of North Carolina Press.

Hilpert, John M. 2015. *American Cyclone: Theodore Roosevelt and His 1900 Whistle-stop Campaign*. Jackson: University Press of Mississippi.

Hoar, George Frisbie. 1903a. *Autobiography of Seventy Years*. Vol. 1. New York: Charles Scribner's Sons.

Hoar, George Frisbie. 1903b. *Autobiography of Seventy Years*. Vol. 2. New York: Charles Scribner's Sons.

Hobsbawm, Eric J. 1982. *The History of Marxism: Marxism in Marx's Day*. Bloomington: Indiana University Press.

Hochfelder, David. 2013. *The Telegraph in America, 1832–1920*. Baltimore, MD: Johns Hopkins University Press.

Hochschild, Adam. 1998. "The King's Lobbyists." *American Scholar* 67 (3): 39–52.

Hoffmann, Charles. 1970. *The Depression of the Nineties: An Economic History*. Westport, CT: Greenwood.

Hofstadter, Richard. 1944. *Social Darwinism in American Thought*. Boston: Beacon Press.

Holmes, George K. 1893. "The Concentration of Wealth." *Political Science Quarterly* 8 (4): 589–600.

Holt, Byron W. 1899. "Trusts—The Rush to Industrial Monopoly." *American Review of Reviews* 19 (6): 675–689.

Holt, Michael F. 1999. *The Rise and Fall of the American Whig Party: Jacksonian Politics and the Onset of the Civil War*. New York: Oxford University Press.

Holt, Michael F. 2008. *By One Vote: The Disputed Presidential Election of 1876*. Lawrence: University Press of Kansas.

Holzer, Harold, and David Herbert Donald. 2005. *Lincoln in the Times: The Life of Abraham Lincoln, as Originally Reported in the New York Times*. New York: St. Martin's Press.

Homberger, Eric. 2004. *Mrs. Astor's New York: Money and Social Power in a Gilded Age*. New Haven, CT: Yale University Press.

Hoogenboom, Ari A. 1961. *Outlawing the Spoils: A History of the Civil Service Reform Movement, 1865–1883*. Urbana: University of Illinois Press.

Hoogenboom, Ari. 1988. *The Presidency of Rutherford B. Hayes*. Lawrence: University Press of Kansas.

Hoogenboom, Ari. 2014. "Hayes and Civil Service Reform." In *A Companion to the Reconstruction Presidents, 1865–1881*, edited by Edward O. Frantz, 431–451. West Sussex: John Wiley & Sons.

Hoogenboom, Ari A., and Olive Hoogenboom. 1976. *A History of the ICC: From Panacea to Palliative*. New York: Norton.

Hooper, Candice Shy. 2012. "The War That Made Hollywood: How the Spanish-American War Saved the US Film Industry." *Journal of Military History* 76 (1): 69–97.

Horner, William T. 2010. *Ohio's Kingmaker: Mark Hanna, Man and Myth*. Athens: Ohio University Press.

Horton, S. Dana, ed. 1891. *A Survey of the Diplomatic Aspects of the Silver Question*. New York: privately printed.

Hounshell, David A. 1984. *From the American System to Mass Production, 1800–1932: The Development of Manufacturing Technology in the United States*. Baltimore, MD: Johns Hopkins University Press.

Hovenkamp, Herbert. 2015. *The Opening of American Law: Neoclassical Legal Thought, 1870–1970*. New York: Oxford University Press.

Howard, James Quay. 1876. *The Life, Public Services and Select Speeches of Rutherford B. Hayes*. Cincinnati, OH: Robert Clarke.

Howard, M. W. 1895. *The American Plutocracy*. New York: Holland.

Howe, Daniel Walker. 1979. *The Political Culture of the American Whigs*. Chicago: University of Chicago Press.

Howe, Daniel W. 2007. *What Hath God Wrought: The Transformation of America, 1815–1848*. New York: Oxford University Press.

Howell, William G. 2001. "Unilateral Powers: A Brief Overview." *Presidential Studies Quarterly* 35 (3): 417–439.

Howell, William G. 2003. *Power without Persuasion: The Politics of Direct Presidential Action*. Princeton, NJ: Princeton University Press.

Howell, William G., and Terry M. Moe. 2016. *Relic: How Our Constitution Undermines Effective Government and Why We Need a More Powerful Presidency*. New York: Basic Books.

Howells, William Dean. 1894. "Are We a Plutocracy?" *North American Review* 158 (447): 185–196.

Hoy, Suellen, and Walter Nugent. 1989. "Public Health or Protectionism? The German-American Pork War, 1880–1891." *Bulletin of the History of Medicine* 63 (2): 198–224.

Hudson, William C. 1911. *Random Recollections of an Old Political Reporter*. New York: Cupples & Leon.

Hughes, Thomas P. 1983. *Networks of Power: Electrification in Western Society, 1880–1930*. Baltimore, MD: Johns Hopkins University Press.

Hugins, Roland. 1922. *Grover Cleveland: A Study in Political Courage*. Washington, DC: Anchor-Lee.

Hunt, Bruce J. 1991. *The Maxwellians*. Ithaca, NY: Cornell University Press.

Huntzicker, William. 1999. *The Popular Press, 1833–1865*. Westport, CT: Greenwood Press.

Huston, Alexander B. 1900. *Historical Sketch of Farmers' College*. Cincinnati, OH: Students' Association of Farmers' College.

Interstate Commerce Commission. 1892–1902. *Annual Report on the Statistics of Railways in the United States*. Vols. 5–15. Washington, DC: Government Printing Office.

Irwin, Douglas A. 2000. "Did Late-Nineteenth-Century U.S. Tariffs Promote Infant Industries? Evidence from the Tinplate Industry." *Journal of Economic History*. 60 (2): 335–361.

Irwin, Douglas A. 2017. *Clashing over Commerce: A History of US Trade Policy*. Chicago: University of Chicago Press.

Irwin, Neil. 2017. "Presidents Have Less Power over the Economy Than You Might Think." *New York Times*, January 17. https://www.nytimes.com/2017/01/17/upshot/preside nts-have-less-power-over-the-economy-than-you-might-think.html.

Jacks, David S., and Martin Stuermer. 2021. "Dry Bulk Shipping and the Evolution of Maritime Transport Costs, 1850–2020." Working Paper 28627. Cambridge, MA: NBER.

Jacoby, Karl. 2014. *Crimes against Nature: Squatters, Poachers, Thieves, and the Hidden History of American Conservation*. Berkeley: University of California Press.

James, John A., and Jonathan S. Skinner. 1985. "The Resolution of the Labor-Scarcity Paradox." *Journal of Economic History* 45: 513–550.

Jaques, Mary J. 1889. *Texan Ranch Life*. London: H. Cox.

Jeal, Tim. 2007. *Stanley: The Impossible Life of Africa's Greatest Explorer*. New Haven, CT: Yale University Press.

Jenks, Jeremiah W. 1900. *The Trust Problem*. New York: McClure, Phillips.

Jennings, Julie, and Jared C. Nagel. 2019. "Federal Workforce Statistics Sources: OPM and OMB." CRS Report R43590. Washington, DC: Congressional Research Service.

Johnson, C. Donald. 2018. *The Wealth of a Nation: A History of Trade Politics in America*. New York: Oxford University Press.

Johnson, David R. 1995. *Illegal Tender: Counterfeiting and the Secret Service in Nineteenth-century America*. Washington, DC: Smithsonian Institution Press.

Johnson, Ronald N., and Gary D. Liebcap. 1994. *The Federal Civil Service System and the Problem of Bureaucracy: The Economics and Politics of Institutional Change*. Chicago: University of Chicago Press.

Johnson, Willis Fletcher. 1889. *History of the Johnstown Flood*. Philadelphia, PA: Edgewood.

Johnstown Area Heritage Association. 1889. "1889 Flood Materials." https://www.jaha. org/about-jaha/archives-research/collections/1889-flood-resources/.

Jones, Benjamin F., and Benjamin A. Olken. 2005. "Do Leaders Matter? National Leadership and Growth since World War II." *Quarterly Journal of Economics* 120 (3): 835–864.

Jones, Charles. 1998. *Introduction to Economic Growth*. New York: W. W. Norton.

Jones, Charles O. 1994. *The Presidency in a Separated System*. Washington, DC: Brookings Institution Press.

Jones, Charles O. 1999. *Separate but Equal Branches: Congress and the Presidency*. 2nd ed. New York: Chatham House.

Jonnes, Jill. 2003. *Empires of Light: Edison, Tesla, Westinghouse, and the Race to Electrify the World*. New York: Random House.

Jordan, David M. 1971. *Roscoe Conkling of New York: Voice in the Senate*. Ithaca, NY: Cornell University Press.

Josephson, Matthew. 1938. *The Politicos*. New York: Harcourt Brace.

Justesen, Benjamin R. 2020. *Forgotten Legacy: William McKinley, George Henry White, and the Struggle for Black Equality*. Baton Rouge: Louisiana State University Press.

Kaczorowski, Robert J. 2005. *The Politics of Judicial Interpretation: The Federal Courts, Department of Justice, and Civil Rights, 1866–1876*. New York: Fordham University Press.

Kagan, Elena. 2001. "Presidential Administration." *Harvard Law Review* 114 (8): 2245–2385.

Kahan, Michael B. 2017. "Urban America." In *A Companion to the Gilded Age and Progressive Era*, edited by Christopher McKnight Nichols and Nancy C. Unger, 31–43. New York: John Wiley & Sons.

Kalla, Joshua L., and David E. Broockman. 2016. "Campaign Contributions Facilitate Access to Congressional Officials: A Randomized Field Experiment." *American Journal of Political Science* 60 (3): 545–558.

Kamarck, Elaine. 2016. *Why Presidents Fail and How They Can Succeed Again*. Washington, DC: Brookings Institution Press.

Kammer, Sean M. 2017. "Railroad Land Grants in an Incongruous Legal System: Corporate Subsidies, Bureaucratic Governance, and Legal Conflict in the United States, 1850–1903." *Law and History Review* 35 (2): 391–432.

Kaplan, Richard L. 2002. *Politics and the American Press: The Rise of Objectivity, 1865–1920*. New York: Cambridge University Press.

Kapur, Nick. 2011. "William McKinley's Values and the Origins of the Spanish-American War: A Reinterpretation." *Presidential Studies Quarterly* 41 (1): 18–38.

Karabell, Zachary. 2004. *Chester Alan Arthur*. New York: Henry Holt.

Kaufman, Stuart Bruce. 1973. *Samuel Gompers and the Origins of the American Federation of Labor, 1848–1896*. Westport, CT: Greenwood Press.

Kazin, Michael. 2008. *William McKinley and the Republican Party*. Alexandria, VA: Alexander Street Press.

Keegan, John. 2009. *The American Civil War: A Military History*. New York: Alfred A. Knopf.

Keele, Luke. 2005. "The Authorities Really Do Matter: Party Control and Trust in Government." *Journal of Politics* 67 (3): 873–886.

Keele, Luke. 2007. "Social Capital and the Dynamics of Trust in Government." *American Journal of Political Science* 51 (2): 241–254.

Keen, William W. 1917. "The Surgical Operations on President Cleveland in 1893." *Saturday Evening Post*, September 22.

Kellerman, Barbara. 2016. "Leadership—It's a System, Not a Person!" *Daedalus* 145 (3): 83–94.

Kennedy, Duncan. 2006. *The Rise and Fall of Classical Legal Thought*. Washington, DC: Beard Books.

Kennedy, Paul M. 1987. *The Rise and Fall of the Great Powers: Economic Change and Military Conflict from 1500 to 2000*. New York: Vintage Books.

Kernell, Samuel H. 2006. *Going Public: New Strategies of Presidential Leadership*. Washington, DC: CQ Press.

Keynes, John Maynard. 1936. *The General Theory of Employment, Interest, and Money*. New York: Palgrave Macmillan.

King, Clarence. 1880. *First Annual Report of the United States Geological Survey*. Washington, DC: Government Printing Office.

Kirshner, Jonathan. 2007. *Appeasing Bankers: Financial Caution on the Road to War*. Princeton, NJ: Princeton University Press.

Klein, Ezra. 2014. "The Green Lantern Theory of the Presidency." *Vox*, May 20. https://www.vox.com/2014/5/20/5732208/the-green-lantern-theory-of-the-presidency-explained.

Klein, Herbert S. 2012. *A Population History of the United States*. 2nd ed. New York: Cambridge University Press.

Klein, Maury. 2007. *The Genesis of Industrial America, 1870–1920*. Cambridge: Cambridge University Press.

Klinghard, Daniel P. 2005. "Grover Cleveland, William McKinley, and the Emergence of the President as Party Leader." *Presidential Studies Quarterly* 35 (4): 736–760.

Klinghard, Daniel. 2010. *The Nationalization of American Political Parties, 1880–1896*. New York: Cambridge University Press.

Knack, Stephen, and Philip Keefer. 1997. "Does Social Capital Have an Economic Payoff? A Cross-Country Investigation." *Quarterly Journal of Economics* 112 (4): 1251–1288.

Knack, Stephen, and Paul J. Zak. 2003. "Building Trust: Public Policy, Interpersonal Trust, and Economic Development." *Supreme Court Economic Review* 10: 91–107.

Knight, Jack. 2001. "Social Norms and the Rule of Law: Fostering Trust in a Socially Diverse Society." In *Trust in Society*, edited by Karen S. Cook, 354–373. New York: Russell Sage Foundation.

Knight, Peter. 2016. *Reading the Market Genres of Financial Capitalism in Gilded Age America*. Baltimore, MD: Johns Hopkins University Press.

Knoles, George H. 1942. *The Presidential Campaign and Election of 1892*. Stanford, CA: Stanford University Press.

Knott, Stephen F. 2019. *The Lost Soul of the American Presidency: The Decline into Demagoguery and the Prospects for Renewal*. Lawrence: University Press of Kansas.

Knox, John Jay. 1900. *A History of Banking in the United States*. New York: Bradford Rhodes.

Kobel, Peter. 2009. *Silent Movies: The Birth of Film and the Triumph of Movie Culture*. New York: Little, Brown.

Kocka, Jürgen. 1980. *White Collar Workers in America, 1890–1940: A Social-Political History in International Perspective*. Beverly Hills, CA: Sage.

Koistinen, Paul A. C. 1996. *Beating Plowshares into Swords: Political Economy of American Warfare, 1606–1865*. Lawrence: University Press of Kansas.

Koistinen, Paul A. C. 1997. *Mobilizing for Modern War: The Political Economy of American Warfare, 1865–1919*. Lawrence: University Press of Kansas.

Kolko, Gabriel. 1965. *Railroads and Regulations, 1877–1916*. Princeton, NJ: Princeton University Press.

Konings, Martijn. 2011. *The Development of American Finance*. New York: Cambridge University Press.

Kornblith, Gary J., and Michael Zakim, eds. 2011. *Capitalism Takes Command: The Social Transformation of Nineteenth-Century America*. Chicago: University of Chicago Press.

Kousser, J. Morgan. 1974. *The Shaping of Southern Politics: Suffrage Restriction and the Establishment of the One-Party South, 1880–1910*. New Haven, CT: Yale University Press.

Kovacic, W. E. 2010. "Dominance, Duopoly and Oligopoly: The United States and the Development of Global Competition Policy." *Global Competition Review* 14: 39–42.

Kraeussl, Roman, Andre Lucas, David R. Rijsbergen, and Pieter Jelle van der Sluis. 2014. "Washington Meets Wall Street: A Closer Examination of the Presidential Cycle Puzzle." *Journal of International Money and Finance* 43: 50–69.

Krause, Paul. 1992. *The Battle for Homestead, 1880–1892: Politics, Culture, and Steel*. Pittsburgh, PA: University of Pittsburgh Press.

Krcmaric, Daniel, Stephen C. Nelson, and Andrew Roberts. 2020. "Studying Leaders and Elites: The Personal Biography Approach." *Annual Review of Political Science* 23: 133–151.

Krell, Alan. 2002. *The Devil's Rope: A Cultural History of Barbed Wire*. Chicago: University of Chicago Press.

Kuhn, Thomas S. 1962. *The Structure of Scientific Revolutions*. Chicago: University of Chicago Press.

Lachman, Charles. 2011. *A Secret Life: The Lies and Scandals of President Grover Cleveland*. New York: Skyhorse.

Laing, Matthew, and Brendan McCaffrie. 2017. "The Impossible Leadership Situation? Analyzing Success for Disjunctive Presidents." *Presidential Studies Quarterly* 47 (2): 255–276.

Lamoreaux, Naomi R. 1985. *The Great Merger Movement in American Business, 1895–1904*. New York: Cambridge University Press.

Lamoreaux, Naomi, Margaret Levenstein, and Kenneth L. Sokoloff. 2007. "Financing Invention during the Second Industrial Revolution: Cleveland, Ohio 1870–1920." In *Financing Innovation in the United States 1870 to the Present*, edited by Naomi Lamoreaux and Kenneth L. Sokoloff, 39–84. Cambridge, MA: MIT Press.

Lapinski, John S. 2013. *The Substance of Representation: Congress, American Political Development, and Lawmaking*. Princeton, NJ: Princeton University Press.

LaPorta, Rafael, Florencio Lopez-de-Silanes, Andrei Shleifer, and Robert W. Vishny. 1997. "Trust in Large Organizations." *American Economic Review Papers and Proceedings* 87: 333–38.

Laracey, Melvin. 1998. "The Presidential Newspaper." In *Speaking to the People: The Rhetorical Presidency in Historical Perspective*, edited by Richard J. Ellis, 66–86. Amherst: University of Massachusetts Press.

Laracey, Melvin C. 2002. *Presidents and the People: The Partisan Story of Going Public*. College Station: Texas A&M University Press.

Larkin, Oliver W. 1949. *Art and Life in America*. New York: Rinehart.

Larson, Erik. 2003. *The Devil in the White City: Murder, Magic and Madness at the Fair That Changed America*. New York: Crown.

Latham, Charles G. 1939. "Benjamin Harrison in the Senate, 1881–87." Senior thesis, Princeton University.

Lauck, William. J. 1907. *The Causes of the Panic of 1893*. New York: Houghton, Mifflin.

Laughlin, J. Laurence. 1882. "The Refunding Bill of 1881." *Atlantic Monthly* 49 (292): 195–205.

Laughlin, J. Laurence, ed. 1898. *Report of the Monetary Commission of the Indianapolis Convention*. Chicago: University of Chicago Press.

Laurie, Bruce. 1989. *Artisans into Workers: Labor in Nineteenth-Century America*. New York: Noonday.

Lause, Mark A. 2001. *The Civil War's Last Campaign: James B. Weaver, the Greenback-Labor Party and the Politics of Race and Section*. Lanham, MD: University Press of America.

Laver, Harry S. 2013. *The Leadership of Ulysses S. Grant: A General Who Will Fight*. Lexington: University Press of Kentucky.

Law, James. 1874. "Influenza in Horses." In *Report of the Commissioner of Agriculture for the Year 1872*, edited by the US Department of Agriculture, 203–247. Washington, DC: Government Printing Office.

Lawver, Anthony. 1998. "National Grange: A Paradox between Founding Principles and Political Activities." ALM thesis, Harvard University.

Lebergott, Stanley. 1980. "The Returns to US Imperialism." *Journal of Economic History* 40 (2): 229–252.

Lee, Chulhee. 2005. "Wealth Accumulation and the Health of Union Army Veterans, 1860–1870." *Journal of Economic History* 65 (2): 352–385.

Lee, Erika. 2003. *At America's Gates: Chinese Immigration during the Exclusion Era, 1882–1943*. Raleigh: University of North Carolina Press.

Lee, Francis E. 2016. "Patronage, Logrolls, and Polarization: Congressional Parties of the Gilded Age, 1876–1896." *Studies in American Political Development* 30 (2): 116–127.

Leech, Margaret. 1959. *In the Days of McKinley*. New York: Harper Brothers.

Leech, Margaret, and Harry J. Brown. 1978. *The Garfield Orbit*. New York: Harper and Row.

Leff, Michael. 2008. "Grover Cleveland and the Non-Rhetorical Presidency." In *Before the Rhetorical Presidency*, edited by Martin J. Medhurst, 289–306. College Station: Texas A&M University Press.

Lehman, Tim. 2018. *Up the Trail: How Texas Cowboys Herded Longhorns and Became an American Icon*. Baltimore, MD: Johns Hopkins University Press.

LeMay, Michael C., ed. 2012. *Transforming America: Perspectives on U.S. Immigration*. Vol. 3. Santa Barbara, CA: Praeger.

Lesley, J. P. 1886. "An Obituary Notice of James Macfarlane." *Proceedings of the American Philosophical Society* 23 (122): 287–289.

Levin, Martin A., Daniel DiSalvo, and Martin M. Shapiro. 2012. *Building Coalitions, Making Policy: The Politics of the Clinton, Bush, and Obama Presidencies*. Baltimore, MD: Johns Hopkins University Press.

Levine, Bruce. 2001. "Conservatism, Nativism, and Slavery: Thomas R. Whitney and the Origins of the Know-Nothing Party." *Journal of American History* 88 (2): 455–488.

Lewis, Catherine M., and Richard J. Lewis. 2009. *Jim Crow America: A Documentary History*. Fayetteville: University of Arkansas Press.

Lewis, David E. 2003. *Presidents and the Politics of Agency Design: Political Insulation in the United States Government Bureaucracy, 1946–1997*. Stanford, CA: Stanford University Press.

Lewis, Lloyd. 1950. *Captain Sam Grant*. Boston: Little, Brown.

Lewis, Verlan. 2019. *Ideas of Power: The Politics of American Party Ideology Development*. New York: Cambridge University Press.

Lewis, W. Arthur. 2010. *Growth and Fluctuations 1870–1913*. 3rd ed. New York: Routledge.

Link, Stefan, and Noam Maggor. 2020. "The United States as a Developing Nation: Revisiting the Peculiarities of American History." *Past & Present* 246 (1): 269–306.

Linn, Brian McAllister. 2000. *The Philippine War, 1899–1902*. Lawrence: University Press of Kansas.

Lipset, Seymour M., and Gary Marks. 2000. *It Didn't Happen Here: Why Socialism Failed in the United States*. New York: W. W. Norton.

Liu, Cheol, Tima T. Moldogaziev, and John L. Mikesell. 2017. "Corruption and State and Local Government Debt Expansion." *Public Administration Review* 77 (5): 681–690.

Livingston, James. 1986. *Origins of the Federal Reserve System: Money, Class, and Corporate Capitalism, 1890–1913*. Ithaca, NY: Cornell University Press.

Livingston, James. 1994. *Pragmatism and the Political Economy of Cultural Revolution, 1850–1940*. Chapel Hill: University of North Carolina Press.

Livingston, James. 2016. "The Myth of a 'Second Gilded Age.'" *Chronicle of Higher Education*, January 31.

Lloyd, Henry Demarest. 1894. *Wealth against Commonwealth*. New York: Harper & Brothers.

Long, Priscilla. 1989. *Where the Sun Never Shines: A History of America's Bloodied Coal Industry*. New York: Paragon House.

Long, Jason, and Joseph Ferrie. 2013. "Intergenerational Occupational Mobility in Great Britain and the United States Since 1850." *The American Economic Review* 103 (4): 1109–1137.

Lovett, John, Shaun Bevan, and Frank R. Baumgartner. 2015. "Popular Presidents Can Affect Congressional Attention, for a Little While." *Policy Studies Journal* 43 (1): 22–43.

Lowenthal, David. 2000. *George Perkins Marsh, Prophet of Conservation*. Seattle: University of Washington Press.

Lowi, Theodore J. 1985. *The Personal President Power Invested, Promise Unfulfilled*. Cornell: Cornell University Press.

Lubetkin, M. John. 2006. *Jay Cooke's Gamble: The Northern Pacific Railroad, the Sioux, and the Panic of 1873*. Norman: University of Oklahoma Press.

Lucas, Christopher J. 1994. *American Higher Education: A History*. New York: St. Martin's Press.

Luckey, John R. 2003. "A History of Federal Estate, Gift, and Generation-Skipping Taxes." Washington, DC: Congressional Research Service.

Luconi, Stefano. 2007. "Italian Americans for Ulysses S. Grant: The 1872 Campaign as a Case Study of Political Mobilization before Mass Migration." *Proceedings of the American Italian Historical Association* 37: 3–16.

Lucy, Ernest W. 1882. *The Molly Maguires of Pennsylvania, or Ireland in America: A True Narrative*. London: George Bell and Sons.

Luhmann, Niklas. 2017. *Trust and Power*. Medford, MA: Polity Press.

Lundberg, James M. 2019. *Horace Greeley: Print, Politics, and the American Conflict*. Baltimore, MD: Johns Hopkins University Press.

Lyons, Russell. 1954. *The Tastemakers*. New York: Grosset and Dunlap.

MacFarlane, James. 1873. *The Coal Regions of America*. New York: D. Appleton.

Maggor, Noam. 2017. *Brahmin Capitalism: Frontiers of Wealth and Populism in America's First Gilded Age*. Cambridge, MA: Harvard University Press.

Magie, David. 1910. *Life of Garret Augustus Hobart: Twenty-fourth Vice-President of the United States*. New York: G. P. Putnam's Sons.

Maihafer, Harry J. 1998. *The General and the Journalists: Ulysses S. Grant, Horace Greeley, and Charles Dana*. Washington, DC: Brassey's.

Mankiw, N. Gregory. 2018. *Principles of Macroeconomics*. 8th ed. Boston: Cengage Learning.

Mannen, William. 2018. *Efficient Macro Concept: U.S. Monetary, Industrial, and Foreign Exchange Policies*. Lanham, MD: Lexington Books.

Marchant-Shapiro, Theresa. 2015. *Professional Pathways to the Presidency*. New York: Palgrave Macmillan.

Markel, Howard. 1997. *Quarantine! East European Jewish Immigrants and the New York City Epidemics of 1892*. Baltimore, MD: Johns Hopkins University Press.

Markham, Jerry W. 2002. *A Financial History of the United States: From Christopher Columbus to the Robber Barons (1492–1900)*. Vol. 1. Armonk, NY: M. E. Sharpe.

Marshall, Alfred. 1898. *Principles of Economics*. Vol. I. New York: Macmillan.

Marshall, Monty G., and Ted Gurr. 2018. "Polity V Database: Political Regime Characteristics and Transitions, 1800–2018." Vienna, VA: Center for Systemic Peace. www.systemicpeace.org.

Marshall, Peter H. 2010. *Demanding the Impossible: A History of Anarchism*. Oakland, CA: PM Press.

Marten, James, and Caroline E. Janney. 2021. *Buying and Selling Civil War Memory in Gilded Age America*. Athens: University of Georgia Press.

Martin, Albro. 1992. *Railroads Triumphant: The Growth, Rejection, and Rebirth of a Vital American Force*. New York: Oxford University Press.

Martin, Susan F. 2011. *A Nation of Immigrants*. New York: Cambridge University Press.

Martis, Kenneth C., Ruth Anderson Rowles, and Gyula Pauer, eds. 1989. *The Historical Atlas of Political Parties in the United States Congress, 1789–1989*. New York: Macmillan.

Mason, Edward S., and Thomas S. Lamont. 1982. "The Harvard Department of Economics from the Beginning to World War II." *Quarterly Journal of Economics* 97 (3): 383–433.

Massachusetts Board of Railroad Commissioners. 1870. *First Annual Report of the Board of Railroad Commissioners*. Boston: Wright & Potter.

Mattozzi, Andrea, and Antonio Merlo. 2008. "Political Careers or Career Politicians?" *Journal of Public Economics* 92 (3–4): 597–608.

Mauro, Paolo. 1995. "Corruption and Growth." *Quarterly Journal of Economics* 110 (3): 681–712.

May, Ernest R. 1961. *Imperial Democracy: The Emergence of America as a Great Power*. New York: Harcourt, Brace & World.

Mayer, George H. 1964. *The Republican Party, 1854–1964*. New York: Oxford University Press.

Mayer, Kenneth R. 2001. *With the Stroke of a Pen: Executive Orders and Presidential Power*. Princeton, NJ: Princeton University Press.

McAlevey, Jane F. 2016. *No Shortcuts: Organizing for Power in the New Gilded Age*. New York: Oxford University Press.

McCabe, James D. 1873. *History of the Grange Movement, or The Farmer's War against Monopolies*. Philadelphia, PA: National Publishing Company.

McCabe, James D. 1880. *From the Farm to the Presidential Chair*. Philadelphia, PA: National Publishing Co.

McCaffrey, James M. 2009. *Inside the Spanish-American War: A History Based on First-Person Accounts*. Jefferson, NC: McFarland.

McClintock, John S. 2000. *Pioneer Days in the Black Hills: Accurate History and Facts Related by One of the Early Day Pioneers*. Norman: University of Oklahoma Press.

McClure, Alexander Kelly. 1892. *Abraham Lincoln and Men of War-Times*. Philadelphia, PA: Times Publishing Company.

McClure, J. B. 1880. *Stories and Sketches of Gen. Garfield*. Chicago: Rhodes & McClure.

McCoy, Drew R. 1980. *The Elusive Republic: Political Economy in Jeffersonian America*. Chapel Hill: University of North Carolina Press.

McCraw, Thomas K. 1984. *Prophets of Regulation: Charles Francis Adams, Louis D. Brandeis, James M. Landis, Alfred E. Kahn*. Cambridge, MA: Belknap Press of Harvard University Press.

McCulley, Richard T. 1992. *Banks and Politics during the Progressive Era: The Origins of the Federal Reserve System, 1897–1913*. New York: Garland.

McCullough, David. 1987. *The Johnstown Flood*. 2nd ed. New York: Simon and Schuster.

McCullough, Stephen. 2014. "Avoiding War: The Foreign Policy of Ulysses S. Grant and Hamilton Fish." In *A Companion to the Reconstruction Presidents 1865–1881*, edited by Edward O. Frantz, 311–327. West Sussex: John Wiley & Sons.

McCurry, Stephanie. 2019. *Women's War: Fighting and Surviving the American Civil War*. Cambridge, MA: Harvard University Press.

McElroy, Robert McNutt. 1923. *Grover Cleveland: The Man and the Statesman: An Authorized Biography*. Vols. 1–2. New York: Harper & Brothers.

McFeely, William S. 1981. *Grant: A Biography*. New York: W. W. Norton.

McKeown, Adam. 2010. "Chinese Emigration in Global Context, 1850–1940." *Journal of Global History* 5: 95–124.

McKinley, William. 1893. *Speeches and Addresses of William McKinley, from His Election to Congress to the Present Time*. New York: D. Appleton.

McKinley, William. 1896. *The Tariff in the Days of Henry Clay and Since*. New York: Henry Clay Publishing.

McKinley, William. 1900. *Speeches and Addresses of William McKinley, from March 1, 1897, to May 30, 1900*. New York: Doubleday & McCure.

McKitrick, Eric. 1960. *Andrew Johnson and Reconstruction*. New York: Oxford University Press.

McKnight Nichols, Christopher, and Nancy C. Unger, eds. 2017. *A Companion to the Gilded Age and Progressive Era*. Malden, MA: John Wiley & Sons.

McNeill, George E., ed. 1887. *The Labor Movement: The Problem of To-day*. Boston: A. M. Bridgman.

McPherson, Edward. 1880. *The Political History of the United States of America during Reconstruction*. 3rd ed. Washington, DC: James J. Chapman.

McPherson, James M. 1965. "Abolitionists and the Civil Rights Act of 1875." *Journal of American History* 52 (3): 493–510.

McPherson, James M. 1988. *Battle Cry of Freedom: The Civil War Era*. New York: Oxford University Press.

McSeveney, Samuel. 1972. *The Politics of Depression, Political Behavior in the Northeast, 1893–1896*. New York: Oxford University Press.

Means, Gardiner C. 1930. "The Diffusion of Stock Ownership in the United States." *Quarterly Journal of Economics* 44 (4): 561–600.

Medhurst, Martin J. ed. 1996. *Beyond the Rhetorical Presidency*. College Station, TX: Texas A&M University Press.

Medhurst, Martin J., ed. 2008. *Before the Rhetorical Presidency*. College Station: Texas A&M University Press.

Meissner, Christopher M. 2005. "A New World Order: Explaining the International Diffusion of the Gold Standard, 1870–1913." *Journal of International Economics* 66: 385–406.

Mellon, Thomas. 1885. *Thomas Mellon and His Times*. Pittsburgh, PA: Wm. G. Johnston.

Merry, Robert W. 2012. *Where They Stand: The American Presidents in the Eyes of Voters and Historians*. New York: Simon and Schuster.

Merry, Robert W. 2017. *President McKinley: Architect of the American Century*. New York: Simon & Schuster.

Michener, Kris J., and Marc D. Weidenmier. 2008. "The Baring Crisis and the Great Latin American Meltdown of the 1890s." *Journal of Economic History* 68 (2): 462–500.

Middlekauf, Bradford. 1991. "Twisting the President's Arm: The Impoundment Control Act as a Tool for Enforcing the Principle of Appropriation Expenditure." *Yale Law Journal* 100 (1): 209–228.

Milkis, Sidney M., and Michael Nelson. 2008. *The American Presidency: Origins and Development, 1776–2007*. 5th ed. Washington, DC: CQ Press.

Milkis, Sidney, and Michael Nelson. 2019. *The American Presidency: Origins and Development 1776–2018*. 8th ed. Washington, DC: CQ Press.

Milkis, Sidney M., and Daniel J. Tichenor. 2019. *Rivalry and Reform: Presidents, Social Movements, and the Transformation of American Politics*. Chicago: University of Chicago Press.

Mill, John Stuart. 1870. *Chapters and Speeches on the Irish Land Question*. 2nd ed. London: Longmans, Green, Reader, and Dyer.

Millard, Candice. 2011. *Destiny of the Republic: A Tale of Madness, Medicine, and the Murder of a President*. New York: Anchor Books.

Miller, Charles Ransom. 1897. "Grover Cleveland as President." *New York Times*, March 2.

Miller, Joshua. 2019. "The Politics of Race and the Development of the Law and Order President, 1790–1974." PhD dissertation, Catholic University.

Miroff, Bruce. 2016. *Presidents on Political Ground: Leaders in Action and What They Face*. Lawrence: University Press of Kansas.

Mitchell, Brian R. 2003a. *International Historical Statistics: Europe, 1750–2000*. 5th ed. New York: Stockton Press.

Mitchell, Brian R. 2003b. *International Historical Statistics: The Americas, 1750-2000*. 5th ed. New York: Stockton Press.

Mitchell, Robert B. 2018. *Congress and the King of Frauds: Corruption and the Credit Mobilier Scandal at the Dawn of the Gilded Age*. Roseville, MN: Edinborough Press.

Mitchell, Wesley C. 1908. *Gold, Prices, and Wages under the Greenback Standard*. Berkeley, CA: University Press.

Mnasri, Ayman, and Naceur Essaddam. 2021. "Impact of US Presidential Elections on Stock Markets' Volatility: Does Incumbent President's Party Matter?" *Finance Research Letters* 39 (9): 101622.

Mock, Cary J. 2000. "Rainfall in the Garden of the United States Great Plains, 1870–1889." *Climatic Change* 44 (1): 173–195.

Moe, Terry M., and William G. Howell. 1999a. "The Presidential Power of Unilateral Action." *Journal of Law, Economics, and Organization* 15: 132–179.

Moe, Terry M., and William G. Howell. 1999b. "Unilateral Action and Presidential Power: A Theory." *Presidential Studies Quarterly* 29 (4): 850–873.

Mohl, Raymond A. 1997. *The Making of Urban America*. Lanham, MD: Rowman & Littlefield.

Montrie, Chad. 2011. *A People's History of Environmentalism in the United States*. London: Continuum International.

Moody, John. 1904. *The Truth about the Trusts: A Description and Analysis of the American Trust Movement*. New York: Moody.

Moore, Anne Chieko. 2006. *Benjamin Harrison: Centennial President*. New York: Nova Science.

Morgan, H. Wayne. 2003. *William McKinley and His America*. Kent, OH: Kent State University Press.

Morgan, James. 1969. *Our Presidents: Chapters on Kennedy and Johnson*. New York: Macmillan.

Morris, Charles R. 2005. *The Tycoons*. New York: Henry Holt.

Morris, Edmund. 1979. *The Rise of Theodore Roosevelt*. New York: Random House.

Morris, Roy. 2003. *Fraud of the Century: Rutherford B. Hayes, Samuel Tilden, and the Stolen Election of 1876*. New York: Simon & Schuster.

Morrison, James L. 1998. *The Best School: West Point, 1833–1866*. Kent, OH: Kent State University Press.

Morrison, Rodney J. 1986. *Henry C. Carey and American Economic Development.* Philadelphia, PA: American Philosophical Society.

Muccigrosso, Robert. 1993. *Celebrating the New World: Chicago's Columbian Exposition of 1893.* Chicago: I. R. Dee.

Muir, John. 1901. *Our National Parks.* Boston: Houghton Mifflin.

Mukunda, Gautam. 2012. *Indispensable: When Leaders Really Matter.* Boston: Harvard Business Review Press.

Mukunda, Gautam. 2022. *Picking Presidents: How to Make the Most Consequential Decision in the World.* Oakland: University of California Press.

Mumford, Lewis. 1931. *The Brown Decades.* New York: Harcourt Brace.

Murray, William H. H. 1869. *Adventures in the Wilderness.* Boston: Fields, Osgood.

Murtazashvili, Ilia. 2013. *The Political Economy of the American Frontier.* New York: Cambridge University Press.

Musicant, Ivan. 1998. *Empire by Default: The Spanish-American War and the Dawn of the American Century.* New York: Henry Holt.

Mutch, Robert E. 2014. *Buying the Vote: A History of Campaign Finance Reform.* New York: Oxford University Press.

Mycoff, Jason D., Joseph A. Pika, and James R. Sole. 2008. *Confrontation and Compromise: Presidential and Congressional Leadership, 2001–2006.* Latham, MD: Rowman & Littlefield.

Myers, Gustavus. 1971. *The History of Tammany Hall.* 2nd ed. New York: Dover.

Myers, Margaret G. 1970. *A Financial History of the United States.* New York: Columbia University Press.

National Bureau of Economic Research. 2021. "US Business Cycle Expansions and Contractions." Cambridge, MA: NBER. https://www.nber.org/research/data/us-busin ess-cycle-expansions-and-contractions.

National Portrait Gallery. 2008. "The Politics of Personality: Horace Greeley." May 20, https://npg.si.edu/blog/politics-personality-horace-greeley.

National Research Council. 1995. *Colleges of Agriculture at the Land Grant Universities: A Profile.* Washington, DC: National Academies Press.

Navin, Thomas R., and Marian V. Sears. 1955. "The Rise of a Market for Industrial Securities, 1887–1902." *Business History Review* 29 (2): 105–138.

Nelson, Scott Reynolds. 2011. "A Storm of Cheap Goods: New American Commodities and the Panic of 1873." *Journal of the Gilded Age and Progressive Era* 10 (4): 447–453.

Neumeier, Florian. 2018. "Do Businessmen Make Good Governors?" *Economic Inquiry* 56 (4): 2116–2136.

Neustadt, Richard E. 1960. *Presidential Power: The Politics of Leadership.* New York: Wiley.

Nevins, Allan. 1927. *The Emergence of Modern America, 1865–1878.* New York: Macmillan.

Nevins, Allan. 1932. *Grover Cleveland: A Study In Courage.* Vols. 1–2. Newton, CT: American Political Biography Press.

Nevins, Alan, ed. 1933. *Letters of Grover Cleveland, 1850–1908.* Boston: Houghton Mifflin.

Ngai, Mae. 2021. *The Chinese Question: The Gold Rushes and Global Politics.* New York: W. W. Norton.

Nichols, David K. 1994. *The Myth of the Modern Presidency.* University Park: Pennsylvania State University Press.

Nitschke, Christoph. 2018. "Theory and History of Financial Crises: Explaining the Panic of 1873." *Journal of the Gilded Age and Progressive Era* 17: 221–240.

Niven, John. 1993. *John C. Calhoun and the Price of Union: A Biography*. Baton Rouge: Louisiana State University Press

Nordhaus, William D. 1975. "The Political Business Cycle." *Review of Economic Studies* 42 (2): 169–190.

Nordin, Dennis S. 1974. *Rich Harvest: A History of the Grange, 1867–1900*. Jackson: University Press of Mississippi.

Norwood, Janet L. 1985. "One Hundred Years of the Bureau of Labor Statistics." *Monthly Labor Review*, July.

Novak, Daniel A. 1978. *The Wheel of Servitude: Black Forced Labor after Slavery*. Lexington: University Press of Kentucky.

Novak, William J. 1996. *The People's Welfare: Law and Regulation in Nineteenth-Century America*. Chapel Hill: University of North Carolina Press.

Numbers, Ronald L. 1998. *Darwinism Comes to America*. Cambridge, MA: Harvard University Press.

Nutter, G. Warren. 1951. *The Extent of Enterprise Monopoly in the United States, 1899–1939*. Chicago: University of Chicago Press.

Nyhan, Brendan. 2009. "The Green Lantern Theory of the Presidency Explained." December 14. https://www.brendan-nyhan.com/blog/2009/12/the-green-lantern-the ory-of-the-presidency.html.

Nye, David E. 2018. *American Illuminations: Urban Lighting, 1800–1920*. Cambridge, MA: MIT Press.

Oberholtzer, Ellis Paxson. 1907. *Jay Cooke: Financier of the Civil War*. Vol. 1. Philadelphia, PA: George W. Jacobs.

O'Brien, Patrick Robert. 2017. "A Theoretical Critique of the Unitary Executive Framework: Rethinking the First-Mover Advantage, Collective-Action Advantage, and Informational Advantage." *Presidential Studies Quarterly* 47 (1): 169–185.

O'Brien, Patrick Robert. 2018. "Presidential Control and Public Finance: The Unitary Executive as an Historical Variable." PhD dissertation, Yale University.

O'Connor, Marion A. 1970. "World Wheat Supplies 1865–1913." Discussion Paper No. 12. Princeton, NJ: Research Program in Economic Development. Woodrow Wilson School, Princeton University.

O'Donnell, Edward T. 2015. *Henry George and the Crisis of Inequality: Progress and Poverty in the Gilded Age*. New York: Columbia University Press.

Oestreicher, Richard. 1988. "Urban Working-Class Political Behavior and Theories of American Electoral Politics, 1870–1940." *Journal of American History* 74 (4): 1257–1286.

Ogilvie, J. S., ed. 1896. *Life and Speeches of William McKinley*. New York: J. S. Ogilvie Publishing Company.

Ogle, Maureen. 1996. *All the Modern Conveniences: American Household Plumbing, 1840–1890*. Baltimore, MD: Johns Hopkins University Press.

Olcott, Charles Sumner. 1916. *The Life of William McKinley*. Vol. 1. Boston: Houghton Mifflin.

Oldfield, Arthur. 1891. "A Very Costly Comma." *Printing World* 1 (4): 116.

Oliphant, J. Orin. 1932. "Winter Losses of Cattle in the Oregon Country, 1847–1890." *Washington Historical Quarterly* 23 (1): 8–10.

Olmstead, Alan L., and Paul Rhode. 1988. "An Overview of California Agricultural Mechanization, 1870–1930." *Agricultural History* 62 (3): 86–112.

O'Malley, Michael. 2008. "Rags, Blacking, and Paper Soldiers: Money and Race in the Civil War." In *The Cultural Turn in U. S. History: Past, Present, and Future*, edited by James W. Cook, Lawrence B. Glickman, and Michael O'Malley, 95–120. Chicago: University of Chicago Press.

Osterbrock, Donald E. 1997. *Yerkes Observatory, 1892–1950: The Birth, Near Death, and Resurrection of a Scientific Research Institution*. Chicago: University of Chicago Press.

O'Sullivan, Mary. 2007. "The Expansion of the U.S. Stock Market, 1885–1930: Historical Facts and Theoretical Fashions." *Enterprise & Society* 8 (3): 489–542.

O'Sullivan, Mary A. 2016. *Dividends of Development: Securities Markets in the History of US Capitalism 1866–1922*. New York: Oxford University Press.

O'Toole, George J. A. 1984. *The Spanish War: An American Epic—1898*. New York: W. W. Norton.

Ouida. 1894. "The New Woman." *North American Review* 158 (450): 610–619.

Outlook. 1909. "Grover Cleveland." December 11.

Palen, Marc-William. 2014. Election of 1876/Compromise of 1877. In *A Companion to the Reconstruction Presidents 1865–1881*, edited by Edward O. Frantz, 415–430. West Sussex: John Wiley & Sons.

Palen, Marc-William. 2016. *The "Conspiracy" of Free Trade: The Anglo-American Struggle over Empire and Economic Globalization, 1846–1896*. New York: Cambridge University Press.

Papagapitos, Agapitos, and Robert Riley. 2009. "Social Trust and Human Capital Formation." *Economics Letters* 102 (3): 158–160.

Papke, David Ray. 1999. *The Pullman Case: The Clash of Labor and Capital in Industrial America*. Lawrence: University Press of Kansas.

Parker, David C. W. 2008. *The Power of Money in Congressional Campaigns, 1880–2006*. Norman: University of Oklahoma Press.

Parker, George E., ed. 1892. *The Writings and Speeches of Grover Cleveland*. New York: Cassell.

Parker, George F. 1909. *Recollections of Grover Cleveland*. New York: Century.

Parker, Kunal M. 2015. *Making Foreigners: Immigration and Citizenship Law in America, 1600–2000*. New York: Cambridge University Press.

Parsons, Albert. 1887. *The Autobiography of Albert Parsons*. Washington, DC: US Library of Congress. http://memory.loc.gov/award/ichihay/m07/m07.htm.

Parsons, Elaine Frantz. 2015. *Ku-Klux: The Birth of the Klan during Reconstruction*. Chapel Hill: University of North Carolina Press.

Pastor, Lubos, and Pietro Veronesi. 2020. "Political Cycles and Stock Returns." *Journal of Political Economy* 128 (11): 4011–4045.

Patai, Daphne, ed. 1988. *Looking Backward, 1988–1888: Essays on Edward Bellamy*. Amherst: University of Massachusetts Press.

Patterson, Martha H. 2008. *Beyond the Gibson Girl: Re-imagining the American New Woman 1895–1915*. Chicago: University of Illinois Press.

Patterson, Robert T. 1952. "A Major Error in Refunding." *Journal of Finance* 7 (3): 421–433.

Peck, Harry Thurston. 1906. *Twenty Years of the Republic, 1885–1905*. New York: Dodd, Mead.

Peltzman, Sam. 1977. "The Gains and Losses from Industrial Concentration." *Journal of Law & Economics* 20 (2): 229–263.

Pendel, Thomas F. 1902. *Thirty-six Years in the White House*. Washington, DC: Neale.

Perez, Santiago. 2021. "Southern (American) Hospitality: Italians in Argentina and the United States during the Age of Mass Migration." *Economic Journal* 131 (638): 2613–2628.

Peritz, Rudolph J. R. 2001. *Competition Policy in America, 1888–1992*. New York: Oxford University Press.

Perret, Geoffrey. 1997. *Ulysses S. Grant: Soldier and President*. New York: Random House.

Perrow, Charles. 2002. *Organizing America: Wealth, Power, and the Origins of Corporate Capitalism*. Princeton, NJ: Princeton University Press.

Peskin, Allan. 1978. *Garfield*. Kent, OH: Kent State University Press.

Peskin, Allan. 1984–1985. "Who Were the Stalwarts? Who Were Their Rivals? Republican Factions in the Gilded Age." *Political Science Quarterly* 99 (4): 703–716.

Peskin, Alan. 1991. "James Garfield." In *The Reader's Companion to American History*, edited by Eric Foner and John A. Garraty, 437–439. Boston: Houghton-Mifflin.

Peterson, Geoff, and J. Mark Wrighton. 1998. "Expressions of Distrust: Third-Party Voting and Cynicism in Government." *Political Behavior* 20 (1): 17–34.

Peterson, Mark A. 1993. *Legislating Together: The White House and Capitol Hill from Eisenhower to Reagan*. Cambridge, MA: Harvard University Press.

Pfiffner, James P. 1999. *The Managerial Presidency*. College Station: Texas A&M University Press.

Pfiffner, James P. 2003. "Ranking the Presidents: Continuity and Volatility." In *The Uses and Abuses of Presidential Ratings*, edited by Meena Bose and Mark Landis, 27–42. New York: Nova Science.

Pfiffner, James P. 2004. *The Character Factor: How We Judge America's Presidents*. College Station: Texas A&M University Press.

Phelan, Craig. 2000. *Grand Master Workman: Terence Powderly and the Knights of Labor*. Westport, CT: Praeger.

Phillips, Ray. 1997. *Edison's Kinetoscope and Its Films: A History to 1896*. Westport, CT: Greenwood Press.

Pickenpaugh, Roger. 2016. *McKinley, Murder and the Pan-American Exposition: A History of the Presidential Assassination, September 6, 1901*. Jefferson, NC: McFarland.

Pika, Joseph A., John Maltese, and Andrew Rudalevige. 2017. *The Politics of the Presidency*. 9th ed. Washington, DC: CQ Press.

Pike, James S. 1874. *The Prostrate State: South Carolina under Negro Government*. New York: D. Appleton.

Piketty, Thomas, and Gabriel Zucman. 2014. "Capital Is Back: Wealth-Income Ratios in Rich Countries 1700–2010." *Quarterly Journal of Economics* 129 (3): 1255–1310.

Pious, Richard M. 2008. *Why Presidents Fail*. Latham, MD: Rowman & Littlefield.

Platt, D. C. M. 1984. *Foreign Finance in Continental Europe and the United States*. Boston: George Allen & Unwin.

Platt, John D. R. 1968. *The United States Independent Treasury System*. Washington, DC: Division of History, US Office of Archeology and Historic Preservation.

Pletcher, David M. 1998. *The Diplomacy of Trade and Investment in the Hemisphere, 1865–1900*. Columbia: University of Missouri Press.

Pocalyko, Michael. 2017. "The Businessman President." *Survival* 59 (1): 51–57.

Ponder, Daniel E. 2017. *Presidential Leverage: Presidents, Approval, and the American State*. Stanford, CA: Stanford University Press.

Ponder, Stephen. 1994. "The President Makes News: William McKinley and the First Presidential Press Corps, 1897–1901." *Presidential Studies Quarterly* 24 (4): 823–836.

Ponder, Stephen. 1998. *Managing the Press: Origins of the Media Presidency, 1897–1933.* New York: St. Martin's.

Poole, Keith T., and Howard Rosenthal. 2007. *Ideology and Congress.* 2nd revised ed. New Brunswick, NJ: Transaction.

Porter, Glenn. 2006a. "Industrialization and the Rise of Big Business." In *The Gilded Age: Perspectives on the Origins of Modern America,* 2nd ed., edited by Charles W. Calhoun, 11–28. New York: Rowman & Littlefield.

Porter, Glenn. 2006b. *The Rise of Big Business, 1860–1920.* West Sussex: John Wiley & Sons.

Posner, Eric A., and Adrian Vermeule. 2010. *The Executive Unbound: After the Madisonian Republic.* New York: Oxford University Press.

Post, Louis F. 1976. *Henry George's 1886 Campaign: An Account of the George-Hewitt Campaign in the New York Municipal Election of 1886.* Westport, CT: Hyperion Press.

Potter, David Morris. 1976. *The Impending Crisis, 1848–1861.* New York: Harper & Row.

Potter, Philip B. K. 2007. "Does Experience Matter? American Presidential Experience, Age, and International Conflict." *Journal of Conflict Resolution* 51 (3): 351–78.

Potter, Rachel Augustine. 2019. *Bending the Rules: Procedural Politicking in the Bureaucracy.* Chicago: University of Chicago Press.

Powers, Samuel L. 1925. *Portraits of a Half Century.* Boston: Little, Brown.

Prakash, Saikrishna Bangalore. 2015. *Imperial from the Beginning: The Constitution of the Original Executive.* New Haven, CT: Yale University Press.

Pratt, Fletcher. 1938. *The Navy, a History: The Story of a Service in Action.* New York: Garden City.

Pratt, Sereno Stansbury. 1903. *The Work of Wall Street.* New York: D. Appleton.

Presbrey, Frank. 1929. *The History and Development of Advertising.* Garden City, NY: Doubleday.

Prince, Carl E., and Mollie Keller. 1989. *The U.S. Customs Service: A Bicentennial History.* Washington, DC: Treasury Department, US Customs Service.

Prymak, Andrew. 2014. "The 1868 and 1872 Elections." In *A Companion to the Reconstruction Presidents 1865–1881,* edited by Edward O. Franz, 235–256. West Sussex: John Wiley & Sons.

Pulitzer, Joseph. 1899. "Has Congress Abdicated?" *North American Review* 169 (517): 885–893.

Pursell, Carroll W., Jr. 1962. "Tariff and Technology: The Foundation and Development of the American Tin-Plate Industry, 1872–1900." *Technology & Culture.* 3 (3): 267–284.

Putnam, Robert D. 2001. *Bowling Alone: The Collapse and Revival of American Community.* New York: Touchstone.

Rable, George C. 2015. *Damn Yankees: Demonization and Defiance in the Confederate South.* Baton Rouge: Louisiana State University Press.

Ramírez, Carlos D. 2009. "Bank Fragility, 'Money under the Mattress,' and Long-Run Growth: US Evidence from the 'Perfect' Panic of 1893." *Journal of Banking & Finance* 33: 2185–2198.

Randall, James G. 1926. *Constitutional Problems under Lincoln.* New York: D. Appleton.

Ransom, Roger. 2018. "The Civil War in American Economic History." In *Oxford Handbook of American Economic History,* Vol. 2. edited by Louis P. Cain, Price V. Fishback, and Paul W. Rhode, 371–390. New York: Oxford University Press.

Ransom, Roger, and Richard Sutch. 1988. "Capitalists without Capital: The Burden of Slavery and the Impact of Emancipation." *Agricultural History* 62 (3): 133–160.

Rawlins, John A. 1868. *Speech of Major Gen'l John A. Rawlins, Chief of Staff, U.S.A.; General Grant's Views in Harmony with Congress*. Washington, DC: Chronicle.

Rayner, Richard. 2009. *The Associates: Four Capitalists Who Created California*. New York: W. W. Norton.

Razac, Olivier. 2002. *Barbed Wire: A Political History*. New York: New Press.

Reddy, Marlita A. 1993. *Statistical Record of Native North Americans*. Detroit, MI: Gale.

Redish, Angela. 1993. *The Latin Monetary Union and the Emergence of the International Gold Standard*. Cambridge: Cambridge University Press.

Rees, Jonathan. 2013. *Refrigeration Nation: A History of Ice, Appliances, and Enterprise in America*. Baltimore, MD: Johns Hopkins University Press.

Reeves, Thomas C. 1975. *Gentleman Boss: The Life of Chester Alan Arthur*. New York: Knopf.

Reid, Whitelaw. 1895. *History of Ohio during the War, and the Lives of Her Generals*. Vol. I. Cincinnati, OH: Robert Clarke.

Remini, Robert V., ed. 1972. *The Age of Jackson*. Columbia: University of South Carolina Press.

Remini, Robert V. 2006. *The House: The History of the House of Representatives*. New York: HarperCollins.

Resch, Andreas, and Dieter Stiefel. 2011. "Vienna: The Eventful History of a Financial Center." In *Global Austria: Austria's Place in Europe and the World*, edited by Günter Bischof, Fritz Plasser, Anton Pelinka, and Alexander Smith, 117–146. New Orleans, LA: University of New Orleans Press.

Reti, Stephen P. 1998. *Silver and Gold: The Political Economy of International Monetary Conferences, 1867–1892*. Westport, CT: Greenwood Press.

Rezneck. Samuel. 1956. "Patterns of Thought and Action in an American Depression, 1882–1886." *American Historical Review* 6 (2): 284–307.

Richardson, Albert Deane. 1868. *A Personal History of Ulysses S. Grant*. Hartford, CT: American Publishing.

Richardson, Heather Cox. 2017. "Reconstructing the Gilded Age and Progressive Era." In *A Companion to the Gilded Age and Progressive Era*, edited by Christopher M. Nichols and Nancy C. Unger, 7–20. Malden, MA: John Wiley & Sons.

Richardson, Heather Cox. 2020. *How the South Won the Civil War: Oligarchy, Democracy, and the Continuing Fight for the Soul of America*. New York: Oxford University Press.

Richardson, James D. 1905. *A Compilation of the Messages and Papers of the Confederacy*. Nashville, TN: United States Publishing Company.

Richardson, William A. 1869. *Statement of the Public Debt of the United States*. June 1. Washington, DC: US Department of the Treasury, Bureau of the Fiscal Service.

Richardson, William A. 1870. *Statement of the Public Debt of the United States*. January 1. Washington, DC: US Department of the Treasury, Bureau of the Fiscal Service.

Ridpat, John Clark. 1881. *The Life and Work of James A. Garfield*. Cincinnati, OH: Walden & Stowe.

Righter, Robert W. 1996. *Wind Energy in America: A History*. Norman: University of Oklahoma Press.

Riis, Jacob A. 1890. *How the Other Half Lives: Studies among the Tenements of New York*. New York: Charles Scribner's Sons.

Ringenberg, William C. 1986. "Benjamin Harrison: The Religious Thought and Practice of a Presbyterian President." *American Presbyterians* 64 (3): 175–189.

Riordon, William L. 1905. *Plunkitt of Tammany Hall*. New York: McClure, Phillips.

Ritter, Gretchen. 1997. *Goldbugs and Greenbacks*. New York: Cambridge University Press.

Robbins, William G. 1994. *Colony and Empire: The Capitalist Transformation of the American West*. Lawrence: University Press of Kansas.

Rockoff, Hugh. 2008. "Great Fortunes of the Gilded Age." Working Paper No. 14555. Cambridge, MA: NBER.

Rockoff, Hugh. 2012. *America's Economic Way of War*. New York: Cambridge University Press.

Rodabaugh, James H. 1935. *Robert Hamilton Bishop*. Vol. 4. Columbus: Ohio State Archaeological and Historical Society.

Rodrik, Dan. 2007. *One Economics, Many Recipes: Globalization, Institutions, and Economic Growth*. Princeton, NJ: Princeton University Press.

Rodrik, Dani, Arvind Subramanian, and Francesco Trebbi. 2004. "Institutions Rule: The Primacy of Institutions over Geography and Integration in Economic Development." *Journal of Economic Growth* 9: 131–165.

Rogowski, Jon C. 2016. "Presidential Influence in an Era of Congressional Dominance." *American Political Science Review* 110 (2): 325–341.

Rohlfs, Chris, Ryan S. Sullivan, and Robert McNab. 2015. "Can the President Really Affect Economic Growth? Presidential Effort and the Political Business Cycle." *Economic Inquiry* 53 (1): 240–257.

Rood, Henry, ed. 1911. *Memories of the White House: Personal Recollections of Colonel W. H. Crook*. Boston: Little, Brown.

Root, Elihu. 1917. *Miscellaneous Addresses*. Cambridge, MA: Harvard University Press.

Rose, Anne C. 1992. *Victorian America and the Civil War*. New York: Cambridge University Press.

Rose-Ackerman, Susan. 2016. *Corruption and Government: Causes, Consequences, and Reform*. New York: Cambridge University Press.

Rosenberg, Chaim M. 2008. *America at the Fair: Chicago's 1893 World's Columbian Exposition*. Charleston, SC: Arcadia.

Rosenberg, Dorothy. 1962. "The Dirtiest Election." *American History* 13 (5): 4–100.

Rosenberg, Emily S. 1985. "Foundations of United States International Financial Power: Gold Standard Diplomacy, 1900–1905." *Business History Review* 59 (2): 169–202.

Rosenthal, Howard. 2007. *Ideology and Congress: A Political Economic History of Roll Call Voting*. New Brunswick, NJ: Transaction.

Ross, Edward A. 1892. "Sinking Funds." *Publications of the American Economic Association* 7 (4–5): 9–106.

Rothbard, Murray N. 1995. *An Austrian Perspective on the History of Economic Thought*. Brookfield, VT: Edward Elgar.

Rothbard, Murray Newton. 2002. *History of Money and Banking in the United States: The Colonial Era to World War II*. Auburn, AL: Ludwig von Mises Institute.

Rothstein, Bo. 2000. "Trust, Social Dilemmas and Collective Memories." *Journal of Theoretical Politics* 12 (4): 477–501.

Rothstein, Bo, and Dietlind Stolle. 2008. "The State and Social Capital: An Institutional Theory of Generalized Trust." *Comparative Politics* 40 (4): 441–459.

Rudalevige, Andrew. 2002. *Managing the President's Program: Presidential Leadership and Legislative Policy Formulation*. Princeton, NJ: Princeton University Press.

Rudalevige, Andrew. 2005a. *The New Imperial Presidency: Renewing Presidential Power after Watergate*. Ann Arbor: University of Michigan Press.

Rudalevige, Andrew. 2005b. "The Structure of Leadership: Presidents, Hierarchies, and Information Flow." *Presidential Studies Quarterly* 35: 333–360.

Rudalevige, Andrew. 2009. "'Therefore, Get Wisdom': What Should the President Know, and How Can He Know It?" *Governance* 22: 177–187.

Rudolph, Frederick. 1990. *The American College and University: A History.* 2nd ed. Athens: University of Georgia Press.

Russell, Henry B. 1896. *The Lives of William McKinley and Garret A. Hobart.* Hartford, CT: A. D. Worthington.

Rutkow, Ira. 2006. *James A. Garfield.* New York: Henry Holt.

Rutkow, Ira. 2013. "Joseph Lister and His 1876 Tour of America." *Annals of Surgery* 257 (6): 1181–1187.

Sachsman, David B., and Gregory A. Borchard. 2019. *The Antebellum Press: Setting the Stage for Civil War.* New York: Taylor & Francis.

Sage, Agnes Carr. 1909. *The Boys and Girls of the White House.* New York: Frederick A. Stokes.

Salisbury, Robert Seward. 1993. *William Windom: Apostle of Positive Government.* Lanham, MD: University Press of America.

Salvatore, Nick. 1982. *Eugene V. Debs: Citizen and Socialist.* Urbana: University of Illinois Press.

Samuels, David. 2004. "Presidentialism and Accountability for the Economy in Comparative Perspective." *American Political Science Review* 98 (3): 425–436.

Samuels, Peggy, and Harold Samuels. 1995. *Remembering the Maine.* Washington, DC: Smithsonian Institution Press.

Samuels, Warren J., Jeff E. Biddle, and John B. Davis, eds. 2003. *A Companion to the History of Economic Thought.* Malden, MA: Blackwell.

Sanders, Elizabeth. 1999. *Roots of Reform: Farmers, Workers, and the American State, 1877–1917.* Chicago: University of Chicago.

Santa-Clara, Pedro, and Rossen Valkanov. 2003. "The Presidential Puzzle: Political Cycles and the Stock Market." *Journal of Finance* 58 (5): 1841–1872.

Sarada, Sarada, Michael J. Andrews, and Nicolas L. Ziebarth. 2019. "Changes in the Demographics of American Inventors, 1870–1940." *Explorations in Economic History* 74: 101–275.

Saunders, Elizabeth. 2017. "No Substitute for Experience: Presidents, Advisers, and Information in Group Decision Making." *International Organization* 71 (S1): 219–247.

Scaturro, Frank J. 1998. *President Grant Reconsidered.* Lanham, MD: University Press of America.

Schaack, Michael J. 1889. *Anarchy and Anarchists: A History of the Red Terror and the Social Revolution in America and Europe.* Chicago: F. J. Schulte.

Schlesinger, Arthur M., Jr. 1973. *The Imperial Presidency.* New York: Houghton Mifflin.

Schlozman, Kay Lehman, Henry E. Brady, and Sidney Verba. 2018. *Unequal and Unrepresented: Political Inequality and the People's Voice in the New Gilded Age.* Princeton, NJ: Princeton University Press.

Schlup, Leonard. 1978. "Henry C. Hansbrough and the Fight against the Tariff in 1894." *North Dakota History* 45 (1): 4–9.

Schneirov, Richard. 2006. "Thoughts on Periodizing the Gilded Age: Capital Accumulation, Society, and Politics, 1873–1898." *Journal of the Gilded Age and Progressive Era* 5 (3): 189–224.

Schneirov, Richard, Shelton Stromquist, and Nick Salvatore, eds. 1999. *The Pullman Strike and the Crisis of the 1890s: Essays on Labor and Politics*. Urbana: University of Illinois Press.

Schoultz, Lars. 1998. *Beneath the United States: A History of U.S. Policy toward Latin America*. Cambridge, MA: Harvard University Press.

Schudson, Michael, and Susan E. Tifft. 2005. "American Journalism in Historical Perspective." In *The Press*, edited by Geneva Overholser and Kathleen Hall Jamieson, 17–47. New York: Oxford University Press.

Schultz, George P. 2020. "The 10 Most Important Things I've Learned about Trust over My 100 Years." *Washington Post*, December 11.

Schurz, Carl. 1884. "Why James G. Blaine Should Not Be President." Speech at Brooklyn, New York, August 5. In *Speeches, Correspondence and Political Papers of Carl Schurz*. Vol. 4: *1913*, edited by Frederic Bancroft, 224–272. New York: G. P. Putnam's Sons.

Schurz, Carl. 1897. "Grover Cleveland's Second Administration." *McClure's Magazine* 9 (1): 632–644.

Schwantes, Carlos A. 1985. *Coxey's Army: An American Odyssey*. Lincoln: University of Nebraska Press.

Schwartz, Bernard. 1974. *The Law in America: A History*. New York: McGraw-Hill.

Schwartzman, Felipe. 2020. "The Benefits of Commitment to a Currency Peg: Aggregate Lessons from the Regional Effects of the 1896 US Presidential Election." *Review of Economics and Statistics* 102 (3): 600–616.

Screpanti, Ernesto, and Stefano Zamagni. 2005. *An Outline of the History of Economic Thought*. 2nd ed. New York: Oxford University Press.

Scully, Mark A. 2018. "Principled Rhetoric as Coalition Management: Speech in the Reconstructive Presidencies of Franklin Roosevelt and Ronald Reagan." *Polity* 50 (1): 129–157.

Seale, William. 2008. *The President's House*. 2nd ed. Washington, DC: White House Historical Association.

Seavoy, Ronald E. 2006. *An Economic History of the United States: From 1607 to the Present*. New York: Routledge.

Selgin, George, 2000. "The Suppression of State Banknotes: A Reconsideration." *Economic Inquiry* 38 (4): 600–615.

Sequeira, Sandra, Nathan Nunn, and Nancy Qian. 2020. "Immigrants and the Making of America." *Review of Economic Studies* 87 (1): 382–419.

Serritzlew, Soren, Kim Sonderskov, and Gert Svendsen. 2014. "Do Corruption and Social Trust Affect Economic Growth? A Review." *Journal of Comparative Policy Analysis* 16 (2 SI): 121–139.

Shannon, Fred A. 1977. *The Farmer's Last Frontier: Agriculture, 1860–1897*. White Plains, NY: M. E. Sharpe.

Shaw, George Bernard. 1905. "Tribute to the Work of Henry George: Letter to the Progress and Poverty Dinner." *Single Tax Review* 4 (4): 27.

Shaw, William B. 1894. "Social and Economic Legislation of the States in 1893." *Quarterly Journal of Economics* 8 (2): 230–240.

Sheldon, Winthrop D. 1892. "College-Bred Men in the Business World." *New Englander and Yale Review* 264: 189–209.

Sherman, John. 1896. *Recollections of Forty Years in the House, Senate, and Cabinet: An Autobiography*. Chicago: Werner.

Shiller, Robert J. 2015. *Irrational Exuberance.* Princeton, NJ: Princeton University Press. http://www.econ.yale.edu/~shiller/data.htm.

Shogan, Robert. 1999. *The Double-Edged Sword: How Character Makes and Ruins Presidents, from Washington to Clinton.* Boulder, CO: Westview Press.

Shugerman, Jed Handelsman. 2014. "The Creation of the Department of Justice: Professionalization without Civil Rights or Civil Service." *Stanford Law Review* 66 (1): 121–172.

Sievers, Harry J. 1959. *Benjamin Harrison: Hoosier Statesman—From the Civil War to the White House, 1865–1888.* New York: University Publishers.

Sievers, Harry J. 1960. *Benjamin Harrison: Hoosier Warrior, 1833–1865.* Chicago: H. Regnery.

Sievers, Harry J. 1968. *Benjamin Harrison: Hoosier President.* Newtown, CT: American Political Biography Press.

Silber, William L. 2019. *The Story of Silver: How the White Metal Shaped America and the Modern World.* Princeton, NJ: Princeton University Press.

Silberman, C. E. 1970. "President as Educator." *Fortune* 81 (5): 150.

Silbey, David J. 2007. *War of Frontier and Empire: The Philippine-American War, 1899–1902.* New York: Hill and Wang.

Silla, Cesare. 2018. *The Rise of Consumer Capitalism in America, 1880–1930.* New York: Routledge.

Simon, Arthur M., and Joseph E. Uscinski. 2012. "Prior Experience Predicts Presidential Performance." *Presidential Studies Quarterly* 42 (3): 514–548.

Simon, James Y. 1995. *The Papers of Ulysses S. Grant.* Carbondale: Southern Illinois University Press.

Simonton, D. K. 2018. "Intellectual Brilliance and Presidential Performance: Why Pure Intelligence (or Openness) Doesn't Suffice." *Journal of Intelligence* 6 (2): 18.

Simonton, Dean K. 1987. *Why Presidents Succeed: A Political Psychology of Leadership.* New Haven, CT: Yale University Press.

Simonton, Dean Keith. 1988. "Presidential Style: Personality, Biography, and Performance." *Journal of Personality and Social Psychology* 55 (6): 928–936.

Simonton, Dean Keith. 2006. "Presidential IQ, Openness, Intellectual Brilliance, and Leadership: Estimates and Correlations for 41 U.S. Chief Executives." *Political Psychology* 27 (4): 511–526.

Simpson, Brooks D. 1990. "'The Doom of Slavery': Ulysses S. Grant, War Aims, and Emancipation, 1861–1863." *Civil War History* 36 (1): 36–56.

Simpson, Brooks D. 1991. *Let Us Have Peace: Ulysses S. Grant and the Politics of War and Reconstruction 1861–1868.* Chapel Hill: University of North Carolina Press.

Simpson, Brooks D. 1998. *The Reconstruction Presidents.* Lawrence: University Press of Kansas.

Simpson, Brooks D. 2000. *Ulysses S. Grant: Triumph over Adversity, 1822–1865.* Boston: Houghton Mifflin.

Sinclair, Andrew. 1981. *Corsair: The Life of J. Pierpont Morgan.* Boston: Little, Brown.

Skeel, David A. 2001. *Debt's Dominion: A History of Bankruptcy Law in America.* Princeton, NJ: Princeton University Press.

Skidmore, Max J. 2014. *Maligned Presidents: The Late 19th Century.* New York: Palgrave Macmillan.

Sklansky, Jeffrey. 2002. *The Soul's Economy: Market Society and Selfhood in American Thought, 1820–1920.* Chapel Hill: University of North Carolina Press.

Sklar, Martin J. 1988. *The Corporate Reconstruction of American Capitalism, 1890–1916*. New York: Cambridge University Press.

Skocpol, Theda. 1992. *Protecting Soldiers and Mothers: The Political Origins of Social Policy in the United States*. Cambridge, MA: Belknap Press of Harvard University Press.

Skocpol, Theda. 1993. "America's First Social Security System: The Expansion of Benefits for Civil War Veterans." *Political Science Quarterly* 108 (1): 85–116.

Skocpol, Theda, and Alexander Hertel-Fernandez. 2016. "The Koch Network and Republican Party Extremism." *Perspectives on Politics* 14 (3): 681–699.

Skowronek, Stephen. 1982. *Building a New American State: The Expansion of National Administrative Capacities, 1877–1920*. New York: Cambridge University Press.

Skowronek, Stephen. 1997. *The Politics Presidents Make: Leadership from John Adams to Bill Clinton*. Cambridge, MA: Harvard University Press.

Skowronek, Stephen. 2015. "The Unsettled State of Presidential History." In *Recapturing the Oval Office: New Historical Approaches to the American Presidency*, edited by Brian Balogh and Bruce J. Schulman, 13–33. Ithaca, NY: Cornell University Press.

Skrabec, Quentin R. 2008. *William McKinley: Apostle of Protectionism*. New York: Algora.

Skrabec, Quentin R. 2015. *The 100 Most Important American Financial Crises: An Encyclopedia of the Lowest Points in American Economic History*. Santa Barbara, CA: Greenwood Press.

Skrabec, Quentin R. 2018. *The Ohio Presidents: Eight Men and a Binding Political Philosophy in the White House, 1841–1923*. Jefferson, NC: McFarland.

Slap, Andrew L. 2006. *The Doom of Reconstruction: The Liberal Republicans in the Civil War Era*. New York: Fordham University Press.

Smith, Crosbie. 2018. *Coal, Steam and Ships: Engineering, Enterprise and Empire on the Nineteenth-Century Seas*. New York: Cambridge University Press,

Smith, Gary Scott. 2015. *Religion in the Oval Office: The Religious Lives of American Presidents*. New York: Oxford University Press.

Smith, Henry Nash. 1947. "Rain Follows the Plow: The Notion of Increased Rainfall for the Great Plains, 1844–1880." *Huntington Library Quarterly* 10 (2): 169–193.

Smith, Jean Edward. 2001. *Grant*. New York: Simon and Schuster.

Smith, Michael P. 1973. *American Politics and Public Policy*. New York: Random House.

Smith, Neil. 2018. "A Riot Is Now in Progress in Tompkins Square Park" (1874). In *Revolting New York: How 400 Years of Riot, Rebellion, Uprising, and Revolution Shaped a City*, edited by Neil Smith and Don Mitchell, 105–113. Athens: University of Georgia Press.

Smith, Robert J. 2005. "Man Proposes and God Disposes: The Religious Faith of Ulysses S. Grant." *Perspectives in History* 20: 49–70.

Smith, Theodore Clarke. 1968. *The Life and Letters of James Abram Garfield: 1831–1877*. Vol. 1. Hamden, CT: Archon Books.

Smythe, Ted Curtis. 2003. *The Gilded Age Press: 1865–1900*. Westport, CT: Praeger.

Socolofsky, Homer E., and Allan B. Spetter. 1987. *The Presidency of Benjamin Harrison*. Lawrence: University Press of Kansas.

Sorkin, Alan. 1997. "The Depression of 1882–1885." In *Business Cycles and Depressions: An Encyclopedia*, edited by David Glasner, 149–151. New York: Garland.

Southern Poverty Law Center. 1998. *The Ku Klux Klan: A History of Racism and Violence*. Montgomery, AL: Southern Poverty Law Center.

Sowerbutts, Rhiannon, and Marco Schneebalg. 2016. "The Demise of Overend Gurney." *Bank of England Quarterly Bulletin*, 2nd quarter: 94–106.

Spencer, David Ralph, and Judith Spencer. 2007. *The Yellow Journalism: The Press and America's Emergence as a World Power*. Evanston, IL: Northwestern University Press.

Spencer, Herbert. 1851. *Social Statics, or the Conditions Essential to Happiness Specified and the First of Them Developed*. London: John Chapman.

Spencer, Herbert. 1862. *First Principles*. London: Williams and Norgate.

Spies, August. 1886. "Speech to Haymarket Rally." In *The Great Anarchist Trial: The Haymarket Speeches*, edited by August Spies and Albert R. Parsons, 3–5. Chicago: Chicago Labor Press Association.

Sprague, Oliver M. W. 1910. *History of Crises under the National Banking System*. Washington, DC: Government Printing Office.

St. Martin, Thomas. 2009. "With a Bang: Not a Whimper—The Winter of 1887–1888." Unpublished manuscript. https://files.dnr.state.mn.us/natural_resources/climate/summaries_and_publications/mn_winter_1887-1888_revised.pdf.

Stam, Daan Alexander, Daan Van Knippenberg, and Barbara Wisse. 2010. "The Role of Regulatory Fit in Visionary Leadership." *Journal of Organizational Behavior* 31 (4): 499–518.

Stamper, Anita, Jill Condra, and Joan Severa. 2010. *Clothing through American History: The Civil War through the Gilded Age, 1861–1899*. Santa Barbara, CA: ABC-CLIO.

Stanton, Nile. 1974. "History and Practice of Executive Impoundment of Appropriated Funds." *Nebraska Law Review* 53 (1): 1–30.

Starr, Gerald Frank. 1993. *Minimum Wage Fixing: An International Review of Practices and Problems*. 2nd ed. Geneva: International Labour Office.

Stead. W. T. 1894. *Chicago To-day: The Labour War in America*. London: "Review of Reviews" Office.

Steeples, Douglas, and David O. Whitten. 1998. *Democracy in Desperation: The Depression of 1893*. Westport, CT: Greenwood Press.

Stern, Eric K. 2009. "Crisis Navigation: Lessons from History for the Crisis Manager in Chief." *Governance* 22 (2): 189–202.

Stewart, Frank H., and Robert J. Townsend. 1966. "Strike Violence: The Need for Federal Injunctions." *University of Pennsylvania Law Review* 114 (4): 459–486.

Stewart, David O. 2009. *Impeached: The Trial of President Andrew Johnson and the Fight for Lincoln's Legacy*. New York: Simon & Schuster.

Stoddard, Henry L. 1927. *As I Knew Them: Presidents and Politics from Grant to Coolidge*. New York: Harper & Brothers.

Stowell, David O. 2008. *The Great Strikes of 1877*. Chicago: University of Illinois Press.

Strom, Claire. 2003. *Profiting from the Plains: The Great Northern Railway and Corporate Development of the American West*. Seattle: University of Washington Press.

Strong, George Templeton. 1952. *Diary of George Templeton Strong, Post-war Years, 1865–1875*. Edited by Allan Nevins and Milton Halsey Thomas. New York: Macmillan.

Stuart, Paul. 1987. *Nations within a Nation: Historical Statistics of American Indians*. New York: Greenwood Press.

Studenski, Paul, and Herman E. Krooss. 1963. *Financial History of the United States*. 2nd ed. New York: McGraw-Hill.

Summers, Mark W. 1984. *Railroads, Reconstruction, and the Gospel of Prosperity: Aid under the Radical Republicans 1865–1877*. Princeton, NJ: Princeton University Press.

Summers, Mark Wahlgren. 1993. *The Era of Good Stealings*. New York: Oxford University Press.

Summers, Mark Wahlgren. 1994. *The Press Gang: Newspapers and Politics, 1865–1878.* Chapel Hill: University of North Carolina Press.

Summers, Mark Wahlgren. 2000. *Rum, Romanism, and Rebellion: The Making of a President, 1884.* Chapel Hill: University of North Carolina Press.

Summers, Mark Wahlgren. 2004. *Party Games: Getting, Keeping, and Using Power in Gilded Age Politics.* Chapel Hill: University of North Carolina Press.

Summers, Mark Wahlgren. 2008. "A Good Man Is Hard to Take: Grover Cleveland—Man of Destiny." Lecture presented at the 19th Annual Hayes Lecture on the Presidency, Spiegel Grove, Fremont, OH, Rutherford B. Hayes Presidential Library & Museums, February 17. https://www.rbhayes.org/hayes/a-good-man-is-hard-to-take-grover-cleveland-man-of-destiny/.

Summers, Mark Wahlgren. 2014. *The Ordeal of the Reunion: A New History of Reconstruction.* Chapel Hill: University of North Carolina Press.

Summers, Mark Wahlgren. 2017. "Congress in the Gilded Age and Progressive Era." In *A Companion to the Gilded Age and Progressive Era,* edited by Christopher McKnight Nichols and Nancy C. Unger, 339–349. Malden, MA: John Wiley & Sons.

Sumner, Charles. 1872. *Republicanism vs. Grantism: Speech to the Senate.* Washington, DC: F. & J. Rives & G. A. Bailey.

Sumner, William Graham. 1874. *A History of American Currency.* New York: H. Holt.

Sumner, William Graham. 1877. *Lectures on the History of Protectionism in the United States.* New York: G. P. Putnam's Sons.

Sumner, William Graham. 1883. *What Social Classes Owe to Each Other.* New York: Harper & Brothers.

Sumner, William Graham. 1901. "The Economics of Trusts." *New York Journal of Commerce,* June 24.

Sumner, William G. 1913. *Earth Hunger, and Other Essays.* New Haven, CT: Yale University Press.

Sutherland, Daniel E. 1989. *The Expansion of Everyday Life 1860–1876.* New York: Harper and Row.

Sylla, Richard, and David J. Cowen. 2018. *Alexander Hamilton on Finance, Credit, and Debt.* New York: Columbia University Press.

Sztompka, Piotr. 1999. *Trust: A Sociological Theory.* New York: Cambridge University Press.

Tarbell, Ida. 1911. *The Tariff and Our Times.* New York: Macmillan.

Taussig, Frank W. 1915. *Some Aspects of the Tariff Question.* Cambridge, MA: Harvard University Press.

Taylor, Dorceta E. 2016. *The Rise of the American Conservation Movement: Power, Privilege, and Environmental Protection.* Durham, NC: Duke University Press.

Taylor, Mark Z. 2012. "An Economic Ranking of the US Presidents, 1789–2009: A Data-Based Approach." *PS: Politics & Political Science* 45 (4): 596–604.

Taylor, Mark Z. 2016. *The Politics of Innovation: Why Some Countries Are Better Than Others at Science and Technology.* New York: Oxford University Press.

Taylor, Mark Z. 2021a. "The Gilded Age Presidents and the Economy." *Presidential Studies Quarterly* 51 (4): 860–883.

Taylor, Mark Z. 2021b. "Ideas and Their Consequences: Benjamin Harrison and the Seeds of Economic Crisis, 1889–1893." *Critical Review* 33 (1): 102–127.

Thayer, William Roscoe. 1915. *The Life and Letters of John Hay.* Vol. 2. Boston: Houghton Mifflin.

Thomas, Emory M. 2011. *The Dogs of War: 1861.* New York: Oxford University Press.

Thompson, Dennis F. 2010. "Constitutional Character: Virtues and Vices in Presidential Leadership." *Presidential Studies Quarterly* 40: 23–37.

Thompson, John B. 2000. *Political Scandal: Power and Visability in the Media Age.* Oxford: Polity Press.

Thompson, Kristin, and David Bordwell. 2019. *Film History: An Introduction.* 4th ed. Boston: McGraw-Hill.

Thompson, Robert Luther. 1947. *Wiring a Continent: The History of the Telegraph Industry in the United States, 1832–1866.* Princeton, NJ: Princeton University Press.

Thomson, David K. 2016. "'Like a Cord through the Whole Country': Union Bonds and Financial Mobilization for Victory." *Journal of the Civil War* 6 (3): 347–375.

Thorndike, Joseph J. 2004. "Historical Perspective: The Unhappy History of Private Tax Collection." *Tax History Project,* September 20. https://www.taxnotes.com/tax-hist ory-project/historical-perspective-unhappy-history-private-tax-collection/2004/09/ 20/yscr.

Thrower, Sharece. 2019. "The Study of Executive Policy Making in the US States." *Journal of Politics* 81 (1): 364–370.

Tilley, James, and Sara B. Hobolt. 2011. "Is the Government to Blame? An Experimental Test of How Partisanship Shapes Perceptions of Performance and Responsibility." *Journal of Politics* 73 (2): 316–330.

Timberlake, Richard H. 1975. "The Resumption Act and the Money Supply." *Journal of Monetary Economics* 1 (3): 343–354.

Timberlake, Richard H. 1993. *Monetary Policy in the United States: An Intellectual and Institutional History.* Chicago: University of Chicago Press.

Tipple, John. 1959. "The Anatomy of Prejudice: Origins of the Robber Baron Legend." *Business History Review* 33 (4): 510–523.

Todd, Richard Cecil. 1954. *Confederate Finance.* Athens: University of Georgia Press.

Tolliday, Steven. 2001. *The Economic Development of Modern Japan, 1868–1945: From the Meiji Restoration to the Second World War.* Northampton, MA: Edward Elgar.

Tolstoi, Lyof. 1886. *Anna Karenina.* Translated by Nathan Haskell Dole. New York: Thomas Y Crowell.

Tomory, Leslie. 2012. *Progressive Enlightenment: The Origins of the Gaslight Industry, 1780–1820.* Cambridge, MA: MIT Press.

Trachtenberg, Alan. 1982. *The Incorporation of America: Culture and Society in the Gilded Age.* New York: Hill and Wang.

Traubel, Horace. 1906. *With Walt Whitman in Camden.* Vol. 2. Boston: Small, Maynard.

Trefousse, Hans Louis. 1968. *The Radical Republicans: Lincoln's Vanguard for Racial Justice.* New York: Knopf.

Trefousse, Hans L. 1989. *Andrew Johnson: A Biography.* New York: Norton.

Trefousse, Hans L. 2002. *Rutherford B. Hayes.* New York: Henry Holt.

Troy, Gil. 1996. *See How They Ran: The Changing Role of the Presidential Candidate.* Cambridge, MA: Harvard University Press.

Tsebelis, G. 2002. *Veto Players: How Political Institutions Work.* Princeton, NJ: Princeton University Press.

Tuchman, Barbara. 1966. *The Proud Tower: A Portrait of the World before the War, 1890–1914.* New York: Macmillan.

Tucker, Spencer C., ed. 2013. *The Encyclopedia of the Mexican-American War: A Political, Social, and Military History.* Vol. 1. Santa Barbara, CA: ABC-CLIO.

Tugwell, Rexford G. 1968. *Grover Cleveland*. New York: Macmillan.

Tulis, Jeffrey K. 1987. *The Rhetorical Presidency*. Princeton, NJ: Princeton University Press.

Turner, Frederick Jackson. 1894. "The Significance of the Frontier in American History." In *Proceedings of the Forty-first Annual Meeting of the State Historical Society of Wisconsin*, edited by the State Historical Society of Wisconsin, 79–112. Madison, WI: Democrat Printing Company, State Printer.

Twede, Diana. 2012. "The Birth of Modern Packaging: Cartons, Cans and Bottles." *Journal of Historical Research in Marketing* 4 (2): 245–272.

Twede, Diana. 2015. "History of Packaging." In *The Routledge Companion to Marketing History*, edited by Mark Tadajewski and D. G. Brian Jones, 115–129. New York: Routledge, Taylor & Francis Group.

Twiss, Benjamin R. 1942. *Lawyers and the Constitution: How Laissez Faire Came to the Supreme Court*. Princeton, NJ: Princeton University Press.

US Census Bureau. 1864. *Population of the United States in 1860: The Eighth Census*. Washington, DC: Government Printing Office.

US Census Bureau. 1872. *1870 Census: The Statistics of the Population of the United States*. Vol 1. https://www.census.gov/library/publications/1872/dec/1870a.html.

US Census Bureau. 1883. *1880 Census: The Statistics of the Population of the United States*. Vol 1. https://www.census.gov/library/publications/1883/dec/vol-01-population.html.

US Census Office. 1885. *Compendium of the Tenth Census—1880*. Washington, DC: Government Printing Office.

US Census Bureau. 1895. *1890 Census: Report on the Population of the United States*. Vol 1. https://www.census.gov/library/publications/1895/dec/volume-1.html.

US Census Bureau. 1902. *1900 Census: Report on the Population of the United States*. Vol 2. https://www.census.gov/library/publications/1902/dec/vol-02-population-age.html.

Uscinski, Joseph, and Arthur Simon. 2011. "Partisanship as a Source of Presidential Rankings." *White House Studies* 11 (1): 79–92.

US Congress. 1875. *Congressional Record*. 43rd Congress, 2nd sess., Vol 3, pt.I. Washington: GPO.

US Department of Agriculture. 2019. *America's Diverse Family Farms*. Economic Information Bulletin #214. Washington, DC: Economic Research Service.

US Department of Commerce. 1975. *Historical Statistics of the United States, Colonial Times to 1970*. Washington, DC: Bureau of the Census.

US Department of Commerce and Labor. 1908. *Statistical Abstract of the United States, 1907*. Washington, DC: Government Printing Office.

US House of Representatives. 1868. "Articles of Impeachment against President Andrew Johnson." 40th Congress, 2nd Session, March 2. (Article 10).

US House of Representatives. 1870. *Investigation into the Causes of the Gold Panic: Report of the Majority*. Report No. 31. 41st Congress, 2nd Session, March 1. Washington, DC: Government Printing Office.

Uslaner, Eric M., ed. 2018. *The Oxford Handbook of Social and Political Trust*. New York: Oxford University Press.

Usselman, Steven W. 2002. *Regulating Railroad Innovation: Business, Technology, and Politics in America, 1840–1920*. New York: Cambridge University Press.

US Senate. 1885. *Report of the Committee of the Senate upon the Relations between Labor and Capital*. Vol. 1. 48th Congress, 2nd Session. Washington, DC: Government Printing Office.

US Treasury. 1861. *Annual Report of the Secretary of the Treasury on the State of the Finances for the Year*. Washington, DC: Government Printing Office.

US Treasury. 1869. *Annual Report of the Secretary of the Treasury on the State of the Finances for the Year*. Washington, DC: Government Printing Office.

US Treasury. 1872. *Annual Report of the Secretary of the Treasury on the State of the Finances for the Year*. Washington, DC: Government Printing Office.

US Treasury. 1873. *Annual Report of the Secretary of the Treasury on the State of the Finances for the Year*. Washington, DC: Government Printing Office.

US Treasury. 1874. *Annual Report of the Secretary of the Treasury on the State of the Finances for the Year*. Washington, DC: Government Printing Office.

US Treasury. 1876. *Annual Report of the Secretary of the Treasury on the State of the Finances for the Year*. Washington, DC: Government Printing Office.

US Treasury. 1877. *Annual Report of the Secretary of the Treasury on the State of the Finances for the Year*. Washington, DC: Government Printing Office.

US Treasury. 1878. *Annual Report of the Secretary of the Treasury on the State of the Finances for the Year*. Washington, DC: Government Printing Office.

US Treasury. 1897. *Annual Report of the Secretary of the Treasury on the State of the Finances for the Year*. Washington, DC: Government Printing Office.

US Treasury. 1900. *Annual Report of the Secretary of the Treasury on the State of the Finances for the Year*. Washington, DC: Government Printing Office.

US Treasury. 1901. *Annual Report of the Secretary of the Treasury on the State of the Finances for the Year*. Washington, DC: Government Printing Office.

US Treasury Department. 1927. *Annual Report of the Director of the Mint*. Bureau of the Mint. Washington, DC: Government Printing Office.

US War Department. 1887. *Monthly Weather Review*. Washington City: Signal Office.

Unger, Irwin. 1964. *The Greenback Era: A Social and Political History of American Finance, 1865-1879*. Princeton NJ: Princeton University Press.

Union Pacific Railroad Company. 2020. "Union Pacific Timeline 1994-2020." https://www.up.com/timeline/index.cfm.

Utley, Robert Marshall. 1984. *Frontier Regulars: The United States Army and the Indian, 1866-1891*. Lincoln: University of Nebraska Press.

Utley, Robert M. 2003. *The Indian Frontier, 1846-1890*. Albuquerque: University of New Mexico Press.

Vaaler, Paul, Burkhard N. Schrage, and Steven Block. 2005. "Counting the Investor Vote: Political Business Cycle Effects on Sovereign Bond Spreads in Developing Countries." *Journal of International Business Studies* 36 (1): 62–88.

Valeonti, Sofia. 2020. "Simon Newcomb's Monetary Theory: A Reappraisal." *European Journal of the History of Economic Thought* 27 (6): 837–852.

Vaughn, Justin S., and Jose D. Villalobos. 2006. "Conceptualizing and Measuring White House Staff Influence on Presidential Rhetoric." *Presidential Studies Quarterly* 36 (4): 681–688.

Veblen, Thorstein B. 1892. "The Price of Wheat since 1867." *Journal of Political Economy* 1 (1): 68–103.

Vedder, Richard, and Lowell Gallaway. 2001. "Rating Presidential Performance." In *Reassessing the Presidency: The Rise of the Executive State and the Decline of Freedom*, edited by John V. Denson, 1–32. Auburn, AL: Ludwig von Mises Institute.

Veenendaal, Augustus J., Jr. 2002. *American Railroads in the Nineteenth Century*. Westport, CT: Greenwood Press.

Velde, François R. 2002. "The Crime of 1873: Back to the Scene." Working Paper WP 2002–29. Chicago: Federal Reserve Bank of Chicago.

Villard, Henry. 1904. *Memoirs of Henry Villard, Journalist and Financier, 1835–1900*. Vol. 2. Boston: Houghton, Mifflin.

Waisman, Maya, Pengfei Ye, and Yun Zhu. 2015. "The Effect of Political Uncertainty on the Cost of Corporate Debt." *Journal of Financial Stability* 16: 106–117.

Walker, Francis Amasa. 1876. *The Wages Question: A Treatise on Wages and the Wage Class*. New York: H. Holt.

Walker, Francis A. 1896. "The Restriction of Immigration." *Atlantic Monthly* 77 (464): 822–829.

Wallace, Lew. 1888. *Life of Gen. Ben Harrison*. Cleveland, OH: N. G. Hamilton.

Wallace, Lew, and Murat Halstead. 1892. *Life and Public Services of Hon. Benjamin Harrison, President of the U.S.* Philadelphia: Edgewood.

Ward, Geoffrey C. 2012. *A Disposition to Be Rich: How a Small-Town Pastor's Son Ruined an American President, Brought on a Wall Street Crash, and Made Himself the Best-Hated Man in the United States*. New York: Alfred A. Knopf.

Ward, Zachary. 2020. "The Not-So-Hot Melting Pot: The Persistence of Outcomes for Descendants of the Age of Mass Migration." *American Economic Journal—Applied Economics* 12 (4): 73–102.

Ware, Alan. 2006. *The Democratic Party Heads North, 1877–1962*. New York: Cambridge University Press.

Watson, James E. 1936. *As I Knew Them: Memoirs of James Watson*. Indianapolis, IN: Bobbs-Merrill.

Waugh, Joan. 2009. *U. S. Grant: American Hero, American Myth*. Chapel Hill: University of North Carolina Press.

Weatherford, M. Stephen. 2009. "Comparing Presidents' Economic Policy Leadership." *Perspectives on Politics* 1 (3): 537–560.

Weaver, John B. 1987. "John Sherman and the Politics of Economic Change." *Hayes Historical Journal* 6 (3). https://www.rbhayes.org/research/hayes-historical-journal-john-sherman/.

Webb, Ross A. 1969. *Benjamin Helm Bristow: Border State Politician*. Lexington: University Press of Kentucky.

Webb, Steven B. 1982. "Agricultural Protection in Wilhelminian Germany: Forging an Empire with Pork and Rye." *Journal of Economic History* 42 (2): 309–326.

Wegge, Simone A. 2002. "Occupational Self-Selection of European Emigrants: Evidence from Nineteenth-Century Hesse-Cassel." *European Review of Economic History* 6 (3): 365–394.

Weinstein, Allen. 1967. "Was There a 'Crime of 1873'? The Case of the Demonetized Dollar." *Journal of American History* 54: 307–326.

Weinstein, James. 2003. *The Long Detour: The History and Future of the American Left*. Boulder, CO: Westview Press.

Weir, Robert E. 1996. *Beyond Labor's Veil: The Culture of the Knights of Labor*. University Park: Pennsylvania State University Press.

Weissing, Franz. 2011. "Animal Behavior: Born Leaders." *Nature* 474 (7351): 288–289.

Welch, Richard E., Jr. 1988. *The Presidencies of Grover Cleveland*. Lawrence: University Press of Kansas.

Welles, Gideon. 1911. *Diary of Gideon Wells*. Vol. 3. Boston: Houghton Mifflin.

Wells, David A. 1864. *Our Burden and Our Strength*. Boston: Gould & Lincoln.

Wells, David. 1889. *Recent Economic Changes and Their Effect on the Production and Distribution of Wealth and the Well-being of Society*. New York: D. Appleton.

Werbel, Amy. 2018. *Lust on Trial: Censorship and the Rise of American Obscenity in the Age of Anthony Comstock*. New York: Columbia University Press.

Wert, Jeffry D. 2018. *Civil War Barons: The Tycoons, Entrepreneurs, Inventors, and Visionaries Who Forged Victory and Shaped a Nation*. New York: DeCapo Press.

West, Henry Litchfield. 1901. "The Growing Powers of the President." *Forum* 31 (March): 23–24.

Wheeler, Tom. 2018. *Who Makes the Rules in the New Gilded Age? Lessons from the Industrial Age Inform the Information Age*. Washington, DC: Brookings Institute.

Whitcomb, John, and Claire Whitcomb. 2000. *Real Life at the White House: Two Hundred Years of Daily Life at America's Most Famous Residence*. New York: Routledge.

White, Gerald T. 1982. *The United States and the Problem of Recovery after 1893*. Tuscaloosa: University of Alabama Press.

White, Horace. 1884. "State of Trade." *The Nation*, February 7.

White, John H. 1993. *The American Railroad Freight Car: From the Wood-Car Era to the Coming of Steel*. Baltimore, MD: Johns Hopkins University Press.

White, Richard. 2011. *Railroaded: The Transcontinentals and the Making of Modern America*. New York: W. W. Norton.

White, Richard. 2017. *The Republic for Which It Stands: The United States during Reconstruction and the Gilded Age, 1865–1896*. New York: Oxford University Press.

White, Ronald C. 2016. *American Ulysses: A Life of Ulysses S. Grant*. New York: Random House.

Wicker, Elmus. 2000. *Banking Panics of the Gilded Age*. New York: Cambridge University Press.

Wiebe, Robert. 1967. *The Search for Order, 1877–1920*. New York: Hill and Wang.

Wilkins, Mira. 1989. *The History of Foreign Investment in the United States to 1914*. Cambridge, MA: Harvard University Press.

Wilkins, Mira. 1992. "Foreign Banks and Foreign Investment in the United States." In *International Banking 1870–1914*, edited by Rondo Cameron and V. I. Bovykin, 233–252. New York: Oxford University Press.

Willard, Frances. 1893. *Address before the Second Biennial Convention of the World's Woman's Christian Temperance Union, and the Twentieth Annual Convention of the National Women's Christian Temperance Union*. London: White Ribbon.

Willard, Kristen L., Timothy W. Guinnane, and Harvey S. Rosen. 1996. "Turning Points in the Civil War: Views from the Greenback Market." *American Economic Review* 86 (4): 1001–1018.

Williams, Charles Richard, ed. 1922. *The Diary and Letters of Rutherford B. Hayes, Nineteenth President of the United States*. Columbus: Ohio State Archeological and Historical Society.

Williams, Charles R. 1928. *The Life of Rutherford B. Hayes*. Vol. 2. Columbus: Ohio State Archaeological and Historical Society.

Williams, David M., and John Armstrong. 2012. "An Appraisal of the Progress of the Steamship in the Nineteenth Century." In *The World's Key Industry: History and Economics of International Shipping*, edited by Harlaftis Gelina, Stig Tenold, and Jesús M. Valdaliso, 43–63. Basingstoke: Palgrave Macmillan.

Williams, John Alexander. 1973. "The Bituminous Coal Lobby and the Wilson-Gorman Tariff of 1894." *Maryland Historical Magazine* 68 (3): 273–287.

Williams, L. Pearce. 1966. *The Origins of Field Theory*. New York: Random House.

Williams, R. Hal. 2010. *Realigning America: McKinley, Bryan, and the Remarkable Election of 1896*. Lawrence: University Press of Kansas.

Williams, Robert C. 2006. *Horace Greeley: Champion of American Freedom*. New York: New York University Press.

Williamson, Samuel H. 2022. "Daily Closing Values of the DJA in the United States, 1885 to Present." *MeasuringWorth*. http://www.measuringworth.com/datasets/DJA/.

Wilson, Mark R. 2003. "The Business of Civil War: Military Enterprise, the State, and Political Economy in the United States, 1850–1880." *Enterprise and Society* 4 (4): 599–605.

Wilson, Mark R. 2006. *The Business of Civil War: Military Mobilization and the State, 1861–1865*. Baltimore, MD: Johns Hopkins University Press.

Wilson, Theodore Brantner. 1965. *The Black Codes of the South*. Tuscaloosa: University of Alabama Press.

Wilson, Thomas Woodrow. 1879. "Cabinet Government in the United States." *International Review* 7: 146–163.

Wilson, Woodrow. 1885. *Congressional Government: A Study in American Politics*. Boston: Houghton Mifflin.

Wilson, Woodrow. 1897. "Mr. Cleveland as President." *Atlantic Monthly* 79 (473): 289–300.

Wimmer, Larry T. 1975. "The Gold Crisis of 1869: Stabilizing or Destabilizing Speculation under Floating Exchange Rates?" *Explorations in Economic History* 12 (2): 105–122.

Winsor, Justin. 1887. *A Record of the Commemoration, November Fifth to Eight, 1886, on the Two Hundred and Fiftieth Anniversary of the Founding of Harvard College*. Cambridge, MA: J. Wilson and Son, University Press.

Wirth, Max. 1893. "The Crisis of 1890." *Journal of Political Economy* 1 (2): 234.

Witcover, Jules. 2003. *Party of the People: A History of the Democrats*. New York: Random House.

Witkowski, Terrence H. 2018. *A History of American Consumption: Threads of Meaning, Gender, and Resistance*. New York: Routledge.

Wolf, Eric R. 1982. *Europe and the People without History*. Berkeley: University of California Press.

Wolf, Michael R., J. Cherie Strachan, and Daniel M. Shea. 2012. "Forget the Good of the Game: Political Incivility and Lack of Compromise as a Second Layer of Party Polarization." *American Behavioral Scientist* 56 (12): SI 1677–1695.

Wolfe, Thomas. 1934. "The Four Lost Men." *Scribner's Magazine*, February.

Wolff, Leon. 1965. *Lockout: The Story of the Homestead Strike of 1892*. New York: Harper & Row.

Wolman, Paul. 1992. *Most Favored Nation: The Republican Revisionists and US Tariff Policy 1897–1912*. Chapel Hill: University of North Carolina Press.

Wolmar, Christian. 2012. *The Great Railway Revolution: The Epic Story of the American Railroad*. London: Atlantic Books.

Wong, Ho-Po C., J. R. Clark, and Joshua C. Hall. 2018. "Immigrant Ethnic Composition and the Adoption of Women's Suffrage in the United States." *Public Choice Analyses of American Economic History* 2 (37): 167–178.

Woo-Cumings, Meredith, ed. 1999. *The Developmental State*. Ithaca, NY: Cornell University Press.

Wood, Dan. 2007. *The Politics of Economic Leadership: The Causes and Consequences of Presidential Rhetoric*. Princeton, NJ: Princeton University Press.

Woodworth, John M. 1875. *The Cholera Epidemic of 1873 in the United States*. Washington, DC: Government Printing Office.

Wright, Carroll D. 1886. *Industrial Depressions: The First Annual Report of the Commissioner of Labor. United States*. Washington, DC: Government Printing Office.

Wright, Gavin. 1986. *Old South, New South: Revolutions in the Southern Economy since the Civil War*. New York: Basic Books.

Yergin, Daniel. 2008. *The Prize: The Epic Quest for Oil, Money and Power*. New York: Free Press.

Yglesias, Matthew. 2006. "The Green Lantern Theory of Geopolitics." TPM Café, July 10. http://www.smirkingchimp.com/thread/845.

Yonce, Adam. 2015. "US Corporate Investment over the Political Cycle." *Quarterly Journal of Finance* 5 (1): 1–37.

Young, James A. 2017. "The President, His Assassin, and the Court-Martial of Sergeant John A. Mason." *Air Force Law Review* 77: 1–50.

Young, John Russell. 1879. *Around the World with General Grant*. New York: American News Company.

Zais, Barrie Emert. 1974. *President McKinley's Dodge Commission: A Prelude to Army Reform, 1898–1899*. Durham, NC: Duke University Press.

Zak, Paul J., and Stephen Knack. 2001. "Trust and Growth." *Economic Journal* 111 (470): 295–321.

Zakaria, Fareed. 1998. *From Wealth to Power: The Unusual Origins of America's World Role*. Princeton, NJ: Princeton University Press.

Zeidel, Robert F. 2020. *Robber Barons and Wretched Refuse: Ethnic and Class Dynamics during the Era of American Industrialization*. Ithaca, NY: Cornell University Press.

Zelizer, Julian E., ed. 2004. *The American Congress: The Building of Democracy*. Boston: Houghton Mifflin.

Zhylyevskyy, Oleksandr. 2010. "The Paradox of Interest Rates of the Greenback Era: A Reexamination." *Journal of Monetary Economics* 57 (8): 1026–1037.

Zirin, David. 2008. *A People's History of Sports in the United States: 250 Years of Politics, Protest, People, and Play*. New York: Free Press.

Zmerli, Sonja, and Tom W. G. van der Meer, eds. 2017. *Handbook of Political Trust*. Cheltenham: Edward Elgar.

Zolberg, Aristide R. 2009. *A Nation by Design: Immigration Policy in the Fashioning of America*. Cambridge, MA: Harvard University Press.

Zunz, Olivier. 1990. *Making America Corporate, 1870–1920*. Chicago: University of Chicago Press.

Index